# The
# BEST
# AMERICAN
# SPORTS
# WRITING
## of the Century

# The
# BEST
# AMERICAN
# SPORTS
# WRITING
# of the Century

David Halberstam · EDITOR

Glenn Stout · SERIES EDITOR

HOUGHTON MIFFLIN COMPANY

BOSTON · NEW YORK 1999

ISSN 1056-8034
ISBN 0-395-94513-5
ISBN 0-395-94514-3 (pbk.)

Book design by Robert Overholtzer

Printed in the United States of America

QUM 10 9 8 7 6 5 4 3 2 1

# Contents

# Foreword

One hundred years ago, a book of this title would have made about as much sense as one that extolled the virtues of the home run, slam dunk, slap shot or forward pass. For neither sports writing nor these now common scoring methods were necessary for the enjoyment of their attendant games.

What little sports writing there was at the time was either accidental, derivative, or mired in the lustful muck of adventure stories. Sports, at least in any contemporary sense, was still new. Hunting and fishing were the province of either the genuinely hungry or the gentile. Boxing, horse racing and baseball operated on the fringes of the national consciousness. Participation or attendance was not without a certain kind of social risk. Football was a collegiate curiosity, golf a pastime of those with nothing else to do. Basketball and hockey were in their infancy, played in a cage and on a pond. "Amateur" athletes were those who didn't need to work. Reading and writing about sports was absurd. Whatever for?

Newspapers covered most sporting events grudgingly, if at all. When they did, they were reviewed like performances, and often covered by theater writers. The few existing sporting periodicals, like *Sporting Life* and the *Sporting News,* were essentially trade papers more interested in the political maneuvering of sporting institutions than in either personalities or the play itself, beyond a simple recitation of facts. Other magazines of the era included sport only for its ability to provide earnest thrills, and when it didn't, overwrought wordsmiths wrang out the hyperbole. Ernest L. Thayer's "Casey at the Bat" — a poem, for crying out loud — was unquestionably the single best example of sports writing yet produced in America.

I'll leave it to others to speculate precisely why and how this came to change. The effects of the industrial revolution, the growth of gambling and a host of other factors all played significant roles, I'm sure. But by 1910 almost every daily paper in the country had a sports section. By 1920 sports writing was regularly appearing in the general interest magazines of the day, and sports magazines were common. "Serious" writers like Hemingway, Fitzgerald, Jack London, and others embraced sport as part of their creative landscape, while sports writers like Damon Runyon and Ring Lardner crossed over into literature. By the 1930s sports writers were becoming celebrities and serious writers of other genres were making regular forays into the sports pages in search of subjects. During World War II many of the best war correspondents were culled from the sports page.

Sports writing was beginning to flourish. In 1944 Dutton began publishing Irving Marsh and Edward Ehre's annual *Best Sports Stories*. Selections were made through a judged competition according to category and sport. Some incorrectly believe *The Best American Sports Writing* is a continuation of that series. Not so, but more on that later.

*Best Sports Stories,* rather accidentally, elevated the field. For the first time, readers, and, just as significantly, writers from around the country had ready access to the work of writers other than those in their own city.

The small library in the town where I grew up had nearly every volume, which was published, with one brief hiatus, until 1990, when the *Sporting News,* who had taken over as publisher, dropped it. I made its discovery at about age twelve and read backward and forward from 1970. Since then, I'm certain I've read every story in each and every volume.

Reading the best stories in these books did not make me want to be a sports writer. They made me want to be a writer, period, just as reading Whitman and Kerouac did.

The series was enormously important, not just to me, but for anyone who either wrote about sports or was the least bit interested in the topic. At least once or twice in every edition it was proven, unquestionably, that the best "sports writing" was, on occasion, just good writing that happened to be about sports. And the contrast between these few stories and the remainder of each collection proved there was plenty of room at the table.

After the Dutton series debuted, other anthologies of sports writing began to appear more or less regularly, sport-specific collections like the old Fireside series and a hundred imitators. *Sport* magazine and *Sports Illustrated* soon followed, periodicals that seemed to acknowledge a similar realization.

Since then, sports writing has become something of a respected genre of American literature. With hundreds of sports-specific and general interest magazines that regularly feature distinguished sports writing, there is a wider market for work of this kind than ever before. And even though the number of daily newspapers in this country has dropped dramatically, newspaper sports writers, who have always been the backbone of the genre, fight the good fight. For in spite of meddlesome editors and increasing demands on their space, they continue to produce memorable work.

Which brings me around to say what may surprise some. As far as I can tell, we're still in the midst of a golden age. The writers who have contributed to *The Best American Sports Writing* continue to enlarge and expand the field in new and vibrant ways, building on those who have come before, but not depending on them. I am now at work on the ninth annual edition of this series and am not yet bored. Neither, I hope, are the readers.

My task in putting this collection together necessarily has led me into the past, to all the aforementioned sources. I was surprised, as I reread some forty-plus years of *Best Sports Stories* and dozens of other anthologies and collections, that much of the material I've read since this series was first conceived in 1991 is just plain better. Writers are doing better work now than ever before. While there are unquestionably standout stories from earlier eras, many of which follow in this collection, the bulk of the award-winning stories of the past, while often examples of excellent reporting, would never be reprinted today in any collection that honors writing. They are too often too tame, too false, too safe, or too afraid. The wise know nostalgia for what it is.

As I noted earlier, the old *Best Sports Stories* annual collection was the result of a competition. If a publication didn't enter a writer's work, he or she had little chance to appear in the book, leaving the work almost certain to disappear forever. When a "best of the best" of *Best Sports Stories* appeared in 1974, the editors boasted that in thirty years they had considered more than seven thousand entries.

*The Best American Sports Writing,* born a year after the earlier series ceased to be, is quite different. The annual is not the result of a judged competition, a process that tends to reward the safe and predictable at the expense of writing that takes more chances. While writers and editors are encouraged to submit material to *The Best American Sports Writing,* most selections by far stem from my ongoing survey of publications throughout the year. Seven thousand stories would be a conservative estimate of the number of stories read each year in search of *The Best American Sports Writing,* not including perhaps another five hundred stories that are individually submitted. Likewise, unlike *Best Sports Stories, The Best American Sports Writing* is not bound by category, subject, or other criteria.

That is also one of the reasons why this series elects to refer to "sports writing," where "sports" is an adjective, rather than that compound word "sportswriting." For, first and foremost, this series is a collection of writing, and that's why I also use the largest possible definition of "sports." My goal with this series has always been to push those borders as far and wide as possible, for I think little good ever comes from narrowness. The "best" is simply what I read each year and want to read again, and from that group, what our guest editor selects and adds to.

This volume had to be put together in a slightly different way, for it is clearly impossible to survey a century's worth of periodicals and newspapers without taking another century to finish the task. To cover the first ninety years of this century I was forced to look to other collections — the entire *Best Sports Stories* and nearly another hundred anthologies or other collections that seemed a potential source of material, including, of course, the first nine years of *The Best American Sports Writing.* I also asked friends and acquaintances for their input, scoured a number of libraries, and got up to my knees and elbows in the boxes in my basement that represent material I've collected over my lifetime.

The criteria for consideration in this volume are nearly the same as for the annual edition. Each nonfiction story had to appear in either the United States or Canada during this century and had to be column-length or longer. Book excerpts were not eligible, although stories that later spawned books or appeared in anthologies were not excluded. That is why some pieces that may be familiar to the reader from other collections, such as Ring Lardner's short story "Alibi Ike," are not included here.

Yet that is also why this book is unique. A number of other comprehensive sports writing anthologies have been published before, yet none have placed their trust solely in work from newspapers and magazines. Book excerpts, fiction, and poetry have usually appeared side by side with newspaper and magazine pieces. While the results have in some ways been satisfying, they have also been predictable, for the same works have tended to appear over and over again with the most recent work being ignored altogether. Although a number of those already familiar pieces that first appeared in newspapers and magazines are correctly included in this book, the reader will also find writing and writers he or she has either never read before, or has forgotten. Some work once too risky in subject or tone to ever win a competition has, I think, been restored to its rightful place in these pages.

My initial survey of the product of the century resulted in ninety-four preliminary selections, all of which were forwarded to David Halberstam, who made the final selection of the contents of *The Best American Sports Writing of the Century*. Happily, he added a number of stories I had either missed or forgotten myself. His generous contribution in these pages cannot be overstated, for he has approached this project with the same dedication and alacrity that has always distinguished his work. It has been my pleasure to share his delight in reading the stories in this collection.

One hundred years from now, some subsequent series editor may well sit down to create, in some fashion, *The Best American Sports Writing of the Century*. If we've done our job, he or she will have to look no further than the next hundred years of this series, have a damn hard time deciding what's in and what's out, and, hopefully, will have to find another way to begin the Foreword of the second edition of *The Best American Sports Writing of the Century*.

I think any book that purports to be the "best" of anything always feels a little unfinished. My only regret is that we couldn't include fifty or a hundred stories more, for I believe this volume has *just* tapped the wealth of worthy material that might have made its way inside. How to select, in most cases, only a single story by so many writers who deserve their own volume is not a satisfying experience. Neither is the necessity of excluding so many more writers entirely. Considerations of space made an otherwise infinite quest distressingly finite. For that reason I urge readers not to ignore the list of Notable Sports Writing and Sports Writers that appears at the end of this volume, for there I have tried to honor both individual writers and stories of note that otherwise escaped this collection. They are the reasons libraries exist. The writing and the work continue far beyond these pages. The good men and women who gather together inside these pages have seen to that.

A project of this scope could never be completed without the help and assistance of others. Early on I asked for the input and suggestions of trusted friends and colleagues, many of whom I've met during the process of creating this series each year. I'd like to offer my thanks to those who honored me with their suggestions and apologize in advance to those whose help I may have forgotten. Joe Farara, Pat Forde, Ron Pollack, Frank Deford, Lew Freedman, Linda Robertson, Bill Littlefield, Dick Johnson, Tom Farrey and Joel Reese were all generous with their recommendations. Marnie Cochran deserves credit and my unending gratitude for shepherding this series through its formative years and pressing for this volume, while Christine Corcoran Cox deserves similar thanks for coming aboard in the middle innings and putting up with a couple of guys who didn't want to stop tossing the ball around. The staffs of the Milford Public Library, Thayer Memorial Library of Uxbridge, Massachusetts, and Boston Public Library were invaluable for their help, as were Dick Johnson, curator of the Sports Museum of New England, and John Dorsey, both of whom made great plays to prevent this project from being called by darkness. Siobhan and Saorla, as usual, have understood why we live in a house of books and paper.

Writers, readers, and editors who wish to submit material for the annual volume according to the usual criteria are encouraged to do so by February 1 following the calendar year in which the story first appeared. Submissions, including author name, date and place of publication, may be sent to Glenn Stout, Series Editor, The Best American Sports Writing, P.O. Box 381, Uxbridge, MA 01569.

GLENN STOUT

# Introduction

IN OCTOBER 1965, Gay Talese, a young writer recently departed from the more confining pages of the *New York Times,* suggested to his editors at *Esquire* that the next piece he wanted to write was about Joe DiMaggio. DiMaggio was by then the mythic baseball hero to two generations of Americans, a figure of epic proportions, albeit an almost completely unexamined one, and Talese wanted to do a portrait of DiMaggio some fourteen years after his last game. What happens, Talese wondered, to a great figure after the cheering stops, and what kind of man was DiMaggio anyway? He knew the legend but not the man, and DiMaggio had always been treated by writers as a legend rather than a man. Off he set for San Francisco, Fisherman's Wharf, and the DiMaggio family restaurant. It would turn out to be the perfect union of reporter, magazine, and subject matter at a critical time in the history of nonfiction journalism.

At thirty-three years old Talese was already something of a star in the world of journalism and nonfiction letters. The *Times* in those days was still a place where the copy editors were all-powerful, on red alert for any departure from the strictest adherence to traditional journalistic form, and his tenure there had not been a particularly happy one. But if he had wrestled constantly with the paper's copy editors, his work was greatly admired elsewhere, particularly by reporters of his own generation in city rooms around the country who were, like him, struggling to break out of the narrow confines of traditional journalism and bring to their work both a greater sense of realism as well as a greater literary touch. As such, his reporting first at the *Times,* and then his early magazine writing for *Esquire,* had already gained him a considerable following, particularly among his peers as a rising star from whom a great deal could be learned stylistically. His particular strength, he liked to say, was not so much in interviewing, but in observing, in studying his subjects in their natural habitat; he had already displayed the strength of that style in a piece just completed but not yet published in *Esquire*. This was a piece on Frank Sinatra, and in the previous fall he had bided his time in Las Vegas until a reluctant Sinatra finally let him across the moat. In time, waiting patiently for the right moment, he had captured a marvelous sense of Sinatra in his own environment, a gifted man hardly at peace with himself, surrounded largely by flunkies. The Sinatra piece would establish Talese's credentials as the point man in a constantly changing form, certainly the most daring and talented practitioner of a form which was now rivaling fiction for its capacity to capture moments of reality.

What came through in Talese's work was a kind of journalism verité, reporting profoundly influenced by cinema verite — the reporter as camera. American nonfiction journalism was changing at an accelerating rate in those days, and *Esquire* in the early sixties was very much the leader in the changes taking place, the magazine where young restless writers wanting to challenge these archaic professional formulas were coming together under the talented leadership of two exceptional editors, Harold Hayes and Clay Felker. It had become the most exciting magazine in the country, and at a time when print reporting and magazines were far more important than they were to be only thirty years later, young ambitious journalists could not wait for the next issue of *Esquire* to see which colleague had gone a little further in pushing forward the barriers of the trade.

So Talese working for Hayes at *Esquire* was already a formidable combination — arguably the most talented young magazine writer in the country, progenitor of a new type of reporting, working for the most adventurous magazine editor of his time. In addition the subject, DiMaggio, was perfect — because of the almost unique degree of difficulty he presented to the writer, for in truth he was a man who could not be reported on with any degree of accuracy under the old rules. The premise of what both Talese and Hayes were pushing at, and what would eventually be called the New Journalism, demanded a new journalistic realism, and at its best it stripped away the facade with which most celebrities protected themselves as they presented themselves to the public. In this new kind of journalism just coming of age the journalist was able to see these celebrities as they really were, not as they had so carefully presented themselves over the years.

And perhaps no celebrity was a better subject for that kind of report-ing than Joe DiMaggio. At that moment he remained not merely in the world of sports, but to all Americans, a kind of icon of icons, the most celebrated athlete of his age, the best big game player of his era and a man who because of his deeds, looks, and marriage to the actress Marilyn Monroe, had transcended the barriers of sports in terms of the breadth of his fame. But in journalistic terms, he remained a man about whom a great deal had been written but also, about whom very little real reporting had ever been done, and about whom very little was known.

Because the Yankees almost always won and because DiMaggio was the best player on those dominating teams and played with a certain athletic elegance (in the media capital of the world no less), and because it was a decidedly less iconoclastic era, he had always been treated with great delicacy by an adoring New York and thus national press corps. The essential portrait of DiMaggio which had emerged over the years was of someone as attractive and graceful off the field as he was on it. DiMaggio had rather skillfully contributed to this image — he was extremely forceful and icy in his control of his own image, as attentive and purposeful in controlling it as he was in excelling on the field, and he quickly and ruthlessly cut off any reporter who threatened to go beyond the accepted journalistic limits. Those limits were, of course, set by Joe DiMaggio. At the same time he was deft at offering just enough access — access under which he set all the ground rules — to a few favored reporters and he was particularly good with a number of col-umnists who were unusually influential in those days, most notably Jimmy Cannon, then of the *New York Post,* who often hung out with him. If you were influential enough, you were on occasion allowed to pal around with him, but if you palled around with him, you could not write about what he did or said when you palled around together. Over the years Cannon and a handful of others had created an image of a graceful, admirable, thoroughly likeable DiMaggio. No one had ever been allowed enough access to dispute that image.

Yet the truth among those who knew him relatively well was some-what different: he was said (privately by people who did not want to go on the record) to be an unusually self-absorbed man, suspicious, often hostile, and largely devoid of charm. By and large those who were close to him, it was said, tended to be sycophants, people whose principal importance came from their proximity to him, men who were always aware that if they displeased him he would quickly hit the ejector button on them. Their job was to be with him when he needed them and to keep him from being alone — although he was in truth a man who was almost always alone, even when they were with him. Like many celebrities he wanted to have his fame both ways — to enjoy the benefits of his celebrity and yet to hold on to his privacy; unlike many celebrities, he had been surprisingly successful at having it both ways for most of his life, and he had successfully controlled what was written about him.

Therefore Talese was taking on an immensely difficult subject. But that made the challenge all the more interesting, because the territory was virginal — a great figure who was said to be very different from his carefully constructed public image and who therefore had not in any real way been written about before.

Talese had tried to make a connection to DiMaggio even before he set out for San Francisco. He was friendly with Ernie Sisto, a veteran *Times* photographer who was said to be a DiMaggio pal, and Sisto had volunteered to make the introduction, and in time at an Old Timers game at Yankee Stadium Sisto introduced Talese to DiMaggio. Talese explained the idea, and DiMaggio seemed to give his consent. (Here I should make my own confession of some degree of bias: some twenty-four years later, I was working on a book about the 1949 pennant race between the Yankees and the Red Sox. I wanted to interview DiMaggio for it, and a good deal of time and effort went into the approach, principally through Edward Bennett Williams, allegedly one of the Yankee star's closest friends, a man quite enthusiastic about my project. Finally, after weeks of negotiations, Williams had called me one night and said it was all arranged and I was to call DiMaggio immediately and that Yankee great would see me very soon. I did, and though DiMaggio said he would see me, it was also true that no one has ever been so gratuitously rude to me over the phone in my forty-odd-year career as a reporter. I was stunned by the undertow of rage my rather simple request had produced and his intense wariness. "How come you know so many important and powerful men?" he had asked me, and he had done that with self-evident anger. Though he promised he would see me, I knew as I put down the phone that he was never going to talk to me. When my book came out, some of it a rather generous celebration of his own athletic deeds in that magical year, he referred to it as "garbage" to friends.)

Talese in time showed up to meet with him. DiMaggio, it turned out, was not happy to see him despite his earlier promise, and for several days did not return his phone calls. After almost a week of waiting, his calls still unanswered, Talese set off for the DiMaggio family restaurant. What happened then — DiMaggio's almost lethal rejection of him — is what makes the piece so powerful — DiMaggio, dodging him in the restaurant and then calling him on the phone — both of them still inside the restaurant: *"You are invading my rights. I did not ask you to come. I assume you have a lawyer, you must have a lawyer, get your lawyer!"* All of this was shouted at him by one of the most famous and most admired men in America. It is the reader as well as the writer who feels buffeted and beaten up at this point, the reader who, like the writer, has dropped in on a much admired hero, ready to like him even more but finds that he is a very ordinary and not particularly likeable man; it is the reader who has his face slapped in the piece. The particulars seem to flow from that first scene, DiMaggio angrily handing back Talese the letter he had written about an interview they had agreed on, the letter still unopened. Talese, it should be noted, did not bend under DiMaggio's assault. He managed to ask for permission to hang out with Lefty O'Doul, an old DiMaggio pal and the most independent of the men around him. DiMaggio assented, and through O'Doul, Talese finally began to connect to DiMaggio and his inner group. What we end up with is an evocative portrait of a great ballplayer long after his last game is over, and we have a powerful sense of his loneliness and his essential separation from almost everyone around him. There is one particular anecdote that is uniquely powerful, DiMaggio and Marilyn Monroe honeymooning in Japan, she being asked to entertain the troops in Korea, and later returning to tell him excitedly that he had never heard such cheering. "Yes, I have," he says.

All of us who do this for a living bring different strengths to our work. Talese, in my mind the most important nonfiction writer of his generation, the person whose work most influenced at least two generations of other reporters, is classically a cinematic journalist: he becomes something of a camera as this piece shows, hanging around, gradually blending into the woodwork, capturing a series of scenes in a form which constitutes a great nonfiction short story. DiMaggio hated the piece. Thirty-one years after it came out, Talese and DiMaggio were both at the seventy-fifth anniversary of the birth of *Time* magazine. Talese spotted DiMaggio coming in the direction of a small group he was standing with. As DiMaggio arrived, he reintroduced himself. "Are you still writing for that rag?" DiMaggio immediately asked. "You mean

*Esquire?*" Talese asked. No, Talese answered, he had not written for
*Esquire* in a number of years.

We who edit this book are, mercifully, not giving out any awards —
best sports story of the century, or anything like this — but more than
thirty years after it was printed, I still believe this is the best magazine
piece I have ever read. I have not merely included the DiMaggio piece in
this collection but have used it as the opening piece — American magazine writing at its very best. Talese's pieces, particularly his articles on
DiMaggio and Frank Sinatra, as well as his book on the *New York Times,*
*The Kingdom and the Power,* remain the most influential work at a time
when nonfiction writing was undergoing profound change. His impact
on his contemporaries was simply stunning, and here I speak not
merely for my generation but for myself. I can remember distinctly
reading the DiMaggio piece — it was the spring of 1966 and I was still
working in the Paris bureau of the *New York Times* after being expelled
from Eastern Europe — I simply devoured it. By the time I finished
reading it I had decided to get out of daily journalism. That one piece, it
struck me, was worth everything I had written in the past year. Within a
year I had left the *Times* to become a contract magazine reporter for
Willie Morris at *Harper's,* an editor who was trying to emulate what
Harold Hayes and a number of other editors were then doing with what
had been up until then a rather stodgy magazine.

It strikes me that the Talese piece reflects a number of things that
were taking place in American journalism at the time — some twenty
years after the end of World War II. The first thing is that the level of
education was going up significantly, both among writers and among
readers. That mandated better, more concise writing. It also meant that
because of a burgeoning and growing paperback market, the economics
of the profession were getting better: self-employed writers were doing
better financially and could take more time to stake out a piece. In the
previous era, a freelance writer had to scrounge harder to make a living,
fighting constantly against the limits of time, more often than not
writing pieces he or she did not particularly want to write in order to
subsidize the one or two pieces the writer did want to do. Now, increased book advances and better payment from magazines were allowing writers the luxury of time, and Talese was one of the first to take
maximum advantage of it. He was then, as now, obsessed with doing his
best work, of doing fewer but better pieces. When he had gone to *Esquire* the previous year it had been for $15,000 for a handful of pieces
each year, somewhat less than he had been making at the *Times,* but a

figure that allowed him, a young talented reporter on the ascent, the greatest indulgence of all for a journalist, the luxury of time.

He used his time well. One thing which set him apart from any number of imitators who eventually followed him is the saturation quality of his legwork: he would wait and wait until he caught the moment he knew he wanted; he would do this even if it meant staking out a piece for several weeks. The DiMaggio piece took some six weeks of legwork. By contrast some of his lineal successors picked up the form but not the substance of what he did; they did not put in the man hours, and as such their work was always notably thinner, and seemed to lack the density and thus the grace of his work.

Let me, if I may, go back a little further in the century and trace the origins of the kind of reporting Talese's work exemplified. Talese was very much the beneficiary of an infinitely more affluent economy that allowed him more time — he was working at *Esquire* on a contract that gave him a considerable safety net. His most important lineal predecessor as a magazine writer in breaking down form and giving readers a sense of what their sports heroes were really like was a writer named Bill Heinz (byline W. C. Heinz), whose work dazzled his peers in the period of the forties and fifties. Heinz, it should be noted, was about fifty and at the top of his game, when he read Talese on DiMaggio and thought it was the best magazine piece he had ever seen. It was, he thought, the almost perfect piece of writing, made even better by what he as a professional knew was the special degree of difficulty created by the subject matter. "I had been around DiMaggio a good deal, I knew how most of the reporters played up to him, I knew how difficult he could be, and how coldly he could treat writers and how he would cut them off if he was displeased. So doing that piece couldn't have presented a tougher challenge. For a writer it was everything you've always been warned against — like a boxer going into Philly and fighting a southpaw from Philly and the referee is from Philly," he said. "And Talese did it almost perfectly — the great thing about the piece is how deft it is, how he gives the reader a sense of who DiMaggio is and what he's like — how he doesn't force his own opinion on you. He lets the reader meet DiMaggio and see him for himself."

Some eight years ago, when I edited the first edition of the Houghton Mifflin collection of the year's best sports writing, I dedicated my share of the book to Bill Heinz. That was a kind of generational homage on my part — because when I was young and still in college his work affected me profoundly, the sense that what he did had a greater sense of truth to it than that of most of his colleagues. I mentioned in particular a piece he had written some forty years earlier which I had remembered as if yesterday about Pete Reiser, the great Dodger center fielder, who was famed for running into outfield walls and spending much of the season on the disabled list. One preseason a bunch of Dodger players were being asked where they thought they would end up. Most said first place. When it was Reiser's turn he told Heinz, "Brooklyn Memorial Hospital."

My homage to him in this new collection is somewhat different. We are including three of his pieces, including the Reiser one, which sets him apart from any other magazine writer. (We are only running two by the immensely gifted Frank Deford.) One of the other Heinz pieces is a much admired piece he did on a fighter named Bummy Davis. My colleague Jimmy Breslin, whose work also appears in this collection, was a huge Heinz fan. Breslin was fond of proclaiming to any and all that the Bummy Davis piece was the best sports story of all time. One night years ago, sitting in a Manhattan bar, he was making this point with considerable enthusiasm to another writer who was clearly a disbeliever. "Hey Rosemary," he yelled to his first wife, then at the other end of the bar, "What's the best sports magazine piece of all time?" "Bummy Davis by Bill Heinz," she immediately and correctly answered back. The third Heinz piece is a lovely bit of reportage about Red Grange that captures a certain innocence about sports and its superstars from an earlier time in the century. It is interesting to compare the innate modesty of Grange with the immodesty reflected in an athlete in another article in this book — Reggie Jackson as chronicled by the marvelously talented David Remnick.

If the generation that Gay Talese and Tom Wolfe and Jimmy Breslin and others represent produced a new kind of superstar of magazine writing, then Bill Heinz was one of the pioneers who helped break down the existing form and did it in a less affluent era, against significant economic odds. That meant that finding the time to do your best work was much more difficult than it was for members of the generation that followed, where the material rewards tended to be far greater as America became more of a media society and, in time, an entertainment society.

Bill Heinz was born in 1915, which makes him about twenty years older than many of the younger writers who admired him so much and followed his lead. He had grown up in Mt. Vernon, New York, in suburban Westchester County, the son of a salesman who told him one particular thing which would be of value in his profession — "always believe in your product" — that is, always do your best work. He went to Middlebury College in Vermont, which would set him apart from many of the sports writers of his generation, most of whom had never been to college and had little in the way of literary ambitions. He loved sports, had read the sports pages avidly as a boy, and not being good enough to be an athlete on his own, he had decided early on to be a sports writer because it seemed so romantic — traveling on trains (plane travel did not exist in his childhood), moving around in the locker rooms among these gifted, wonderful men, and getting to know the ballplayers up close. If as he noted some sixty-five years later, "I eventually discovered that there was a lot more dandruff to that world than stardust," it proved to be an exciting if not exactly romantic world and he was never bored. He did not have to work nine to five, there was, as he had hoped, a good deal of travel, and if the athletes themselves were less romantic than he had envisioned as a boy, that did not mean that there was any less humanity to it — indeed, the tarnish, the very imperfections, and the humanity were much the same thing.

He had arrived in New York after his college graduation in 1937, when the Depression was still at its height and he had gotten a job as a copy boy for the old *New York Sun*. He stayed there thirteen years, first as a reporter then as a sports columnist. His work immediately attracted the attention of his peers. It was clean and understated, a reflection of a new generation of journalists who also wanted to be writers. He was, as he later noted, like most young writers of his generation, profoundly influenced by Hemingway who had done so much to simplify and modernize the language, and in particular, by a sports writer of a previous generation named Frank Graham.

Graham (whose work is also represented here with a beautiful and quite understated piece on the funeral of a fight manager) was the beau ideal of his time, a man about twenty years older than Heinz. He had never gone to college, but he had a wonderful technique, a pre-Talese fly on the wall style; he too had been strongly influenced by Hemingway, and he had figured out how to be a sports columnist, to get to the scene, to listen, and then to take himself out of the column. The sum of that style was a new kind of realism, an ability to give the reader a sense of

being on location. (Heinz pointed out that as Graham became better and better known, his style became harder to pull off, because
his subjects inevitably became aware of him and what he was doing,
and they changed — it was harder to get them to be natural — a phenomenon not unlike what happens these days when a television camera comes into a dressing room.) Graham taught the young Heinz
how to listen, how to write — by underwriting — and how to craft a
column.

When in 1950 the *Sun,* a paper noted for the talent of its writers, went
under as an early victim of the circulation wars, Bill Heinz had a
number of offers. The principal among them was one from the *New
York Daily News,* then the most successful tabloid in the nation with a
circulation of some 4 million on Sunday, a paper with some good
reporters like Dick Young (also represented here) but desperately in
need of a star columnist. The lead columnist at the time was a man
named Jimmy Powers, the paper's sports editor, a man with the most
marginal literary ambitions and ability. In 1950, when Powers went on
vacation, a man named Bob Shand, the *News'*s managing editor, called
Heinz and asked if he would like to write a column for a month while
Powers was away. Does Powers know you're asking me? Heinz asked.
No, but what difference does that make, Shand answered, which intrigued Heinz, since Powers made such a big thing of how tightly he was
connected to the paper's publisher, Colonel Patterson.

He tried the column for a month and it was a huge success — the
paper was deluged with mail about the appearance of a fresh, lively
writer who always seemed to be at the right place and to give them a
glimpse of an inner world heretofore closed off to them. When the trial
period was over, Shand offered him a column, six times a week, to
appear alongside that of Powers. Given the competition — or the lack
thereof — for his work would effectively dominate that of rather mun-
dane Powers every day — it was an enticing offer. There were two
problems. First was the salary, some $12,000 a year, not even in those
days an enviable figure, particularly for a paper that was virtually coin-
ing money. The second thing was that Heinz longed to break out of the
form, even that of the column. Being a columnist was certainly far more
rewarding than being a straight sports reporter, but a column had its
own limitations, based on space and in a different way from daily
reporting, form. Much of the good stuff which he picked up by hanging
around the different venues, the little tidbits and anecdotes that allowed
a writer to capture a scene and to penetrate the psyche and character of

an athlete, was often excluded simply because of space limitations. He was tired of writing 750 words each time he sat down.

So he took a big risk and gave up the chance to be the star columnist for the most powerful tabloid in the city and went out on his own. He was betting on himself — and his desire to be a writer. This was not yet America in the media age: The economics would be difficult — the communications world of America was not nearly as affluent as it was to become some fifteen years later when the generation I belong to began to leave daily journalism for magazine and book writing, driven by much the same sense of frustration. Heinz took the jump when being self-employed was still a risky venture. The first piece he did was the Bummy Davis piece, for all of $500 for *True*, but it was a singular piece, a marvelous journalist on a world-class rogue. For the first time he had space enough and time enough and it became a signature piece. Everyone took notice. Soon he picked up a very good agent, Helen Strauss, one of the most high powered agents of the time, a woman who represented Arthur Miller and James Michener, among others, and his price went up accordingly, $1,500 and $2,000 writing for *True* and *Sport* and the *Saturday Evening Post, Collier's, Look,* and *Life.*

He was doing very well in those years, making far more than he might have made if he had stayed in daily journalism. But the problem he next dealt with was one which had existed from time immemorial for writers, that the freedom of time and space which he discovered working for magazines fed an even greater hunger, to write a book, particularly a novel. He had the idea for a novel about the fight game, based on a fighter named Billy Graham, a much admired white fighter of that day, a connoisseur's fighter whom he had grown close to. Working closely with the jockey Eddie Arcaro, Heinz did a long two-part series around 1957 for *Look,* for which he was paid the immense sum of $11,500. The paycheck was the biggest that had ever come in the house. That meant for the first time he was ahead of the game. His wife, he remembered with great fondness, did not ask for a new car, a new coat, or anything for the house. "Well," she had said, "you've always been saying how you wanted to write a novel if we only could get ahead — and now we're ahead, so here's your chance." So he went to work, and a year later he finished *The Professional,* an almost perfect novel about the fight game. Harper and Row published it with great enthusiasm (if not with great skill). Hemingway, at the peak of his powers, sent in a jacket quote, which was quite rare (although it arrived after publication). The book received wonderful reviews, but it never took off, selling some 14,000 copies. *The Professional* had an interesting shelf life — a few years ago George Plimpton (who is also represented in this book) wrote an introduction for a new edition in a paperback line, and the book has been optioned by the movies four or five times; Walter Matthau, the actor, apparently saw one version of the screenplay and was heard to say that the script was far too good — "there's no way you can screw this one up." So it is a particular pleasure to reintroduce some of the best work of Bill Heinz to a new generation of readers.

Better known than Bill Heinz, and influential in a somewhat different way, is Red Smith, and we have included a kind of Red Smith sampler in the book. He was far and away the best sports columnist of his time, and he stayed at the top of his game for more than thirty years: his columns at their best were like miniature short stories. They were deftly crafted and at a time when most sports writers still indulged a tendency to overwrite, Smith tended to underwrite. His work if anything got better over the years, and unlike many sports writers whose work reflected the prejudices of their day, he was strikingly open to new ideas: his ability to change his mind about Cassius Clay/Muhammad Ali when most men of his generation were so offended by Ali's style, theatrics, and politics that they did not deign to see the brilliance of him as a fighter and the originality of him as a man, is part of his enduring legacy. When Clay became a champion and then changed his name, the division within the ranks of sports writers was something of a chasm, a division which among other things seemed to fall along generational lines. Red Smith, it would turn out, was generational prejudice–immune. His own innate decency and intelligence guided him to the larger truth about Ali, in spite of what might have been his own natural prejudices.

Although this collection is not intended as a work of history, it is not without a certain historical legitimacy. In the background as we track the century from beginning to end, the reader should be able to sense the changes being wrought in the society by a number of forces: racial change, the coming of stunning new material affluence, the growing importance of sports in what is increasingly an entertainment age, and finally the effect of other forms of communications on print. That last is particularly important, because the coming and then the growth of the broadcast media, first radio, and then far more importantly, television, dramatically changed the role of print. Not only was the audience growing at an astonishing rate because people were hearing and seeing games in their homes, but the role of print was changing — it was no longer the fastest or the most important means of communication. Instead by the late fifties reporters had to assume that in most cases their readers knew the score and the essentials of what had taken place; increasingly their job was to *explain* what happened and why it had happened, and what these athletes whom they had seen play were really like.

This was particularly true of the coming of television and it is one reason why I think there was such a flowering of print in the early sixties. The first thing television did was to whet the appetite for good nonfiction reporting; more people were buying more books and magazines because they wanted to know more about the public figures whom they had just seen flash on the screen in their living rooms. In addition it was increasingly obvious (if often to reporters before some of their editors) that television was with some degree of finality changing the nature and the mission of print journalism. Not only was television quickly becoming the dominant means of communication — the first Kennedy-Nixon debate had shown that, and the coverage of Kennedy's assassination had driven the point home even more clearly — not only was it faster, but it was also becoming more powerful. That meant that talented print journalists, to remain viable and be of value, had to go where the television cameras could not go (or where television executives were too lazy to send them) and answer questions that were posed by what readers had already seen on television.

Therefore, for print to survive, the reporting had to be better, and more thoughtful, the writing had to be better, and above all — the story telling itself had to be better. Print people were being forced to become not merely journalists, but in the best sense it seems to me, dramatists as well. I think that is what began to happen in the sixties: Talese's piece on DiMaggio is a signature piece, and it was printed some four years after both CBS and NBC went from fifteen-minute news shows to half-hour ones.

I think that for these reasons much of the magazine writing from the sixties and seventies is exceptionally good, a kind of golden age in magazine writing. Television had made the style of reporting better, but its presence had not yet begun to undermine some of the magazines which later came on harder days because of their lack of advertising and their diminished role. Because the society at large was becoming ever more affluent, a number of magazines were still relatively affluent and because they were relatively affluent, they paid reporters better, which allowed them the luxury of time on their pieces. Reporters who had been given one or two days to work a piece in city rooms now had six weeks to two months to do them for *Esquire* or *Harper's* or *Playboy*.

I have begun this book with four favorite pieces from that general era, two of them already celebrated among connoisseurs, Talese on DiMaggio, Tom Wolfe on Junior Johnson, the stock car driver, and two others perhaps not quite as well known, Richard Ben Cramer on Ted Williams and Brad Darrach on Bobby Fischer, the chess champion. The first three were done for *Esquire* which was the leader in breaking the barriers, the fourth for *Playboy* which also published exceptional reportage in that period.

In putting together this collection, along with my colleague Glenn Stout (who, it should be noted, does most of the heavy lifting), I am struck by the vast, indeed dramatic, improvement in the quality of writing which took place in the second half of the century. Much of the sports writing earlier in the century seemed to me, as I went through old clips and Xeroxes, as being heavy and florid. A certain style, self-consciously arch, was often believed to be a sign of good writing. There are exceptions to that, of course, but it is obvious that in the middle of the century, driven by a variety of societal forces, and with Hemingway as the principal literary exemplar, the writing became clearer and simpler.

Glenn Stout and I have worked very hard to make this an exceptional collection. Our ground rules were reasonably flexible — the work has to be published originally in magazine or newspaper form and therefore we do not use book excerpts. A number of prominent writers are included but we have worked assiduously to feature well-known writers at their best, and not, as sometimes happens in collections, to exploit name writers even if it is their lesser work. We have tried to emphasize very good writing and the human element of sports; as such there is less writing about teams' winning varying championships as there is about the human complexity of the world of sports. Typically, we have chosen to run a column by the much revered Murray Kempton on an unusually dramatic day in baseball, the day Don Larsen pitched a World Series perfect game against the Dodgers. Kempton, of course, went to the losers' locker room and did a beautiful piece on Sal Maglie, who pitched for the Dodgers.

We have tried to throw a wide net: John Krakauer with his brilliant reporting on a fatal mountain climb, William Nack on Secretariat, Frank Deford on both Bobby Knight and Billy Conn, John McPhee with a lovely report on Wimbledon, Hunter Thompson with a truly zany piece on the Kentucky Derby, Ira Berkow on Jake LaMotta's sixth marriage, George Plimpton on taking his young daughter to a Harvard-Yale game, Mark Kram on the Ali-Frazier fight in Manila. We've tried to be fair to a wide variety of sports — obviously boxing and baseball, the dominating American sports through much of the century, for a variety of reasons lent themselves to more exceptional pieces than did football and basketball. I suspect that happened for two reasons — they were deeper in the American grain earlier in this century, and both sports by their nature produced athletes who were exceptionally accessible to writers. Basketball and football strike me as probably being slightly underrepresented, but we went with what we liked and in many cases loved.

Obviously no one can write about sports in America in this century without writing about race as well, given the terrible prejudice inflicted on blacks earlier in the century and their immense contributions in the second half of the century. So we have presented here among other things, a portrait, however incomplete, of the rise of the black athlete in America; we watch Joe Louis beat Schmeling, we see the coming of Jackie Robinson and the commissioner of baseball slapping down a would-be strike, and we watch with fascination the ascent of one of the two or three most charismatic and historically most important athletes of the century, Muhammad Ali. The editors deliberately chose to look at Ali from several different viewpoints at different moments in his career.

Somehow and somewhere in this book, though the pieces are written at random for a vast variety of newspapers and magazines in very different eras, we watch the country change and we watch its athletes change. We watch the rise of sports in terms of societal importance, as America, because of the explosion in communications and the quantum leap in affluence, becomes less of a Calvinist society and more of an entertainment society, with athletes among its leading entertainers. In the end what Glenn Stout and I think we have managed to do is present not just a portrait of sports in America in this century, but of the nation itself during that explosive period.

DAVID HALBERSTAM

# The Best of the Best

......................................................................................

1966

## Gay Talese

........................................................................................................................

# The Silent Season of a Hero

FROM *Esquire*

> "I would like to take the great DiMaggio fishing," the old man said.
> "They say his father was a fisherman. Maybe he was as poor as we
> are and would understand."
>
> — ERNEST HEMINGWAY, *The Old Man and the Sea*

IT WAS NOT quite spring, the silent season before the search for salmon, and the old fishermen of San Francisco were either painting their
boats or repairing their nets along the pier or sitting in the sun talking
quietly among themselves, watching the tourists come and go, and
smiling, now, as a pretty girl paused to take their picture. She was about
25, healthy and blue-eyed and wearing a turtleneck sweater, and she had
long, flowing blonde hair that she brushed back a few times before
clicking her camera. The fishermen, looking at her, made admiring
comments, but she did not understand because they spoke a Sicilian
dialect; nor did she understand the tall gray-haired man in a dark suit
who stood watching her from behind a big bay window on the second
floor of DiMaggio's Restaurant that overlooks the pier.

He watched until she left, lost in the crowd of newly arrived tourists
that had just come down the hill by cable car. Then he sat down again at
the table in the restaurant, finishing his tea and lighting another cigarette, his fifth in the last half hour. It was 11:30 in the morning. None of
the other tables was occupied, and the only sounds came from the bar,
where a liquor salesman was laughing at something the headwaiter had
said. But then the salesman, his briefcase under his arm, headed for the
door, stopping briefly to peek into the dining room and call out, "See
you later, Joe." Joe DiMaggio turned and waved at the salesman. Then
the room was quiet again.

At 51, DiMaggio was a most distinguished-looking man, aging as gracefully as he had played on the ball field, impeccable in his tailoring, his nails manicured, his 6-foot-2 body seeming as lean and capable as when he posed for the portrait that hangs in the restaurant and shows him in Yankee Stadium, swinging from the heels at a pitch thrown 20 years ago. His gray hair was thinning at the crown, but just barely, and his face was lined in the right places, and his expression, once as sad and haunted as a matador's, was more in repose these days, though, as now, tension had returned and he chain-smoked and occasionally paced the floor and looked out the window at the people below. In the crowd was a man he did not wish to see.

The man had met DiMaggio in New York. This week he had come to San Francisco and had telephoned several times, but none of the calls had been returned because DiMaggio suspected that the man, who had said he was doing research on some vague sociological project, really wanted to delve into DiMaggio's private life and that of DiMaggio's former wife, Marilyn Monroe. DiMaggio would never tolerate this. The memory of her death is still very painful to him, and yet, because he keeps it to himself, some people are not sensitive to it. One night in a supper club, a woman who had been drinking approached his table, and when he did not ask her to join him, she snapped:

"All right, I guess I'm *not* Marilyn Monroe."

He ignored her remark, but when she repeated it, he replied, barely controlling his anger, "No — I wish you were, but you're not."

The tone of his voice softened her, and she asked, "Am I saying something wrong?"

"You already have," he said. "Now will you please leave me alone?"

His friends on the wharf, understanding him as they do, are very careful when discussing him with strangers, knowing that should they inadvertently betray a confidence, he will not denounce them but rather will never speak to them again; this comes from a sense of propriety not inconsistent in the man who also, after Marilyn Monroe's death, directed that fresh flowers be placed on her grave "forever."

Some of the older fishermen who have known DiMaggio all his life remember him as a small boy who helped clean his father's boat, and as a young man who sneaked away and used a broken oar as a bat on the sandlots nearby. His father, a small mustachioed man known as Zio Pepe, would become infuriated and call him *lagnuso*, lazy, *meschino*, good-for-nothing, but in 1936 Zio Pepe was among those who cheered when Joe DiMaggio returned to San Francisco after his first season with the New York Yankees and was carried along the wharf on the shoulders of the fishermen.

The fishermen also remember how, after his retirement in 1951, Di-Maggio brought his second wife, Marilyn, to live near the wharf, and sometimes they would be seen early in the morning fishing off DiMaggio's boat, the *Yankee Clipper*, now docked quietly in the marina, and in the evening they would be sitting and talking on the pier. They had arguments, too, the fishermen knew, and one night Marilyn was seen running hysterically, crying, as she ran, along the road away from the pier, with Joe following. But the fishermen pretended they did not see this; it was none of their affair. They knew that Joe wanted her to stay in San Francisco and avoid the sharks in Hollywood, but she was confused and torn then — "She was a child," they said — and even today DiMaggio loathes Los Angeles and many of the people in it. He no longer speaks to his onetime friend, Frank Sinatra, who had befriended Marilyn in her final years, and he also is cool to Dean Martin and Peter Lawford and Lawford's former wife, Pat, who once gave a party at which she introduced Marilyn Monroe to Robert Kennedy, and the two of them danced often that night, Joe heard, and he did not take it well. He was possessive of her that year, his close friends say, because Marilyn and he had planned to remarry; but before they could she was dead, and DiMaggio banned the Lawfords and Sinatra and many Hollywood people from her funeral. When Marilyn Monroe's attorney complained that DiMaggio was keeping her friends away, DiMaggio answered coldly, "If it weren't for those friends persuading her to stay in Hollywood, she would still be alive."

Joe DiMaggio now spends most of the year in San Francisco, and each day tourists, noticing the name on the restaurant, ask the men on the wharf if they ever see him. Oh, yes, the men say, they see him nearly every day; they have not seen him yet this morning, they add, but he should be arriving shortly. So the tourists continue to walk along the piers past the crab vendors, under the circling sea gulls, past the fish-'n'-chip stands, sometimes stopping to watch a large vessel steaming toward the Golden Gate Bridge, which, to their dismay, is painted red. Then they visit the Wax Museum, where there is a life-size figure of DiMaggio in uniform, and walk across the street and spend a quarter to peer through the silver telescopes focused on the island of Alcatraz, which is no longer a federal prison. Then they return to ask the men if DiMaggio has been seen. Not yet, the men say, although they notice his blue Impala parked in the lot next to the restaurant. Sometimes tourists will walk into the restaurant and have lunch and will see him sitting calmly in a corner signing autographs and being extremely gracious with everyone. At other times, as on this particular morning when the man from New York chose to visit, DiMaggio was tense and suspicious.

When the man entered the restaurant from the side steps leading to the dining room, he saw DiMaggio standing near the window, talking with an elderly maître d' named Charles Friscia. Not wanting to walk in and risk intrusion, the man asked one of DiMaggio's nephews to inform Joe of his presence. When DiMaggio got the message, he quickly turned and left Friscia and disappeared through an exit leading down to the kitchen.

Astonished and confused, the visitor stood in the hall. A moment later Friscia appeared and the man asked, "Did Joe leave?"

"Joe who?" Friscia replied.

"Joe DiMaggio!"

"Haven't seen him," Friscia said.

"You haven't *seen* him! He was standing right next to you a second ago!"

"It wasn't me," Friscia said.

"You were standing next to him. I saw you. In the dining room."

"You must be mistaken," Friscia said, softly, seriously. "It wasn't me."

"You *must* be kidding," the man said angrily, turning and leaving the restaurant. Before he could get to his car, however, DiMaggio's nephew came running after him and said, "Joe wants to see you."

He returned, expecting to see DiMaggio waiting for him. Instead, he was handed a telephone. The voice was powerful and deep and so tense that the quick sentences ran together.

*"You are invading my rights. I did not ask you to come. I assume you have a lawyer. You must have a lawyer, get your lawyer!"*

"I came as a friend," the man interrupted.

"That's beside the point," DiMaggio said. "I have my privacy. I do not want it violated. You'd better get a lawyer. . . ." Then, pausing, DiMaggio asked, "Is my nephew there?"

He was not.

"Then wait where you are."

A moment later DiMaggio appeared, tall and red-faced, erect and beautifully dressed in his dark suit and white shirt with the gray silk tie and the gleaming silver cuff links. He moved with his big steps toward the man and handed him an airmail envelope unopened that the man had written from New York.

"Here," DiMaggio said. "This is yours."

Then DiMaggio sat down at a small table. He said nothing, just lit a cigarette and waited, legs crossed, his head held high and back so as to reveal the intricate construction of his nose, a fine sharp tip above the big nostrils and tiny bones built out from the bridge, a great nose.

"Look," DiMaggio said, more calmly, "I do not interfere with other people's lives. And I do not expect them to interfere with mine. There are things about my life, personal things, that I refuse to talk about. And even if you asked my brothers, they would be unable to tell you about them because they do not know. There are things about me, so many things, that they simply do not know. . . ."

"I don't want to cause trouble," the man said. "I think you're a great man, and . . ."

"I'm not great," DiMaggio cut in. "I'm not great," he repeated softly. "I'm just a man trying to get along."

Then DiMaggio, as if realizing that he was intruding upon his own privacy, abruptly stood up. He looked at his watch.

"I'm late," he said, very formal again. "I'm 10 minutes late. You're making me late."

The man left the restaurant. He crossed the street and wandered over to the pier, briefly watching the fishermen hauling their nets and talking in the sun, seemingly very calm and contented. Then, after he turned and was headed back toward the parking lot, a blue Impala stopped in front of him and Joe DiMaggio leaned out the window and asked, "Do you have a car?" His voice was very gentle.

"Yes," the man said.

"Oh," DiMaggio said. "I would have given you a ride."

Joe DiMaggio was not born in San Francisco but in Martinez, a small fishing village 25 miles northeast of the Golden Gate. Zio Pepe had settled there after leaving Isola delle Femmine, an islet off Palermo where the DiMaggios had been fishermen for generations. But in 1915, hearing of the luckier waters off San Francisco's wharf, Zio Pepe left Martinez, packing his boat with furniture and family, including Joe, who was one year old.

San Francisco was placid and picturesque when the DiMaggios arrived, but there was a competitive undercurrent and struggle for power along the pier. At dawn the boats would sail out to where the bay meets the ocean and the sea is rough, and later the men would race back with their hauls, hoping to beat their fellow fishermen to shore and sell it while they could. Twenty or 30 boats would sometimes be trying to gain the channel shoreward at the same time, and a fisherman had to know every rock in the water, and later know every bargaining trick along the shore, because the dealers and restaurateurs would play one fisherman off against the other, keeping the prices down. Later the fishermen became wiser and organized, predetermining the maximum amount each fisherman would catch, but there were always some men who, like the fish, never learned, and so heads would sometimes be broken, nets slashed, gasoline poured onto their fish, flowers of warning placed outside their doors.

But these days were ending when Zio Pepe arrived, and he expected his five sons to succeed him as fishermen, and the first two, Tom and Michael, did; but a third, Vincent, wanted to sing. He sang with such magnificent power as a young man that he came to the attention of the great banker, A. P. Giannini, and there were plans to send him to Italy for tutoring and the opera. But there was hesitation around the DiMaggio household and Vince never went; instead, he played ball with the San Francisco seals and sports writers misspelled his name.

It was DiMaggio until Joe, at Vince's recommendation, joined the team and became a sensation, being followed later by the youngest brother, Dominic, who was also outstanding. All three later played in the big leagues, and some writers like to say that Joe was the best hitter, Dom the best fielder, Vince the best singer, and Casey Stengel once said: "Vince is the only player I ever saw who could strike out three times in one game and not be embarrassed. He'd walk into the clubhouse whistling. Everybody would be feeling sorry for him, but Vince always thought he was doing good."

After he retired from baseball Vince became a bartender, then a milkman, now a carpenter. He lives 40 miles north of San Francisco in a house he partly built, has been happily married for 34 years, has four grandchildren, has in the closet one of Joe's tailor-made suits that he has never had altered to fit, and when people ask him if he envies Joe he always says, "No, maybe Joe would like to have what I have." The brother Vincent most admired was Michael, "a big earthy man, a dreamer, a fisherman who wanted things but didn't want to take from Joe, or to work in the restaurant. He wanted a bigger boat, but wanted to earn it on his own. He never got it." In 1953, at the age of 44, Michael fell from his boat and drowned.

Since Zio Pepe's death at 77 in 1949, Tom at 62, the oldest brother — two of his four sisters are older — has become nominal head of the family and manages the restaurant that was opened in 1937 as Joe

DiMaggio's Grotto. Later Joe sold out his share, and now Tom is the co-owner with Dominic. Of all the brothers, Dominic, who was known as the "Little Professor" when he played with the Boston Red Sox, is the most successful in business. He lives in a fashionable Boston suburb with his wife and three children and is president of a firm that manufactures fiber cushion materials and grossed more than $3,500,000 last year.

Joe DiMaggio lives with his widowed sister, Marie, in a tan stone house on a quiet residential street not far from Fisherman's Wharf. He bought the house almost 30 years ago for his parents, and after their deaths he lived there with Marilyn Monroe. Now it is cared for by Marie, a slim and handsome dark-eyed woman who has an apartment on the second floor, Joe on the third. There are some baseball trophies and plaques in the small room off DiMaggio's bedroom, and on his dresser are photographs of Marilyn Monroe, and in the living room downstairs is a small painting of her that DiMaggio likes very much; it reveals only her face and shoulders and she is wearing a wide-brimmed sun hat, and there is a soft, sweet smile on her lips, an innocent curiosity about her that is the way he saw her and the way he wanted her to be seen by others — a simple girl, "a warm, big-hearted girl," he once described her, "that everybody took advantage of."

The publicity photographs emphasizing her sex appeal often offend him, and a memorable moment for Billy Wilder, who directed her in *The Seven-Year Itch*, occurred when he spotted DiMaggio in a large crowd of people gathered on Lexington Avenue in New York to watch a scene in which Marilyn, standing over a subway grating to cool herself, had her skirts blown high by a sudden wind blow. "What the hell is going on here?" DiMaggio was overheard to have said in the crowd, and Wilder recalled, "I shall never forget the look of death on Joe's face."

He was then 39, she was 27. They had been married in January of that year, 1954, despite disharmony in temperament and time; he was tired of publicity, she was thriving on it; he was intolerant of tardiness, she was always late. During their honeymoon in Tokyo an American general had introduced himself and asked if, as a patriotic gesture, she would visit the troops in Korea. She looked at Joe. "It's your honeymoon," he said, shrugging, "go ahead if you want to."

She appeared on 10 occasions before 100,000 servicemen, and when she returned, she said, "It was so wonderful, Joe. You never heard such cheering."

"Yes, I have," he said.

Across from her portrait in the living room, on a coffee table in front of a sofa, is a sterling-silver humidor that was presented to him by his Yankee teammates at a time when he was the most talked-about man in America, and when Les Brown's band had recorded a hit that was heard day and night on the radio.

> From Coast to Coast, that's all you hear
> Of Joe the One-Man Show.
> He's glorified the horsehide sphere,
> Jolting Joe DiMaggio . . .
> Joe . . . Joe . . . DiMaggio . . . we
> want you on our side . . .

The year was 1941, and it began for DiMaggio in the middle of May after the Yankees had lost four games in a row, seven of their last nine, and were in fourth place, five and a half games behind the leading Cleveland Indians. On May 15, DiMaggio hit only a first-inning single in a game that New York lost to Chicago 13–1; he was barely hitting .300, and had greatly disappointed the crowds that had seen him finish with a .352 average the year before and .381 in 1939.

He got a hit in the next game, and the next, and the next. On May 24, with the Yankees losing 6–5 to Boston, DiMaggio came up with runners on second and third and singled them home, winning the game, extending his streak to 10 games. But it went largely unnoticed. Even DiMaggio was not conscious of it until it had reached 29 games in mid-June. Then the newspapers began to dramatize it, the public became aroused, they sent him good-luck charms of every description, and DiMaggio kept hitting, and radio announcers would interrupt programs to announce the news, and then the song again: "Joe . . . Joe . . . DiMaggio . . . we want you on our side . . ."

Sometimes DiMaggio would be hitless his first three times up, the tension would build, it would appear that the game would end without his getting another chance — but he always would, and then he would hit the ball against the left-field wall, or through the pitcher's legs, or between two leaping infielders. In the forty-first game, the first of a doubleheader in Washington, DiMaggio tied an American League record that George Sisler had set in 1922. But before the second game began, a spectator sneaked onto the field and into the Yankees' dugout and stole DiMaggio's favorite bat. In the second game, using another of his bats, DiMaggio lined out twice and flied out. But in the seventh inning, borrowing one of his old bats that a teammate was using, he singled and broke Sisler's record, and he was only three games away from surpassing the major-league record of 44 set in 1897 by Willie Keeler while playing for Baltimore when it was a National League franchise.

An appeal for the missing bat was made through the newspapers. A man from Newark admitted the crime and returned it with regrets. And on July 2 at Yankee Stadium, DiMaggio hit a home run into the left-field stands. The record was broken.

He also got hits on the next 11 games, but on July 17 in Cleveland, at a night game attended by 67,468, he failed against two pitchers, Al Smith and Jim Bagby, Jr., although Cleveland's hero was really its third baseman, Ken Keltner, who in the first inning lunged to his right to make a spectacular backhanded stop of a drive and, from the foul line behind third base, threw DiMaggio out. DiMaggio received a walk in the fourth inning. But in the seventh he again hit a hard shot at Keltner, who again stopped it and threw him out. DiMaggio hit sharply toward the shortstop in the eighth inning, the ball taking a bad hop, but Lou Boudreau speared it off his shoulder and threw to the second baseman to start a double play and DiMaggio's streak was stopped at 56 games. But the New York Yankees were on their way to winning the pennant by 17 games, and the World Series too, and so in August, in a hotel suite in Washington, the players threw a surprise party for DiMaggio and toasted him with champagne and presented him with his Tiffany silver humidor that is now in San Francisco in his living room. . . .

Marie was in the kitchen making toast and tea when DiMaggio came down for breakfast; his gray hair was uncombed but, since he wears it short, it was not untidy. He said good morning to Marie, sat down, and yawned. He lit a cigarette. He wore a blue wool bathrobe over his pajamas. It was 8:00 A.M. He had many things to do today and he seemed cheerful. He had a conference with the president of Continental Television, Inc., a large retail chain in California of which he is a partner and vice-president; later he had a golf date, and then a big banquet to attend, and, if that did not go on too long and if he were not too tired afterward, he might have a date.

Picking up the morning paper, not rushing to the sports page, DiMaggio read the front-page news, the people problems of 1966; Kwame Nkrumah was overthrown in Ghana, students were burning their draft cards (DiMaggio shook his head), the flu epidemic was spreading through the whole state of California. Then he flipped inside through the gossip columns, thankful they did not have him in there today — they had printed an item about his dating "an electrifying airline hostess" not long ago, and they also spotted him at dinner with Dori Lane, "the frantic frugger" in Whisky à Go Go's glass cage — and then he turned to the sports page and read a story about how the injured Mickey Mantle may never regain his form.

It happened all so quickly, the passing of Mantle, or so it seemed; he had succeeded DiMaggio, who had succeeded Ruth, but now there was no great young power hitter coming up, and the Yankee management, almost desperate, had talked Mantle out of retirement, and on September 18, 1965, they gave him a "day" in New York during which he received several thousand dollars' worth of gifts — an automobile, two quarter horses, free vacation trips to Rome, Nassau, Puerto Rico — and DiMaggio had flown to New York to make the introduction before 50,000: it had been a dramatic day, an almost holy day for the believers who had jammed the grandstands early to witness the canonization of a new stadium saint. Cardinal Spellman was on the committee, President Johnson sent a telegram, the day was officially proclaimed by the Mayor of New York, an orchestra assembled in the center field in front of the trinity of monuments to Ruth, Gehrig, Huggins; and high in the grandstands, billowing in the breeze of early autumn, were white banners that read: "Don't Quit, Mick," "We Love the Mick."

The banner had been held by hundreds of young boys whose dreams had been fulfilled so often by Mantle, but also seated in the grandstands were older men, paunchy and balding, in whose middle-aged minds DiMaggio was still vivid and invincible, and some of them remembered how one month before, during a pregame exhibition at Old-Timers' Day in Yankee Stadium, DiMaggio had hit a pitch into the left-field seats, and suddenly thousands of people had jumped wildly to their feet, joyously screaming — the great DiMaggio had returned, they were young again, it was yesterday.

But on this sunny September day at the stadium, the feast day of Mickey Mantle, DiMaggio was not wearing No. 5 on his back or a black cap to cover his graying hair; he was wearing a black suit and white shirt and blue tie, and he stood in one corner of the Yankees' dugout waiting to be introduced by Red Barber, who was standing near home plate behind a silver microphone. In the outfield Guy Lombardo's Royal Canadians were playing soothing, soft music; and moving slowly back and forth over the sprawling green grass between the left-field bullpen and the infield were two carts driven by grounds keepers and containing dozens and dozens of large gifts for Mantle — a 6-foot, 100-pound Hebrew National salami, a Winchester rifle, a mink coat for Mrs. Mantle, a set of Wilson golf clubs, a year's supply of Chunky Candy. DiMaggio smoked a cigarette, but cupped it in his hands as if not wanting to be caught in the act by teen-aged boys near enough to peek down into the dugout. Then, edging forward a step, DiMaggio poked his head out and looked up. He could see nothing above except the packed, towering green grandstands that seemed a mile high and moving, and he could see no clouds or blue sky, only a sky of faces. Then the announcer called out his name — *"Joe DiMaggio!"* — and suddenly there was a blast of cheering that grew louder and louder, echoing and reechoing within the big steel canyon, and DiMaggio stomped out his cigarette and climbed up the dugout steps and onto the soft green grass, the noise resounding in his ears, he could almost feel the breeze, the breath of 50,000 lungs upon him, 100,000 eyes watching his every move, and for the briefest instant as he walked he closed his eyes.

Then in his path he saw Mickey Mantle's mother, a smiling woman wearing an orchid, and he gently reached out for her elbow, holding it as he led her toward the microphone next to the other dignitaries lined up on the infield. Then he stood, very erect and without expression as the cheers softened and the stadium settled down.

Mantle was still in the dugout, in uniform, standing with one leg on the top step, and lined on both sides of him were the other Yankees who, when the ceremony was over, would play the Detroit Tigers. Then into the dugout, smiling, came Senator Robert Kennedy, accompanied by two tall curly-haired assistants with blue eyes, Fordham freckles. Jim Farley was the first on the field to notice the Senator, and Farley muttered, loud enough for others to hear, "Who the hell invited *him?*"

Toots Shor and some of the other committeemen standing near Farley looked into the dugout, and so did DiMaggio, his glance seeming cold, but he remained silent. Kennedy walked up and down within the dugout, shaking hands with the Yankees, but he did not walk onto the field.

"Senator," said Yankees' manager Johnny Keane, "why don't you sit down?" Kennedy quickly shook his head, smiled. He remained standing, and then one Yankee came over and asked about getting relatives out of Cuba, and Kennedy called over one of his aides to take down the details in a notebook.

On the infield the ceremony went on, Mantle's gifts continued to pile up — a Mobilette motorbike, a Sooner Schooner wagon barbecue, a year's supply of Chock Full O' Nuts coffee, a year's supply of Topps Chewing Gum — and the Yankee players watched, and Maris seemed glum.

"Hey, Rog," yelled a man with a tape recorder, Murray Olderman, "I want to do a 30-second tape with you."

Maris swore angrily, shook his head.

"Why don't you ask Richardson? He's a better talker than me."

"Yes, but the fact that it comes from you . . ."

Maris swore again. But finally he went over and said in an interview that Mantle was the finest player of his era, a great competitor, a great hitter.

Fifteen minutes later, standing behind the microphone at home plate, DiMaggio was telling the crowd, "I'm proud to introduce the man who succeeded me in center field in 1951," and from every corner of the stadium, the cheering, whistling, clapping came down. Mantle stepped forward. He stood with his wife and children, posed for the photographers kneeling in front. Then he thanked the crowd in a short speech, and, turning, shook hands with the dignitaries standing nearby. Among them now was Senator Kennedy, who had been spotted in the dugout five minutes before by Red Barber, and been called out and introduced. Kennedy posed with Mantle for a photographer, then shook hands with the Mantle children, and with Toots Shor and James Farley and others. DiMaggio saw him coming down the line and at the last second he backed away, casually, hardly anybody noticing it, and Kennedy seemed not to notice it either, just swept past, shaking more hands. . . .

Finishing his tea, putting aside the newspaper, DiMaggio went upstairs to dress, and soon he was waving good-bye to Marie and driving toward his business appointment in downtown San Francisco with his partners in the retail television business. DiMaggio, while not a millionaire, has invested wisely and has always had, since his retirement from baseball, executive positions with big companies that have paid him well. He also was among the organizers of the Fisherman's National Bank of San Francisco last year, and, though it never came about, he demonstrated an acuteness that impressed those businessmen who had thought of him only in terms of baseball. He has had offers to manage big-league baseball teams but always has rejected them, saying, "I have enough trouble taking care of my own problems without taking on the responsibilities of 25 ball players."

So his only contact with baseball these days, excluding public appearances, is his unsalaried job as a batting coach each spring in Florida with the New York Yankees, a trip he would make once again on the following Sunday, three days away, if he could accomplish what for him is always the dreaded responsibility of packing, a task made no easier by the fact that he lately had fallen into the habit of keeping his clothes in two places — some hang in his closet at home, some hang in the back room of a saloon called Reno's.

Reno's is a dimly lit bar in the center of San Francisco. A portrait of DiMaggio swinging a bat hangs on the wall, in addition to portraits of other star athletes, and the clientele consists mainly of the sporting crowd and newspapermen, people who know DiMaggio quite well and around whom he speaks freely on a number of subjects and relaxes as he can in few other places. The owner of the bar is Reno Barsocchini, a broad-shouldered and handsome man of 51 with graying wavy hair who began as a fiddler in Dago Mary's tavern 35 years ago. He later became a bartender there and elsewhere, including DiMaggio's Restaurant, and now he is probably DiMaggio's closest friend. He was the best man at the DiMaggio-Monroe wedding in 1954, and when they separated nine months later in Los Angeles, Reno rushed down to help DiMaggio with the packing and drove him back to San Francisco. Reno will never forget the day.

Hundreds of people were gathered around the Beverly Hills home that DiMaggio and Marilyn had rented, and photographers were perched in the trees watching the windows, and others stood on the lawn and behind the rose bushes waiting to snap pictures of anybody who walked out of the house. The newspapers that day played all the puns — "Joe Fanned on Jealousy"; "Marilyn and Joe — Out at Home" — and the Hollywood columnists, to whom DiMaggio was never an idol, never a gracious host, recounted instances of incompatibility, and Oscar Levant said it all proved that no man could be a success in two national pastimes. When Reno Barsocchini arrived, he had to push his way through the mob, then bang on the door for several minutes before being admitted. Marilyn Monroe was upstairs in bed. Joe DiMaggio was downstairs with his suitcases, tense and pale, his eyes bloodshot.

Reno took the suitcase and golf clubs out to DiMaggio's car, and then DiMaggio came out of the house, the reporters moving toward him, the lights flashing.

"Where are you going?" they yelled.

"I'm driving to San Francisco," he said, walking quickly.

"Is that going to be your home?"

"That is my home and always has been."

"Are you coming back?"

DiMaggio turned for a moment, looking up at the house.

"No," he said, "I'll never be back."

Reno Barsocchini, except for a brief falling-out over something he will not discuss, has been DiMaggio's trusted companion ever since, joining him whenever he can on the golf course or on the town, otherwise waiting for him in the bar with other middle-aged men. They may wait for hours sometimes, waiting and knowing that when he arrives he may wish to be alone; but it does not seem to matter, they are endlessly awed by him, moved by the mystique, he is a kind of male Garbo. They know that he can be warm and loyal if they are sensitive to his wishes, but they must never be late for an appointment to meet him. One man, unable to find a parking place, arrived a half hour late once, and DiMaggio did not talk to him again for three months. They know, too, when dining at night with DiMaggio, that he generally prefers male companions and occasionally one or two young women, but never wives; wives gossip, wives complain, wives are trouble, and men wishing to remain close to DiMaggio must keep their wives at home.

When DiMaggio strolls into Reno's bar, the men wave and call out his name and Reno Barsocchini smiles and announces, "Here's the Clipper!" — the "Yankee Clipper" being a nickname from his baseball days.

"Hey Clipper, Clipper," Reno had said two nights before, "where you been, Clipper? . . . Clipper, how 'bout a belt?"

DiMaggio refused the offer of a drink, ordering instead a pot of tea, which he prefers to all other beverages except before a date, when he will switch to vodka.

"Hey, Joe," a sports writer asked, a man researching a magazine piece on golf, "why is it that a golfer, when he starts getting older, loses his putting touch first? Like Snead and Hogan, they can still hit a ball well off the tee, but on the greens they lose the strokes."

"It's the pressure of age," DiMaggio said, turning around on his barstool. "With age you get jittery. It's true of golfers, it's true of any man when he gets into his 50s. He doesn't take chances like he used to. The younger golfer, on the greens, he'll stroke his putts better. The older man, he becomes hesitant. A little uncertain. Shaky. When it comes to taking chances, the younger man, even when driving a car, will take chances that the older man won't."

"Speaking of chances," another man said, one of the group that had gathered around DiMaggio, "did you see that guy on crutches in here last night?"

"Yeah, had his leg in a cast," a third said. "Skiing."

"I would never ski," DiMaggio said. "Men who ski must be doing it to impress a broad. You see these men, some of them 40, 50, getting onto skis. And later you see them all bandaged up, broken legs."

"But skiing's a very sexy sport, Joe. All the clothes, the tight pants, the fireplaces in the ski lodge, the bear rug — Christ nobody goes to ski. They just go out there to get it cold so they can warm it up."

"Maybe you're right," DiMaggio said. "I might be persuaded."

"Want a belt, Clipper?" Reno asked.

DiMaggio thought for a second, then said, "All right — first belt tonight."

Now it was noon, a warm sunny day. DiMaggio's business meeting with the television retailers had gone well; he had made a strong appeal to George Shahood, president of Continental Television, Inc., which has eight retail outlets in Northern California, to put prices on color television sets and increase the sales volume, and Shahood had conceded it was worth a try. Then DiMaggio called Reno's bar to see if there were any messages, and now he was in Lefty O'Doul's car being driven along Fisherman's Wharf toward the Golden Gate Bridge en route to a golf course 30 miles upstate. Lefty O'Doul was one of the great hitters in the National League in the early thirties, and later he managed the San Francisco Seals when DiMaggio was the shining star. Though O'Doul is now 69, 18 years older than DiMaggio, he nevertheless possesses great energy and spirit, is a hard-drinking, boisterous man with a big belly and roving eye; and when DiMaggio, as they drove along the highway toward the golf club, noticed a lovely blonde at the wheel of a car nearby and exclaimed, "Look at *that* tomato!" O'Doul's head suddenly spun around, he took his eyes off the road, and yelled, "Where, *where?*" O'Doul's golf game is less than what it was — he used to have a two-handicap — but he still shoots in the 80s, as does DiMaggio.

DiMaggio's drives range between 250 and 280 yards when he doesn't sky them, and his putting is good, but he is distracted by a bad back that both pains him and hinders the fullness of his swing. On the first hole, waiting to tee off, DiMaggio sat back watching a foursome of college boys ahead swinging with such freedom. "Oh," he said with a sigh, "to have *their* backs."

DiMaggio and O'Doul were accompanied around the golf course by Ernie Nevers, the former football star, and two brothers who are in the hotel and movie-distribution business. They moved quickly up and down the green hills in electric golf carts, and DiMaggio's game was exceptionally good for the first nine holes. But then he seemed distracted, perhaps tired, perhaps even reacting to a conversation of a few minutes before. One of the movie men was praising the film *Boeing, Boeing,* starring Tony Curtis and Jerry Lewis, and the man asked DiMaggio if he had seen it.

"No," DiMaggio said. Then he added, swiftly, "I haven't seen a film in eight years."

DiMaggio hooked a few shots, was in the woods. He took a No. 9 iron and tried to chip out. But O'Doul interrupted DiMaggio's concentration to remind him to keep the face of the club closed. DiMaggio hit the ball. It caromed off the side of his club, went skipping like a rabbit through the high grass down toward a pond. DiMaggio rarely displays any emotion on a golf course, but now, without saying a word, he took his No. 9 iron and flung it into the air. The club landed in a tree and stayed up there.

"Well," O'Doul said casually, "there goes *that* set of clubs."

DiMaggio walked to the tree. Fortunately the club had slipped to the lower branch, and DiMaggio could stretch up on the cart and get it back.

"Every time I get advice," DiMaggio muttered to himself, shaking his head slowly and walking toward the pond, "I shank it."

Later, showered and dressed, DiMaggio and the others drove to a banquet about 10 miles from the golf course. Somebody had said it was going to be an elegant dinner, but when they arrived they could see it was more like a county fair; farmers were gathered outside a big barn-like building, a candidate for sheriff was distributing leaflets at the front door, and a chorus of homely ladies was inside singing "You Are My Sunshine."

"How did we get sucked into this?" DiMaggio asked, talking out of the side of his mouth, as they approached the building.

"O'Doul," one of the men said. "It's his fault. Damned O'Doul can't turn *anything* down."

"Go to hell," O'Doul said.

Soon DiMaggio and O'Doul and Ernie Nevers were surrounded by the crowd, and the woman who had been leading the chorus came rushing over and said, "Oh, Mr. DiMaggio, it certainly is a pleasure having you."

"It's a pleasure being here, ma'am," he said, forcing a smile.

"It's too bad you didn't arrive a moment sooner. You'd have heard our singing."

"Oh, I heard it," he said, "and I enjoyed it very much."

"Good, good," she said. "And how are your brothers, Dom and Vic?"

"Fine. Dom lives near Boston. Vince is in Pittsburgh."

"Why, *hello* there, Joe," interrupted a man with wine on his breath, patting DiMaggio on the back, feeling his arm. "Who's gonna take it this year, Joe?"

"Well, I have no idea," DiMaggio said.

"What about the Giants?"

"Your guess is as good as mine."

"Well, you can't count the Dodgers out," the man said.

"You sure can't," DiMaggio said.

"Not with all that pitching."

"Pitching is certainly important," DiMaggio said.

Everywhere he goes the question seems the same, as if he has some special vision into the future of new heroes, and everywhere he goes, too, older men grab his hand and feel his arm and predict that he could still go out there and hit one, and the smile on DiMaggio's face is genuine. He tries hard to remain as he was — he diets, he takes steambaths, he is careful; and flabby men in the locker rooms of golf clubs sometimes steal peeks at him when he steps out of the shower, observing the tight muscles across his chest, the flat stomach, the long sinewy legs. He has a young man's body, very pale and little hair; his face is dark and lined, however, parched by the sun of several seasons. Still he is always an impressive figure at banquets such as this — an "immortal" sports writers called him, and that is how they have written about him and others like him, rarely suggesting that such heroes might ever be prone to the ills of mortal men, carousing, drinking, scheming; to suggest this would destroy the myth, would disillusion small boys, would infuriate rich men who own ball clubs and to whom baseball is a business dedicated to profit and in pursuit of which they trade mediocre players' flesh as casually as boys trade players' pictures on bubble-gum cards. And so the baseball hero must always act the part, must preserve the myth, and none does it better than DiMaggio, none is more patient when drunken old men grab an arm and ask, "Who's gonna take it this year, Joe?"

Two hours later, dinner and the speeches over, DiMaggio was slumped in O'Doul's car headed back to San Francisco. He edged himself up, however, when O'Doul pulled into a gas station in which a pretty red-haired girl sat on a stool, legs crossed, filing her fingernails. She was about 22, wore a tight black skirt and tighter white blouse.

"Look at *that*," DiMaggio said.

"Yeah," O'Doul said.

O'Doul turned away when a young man approached, opened the gas tank, began wiping the windshield. The young man wore a greasy white uniform on the front of which was printed the name "Burt." DiMaggio kept looking at the girl, but she was not distracted from her fingernails. Then he looked at Burt, who did not recognize him. When the tank was full, O'Doul paid and drove off. Burt returned to his girl; DiMaggio slumped down in the front seat and did not open his eyes again until they arrived in San Francisco.

"Let's go see Reno," DiMaggio said.

"No, I gotta go see my old lady," O'Doul said. So he dropped DiMaggio off in front of the bar, and a moment later Reno's voice was announcing in the smoky room, "Hey, here's the Clipper!" The men waved and offered to buy him a drink. DiMaggio ordered a vodka and sat for an hour at the bar talking to a half-dozen men around him. Then a blonde girl who had been with friends at the other end of the bar came over, and somebody introduced her to DiMaggio. He bought her a drink, offered her a cigarette. Then he struck a match and held it. His hand was unsteady.

"Is that me that's shaking?" he asked.

"It must be," said the blonde. "I'm calm."

Two nights later, having collected his clothes out of Reno's back room, DiMaggio boarded a jet; he slept crossways on three seats, then came down the steps as the sun began to rise in Miami. He claimed his luggage and golf clubs, put them into the trunk of a waiting automobile, and less than an hour later he was being driven into Fort Lauderdale, past palm-lined streets, toward the Yankee Clipper Hotel.

"All my life it seems I've been on the road traveling," he said, squinting through the windshield into the sun. "I never get a sense of being in any one place."

Arriving at the Yankee Clipper Hotel, DiMaggio checked into the largest suite. People rushed through the lobby to shake hands with him, to ask for his autograph, to say, "Joe, you look great." And early the next morning, and for the next 30 mornings, DiMaggio arrived punctually at the baseball park and wore his uniform with the famous No. 5, and the tourists seated in the sunny grandstands clapped when he first appeared on the field each time, and then they watched with nostalgia as he picked up a bat and played "pepper" with the younger Yankees, some of whom were not even born when, 25 years ago this summer, he hit in 56 straight games and became the most celebrated man in America.

But the younger spectators in the Fort Lauderdale park, and the sports writers, too, were more interested in Mantle and Maris, and nearly every day there were news dispatches reporting how Mantle and Maris felt, what they did, what they said, even though they said and did very little except walk around the field frowning when photographers asked for another picture and when sports writers asked how they felt.

After seven days of this, the big day arrived — Mantle and Maris would swing a bat — and a dozen sports writers were gathered around the big batting cage that was situated beyond the left-field fence; it was completely enclosed in wire, meaning that no baseball could travel more than 30 or 40 feet before being trapped in rope; still Mantle and Maris would be swinging, and this, in spring, makes news.

Mantle stepped in first. He wore black gloves to help prevent blisters. He hit right-handed against the pitching of a coach named Vern Benson, and soon Mantle was swinging hard, smashing line drives against the nets, going *ahhh ahhh* as he followed through with his mouth open.

Then Mantle, not wanting to overdo it on his first day, dropped his bat in the dirt and walked out of the batting cage. Roger Maris stepped in. He picked up Mantle's bat.

"This damn thing must be 38 ounces," Maris said. He threw the bat down into the dirt, left the cage, and walked toward the dugout on the other side of the field to get a lighter bat.

DiMaggio stood among the sports writers behind the cage, then turned when Vern Benson, inside the cage, yelled, "Joe, wanna hit some?"

"No chance," DiMaggio said.

"Com'on Joe," Benson said.

The reporters waited silently. Then DiMaggio walked slowly into the cage and picked up Mantle's bat. He took his position at the plate but obviously it was not the classic DiMaggio stance; he was holding the bat about two inches from the knob, his feet were not so far apart, and when DiMaggio took a cut at Benson's first pitch, fouling it, there was none of that ferocious follow-through, the blurred bat did not come whipping all the way around, the No. 5 was not stretched full across his broad back.

DiMaggio fouled Benson's second pitch, then he connected solidly with the third, the fourth, the fifth. He was just meeting the ball easily, however, not smashing it, and Benson called out, "I didn't know you were a choke hitter, Joe."

"I am now," DiMaggio said, getting ready for another pitch.

He hit three more squarely enough, and then he swung again and there was a hollow sound.

"Ohhh," DiMaggio yelled, dropping his bat, his fingers stung. "I was waiting for that one." He left the batting cage, rubbing his hands together. The reporters watched him. Nobody said anything. Then Di-Maggio said to one of them, not in anger or in sadness, but merely as a simply stated fact, "There was a time when you couldn't get me out of there."

1965

## Tom Wolfe

..................................................................................................

# The Last American Hero

FROM *Esquire*

TEN O'CLOCK Sunday morning in the hills of North Carolina. Cars, miles of cars, in every direction, millions of cars, pastel cars, aqua green, aqua blue, aqua beige, aqua buff, aqua dawn, aqua dusk, aqua Malacca, Malacca lacquer, Cloud lavender, Assassin pink, Rake-a-Cheek raspberry, Nude Strand coral, Honest Thrill orange, and Baby Fawn Lust cream-colored cars are all going to the stock car races, and that old mothering North Carolina sun keeps exploding off the windshields.

Seventeen thousand people, me included, all of us driving out Route 421, out to the stock car races at the North Wilkesboro Speedway, 17,000 going out to a five-eighths-mile stock car track with a Coca-Cola sign out front. This is not to say there is no preaching and shouting in the South this morning. There is preaching and shouting. Any of us can turn on the old automobile transistor radio and get all we want:

"They are greedy dogs. Yeah! They ride around in big cars. Unnh-hunh! And chase women. Yeah! And drink liquor. Unnh-hunh! And smoke cigars. Oh yes! And they are greedy dogs. Yeah! Unh-hunh! Oh yes! Amen!"

There are also some commercials on the radio for Aunt Jemima grits, which cost ten cents a pound. There are also the Gospel Harmonettes, singing: "If you dig a ditch, you better dig two. . . ."

There are also three fools in a panel discussion on the New South, which they seem to conceive of as General Lee running the new Dulcidreme Labial Cream factory down at Griffin, Georgia.

And suddenly my car is stopped still on Sunday morning in the middle of the biggest traffic jam in the history of the world. It goes for ten miles in every direction from the North Wilkesboro Speedway. And right there it dawns on me that as far as this situation is concerned, anyway, all the conventional notions about the South are confined to . . . the Sunday radio. The South has preaching and shouting, the South has grits, the South has country songs, old mimosa traditions, clay dust, Old Bigots, New Liberals — and all of it, all of that old mental cholesterol, is confined to the Sunday radio. What I was in the middle of — well, it wasn't anything one hears about in panels about the South today. Miles and miles of eyebusting pastel cars on the expressway, which roar right up into the hills, going to the stock car races. Fifteen years of stock car racing, and baseball — and the state of North Carolina alone used to have forty-four professional baseball teams — baseball is all over with in the South. We were all in the middle of a wild new thing, the southern car world, and heading down the road on my way to see a breed such as sports never saw before, southern stock car drivers, all lined up in these two-ton mothers that go over 175 m.p.h., Fireball Roberts, Freddie Lorenzen, Ned Jarrett, Richard Petty, and — the hardest of all the hard chargers, one of the fastest automobile racing drivers in history — yes! Junior Johnson.

The legend of Junior Johnson! In this legend, here is a country boy, Junior Johnson, who learns to drive by running whiskey for his father, Johnson Senior, one of the biggest copper-still operators of all time, up in Ingle Hollow, near North Wilkesboro, in northwestern North Carolina, and grows up to be a famous stock car racing driver, rich, grossing $100,000 in 1963, for example, respected, solid, idolized in his hometown and throughout the rural South. There is all this about how good old boys would wake up in the middle of the night in the apple shacks and hear a supercharged Oldsmobile engine roaring over Brushy Mountain and say, "Listen at him — there he goes!" although that part is doubtful, since some nights there were so many good old boys taking off down the road in supercharged automobiles out of Wilkes County, and running loads to Charlotte, Salisbury, Greensboro, Winston-Salem, High Point, or wherever, it would be pretty hard to pick out one. It was Junior Johnson specifically, however, who was famous for the "bootleg turn" or "about-face," in which, if the Alcohol Tax agents had a roadblock up for you or were too close behind, you threw the car up into second gear, cocked the wheel, stepped on the accelerator and made the car's rear end skid around in a complete 180-degree arc, a complete about-face, and tore on back up the road exactly the way you came from. God! The Alcohol Tax agents used to burn over Junior Johnson.

Practically every good old boy in town in Wilkesboro, the county seat, got to know the agents by sight in a very short time. They would rag them practically to their faces on the subject of Junior Johnson, so that it got to be an obsession. Finally, one night they had Junior trapped on the road up toward the bridge around Millersville, there's no way out of there, they had the barricades up and they could hear this souped-up car roaring around the bend, and here it comes — but suddenly they can hear a siren and see a red light flashing in the grille, so they think it's another agent, and boy, they run out like ants and pull those barrels and boards and sawhorses out of the way, and then — Ggghhzzzzzzz-hhhhhhgggggggzzzzzzzeeeeeong! — gawdam! there he goes again, it was him, Junior Johnson! with a gawdam agent's si-reen and a red light in his grille!

I wasn't in the South five minutes before people started making oaths, having visions, telling these hulking great stories, all on the subject of Junior Johnson. At the Greensboro, North Carolina, Airport there was one good old boy who vowed he would have eaten "a bucket of it" if that would have kept Junior Johnson from switching from a Dodge racer to a Ford. Hell yes, and after that — God-almighty, remember that 1963 Chevrolet of Junior's? Whatever happened to that car? A couple of more good old boys join in. A good old boy, I ought to explain, is a generic term in the rural South referring to a man, of any age, but more often young than not, who fits in with the status system of the region. It usually means he has a good sense of humor and enjoys ironic jokes, is tolerant and easygoing enough to get along in long conversations at places like on the corner, and has a reasonable amount of physical courage. The term is usually heard in some such form as: "Lud? He's a good old boy from over at Crozet." These good old boys in the airport, by the way, were in their twenties, except for one fellow who was a cabdriver and was about forty-five, I would say. Except for the cabdriver, they all wore neo-Brummellian clothes such as Lacoste tennis shirts, Slim Jim pants, windbreakers with the collars turned up, "fast" shoes of the winkle-picker genre, and so on. I mention these details just by way of pointing out that very few grits, Iron Boy overalls, clodhoppers or hats with ventilation holes up near the crown enter into this story. Anyway, these good old boys are talking about Junior Johnson and how he has switched to Ford. This they unanimously regard as some kind of betrayal on Johnson's part. Ford, it seems, they regard as the car symbolizing the established power structure. Dodge is kind of a middle ground. Dodge is at least a challenger, not a ruler. But the Junior

Johnson they like to remember is the Junior Johnson of 1963, who took on the whole field of NASCAR (National Association For Stock Car Auto Racing) Grand National racing with a Chevrolet. All the other drivers, the drivers driving Fords, Mercurys, Plymouths, Dodges, had millions, literally millions when it is all added up, millions of dollars in backing from the Ford and Chrysler Corporations. Junior Johnson took them all on in a Chevrolet without one cent of backing from Detroit. Chevrolet had pulled out of stock car racing. Yet every race it was the same. It was never a question of whether anybody was going to *outrun* Junior Johnson. It was just a question of whether he was going to win or his car was going to break down, since, for one thing, half the time he had to make his own racing parts. God! Junior Johnson was like Robin Hood or Jesse James or Little David or something. Every time that Chevrolet, No. 3, appeared on the track, wild curdled yells, "Rebel" yells, they still have those, would rise up. At Daytona, at Atlanta, at Charlotte, at Darlington, South Carolina; Bristol, Tennessee; Martinsville, Virginia — Junior Johnson!

And then the good old boys get to talking about whatever happened to that Chevrolet of Junior's, and the cabdriver says he knows. He says Junior Johnson is using that car to run liquor out of Wilkes County. What does he mean? For Junior Johnson ever to go near another load of bootleg whiskey again — he would have to be insane. He has this huge racing income. He has two other businesses, a whole automated chicken farm with 42,000 chickens, a road-grading business — but the cab-driver says he has this dream Junior is still roaring down from Wilkes County, down through the clay cuts, with the Atlas Arc Lip jars full in the back of that Chevrolet. It is in Junior's blood — and then at this point he puts his right hand up in front of him as if he is groping through fog, and his eyeballs glaze over and he looks out in the distance and he describes Junior Johnson roaring over the ridges of Wilkes County as if it is the ghost of Zapata he is describing, bounding over the Sierras on a white horse to rouse the peasants.

A stubborn notion! A crazy notion! Yet Junior Johnson has followers who need to keep him, symbolically, riding through nighttime like a demon. Madness! But Junior Johnson is one of the last of those sports stars who is not just an ace at the game itself, but a hero a whole people or class of people can identify with. Other, older examples are the way Jack Dempsey stirred up the Irish or the way Joe Louis stirred up the Negroes. Junior Johnson is a modern figure. He is only thirty-three years old and still racing. He should be compared to two other sports heroes whose cultural impact is not too well known. One is Antonino Rocca, the professional wrestler, whose triumphs mean so much to New York City's Puerto Ricans that he can fill Madison Square Garden, despite the fact that everybody, the Puerto Ricans included, knows that wrestling is nothing but a crude form of folk theatre. The other is Ingemar Johanssen, who had a tremendous meaning to the Swedish masses — they were tired of that old king who played tennis all the time and all his friends who keep on drinking Cointreau behind the screen of socialism. Junior Johnson is a modern hero, all involved with car culture and car symbolism in the South. A wild new thing —

Wild — gone wild, Fireball Roberts' Ford spins out on the first turn at the North Wilkesboro Speedway, spinning, spinning, the spin seems almost like slow motion — and then it smashes into the wooden guard-rail. It lies up there with the frame bent. Roberts is all right. There is a new layer of asphalt on the track, it is like glass, the cars keep spinning off the first turn. Ned Jarrett spins, smashes through the wood. "Now, boys, this ice ain't gonna get one goddamn bit better, so you can either line up and qualify or pack up and go home — "

I had driven from the Greensboro Airport up to Wilkes County to see Junior Johnson on the occasion of one of the two yearly NASCAR Grand National stock car races at the North Wilkesboro Speedway.

It is a long, very gradual climb from Greensboro to Wilkes County. Wilkes County is all hills, ridges, woods and underbrush, full of pin oaks, sweet-gum maples, ash, birch, apple trees, rhododendron, rocks, vines, tin roofs, little clapboard places like the Mount Olive Baptist Church, signs for things like Double Cola, Sherrill's Ice Cream, Eckard's Grocery, Dr. Pepper, Diel's Apples, Google's Place, Suddith's Place and — yes! — cars. Up onto the highway, out of a side road from a hollow, here comes a 1947 Hudson. To almost anybody it would look like just some old piece of junk left over from God knows when, rolling down a country road . . . the 1947 Hudson was one of the first real "hot" cars made after the war. Some of the others were the 1946 Chrysler, which had a "kick-down" gear for sudden bursts of speed, the 1955 Pontiac and a lot of the Fords. To a great many good old boys a hot car was a symbol of heating up life itself. The war! Money even for country boys! And the money bought cars. In California they suddenly found kids of all sorts involved in vast drag racing orgies and couldn't figure out what was going on. But in the South the mania for cars was even more intense, although much less publicized. To millions of good old boys, and girls, the automobile represented not only liberation from what was still pretty much a land-bound form of social organization but also a great leap forward into twentieth-century glamour, an idea that was being dinned in on the South like everywhere else. It got so that one of the typical rural sights, in addition to the red rooster, the gray split-rail fence, the Edgeworth Tobacco sign and the rusted-out harrow, one of the typical rural sights would be . . . you would be driving along the dirt roads and there beside the house would be an automobile up on blocks or something, with a rope over the tree for hoisting up the motor or some other heavy part, and a couple of good old boys would be practically disappearing into its innards, from below and from above, draped over the side under the hood. It got so that on Sundays there wouldn't be a safe straight stretch of road in the county, because so many wild country boys would be out racing or just raising hell on the roads. A lot of other kids, who weren't basically wild, would be driving like hell every morning and every night, driving to jobs perhaps thirty or forty miles away, jobs that were available only because of automobiles. In the morning they would be driving through the dapple shadows like madmen. In the hollows, sometimes one would come upon the most incredible tar-paper hovels, down near the stream, and out front would be an incredible automobile creation, a late-model car with aerials, Continental kit overhangs in the back, mudguards studded with reflectors, fender skirts, spotlights, God knows what all, with a girl and perhaps a couple of good old boys communing over it and giving you rotten looks as you drive by. On Saturday night everybody would drive into town and park under the lights on the main street and neck. Yes! There was something about being right in there in town underneath the lights and having them reflecting off the baked enamel on the hood. Then if a good old boy insinuated his hands here and there on the front seat with a girl and began . . . necking . . . somehow it was all more *complete*. After the war there was a great deal of stout-burgher talk about people who lived in hovels and bought big-yacht cars to park out front. This was one of the symbols of a new, spendthrift age. But there was a great deal of unconscious resentment buried in the talk. It was resentment against (a) the fact that the good old boy had his money at all and (b) the fact that the car symbolized freedom, a slightly wild, careening emancipation from the old social order. Stock car racing got started about this time, right after the war, and it was immediately regarded as some kind of manifestation of the animal irresponsibility of the lower orders. It had a truly terrible reputation. It was — well, it looked *rowdy* or something. The cars were likely to be used cars, the tracks were dirt, the stands were rickety wood, the drivers were country boys, and they had regular feuds out there, putting each other "up against the wall" and "cutting tires" and everything else. Those country boys would drive into the curves full tilt, then slide maniacally, sometimes coming around the curve sideways, with red dirt showering up. Sometimes they would race at night, under those weak-eyed yellow-ochre lights they have at small tracks and baseball fields, and the clay dust would start showering up in the air, where the evening dew would catch it, and all evening long you would be sitting in the stands or standing out in the infield with a fine clay-mud drizzle coming down on you, not that anybody gave a damn — except for the Southern upper and middle classes, who never attended in those days, but spoke of the "rowdiness."

But mainly it was the fact that stock car racing was something that was welling up out of the lower orders. From somewhere these country boys and urban proles were getting the money and starting this hellish sport.

Stock car racing was beginning all over the country, at places like Allentown, Langhorne, and Lancaster, Pennsylvania, and out in California and even out on Long Island, but wherever it cropped up, the Establishment tried to wish it away, largely, and stock car racing went on in a kind of underground world of tracks built on cheap stretches of land well out from the town or the city, a world of diners, drive-ins, motels, gasoline stations, and the good burghers might drive by from time to time, happen by on a Sunday or something, and see the crowd gathered from out of nowhere, the cars coming in, crowding up the highway a little, but Monday morning they would be all gone, and all would be as it was.

Stock car racing was building up a terrific following in the South during the early fifties. Here was a sport not using any abstract devices, any *bat* and *ball*, but the same automobile that was changing a man's own life, his own symbol of liberation, and it didn't require size, strength, and all that, all it required was a taste for speed, and the guts. The newspapers in the South didn't seem to catch onto what was happening until late in the game. Of course, newspapers all over the country have looked backward over the tremendous rise in automobile sports, now the second-biggest type of sports in the country in terms of attendance. The sports pages generally have an inexorable lower-middle-class outlook. The sportswriter's "zest for life" usually amounts, in the end, to some sort of gruff Mom's Pie sentimentality at a hideously cozy bar somewhere. The sportswriters caught onto Grand Prix racing first because it had "tone," a touch of defrocked European nobility about it, what with a few counts racing here and there, although, in fact, it is the least popular form of racing in the United States. What finally put stock car racing onto the sports pages in the South was the intervention of the Detroit automobile firms. Detroit began putting so much money into the sport that it took on a kind of massive economic respectability and thereby, in the lower-middle-class brain, status.

What Detroit discovered was that thousands of good old boys in the South were starting to form allegiances to brands of automobiles, according to which were hottest on the stock car circuits, the way they used to have them for the hometown baseball team. The South was one of the hottest car-buying areas in the country. Cars like Hudsons, Oldsmobiles and Lincolns, not the cheapest automobiles by any means, were selling in disproportionate numbers in the South, and a lot of young good old boys were buying them. In 1955, Pontiac started easing into stock car racing, and suddenly the big surge was on. Everybody jumped into the sport to grab for themselves The Speed Image. Suddenly, where a good old boy used to have to bring his gasoline to the track in old filling-station pails and pour it into the tank through a funnel when he made a pit stop, and change his tires with a hand wrench, suddenly, now, he had these "gravity" tanks of gasoline that you just jam into the gas pipe, and air wrenches to take the wheels off, and whole crews of men in white coveralls to leap all over a car when it came rolling into the pit, just like they do at Indianapolis, as if they are mechanical apparati *merging* with the machine as it rolls in, forcing water into the radiator, jacking up the car, taking off wheels, wiping off the windshield, handing the driver a cup of orange juice, all in one synchronized operation. And now, today, the *big money* starts descending on this little place, the North Wilkesboro, North Carolina, Speedway, a little five-eighths-of-a-mile stock car track with a Coca-Cola sign out by the highway where the road in starts.

The private planes start landing out at the Wilkesboro Airport. Freddie Lorenzen, the driver, the biggest money winner last year in stock car racing, comes sailing in out of the sky in a twin-engine Aero Commander, and there are a few good old boys out there in the tall grass by the runway already with their heads sticking up watching this hero of the modern age come in and taxi up and get out of that twin-engine airplane with his blonde hair swept back as if by the mother internal combustion engine of them all. And then Paul Goldsmith, the driver, comes in in a 310 Cessna, and *he* gets out, all these tall, lanky hard-boned Americans in their thirties with these great profiles like a comic-strip hero or something, and then Glenn (Fireball) Roberts — Fireball Roberts! — Fireball is *hard*— he comes in in a Comanche 250, like a flying yacht, and then Ray Nichels and Ray Fox, the chief mechanics, who run big racing crews for the Chrysler Corporation, this being Fox's last race for Junior as his mechanic, before Junior switches over to Ford, they come in in two-engine planes. And even old Buck Baker — hell, Buck Baker is a middling driver for Dodge, but even he comes rolling in down the landing strip at two hundred miles an hour with his South-ern-hero face at the window of the cockpit of a twin-engine Apache, traveling first class in the big status boat that has replaced the yacht in America, the private plane.

And then the Firestone and Goodyear vans pull in, huge mothers, bringing in huge stacks of racing tires for the race, big wide ones, 8.20's, with special treads, which are like a lot of bumps on the tire instead of grooves. They even have special tires for qualifying, soft tires, called "gumballs," they wouldn't last more than ten times around the track in a race, but for qualifying, which is generally three laps, one to pick up speed and two to race against the clock, they are great, because they hold tight on the corners. And on a hot day, when somebody like Junior Johnson, one of the fastest qualifying runners in the history of the sport, 170.777 m.p.h. in a one-hundred-mile qualifying race at Daytona in 1964, when somebody like Junior Johnson really pushes it on a qualifying run, there will be a ring of blue smoke up over the whole goddamned track, a ring like an oval halo over the whole thing from the gumballs burning, and some good old boy will say, "Great smokin' blue gumballs god almighty dog! There goes Junior Johnson!"

The thing is, each one of these tires costs fifty-five to sixty dollars, and on a track that is fast and hard on tires, like Atlanta, one car might go through ten complete tire changes, easily, forty tires, or almost $2500 worth of tires just for one race. And he may even be out of the money. And then the Ford van and the Dodge van and the Mercury van and the Plymouth van roll in with new motors, a whole new motor every few races, a 427-cubic-inch stock car racing motor, 600 horsepower, the largest and most powerful allowed on the track, that probably costs the company $1000 or more, when you consider that they are not mass produced. And still the advertising appeal. You can buy the very same car that these fabulous wild men drive every week at these fabulous wild speeds, and some of their power and charisma is yours. After every

NASCAR Grand National stock car race, whichever company has the car that wins, this company will put big ads in the Southern papers, and papers all over the country if it is a very big race, like the Daytona 500, the Daytona Firecracker 400 or the Atlanta and Charlotte races. They sell a certain number of these 427-cubic-inch cars to the general public, a couple of hundred a year, perhaps, at eight or nine thousand dollars apiece, but it is no secret that these motors are specially reworked just for stock car racing. Down at Charlotte there is a company called Holman & Moody that is supposed to be the "garage" or "automotive-engineering" concern that prepares automobiles for Freddie Lorenzen and some of the other Ford drivers. But if you go by Holman & Moody out by the airport and Charlotte, suddenly you come upon a huge place that is a *factory*, for godsake, a big long thing, devoted mainly to the business of turning out stock car racers. A whole lot of other parts in stock car racers are heavier than the same parts on a street automobile, although they are made to the same scale. The shock absorbers are bigger, the wheels are wider and bulkier, the swaybars and steering mechanisms are heavier, the axles are much heavier, they have double sets of wheel bearings, and so forth and so on. The bodies of the cars are pretty much the same, except that they use lighter sheet metal, practically tinfoil. Inside, there is only the driver's seat and a heavy set of roll bars and diagonal struts that turn the inside of the car into a rigid cage, actually. That is why the drivers can walk away unhurt — most of the time — from the most spectacular crackups. The gearshift is the floor kind, although it doesn't make much difference, as there is almost no shifting gears in stock car racing. You just get into high gear and go. The dashboard has no speedometer, the main thing being the dial for engine revolutions per minute. So, anyway, it costs about $15,000 to prepare a stock car racer in the first place and another three or four thousand for each new race and this does not even count the costs of mechanics' work and transportation. All in all, Detroit will throw around a quarter of a million dollars into it every week while the season is on, and the season runs, roughly, from February to October, with a few big races after that. And all this turns up even out at the North Wilkesboro Speedway in the up-country of Wilkes County, North Carolina.

Sunday! Racing day! There is the Coca-Cola sign out where the road leads in from the highway, and hills and trees, but here are long concrete grandstands for about 17,000 and a paved five-eighths-mile oval. Practically all the drivers are out there with their cars and their crews, a lot of guys in white coveralls. The cars look huge . . . and curiously nude and blind. All the chrome is stripped off, except for the grilles. The headlights are blanked out. Most of the cars are in the pits. The so-called "pit" is a paved cutoff on the edge of the infield. It cuts off from the track itself like a service road off an expressway at the shopping center. Every now and then a car splutters, hacks, coughs, hocks a lunga, rumbles out onto the track itself for a practice run. There is a lot of esoteric conversation going on, speculation, worries, memoirs:

"What happened?"

"Mother— condensed on me. Al brought it up here with him. Water in the line."

"Better keep Al away from a stable, he'll fill you up with horse manure."

". . . they told me to give him one, a creampuff, so I give him one, a creampuff. One goddam race and the son of a bitch, he *melted* it. . . ."

". . . he's down there right now pettin' and rubbin' and huggin' that car just like those guys do a horse at the Kentucky Derby. . . ."

". . . They'll blow you right out of the tub. . . ."

". . . No, the quarter inch, and go on over and see if you can get Ned's blowtorch. . . ."

". . . Rear end's loose. . . ."

". . . I don't reckon this right here's got nothing to do with it, do you? . . ."

". . . Aw, I don't know, about yea big. . . ."

". . . Who the hell stacked them gumballs on the bottom? . . ."

". . . th'owing rocks. . . ."

". . . won't turn seven thousand. . . ."

". . . strokin' it. . . ."

". . . blistered. . . ."

". . . spun out. . . ."

". . . muvva. . . ."

Then, finally, here comes Junior Johnson. How he does come on. He comes tooling across the infield in a big white dreamboat, a brand-new white Pontiac Catalina four-door hard-top sedan. He pulls up and as he gets out he seems to get more and more huge. First his crew-cut head and then a big jaw and then a bigger neck and then a huge torso, like a wrestler's, all done up rather modish and California modern, with a red-and-white candy-striped sport shirt, white ducks and loafers.

"How you doing?" says Junior Johnson, shaking hands, and then he says, "Hot enough for ye'uns?"

Junior is in an amiable mood. Like most up-hollow people, it turns out, Junior is reserved. His face seldom shows an emotion. He has three basic looks: amiable, amiable and a little shy, and dead serious. To a lot of people, apparently, Junior's dead-serious look seems menacing. There are no cowards left in stock car racing, but a couple of drivers tell me that one of the things that can shake you up is to look into your rear-view mirror going around a curve and see Junior Johnson's car on your tail trying to "root you out of the groove," and then get a glimpse of Junior's dead-serious look. I think some of the sportswriters are afraid of him. One of them tells me Junior is strong, silent — and explosive. Junior will only give you three answers, "Uh-huh," "Uh-unh," and "I don' know," and so forth and so on. Actually, I found he handles questions easily. He has a great technical knowledge of automobiles and the physics of speed, including things he never fools with, such as Offenhauser engines. What he never does offer, however, is small talk. This gives him a built-in poise, since it deprives him of the chance to say anything asinine. "Ye'uns," "we'uns," "H'it" for "it," "growed" for "grew" and a lot of other unusual past participles — Junior uses certain older forms of English, not exactly "Elizabethan," as they are sometimes called, but older forms of English preserved up-country in his territory, Ingle Hollow.

Kids keep coming up for Junior's autograph and others are just hanging around and one little boy comes up, he is about thirteen, and Junior says: "This boy here goes coon hunting with me."

One of the sportswriters is standing around, saying: "What do you shoot a coon with?"

"Don't shoot 'em. The dogs tree 'em and then you flush 'em out and the dogs fight 'em."

"Flush 'em out?"

"Yeah. This boy right here can flush 'em out better than anybody you ever did see. You go out at night with the dogs, and soon as they get the scent, they start barking. They go on out ahead of you and when they tree a coon, you can tell it, by the way they sound. They all start baying up at that coon — h'it sounds like, I don't know, you hear it once and you not likely to forget it. Then you send a little old boy up to flush him out and he jumps down and the dogs fight him."

"How does a boy flush him out?"

"Aw, he just climbs up there to the limb he's on and starts shaking h'it and the coon'll jump."

"What happens if the coon decides he'd rather come back after the boy instead of jumping down to a bunch of dogs?"

"He won't do that. A coon's afraid of a person, but he can kill a dog. A coon can take any dog you set against him if they's just the two of them fighting. The coon jumps down on the ground and he rolls right over on his back with his feet up, and he's *got* claws about like this. All he has to do is get a dog once in the throat or in the belly, and he can kill him, cut him wide open just like you took a knife and did it. Won't any dog even fight a coon except a coon dog."

"What kind of dogs are they?"

"*Coon* dogs, I guess. Black and tans they call 'em sometimes. They's bred for it. If his mammy and pappy wasn't coon dogs, he ain't likely to be one either. After you got one, you got to train him. You trap a coon, live, and then you put him in a pen and tie him to a post with a rope on him and then you put your dog in there and he has to fight him. Sometimes you get a dog just don't have any fight in him and he ain't no good to you."

Junior is in the pit area, standing around with his brother Fred, who is part of his crew, and Ray Fox and some other good old boys, in a general atmosphere of big stock car money, a big ramp truck for his car, a white Dodge, number 3, a big crew in white coveralls, huge stacks of racing tires, a Dodge P.R. man, big portable cans of gasoline, compressed air hoses, compressed water hoses, the whole business. Herb Nab, Freddie Lorenzen's chief mechanic, comes over and sits down on his haunches and Junior sits down on his haunches and Nab says:

"So Junior Johnson's going to drive a Ford."

Junior is switching from Dodge to Ford mainly because he hasn't been winning with the Dodge. Lorenzen drives a Ford, too, and the last year, when Junior was driving the Chevrolet, their duels were the biggest excitement in stock car racing.

"Well," says Nab, "I'll tell you, Junior. My ambition is going to be to outrun your ass every goddamned time we go out."

"That was your ambition last year," says Junior.

"I know it was," says Nab. "and you took all the money, didn't you? You know what my strategy was. I was going to outrun everybody else and outlast Junior, that was my strategy."

Setting off his California modern sport shirt and white ducks Junior has on a pair of twenty-dollar rimless sunglasses and a big gold Timex watch, and Flossie, his fiancée, is out there in the infield somewhere with the white Pontiac, and the white Dodge that Dodge gave Junior is parked up near the pit area — and then a little thing happens that brings the whole thing right back there to Wilkes County, North Carolina, to Ingle Hollow and to hard muscle in the clay gulches. A couple of good old boys come down to the front of the stands with the screen and the width of the track between them and Junior, and one of the good old boys comes down and yells out in the age-old baritone raw-curdle yell of the Southern hills:

"Hey! Hog jaw!"

Everybody gets quiet. They know he's yelling at Junior, but nobody says a thing. Junior doesn't even turn around.

"Hey, hog jaw! . . ."

Junior, he does nothing.

"Hey, hog jaw, I'm gonna get me one of them fastback roosters, too, and come down there and get you!"

Fastback rooster refers to the Ford — it has a "fastback" design — Junior is switching to.

"Hey, hog jaw, I'm gonna get me one of them fastback roosters and run you right out of here, you hear me, hog jaw!"

One of the good old boys alongside Junior says, "Junior, go on up there and clear out those stands."

Then everybody stares at Junior to see what he's gonna do. Junior, he don't even look around. He just looks a bit dead serious.

"Hey, hog jaw, you got six cases of whiskey in the back of that car you want to let me have?"

"What you hauling in that car, hog jaw!"

"Tell him you're out of that business, Junior," one of the good old boys says.

"Go on up there and clean house, Junior," says another good old boy.

Then Junior looks up, without looking at the stands, and smiles a little and says, "You flush him down here out of that tree — and I'll take keer of him."

Such a howl goes up from the good old boys! It is almost a blood curdle —

"Goddamn, he *will*, too!"

"Lord, he better know how to do an *about-face* hissef if he comes down here!"

"Goddam, get him, Junior!"

"Whooeeee!"

"Mother dog!"

— a kind of orgy of reminiscence of the old Junior before the Detroit money started flowing, wild *combats d'honneur* up-hollow — and, suddenly, when he heard that unearthly baying coming up from the good old boys in the pits, the good old boy retreated from the edge of the stands and never came back.

Later on Junior told me, sort of apologetically, "H'it used to be, if a fellow crowded me just a little bit, I was ready to crawl him. I reckon that was one good thing about Chillicothe.

"I don't want to pull any more time," Junior tells me, "but I wouldn't take anything in the world for the experience I had in prison. If a man needed to change, that was the place to change. H'it's not a waste of time there, h'it's good experience.

"H'it's that they's so many people in the world that feel that nobody is going to tell them what to do. I had quite a temper, I reckon. I always had the idea that I had as much sense as the other person and I didn't want them to tell me what to do. In the penitentiary there I found out that I could listen to another fellow and be told what to do and h'it wouldn't kill me."

Starting time! Linda Vaughn, with the big blonde hair and blossomy breasts, puts down her Coca-Cola and the potato chips and slips off her red stretch pants and her white blouse and walks out of the officials' booth in her Rake-a-cheek red show-girl's costume with her long honeydew legs in net stockings and climbs up on the red Firebird float. The Life Symbol of stock car racing! Yes! Linda, every luscious morsel of Linda, is a good old girl from Atlanta who was made Miss Atlanta International Raceway one year and was paraded around the track on a float and she liked it so much and all the good old boys liked it so much, Linda's flowing hair and blossomy breasts and honeydew legs, that she became the permanent glamor symbol of stock car racing, and never mind this other modeling she was doing . . . this, she liked it. Right before practically every race on the Grand National circuit Linda Vaughn puts down her Coca-Cola and potato chips. Her momma is there, she generally comes around to see Linda go around the track on the float, it's such a nice spectacle seeing Linda looking so lovely, and the applause and all. "Linda, I'm thirstin', would you bring me a Coca-Cola?" "A lot of them think I'm Freddie Lorenzen's girl friend, but I'm not any of 'em's girl friend, I'm real good friends with 'em all, even Wendell," he being Wendell Scott, the only Negro in big-league stock car racing. Linda gets up on the Firebird float. This is an extraordinary object, made of wood, about twenty feet tall, in the shape of a huge bird, an eagle or something, blazing red, and Linda, with her red show-girl's suit on, gets up on the seat, which is up between the wings, like a saddle, high enough so her long honeydew legs stretch down, and a new car pulls her — Miss Firebird! — slowly once around the track just before the race. It is more of a ceremony by now than the national anthem. Miss Firebird sails slowly in front of the stands and the good old boys let out some real curdle Rebel yells, "Yaaaaaaaaaaaaaghhhhoooooo! Let me at that car!" "Honey, you sure do start my motor, I swear to God!" "Great God and Poonadingdong, I mean!"

And suddenly there's a big roar from behind, down in the infield, and then I see one of the great sights in stock car racing. That infield! The cars have been piling into the infield by the hundreds, parking in there on the clay and the grass, every which way, angled down and angled up, this way and that, where the ground is uneven, these beautiful blazing brand-new cars with the sun exploding off the windshields and the baked enamel and the glassy lacquer, hundreds, thousands of cars stacked this way and that in the infield with the sun bolting down and no shade, none at all, just a couple of Coca-Cola stands out there. And already the good old boys and girls are out beside the cars, with all these beautiful little buds in short shorts already spread-eagled out on top of the car roofs, pressing down on good hard slick automobile sheet metal, their little cupcake bottoms aimed up at the sun. The good old boys are lollygagging around with their shirts off and straw hats on that have miniature beer cans on the brims and buttons that read, "Girls Wanted — No Experience Required." And everybody, good old boys and girls of all ages, is out there with portable charcoal barbecue ovens set up, and folding tubular steel terrace furniture, deck chairs and things, and Thermos jugs and coolers full of beer — and suddenly it is not the up-country South at all but a concentration of the modern suburbs, all jammed into that one space, from all over America, with blazing cars and instant goodies, all cooking under the bare blaze — inside a strange bowl. The infield is like the bottom of a bowl. The track around it is banked so steeply at the corners and even on the straightaways, it is like the steep sides of a bowl. The wall around the track, and the stands and the bleachers are like the rim of a bowl. And from the infield, in this great incredible press of blazing new cars, there is no horizon but the bowl, up above only that cobalt-blue North Carolina sky. And then suddenly, on a signal, thirty stock car engines start up where they are lined up in front of the stands. The roar of these engines is impossible to describe. They have a simultaneous rasp, thunder and rumble that goes right through a body and fills the whole bowl with a noise of internal combustion. Then they start around on two buildup runs, just to build up speed, and then they come around the fourth turn and onto the straightaway in front of the stands at — here, 130 miles an hour, in Atlanta, 160 miles an hour, at Daytona, 180 miles an hour — and the flag goes down and everybody in the infield and in the stands is up on their feet going mad, and suddenly here is a bowl that is one great orgy of everything in the way of excitement and liberation the automobile has meant to Americans. An orgy!

The first lap of a stock car race is a horrendous, a wildly horrendous spectacle such as no other sport approaches. Twenty, thirty, forty automobiles, each of them weighing almost two tons, 3700 pounds, with 427-cubic-inch engines, 600 horsepower, are practically locked together, side to side and tail to nose, on a narrow band of asphalt at 130, 160, 180 miles an hour, hitting the curves so hard the rubber burns off the tires in front of your eyes. To the driver, it is like being inside a car going down the West Side Highway in New York City at rush hour, only with everybody going literally three to four times as fast, at speeds a man who has gone eighty-five miles an hour down a highway cannot conceive of, and with every other driver an enemy who is willing to cut inside of you, around you or in front of you, or ricochet off your side in the battle to get into a curve first.

The speeds are faster than those in the Indianapolis 500 race, the cars are more powerful and much heavier. The prize money in Southern stock car racing is far greater than that in Indianapolis-style or European Grand Prix racing, but few Indianapolis or Grand Prix drivers have the raw nerve required to succeed at it.

Although they will deny it, it is still true that stock-car drivers will put each other "up against the wall" — cut inside on the left of another car and ram it into a spin — if they get mad enough. Crashes are not the only danger, however. The cars are now literally too fast for their own parts, especially the tires. Firestone and Goodyear have poured millions into stock car racing, but neither they nor anybody so far has been able to come up with a tire for this kind of racing at the current speeds. Three well-known stock car drivers were killed last year, two of them champion drivers, Joe Weatherly and Fireball Roberts, and another, one of the best new drivers, Jimmy Pardue, from Junior Johnson's own home territory, Wilkes County, North Carolina. Roberts was the only one killed in a crash. Junior Johnson was in the crash but was not injured. Weatherly and Pardue both lost control on curves. Pardue's death

came during a tire test. In a tire test, engineers from Firestone or Goodyear try out various tires on a car, and the driver, always one of the top
competitors, tests them at top speed, usually on the Atlanta track. The
drivers are paid three dollars a mile and may drive as much as five or six
hundred miles in a single day. At 145 miles an hour average that does not
take very long. Anyway, these drivers are going at speeds that, on curves,
can tear tires off their casings or break axles. They practically run off
from over their own wheels.

Junior Johnson was over in the garden by the house some years ago,
plowing the garden barefooted, behind a mule, just wearing an old pair
of overalls, when a couple of good old boys drove up and told him to
come on up to the speedway and get in a stock car race. They wanted
some local boys to race, as a preliminary to the main race, "as a kind of
side show," as Junior remembers it.

"So I just put the reins down," Junior is telling me, "and rode on over
'ere with them. They didn't give us seat belts or nothing, they just roped
us in. H'it was a dirt track then. I come in second."

Junior was a sensation in dirt-track racing right from the start. Instead of going into the curves and just sliding and holding on for dear
life like the other drivers, Junior developed the technique of throwing
himself into a slide about seventy-five feet before the curve by cock-
ing the wheel to the left slightly and gunning it, using the slide, not
the brake, to slow down, so that he could pick up speed again halfway
through the curve and come out of it like a shot. This was known as his
"power slide," and — yes! of course! — every good old boy in North
Carolina started saying Junior Johnson had learned that stunt doing
those goddamned *about-faces* running away from the Alcohol Tax
agents. Junior put on such a show one night on a dirt track in Charlotte
that he broke two axles, and he thought he was out of the race because
he didn't have any more axles, when a good old boy came running up
out of the infield and said, "Goddamn it, Junior Johnson, you take the
axle off my car here, I got a Pontiac just like yours," and Junior took it
off and put it on his and went out and broke *it* too. Mother dog! To this
day Junior Johnson loves dirt track racing like nothing else in this
world, even though there is not much money in it. Every year he sets
new dirt track speed records, such as at Hickory, North Carolina, one of
the most popular dirt tracks, last spring. As far as Junior is concerned,
dirt track racing is not so much of a mechanical test for the car as those
long five- and six-hundred-mile races on asphalt are. Gasoline, tire and

engine wear aren't so much of a problem. It is all the driver, his skill, his courage — his willingness to mix it up with the other cars, smash and carom off of them at a hundred miles an hour or so to get into the curves first. Junior has a lot of fond recollections of mixing it up at places like Bowman Gray Stadium in Winston-Salem, one of the minor league tracks, a very narrow track, hardly wide enough for two cars. "You could always figure Bowman Gray was gonna cost you two fenders, two doors and two quarter panels," Junior tells me with nostalgia.

Anyway, at Hickory, which was a Saturday night race, all the good old boys started pouring into the stands before sundown, so they wouldn't miss anything, the practice runs or the qualifying or anything. And pretty soon, the dew hasn't even started falling before Junior Johnson and David Pearson, one of Dodge's best drivers, are out there on practice runs, just warming up, and they happen to come up alongside each other on the second curve, and — the thing is, here are two men, each of them driving $15,000 automobiles, each of them standing to make $50,000 to $100,000 for the season if they don't get themselves killed, and they meet on a curve on a goddamned practice run on a dirt track, and neither of them can resist it. Coming out of the turn they go into a wildass race down the backstretch, both of them trying to get into the third turn first, and all the way across the infield you can hear them ricocheting off each other and bouncing at a hundred miles an hour on loose dirt, and then they go into ferocious power slides, red dust all over the goddamned place, and then out of this goddamned red-dust cloud, out of the fourth turn, here comes Junior Johnson first, like a shot, with Pearson right on his tail, and the good old boys in the stands going wild, and the *qualifying* runs haven't started yet, let alone the race.

Junior worked his way up through the minor leagues, the Sportsman and Modified classifications, as they are called, winning championships in both, and won his first Grand National race, the big leagues, in 1955 at Hickory, on dirt. He was becoming known as "the hardest of the hard-chargers," power sliding, rooting them out of the groove, raising hell, and already the Junior Johnson legend was beginning.

He kept hard-charging, power sliding, going after other drivers as though there wasn't room on the track but for one, and became the most popular driver in stock car racing by 1959. The presence of Detroit and Detroit's big money had begun to calm the drivers down a little. Detroit was concerned about Image. The last great duel of the dying dog-eat-dog era of stock car racing came in 1959, when Junior and Lee

Petty, who was then leading the league in points, had it out on the Charlotte raceway. Junior was in the lead, and Petty was right on his tail, but couldn't get by Junior. Junior kept coming out of the curves faster. So every chance he got, Petty would get up right on Junior's rear bumper and start banging it, gradually forcing the fender in to where the metal would cut Junior's rear tire. With only a few laps to go, Junior had a blowout and spun out up against the guardrail. That is Junior's version. Petty claimed Junior hit a pop bottle and spun out. The fans in Charlotte were always throwing pop bottles and other stuff onto the track late in the race, looking for blood. In any case, Junior eased back into the pits, had the tire changed, and charged out after Petty. He caught him on a curve and — well, whatever really happened, Petty was suddenly "up against the wall" and out of the race, and Junior won.

What a howl went up. The Charlotte chief of police charged out onto the track after the race, according to Petty, and offered to have Junior arrested for "assault with a dangerous weapon," the hassling went on for weeks —

"Back then," Junior tells me, "when you got into a guy and racked him up, you might as well get ready, because he's coming back for you. H'it was dog eat dog. That straightened Lee Petty out right smart. They don't do stuff like that anymore, though, because the guys don't stand for it."

Anyway, the Junior Johnson legend kept building up and building up, and in 1960 it got hotter than ever when Junior won the biggest race of the year, the Daytona 500, by discovering a new technique called "drafting." That year stock car racing was full of big powerful Pontiacs manned by top drivers, and they would go like nothing else anybody ever saw. Junior went down to Daytona with a Chevrolet.

"My car was about ten miles an hour slower than the rest of the cars, the Pontiacs," Junior tells me. "In the preliminary races, the warm-ups and stuff like that, they was smoking me off the track. Then I remember once I went out for a practice run, and Fireball Roberts was out there in a Pontiac and I got in right behind him on a curve, right on his bumper. I knew I couldn't stay with him on the straightaway, but I came out of the curve fast, right in behind him, running flat out, and then I noticed a funny thing. As long as I stayed right in behind him, I noticed I picked up speed and stayed right with him and my car was going faster than it had ever gone before. I could tell on the tachometer. My car wasn't turning no more than 6000 before, but when I got into this drafting position, I was turning 6800 to 7000. H'it felt like the car was plumb off the ground, floating along."

"Drafting," it was discovered at Daytona, created a vacuum behind the lead car and both cars would go faster than they normally would. Junior "hitched rides" on the Pontiacs most of the afternoon, but was still second to Bobby Johns, the lead Pontiac. Then, late in the race, Johns got into a drafting position with a fellow Pontiac that was actually one lap behind him and the vacuum got so intense that the rear window blew out of Johns' car and he spun out and crashed and Junior won.

This made Junior the Lion Killer, the Little David of stock car racing, and his performance in the 1963 season made him even more so.

Junior raced for Chevrolet at Daytona in February, 1963, and set the all-time stock car speed record in a hundred-mile qualifying race, 164.083 miles an hour, twenty-one miles an hour faster than Parnelli Jones's winning time at Indianapolis that year. Junior topped that at Daytona in July of 1963, qualifying at 166.005 miles per hour in a five-mile run, the fastest that anyone had ever averaged that distance in a racing car of any type. Junior's Chevrolet lasted only twenty-six laps in the Daytona 500 in 1963, however. He went out with a broken push rod. Although Chevrolet announced they were pulling out of racing at this time, Junior took his car and started out on the wildest performance in the history of stock car racing. Chevrolet wouldn't give him a cent of backing. They wouldn't even speak to him on the telephone. Half the time he had to have his own parts made. Plymouth, Mercury, Dodge and Ford, meantime, were pouring more money than ever into stock car racing. Yet Junior won seven Grand National races out of the thirty-three he entered and led most others before mechanical trouble forced him out.

All the while, Junior was making record qualifying runs, year after year. In the usual type of qualifying run, a driver has the track to himself and makes two circuits, with the driver with the fastest average time getting the "pole" position for the start of the race. In a way this presents stock car danger in its purest form. Driving a stock car does not require much handling ability, at least not as compared to Grand Prix racing, because the tracks are simple banked ovals and there is almost no shifting of gears. So qualifying becomes a test of raw nerve — of how fast a man is willing to take a curve. Many of the top drivers in competition are poor at qualifying. In effect, they are willing to calculate their risks only against the risks the other drivers are taking. Junior takes the pure risk as no other driver has ever taken it.

"Pure" risk or total risk, whichever, Indianapolis and Grand Prix drivers have seldom been willing to face the challenge of Southern stock car drivers. A. J. Foyt, last year's winner at Indianapolis, is one exception. He has raced against the Southerners and beaten them. Parnelli Jones has tried and fared badly. Driving "Southern style" has a quality that shakes a man up. The Southerners went on a tour of northern tracks last fall. They raced at Bridgehampton, New York, and went into the corners so hard the marshals stationed at each corner kept radioing frantically to the control booth: "They're going off the track. They're all going off the track!"

But this, Junior Johnson's last race in a Dodge, was not his day, neither for qualifying or racing. Lorenzen took the lead early and won the 250-mile race a lap ahead of the field. Junior finished third, but was never in contention for the lead.

"Come on, Junior, do my hand — "

Two or three hundred people come out of the stands and up out of the infield and onto the track to be around Junior Johnson. Junior is signing autographs in a neat left-handed script he has. It looks like it came right out of the Locker book. The girls! Levis, stretch pants, sneaky shorts, stretch jeans, they press into the crowd with lively narbs and try to get their hands up in front of Junior and say:

"Come on, Junior, do my hand!"

In order to do a hand, Junior has to hold the girl's hand in his right hand and then sign his name with a ball-point on the back of her hand.

"Junior, you got to do mine, too!"

"Put it on up here."

All the girls break into . . . smiles. Junior Johnson does a hand. Ah, sweet little cigarette-ad blonde! She says:

"Junior, why don't you ever call me up?"

"I 'spect you got plenty of calls 'thout me."

"Oh, Junior! You call me up, you hear now?"

But also a great many older people crowd in, and they say:

"Junior, you're doing a real good job out there, you're driving real good."

"Junior, when you get in that Ford, I want to see you pass that Freddie Lorenzen, you hear now?"

"Junior, you like that Ford better than that Dodge?"

And:

"Junior, here's a young man that's been waiting some time and wanting to see you — " and the man lifts up his little boy in the middle of the crowd and says: "I told you you'd see Junior Johnson. This here's Junior Johnson!"

The boy has a souvenir racing helmet on his head. He stares at Junior through a buttery face. Junior signs the program he has in his hand, and then the boy's mother says:

"Junior, I tell you right now, he's beside you all the way. He can't be moved."

And then:

"Junior, I want you to meet the meanest little girl in Wilkes County."

"She don't look mean to me."

Junior keeps signing autographs and over by the pits the other kids are all over his car, the Dodge. They start pulling off the decals, the ones saying Holly Farms Poultry and Autolite and God knows whatall. They fight over the strips, the shreds of decal, as if they were totems.

All this homage to Junior Johnson lasts about forty minutes. He must be signing about 250 autographs, but he is not a happy man. By and by the crowd is thinning out, the sun is going down, wind is blowing the Coca-Cola cups around, all one can hear, mostly, is a stock car engine starting up every now and then as somebody drives it up onto a truck or something, and Junior looks around and says:

"I'd rather lead one lap and fall out of the race than stroke it and finish in the money."

"Stroking it" is driving carefully in hopes of outlasting faster and more reckless cars. The opposite of stroking it is "hard-charging." Then Junior says:

"I hate to get whipped up here in Wilkes County, North Carolina."

Wilkes County, North Carolina! Who was it tried to pin the name on Wilkes County, "The bootleg capital of America"? This fellow Vance Packard. But just a minute . . .

The night after the race Junior and his fiancée, Flossie Clark, and myself went in North Wilkesboro to have dinner. Junior and Flossie came by Lowes Motel and picked us up in the dreamboat white Pontiac. Flossie is a bright, attractive woman, *saftig,* well-organized. She and Junior have been going together since they were in high school. They are going to get married as soon as Junior gets his new house built. Flossie has been doing the decor. Junior Johnson, in the second-highest income bracket in the United States for the past five years, is moving out of his father's white frame house in Ingle Hollow at last. About three hundred yards down the road. Overlooking a lot of good green land and Anderson's grocery. Junior shows me through the house, it is almost finished, and when we get to the front door, I ask him, "How much of this land is yours?"

Junior looks around for a minute, and then back up the hill, up past his three automated chicken houses, and then down into the hollow over the pasture where his $3100 Santa Gertrudis bull is grazing, and then he says:

"Everything that's green is mine."

Junior Johnson's house is going to be one of the handsomest homes in Wilkes County. Yes. And — such complicated problems of class and status. Junior is not only a legendary figure as a backwoods boy with guts who made good, he is also popular personally, he is still a good old boy, rich as he is. He is also respected for the sound and sober way he has invested his money. He also has one of the best business connections in town, Holly Farms Poultry. What complicates it is that half the county, anyway, reveres him as the greatest, most fabled night-road driver in the history of Southern bootlegging. There is hardly a living soul in the hollows who can conjure up two seconds' honest moral indignation over "the whiskey business." That is what they call it, "the whiskey business." The fact is, it has some positive political overtones, sort of like the I.R.A. in Ireland. The other half of the county — well, North Wilkesboro itself is a prosperous, good-looking town of 5,000, where a lot of hearty modern business burghers are making money the modern way, like everywhere else in the U.S.A., in things like banking, poultry processing, furniture, mirror, and carpet manufacture, apple growing, and so forth and so on. And one thing these men are tired of is Wilkes County's reputation as a center of moonshining. The U.S. Alcohol and Tobacco Tax agents sit over there in Wilkesboro, right next to North Wilkesboro, year in and year out, and they have been there since God knows when, like an Institution in the land, and every day that they are there, it is like a sign saying, Moonshine County. And even that is not so *bad* — it has nothing to do with it being immoral and only a little to do with it being illegal. The real thing is, it is — raw and hillbilly. And one thing thriving modern Industry is not is hillbilly. And one thing the burghers of North Wilkesboro are not about to be is hillbilly. They have split-level homes that would knock your eyes out. Also swimming pools, white Buick Snatchwagons, flagstone *terrasse*-porches enclosed with louvered glass that opens wide in the summertime, and built-in brick barbecue pits and they give parties where they wear Bermuda shorts and Jax stretch pants and serve rum collins and play twist and bossa nova records on the hi-fi and tell Shaggy Dog jokes about strange people ordering martinis. Moonshining . . . just a minute — the truth is, North Wilkesboro . . .

So we are all having dinner at one of the fine new restaurants in North Wilkesboro, a place of suburban plate-glass elegance. The manager knows Junior and gives us the best table in the place and comes over and talks to Junior a while about the race. A couple of men get up and come over and get Junior's autograph to take home to their sons and so forth. Then toward the end of the meal a couple of North Wilkesboro businessmen come over ("Junior, how are you, Junior. You think you're going to like that fast-backed Ford?") and Junior introduces them to me.

"You're not going to do like that fellow Vance Packard did, are you?"

"Vance Packard?"

"Yeah, I think it was Vance Packard wrote it. He wrote an article and called Wilkes County the bootleg capital of America. Don't pull any of that stuff. I think it was in *American* magazine. The bootleg capital of America. Don't pull any of that stuff on us."

I looked over at Junior and Flossie. Neither one of them said anything. They didn't even change their expressions.

The next morning I met Junior down in Ingle Hollow at Anderson's Store. That's about fifteen miles out of North Wilkesboro on County Road No. 2400. Junior is known in a lot of Southern newspapers as "the wild man from Ronda" or "the lead-footed chicken farmer from Ronda," but Ronda is only his post-office-box address. His telephone exchange, with the Wilkes Telephone Membership Corporation, is Clingman, North Carolina, and that isn't really where he lives either. Where he lives is just Ingle Hollow, and one of the communal centers of Ingle Hollow is Anderson's Store. Anderson's is not exactly a grocery store. Out front there are two gasoline pumps under an overhanging roof. Inside there are a lot of things like a soda-pop cooler filled with ice, Coca-Colas, Nehi drinks, Dr. Pepper, Double Cola, and a gumball machine, a lot of racks of Red Man chewing tobacco, Price's potato chips, OKay peanuts, cloth hats for working outdoors in, dried sausages, cigarettes, canned goods, a little bit of meal and flour, fly swatters, and I don't know what all. Inside and outside of Anderson's there are good old boys. The young ones tend to be inside, talking, and the old ones tend to be outside, sitting under the roof by the gasoline pumps, talking. And on both sides, cars; most of them new and pastel.

Junior drives up and gets out and looks up over the door where there is a row of twelve coon tails. Junior says:

"Two of them gone, ain't they?"

One of the good old boys says, "Yeah," and sighs.

A pause, and the other one says, "Somebody stole 'em."

Then the first one says, "Junior, that dog of yours ever come back?"

Junior says, "Not yet."

The second good old boy says, "You looking for her to come back?"

Junior says, "I reckon she'll come back."

The good old boy says, "I had a coon dog went off like that. They don't ever come back. I went out 'ere one day, back over yonder, and there he was, cut right from here to here. I swear if it don't look like a coon got him. Something. H'it must of turned him every way but loose."

Junior goes inside and gets a Coca-Cola and rings up the till himself, like everybody who goes into Anderson's does, it seems like. It is dead quiet in the hollow except for every now and then a car grinds over the dirt road and down the way. One coon dog missing. But he still has a lot of the black and tans, named Rock. . . .

. . . Rock, Whitey, Red, Buster are in the pen out back of the Johnson house, the old frame house. They have scars all over their faces from fighting coons. Gypsy has one huge gash in her back from fighting something. A red rooster crosses the lawn. That's a big rooster. Shirley, one of Junior's two younger sisters, pretty girls, is out by the fence in shorts, pulling weeds. Annie May is inside the house with Mrs. Johnson. Shirley has the radio outside on the porch aimed at her, The Four Seasons! "Dawn! — ahhhh, ahhhhh, ahhhhhh!" Then a lot of electronic wheeps and lulus and a screaming disc jockey, yessss! WTOB, the Vibrant Mothering Voice of Winston-Salem, North Carolina. It sounds like WABC in New York. Junior's mother, Mrs. Johnson, is a big, good-natured woman. She comes out and says, "Did you ever see anything like that in your life? Pullin' weeds listenin' to the radio." Junior's father, Robert Glenn Johnson, Sr. — he built this frame house about thirty-five years ago, up here where the gravel road ends and the woods starts. The road just peters out into the woods up a hill. The house has a living room, four bedrooms and a big kitchen. The living room is full of Junior's racing trophies, and so is the piano in Shirley's room. Junior was born and raised here with his older brothers, L. P., the oldest, and Fred, and his older sister, Ruth. Over yonder, up by that house, there's a man with a mule and a little plow. That's L. P. The Johnsons still keep that old mule around to plow the vegetable gardens. And all around, on all sides, like a rim are the ridges and the woods. Well, what about those woods, where Vance Packard said the agents come stealing over the ridges and good old boys go crashing through the underbrush to get away from the still and the women start "calling the cows" up and down the hollows as the signal *they were coming. . . .*

Junior motions his hand out toward the hills and says, "I'd say nearly everybody in a fifty-mile radius of here was in the whiskey business at one time or another. When we growed up here, everybody seemed to be more or less messing with whiskey, and myself and my two brothers did quite a bit of transporting. H'it was just a business, like any other business, far as we was concerned. H'it was a matter of survival. During the Depression here, people either had to do that or starve to death. H'it wasn't no gangster type of business or nothing. They's nobody that ever messed with it here that was ever out to hurt anybody. Even if they got caught, they never tried to shoot anybody or anything like that. Getting caught and pulling time, that was just part of it. H'it was just a business, like any other business. Me and my brothers, when we went out on the road at night, h'it was just like a milk run, far as we was concerned. They was certain deliveries to be made and. . . ."

A milk run — yes! Well, it was a business, all right. In fact, it was a regional industry, all up and down the Appalachian slopes. But never mind the Depression. It goes back a long way before that. The Scotch-Irish settled the mountains from Pennsylvania down to Alabama, and they have been making whiskey out there as long as anybody can remember. At first it was a simple matter of economics. The land had a low crop yield, compared to the lowlands, and even after a man struggled to grow his corn, or whatever, the cost of transporting it to the markets from down out of the hills was so great, it wasn't worth it. It was much more profitable to convert the corn into whiskey and sell that. The trouble started with the Federal Government on that score almost the moment the Republic was founded. Alexander Hamilton put a high excise tax on whiskey in 1791, almost as soon as the Constitution was ratified. The "Whiskey Rebellion" broke out in the mountains of western Pennsylvania in 1794. The farmers were mad as hell over the tax. Fifteen thousand Federal troops marched out to the mountains and suppressed them. Almost at once, however, the trouble over the whiskey tax became a symbol of something bigger. This was a general enmity between the western and eastern sections of practically every seaboard state. Part of it was political. The eastern sections tended to control the legislatures, the economy and the law courts, and the western sections felt shortchanged. Part of it was cultural. Life in the western sections was rougher. Religions, codes and styles of life were sterner. Life in the eastern capitals seemed to give off the odor of Europe and decadence. Shays's Rebellion broke out in the Berkshire hills of western Massachusetts in 1786 in an attempt to shake off the yoke of Boston, which seemed as bad as George III's. To this day people in western Massachusetts make proposals, earnestly or with down-in-the-mouth humor, that they all ought to split off from "Boston." Whiskey — the mountain people went right on making it. Whole sections of the Appalachians were a whiskey belt, just as sections of Georgia, Alabama, and Mississippi were a cotton belt. Nobody on either side ever had any moral delusions about why the Federal Government was against it. It was always the tax, pure and simple. Today the price of liquor is 60 percent tax. Today, of course, with everybody gone wild over the subject of science and health, it has been much easier for the federals to persuade people that they crack down on moonshine whiskey because it is dangerous, it poisons, kills, and blinds people. The statistics are usually specious.

Moonshining was *illegal,* however; that was also the unvarnished truth. And that had a side effect in the whiskey belt. The people there were already isolated, geographically, by the mountains and had strong clan ties because they were all from the same stock, Scotch-Irish. Moonshining isolated them even more. They always had to be careful who came up there. There are plenty of hollows to this day where if you drive in and ask some good old boy where so-and-so is, he'll tell you he never heard of the fellow. Then the next minute, if you identify yourself and give some idea of why you want to see him, and he believes you, he'll suddenly say, "Aw, you're talking about *so-and-so.* I thought you said —" With all this isolation, the mountain people began to take on certain characteristics normally associated, by the diffident civilizations of today, with tribes. There was a strong sense of family, clan and honor. People would cut and shoot each other up over honor. And physical courage! They were almost like Turks that way.

In the Korean War, there were seventy-eight Medal of Honor winners. Thirty-two of them were from the South, and practically all of the thirty-two were from small towns in or near the Appalachians. The New

York metropolitan area, which has more people than all these towns put together, had three Medal of Honor winners, and one of them had just moved to New York from the Appalachian region of West Virginia. Three of the Medal of Honor winners came from within fifty miles of Junior Johnson's side porch.

Detroit had discovered these pockets of courage, almost like a natural resource, in the form of Junior Johnson and about twenty other drivers. There is something exquisitely ironic about it. Detroit is now engaged in the highly sophisticated business of offering the illusion of Speed for Everyman — making their cars go 175 miles an hour on racetracks — by discovering and putting behind the wheel a breed of mountain men who are living vestiges of a degree of physical courage that became extinct in most other sections of the country by 1900. Of course, very few stock car drivers have ever had anything to do with the whiskey business. A great many always lead quiet lives off the track. But it is the same strong people among whom the whiskey business developed who produced the kind of men who could drive the stock cars. There are a few exceptions, Freddie Lorenzen, from Elmhurst, Illinois, being the most notable. But, by and large, it is the rural Southern code of honor and courage that has produced these, the most daring men in sports.

Cars and bravery! The mountain-still operators had been running white liquor with hopped-up automobiles all during the thirties. But it was during the war that the business was so hot out of Wilkes County, down to Charlotte, High Point, Greensboro, Winston-Salem, Salisbury, places like that; a night's run, by one car, would bring anywhere from $500 to $1000. People had money all of a sudden. One car could carry twenty-two to twenty-five cases of white liquor. There were twelve half-gallon fruit jars full per case, so each load would have 132 gallons or more. It would sell to the distributor in the city for about ten dollars a gallon, when the market was good, of which the driver would get two dollars, as much as $300 for the night's work.

The usual arrangement in the white liquor industry was for the elders to design the distillery, supervise the formulas and the whole distilling process and take care of the business end of the operation. The young men did the heavy work, carrying the copper and other heavy goods out into the woods, building the still, hauling in fuel — and driving. Junior and his older brothers, L. P. and Fred, worked that way with their father, Robert Glenn Johnson, Sr.

Johnson, Senior, was one of the biggest individual copper-still operators in the area. The fourth time he was arrested, the agents found a
small fortune in working corn mash bubbling in the vats.

"My Daddy was always a hard worker," Junior is telling me. "He
always wanted something a little bit better. A lot of people resented that
and held that against him, but what he got, he always got h'it by hard
work. There ain't no harder work in the world than making whiskey. I
don't know of any other business that compels you to get up at all times
of night and go outdoors in the snow and everything else and work.
H'it's the hardest way in the world to make a living, and I don't think
anybody'd do it unless they had to."

Working mash wouldn't wait for a man. It started coming to a head
when it got ready to and a man had to be there to take it off, out there in
the woods, in the brush, in the brambles, in the muck, in the snow.
Wouldn't it have been something if you could have just set it all up
inside a good old shed with a corrugated metal roof and order those
parts like you want them and not have to smuggle all that copper and all
that sugar and all that everything out here in the woods and be a
coppersmith and a plumber and a copper and a carpenter and a pack
horse and every other goddamned thing God ever saw in this world, all
at once.

And live decent hours — Junior and his brothers, about two o'clock
in the morning they'd head out to the stash, the place where the liquor
was hidden after it was made. Sometimes it would be somebody's house
or an old shed or someplace just out in the woods, and they'd make
their arrangements out there, what the route was and who was getting
how much liquor. There wasn't anything ever written down. Everything
was cash on the spot. Different drivers liked to make the run at different
times, but Junior and his brother always liked to start out from 3 to 4
A.M. But it got so no matter when you started out you didn't have those
roads to yourself.

"Some guys liked one time and some guys liked another time," Junior
is saying, "but starting about midnight they'd be coming out of the
woods from every direction. Some nights the whole road was full of
bootleggers. It got so some nights they'd be somebody following you
going just as fast as you were and you didn't know who h'it was, the law
or somebody else hauling whiskey."

And it was just a business, like any other business, just like a milk
route — but this funny thing was happening. In those wild-ass times,
with the money flush and good old boys from all over the country run-

ning that white liquor down the road ninety miles an hour and more than that if you try to crowd them a little bit — well, the funny thing was, it got to be competitive in an almost aesthetic, a pure sporting way. The way the good old boys got to hopping up their automobiles — it got to be a science practically. Everybody was looking to build a car faster than anybody ever had before. They practically got into industrial espionage over it. They'd come up behind one another on those wild-ass nights on the highway, roaring through the black gulches between the clay cuts and the trees, pretending like they were officers, just to challenge them, test them out, race . . . *pour le sport*, you mothers, careening through the darkness, old Carolina moon. All these cars were registered in phony names. If a man had to abandon one, they would find license plates that traced back to . . . nobody at all. It wasn't anything, particularly, to go down to the Motor Vehicle Bureau and get some license plates, as long as you paid your money. Of course, it's rougher now, with compulsory insurance. You have to have your insurance before you can get your license plates, and that leads to a lot of complications. Junior doesn't know what they do about that now. Anyway, all these cars with the magnificent engines were plain on the outside, so they wouldn't attract attention, but they couldn't disguise them altogether. They were jacked up a little in the back and had 8.00 or 8.20 tires, for the heavy loads, and the sound —

"They wasn't no way you could make it sound like an ordinary car," says Junior.

God-almighty, that sound in the middle of the night, groaning, roaring, humming down into the hollows, through the clay gulches — yes! And all over the rural South, hell, all over the South, the legends of wild-driving whiskey running got started. And it wasn't just the plain excitement of it. It was something deeper, the symbolism. It brought into a modern focus the whole business, one and a half centuries old, of the country people's rebellion against the Federals, against the seaboard establishment, their independence, their defiance of the outside world. And it was like a mythology for that and for something else that was happening, the whole wild thing of the car as the symbol of liberation in the postwar South.

"They was out about every night, patroling, the agents and the State Police was," Junior is saying, "but they seldom caught anybody. H'it was like the dogs chasing the fox. The dogs can't catch a fox, he'll just take 'em around in a circle all night long. I was never caught for transporting. We never lost but one car and the axle broke on h'it."

The fox and the dogs! Whiskey running certainly had a crazy game-like quality about it, considering that a boy might be sent up for two years or more if he were caught transporting. But these boys were just wild enough for that. There got to be a code about the chase. In Wilkes County nobody, neither the good old boys nor the agents, ever did anything that was going to hurt the other side physically. There was supposed to be some parts of the South where the boys used smoke screens and tack buckets. They had attachments in the rear of the cars, and if the agents got too close they would let loose a smoke screen to blind them or a slew of tacks to make them blow a tire. But nobody in Wilkes County ever did that because that was a good way for somebody to get killed. Part of it was that whenever an agent did get killed in the South, whole hordes of agents would come in from Washington and pretty soon they would be tramping along the ridges practically inch by inch, smoking out the stills. But mainly it was — well, the code. If you got caught, you went along peaceably, and the agents never used their guns. There were some tense times. Once was when the agents started using tack belts in Iredell County. This was a long strip of leather studded with nails that the agents would lay across the road in the dark. A man couldn't see it until it was too late and he stood a good chance of getting killed if it got his tires and spun him out. The other was the time the State Police put a roadblock down there at that damned bridge at Millersville to catch a couple of escaped convicts. Well, a couple of good old boys rode up with a load, and there was the roadblock and they were already on the bridge, so they jumped out and dove into the water. The police saw two men jump out of their car and dive in the water, so they opened fire and they shot one good old boy in the backside. As they pulled him out, he kept saying:

"What did you have to shoot at me for? What did you have to shoot at me for?"

It wasn't pain, it wasn't anguish, it wasn't anger. It was consternation. The bastards had broken the code.

Then the Federals started getting radio cars.

"The radios didn't do them any good," Junior says. "As soon as the officers got radios, then *they* got radios. They'd go out and get the same radio. H'it was an awful hard thing for them to radio them down. They'd just listen in on the radio and see where they're setting up the roadblocks and go a different way."

And such different ways. The good old boys knew back roads, dirt roads, up people's backlanes and every which way, and an agent would have to live in the North Carolina hills a lifetime to get to know them. There wasn't hardly a stretch of road on any of the routes where a good old boy couldn't duck off the road and into the backcountry if he had to. They had wild detours around practically every town and every intersection in the region. And for tight spots — the legendary devices, the "bootleg slide," the siren and the red light. . . .

It was just a matter of keeping up with the competition. You always have to have the latest equipment. It was a business thing, like any other business, you have to stay on top — "They was some guys who was more dependable, they done a better job" — and it may have been business to Junior, but it wasn't business to a generation of good old boys growing up all over the South. The Wilkes County bootleg cars started picking up popular names in a kind of folk hero worship — "The Black Ghost," "The Grey Ghost," which were two of Junior's, "Old Mother Goose," "The Midnight Traveler," "Old Faithful."

And then one day in 1955 some agents snuck over the ridges and caught Junior Johnson at his daddy's still. Junior Johnson, the man couldn't *any*body catch!

The arrest caught Junior just as he was ready to really take off in his career as a stock car driver. Junior says he hadn't been in the whiskey business in any shape or form, hadn't run a load of whiskey for two or three years, when he was arrested. He says he didn't need to fool around with running whiskey after he got into stock car racing, he was making enough money at that. He was just out there at the still helping his daddy with some of the heavy labor, there wasn't a good old boy in Ingle Hollow who wouldn't help his daddy lug those big old cords of ash wood, it doesn't give off much smoke, out in the woods. Junior was sentenced to two years in the federal reformatory in Chillicothe, Ohio.

"If the law felt I should have gone to jail, that's fine and dandy," Junior tells me. "But I don't think the true facts of the case justified the sentence I got. I never had been arrested in my life. I think they was punishing me for the past. People get a kick out of it because the officers can't catch somebody, and this angers them. Soon as I started getting publicity for racing, they started making it real hot for my family. I was out of the whiskey business, and they knew that, but they was just waiting to catch me on something. I got out after serving ten months and three days of the sentence, but h'it was two or three years I was set back, about half of fifty-six and every bit of fifty-seven. H'it takes a year to really get back into h'it after something like that. I think I lost the prime of my racing career. I feel that if I had been given the chance I feel

I was due, rather than the sentence I got, my life would have got a real boost."

But, if anything, the arrest only made the Junior Johnson legend hotter.

And all the while Detroit kept edging the speeds up, from 150 m.p.h. in 1960 to 155 to 165 to 175 to 180 flat out on the longest straightaway, and the good old boys of Southern stock car racing stuck right with it. Any speed Detroit would give them they would take right with them into the curve, hard-charging even though they began to feel strange things such as the rubber starting to pull right off the tire casing. And God! Good old boys from all over the South roared together after the Stanchion — Speed! Guts! — pouring into Birmingham, Daytona Beach, Randleman, North Carolina; Spartanburg, South Carolina; Weaver-ville, Hillsboro, North Carolina; Atlanta, Hickory, Bristol, Tennessee; Augusta, Georgia; Richmond, Virginia; Asheville, North Carolina; Char-lotte, Myrtle Beach — tens of thousands of them. And still upper- and middle-class America, even in the South, keeps its eyes averted. Who cares! They kept on heading out where we all live, after all, out amongst the Drive-ins, white-enameled filling stations, concrete aprons, shop-ping-plaza apothecaries, show-window steak houses, Burger-Ramas, Bar-B-Cubicles and Miami aqua-swimming-pool motor inns, on out the highway . . . even outside a town like Darlington, a town of 10,000 souls, God, here they come, down Route 52, up 401, on 340, 151 and 34, on through the South Carolina lespedeza fields. By Friday night already the good old boys are pulling the infield of the Darlington raceway with those blazing pastel dreamboats stacked this way and that on the clay flat and the tubular terrace furniture and the sleeping bags and the thermos jugs and the brown whiskey bottles coming on out. By Sunday — the race! — there are 65,000 piled into the racetrack at Darlington. The sheriff, as always, sets up the jail right there in the infield. No use trying to haul them out of there. And now — the *sound* rises up inside the raceway, and a good ole boy named Ralph goes mad and starts selling chances on his Dodge. Twenty-five cents and you can take the sledge he has and smash his car anywhere you want. How they roar when the windshield breaks! The police could interfere, you know, but they are busy chasing a good old girl who is playing Lady Godiva on a hogbacked motorcycle, naked as sin, hauling around and in and out of the clay ruts.

Eyes averted, happy burghers. On Monday the ads start appearing — for Ford, for Plymouth, for Dodge — announcing that we gave it to you, speed such as you never saw. There it was! At Darlington, Daytona, Atlanta — and not merely in the Southern papers but in the albino pages of the suburban women's magazines, such as *The New Yorker*, in color — the Ford winners, such as Fireball Roberts, grinning with a cigar in his mouth in *The New Yorker* magazine. And somewhere, some Monday morning, Jim Pascal of High Point, Ned Jarrett of Boykin, Cale Yarborough of Timmonsville and Curtis Crider from Charlotte, Bobby Isaac of Catawba, E. J. Trivette of Deep Gap, Richard Petty of Randleman, Tiny Lund of Cross, South Carolina; Stick Elliott of Shelby — and from out of Ingle Hollow —

And all the while, standing by in full Shy, in alumicron suits — there is Detroit, hardly able to believe itself what it has discovered, a breed of good old boys from the fastness of the Appalachian hills and flats — a handful from this rare breed — who have given Detroit . . . speed . . . and the industry can present it to a whole generation as . . . yours. And the Detroit P.R. men themselves come to the tracks like folk worshipers and the millions go giddy with the thrill of speed. Only Junior Johnson goes about it as if it were . . . the usual. Junior goes on down to Atlanta for the Dixie 400 and drops by the federal penitentiary to see his Daddy. His Daddy is in on his fifth illegal distillery conviction; in the whiskey business that's just part of it; an able craftsman, an able businessman, and the law kept hounding him, that was all. So Junior drops by and then goes on out to the track and gets in his new Ford and sets the qualifying speed record for Atlanta Dixie 400, 146.301 m.p.h.; later on he tools on back up the road to Ingle Hollow to tend to the automatic chicken houses and the road-grading operation. Yes.

Yet how can you tell that to . . . anybody . . . out on the bottom of that bowl as the motor thunder begins to lift up through him like a sigh and his eyeballs glaze over and his hands reach up and there, riding the rim of the bowl, soaring over the ridges, is Junior's yellow Ford . . . which is his white Chevrolet . . . which is a White Ghost, forever rousing the good old boys . . . hard-charging! . . . up with the automobile into their America, and the hell with arteriosclerotic old boys trying to hold onto the whole pot with arms of cotton seersucker. Junior!

1986

Richard Ben Cramer

.......................................................................................................................................................

# What Do You Think
# of Ted Williams Now?

FEW MEN TRY for best ever, and Ted Williams is one of those. There's a story about him I think of now. This is not about baseball but fishing. He meant to be the best there, too. One day he says to a Boston writer: "Ain't no one in heaven or earth ever knew more about fishing."

"Sure there is," says the scribe.

"Oh, yeah? Who?"

"Well, God made the fish."

"Yeah, awright," Ted says. "But you had to go pretty far back."

It was forty-five years ago, when achievements with a bat first brought him to the nation's notice, that Ted Williams began work on his defense. He wanted fame, and wanted it with a pure, hot eagerness that would have been embarrassing in a smaller man. But he could not stand celebrity. This is a bitch of a line to draw in America's dust.

Ted was never the kind to quail. In this epic battle, as in the million smaller face-offs that are his history, his instinct called for exertion, for a show of force that would *shut those bastards up.* That was always his method as he fought opposing pitchers, and fielders who bunched up on him, eight on one half of the field; as he fought off the few fans who booed him and thousands who thought he ought to love them, too; as he fought through, alas, three marriages; as he fought to a bloody standoff a Boston press that covered, with comment, his every sneeze and snort. He meant to *dominate,* and to an amazing extent, he did. But he came to know, better than most men, the value of his time. So over the years, Ted Williams learned to avoid annoyance. Now in his seventh decade, he has girded his penchants for privacy and ease with a bristle of dos and don'ts that defeat casual intrusion. He is a hard man to meet.

This is not to paint him as a hermit or a shrinking flower, Garbo with a baseball bat. No, in his home town of Islamorada, on the Florida Keys, Ted is not hard to *see.* He's out every day, out early and out loud. You might spot him at a coffee bar where the guides breakfast, quizzing them on their catches and telling them what *he* thinks of fishing here lately, which is, "IT'S HORSESHIT." Or you might notice him in a crowded but quiet tackle shop, poking at a reel that he's seen before, opining that it's not been sold because "THE PRICE IS TOO DAMN HIGH," after which Ted advises his friend, the proprietor, across the room: "YOU MIGHT AS WELL QUIT USING THAT HAIR DYE. YOU'RE GOING BALD ANYWAY."

He's always first, 8:00 A.M., at the tennis club. He's been up for hours, he's ready. He fidgets, awaiting appearance by some other, any other, man with a racket, whereupon Ted bellows, before the newcomer can say hello: "WELL, YOU WANNA PLAY?" Ted's voice normally emanates with gale force, even at close range. Apologists attribute this to the ear injury that sent him home from Korea and ended his combat flying career. But Ted can speak softly and hear himself fine, if it's only one friend around. The roar with which he speaks in a public place, or to anyone else, has nothing to do with his hearing. It's your hearing he's worried about.

Ted Williams can hush a room just by entering. There is a force that boils up from him and commands attention. This he has come to accept as his destiny and his due, just as he came to accept the maddening, if respectful, way that opponents pitched around him (he always seemed to be leading the league in bases on balls), or the way every fan in the ball park seemed always to watch (and comment upon) T. Williams's every move. It was often said Ted would rather play ball in a lab, where fans couldn't see. But he never blamed fans for watching him. His hate was for those who couldn't or wouldn't *feel* with him, his effort, his exultation, pride, rage, or sorrow. If they wouldn't share those, then there was his scorn, and he'd make them feel that, by God. These days, there are no crowds, but Ted is watched, and why not? What other match could draw a kibitzer's eye when Ted, on the near court, pounds toward the net, slashing the air with his big racket, laughing in triumphant derision as he scores with his killer drop shot, or smacking the ball twenty feet long and roaring, "SYPHILITIC SONOFABITCH!" as he hurls his racket to the clay at his feet?

And who could say Ted does not mean to be seen when he stops in front of the kibitzers as he and his opponent change sides? "YOU OKAY?" Ted wheezes as he yells at his foe. "HOW D'YA FEEL? . . . HOW OLD ARE YOU? . . . JUST WORRIED ABOUT YOUR HEART HA HA HAW." Ted turns and winks, mops his face. A kibitzer says mildly: "How are you, Ted?" And Ted drops the towel, swells with Florida air, grins gloriously, and booms back: "WELL, HOW DO I LOOK? . . . HUH? . . . *WHAT DO YOU THINK OF TED WILLIAMS NOW?*"

It is another matter, though, to interrupt his tour of life and force yourself on his attention. This is where the dos and don'ts come in. The dos fall to you. They concern your conduct, habits, schedule, attitude, and grooming. It's too long a list to go into, but suffice it to recall the one thing Ted liked about managing the Washington Senators: "I was in a position where people had to by God *listen.*"

The don'ts, on the other hand, pertain to Ted, and they are probably summed up best by Jimmy Albright, the famous fishing guide, Ted's friend since 1947 and Islamorada neighbor. "Ted don't do," Jimmy says, "mucha anything he don't want to."

He does not wait or bend his schedule: "I haven't got my whole career to screw around with you, bush!" He does not screw around with anything for long, unless it's hunting fish, and then he'll spend all day with perfect equanimity. He does not reminisce, except in rare moods of ease. He does not talk about his personal life. "Why the hell should I?"

His standing in the worlds of baseball and fishing would net him an invitation a night, but he does not go to dinners. One reason is he does not wear ties, and probably hasn't suffered one five times in a quarter century. Neither does he go to parties, where he'd have to stand around with a drink in his hand, "listening to a lot of bullshit." No, he'd rather watch TV.

He does not go to restaurants, and the reasons are several: They make a fuss, and the owner or cook's on his neck like a gnat. Or worse, it's a stream of *sportsfans* (still Ted's worst epithet) with napkins to sign. At restaurants you wait, wait, *wait.* Restaurants have little chairs and tables, no place for elbows, arms, knees, feet. At restaurants there's never enough food. Lastly, restaurants charge a lot, and Ted doesn't toss money around. (A few years ago he decided $2.38 was top price for a pound of beef. For more than a year, he honed his technique on chuck roast and stew meat. Only an incipient boycott by his friends, frequent dinner guests, finally shook his resolve.)

The last reason is seized upon unkindly by restaurateurs in Islamorada and nearby Keys: "No, he doesn't come in. He's too cheap. He'd go all over town, sonofabitch, and he'd pay by check, hoping they wouldn't cash the check, they'd put it on the wall."

But this is resentment speaking, and it is Ted's lot in life to be misunderstood. Some are put off, for instance, by the unlisted phone, by the steel fence, the burglar alarm, and KEEP OUT signs that stud his gates when he swings them shut with the carbon-steel chain and the padlock. But friends think nothing of it. A few have his number, but they don't call, as they know he's got the phone off the hook. No, they'll cruise by; if the gates are unchained, if they see his faded blue truck with the bumper sign IF GUNS ARE OUTLAWED ONLY OUTLAWS WILL HAVE GUNS, if it's not mealtime and not too late and there's nothing they know of that's pissing Ted off, well, then . . . they drive right in.

And this is the way to meet Ted: by introduction of an old friend, like Jimmy Albright. It's Jimmy who knows where to park the car so it won't annoy Ted. It's Jimmy who cautions, as we throw away our cigarettes, that Ted won't allow any smoke in his house. It's Jimmy who starts the ball rolling, calls out "Hiya, Ted!" as the big guy launches himself from his chair and stalks across the living room, muttering in the stentorian growl that passes with him as sotto voce: "Now who the hell is THIS?"

He fills the door. "Awright, come on in. WELL, GET THE HELL IN HERE." He sticks out a hand, but his nose twitches, lip curls at a lingering scent of smoke. Ted's got my hand now, but he says to Jimmy: "S'that you who stinks, or this other one, too? Jesus! Awright, sit down. Sit over there."

Ted wants to keep this short and sweet. He's in the kitchen filling tumblers with fresh lemonade. Still, his voice rattles the living room: "D'YOU READ THE BOOK?" He means his memoir, *My Turn at Bat.* "Anything you're gonna ask, I guarantee it's in the goddamn book . . . Yeah, awright. I only got one copy myself.

"Where's the BOOK?" he yells to Louise Kaufman, his mate. Ted thinks that Lou knows the location of everything he wants. "HEY SWEETIE, WHERE'S THAT GODDAMN BOOK?"

Lou has raised three sons, so no man, not even Ted, is going to fluster her. She comes downstairs bearing the book, which she hands to Ted, and which he throws to the floor at my feet. He growls: "Now, I want you to read that. And then I'm gonna ask you a *key question.*"

I ask: "Tomorrow? Should I call?"

"HELL NO."

Jimmy says he'll arrange a meeting.

Ted says: "HOW'S THAT LEMONADE?"

"Good."

"HUH? IS IT? . . . WELL, WHAT DO YOU THINK OF ME?"

In the car, minutes later, Jimmy explains that Ted won't talk on the phone. "Ted gimme his number twenty-five years ago," Jimmy says. "And I never give it yet to any asshole." We both nod solemnly as this fact settles, and we muse on the subject of trust. I'm thinking of the fine camaraderie between sportsmen and . . . wait a minute. Jimmy and Ted have been friends forty years now.

Does that make fifteen years Ted *didn't* give him the number?

> I'm glad it's over. Before anything else, understand that I am glad it's over. . . . I wouldn't go back to being eighteen or nineteen years old knowing what was in store, the sourness and the bitterness, knowing how I thought the weight of the damn world was always on my neck, grinding on me. I wouldn't go back to that for anything. I wouldn't *want* to go back. . . . I wanted to be the greatest hitter who ever lived.
> — Ted Williams, with John Underwood: *My Turn at Bat*

San Diego was a small town, and the Williams house was a small box of wood, one story like the rest on Utah Street. It was a workingman's neighborhood, but at the bottom of the Great Depression a lot of men weren't working. Ted's father was a photographer with a little shop downtown. Later he got a U.S. marshal's job, in gratitude for some election favors he'd done for Governor Merriam, and that remained his claim to fame. Ted never saw much of him. His mother was the strength in the family, a small woman with a will of steel who gave her life to the Salvation Army. She was always out on the streets, San Diego or south of the border, the Angel of Tijuana, out fighting the devil drink, selling the *War Cry* or playing on a cornet, and God-blessing those who vouchsafed a nickel. Sometimes she'd take along her elder boy, and Ted hated it, but he didn't disobey. He was a scrawny kid and shy, and he tried to shrink behind the bass drum so none of his friends would see. There was school, but he wasn't much good there. History was the only part he liked. And then he'd come home, and his mother was out, and sometimes it was ten at night, and Ted and his brother, Danny, were still on the porch on Utah Street, waiting for someone to let them in.

Soon home lost its place at the center of Ted's life. There wasn't much in the little house that could make him feel special. It wasn't the place where he could be the Ted Williams he wanted to be. North Park playground was a block away, and there, with one friend, a bat, and a ball, Ted could be the biggest man in the majors. The game he played was called Big League: one kid pitched, the other hit to a backstop screen. "O.K., here's the great Charlie Gehringer," Ted would announce as he took his stance. Or sometimes it was Bill Terry, Hack Wilson, or another great man he'd never seen. "Last of the ninth, two men on, two out, here's the pitch . . . *Gehringer swings!*" Ted swung. *Crack!* Another game-winning shot for the great . . . *the Great Ted Williams.*

They were just the dreams of a kid, that's all. But Ted went back to the playground every day. First it was with a friend his own age, then the playground director, Rod Luscomb, a grown man, a two-hundred-pounder who'd made it to the Cal State League. Ted pitched to Luscomb, Luscomb to Ted. At first they'd always tell each other when they were going to throw a curve. But then Ted started calling out: "Don't tell me, just see if I can hit it." *Crack!* Ted could hit it. "Listen, Lusk," Ted used to say. "Someday I'm going to build myself a ball park with cardboard fences. Then, I'm going to knock 'em all down, every darn one, with home runs." But Ted wasn't hitting homers with his scrawny chest, those skinny arms. Luscomb set him to push-ups, twenty, then forty, fifty, then a hundred, then fingertip push-ups. Ted did them at home on Utah Street. He picked his high school, Herbert Hoover High, because it was new and he'd have a better chance to make the team. When he made it, he came to school with his glove hung like a badge on his belt. He carried a bat to class. And after his last class (or before), it was back to the playground. Then in darkness, home for dinner, the push-ups, and the dreams.

There were no major leagues in San Diego. There was no TV. He had no more idea of the life he sought than we have of life on the moon. Maybe less, for we've seen the replays. Ted had to dream it all himself. And how could he measure what he'd give up? He wasn't interested in school, didn't care about cars, or money, or girls. He felt so awkward, except on the field. There, he'd show what Ted Williams could do. Now Hoover High went to the state tourney, traveled all the way to Pomona for a double-header, and Ted pitched the first game, played outfield in the second, and hit and hit, and Hoover won, and wasn't it great? There was an ice cream cart, and Ted ate eighteen Popsicles. His teammates started counting when he got to ten. But Ted didn't mind them making fun. That's how good he felt: him hitting, and Hoover winning, and the big crowd. Gee, that's the governor! And Ted found himself in the governor's path, the man who'd tossed his father a job, and he had to say something, and the awkwardness came flooding back, he felt the red in his face. So Ted grabbed tighter on his bat and he barked at Merriam: "HIYA, GOV!"

Of course people called him cocky. But he only wondered: was he good enough? At seventeen, as high school closed, he signed with the local team, the Coast League Padres. They offered $150 a month and said they'd pay for the whole month of June, even though this was already June 20. So that was Ted's bonus — twenty days' pay. He didn't care: he was a step closer, and each day was a new wonder.

He rode the trains, farther from home than he'd ever been. He stayed in hotels with big mirrors, and Ted would stand at a mirror with a bat or a rolled-up paper, anything — just to see his swing, how he looked: he had to look good. He got balls from the club, so many that his manager, Frank Shellenback, thought Ted must be selling them. No, Ted took them to his playground, got Lusk and maybe a kid to shag flies, and hit the covers off those balls.

Best of all, there were major leaguers, real ones, to see. They were old by the time they came to the Coast League, but Ted watched them, almost ate them with his eyes, measured himself against their size. Lefty O'Doul was managing the San Francisco Seals, and he was one of the greats. Ted stopped Lefty on the field one day. He had to know: "Mr. O'Doul, please . . . What should I do to be a good hitter?" And Lefty said: "Kid, best advice I can give you is don't let anybody change you." Ted walked around on air. After that, in bad times, he'd hear O'Doul's voice telling him he'd be O.K. The bad times were slumps. If Ted couldn't hit, the world went gray. In his second year with San Diego, Ted hit a stretch of oh-for-eighteen. He hung around the hotel in San Francisco, moping. He didn't know what to do with himself. He got a paper and turned to the sports. There was an interview with O'Doul. The headline said: WILLIAMS GREATEST HITTER SINCE WANER. And Ted thought: I wonder who this Williams is?

It was a newspaper that told him, too, about Boston buying his contract. The Red Sox! Ted's heart sank. It was a fifth-place club and as far away as any team could be: cold, northerly, foreign. Still, it was big league, wasn't it?

He had to borrow $200 for the trip east; there were floods that spring of 1938. He got to Sarasota, Florida, about a week late. And when he walked into the clubhouse, all the players were on the field.

"Well, so you're the kid."

It was Johnny Orlando, clubhouse boy. The way Johnny told it, he'd been waiting for this Williams. "Then, one morning, this Li'l Abner walks into the clubhouse. He's got a red sweater on, his shirt open at the neck, a raggedy duffle bag. His hair's on end like he's attached to an electric switch . . . 'Where you been, Kid?' I asked him. 'Don't you know we been working out almost a whole week? Who you supposed to be, Ronald Colman or somebody you can't get here in time?" Johnny gave Ted a uniform, the biggest he had in stock. But as Ted grabbed a couple of bats, his arms and legs stuck out, the shirttail wouldn't stay in the pants.

"Well, come on, Kid," Johnny said, and he led the bean pole out to the field. From the first-base stands, a voice yelled: "Hey, busher, tuck your shirt in! You're in the big leagues now."

Ted wheeled around, face red. "Who's that wise guy up in the stands?" Johnny told him: "That's Joe Cronin, Kid, your manager." Ted put his head down and made for the outfield. It wasn't the reception he'd expected, but at least he had his nickname. Everyone heard Johnny show him around: "Look here, Kid. Go over there, Kid." It stuck right away; it was a role, he knew. And soon Joe Cronin would fill the spot Rod Luscomb had held in Ted's life. Cronin was only thirty-one, but that was old enough. He was a hitter and a teacher, a manager, a counselor, and Ted was ever the Kid.

Cronin had come from Washington, one of the Red Sox's imported stars. The owner, Tom Yawkey, was buying a contender. Along with Cronin, the Hall of Fame shortstop, Yawkey raided Washington for Ben Chapman, a speedy right fielder and .300 hitter. From the Browns, Yawkey got Joe Vosmik, a left fielder who would hit .324. From the A's, Yawkey bought two old greats, Lefty Grove and Jimmy Foxx, along with Doc Cramer, another .300 hitter, for center field.

These were the finest hitters Ted had seen. He couldn't take his eyes off the batter's box. But the presence of all those hitters in camp meant one thing of terrible import to Ted: no nineteen-year-old outfielder was breaking in, not that year, and the veterans let Ted know it. Vosmik, Chapman, and Cramer, rough old boys all of them, made sure he had his share of insults. He lasted about a week, until the club broke camp for the first game in Tampa.

Ted wasn't going to Tampa. He was headed to Daytona Beach, where the Minneapolis farm team trained. Ted saw the list and the shame welled up, turned to rage. He yelled to the veteran outfielders: "*I'll be back. And I'll make more money in this fucking game than all three of you combined.*" When he walked to the bus stop with Johnny Orlando, he asked: "How much you think those guys make?" And Johnny said: "I don't know, maybe fifteen thousand apiece." Ted nodded, his mouth set in a grim line. He had his salary goal now. Then he borrowed $2.50 from Johnny for the bus trip to the minors.

In Minneapolis, Ted led the league in everything: average, home runs, runs batted in, screwball stunts . . . There were tales of his conduct in the outfield, where he'd sit down between batters or practice swinging an imaginary bat, watching his leg-stride, watching his wrist-break, watching everything except balls hit to him. If he did notice a fly ball, he'd gallop after it, slapping his ass and yelling, "HI HO SILVER!" He was nineteen, and fans loved him. But if there was one boo, the Kid would hear it, and he'd try to shut that sonofabitch up for good. Once, when a heckler got to him, Ted fired a ball into the stands — and hit the wrong guy. That was more than the manager, poor old Donie Bush, could stand. He went to the owner, Mike Kelley, and announced: "That's it. One of us goes. Him or me." Kelley replied, quick and firm: "Well, then, Donie, it'll have to be you."

By the time Ted came back to Sarasota, the Red Sox were banking on him, too. They traded Ben Chapman, the right fielder who'd hit .340 the year before. Ted told himself: "I guess that shows what they think of ME." It was like he had to convince himself he was really big league now. Even after a good day, three-for-four, he'd sit alone in the hotel with the canker of one failure eating at him. If he screwed up, or looked bad, the awkwardness turned to shame, the shame to rage. As the team headed north, Ted was hitting a ton, but it wasn't enough. At the first stop, Atlanta, Johnny Orlando pointed out the strange right-field wall — three parallel fences, one behind the other. Johnny said: "I saw Babe Ruth hit one over that last fence . . ." Ted vowed right there he'd do it, too. But next day, he couldn't clear one fence. Worse still, he made an error. In the seventh, he put the Sox up with a three-run triple, but it wasn't enough. He had to show what Ted Williams could do! When he struck out in the eighth, he went to right field seething. Then a pop-up twisted toward his foul line. He ran and ran, dropped the ball, then booted it trying to pick it up. Rage was pounding in him. He grabbed the ball and fired it over those right-field walls. By the time the ball hit Ponce de Leon Avenue and bounced up at a Sears store, Cronin had yanked Ted out of the game.

Even Ted couldn't understand what that rage was to him, why he fed it, wouldn't let it go. He only knew that the next day in Atlanta he smashed a ball over those three walls and trotted to the bench with a hard stare that asked Johnny Orlando and anyone else who cared to look: Well, what do you think of the Kid now?

He had a great first year in the bigs. On his first Sunday at Fenway Park, he was four-for-five with his first home run, a shot to the bleachers in right-center, where only five balls had landed the whole year before. There were nine Boston dailies that vied in hyperbole on the new hero. TED WILLIAMS REVIVES FEATS OF BABE RUTH, said the *Globe* after Ted's fourth game.

From every town he wrote a letter to Rod Luscomb with a layout of the ball park and a proud X where his homer hit. He was always first to the stadium and last to leave after a game. He took his bats to the post office to make sure they were the proper weight. He quizzed the veterans mercilessly about the pitchers coming up. "What does Newsom throw in a jam? How about Ruffing's curve?" It was as if he meant to ingest the game. He only thought baseball. On trains, he'd never join the older guys in poker games or drinking bouts. At hotels, it was always room service, and Ted in his shorts, with a bat, at a mirror.

His roomie was Broadway Charlie Wagner, a pitcher with a taste for fancy suits and an occasional night on the town. One night, at four A.M., Wagner was sleeping the sleep of the just when, *wham, CRASH,* he's on the floor with the bed around his ears, and he figures it's the end. He opens his eyes to see the bean-pole legs, then the shorts, and then the bat. Ted's been practicing and he hit the bedpost. Does he say he's sorry? No, doesn't say a damn thing to Wagner. He's got a little dream-child smile on his face and he murmurs to himself: "Boy, what power!"

He ended up hitting .327 and leading the league in runs batted in, the first time a rookie ever won that crown. He finished with thirty-one home runs, at least one in each American league park. There was no Rookie of the Year award, but Babe Ruth himself put the title on Ted, and that seemed good enough.

And after the season, he didn't go home. San Diego had lost its hold. His parents were getting a divorce, and that was pain he didn't want to face. He didn't want to see his troubled brother. He didn't want to see the crummy little house with the stained carpet and the chair with the hole where the mice ate through. He had a car now, a green Buick worth a thousand bucks. He went to Minnesota. There was a girl there he might want to see. Her dad was a hunting guide, and he could talk to her. And there was duck to hunt. As many as he wanted. And he could go where he wanted. And do what he wanted. He was twenty-one. And Big League.

Everybody knew 1940 would be a great year. Ted knew he'd be better: now he'd seen the pitchers, he knew he could do it. Tom Yawkey sent him a contract for $10,000, double his rookie pay. "I guess that shows what they think of ME."

No one thought about this, but pitchers had seen Ted, too. And this time around, no one was going to try to blow a fastball by him. Cronin was having an off year and Double-X Foxx was getting old and would never again be batting champ. So the pressure fell to Ted. If they pitched around him and he got a walk, that wasn't enough; the Sox needed hits. If he got a hit, it should have been a homer. A coven of bleacherites started riding Ted. And why not? They could always get a rise. Sometimes he'd yell back. Or he'd tell the writers: "I'm gonna take raw hamburger out to feed those wolves." The papers rode the story hard: O Unhappy Star! Then he told the writers: "Aw, Boston's a shitty town. Fans are lousy." Now the papers added commentary, pious truths about the Boston fans as the source of Ted's fine income. So Ted let them have it again: "My salary is peanuts. I'd rather be traded to New York." That did it. Now it wasn't just a left-field crowd riding Ted. It was civic sport: *He doesn't like Boston, huh? Who does he think he is?*

Writers worked the clubhouse, trying to *explain* the Kid. Big Jimmy Foxx, a hero to Ted, said: "Aw, he's just bein' a spoiled boy." The great Lefty Grove said if Williams didn't hustle, he'd punch him in the nose. Of course, all that made the papers. Now when writers came to his locker, Ted didn't wait for questions. "HEY, WHAT STINKS?" he'd yell in their faces. "HEY! SOMETHING STINK IN HERE? OH, IT'S YOU. WELL, NO WONDER WITH THAT SHIT YOU WROTE." So they made new nicknames for him: Terrible Ted, the Screwball, the Problem Child. Fans picked it up and gave him hell. It didn't seem to matter what he *did* anymore. And Ted read the stories in his hotel room and knew he was alone. Sure, he read the papers, though he always said he didn't. He read the stories twenty times, he'd recite them word for word. He'd pace the room and seethe, want to shut them up, want to hit them back. But he didn't know how.

And Ted would sit alone in the locker room boning his bats, not just the handle, like other guys did, but the whole bat, grinding down on the wood, compressing the fiber tighter, making it tougher, harder, tighter.

He would sting the ball. He'd show them. He'd shut them up. Jesus, he was trying. And he was hitting. Wasn't his average up? Wasn't he leading the league in runs? He was doing it like he'd taught himself, like he'd dreamed. Wasn't that enough? What the hell did they want him to be?

What else could he be? Some players tried to help, to ease him up a bit. Once, Ted gave Doc Cramer a ride, and they were talking hitting, as Ted always did. It was at Kenmore Square that Cramer said: "You know who's the best, don't you? You know who's the best in the league? You are." And Ted never forgot those words. But neither could he forget what was written, just as he couldn't forget one boo, just as he'd never forget the curve that struck him out a year before. Why didn't they understand? He could never forget.

And one day he made an error, and then struck out, and it sounded like all of Fenway was booing, and he ran to the bench with his head down, the red rising in his face, the shame in his belly, and the rage. Ted thought: These are the ones who cheered, the fans I waved my cap to? Well, never again. He vowed to himself: Never again. And he could not forget that either.

Lou is in a Miami hospital for heart tests. Ted says I can drive up with him. He figures we'll talk, and he'll have me out of his hair. We start from his house and I wait for him on the porch, where a weary woman irons. The woman is trying to fill in for Lou and she's been ironing for hours. Ted may wear a T-shirt until it's half holes and no color at all, but he wants it just so. The woman casts a look of despair at the pile and announces: "She irons his *underpants*."

Ted blows through the back door and makes for the car, Lou's Ford, which he proclaims "a honey of a little car, boys!" When Ted puts his seal of judgment on a thing or person, by habit he alerts the whole dugout. We are out of Islamorada on the crowded highway, U.S. 1, the only road that perseveres to these islets off the corner of the country, when Ted springs his key question. "You read the book? Awright. Now we're going to see how smart YOU are. What would YOU do to start, I mean, the first goddamn thing now, the first thing you see when you're sitting in the seats and the lights go off, how would YOU start the movie?"

Ted is considering a film deal for *My Turn at Bat*. He is working the topic of moviedom, as he does anything he wants to know. Now as he pilots the Ford through Key Largo, he listens with a grave frown to some possible first scenes. "Awright. Now I'll tell you how it's supposed to start, I mean how the guy's doing it said . . . It's in a fighter plane, see, flying, from the pilot's eye, over KOREA, Seoul. And it's flying, slow and sunny and then *bang WHAM BOOOOMMM the biggest goddamn explosion ever on the screen,* I mean *BOOOOOMMM.* And the screen goes dark. Dark. For maybe ten seconds there's NOTHING. *NOTHING.* And then when it comes back, there's the ball park and the crowd ROARING . . . and that's the beginning."

"Sounds great, Ted."

"Does it? LOOKIT THIS NOW. I wonder where he's goin'. Well, O.K., he's gonna do *that.* Well, O.K. — I'm passing too. Fuck it." Ted is pushing traffic hard to be at the hospital by two, when Lou's doctors have promised results from the heart tests. He is trying to be helpful, but he's edgy.

"How long have you and Lou been together?"

"Oh, I've known Lou for thirty-five years. You shouldn't put any of that shit in there. Say I have a wonderful friend, that's all."

"Yeah, but it makes a difference in how a man lives, Ted, whether he's got a woman or not — "

"Boy, that Sylvester Stallone, he's really made something out of that Rocky, hasn't he? . . ."

"So Ted, let me ask you what — "

"LOOK, I don't wanta go through my personal life with YOU, for Christ's sake. I won't talk to you about Lou, I won't talk to you about any of it. You came down here and you're talkin' about me, as I'm supposed to be different and all that . . ."

"Do you think you're different?"

"NO, not a damn bit. I'm in a little bit different POSITION. I mean, I've had things happen to me that have, uh, made it possible for me to be different. DAMN DIFFERENT in some ways. Everybody's not a big league ball player, everybody doesn't have, uh, coupla hitches in the service, everybody hasn't had, uh, as much notoriety about 'em as I had ALL MY LIFE, so . . ."

"So . . ."

"I wanna go NORTH. I'm gonna go up here and go farther down. I made a mistake there, GODDAMNIT, HOW THE HELL DO I GET ON THE FUCKIN' THING? I'll make a U-turn . . ."

"Ted, I think you were more serious about living life on your own terms . . ."

"Well, I wanted to be alone at times. It was the hustle and the bustle of the crowd for seven months a year. So sure, I wanted a little more privacy, a little more quiet, a little more tranquility. This is the fucking left we wanted."

"Yeah, but it's not just privacy, Ted. I'm not trying to make it seem unnatural. But what you toss off as a little more privacy led you *off* the continent, so far off in a corner that — "

"Well, lemme tell you about Koufax. He got through playin' baseball, he went to a fuckin' little shitty remote town in Maine, and that's where he was for five years. Everybody thought he was a recluse, he wasn't very popular just 'cause he wanted to be alone and he finally moved out. Lemme tell you about Sterling Hayward, Hayden. HELL of an actor. And still he wanted to be ALONE, he wanted to TRAVEL, he wanted to be on his BOAT GOIN' TO THE SOUTH SEAS. So, see, that's not way outa line! . . . I guess I'll take a right, that oughta do it. Eight seventy-four, do you see eight seventy-four anyplace? Go down here till I get to Gilliam Road, or some goddamn thing . . . Fuck, eight seventy-four's where I wanted to go, but looked like it was puttin' me back on the fuckin' turnpike, shit. So, you know, seeking privacy and, uh, seeking that kind of thing . . . what road is this?"

"We're on Killian . . . So privacy, you don't think that's what?"

"*Unusual*, for Christ's sake. Shit."

"I don't think it's unusual either."

"WELL, YOU'RE MAKIN' A PROJECT OUT OF IT!"

"No, I don't think it's unusual . . . You don't think you're exceptionally combative?"

"Nahh, me? Not a bit. Hell, no. THAT SAY KENDALL? Does it? Well, I made a hell of a move here. HELL of a move! See, eight seventy-four is right off there, hospital's down here . . ."

"You're a half-hour early, too."

"Here it is, right here, too. Best hospital in Miami. Expensive sonofabitch, boy. Christ. I'm all for Medicare. And I've always thought that, ALWAYS thought that. Shit. WELL, WHERE ARE YOU GOING? Where ARE you going, lady? *Cunt!*" Ted takes the parking space vacated by the lady and tells me he'll be back in an hour.

When he comes back he has good news about Lou: all tests are negative, her heart is fine. "Gee, I met the big cardiovascular man, he came in and I met him." Ted sounds twenty years younger.

He's walking to the car when a nurse passes. "GEE, WASN'T IT A

SHAME," Ted suddenly booms. "THAT ALLIGATOR BIT THAT LIT-
TLE GIRL'S LEG OFF?" He casts a sly sideward glance at the nurse to
see if she's fallen for his favorite joke.

"Honey of a little shittin' car!" he sings out as we hit the road. Now
there is no fretting with traffic. Ted makes all the turns. Along the way,
he sings forth a monologue about cars, this car, this road, this town of
Homestead, that house, his house, the new house he's planning in
central Florida, up on a hill, just about the highest point in the whole
goddamn state, what a deal he's getting there, Citrus Hills, HELL of a
deal; about his hopes for his kids, his daughter Claudia, only fourteen,
who lives in Vermont with her mother. Ted's third wife, who was too
much of a pain in the ass to live with, but gee, she's done a hell of a job
with those kids, HELL of a job, the little girl is an actress, she had the
lead in the Christmas play and she was so good, the papers up there all
said she bears watching, SHE BEARS WATCHING, and her brother,
Ted's boy, John Henry, he's picking colleges now, he's a good boy and
Ted's critical, but he can't see too much wrong with that boy, and even
the big daughter, Bobby Jo, she's thirty-eight already, still can bust Ted's
chops pretty good, boys, but she's straightening out now; and these
islands, there's bonefish here, used to be wonderful, years ago, there
was NOTHING, NOTHING except a few of the best fishermen God
ever made, and a narrow road between bay and sea, just a little shittin'
road, and some women who weren't half bad on the water or off it
either, and the world here was empty and the water was clear and
you could have a few pops of rum, maybe get a little horny, go see
friends, that's all there was here, a few friends, thirty, thirty-five years
ago, when this place was young, when he first fished with Jimmy and
he met Lou . . .

"Gee, I'm so fuckin' happy about Louise," Ted says. "Goddamn, she's
a great person. Have more fun with her than . . . Goddamn."

They booed in Boston? Well, not in Detroit, the 1941 All-Star Game,
with all the nation listening in. Ted doubled in a run in the fourth, but
the National League still led, 5–3, going into the ninth. Then an infield
hit, a single, a walk, a botched double play, and here it was: two out, two
on, bottom of the ninth. *Here's the great Ted Williams.* Claude Passeau,
the Cubbie on the mound, sends a mean fastball in on his fists. *Williams
swings!* When the ball made the seats, Ted started jumping on the base
path. DiMaggio met him at home plate. Bob Feller ran out in street
clothes, Cronin jumped the box-seat rail, the dugout emptied. The

manager, Del Baker, kissed him on the forehead. They carried the Kid off the field.

He was showing them all now: after the All-Star break, Ted was still hitting more than .400. Sure, guys hit like that for a month, but then tailed off. No one in the league hit like that for a year, not since the twenties, and each day the whole country watched. Writers from New York joined the Sox. *Life* brought its new strobe-light camera to photograph Ted in his shorts, swinging like he did in front of the mirror. Ted was on national radio: "Can you keep it up, Kid?" It was murderous pressure. By September, he was slipping, almost a point a day. On the last day, the Sox would have two games in Philadelphia. Ted had slipped to .39955. The way they round off averages, that's still .400. Cronin came to Ted on the eve of the twin bill and offered: "You could sit it out, Kid, have it made." But Ted said he'd play.

That night, he and Johnny Orlando walked Philadelphia. Ted stopped for milk shakes, Johnny for whiskey. Ten thousand people came to Shibe Park, though the games meant nothing. Connie Mack, the dour and penurious owner of the A's, threatened his men with fines if they eased up on Williams. But Ted didn't need help. First game, he got a single, then a home run, then two more singles. Second game, two more hits: one a screaming double that hit Mr. Mack's right-field loudspeaker so hard that the old man had to buy a new horn. In all, Ted went six-for-eight, and .406 for his third season. That night, he went out for chocolate ice cream.

Who could tell what he'd do the next year: maybe .450, the best *ever*, or break the Babe's record of sixty homers. He got a contract for $30,000 and he meant to fix up his mother's house. He'd have more money than he'd ever expected. He was the toast of the nation. But then the nation went to war.

Ted wanted to play. He'd read where some admiral said we'd kick the Japs back to Tokyo in six months. What was that compared to hitting? A lawyer in Minnesota drew up a plea for deferment, and Ted O.K.'d the request: he was entitled, as his mother's support. When the local board refused deferment, the lawyer sent it up for review by the presidential board. That's when the papers got it. In headlines the size of howitzer shells, they said Ted didn't want to fight for his country. Teddy Ballgame just wanted to play.

Tom Yawkey called to say he could be making the mistake of his life. The league president told Ted to go ahead and play. Papers ran man-on-the-street polls. In Boston, Ted was bigger news than war in the Pacific. At spring training, Joe Cronin said he'd be on his own with fans. "To hell with them," Ted spat. "I've heard plenty of boos." Still, he remembered the venomous letters that said he was an ingrate or a traitor. The one that hurt most said nothing at all: it was just a blank sheet of paper, *yellow* paper.

Opening day in Boston, reporters sat in the left-field stands, out there with soldiers and sailors, to record reaction to Ted. The Kid treated the day as a personal challenge. His first time up, two on, two strikes, he got a waist-high fast ball and drilled it into the bleachers. All the fans rose to cheer, servicemen among them. The Kid was back, and Fenway was with him. "Yeah, ninety-eight percent were for me," Ted said later as he scraped his bat. A writer said: "You mean one hundred percent. I didn't hear a boo." Ted said: "Yeah, they were for me, except a couple of kids in the left-field stand, and a guy out in right. I could hear them."

In May, he enlisted for Navy wings and that shut up most of the hecklers. Still, he was always in a stew of contempt for some joker who said something unfair. It seemed Ted courted the rage now, used it to bone his own fiber. Now there was no awkwardness, no blushing before he blew. It was automatic, a switch in his gut that snapped on and then, watch out for the Kid. One day in July, a fan in left was riding Ted pretty hard. Ted came to bat in the fifth: he took a strange stance and swung late, hit a line drive, but well foul into the left-field seats. Next pitch, again he swung late, hit another liner, but this stayed fair — and Ted didn't run, barely made it to second. Cronin yanked him out of the game, fined him $250 for loafing. But Ted wasn't loafing; the hit caught him by surprise. He'd been trying to kill the heckler with a line drive foul.

Ted loved the service, its certainty and ease. He never had a problem with authority. It was drawing his own lines that gave him fits. He had his fears about the mathematics, navigation problems, and instrument work. But at Amherst College, where the Navy started training, he found his mind was able, and he was pleased. And he loved the feel of an airplane. He was good, right from the start. There was coordination in it, and care: those were natural to him. And he was a constant student, always learning in the air. But he was proudest of his gunnery, the way he could hold back until the last pass, then pour out the lead and shred the sleeve. That wasn't study, that was art. He got his wings near the top of his class and signed on as an instructor at Pensacola, Florida. He was happy, and good at his job. Strangely, in uniform, he was freer than before.

On the day he was commissioned (second lieutenant, U.S. Marines), he married that daughter of the hunting guide, Doris Soule from Minnesota. Now, for the first time, he'd have a house, a place on the coast near the base. And now, on off days, he'd scrape up some gas stamps, grab his fly rod, find a lonesome canal, and lose himself in a hunt for snook. Back at the base, Ted would grab a cadet and take him up in his SNJ, and the new guy of course was goggle-eyed, flying with *Ted Williams,* and Ted would make his plane dance over the coast, then he'd dive and point, and yell to the cadet: "*That's where the Kid fished yesterday.*"

Orders came through slowly for him. What base commander would give him up as ornament and outfielder? At last he got combat training and packed up for the Pacific. But Ted was just getting to Hawaii when Japan folded. So he packed up again for Boston, and now he felt he was going to war.

He came back like he owned the game. Opening day, Washington, after a three-year layoff: *crack,* a four-hundred-foot home run. And then another and another, all around the league. By the All-Star break in 1946, he was hitting .365, with twenty-seven home runs. In the All-Star Game, Ted alone ruined the National League: four straight hits, two homers, and five runs batted in.

And the Red Sox were burying the American League. Tom Yawkey's millions were paying off. The team as a whole was hitting .300, and Ted was hammering the right-field walls. In the first game of two in Cleveland, he hit three homers, one a grand slam when the Sox were behind, the second with two on to tie, the third in the bottom of the ninth to win, 11–10. As Ted came up in the second game, Cleveland's manager, Lou Boudreau, started moving men: the right fielder backed toward the corner; the center fielder played the wall in right-center; the third baseman moved behind second; and Boudreau, the shortstop, played a deep second base; the second baseman stood in short right; the first baseman stood behind his bag. There were eight men on one half of the field (the left fielder was alone on the other), and Ted stood at home plate and laughed out loud.

There never had been anything like it. He had bent the nature of the game. But he would not bend his own and slap the ball for singles to left. He hit into the teeth of the Shift (soon copied around the league), and when he slumped, and the Sox with him, the papers started hammering Ted again, his pride, his "attitude." At last, against the Shift in Cleveland, Ted sliced a drive to left-center, and slid across the plate with an inside-the-park home run, first and last of his career. The Sox had their first pennant since 1918. But the headlines didn't say, SOX CLINCH. Instead, eight-column banners cried that Ted stayed away from the champagne party. "Ted Williams," Dave Egan wrote in the *Record*, "is not a team man." And when St. Louis pulled the Shift in the Series and held Ted to singles, five-for-twenty-five, a new banner read: WILLIAMS BUNTS. And the Red Sox lost the Series, first and last of his career, and after the seventh game, in St. Louis, Ted went to the train, closed his compartment, hung his head, and cried. When he looked up, he saw a crowd watching him through the window. The papers wrote: "Ted Williams cannot win the big ones." The Associated Press voted him number two in a poll for Flop of the Year.

It seemed like Ted couldn't laugh anymore, not in a ball park. He said he was going to Florida to fish. He didn't want to see a bat for months. Soon that was a pattern: one year, before spring training, he tucked in a week in the Everglades. Next year, it was a month. Year after that, longer. In early 1948, the papers discovered that Doris was in a Boston hospital to deliver Ted's first child. But where was the big guy? In Florida? FISHING? The mothers of Boston pelted the press with angry letters. "To hell with them," Ted said. He didn't come north for two days. And two days later, he was back fishing. In two years, he'd moved Doris and his daughter, Barbara Joyce, to a house in Miami, the first he'd ever owned. But he never stayed home there either. He heard about some men in the Keys catching bonefish with light fly tackle. When Ted tried this new sport, he found a love that would last longer than any of his marriages.

The Keys were empty, their railroad wrecked by a hurricane in 1935. There were only a few thousand souls on one road that ran for a hundred miles; the rest was just mangrove and mosquitoes, crushed coral islands, and shining water. In Islamorada — a town of one store, a bar, a restaurant, one gas pump — a few fishing guides, led by Jimmy Albright, were poling their skiffs over shallows that only they knew, hunting bonefish and inventing an art as they went along. These were Ted's kind of men, who'd sneer or scream at a chairman of the stock exchange if he made a lousy cast. Islamorada was a strange meritocracy: if you could not play a fish, tie a fly, cast a line through the wind, you were no one in this town.

Ted could do it all brilliantly. The guides didn't make much fuss about his fame, but they loved his fishing. He meticulous detail work, always an oddity at Fenway Park, was respected here as the mark of a fine angler. Ted had the best tackle, best reels, best rods, the perfect line, his lures were impeccable. He'd work for hours at a bench in his house, implanting balsa plugs with lead so they'd sail off a spinning rod just so, then settle in the water slowly like a fly. He could stand on the bow of a skiff all day, watching the water for signs of fish, and soon he was seeing them before the guides. His casts were quick and long, his power was immense. He never seemed to snap a line, never tangled up, his knots were sure, his knowledge grew, and he always wanted to know *more.* He'd question Jimmy relentlessly and argue every point. But if you showed him something once, he never needed showing again. He fished with Jimmy week after week, and one afternoon as he stood on the bow, he asked without turning his head: "Who's the best you ever fished?" Jimmy said a name, Al Mathers. Ted nodded, "Uh-huh," and asked another question, but he vowed to himself: "He don't know it yet, but the best angler he's had is me."

Every winter, he'd fish the flats, then head north to make his appearance at the Boston Sportsmen's Show. He'd spend a few days doing fly-casting stunts and then take a couple of hours, at most, to tell Tom Yawkey what he wanted for a contract. His salary was enormous. He was the first to break Babe Ruth's $80,000. Ted didn't care for the money as much as the record. It was history now that was the burr on his back. The joy was gone, but not the dream.

Every day, every season, he was still first to the ball park, where he'd strip to shorts and bone his bats; still first out to the cage, where he'd bark his imaginary play-by-play: "Awright, Detroit, top of the ninth . . ." Then back to his locker for a clean shirt and up at a trot to the dugout, to clap a hostile eye on the pitcher warming up, to pick apart his delivery, hunting for any weakness. No, Ted would not give up on one game, one time at bat, a single pitch. No one since Ruth had hit so many home runs per times at bat. No one in the league hit like Ted, year after year: .342, .343, .369, .343 . . . It seemed he never broke a bat at the plate, but he broke a hundred in the clubhouse runway. If he failed at the plate he'd scream at himself, "YOU GODDAMN FOOL!" and bash the cement while the Sox in the dugout stared ahead with mute smiles. Once, after a third strike, he smashed the water pipe to the cooler with his bare fists. No one could believe it until the flood began. And on each opening day, Ted would listen to the national anthem and he'd feel the hair rise on the back of his neck, and his hands would clench, and he'd vow to himself: "This year, the best *ever.*"

In the 1950 All-Star Game, he crashed the outfield wall to catch a drive by Ralph Kiner. His elbow was broken, with thirteen chips off the radius. Surgeons thought he was through, but Ted returned in two months. His first game back, once again: home run, and four-for-four. But Ted could tell as weeks went by that the elbow was not the same. The ball didn't jump off his bat. So all next winter, Ted stayed in the Keys, where he poled a skiff, hunting bonefish and rebuilding his arm. He was pushing thirty-three now, just coming to know how short was his time. But then, after the 1951 season, he was called back to the Marines, drafted for a two-year hitch in Korea. It seemed his time was up.

Ted's living room has a wide white armchair, into and out of which he heaves himself twenty times a day; the chair has a wide white ottoman onto which he'll flop, as whim dictates, one or both of his big legs. From this chair, he roars commands and inquiries, administering the house and grounds. Across the room, a big TV shows his *National Geographic* specials. At his side, a table holds his reading and correspondence. At the moment, these piles are topped by *Yeager: An Autobiography,* and teachers' reports on his son, John Henry. To Ted's right, ten feet away, there's a doorway to the kitchen, through which Lou can supply him and let him know who that was on the phone. To his left and behind, a grand window affords a view of a patio, his dock, some mangrove, and some Florida Bay. Finally, ahead and to the right, in a distant semicircle, there are chairs and a couch for visitors.

"NOW WE'RE GONNA SEE HOW MUCH *YOU* KNOW, SON-OFABITCH," Ted is shouting at Jack Brothers. Jimmy Albright is there, too. The shouting is ritual.

"Ru-mer. R-U-M-E-R." Brothers contends he is spelling the name of the first spinning reel. But Ted has hurled himself up to fetch a fishing encyclopedia, and now he's back in the chair, digging through to the section on spinning. Just so things don't get dull, he says: "Where'd you get that HAIRCUT? D'you have to PAY FOR IT?"

Ted and Jimmy began this colloquy in the early Truman years. Jack helped heat it up when he drifted down from Brooklyn a few years after the war, before Islamorada got its second restaurant or first motel, not to mention the other ten motels, the condos, gift shops, Burger King, or the billboard to proclaim this place: SPORTFISHING CAPITAL OF THE WORLD. These elders are responsible for a lot of the history here, as they helped create flats fishing and turn it into a sport/industry (which they now quietly deplore). Jimmy and Jack were teachers of the first generation of salt-water anglers. Ted is the star of that generation, and its most ferocious pupil.

"Here. HERE! 'Mr. Brown began importing SPINNERS, starting with the LUXAR . . .' THE *LUXAR*. WANNA SEE? GO AHEAD, SON-OFABITCH!"

"Yeah, but that don't say the first spinning reel *manufactured*," Brothers grins in triumph. "Sonofabitch, with your books!"

"This is the goddamn HISTORY, Brothers. Not a FUCKING THING about RUMOR, RHEUMER, RHOOOMAN . . . I GUESS YOU DIDN'T KNOW MUCH ABOUT SPINNING REELS, DID YOU?"

Ted is always the one with the books. He wants *answers*, not a lot of bullshit. Ted is always reading history, biography, fact of all kinds. He doesn't like much made of this, as he's tender on the subject of his education. Once in a camp in Africa, while he and his coauthor, John Underwood, gazed at the night sky, Ted turned from the stars and sighed: "Jeez, I wish I was smart like you."

Now he reports to his friends on his college tours with his son, John Henry: "So we get to Babson and I like it, Babson's a pretty good school, boys. HELL of a school, but, uh, they got dorms, boys and girls all in one dorm, see, and I look on the walls and they're written all over, fuck this and fuck that. I'm thinking, gee, right out there on the walls, it just seemed, you know . . ."

"Liberal?" Jimmy suggests.

"Well, I like to see a place with a little more standards than *that*. So we get to Bates. We got this German girl to show us around, see? And she was a smart little shit, two languages, and she's telling us what she's studying, *aw*, a smart little shit! She give us the tour, see, and John Henry loved Bates, LOVED it. We get back to the office and she goes out. I don't know, she musta told someone, told some of her friends, who she just showed around, see? Then somebody *told* her. She didn't know, see . . .

"Well, a minute later, she's back with some kid and he says, OH, Mr. Williams! and OH this and OH that. And *then* we start talking. And how

about *this*, how about *that*, and how would John Henry like to come for
a *weekend*, get the feel of the place, you know . . ."

Ted stops for a moment and thinks to himself. He doesn't really have
to finish the thought for his friends, who can see him beaming in his big
chair. So he just trails off, to himself: ". . . boy mighta thought the old
man wasn't gonna . . . you know, around a college . . . Well!"

The mayor and the Red Sox held a day for Ted when he left for flight
school. Three weeks into the 1952 season, at Fenway, they gave him a
Cadillac and made a donation to the Jimmy Fund, a charity for sick
children that Ted supported. They gave him a *Ted Williams Memory
Book*, with signatures of four hundred thousand fans. For his last at bat,
bottom of the seventh, he gave them a three-run homer to win the
game, 5–3. He threw a party that night at his Boston hotel. The crowd
was mostly cooks and firemen, bellhops, cabbies, ice cream men. Ted
never liked a smart crowd. Smart people too often asked: "Oh, was your
father a ball player?" "Oh, what did your mother do?" Ted didn't like to
talk about that.

He was just Captain Williams, U.S. Marines, at his flight base at
Pohang, Korea. He had a shed for a home and a cot with inner-tube
strips for springs. The base was a sea of mud, the air was misty and cold,
and he was always sick. He was flying close air support, low strafing, and
bombing runs. His plane was a jet now, an F-9 Panther, but he couldn't
take much joy from flying. He was in and out of sick bay. Doctors called
it a virus, then pneumonia, but his squadron was short of pilots, so he
always flew.

On a bombing run, north of the thirty-eighth parallel, Ted lost sight
of the plane ahead. He dropped through clouds, and when he came out,
he was much too low. North Koreans sent up a hail of bullets. Ted's
plane was hit and set afire. The stick stiffened and shook in his hand; his
hydraulics were gone. Every warning light was red. The radio quit. A
Marine in a nearby F-9 was pointing wildly at Ted's plane. He was trying
to signal: "Fire! Bail out!" But Ted's biggest fear was ejecting; at six three,
wedged in as he was, he'd leave his kneecaps under his gauges. So the
other pilot led him to a base. Ted hauled his plane into a turn and he felt
a shudder of explosion. One of his wheel doors had blown out. Now he
was burning below, too. He made for a runway with fire streaming
thirty feet behind. Koreans in a village saw his plane and ran for their
lives. Only one wheel came down; he had no dive breaks, air flaps,
nothing to slow the plane. He hit the concrete at 225 miles an hour and

slid for almost a mile while he mashed the useless brakes and screamed, *"STOP YOU DIRTY SONOFABITCH STOP STOP STOP."* When the F-9 stopped skidding, he somersaulted out the hatch and slammed his helmet to the ground. Two Marines grabbed him on the tarmac and walked him away as the plane burned to char.

He was flying the next day, and the day after. There weren't enough pilots to rest a man. Ted was sicker, weak and gaunt. Soon his ears were so bad he couldn't hear the radio. He had flown thirty-seven missions and won three air medals when they sent him to a hospital ship. Doctors sent him on to Hawaii and then to Bethesda, Maryland, where at last they gave him a discharge. His thirty-fifth birthday was coming up; he was tired and ill. He didn't want to do anything, much less suit up to play. But Ford Frick, the commissioner, asked him to the 1953 All-Star Game, just to throw out the first ball.

So Ted went to Cincinnati, sat in a sport coat in the dugout. Players greeted him like a lost brother; even Ted couldn't hear a boo in the stands. Tom Yawkey was there, and Joe Cronin; they worked on the Kid. The league president asked him to come back; the National League president, too. Branch Rickey sat him down for a talk; Casey Stengel put in a plea. Ted went to Bethesda to ask the doctors, and then he told the waiting press to send a message to the fans at Fenway: "Warm up your lungs." He took ten days of batting practice and returned with the Red Sox to Boston. First game, Fenway Park, bottom of the seventh: pinch-hit home run.

Ted Williams was the greatest old hitter. In two months, upon return from Korea, he batted .407 and hit a home run once in every seven at bats. For the next two years, he led the league (.345 and .356), but injuries and walks robbed him of the titles: he didn't get the minimum four hundred at bats. In 1956, he lost the title in the season's last week to twenty-four-year-old Mickey Mantle (who finished with .353 to Ted's .345). The next year, Mantle had an even better season, but Ted, at age thirty-nine, pulled away and won, at .388, more than twenty pounds ahead of Mantle, more than sixty points ahead of anyone else. With five more hits (say, the leg hits that a younger man would get), it would have been .400. As it was, it stood as the highest average since his own .406, sixteen years before. In 1958, Ted battled for the crown again, this time with a teammate, Pete Runnels. They were even in September, but then, once again, Ted pulled away to win at .328. For the final fifty-five games (including one on his fortieth birthday), he batted .403.

He accomplished these prodigies despite troubles that would have made most men quit. In 1954, he made spring training for the first time in three years, but he wasn't on the field a minute before he fell and broke his collarbone. He was out six weeks and had a steel bar wired into his clavicle. (First day back, twin bill in Detroit: two home runs, eight-for-nine, seven RBIs.) In 1955, Doris alleged in divorce court that he'd treated her with "extreme cruelty" and constant profane abuse. Boston papers ran the story under two-inch headlines: TED GETS DI-VORCE, with a "box score" on the money, the house, the car, and "Mrs. Ted's" custody of Bobby Jo. In 1956, Ted came forth with his Great Expectorations. In a scoreless game with the Yankees, in front of Fenway's biggest crowd since World War II, he was booed for an error, and he let fans know what he thought of them: he spat toward the right-field stands and spat toward the left, and when fans rained more boos on his head, he leaped out of the dugout and sprayed all around. "Oh, no, this is a bad scene," Curt Gowdy, the Sox broadcaster, mourned to his microphone. Tom Yawkey heard the game on radio, and Ted got a $5,000 fine (tying another Babe Ruth record). Boston writers said Ted ought to quit. But Ted was in the next game, on Family Night, and at his appearance, fans gave him a five-minute ovation. (He then hit a home run in the bottom of the eighth and clapped his hand over his mouth as he scored the winning run.) In 1957, grippe knocked him flat and stuck him in his hotel for seventeen days in September. He came back to hit four consecutive home runs. In 1958, ptomaine from bad oysters wrecked opening day, then he injured an ankle, pulled a muscle in his side, and hurt his wrist twice. In September, after a called third strike, Ted threw his bat and watched in horror as it sailed to the stands and clonked a gray-haired lady on the head. Ted sat in tears in the dugout and had to be ordered to his place in left field. But over the next twenty at bats, he hit .500.

Now the switch in his gut was always on. The Red Sox gave him a single room and barred the press from the clubhouse for two hours before each game. But it wasn't outside annoyance that was fueling Ted's rage. He'd wake up in the middle of the night, screaming obscenities in the dark. He kept himself alone and pushed away affection. There were plenty of women who would have loved to help. But Ted would say: "WOMEN?" and then he'd grab his crotch. "ALL THEY WANT IS WHAT I GOT RIGHT HERE." Now the press didn't cover just explosions on the field. The *American* wrote him up for shredding a telephone book all over the floor when a hotel maid failed to clean his room. "Now tell me some more," wrote Austen Lake, "about Ted's big, charitable, long-suffering spirit." Roger Kahn reported a scene when Ted was asked about Billy Klaus, the shortstop who was coming back after a bad year. "You're asking *ME* about a BAD YEAR? . . . OLD T.S.W., HE DON'T HAVE BAD YEARS."

But old Ted had a terrible year in 1959. A pain in his neck turned to stiffness, and he was in traction for three weeks. When he came out, he could barely look at the pitcher. His average languished below .300 for the first time in his career. For the first time, he was benched for not hitting. The sight of the Kid at the plate was pathetic; even the papers softened. They started summing up his career, treating him like an old building menaced by the wrecking ball. He finished at .254 and went to see Tom Yawkey. "Why don't you just wrap it up?" Yawkey said, and Ted started to boil. No one was going to make him retire. Ted said he meant to play, and Yawkey, who loved the Kid, offered to renew his contract: $125,000, the highest ever. No, Ted said, he'd had a lousy year and he wanted a cut. So Ted signed for $90,000 and came back one more time.

Opening day, Washington: a five-hundred-foot home run. Next day, another. He slammed his five hundredth in Cleveland, passed Lou Gehrig and then Mel Ott. Only Foxx and Ruth would top him on the all-time list. At forty-two, Ted finished his year with twenty-nine homers and .316. Talk revived that Ted might be back. But this was really quits. On his last day at Fenway, a headline cried: WHAT WILL WE DO WITHOUT TED? And though the day was dreary and the season without hope, ten thousand came out to cheer him and hear him say goodbye. There was another check for the Jimmy Fund and, this time, a silver bowl. And Ted made a speech that said, despite all, he felt lucky to play for these fans. And when he came up in the eighth and they stood to cheer, he showed them what Ted Williams could do. He hit a Jack Fisher fast ball into the bullpen in right field. And he thought about tipping his cap as he rounded first but he couldn't, even then, couldn't forget, so he ran it straight into the dugout, and wouldn't come out for a bow.

Now it was no hobby: Ted fished harder and fished more than any man around. After his divorce from Doris, he'd made his home in Islamorada, bought a little place on the ocean side, with no phone and just room for one man and gear. He'd wake before dawn and spend the day in his boat, then come in, maybe cook a steak, maybe drive off to a Cuban or Italian joint where they served big portions and left him alone. Then, back home, he'd tie a few flies and be in bed by ten. He kept it very spare. He didn't even have a TV. That's how he met Louise. He wanted to see a Joe Louis fight, so Jimmy took him to Lou's big house. Her husband was a businessman from Ohio, and they had a TV, they had everything. Lou had her five kids, the best home, best furniture, best car, and best guides. Though she wasn't a woman of leisure, she was a pretty good angler, too. She could talk fishing with Ted. Yes, they could talk. And soon, Lou would have a little money of her own, an inheritance that she'd use to buy a divorce. She wanted to do for herself, she said. And there was something else, too. "I met Ted Williams," Louise said. "And he was the most gorgeous thing I ever saw in my life."

Now Ted's life was his to make, too. He signed a six-figure deal with Sears, to lend his name to their line of tackle, hunting gear, and sporting goods. Now, when Hurricane Donna wrecked his little house on the ocean, he bought his three-bedroom place on the bay, near Louise's house. Now he bought a salmon pool on the Miramichi, in New Brunswick, Canada, and he fished the summer season there. In Islamorada, he was out every day, fall, winter, spring. He wanted the most and the biggest — bonefish, tarpon, salmon — he called them the Big Three. He wanted a thousand of each, and kept books on his progress. He thought fishing and talked fishing and taught fishing at shows for Sears. He felt the joy of the sport, still. But now there was something else: the switch that clicked when he'd get a hot fish that ran and broke off his lure. Ted would slam his rod to the deck or break it in half on the boat. "HERE, YOU LOUSY SONOFABITCH . . ." He'd hurl the rod into the bay. "TAKE THAT, TOO."

He married again in 1961, a tall blond model from Chicago, Lee Howard. They'd both been divorced, and they thought they'd make a go. Ted brought her down to the Keys. But he still wasn't staying home: he'd be out at dawn without a word on where he'd go or what he planned, and then he'd come home, sometimes still without words. Sometimes there was only rage, and Lee found she was no match. After two years, she couldn't take it. She said: "I couldn't do anything right. If we went fishing, he would scream at me, call me a —— and kick the tackle box."

So Ted found another woman, one to meet him, fire with fire. Her name was Dolores Wettach, a tall, large-eyed former Miss Vermont. He spotted her across the aisle on a long plane flight. He was coming from fishing in New Zealand. Dolores had been in Australia, on modeling assignment for *Vogue*. He wrote a note: "Who are you?" He wadded it up, tossed it at her. She looked him over, tossed one back: "Who are *you?*" He tossed: "Mr. Williams, a fisherman," and later told her his first name was Sam. It wasn't until their third date that she found out he'd done anything but fish. When he found out she was a farm girl who loved the outdoors as much as he, he figured he'd met his match. In a way, he had. She learned to fish, she could hunt, could drink, could curse like a guide. And when they fought, it was toe to toe and Ted who slammed out of the house. They had a son, John Henry, and daughter, Claudia. But that didn't stop the fights, just as it hadn't with Bobby Jo, the daughter he'd had with Doris. Ted would tell his friends he wasn't cut out for family. He was sick at heart when Bobby Jo left school and didn't go to college. He would seethe when any woman let him know that he'd have to change. What the hell did they want? When Dolores became his third divorce, Ted was through with marriage.

Ted made the Hall of Fame in 1966. His old enemies, the writers, gave him the largest vote ever. So Ted went north to Cooperstown and gave a short speech outside the hall. Then he went back to Florida. He never went inside. They gave him a copy of his plaque. It listed his .406 year, his batting titles, slugging titles, total bases, walks, home runs. It didn't say anything about the wars, the dream, the rage, the cost. But how much can a plaque say?

There are no statistics on fans, how they felt, what they took from the game. How many of their days did Ted turn around? How many days did he turn to occasions? And not just with hits: there was a special sound from a crowd when Ted got his pitch, turned on the ball, whipped his bat in that perfect arc — and missed. It was a murmurous rustle, as thousands at once let breath escape, gathered themselves, and leaned forward again. To see Ted suffer a *third* strike was an event four times more rare, and more remarkable, than seeing him get a hit. When Ted retired, some owners feared for attendance in the *league*. In Boston, where millions came through the years to cheer, to boo, to care what he did, there was an accretion of memory so bright, bittersweet, and strong that when he left, the light was gone. And Fenway was left with a lesser game.

And what was Ted left with? Well, there was pride. He'd done, he felt, the hardest thing in sport: by God, he hit the ball. And there was pride in his new life: he had his name on more rods and reels, hunting guns, tackle boxes, jackets, boots, and bats than any man in the world. He studied fishing like no other man, and lent to it his fame and grace, his discerning eye. He had his tournament wins and trophies, a fishing book and fishing movies, and he got his thousand of the Big Three. Jimmy Albright says to this day: "Best all around, the best is Ted." But soon there were scores of boats on the bay, and not so many fish. And even the Miramichi had no pools with salmon wall to wall. And Ted walked away from the tournaments. There wasn't the feeling of sport in them, or respect for the fish anymore. Somehow it had changed. Or maybe it was Ted.

Last year, Ted and Lou went up to Cooperstown together. This was for the unveiling of a statue of the Kid. There are many plaques in the Hall of Fame, but only two statues: just the Babe and him. And Ted went into the hall this time, pulled the sheet off his statue and looked at his young self in the finish of that perfect swing. He looked and he looked while the crowd got quiet and the strobes stopped flashing. And when he tried to speak, he wept.

"HEY, WHERE THE HELL IS HE?" It's after four and Ted's getting hungry. "I'M GONNA CALL HIM."

Lou says, "Don't be ugly."

"I'm not ugly," Ted insists, but quietly. He dials and bends to look at me. "Hey, if this guy doesn't come, you can eat. You wanna eat here?" Then to the phone: "WHERE THE HELL ARE YOU?"

"Ted, don't be mean."

"I'm not. YEAH, TOMORROW? WELL. O.K., BUDDY." Ted has had a successful phone conversation. Quick and to the point.

"Awright, you can eat. Hey, sweetie, take him up so he can see."

There are no mementos in the living room, but Lou has put a few special things in a little room upstairs. Most of the pictures have to do with Ted, but the warmth of the room, and its character, have to do with Louise. This is no shrine. It is a room for right now, a room they walk through every day, and a handsome little place, too. Now it is filled with her quiet energy. "Here's Ted Williams when I met him," she says. "And if that isn't gorgeous, I'll eat my hat." And here's an old photo of Lou in shorts, with a fly rod, looking fragile next to a tarpon she pulled from Florida Bay. She does not seem fragile now. She is spry and able. She has been with Ted ten years straight, and that speaks volumes for her strength and agility. She gets angry sometimes that people do not credit Ted with tenderness — "You don't know him," she says, and her voice has a surprising edge — but she also knows he'll seldom show it. So here she shows a lonely young Ted with a little suitcase, off to flight school. Here's Ted and Tom Yawkey, and look: Mr. Yawkey has pictures of Ted behind him, too. "Here he is in Korea," says Louise. "You know, when he landed that plane, the blood was pouring from his ears. I have to tell people that . . . because he's *so* loud. Big, too." Lou picks up a cushion of a window seat. There are pictures beneath. "See, he's done so many things . . ."

"Hey, you want a drink?" Ted is calling. "TED WILLIAMS IS GONNA HAVE A DRINK."

Soon he flops into his chair with a tumbler and hands over a video-tape. He wants it in the VCR. He says: "This is the most wonderful guy. Hell of a guy. Bill Ziegler. I got him into the majors . . ." That was when Ted came back in 1969 to manage the Senators. Bill Ziegler was the trainer.

"So he had a son and he named him Ted Williams Ziegler. You're gonna see him now. IS IT IN? HEY, YOU LISTENING?" The tape shows Ziegler's two sons batting. Ziegler sends the tapes for analysis. The sound track sends out a steady percussion: *thwack . . . thwack . . . thwack.* Both boys get wood on the ball. "I'm gonna show you the first tape he sent, and I'm gonna ask what's the difference. See this kid, I told him his hips, he's got to get them OPEN."

From the kitchen, Lou protests: "Ted! Not now. Wait for me!"

"SEE? . . ." *Thwack.* "Ground ball. A little slow with his hands."

From Lou: "O.K., O.K., I don't know nothin'."

"HANDS THROUGH!" *Thwack.* "Center field, always to center, see where his hips are pointed? He's got to [*thwack*] OPEN 'EM UP."

From Lou, coming in, wiping her hands as she watches: "He doesn't step into it like Ted Williams."

Ted pretends he doesn't hear. "Hips come through OPEN . . ."

"He doesn't bring his hands around like you do, honey."

"Yeah, he's got to, GROUND BALL! See, when I'm up" — and now Ted takes his stance in the living room — "I'm grindin' . . ." Now his hands are working. "I got the hands cocked. *COCKED!*" And here's the pitch. "*BAMMMM!*" says Ted as he takes his cut and asks: "We got Bill Ziegler's number? WHERE'S HIS NUMBER?"

Ted is yelling on the phone in the kitchen, and Lou is in the living room, fitting her thoughts to small silences. "When Ted talks [*thwack*] it's always right now . . ."

"BILL, I WANNA SEE HIM ON HIS FRONT FOOT MORE, AND THE HANDS QUICK, *QUICK . . .*"

"You know, the baseball players . . . it's not macho, they're just . . .
athletes, just beautiful boys . . ."

Ted hangs up and throws himself into his chair: "AWRIGHT, MAJOR
LEAGUE! LET'S SET IT UP." That means dinner. Lou's cooking Chinese. Ted's still watching Ziegler's kids. "Ground ball. You don't make
history hittin' 'em on the ground, boys." Now he pulls away from the
TV. "Sweetie," he sings playfully. "We got any sake-o?" Lou sings: "Not
tonight-eo." Ted sings: "Well, where's the wine-o?"

Lou says grace while all hold hands. Then we set to food, and Ted is
major league. "It's good, huh?" he says between mouthfuls. "Well, isn't
it? HEY! Aren't you gonna finish that rice?"

He's finished fast and back in his chair. "We got any sweets?"

A little album on the coffee table has pictures from Christmas. John
Henry gave his letter of acceptance from Bates as his present to Ted. It's
got Ted thinking now about the car he's got to buy so John Henry can
take a car to school. "Got to have a car . . ." He's thinking aloud so
Louise can check this out. "Course, there's gonna have to be rules . . ."
He's working it over in his mind, and he muses: "Maybe say that other
than school . . . he can't take the car if his mother says no . . ." Lou is in
a chair across the room. She's nodding. "HAVE to be rules," Ted says,
"so he doesn't just slam out of the house . . . slam out and JUMP IN
THE CAR . . ."

Something has turned in his gut, and his face is working, growing
harder. There's a mean glitter in his eye, and he's thinking of his elder
daughter, walking away from him . . .

"SLAM OUT . . . LIKE MY DAUGHTER USED TO . . ."

His teeth are clenched and the words are spat. It's like he's turned
inward to face something we cannot see. It is a fearsome sight, this big
man, forward, stiff in his chair, hurling ugly words at his vision of pain
. . . I feel I should leave the room, but too late.

". . . THAT BURNED ME . . ."

The switch is on. Lou calls it the Devil in him.

". . . A PAIN IN MY HAIRY RECTUM!"

"Nice," says Lou. She is fighting for him. She has not flinched.

"Well, DID," he says through clenched teeth. *"AND MAKES YOU
HATE BROADS! . . ."*

"Ted. Stop." But Ted is gone.

". . . *HATE GOD! . . .*"

"TED!"

". . . *HATE LIFE!*"

"TED! . . . JUST . . . STOP!"

"DON'T YOU TELL ME TO STOP. DON'T YOU TELL ME TO STOP."

Lou's mouth twists up slightly, and she snorts: "HAH!"

And that does it. They've beaten it, or Lou has, or it's just gone away. Ted sinks back in his chair. His jaw is unclenched. He grins shyly. "You know, I love this girl like I never . . ."

Lou sits back, too, and laughs.

"SHE'S IN TRAINING," Ted says. "I'M TEACHIN' HER . . ."

"He sure is," Lou says, like it's banter, but her voice is limp. She heads back to the kitchen, and Ted follows her with his eyes.

Then he finds me on his couch, and he tries to sneer through his grin: "WHEN ARE YOU LEAVING? HUH?

". . . JESUS, YOU'RE LIKE THE GODDAMN RUSSIAN SECRET POLICE!

". . . O.K., BYE! YEAH, SURE, GOODBYE!"

Ted walks me out to the doorway. As I start the car, Lou's face is a smile in the window, and Ted is bent at his belly, grabbing their new Dalmatian puppy, tickling it with his big hands while the dog rolls and paws the air. And as I ease the car into gear, I hear Ted's voice behind, cooing, very quiet now: "Do I love this little dog, huh? . . . Yes, this little shittin' dog . . . Yes, yes I love you . . . Yes, I do."

1973

Brad Darrach

......................................................................................................

# The Day Bobby Blew It

FROM *Playboy*

BOBBY FISCHER heard a knock at the door. It was sometime after ten
A.M., Thursday, June 29, 1972. Three days before the first game of his
match with Boris Spassky for the world chess championship. Eleven
hours before the plane left for Iceland. Five nights in a row, he had been
booked on a northbound plane and five nights in a row he had not
shown. Now time was running out. He had to take this flight. He
couldn't fly tomorrow night, because the Sabbath began at sundown on
Friday and for religious reasons he couldn't fly on the Sabbath. That left
Saturday night; yet if he flew up on Saturday night, he would arrive on
Sunday morning dog-tired from the trip just a few hours before the
game began. So it was tonight or never. But he didn't want to think
about that right now. He wanted to rest up. He had slept 20 hours since
arriving in New York about 36 hours before; but even so, he kept slipping deeper into exhaustion.

The knock was repeated. It couldn't be the chambermaid. He had
hung a DO NOT DISTURB sign on his doorknob. Who else? Only his
lawyer and a few friends knew he was staying at the Yale Club.

"Package for Mr. Fischer," a male voice called.

Looking vague and unready, Bobby opened the door and peered out,
expecting to see a Yale Club employee. Instead, he saw a short, heavy-set
middle-aged man in street clothes. Startled, Bobby started to close the
door. The man blocked it with his foot.

"Excuse me, Mr. Fischer," he began smartly. A younger man moved in
behind him. Bobby's eyes went wide.

"Who are you?" he asked in alarm. "What do you want?"

Keeping his foot firmly in the door, the first intruder said he was a

British journalist and wanted an interview. A journalist! The match hadn't even begun and already the press was hounding him! Bobby angrily ordered them to leave. The man with his foot in the door smiled and kept trying to wheedle an interview. Suddenly the stalemate was broken. A husky young fellow named Jackie Beers, who was visiting Bobby, strode to the door and with one strong shove sent the reporter reeling. Bobby slammed the door. Minutes later he was on the phone to one of his lawyers, Andrew Davis. "Don't leave the room," Davis told him firmly. "Someone will come to you as quickly as possible." Later Davis told me: "Bobby was scared. You could hear it in his voice. At a moment when he couldn't stand the slightest shock, he got a bad one. I guess the shock triggered it." What the shock triggered was the wildest day in the world of chess since a Danish earl outplayed King Canute and was hacked to hamburger by His Majesty's bullyboys.

I was 2600 miles northeast of the Yale Club when the crisis broke. I was in Reykjavík, Iceland, waiting for Bobby to fly up for the match. Spassky was waiting, too — he had arrived eight days before — and so were 140–150 newspaper, magazine and television reporters from at least 32 countries. They were getting damn tired of waiting, in fact, and the stories out of Reykjavík were reflecting their irritation.

Why was Bobby dragging his heels? Without ever talking to him, most reporters assumed that since money was the main thing he was demanding of the Icelandic Chess Federation, money was the main thing on his mind. "Greedy little punk" and "spoiled brat" began to be muttered over typewriters and the public bought what it was told. "Is it really possible," a British correspondent asked me indignantly at breakfast Thursday morning, "that this yahoo is going to stand us all up? Either he's the smartest little bugger that ever came out of Brooklyn or he's some sort of nut. He devotes his whole life to chess and then turns up his nose at the world chess championship. He grows up in a slum and then walks away from millions. Does he want money or doesn't he want money? I just can't *believe* what's happening!"

Nobody could. And nobody could believe that the most recondite of games, an intellectual sport about as popular as differential calculus, was making front-page headlines day after day; that half the world was waiting breathlessly for two young men to sit down on a solitary butt of lava in the North Atlantic and push little wooden soldiers across a miniature make-believe battlefield. The pundits explained that there was more to the match than chess. It was a war in effigy between two super-powers, the U.S. and the U.S.S.R. It was a chance to watch Russia lose the championship for the first time in 24 years and a chance to watch America win it for the first time in history. But what more than any-thing else had gripped us all was the downright weird personality and approximately superhuman achievements of Bobby Fischer.

In chess circles, Bobby had been a celebrity for 15 years, ever since he won the U.S. chess championship at the incredible age of 14, but only in the past 14 months had the larger public become aware of him. In May 1971 he defeated Grand Master Mark Taimanov of the Soviet Union, 6–0, the first shutout in more than half a century of recorded grand-master play. He repeated the shutout against a much more dangerous opponent, Grand Master Bent Larsen of Denmark. Then in Buenos Aires in October 1971, he gave a 6½–2½ thrashing to Russia's Tigran Petrosian, a former world champion and, while he was at it, extended his winning streak to 21 games — the longest in chess history and one more than chess officials gave him credit for. The media decided they had better take a good close look at what they had here.

What the press had, or decided to say it had, was something known for more than a decade to his jealous rivals as "the monster": Bobby was often discussed as a sort of paranoid monomaniac who was terrified of girls and Russian spies but worshiped money and Spiro Agnew, as a high school dropout with a genetic kink who combined the general cul-ture of a hard-rock deejay with a genius for spatial thinking that had made him quite possibly the greatest chess player of all time. The mon-ster was at best a caricature of Bobby, but he sure made terrific copy.

Obligingly, he made terrific copy all through the spring of 1972. First he refused to play Spassky where the Fédération Internationale des Echecs (F.I.D.E) told him he had to play — half the match in Yugo-slavia, half in Iceland. Ultimatums crackled across the Atlantic. Finally Yugoslavia withdrew, blaming Bobby's unreliability, and the whole match was ceded to Iceland. But at that point Bobby boggled at "bury-ing" the contest in such a tiny and "primitive" country and he com-plained about the financial terms, too — even though the $125,000 prize money was already ten times as high as any prize ever put up for a chess match. When the Icelanders, after a public outcry against the "arrogant Fischer," swallowed their pride and met his demands, Bobby made new demands. When the Icelanders rejected his new demands, Bobby suddenly disappeared. Ten days before the match was scheduled to begin, nobody east of Los Angeles, not even his own lawyer, knew where he was.

On Monday, June 26, the day after he was supposed to arrive in Iceland, I called Bobby in California, hoping to cut through the contradictions and get my own impression of what he was thinking. I got a number of surprises.

"Hi, Brad! How ya doin'?" I had expected what I usually heard when Bobby picked up the phone: a faint, suspicious "Uuuuh?" that might mean hello or might be just electric clutter on the line. But this voice was startlingly rich and full and confident.

Like a kid calling home and wishing he were there, he wanted to know everything about Reykjavík. Did I like the playing hall? Was it quiet? What was the chess table like? How about the weather? "Sixty degrees! Wow! That's *coooold!*" But the air was great, huh? "How about that *skyr* they got? Better'n yoghurt, huh?"

Then he wanted to know how Spassky looked. "Nervous," I told him, and he guffawed. "And Geller — " I began, intending to say something about Yefim Geller, Spassky's second.

Bobby cut in fast. "Geller," he said disgustedly, "is *stupid!*"

Then it happened. "Geller," we both heard a woman's voice say, in what was obviously an Icelandic attempt to mimic Bobby's Brooklyn accent, "is *stupid!*"

I heard Bobby gasp. Suddenly he went ape. "They're listening in on my calls!" he yelled. "I knew it! They got spies on the line! Did you hear that? They got spies on the line!" His voice, so warm and vital a second before, kicked up one register and jangled like an alarm clock. Then anger came into it as the fright wore off. "That rotten little country! Call the manager, Brad! Call the head of the telephone company! I want that person *found and fired!* . . . Imagine that! Listening in on *my* phone calls! It could be the Russians, y'know. They got Communists in the government up there. They'll do anything to find out what I'm thinking!" The idea amused him and he slowly relaxed.

As I put down the receiver, I thought something like this: "I've just been talking to two Bobbys. The happy, healthy California Bobby has decided to play. But the other Bobby, the Bobby who thinks Iceland is eavesdropping on his phone calls, could still take over and in a moment of fury destroy the match. Which Bobby are we going to get?"

\*   \*   \*

Dr. Anthony Saidy is one of the more gifted and appealing members of Bobby's coterie. He looks like a mad scientist in a comic book. His head is large, wide at the temples, curiously dished in at the back and covered with mounds of blue-black hair. His nose is an angry hook and his eyes, the color of black coffee, bulge and glitter. His credentials are impressive. He is an M.D. and a strong chess player (he once won the American Open Championship) and the author of a first-rate book on chess strategy. Yet the minute he begins to talk, he reveals himself as a diffident man, with an anxious need to please. But there is something determined and even daring about Saidy, too. In the summer of '72, at the age of 35, he made the gutsy decision to stop practicing medicine and establish himself as a chess master and free-lance writer.

Like many of Bobby's friends, Saidy can't quite manage to be himself in Bobby's company. He has hitched his wagon to a star and sometimes he seems afraid he might miss the ride. He seems to feel that in order to keep Bobby's friendship he must agree with almost everything Bobby says. At times, in his anxiety to maintain the relationship, he actually encourages Bobby in his aberrations. I don't think he means to. He is honest and loyal and his aim is always to bring his friend back to good sense and his own best interests.

Saidy is a New Yorker, but he was working for the Los Angeles Health Department when Bobby showed up in Santa Monica to stay with some friends. Saidy began visiting him every couple of days. Like most of Bobby's California friends, he was appalled to see no move being made in the direction of Iceland as the date of the match drew near. So on Sunday, June 25, Saidy called and said casually that he would be flying East on Tuesday to see his father, who was ill. And wouldn't Bobby maybe like to come along? "Yeah, might as well," Bobby said vaguely. "Be nice to have company on the plane." Saidy said he had "a strong feeling that if I hadn't called, Bobby would still be there."

The tanned and vigorous young man who boarded the plane at Los Angeles would stand out as one of the handsome males at any gathering. Bobby is tall and broad-shouldered and his face is clean-cut, masculine, attractive. But on second glance the impression dislocates into a number of rather odd parts.

The head, for instance. That amazing brain is lodged in a smallish oval skull that doesn't actually reach very far above the ears. The forehead is low and makes the jaw look large, at certain angles almost

Neanderthal. The look on his face is primitive, too, the alert but unthinking look of an animal. A big wild animal that hunts for a living. There is a sense of danger about Bobby; in some ways I am as careful with him as I would be with a tiger. His eyes are like a tiger's. They hold the same yellow-green serenity and frightening emptiness. And when he laughs, his wide, full-lipped mouth opens into a huge happy cave filled with bright white teeth. Most of his expressions are rudimentary: direct expressions of fear, hunger, anger, pleasure, pain, suspicion, interest — all the emotions a man or even an animal can have without being involved with any other man or animal. I have rarely seen his face register the social emotions of sympathy, invitation, acknowledgement, humor, tenderness, love.

There is also something primitive in Bobby's body and the way it moves. He wears a business suit about as naturally as a python wears a necktie. Standing about 6'1", he weighs close to 190, and a padded jacket makes his shoulders look so wide his head seems even smaller than it is. "Like a pea sitting on a ruler," somebody said. His movements are direct, vigorous, sometimes comically awkward. He walks literally twice as fast as the average good hiker, but he walks the way a hen runs — and this hen fills a doorway. He comes on head forward, feet wide apart and toes turned in, shoulders lurching from side to side, elbows stuck out like wing joints and fingers flipping like feathers. Fastening his eyes on a point about four miles distant and slightly above everybody's head, he charges unswervably toward that point through the densest crowds, a man in motion with an end in view.

As this systematic awkwardness suggests, there are wild gaps and erratic stammers in the flow of Bobby's life. More than almost anyone I can remember, he functions like Frankenstein's creature, like a man made of fragments connected by wires and animated by a monstrous will. When the will collapses or the wires cross, Bobby sometimes cannot execute the simplest physical acts. When he loses interest in a line of thought or action he has pursued for as little as three minutes, his legs may simply give out, as if he had just hiked 20 miles, and he will shuffle off to bed like an old man. And once, when I asked him a question while he was eating, his control circuits got so befuddled from trying to carry two messages at once that he jabbed his fork into his cheek.

Bobby has the same kind of trouble talking. He is the most single-minded man I have ever known. He seems to keep only one thought in his mind at once, and a simple thought at that. He talks as he thinks, in simple sentences that lead him where he is going like steppingstones, and his voice is the voice of a joke robot programmed to sound like a street voice from Brooklyn: flat, monotonous, the color of asphalt.

I sometimes think it is the voice of a man pretending to be an object, so that people won't notice he is soft and alive and then do things to hurt him. But Bobby is too vital to play dead successfully. Energy again and again short-circuits the robot. Energy like a tiger prowls and glares inside him. Now and then it escapes in a binge of anger. Every night, all night, it escapes into chess. When he sits at the board, a big dangerous cat slips into his skin. His chest swells, his green eyes glow, his sallowness fills with warm blood. All the life in his fragmented body flows and he looks wild and beautiful. When I see Bobby in my mind, I see him sprawled with lazy power at a chessboard, eyes half closed, listening to the imaginary rustle of moving pieces as a tiger lies and listens to the murmur of the moving reeds.

New York always has a bad effect on Bobby. He goes back to it with dread and fascination, like a Jonah slipping back into his whale. Andrew Davis knew that this time he might easily get lost inside the whale and never make it to the plane. So he had prepared the kind of script they used to write for *Mission: Impossible.* The plan was to abduct a man for his own good and do it so sneakily that the victim wouldn't know what was happening to him. It was a job for a genie, but Davis didn't happen to have one in his address book. So he asked Tony Saidy to take Bobby on a shopping trip and rounded up two friends and a professional chauffeur to help him. The friends knew Bobby but had not met Saidy. The chauffeur had never even heard of Bobby. And none of the five had ever abducted anything trickier than a cookie.

Herb Hochstetter and Morris Dubinsky, who turned up at the Yale Club at 9:30 Wednesday morning, were the first members of Davis' crew to stand watch. Hochstetter is a stocky, energetic man of 55 with a hard business mouth and pale amused eyes almost concealed by folds of rough skin that hang down from his eyebrows like worn portieres. A man who has lived a little too hard but isn't a damn bit sorry and would like to shoot off a few more cannon crackers before he buys a condominium in St. Petersburg. He is a well-known marketing consultant and an old friend and client of Andrew Davis', who introduced him to Bobby about 12 years ago.

Morris Dubinsky is an ex-butcher from the Bronx and as independent as a rubber chicken. When the supermarkets took over the meat business, he closed his shop and bought a taxi. Two years later, he traded it in for a $10,500 Cadillac limousine. Not long ago, he bought six limousines, all shiny new, and had enough money in the bank to pay cash — about $81,000, plus tax. "I don't owe nobody," Dubinsky told me. "I pay cash or I don't get it. Payin' cash is my biggest thrill in life. That way nobody's gonna lean on Morris." Dubinsky is the last man anybody would lean on. At 54, he is built (as he is the first to admit) "like an ox." He stands 5'10", weighs 183 pounds and has muscles in his hair. He also has muscles in his lip. When Dubinsky doesn't like something, Dubinsky lets you hear about it — and you don't need an ear trumpet.

By one P.M., Hochstetter and Dubinsky were getting antsy. They had called Davis several times. Davis had called Bobby and heard him mumble with a tongue like a sash weight that it was still too early. So he had urged them to sit shibah till the body resurrected. A little after one o'clock Saidy arrived and by two P.M. he had dug Bobby out. But after that almost nothing happened. Bobby lolled millionairily on Cadillac upholstery, called friends on the radiophone, picked up some traveler's checks, had breakfast at the Stage Delicatessen, ran a couple of minor errands, and then headed back to the Yale Club for a meeting with Davis. In theory, he was getting ready to go to Iceland: in fact, he wasn't. In everything that concerned the match, his energy was so viscous that he moved like a man struggling up out of deep sleep and knowing he wasn't going to like what he saw when he opened his eyes.

Who could blame him? In the past 18 months, Bobby had played one long tournament and three long matches, all of them jackhammering assaults on his nervous system. Now he was facing the longest and most difficult match of his career, a contest that might run to 24 games and last up to 75 days. But Bobby had never quailed at challenges before. Something more than the challenge seemed to be troubling him now.

Andrew Davis is a slim man of middle height with quick dark eyes behind professorial specs, a small head penciled with careful hair and a big unexpected crashing Teddy Roosevelt smile. He is 43 and has the crinkles to prove it, but he also has a squirrely schoolboy brightness and a balloon-popping sense of fun. Davis likes to think of himself, I suspect, as something between an English master at Choate, a hard-haggling jobber in the Garment District and a dwindled Disraeli. He reads voraciously in almost all directions, but the intellectual side subordinates without overmuch regret to the zestful practical man.

At the law Davis is shrewd, precise and so ethical that friends call him Saint Andrew. He doesn't altogether enjoy the tricks of his trade, and there are things he will not do in order to win. He shares with his father a solid unspectacular practice that provides a comfortable living but will never make him rich. He certainly won't get rich off Bobby. People close to Bobby tell me that in 12 years as his lawyer he has never charged him a dime. Why not? "Traditional Jewish awe of intellect," a friend of Davis' said. "Andy sees Bobby as a sort of holy idiot, a frail vessel into which the pure logos has been poured. He will never abandon him."

For weeks now, grating his teeth, Davis had been wishing he could. Bobby took time and energy that other clients needed. But he had hung in there because there was nobody to take his place and because he felt in his bones that Bobby was riding recklessly for a fall that might be fatal. Davis saw black if Bobby backed out of the match. The media, already annoyed and mocking, would gut him: the public, denied a spectacle it was lusting after, would remember him with disgust diminishing slowly to contempt; the chess world would write him off as a second Paul Morphy, a genius too morbid to realize his talent. Chess organizers would hesitate to sign for a major match a man who might not even show up to play.

But what worried Davis most was the potential effect of such mass rejection on Bobby himself. "Being the best chess player in the world is Bobby's only way of relating himself to the world," he once told me. "If he can't function as that, he can't function. So if he doesn't play this match and the consequences are as bad as I'm afraid they'll be, we could see a serious breakdown there." Then he looked me straight in the eye and said: "Maybe suicide."

With such risks in mind, Davis proceeded delicately when he met Bobby at the Yale Club. Bobby greeted him with a big smile, but behind the smile Davis felt wariness and resistance. So he didn't press. When Bobby asked how negotiations with the Icelanders were going, Davis almost casually mentioned the deadlock over his demand that the players get 30 percent of the gate apiece, but he laid the blame tactfully on the Icelandic Chess Federation's New York lawyer and suggested that a direct approach to Gudmundur Thorarinsson, the head of the I.C.F., would produce a better result. His idea was to keep Bobby pliable, to head off a hard statement of principle that Bobby would later feel obliged to stick to.

Davis respected many of Bobby's reasons for not wanting to play in Iceland. Way back in March, Bobby had told me that Iceland was "a stupid place for the match." He said it was too small, too isolated, too primitive. He said the hall was inadequate and he was sure that the problem of lighting a championship chess match was beyond the skills of the local technicians. As for hotels, he said there was only one on the island fit to live in, and he was convinced he would have to share it with the Russians and the press. "All the time I'd be watched. No privacy. And another thing — there's no way for me to relax in Iceland, nothing to do between games. The TV is dull, the movies are all three years old, there's no good restaurants hardly. Not one tennis court on the whole island, not even a bowling alley. Things like that might hurt my playing."

Bobby was also sure that gate receipts would be disastrous because there just weren't enough Icelanders to fill the seats — and who could afford to travel all the way to Iceland and stay there for two months to watch a chess match? But what bothered him most was the problem of coverage. A few reporters might fly in for the start and finish of the match, but the games could not be telecast to North America and Europe — no Intelsat equipment. "And this match ought to be televised. If it is, I predict that chess will become a major sport in the United States practically overnight."

Bobby also had some financial objections. He considered himself a superstar, the strongest chess player in the world, and when it came to money, he wanted what superstars like Joe Frazier and Muhammad Ali are offered. The I.C.F. had already met two of his three conditions: a guarantee of $78,125 to the winner and $46,875 to the loser and a thick slice of the film and television profits — 30 percent to Boris, 30 percent to Bobby. But when Bobby demanded 30 percent of the gate, the I.C.F. had stonewalled. "If we give Bobby 30 percent, we must give Boris 30 percent," said Thorarinsson. "But if we do that, how will we raise the prize money? No, the prize money is Bobby's share of the gate."

At that point, Bobby had stonewalled, too. "If I don't get the gate," he told Davis grimly, "I don't go."

Even before discussions with Thorarinsson began, Bobby had been flirting with the idea of abandoning the match. Right from the start, he had been suspicious of Iceland because it was Spassky's first choice as a site for the match. Brooding alone in his room at Grossinger Hotel in the Catskills, where he had set up his "training camp," he found enemies everywhere. He described Dr. Max Euwe, the president of F.I.D.E., as "a tool of the Russians." He said Ed Edmondson of the U.S. Chess Federation, the man who had spent two years of his life and about $75,000 of the U.S.C.F.'s money to nurse Bobby through the challenge rounds, had "made a deal" and "betrayed" him to the Russians. By the time he left for California, he had decided that the U.S. Government was against him, too. Edmondson and Euwe, he figured, had been persuaded by Washington to sidetrack the match to Reykjavík, where a Fischer victory would be so effectively entombed that it would not disturb the developing *détente* between the U.S. and the Soviet Union.

By the time Bobby returned to New York from California, these speculations had overgrown his mind like vines and may have obscured his view of the real situation around him. He was gripped by the idea that Thorarinsson and Euwe and the I.C.F. and F.I.D.E. must be "punished" for their "arrogance." He told Davis to make sure that the deal they made would prevent the Icelanders from earning a króna on the match and, if possible, would leave them with a loss. Even on those terms, he wasn't sure he would go. He shrugged off the money he would be giving up and seemed unconcerned that the title would relapse by default to his lifelong enemies, the Russians. As for his career, he had no fears. "Everybody knows I'm the best," he said carelessly, "so why bother to play?"

After a few minutes with Bobby, it was clear to Davis that these ideas still had the run of his client's head. It was also clear that reasonable discourse would hardly drive them out in a day. Only a Gordian stroke could unwind his mind, and a little after six P.M., Davis delivered it.

He took Bobby to the Yale Club bar for a meeting with Chester Fox and Richard Stein. Fox was the almost-unknown director the I.C.F. had signed to make a documentary movie of the match, a 37-year-old cherub with an acute case of freckles and a halo of fuzzy orange hair. Stein was his backer, a stocky, capable wheeler-dealer who had made millions in athletic apparel and then started a second career in the law. His eyes twinkled like money and he came from a business where a man was judged by the reputation of his brand name and the size of his cigar. From what he'd heard of Bobby, he was in for some heavy haggling, and that suited him just fine.

They had come, Stein announced, to offer Bobby a deal. Bobby's contract with the I.C.F. guaranteed him 30 percent of all profits from the films of the match. In addition to that, Stein offered him a percentage (Fox later said that it was 12½ percent) of the profits of Chester Fox, Inc. According to Stein, all Bobby had to do in return was go to Iceland and play chess — and maybe read some comments accompanying the film Fox intended to make of the match.

Stein and Davis watched Bobby closely. For different reasons they had both hoped the offer would impress him. Instead, it seemed to confuse him and stir up his suspicions. As Stein gave a rundown on residuals, syndications, costs above and below the line, Bobby sat anxiously twisting and tearing and crushing a paper cup until he had mashed it down to the size of a lima bean. Suddenly, eyes narrow with suspicion, he broke in.

"Yeah, but how much am I gonna make?"

Stein blinked. "I realized then," he told me later, "that deals to Bobby were like chess to me. He hadn't understood a word I'd said."

Patiently, Stein explained that the profits of a complicated venture are hard to predict. "But I wouldn't be involved if I didn't think it would make money. And whatever it makes, you get a share of that."

Bobby's eyes narrowed again. "Are you gonna make more money than me?" he demanded.

Stein looked helplessly at Davis. "What could I do?" he asked his wife afterward. "I was pissing in the wind. About business the guy was a *shlub*."

Stein then explained to Bobby that in the American way of doing business, the people who risk the money are entitled to most of the profit. Bobby knew that, but he wasn't sure that the principle applied when *he* was involved.

"Well," Stein asked finally, "have we got a deal or haven't we?"

Bobby wouldn't say yes, but then, he didn't say no. "You better hurry up," he told Fox earnestly, "or you'll miss that plane to Iceland."

Davis almost cracked up. Bobby telling Fox to get on a plane to Iceland without a nailed-down deal was like Gaston at the guillotine saying, "After you, Alphonse." But if Bobby wanted Fox in Iceland, did that mean he expected to be there, too? Had Stein's offer made the match seem more desirable? Not for long. Ten minutes after they left, Bobby was bad-mouthing the Icelanders again. The Gordian stroke had missed its mark. Some other way would have to be found to get Bobby to the chessboard on time.

Robert Haydock Hallowell III is a big, warm, vital man who goes bounding through life like a Saint Bernard through a blizzard. One look and people know he's loaded with the kind of hearty spirits that keep out the cold. His eyes are bright, his voice is clear, his grin is large and welcoming. He stands 6′2″, weighs 250 pounds and at 34 has the same barging energy that made him a hard-hitting third-string tackle on the worst Harvard team since World War Two. There is nothing third-string about his mind. He is a successful executive — "director of new ventures" for a producer of limited editions of medals, plates and fine-art prints called the Franklin Mint — with an education in the classics and a fine salty turn of phrase.

Hallowell met Bobby in 1966, when he supervised production for the Xerox Corporation of a book called *Bobby Fischer Teaches Chess.* He met Davis at the same time and became his friend and client. "I like Bobby because he fights for his beliefs," Hallowell told me. "I go down the line for him."

When Hallowell showed up at the Yale Club on Thursday morning, he ran head on into a crisis. The story of The Tussle in the Doorway between Bobby and the British reporters was on the wires by 11 A.M. and in a few hours half the newsmen in New York would be camping in the Yale Club's lobby. Bobby had to be yanked out of there fast. But that aggressive reporter and photographer were patrolling the lobby like a couple of jumpy coon dogs with a panther up a tree. Hallowell and Saidy and Hochstetter worked up a scheme to smuggle Bobby through the enemy lines.

Still indignant about the attempt to break into his room, Bobby was delighted at the idea of escape. He promised to get up soon, but three visits and almost two hours later, Hallowell and Saidy found him still stumbling around in his Jockey shorts. While Bobby washed and shaved and dressed and packed, Hallowell, Saidy and Beers sat around in the tiny room, feeling like 16 clowns in a phone booth, making small talk and helpful gestures and wondering how in Christ's name they could ever get Bobby to the plane by 9:30 that night if this was to be the pace of progress. At last, about two P.M., the plan of escape was run off.

Saidy took the front elevator to the lobby. The reporter had left, but the photographer was still there. Principally for his benefit, Saidy informed Hochstetter and Dubinsky in a loud voice: "He's not going out. Let's take off." And off they went in the limousine. But the photographer, smelling a rat, ran to check the freight entrance. He arrived just in time to see the back door swing open and Bobby, Hallowell and Beers walk out.

When Hallowell told the photographer to buzz off, he said OK and headed east on 44th Street. Bobby headed west. Suddenly reversing direction, the photographer ran ahead of Bobby and began snapping shots.

With that, Hallowell recalls, "Bobby wheeled around and took off in the opposite direction like a big-assed bird." He turned at the corner and ran south for two blocks at top speed, dodging cars, startling pedestrians, making heads spin like turnstiles at the height of the lunchtime crush in midtown Manhattan. And after him, knees high and eyes bulging, came Hallowell and Beers. When they reached 42nd Street, they all wound down to a stop. Hallowell and Beers were gasping. Bobby had plenty of wind left. They looked back. No photographer. A big grin spread across Bobby's face. "Really showed *him,* huh? Haw! Haw! Haw!"

Hallowell laughed with him. Why not? He had no way of knowing that in the incident a theme had emerged, a theme of flight that would follow their enterprise all day long like a little cold wind and before the night was over would send him racing after Bobby through rain and darkness under circumstances far more frenzied and bizarre.

The next problem to appear was Dubinsky. After one afternoon in Bobby's company, he had decided that his chief passenger had "a hernia in his head." He was also appalled by the behavior of Bobby's friends. "They didn't treat him like a person. They treated him like some idiot king. I'm telling you, it was disgusting to see the way these educated people crept up his behind."

And then came the incident at Unbelievable Syms. Dubinsky had recommended the store as a great place to buy a suit cheap ("Two hundred dollars is ninety dollars there"), but after about ten minutes, Bobby walked out. Dubinsky was suspicious. On the way to Barney's, a clothing store on the Lower West Side, he sizzled Hallowell for dropping a cigarette ash on his precious carpet. Then he called the salesman at Syms and somehow satisfied himself that Bobby had walked out because he thought Dubinsky was getting a kickback. "And that," as Hochstetter put it, "really started the pissing match."

Bobby bought three expensive ready-made suits at Barney's and then asked to be driven farther uptown to buy a Sony TV set and a digital clock. Smoldering, Dubinsky complied. Meanwhile, Bobby's mood had also been steadily souring. On the way downtown to Unbelievable Syms, he had called Davis and warned him he still hadn't decided to go to Iceland. Then he began telling Saidy he definitely didn't want to go — the deals weren't right and, besides, there was too much to do first.

Saidy's reaction was to make understanding noises that sounded dangerously like agreement. "Saidy figured it was better to ride along with Bobby on the downswings," Hallowell told me, "and then try to carry him over the top on the upswings. But he often came off sounding mealymouthed." Hallowell and Hochstetter reacted more aggressively.

Practiced and confident persuaders, they hit Bobby with pep talks about Iceland every chance they got. Bobby in reply did little more than say "Mm."

Everyone in the car felt a sense of rising emergency. Hochstetter cut out on a brief errand and while he was in the clear, put through a call to his brother, the film lobby's man in Washington, and asked him to persuade Vice-President Agnew, Bobby's favorite politician, to send a telegram wishing Bobby Godspeed. His brother tried, Hochstetter said, but Agnew couldn't be reached.

A little while later, Hallowell got out and went to the Yale Club to pick up Bobby's baggage and check him out. Bobby lives out of two enormous plastic suitcases that look like toasted piano crates. He had one of them in 1003, and hefting it around gave Hallowell his second unexpected workout of the day. Hochstetter joined him at the Yale Club and they both repaired by taxi to Bill's Gay Nineties bar on East 54th Street, the point of rendezvous. At that stage, neither one had a clue if the arrow on Bobby's compass was pointing to Iceland or to California. On the evidence available, it was possible to say only that a man who was running around town getting ready to go to Iceland was probably still considering the trip.

Davis turned up briefly at the Gay Nineties and carried Hallowell off to some legal meetings. A little later the limousine arrived. Bobby had his TV set but no digital clock, and after an hour without pep talks, his mood had become darker. Tuning out the conversation, he buried his head in his chess wallet.

Looking no sweeter, Dubinsky drove Bobby, Saidy and Hochstetter to a house on the Upper West Side where Bobby had left some clothes with a friend. Bobby came out carrying a suitcase with a handle that wouldn't stay on. "And now," said Hochstetter, "the Mack Sennett stuff started."

Basically a sociable man, Dubinsky saw his chance to make up.

"I'll fix it," he said, coming forward helpfully.

"You can't fix it," Bobby told him irritably.

Dubinsky drew himself up. "I can fix anything!" he answered — and proceeded to. When the handle was reattached, he stood back and gestured confidently at his handiwork.

Bobby picked the suitcase up. The handle came off. "See?" Bobby said. Twin jets of steam, Hochstetter assures me, shot out of Dubinsky's ears, and that was the last time that day he had kind words for anybody.

Shortly after 6:30 P.M., while Davis was reading over the agreement

with Stein and persuading him to sign it even though Bobby might refuse, he got an anguished phone call from someone in Bobby's party.
According to Davis, the caller said: "We need you. Get here as fast as you
can. Things look bad. We don't know how long we can hold him."

"Take him to my place right away," Davis answered calmly. "I'll meet
you there."

Bobby arrived at the Davis apartment looking like a grenade about to
go off. "The atmosphere was so tense it was unreal," Hallowell told me
later, and Davis agreed: "It was a touchy moment. You couldn't make
eye contact with him. He was obviously at the point of refusing to take
the plane. I felt like a psychiatrist trying to cool out a patient hanging on
the edge."

Instinctively, Davis played the occasion as a casual evening with old
friends. His apartment is a pleasant old-fashioned straggle of fairly large
rooms in a good unswanky building in the West 70s. Hallowell and
Saidy and Hochstetter sank wearily into some solid nondescript chairs
and a fat sofa grouped around a glass-topped coffee table. Davis' wife,
Jessie, a gentle, dark-haired woman who has made her own career as a
pediatrician, brought them drinks. The three Davis children — Jennie,
14, Margot, 11, and David, 9 — were in and out of the room and the
conversation. Bobby took a chair in the darkest corner and sat there
looking stony. But he brightened a little when he saw one of the Davis
cats, a big, soft fur ball that looked consoling. Jessie brought the cat over
and Bobby began to stroke it firmly and rapidly. "That cat usually likes
to be petted," Hallowell told me. "But for some reason, whenever Bobby
touched it, the cat would wriggle free and run away. Jessie brought it
back several times, but it still wouldn't settle down. Finally Bobby gave
up and just sat there looking peeved." He perked up again when Jessie
brought him a big roast-beef sandwich and a glass of milk, but when the
others tried to include him in the conversation, he just mumbled and
looked away.

Davis was in his bedroom most of the time, packing and dressing for
the trip to Reykjavík, but now and again he came wandering into the
living room to follow the conversation and sneak a look at Bobby.
Bobby didn't seem any happier as time went by, and time went by too
fast for comfort. Take-off was scheduled for 9:30 P.M. and Kennedy
Airport was about an hour away. There was a second flight scheduled to
leave at 9:30 that usually took off a little later and a final flight scheduled
for 10:30, but Davis wanted to keep them as emergency reserves. Eight
o'clock, he figured, was about as late as they could sensibly leave.

Davis checked his watch: 7:20. There was still time to call Thorarinsson and wrangle some more about the gate. As a negotiator, he knew it was the perfect moment to call. He had Thorarinsson over a barrel. With perfect sincerity he could say: No gate, no match. But as the man who had to deliver Bobby to the airport, he didn't want to risk a refusal from Thorarinsson unless he had to. If he was reading Bobby's mood correctly, anything less than a complete capitulation by Thorarinsson might kill the last hope of putting Bobby on the plane. So he dawdled over his packing and put off the phone call. Then promptly at 7:30, he slipped into a baggy tweed jacket, strolled into the living room and, looking at Bobby brightly, inquired: "Well, shall we go?"

It was a cool stroke and, under the circumstances, it had about as good a chance as any of succeeding, but it didn't. The others rolled out of the chairs and moved toward the door, but Bobby looked startled and began to sputter. "Huh? What? I haven't agreed to go! What's the deal? What's the deal? What about those open points?"

"Why don't you guys go on down and wait in the car?" Davis continued calmly. "Bobby and I have some business to do." Then he turned to Bobby. "OK, why don't I call Thorarinsson and see what I can work out? I'll call from the bedroom — want to come in?"

"No," Bobby said quickly. "No, I'll stay out here. You handle it."

"Fine," said Davis. But he knew the situation was anything but fine. Bobby was less interested in making a deal than in keeping his escape routes clear. As long as he stayed in the living room and let Davis handle it, he was free to repudiate any deal that Davis might make. The suicidal impulse was so obvious it was scary — scarier yet because Bobby didn't seem to be aware of it. In order to defeat Thorarinsson, he seemed entirely willing to destroy himself.

The phone call was a disaster. "I am sorry," Thorarinsson said coldly, "but we have gone as far as we can. . . . We have made concession after concession. We have done everything in our power to satisfy Mr. Fischer. But we have begun to wonder if it is *possible* to satisfy Mr. Fischer. We Icelanders are a generous people, Mr. Davis, but we are also a proud people. We will be freely generous, but we will not be forced to be generous."

Davis understood Thorarinsson's position. He was a rising young politician who at 32 was a member of Reykjavík's city council, and his constituents were already hollering that he had given Bobby too much. Certainly he had, if by making concessions he had expected to shut Bobby up. "Even if they turned over the Bank of Iceland to Bobby,"

Davis once told me, "there would still be something he wanted." But now it wasn't really a question of concessions. Somehow Davis had to make Thorarinsson realize, without actually telling him, that their interests at the moment almost exactly coincided, that he was just trying to find a face-saving compromise and rescue the match.

It was 7:55. Whatever he did, it had to be done in the next 95 minutes. Davis needed time to think, but the only time left was the time it took to get to the airport.

Davis walked into the living room briskly, like a man who had just accomplished something. He told Bobby curtly what had happened and suggested that Thorarinsson might take a different stand if he could be sure that this was Bobby's last demand. "Look," Davis concluded, "I think I can make a deal, come to some betterment based on costs. So why don't we go to the airport now? We've got the limousine right here. On the way, we can talk the deal over. I can call Thorarinsson from the airport. We can keep the limousine. If we have to come back, we'll come back. We'll keep all our options open. OK?"

Bobby very hesitantly said OK. Davis asked Jessie to call Loftleidir (Icelandic Airlines) and tell them to hold the 9:30 plane. Jessie and the children wished Bobby good luck and then shyly kissed him goodbye. Embarrassed but pleased, Bobby hurried out to the elevator.

Outside, a light rain was falling — along with some debris from Dubinsky's latest explosion. It seems that while waiting in the car, Hallowell and Hochstetter had realized they were hungry and had run over to Gitlitz' Deli at 70th and Broadway. They came back with three corned-beef sandwiches — one for Saidy, too — and opened the back door of the Cadillac, figuring to get in out of the rain, where they could eat in comfort. Not a chance.

"Just one minute, gentlemen," Dubinsky announced in the triumphant tone of a policeman who has spotted two shady-looking characters sneaking gelignite into a bank. "Not in *my* car you don't eat sandwiches."

"But Morris, it's raining out here and we don't have raincoats. We'll — "

"I don't care if it's a blizzard out there. I been through all this before. Ketchup smears on the upholstery, coffee puddles on the rug. I'm sorry, gentlemen. A car is not a restaurant. No eating in this car."

Hochstetter, Hallowell and Saidy looked at one another, shrugged, crossed the street, sat on somebody's steps and ate in the rain.

Damp but still game, they hurried back to the limousine when Bobby and Davis came down. Dubinsky opened the door of the limousine and waited for Bobby to get in. But he didn't get in. He just stood there, head down and glaring, like a steer at the gate of the butcher's van. Davis' heart fell into his shoe. Bobby whirled at him resentfully. "I mean, what's the deal? I still don't know what the deal is! Why go to the airport now? There's another plane, right? Why should I go if I don't have a deal?"

"All right," Davis said calmly. "Let's walk around the block and talk about the deal." Bobby had no raincoat on and he was carrying his chess magazines, but Davis was afraid that if they went back to the apartment to talk, he would never get Bobby out of there again. So they started off, Bobby tagging along suspiciously.

"What I have in mind," Davis began, flashing his wickedest paw-in-the-cookie-jar grin, "is to structure a deal that gives the players *everything* and doesn't give the Icelanders *anything*."

Putting it like that was an inspiration. Bobby's eyes lit up. Davis went on talking, winging it, flinging it, grabbing ideas out of the air and watching Bobby's face as he built up a dream castle of a deal that made Bobby feel like a king and shut Thorarinsson in a financial dungeon that sounded truly dreadful but in fact had no walls at all. At one stroke Davis robbed Bobby of his main apparent motive for not going to Iceland and gave him an extra inducement to play.

"Well," Davis wound up firmly, "shall I try it on him?" Startled, pleased, suspecting a trick but unable to see it, fighting for a delay any way he could get it, Bobby said ye-e-es. Davis got him back upstairs before he had time to change his mind. When Jessie saw Bobby walk in, her smile was something less than sincere and the cat hid.

The proposal Davis made was simple but subtle: "The players will take *all* the gate above $250,000." The beauty of it was that it seemed to give Bobby plenty but actually gave him nothing. If 1500 people paid five dollars apiece to attend 20 games, the gate would amount to only $150,000 — and Thorarinsson privately figured it would be less. So if he agreed to the proposal, he would merely *seem* to make another concession to Bobby. Thorarinsson was tempted, but he felt that the people of Iceland were so angry with Bobby that even a hollow concession might turn them against the man who made it. He also feared that Moscow might not go along. So he refused.

*   *   *

Davis must have done some tall talking to get Bobby out of that apartment and down to the limousine a second time. Thorarinsson had given him worse than nothing to work with, but somehow he persuaded Bobby that there was a solid chance of getting the deal he wanted before the plane took off.

The limousine pulled away from the apartment house where Davis lives no earlier than 8:45 — that left about 45 minutes before take-off time. Traffic being normal, they would be about 15 minutes late. For that long, Davis was pretty sure, Loftleidir would delay the plane.

But traffic was not normal. Three minutes from home, they were caught in a jam. Dubinsky made a dog-leg and broke free — into another jam. Everywhere he turned, the East Side was a mess. It was raining harder now, too, and that didn't help. Dubinsky's eyes gleamed like red lights in the rearview mirror and he began to mutter.

Bobby was in a foul mood, too. The minute he sat down in the back seat and felt all those big shoulders hemming him in, he began to shallow breathe and dart his eyes around like a setup being taken for a ride. Saidy sensed the problem and force-fed him reassurance. "Man, think of the fantastic deals you've got! The prize money alone is ten times anything there's ever been in chess."

"Yeah," Bobby said, "if I get it."

"You'll get it," Saidy insisted. "It's in trust for you. In trust means it's *there* for you. And on top of that, there's your cut of the film and television sales, the fee you're getting from TelePrompTer for letting them use your name, not to mention the house, the car, a staff of three. And when you're champion, they'll be beating a path to your door with endorsements and TV and film offers. You'll be able to write your own ticket!"

Saidy meant well, but when you're dealing with Bobby, casting bread upon the waters often brings up a crocodile.

"Yeah, that reminds me," Bobby said, turning to Davis, "what about that hundred and twenty-five thousand Paul Marshall said he'd get me from Chester Fox?"

Davis was startled. "What hundred and twenty-five thousand? I don't know anything about it."

Horror filled Bobby's face. "You mean you OK'd the deal with Fox and it didn't include that?"

"I don't know anything about it."

"Oh!" he groaned, looking almost ill with disappointment and a fury that only his respect for Davis restrained. "*Ohhhhh!* How could you *do* that?"

Another crisis. Davis began to feel like the captain of a pea pod in a hurricane. But he held steady.

"OK," he said calmly, picking up the radiophone. "Let's call Marshall and get the facts." Paul Marshall is David Frost's New York attorney, a brilliant negotiator and a specialist in international copyright law who had worked with Bobby until mid-spring, when Bobby repudiated a general agreement that Marshall had patiently teased out of the Icelanders. At that point, Marshall had resigned, but he was still friendly to Bobby's interests in a distant, wary way.

As the phone rang, Davis noted with silent irony that the limousine was still on the Manhattan side of the 59th Street Bridge. At the present rate of progress, there was almost an hour to go before they reached Kennedy, an hour in which Bobby could dream up all sorts of mind-pretzeling problems.

Marshall sounded depressingly relaxed and unconcerned. "I thought you were already up there," he said vaguely. "Well, what can I do for you?" Davis told him and Marshall quickly laid out the terms of an agreement he had worked out some weeks before with Fox. As it turned out, the terms were similar to the ones Davis and Stein had arrived at a few hours earlier. Marshall's agreement was a little better for Bobby, but there was no problem, Marshall and Davis agreed. The text could be altered and Fox could sign it in Reykjavík.

"No! No! I'm not going!" Bobby announced when he heard that. "Not under those conditions!"

Davis handed him the phone.

"Look," Marshall said. "Fox is nothing without you. He's got to go along. What are you worried about? I make deals all day long. I know a deal when I see it. You've got a beautiful deal. What can I tell you? Not even Ali gets that kind of contract with a percentage guarantee."

Bobby muttered some more, but the fire had gone out of his complaints. As often happened when Marshall began to speak, the tightness and suspicion in Bobby's face relaxed. He let the matter drop — for the time being.

Dubinsky knew Queens like a cat knows a trash barrel, and once across the 59th Street Bridge, he struck out through back streets that hadn't seen a Cadillac since the asphalt went down. As the car picked up speed, everybody relaxed a little and Saidy got Bobby involved in a conversation about digital clocks. Bobby said he wanted to take one to Reykjavík, and in this and other remarks, Hallowell sensed an assumption that he was going to Reykjavík that night. The mood in the limousine improved steeply. Davis began explaining his plan to elude the media people when they arrived at Loftleidir. Bobby listened eagerly — like all chess players, he dearly loves a plot. As the limousine skimmed past the first airport buildings, Davis found himself thinking that with a little luck they might just make it.

It was 9:50 P.M. when the limousine entered the traffic bay that led past the Loftleidir passenger terminal. There was a crowd in front of the terminal — passengers or press? As the limousine drifted past, Bobby sat well back in his seat. "Press up the ass," Hallowell told me. "Looked like thirty, maybe forty newspaper and television people waiting on the sidewalk or just inside the glass doors, obviously there for Bobby." Every third newsman wore a necklace of Nikons. Here and there, somebody had a TV camera harnessed to his shoulder. They were all jabbering and looking sharp at the cars that pulled up.

According to plan, the limousine eased to a stop about 30 yards beyond Loftleidir. Davis left the car and walked back toward the crowd. Dubinsky parked about 20 yards farther along and Hallowell doubled back to Loftleidir to let Davis know where the limousine was parked. Davis meanwhile slipped anonymously through the crowd of reporters and cameramen and was soon in close conversation with two young men.

Both were slim, alert, bright-eyed, blond. Tedd Hope stood about 6'1" and looked like Tab Hunter did ten years ago. But behind his almost-too-handsome face, there was a cool, swift executive mind. At 30, he was the manager of Loftleidir's Kennedy operation. Hans Indridason, the other young man, was about an inch shorter and had a bright ice ax of a face. But inside the forceful image, there was a subtle diplomat. At 29, he was head of the reservations department and a trouble shooter for the president of the U.S. branch of the company. Good friends on the job and off, both of these young men were witty, honest, likable and disinclined to swallow anybody's exhaust. Both had the punishing energy that gets things done under pressure. Indridason had been vigorously informed by his superiors that getting Bobby to Iceland was a matter of national concern, and the Loftleidir staff stood ready to move Bobby north by any means short of a viking raid on Dubinsky's limousine.

Davis gave a quick fill-in on the situation in the limousine ("Very touchy. We've got to play along."). Hope listed the remaining flights. The first of the 9:30 flights was already closed, he said, but the second was still open and there was the 10:30 flight, too.

One down, two to go.

Then the three of them put together a simple plan to elude the media and ease Bobby on board the 9:30 plane in the next ten minutes. But there were problems aside from Bobby and the press. The crowds, for one thing. It was June 29, the height of the summer rush to Europe. Cars and buses and stretch limousines, honking and gunning their engines, came whizzing into the traffic bay in front of the terminal and piled up two-deep along the curb. Then they popped open like huge parcels and out fell brightly colored passengers and luggage. People everywhere were kissing and laughing and running around with blank airport faces. A large sour-faced cop kept blowing one of those whistles that go through your head like a bright steel nail. And on top of everything, it was now raining cantaloupes.

The plan was to keep Bobby hidden in the limousine until he could be slipped into a Loftleidir station wagon and driven to the plane. "OK," said Davis, "let's do it." Hope hurried off through the back of the building to get the wagon and drive it to where Bobby was. Davis, Indridason and Hallowell walked slowly back to the limousine. A few minutes later, after a rough passage through the holiday traffic, Hope arrived in a white station wagon, which he double-parked beside Dubinsky's Cadillac. The cop promptly banged on his fender. "Move along, mister," he said. Hope explained the baggage transfer. "Make it quick," the officer ruled. "You see the conditions."

Hope ran to his tailgate and opened it. Doing his duty but not liking it, Dubinsky emerged into the rain and opened his trunk. Then Hope, Hallowell, Dubinsky and a Loftleidir supervisor named Einar Asgeirsson, prodded by a cop who looked night sticks at them every few seconds, hustled Bobby's luggage into the back of the station wagon. Davis checked the bags to make sure they were all there.

"OK," Hope said, "it's ten-fifteen. This plane is already forty-five minutes late. If you want to make it, we have to move now."

"OK," Davis said, "let's see if we can get Bobby to go out with the baggage."

Hallowell opened the back door of the limousine on the curb side and stuck his head in. "Bobby," he began — and stopped. The limousine was empty.

Hallowell spun around. "Where is he?"

"I don't know," Hochstetter answered. "He left while you were in the airline terminal. He said he wanted to go get a digital clock, but Tony said no, he'd get it, but before he got very far, Bobby jumped out and went after him. That's the last I saw of either of them."

Davis turned white. "Can you hold it ten minutes?" he asked Indridason, who nodded. "All right, goddamn it, let's find him!"

Davis, Hallowell and Indridason headed off at a dead run toward the main lobby. Hochstetter waited briefly at the limousine, then decided to join the hunt.

Hope jumped into the station wagon and, in line with Davis' instructions, drove the baggage out to the plane.

Dubinsky stared in disbelief at all this panic over one man's momentary disappearance. Then he flung his arms in the air. "What *is* all this horseshit?" he inquired of nobody in particular.

Davis, Hallowell and Indridason skidded through the duty-free shops like shoplifters on roller skates. All day long, disaster had been hanging over their enterprise like a five-ton chandelier with a maniac sawing at its cable. What a rotten shame, they were thinking, to get this far and then have the roof fall in. Please, God, Davis was praying, don't let the press find him now. The press didn't, but another kind of trouble did. While Davis and his friends were keeping a sharp lookout for the obvious danger, they got blind-sided.

It happened like this: About two minutes after the others had left, Bobby and Saidy spotted the limousine just as Dubinsky, hard pressed by the traffic cop, was drifting it through the traffic bay to the east arcade, an area that includes a taxi stand and a secluded courtyard.

When they arrived at the limousine, Bobby asked Dubinsky to open the trunk so he could stow the clock he had just bought in one of his suitcases. Dubinsky got out of the car and explained that the suitcases were no longer in the trunk. "We moved them into an airline station wagon," he said.

"What!" Bobby gasped, turning pale. "You moved my baggage without my permission? That's not right!" He turned to Saidy. "That's not right!"

Nervously, Saidy agreed — at the moment, it was difficult to do anything else. But that was all the support Bobby needed. "He was beginning to feel his power," Davis said later. "For two days, we had all been catering to him, and now he had the airline people holding up the plane and running around doing his bidding." All this primed his courage, and suddenly the frustration, anxiety, depression, loneliness and panic of the day came surging up and spewed out as bitter bile.

"How dare you!" Bobby burst out, whirling on Dubinsky. "How dare you take my baggage without my permission!"

Dubinsky flushed, but at first he tried to explain the situation calmly. Bobby could not listen. In a surging fury, he began to chew Dubinsky out, demanding to know by what right he had so much as touched the bags, and so on. But Dubinsky is not a man who can be chewed out.

Stocky, muscular, half a head shorter than Bobby but probably half again as strong, he came on like a wrestler, with his arms swinging dangerously and his chin thrust forward. "Listen, mister," he announced in a voice warm with promises of strangulation, "you better keep your mouth shut. If you don't, I'll shut it for you, and if you don't think I can do it, keep talking!"

Bobby went pale, but he stood toe to toe. Saidy was in a panic — if Dubinsky hit Bobby, he might knock him all the way back to California. "And I'll tell you something else," Dubinsky went on. "You may be a genius at chess, but in everything else you're a big jerk!"

Bobby's fury began to collapse. He had pictured himself as the boss raising hell with an employee, but suddenly the boot was on the other foot. "Aaaaaa!" he said, pulling in his horns and edging toward the safety of the Cadillac.

"Me," Dubinsky yelled after him triumphantly. "I'm a genius at *everything* and when I do something, I do it right. What I did with your baggage I did right, and I did it on the instructions of the man who is paying me, which you are not!"

Dubinsky was still letting him have it when Bobby ducked back into the Cadillac, looking badly scared. "That man's dangerous!" he told Saidy, rolling his eyes in alarm. "He's violent. He ought to be put away. Who is he? He looks like some kind of foreigner."

Saidy, who looks approximately like Abdul Abulbul Amir, replied soothingly: "Yeah, we don't need any foreigners around here."

Just as the fracas was ending, Davis, Hallowell and Indridason came hurrying back to the limousine from their wild-goose chase after Bobby. At the spot where the limousine had been parked, they stopped short and looked both ways along the curb. "Christ!" Davis said. Now the limousine was gone, too. Why? Where? Davis hurried over to the sour-faced cop. "Officer, if you were a smart limousine driver, where would you hide?" The cop directed them to the courtyard.

When Davis, Hallowell and Indridason arrived at the limousine, they found Bobby and Saidy sitting very quietly in the back seat and Dubinsky standing grim-faced under a canopy nearby.

"What happened?" Bobby asked in a guarded tone.

Davis said they'd all been looking for him everywhere, because the plane was already an hour late.

"Oh," Bobby said coldly, "is there a decision from Iceland?"

Davis said no.

"So why go?" Bobby asked with a hostile stare. Davis sensed that in the past ten minutes, something had definitely gone wrong.

"Bobby," he began carefully in the soothing, old-friend-of-the-family tone he uses so effectively with Bobby, "I think — "

"I mean," Bobby cut him off sharply, "stop trying to hustle me, right?"

It was time to back off. Bobby's eyes were hard again. Suddenly he came to the point.

"And how about my baggage? Where's my baggage?"

Davis looked blank, thinking vaguely of the station wagon. . . . It was gone! Had Hope gone ahead with the plan? Was the baggage —

Seeing Davis hesitate, Indridason leaned forward and said simply, "It's in the plane."

Bobby was staggered. "What? In the *plane?* Whaddya mean? I never said I'd go. What's going on? I want my baggage! I'm sitting right here — I'm not getting out of this car until my baggage is returned! Do you understand? *I want my baggage!*"

His voice was high, his hands were trembling, his eyes were wide. It was the first time Indridason had seen him and he had the impression of "a man in a very strange state of mind."

Davis hesitated, still hoping to turn the moment around, but Saidy jumped in to support Bobby in his headlong overreaction. "That's terrible, that's terrible!" Saidy said in a shocked voice, tears for some reason welling in his eyes. "You shouldn't have done that. Putting a man's baggage on a plane without his permission! That's really terrible!"

That was all Bobby needed. He had found an all-purpose excuse for delay. With Saidy's support, he rapidly propagated an awkward moment into a nightmare of shadowy motives and sinister potentials.

"That's right!" Bobby rushed on. "How could you *do* that? I never said I'd go. What are you trying to do, shanghai me? Wow! They're stealing my things! Wow! How could you *do* that?"

Davis and Hallowell explained that the bags had been moved with the best intentions. "In fact, we thought you were sitting in the car and watching us move them." But Bobby refused to listen. Turning to Indridason, Davis said in tight-lipped desperation: "All right, bring the fucking bags back! Believe me," he went on, "I know what this is doing to you. But you see what the situation is. I need time. He's exhausted, terribly overstrained. I want to take him upstairs to a restaurant, get some food into him, try to put him in a better mood. I think I can do it. But I can't do anything until you bring the fucking bags back."

It was Mack Sennett time again. Indridason said he would have to have Tedd Hope's approval. So a call was put through to the gate where the plane was being loaded. Hope boggled it further, delaying a flight already an hour late, but Indridason insisted they had to "play along with this character."

Hope had a thought. "Look, let's save time. We'll drive Bobby straight to the plane in his limousine. I'll pick up a Port Authority escort and meet you at the east gate. Bobby can inspect his baggage there. Then the limousine can follow the escort across the field to the plane."

In a few minutes the report came back that Bobby had agreed to the scheme. After complete maneuvers that used up about ten minutes, Hope, Indridason and two airport cops in a Port Authority station wagon showed up at the east gate. Where they all waited for the Cadillac. Which did not come.

Why not? Indridason was driven all the way back to the terminal, a distance of about half a mile, so he could ask if Mr. Fischer would care to drive over and inspect his bags.

"No," Bobby said grimly. "They have to bring them to me here."

In the Cadillac, anxious silence followed this remark. Bobby seemed to blame Davis for the baggage incident and had almost stopped speaking to him. When he had anything to say, he said it to Saidy or Hallowell. Something had to be done to soften his mood. Saidy did it. He was hungry, he said. How about Bobby? Why didn't they go upstairs to the coffee shop and get something to eat?

Davis knew the restaurant was a risk. Reporters and photographers were on the prowl everywhere. But just letting Bobby sit there in the Cadillac and stew seemed a much greater risk. Food was to Bobby what air was to a tire, and it was clear he needed some reinflation. Besides, Saidy was gung-ho to talk to Bobby alone and — who could tell? A firm hand hadn't worked. Maybe a soft voice would. "Good idea," Davis said.

*    *    *

Soaked to the skin and mad as wet hens after hand-carrying Bobby's baggage about 30 yards through an all-out deluge, Hope and Indridason arrived in the coffee shop, where Bobby and Saidy were sitting with Davis, who had just joined them in a booth near the entrance. Determined to be polite to his difficult guests, Indridason explained courteously that the bags — actually, four or five suitcases and packages — were now stacked in a corner of the main lobby of the International Arrivals Building, about 200 steps from the coffee shop, and that Bobby could inspect them any time he liked. Hope, who had more water in his pockets and more at risk in the enterprise, went straight to the heart of the matter as far as he was concerned. "The plane is now almost two hours late," he told Davis briskly. "You or somebody will have to make up his mind right now if he is going on this plane or not."

"Give me a couple of minutes," Davis answered. "I just want to talk to Bobby."

"We've been giving you a couple of minutes all night," Hope said icily and left.

Five minutes later, Davis came down to look the baggage over. "Hey, it's wet," he said. "He's not going to like that."

Somebody ran off to get paper towels, but Bobby arrived before the baggage could be dried off. He went straight to the first bag he saw and picked it up. The handle came off. Davis gulped. "I'll — uh — " he said and snatched the handle away from Bobby.

Then Bobby noticed the carton containing his new Sony television set. "It's wet!" he gasped.

"What do you expect," Hope answered tartly, "coming in out of the rain?"

Bobby was appalled. "You mean this has been standing in the rain? *My TV set!* Oh, no! What kind of a place *is* this? *I want this baggage dried right now!*"

Davis felt it all slipping away. For the first time that night, he looked in his mind for an answer and drew a blank. He found himself feebly wiping the Sony carton with the suitcase handle.

The paper towels arrived and everybody began frantically drying luggage.

Hope asked again if anybody wanted to make this plane. Bobby said coldly, "No, I gotta talk about it some more with Tony." Hope left, glowering, and ordered the 9:30 plane to take off. It left the ramp at 11:29 P.M.

Two gone, one to go.

"OK," Bobby announced when the bags were as dry as five hard-working high-income executives could make them, "From now on, *no-body* touches my bags, understand? I want this baggage in lockers. And *I* want the keys."

Nobody looked at anybody. The nearest lockers were about 90 feet away. Bobby insisted on carrying most of the bags across the lobby himself. Saidy was allowed to carry a few. Then Bobby and Saidy stowed the bags in lockers. Bobby couldn't get the keys out of the locks, but Hallowell showed him how. Finally, with a private smile that seemed to go with feelings of power and possession, Bobby pocketed all the keys. "By that time," Hallowell told me, "Bobby was dead white, obviously exhausted, suitcases under his eyes." Turning to Saidy, Bobby invited him back up to the restaurant. The others he instructed to wait. Then he marched off, stone-faced, and left Davis standing there like an untipped porter.

A bleak little group gathered around Davis. The desperate extremity of the situation was clear to everyone. In chess terms, Bobby was on the verge of surmate. In the next half hour Bobby faced a decision that must crown or crush the hopes of a lifetime, and he was clearly in no mood to make such a decision rationally. To make matters worse, Davis now looked beat. He felt as if he had whipped into a hairpin turn at 90 and all at once found himself clutching a steering wheel that had simply come off in his hands. What now?

Davis and the others went up to the bar next to the coffee shop and knocked back a belt or two. Then Davis squared off, lawyer style, for another look at the problem.

The problem wasn't money, wasn't Thorarinsson, wasn't even pride or principle. Davis suspected that it was fear. Bobby at best was one of the most easily frightened people Davis knew, but he had never seen him as frightened as he was today. Frightened of what? Of losing? Of winning? Of the press and the crowds? Of being jailed by the Icelanders or assassinated by the Russians? He may have been afraid of all these things, but there was something else. Some old terror was slithering around in the bottom of Bobby's mind. What was it? Davis had no idea and there was no time to puzzle it out now. It was midnight. The 10:30 flight, the last plane to Reykjavík, was already 90 minutes late. There was no time for tact; he had to barge in there and see Bobby right this minute.

Unfortunately, somebody else had seen him first.

It was a miracle that somebody hadn't seen him long before. By 11 P.M., shortly after the Port Authority police drove Bobby's bags to the east gate, most of the media people had phoned in a hard report that Bobby was somewhere at Kennedy. Then they scattered to find him. For a full hour dozens of story-starved reporters, photographers and TV camera men ran a fine-meshed dragnet through that airport. Oblivious to all this, seized by his own problem, Bobby sat in the coffee shop stuffing himself with eggs and toast and talking earnestly with Saidy only a few feet off the corridor but somehow too obvious to be seen.

The conversation was going well, Saidy said later. He felt he had finally persuaded Bobby to swallow his pride and take the plane.

And then the chutney hit the propeller.

It was a 12-year-old boy who spotted Bobby. "There was this little blond kid," Hochstetter said. "He'd been hanging around with the newspaper photographers and the TV news crews. You could tell this was the big moment of his life."

Worried at seeing so many press people passing so close to Bobby, Hochstetter "stayed in the hallway between the bar and the coffee shop, where I could keep track of things. This kid came along and I saw him duck into the restaurant where Bobby was eating. A minute later, he came running out and went tearing down the corridor to where most of the press was waiting.

"So I dashed into the restaurant. Bobby and Saidy took off just like that. 'Go into the bar!' I told them. 'Way at the back! They'll never suspect!' So they did. Well, the whole megillah came thundering up, at least twenty of them. Nikons, TV cameras, strobes. They charged into the restaurant, and then out again. And I'm standing there. 'You looking for Bobby Fischer?' I said. 'He went down there!' And I pointed to the stairway that goes down to the lobby on the ground floor. So they all ran down there and I figured that's the end of that."

About two minutes later, they all came charging back up again. "And then that damn kid fooled me," Hochstetter continued. "He went snooping around in the bar and spotted Bobby again and came running out, hollering, 'He's in there! He's in there!' So then they all rushed into the bar."

Hallowell was ready for them. When they hit the end of the bar, they ran into a 34-year-old 250-pound former third-string tackle on the worst Harvard team since World War Two and he threw the greatest block of his career. For about 30 seconds, Hallowell had 20 men piled up in front of him. "I'm sorry, gentlemen," he announced suavely, making like the manager, "but the bar is closed."

"I'm from NBC!" a reporter informed him importantly.

"No shit," Hallowell answered calmly.

Suddenly they all broke through Hallowell, but as they went charging toward Bobby, they met Bobby charging out. Face closed and shoulders twisting, he pushed quickly through the startled pack. There were shouts, flashes, shoving, clutching, cries of "Bobby! Bobby!"

It was a scary moment, and not only to Bobby. "Those guys had been waiting for Bobby in that airport all week," Davis explained. "They looked wild. I had a feeling they'd do violence to get their story. My heart started pounding. But it was worse for Bobby. There's something about strobes, flashbulbs, strong sudden bursts of light. Maybe his eyes are more sensitive. Anyway, it seems to hurt him physically. He'll do anything to get away from it."

Just ahead lay the corridor. As Bobby hit it, he turned left. Hallowell was not far behind him and right behind Hallowell was a TV cameraman, an assistant carrying a battery pack and a rack of lights and the 12-year-old boy who had started it all. The lights were blazing, the camera was whining and the boy was squealing, "Mr. Fischer! Mr. Fischer!" as they all turned left, too.

At that moment, a large male hand covered the TV camera's lens. It belonged to Hochstetter, who had been waiting in the corridor for just such an opportunity. "It was like putting pepper in a Turkish wrestler's jockstrap," Hochstetter told me happily. "The cameraman let out a scream. The lighting man screamed, too. Finally they pushed me out of the way, but as the cameraman went past, I gave him a good swift kick — right in the crack. He gave a yell and turned around and started after me. I backed off. I mean, I'm a devout coward. I didn't want to fight. All I wanted was to give Bobby a chance to take off."

Bobby got it. He ran down the stairs three and four at a time, Hallowell about 20 feet behind him. Indridason, who happened to be standing not far from the bottom of the steps, said Bobby's eyes were wide and blank. After him, yelping with alarm, came the pack of newshounds.

Thanks to Hochstetter's holding action, Davis and Saidy reached the stairs ahead of the press and raced for the bottom, where they turned to make a stand. For about five seconds they body-checked the roaring horde. Somebody threw a punch at Saidy. Davis gave way slowly and as the TV cameraman rushed past him, he stepped accidentally, he insists, on the cord that connected the camera to the battery pack. The camera went dead. The cameraman stared in disbelief. First some son of a bitch had grabbed his lens and kicked him in the slats. Now *this* son of a bitch had unplugged his camera. It was too much. Screeching incoherently, he snatched off his glasses and with his camera still harnessed to his shoulder, pushed a floppy little punch at Davis' head.

By the time the press broke out of the stair well, Bobby and Hallowell were out of sight.

Yelling and cursing, the newsmen closed in on Davis, Saidy and Hochstetter. A Port Authority policeman hurried over.

"What's going on here?" the officer demanded.

"We're here to photograph Bobby Fischer," the offended cameraman began, "and — "

"Who's he?" the officer wanted to know.

Everybody explained at once and then the cameraman indignantly described the first assault on his person. Another cop grabbed Hochstetter by the arm. He indignantly denied the charge. The cameraman then accused Davis of punching *him.* Davis drew himself up and declared with lofty forensic disdain: "You, sir, are a liar and a worm."

The cops knew a lawyer when they heard one. "All right, all right," one of them said. "Break it up. Move along."

Davis, Saidy and Hochstetter stood staring at what was left of one another. Hochstetter had been up since eight that morning and had eaten almost nothing all day. The blue blotches under his eyes were the size of mussel shells. Saidy was pale with shock. For three days running, he had put out a total effort of emotional diplomacy — and now this! Davis looked battered, but there was still plenty of fight in him.

"*Shee-it!*" he said savagely. Then he straightened out his eyes and went on briskly: "OK. Anybody see which way he went?"

Nobody had.

Davis bit his lip. The situation, as Hochstetter described it, was "a three-hundred-and-sixty-degree fuck-up."

Davis turned to Indridason. "How long can you hold the plane?"

"We'll hold it."

For the second time that night, Davis organized a search. First, Saidy broadcast a message to Bobby over the airport's loud-speaker system. No reply. Then Davis, Saidy and Hochstetter ransacked every coffee shop, bar, lounge and men's room in the main terminal building — a vast sprawling structure that covers about 40 acres and runs two thirds of a mile from end to end.

Their ace in the hole was Hallowell. If he was still with Bobby (and if he wasn't, why wasn't he there with the rest of them?), then sooner or later he would get to a phone and tell them where Bobby was. In the meantime, they had to do what they could — and hope they got lucky. They didn't.

Unstoppable, Davis proposed plan B. "Let's call every hotel and motel in the airport area." One by one the hotels answered. Bobby was registered at none of them. It was one A.M. A full hour had passed since Bobby bolted. The last plane to Reykjavík was now two and a half hours late. Hope was going out of his mind. There was no word from Hallowell. It looked as if the jig was up.

Bobby ran down the stairs three and four at a time. Behind him he heard shouts and racing feet. Someone was closing on him, a big man, landing hard and breathing heavily as he ran. At the bottom of the stairs, the main lobby of the International Arrivals Building spread away on both sides. Straight ahead he saw a row of glass doors and beyond the doors a traffic bay. He ran for the nearest door, hitting it with both palms just as the photoelectric cell popped it open automatically. He was on the sidewalk. Which way now?

A wall of rain lay ahead. He turned left and began to sprint. The big man hit the door and came pounding after him. Bobby jerked a glance over his shoulder. It was Hallowell! "Are they still behind us?" he hollered as he ran. "Are they still behind us?" Hallowell glanced back. No pursuit in sight. Relief showed in Bobby's face. They were in the clear! He picked up his knees and really poured it on.

Hallowell raced after him. He was in no shape for this. For the past five years that big body of his had pushed nothing heavier than his chair away from his desk. Now for the second time that day, he was up on his hind legs and moving out after Bobby as he hadn't moved after anything since he turned in his crimson sweat suit.

Remembering his morning workout in mid-Manhattan, he wondered uneasily how long he could keep it up. He was sagging after 14 hours of incessant and increasing nervous tension, but as he watched Bobby blast off in front of him, he had a sinking sensation that he was chasing a man so charged up he might run for an hour before he ran down. He set his will hard. No matter how long and how fast Bobby ran, he'd just have to run right along with him. Losing him now would mean losing everything they had been fighting for. As long as he held on, there was a chance he could talk Bobby back to the plane.

The sidewalk in front of the terminal was about 18 feet wide and Bobby ran straight down the center of it. He was obviously running in a blind burst of emotion — all kinds of emotion. His feet hit the pavement like blows struck in anger and his legs leaped and exulted as if shackles had just been struck off. He was a prisoner breaking for freedom and in his first wild dash, he had no idea where his legs were taking him. Hallowell saw in horror that he was running straight toward the Loftleidir terminal, where the media people had been headquartered all night. The sidewalk was empty now — could they zip by without being seen? They made it halfway. Then Hallowell heard a scurry of running feet.

"Bobby! Bobby!" a newsman shouted. "Wait! Wait! *Please!* I've been here all week!"

It was one of those cries of despair, like the yowls of a cartoon cat when the mouse escapes, that are rightly answered with a raspberry. But this time, inexplicably, the victim apologized for escaping.

"I'm sorry!" Bobby yelled contritely — but kept on running.

Like a scatback heading for the side lines, he veered into the traffic bay. At the farther curb he hesitated an instant, checking the traffic, then darted across the airport's two-lane circular highway. Puffing hard, Hallowell raced after him. Rain engulfed them. Both were coatless and before they hit the other side of the highway, their jackets and thighs were soaked. Together they plunged into the enormous parking lot that covers the airport's infield.

At the third or fourth step, Hallowell landed splat in a huge puddle. Water gushed up through a hole in one shoe. Water spewed up his trouser legs and drenched his knees. Water ran down inside his socks.

"Bobby!" he pleaded. "Slow down!"

Throwing a frightened look over his shoulder, Bobby asked in a high voice, "Is anybody still there?"

"Nobody's there," Hallowell assured him. "We've lost them."

Bobby kept on running. "Stick with me!" he shouted. "I know what I'm doing. Believe me. I know what I'm doing!"

After that, Bobby slowed down a little, but he showed no sign of stopping as he galloped across a black lake inhabited by swimming snakes of light and bouldered with silent empty automobiles. Behind them, the roar of the traffic died to a murmur. Now there was only the noise of their own heavy breathing and the ruckus made by their feet as they pounded blacktop and splashed through puddles.

Bobby ran on for two minutes, three minutes. Hallowell's chest was collapsing, his legs were unliftable. Nothing but will kept him going.

"Hey, Bobby!" he gasped. "Let's go . . . American Airlines . . . VIP Lounge. . . . I'm a member. . . . No press people can . . . find us there."

Bobby fiercely refused. "No. I want to get out of this airport, y'understand? I want to get *out of this airport!* I want to take a cab. I want to take a cab and get out of here!" Then he remembered a restaurant several miles from the airport. "I'm hungry. I want something to eat. We'll get a cab and go there. Nobody'll find me there."

"Anywhere you say, Bobby." But let's get there fast, Hallowell was thinking. If he didn't get to a telephone and call Davis pretty damn quick, they could kiss that plane goodbye and probably the match.

When they hit the circular highway again, Hallowell hailed a passing cab. Bobby told the driver where to go and they drove for seven or eight minutes. Bobby was still jumpy, still teetering on the brink. Hallowell made small talk, giving him time to wind down.

Suddenly the driver remembered that the restaurant wasn't there anymore. It had been wiped out by a cloverleaf. Hallowell groaned — more time wasted.

"Where shall we go?" Bobby asked helplessly. "I don't want to go anywhere those press people can find me."

Hallowell suggested a Howard Johnson's motel and restaurant they had passed on the way. They were on Southern State Parkway now, about four miles from Kennedy, and the next turnaround was a couple of miles ahead, but the driver jumped the island in the middle of the highway and drove them back to Howard Johnson's.

Bobby looked around suspiciously. "We far enough away from the airport? I don't want to be anywhere near that airport." Hallowell reassured him.

There was $6.60 on the meter. Bobby paid, thanked the driver and threw in a quarter tip. Inside, they were told that the restaurant was closed, but the bar was still open. Bobby said he wanted food, so they ran about 100 yards through the rain to the Hilton Motel next door. At the Hilton, both the bar and the restaurant were closed. So they ran back to Howard Johnson's. When they finally got settled in a dark corner of the cocktail lounge, it was close to one A.M.

They ordered drinks — as Hallowell recalls, Bobby asked for a whiskey sour — and Bobby started talking about the press with concentrated hatred. Not a word about Iceland or catching the plane. Hallowell's foot was tapping furiously. He *had* to get to a phone, but he knew Bobby didn't want anybody to know where they were. If he rushed right off, Bobby would suspect what he was doing and when he came back, Bobby might not be there. But he had to chance it. Excusing himself, Hallowell eased away to the men's room.

From a pay phone he called information. The phone rang interminably. Then he asked the operator for Loftleidir's number at Kennedy Airport. In a little while, she said there was no number at Kennedy, there was only the main number in Manhattan. Hallowell called it. The phone rang interminably. Hallowell rolled his eyes. "Come *on!*" Come *on!*" he muttered. Any minute now, Bobby might come looking for him. Then a young woman answered. Hallowell described his problem as quickly and as urgently as he could and asked her to put him through on the tie line to the Loftleidir terminal at Kennedy.

"I'm sorry, sir," the young woman said, "we have no tie line."

Hallowell almost jumped into the mouthpiece. "I *knew* there was a tie line," he told me later. "There *had* to be a tie line. So at that point, I said some extremely forceful things." Shaken up, the girl agreed to call Kennedy and tell somebody there to call Hallowell.

Three minutes later, Hallowell's phone rang. Three minutes after that, Davis was on the line.

"Andy! I'm with Bobby."

"Is he all right?"

"Yes."

"Thank God! Where are you?"

Hallowell explained.

"We'll be right over. And for Christ's sake, don't let him out of your sight!"

Five minutes later, a Loftleidir station wagon roared up to Howard Johnson's. Davis and Saidy jumped out and hurried in. Hope and Indridason followed them. Moments later, Hochstetter arrived in the Cadillac with Dubinsky, who at long last had resolved his two-day conflict between hate and duty.

"Look," Dubinsky told Hochstetter. "when I say I'll do a job, I do a job. But this is ridiculous. I'm going home. I find this Fischer a very depressing person and I no longer wish to have him in my car. I am sure you will have no trouble getting home. I will send you a bill on the first of the month. Good night." Exit Dubinsky.

As Hochstetter walked through the street door into the lobby, he saw Davis, Hallowell, Indridason and Hope walking in from the lounge. "Tony's talking to him," Davis explained. A few minutes later, Saidy came out and beckoned to Davis. While the others stood in the lobby and watched from about 50 feet away, Bobby, Saidy and Davis paced back and forth at one end of the lobby, under a sign that said RUM KEG ROOM. "For the first time that night," Hope told me, "Bobby was really opening up. He was waving his arms and talking. We thought, OK. Somebody finally got through to him. Now we're getting somewhere. Now he'll go."

In fact, Bobby was telling Davis emphatically that he would not go to Iceland. He would not go, he said, until the deal was right. He wanted Davis to go instead and see if he could make it right. "Here are my demands," he said in a cold voice. "Either I get them or I don't go. One: I want a nonplaying referee. Lothar Schmid has to go. Two: I want a better TV deal signed by Chester Fox. Three: I want the loser's share of the prize money *in my hand* when I get off the plane in Iceland. Four: I want thirty percent of the gate. When I've got those demands, I'll *think* about going."

So they were back to the original position — and then some. All of Bobby's unmet demands were in that list, and the one about the loser's share was a grumble that had suddenly matured into a must. Davis looked at Bobby's eyes. They were hard and opaque and they didn't look back. Four people pushing for two full days with all their might had failed to budge Bobby an inch. And now they had run out of time. There was nothing to do but admit defeat — and see what could be salvaged from that defeat. Davis reached down into his bag of lawyer's tricks. After all, there was still the Saturday-night plane. . . .

"OK, Bobby," Davis said firmly. "Suppose I go. Suppose I get a reasonable betterment of the deal. Will you come? I want to know. Will you come? I don't want to go up there on a wild-goose chase."

Bobby looked guarded. "I'll think about it."

Davis looked angry. "Come on, this is no joke for me, Bobby!"

Bobby caved a little. "All right, I'll go, but" — the hard covering fell off his eyes and the scaredness showed through — "but I want Tony to be there, too."

Davis looked at Saidy. Saidy nodded. Then Davis nodded gravely and held out his hand. "On that basis," he said, "I'll go."

And he went.

As the Loftleidir station wagon pulled away, a little grin began at the corners of Bobby's mouth. After that his mood improved rapidly. Saidy could hardly move or even speak, he was so exhausted and depressed by what had happened, and Hallowell and Hochstetter were not much better off. They figured they had just watched Bobby destroy his career. But Bobby spoke firmly and moved confidently, like a man who had just had a major success.

Wearily, Hallowell called for two limousines — one for himself, one for Bobby and the others. When his Cadillac came, Bobby jumped in eagerly. He was going to stay at Saidy's father's house in Douglaston and he liked Saidy's mother's Lebanese cooking. Saidy and Hochstetter eased in after him and slumped in the softly molded, back-supporting seats. In Douglaston, before he got out of the limousine, Bobby shook Hochstetter's hand and said respectfully, "Thank you very much, Mr. Hochstetter."

Bobby and Saidy raided the refrigerator, which was loaded with left-over Lebanese goodies. Bobby put away several pounds of food and then Saidy took him to the third floor. There were three bedrooms there and a bathroom, too. "Nobody else up here," Saidy told him. "You've got it all to yourself." Bobby nodded happily and seemed impatient to be alone. Saidy had the impression he wanted to play chess.

And that is the beginning of the story of how Bobby Fischer caught a plane to Reykjavík. It took four more days and the combined efforts of several hundred people and two governments, as well as a landslide of good luck, to get him actually aboard. For the next two days, Davis put Thorarinsson through the wringer and the Saidys treated Bobby like a sacred rhino, but he accepted their efforts as his due and calmly missed the plane on Saturday night. The match was wrecked.

But Bobby's luck held. On Sunday, Spassky saved everybody's neck with an act of rare courage. Risking the certain disapproval of high officials in Moscow, he allowed the opening of the event to be post-poned until Tuesday. Marshall now re-entered the situation, and in a behind-closed-doors harangue that began at midnight and lasted until four o'clock Monday morning, he pierced the perimeter of Bobby's defenses.

Then came a purely incredible piece of luck. On Monday morning, a London banker and chess buff named James Slater offered to double the $125,000 prize if Bobby would play. "Chicken," he said in a message worded for him by Marshall, "come on out!"

Bobby was tempted, but five hours after the offer reached him he was still holding out. Then Marshall threatened to quit again. At that, Bobby gave in and agreed to go. Just for insurance, Marshall arranged to have Henry Kissinger call and ask Bobby to play the match for the sake of his country. Set up by his talk with Kissinger, Bobby announced to the press that he would fly to Reykjavík that night. He did, and after another week of sometimes Byzantine, sometimes ludicrous maneuvering, the Chess Match of the Century began.

Before it was over, the world had discovered another Bobby. Right to the end he came on from time to time as the bad hat from Brooklyn: but as the games began to claim his attention, the fears and suspicions seeped away like goblins fading with the moon, and the force that had scattered in tantrums moved in behind his will and his talent. He proved to be a grim but dignified loser, a ferocious but courteous winner, a warrior-artist who lives by a discipline as severe as a samurai's.

Victory followed victory and the world eagerly forgave the winner for tearing up the pea patch back in June. Bobby later insisted that when he refused to take the plane, he was fighting for a principle. But wasn't it lucky that fighting for a principle happened to make great publicity for the match? One day in Reykjavík he stood in a needle-point shower and, grinning through the water that ran down his face, asked with the sheepish glee of a small boy smeared with illicit chocolate: "Do you think the match would have got as much attention without all the — you know — fuss?" When I grinned back at him, he began to laugh. The day Bobby blew it wasn't really such a bad day for Bobby after all.

# Columns and
# Writing on Deadline

1921

Heywood Broun

......................................................................................................................

# Sport for Art's Sake

FROM *The New York World*

FOR YEARS WE HAD BEEN HEARING about moral victories and at last
we saw one. This is not intended as an excuse for the fact that we said
before the fight that Carpentier would beat Dempsey. We erred with
Bernard Shaw. The surprising revelation which came to us on this July
afternoon was that a thing may be done well enough to make victory
entirely secondary. We have all heard, of course, of sport for sport's sake
but Georges Carpentier established a still more glamorous ideal. Sport
for art's sake was what he showed us in the big wooden saucer over on
Boyle's dirty acres.

It was the finest tragic performance in the lives of ninety thousand
persons. We hope that Professor George Pierce Baker sent his class in
dramatic composition. We will be disappointed if Eugene O'Neill, the
white hope of the American drama, was not there. Here for once was a
laboratory demonstration of lift. None of the crowds in Greece who
went to somewhat more beautiful stadia in search of Euripides ever saw
the spirit of tragedy more truly presented. And we will wager that
Euripides was not able to lift his crowd up upon its hind legs into a
concerted shout of "Medea! Medea! Medea!" as Carpentier moved the
fight fans over in Jersey City in the second round. In fact it is our contention that the fight between Dempsey and Carpentier was the most
inspiring spectacle which America has seen in a generation.

Personally we would go further back than that. We would not accept
a ticket for David and Goliath as a substitute. We remember that in that
instance the little man won, but it was a spectacle less fine in artistry
from the fact that it was less true to life. The tradition that Jack goes up
the beanstalk and kills his giant, and that Little Red Ridinghood has the
better of the wolf, and many other stories are limited in their inspira-

tional quality by the fact that they are not true. They are stories that man has invented to console himself on winter's evenings for the fact that he is small and the universe is large. Carpentier showed us something far more thrilling. All of us who watched him know now that man cannot beat down Fate, no matter how much his will may flame, but he can rock it back upon its heels when he puts all his heart and his shoulders into a blow.

That is what happened in the second round. Carpentier landed his straight right upon Dempsey's jaw and the champion, who was edging in toward him, shot back and then swayed forward. Dempsey's hands dropped to his side. He was an open target. Carpentier swung a terrific right-hand uppercut and missed. Dempsey fell into a clinch and held on until his head cleared. He kept close to Carpentier during the rest of the fight and wore him down with body blows during the infighting. We know of course that when the first prehistoric creature crawled out of the ooze up to the beaches (see *The Outline of History* by H. G. Wells, some place in the first volume, just a couple of pages after that picture of the big lizard) it was already settled that Carpentier was going to miss that uppercut. And naturally it was inevitable that he should have the worst of it at infighting. Fate gets us all in the clinches, but Eugene O'Neill and all our young writers of tragedy make a great mistake if they think that the poignancy of the fate of man lies in the fact that he is weak, pitiful and helpless. The tragedy of life is not that man loses but that he almost wins. Or, if you are intent on pointing out that his downfall is inevitable, that at least he completes the gesture of being on the eve of victory.

For just eleven seconds on the afternoon of July 2 we felt that we were at the threshold of a miracle. There was such flash and power in that right-hand thrust of Carpentier's that we believed Dempsey would go down, and that fate would go with him and all the plans laid out in the days of the oozy friends of Mr. Wells. No sooner were the men in the ring together than it seemed just as certain that Dempsey would win as that the sun would come up on the morning of July 3. By and by we were not so sure about the sun. It might be down, we thought, and also out. It was included in the scope of Carpentier's punch, we feared. No, we did not exactly fear it. We respect the regularity of the universe by which we live, but we do not love it. If the blow had been as devastating as we first believed, we should have counted the world well lost.

Great circumstances produce great actors. History is largely concerned with arranging good entrances for people; and later exits not always quite as good. Carpentier played his part perfectly down to the last side. People who saw him just as he came before the crowd reported that he was pitifully nervous, drawn, haggard. It was the traditional and becoming nervousness of the actor just before a great performance. It was gone the instant Carpentier came in sight of his ninety thousand. His head was back and his eyes and his smile flamed as he crawled through the ropes. And he gave some curious flick to his bathrobe as he turned to meet the applause. Until that very moment we had been for Dempsey, but suddenly we found ourself up on our feet making silly noises. We shouted, "Carpentier! Carpentier! Carpentier!" and forgot even to be ashamed of our pronunciation. He held his hands up over his head and turned until the whole arena, including the five-dollar seats, had come within the scope of his smile.

Dempsey came in a minute later and we could not cheer, although we liked him. It would have been like cheering for Niagara Falls at the moment somebody was about to go over in a barrel. Actually there is a difference of sixteen pounds between the two men, which is large enough, but it seemed that afternoon as if it might have been a hundred. And we knew for the first time that a man may smile and smile and be an underdog.

We resented at once the law of gravity, the Malthusian theory and the fact that a straight line is the shortest distance between two points. Everything scientific, exact, and inevitable was distasteful. We wanted the man with the curves to win. It seemed impossible throughout the first round. Carpentier was first out of his corner and landed the first blow, a light but stinging left to the face. Then Dempsey closed in and even the people who paid only thirty dollars for their seats could hear the thump, thump of his short hooks as they beat upon the narrow stomach of Carpentier. The challenger was only too evidently tired when the round ended.

Then came the second and, after a moment of fiddling about, he shot his right hand to the jaw. Carpentier did it again, a second time, and this was the blow perfected by a lifetime of training. The time was perfect, the aim was perfect, every ounce of strength was in it. It was the blow which had downed Bombardier Wells, and Joe Beckett. It rocked Dempsey to his heels, but it broken Carpentier's hand. His best was not enough. There was an earthquake in Philistia but then out came the signs "Business as usual!" and Dempsey began to pound Carpentier in the stomach.

The challenger faded quickly in the third round, and in the fourth the end came. We all suffered when he went down the first time, but he was up again, and the second time was much worse. It was in this knock-down that his head sagged suddenly, after he struck the floor, and fell back upon the canvas. He was conscious and his legs moved a little, but they would not obey him. A gorgeous human will had been beaten down to a point where it would no longer function.

If you choose, that can stand as the last moment in a completed piece of art. We are sentimental enough to wish to add the tag that after a few minutes Carpentier came out to the center of the ring and shook hands with Dempsey and at that moment he smiled again the same smile which we had seen at the beginning of the fight when he stood with his hands above his head. Nor is it altogether sentimental. We feel that one of the elements of tragedy lies in the fact that Fate gets nothing but the victories and the championships. Gesture and glamor remain with Man. No infighting can take that away from him.

Jack Dempsey won fairly and squarely. He is a great fighter, perhaps the most efficient the world has ever known, but everybody came away from the arena talking about Carpentier. He wasn't very efficient. The experts say he fought an ill-considered fight and should not have forced it. In using such a plan, they say, he might have lasted the whole twelve rounds. That was not the idea. As somebody has said, "Better four rounds of — " but we can't remember the rest of the quotation.

Dempsey won and Carpentier got all the glory. Perhaps we will have to enlarge our conception of tragedy, for that too is tragic.

1936

## Westbrook Pegler

·······································································································

# The Olympic Army

FROM *Scripps-Howard*

GARMISCH-PARTENKIRCHEN — Everything is said to happen for the best, and whatever anyone may think of the sporting propriety of our taking part in the political, military and sporting activities here in Garmisch, the experience should show a net profit to the United States.

Such shoving around as the populace received at the hands of the young strong-armed squad of Hitler bodyguards appropriately, though ingenuously, named the Black Guards, was never seen in the United States, even in the heyday of Jimmy Walker or Huey P. Long.

American athletes and the journalists of all nations sent to cover the program of sports known as the Winter Olympics, saw a perfect demonstration of military dictatorship, and there were those among the throng who agreed that if this is what Huey was promoting in Louisiana they will be glad to have none of the same.

The dictator held ten thousand people in the grandstand of the rink where the figure skating took place until he was ready to take his leave, and before the event they paved his way with such idolatrous care that it made no difference whether anyone else reached the scene or not.

Thousands of people were herded this way and that in the snow who had bought tickets or were trying to buy tickets to see the sport, and thousands were shunted off and away from the inclosure by long cordons of officious, beefy young Nazis in various uniforms, whose only duty was to flatter and accommodate the house painter who became the head man of the third Reich. It was a magnificent display of strong-arm authority wholly corroborating the old tradition that the German people's favorite sport is to be shoved around by men in uniform.

The road approaching the stadium was held clear by a double cordon of troops in brown uniforms who are supposed not to be soldiers but a civilian labor corps, although they dress like soldiers, with a swastika worn on the left arm, and perform military drill with shovels instead of guns.

At the head of the line near the stadium the Black Guards took their stand. They are a special corps, like the King's Life Guard in England, except that they are all young, athletic, tall and of overbearing demeanor. They wear fine black uniforms which flatter the youthful figure of a man, and wear on the left sleeve in silver embroidery the name "Adolf Hitler." They were wearing black tin hats, and the very atmosphere was vibrant with oppression and a sense of the importance of the Leader.

Your correspondent has seen in his time such men as Edison, Ford, Shaw, Einstein, Mussolini, Clemenceau and Eugene Debs, and therefore might have been a trifle slow to take spark. It seemed a secondary experience, not to say an anticlimax, to witness Adolf Hitler, but to the German government, which had invited the athletes of the world to Garmisch in the name of sport and human brotherhood, it was a tremendous affair.

The Olympics were of secondary importance, if any. This was the dictator's day, and it is a good thing for the Americans present that this was so, because they have nothing important to learn from the athletes, but much to learn about absolute authority in government.

You must picture this town. Ten thousand swastikas stir faintly in the light winter wind along the streets of Garmisch-Partenkirchen. The flag is the color of blood, with a white circle containing an ancient device in black. The swastika flies from every house and store, and some homes are adorned with long ribbons of little pennants strung together from window to window, fifty or a hundred swastikas in a row.

Soldiers are everywhere in Garmisch-Partenkirchen, where the athletes of many nations are competing on ice and snow in the brotherhood of sports. There are soldiers in the old German field gray, soldiers of the labor corps in brown, and special soldiers of the Black Guard in black and silver. All the soldiers wear the swastika, and it is seen again on the red post-office trucks and the army transports, which go tearing through the streets off into the mysterious mountains splashing melted slush onto the narrow footway.

This motor transport gives a strange suggestion of war in the little mountain resort where sportsmen are drawn together in a great demonstration of friendship. When the United States held the winter Olympics at Lake Placid, the only armed force in sight was a small detachment of New York State Police with service pistols and cartridge belts, and they were there only to regulate motor traffic.

I do not know why there are so many troops and so much army transport in Garmisch, and I hesitate to inquire unless that be construed as an effort to obtain military information. I was not interested in military affairs but only in sport, and the great international Olympic ideal of amity through chivalrous competition.

I know the ideal by heart, having heard it many times in speeches and read it in statements by Mr Avery Brundage, the president of the American Athletic Union, who brought the American team over to this armed camp, and by other idealists in the Olympic organization who joined Mr Brundage in the enjoyment of official courtesies and flattery delivered in the elegant style of the Old World.

We ought to treat Mr Brundage's vanity better at home. Perhaps an official dinner at the White House would equalize some of the honor which the Germans have shown him in their campaign to overpower disgust in America and procure the participation of American athletes.

The big army trucks which roar up the hills are painted in camouflage and loaded with soldiers. The little officers' cars built on the design of the old-fashioned low-neck hack are camouflaged too, and the scene is strongly reminiscent of the zone behind the front when divisions were being rushed to the sector of the next offensive.

Up to this time no artillery has been seen. I take it that the brotherhood games of the Winter Olympics run under the auspices of Nazi sportsmanship are only infantry action up to this writing. They may be saving their heavy stuff, their tanks and bombers for the summer program.

Well, I am glad I was here for this particular day, and I insist that as matters turned out it was a good thing to send an American team. If they didn't learn their lesson this time they are beyond teaching. At home we have never found it necessary to mobilize an army for a sport event, and even Huey himself, when he went on tour with his football team, carried only a few selected gunmen whose function was strictly retributive in the end.

1938

## Bob Considine

....................................................................................................................

# Louis Knocks Out Schmeling

FROM *The International News Service*

LISTEN TO this, buddy, for it comes from a guy whose palms are still wet, whose throat is still dry, and whose jaw is still agape from the utter shock of watching Joe Louis knock out Max Schmeling.

It was a shocking thing, that knockout — short, sharp, merciless, complete. Louis was like this:

He was a big lean copper spring, tightened and retightened through weeks of training until he was one pregnant package of coiled venom.

Schmeling hit that spring. He hit it with a whistling right-hand punch in the first minute of the fight — and the spring, tormented with tension, suddenly burst with one brazen spang of activity. Hard brown arms, propelling two unerring fists, blurred beneath the hot white candelabra of the ring lights. And Schmeling was in the path of them, a man caught and mangled in the whirring claws of a mad and feverish machine.

The mob, biggest and most prosperous ever to see a fight in a ball yard, knew that there was the end before the thing had really started. It knew, so it stood up and howled one long shriek. People who had paid as much as $100 for their chairs didn't use them — except perhaps to stand on, the better to let the sight burn forever in their memories.

There were four steps to Schmeling's knockout. A few seconds after he landed his only punch of the fight, Louis caught him with a lethal little left hook that drove him into the ropes so that his right arm was hooked over the top strand, like a drunk hanging to a fence. Louis swarmed over him and hit with everything he had — until Referee Donovan pushed him away and counted one.

Schmeling staggered away from the ropes, dazed and sick. He looked drunkenly toward his corner, and before he had turned his head back

Louis was on him again, first with a left and then that awe-provoking right that made a crunching sound when it hit the German's jaw. Max fell down, hurt and giddy, for a count of three.

He clawed his way up as if the night air were as thick as black water, and Louis — his nostrils like the mouth of a double-barreled shotgun — took a quiet lead and let him have both barrels.

Max fell almost lightly, bereft of his senses, his fingers touching the canvas like a comical stew-bum doing his morning exercises, knees bent and the tongue lolling in his head.

He got up long enough to be knocked down again, this time with his dark unshaven face pushed in the sharp gravel of the resin.

Louis jumped away lightly, a bright and pleased look in his eyes, and as he did the white towel of surrender which Louis' handlers had refused to use two years ago tonight came sailing into the ring in a soggy mess. It was thrown by Max Machon, oblivious to the fact that fights cannot end this way in New York.

The referee snatched it off the floor and flung it backwards. It hit the ropes and hung there, limp as Schmeling. Donovan counted up to five over Max, sensed the futility of it all, and stopped the fight.

The big crowd began to rustle restlessly toward the exits, many only now accepting Louis as champion of the world. There were no eyes for Schmeling, sprawled on his stool in his corner.

He got up eventually, his dirty gray-and-black robe over his shoulders, and wormed through the happy little crowd that hovered around Louis. And he put his arm around the Negro and smiled. They both smiled and could afford to — for Louis had made around $200,000 a minute and Schmeling $100,000 a minute.

But once he crawled down in the belly of the big stadium, Schmeling realized the implications of his defeat. He, who won the title on a partly phony foul, and beat Louis two years ago with the aid of a crushing punch after the bell had sounded, now said Louis had fouled him. That would read better in Germany, whence earlier in the day had come a cable from Hitler, calling on him to win.

It was a low, sneaking trick, but a rather typical last word from Schmeling.

1948

## Grantland Rice

........................................................................................................

# Game Called

FROM *The North American Newspaper Alliance*

> Game called by darkness — let the curtain fall,
> No more remembered thunder sweeps the field.
> No more the ancient echoes hear the call
> To one who wore so well both sword and shield.
> The Big Guy's left us with the night to face,
> And there is no one who can take his place.
> Game called — and silence settles on the plain.
> Where is the crash of ash against the sphere?
> Where is the mighty music, the refrain
> That once brought joy to every waiting ear?
> The Big Guy's left us, lonely in the dark,
> Forever waiting for the flaming spark.
> Game called — what more is there for one to say?
> How dull and drab the field looks to the eye.
> For one who rules it in a golden day
> Has waved his cap to bid us all good-bye.
> The Big Guy's gone — by land or sky or foam
> May the Great Umpire call him "safe at home."

THE GREATEST FIGURE the world of sport has ever known has passed from the field. Game called on account of darkness. Babe Ruth is dead.

There have been mighty champions in their day and time from John L. Sullivan to Jack Dempsey — such stars as Bobby Jones, Ty Cobb, Walter Johnson, on and on, who walked along the pathway of fame.

But there has been only one Babe Ruth — one Bambino, who caught and held the love and admiration of countless millions around the world.

From the time he appeared on the big league scene with the Boston Red Sox in 1914, to the day his playing career ended more than 20 years later, Ruth was the greatest all-around ballplayer in the history of the game. He was a brilliant left-handed pitcher — the top power hitter of all time — a star defensive outfielder who could be rated with the best.

He was the one ballplayer who was a master of offense and defense — the nonpareil in both.

But Ruth was something more than a great ballplayer. He was an emblem, a symbol. No other athlete ever approached his color, not even the colorful Jack Dempsey, who had more than his share.

Babe Ruth's appeal to the kids of this nation was something beyond belief. He loved them and the kids knew it. There was nothing phony about his act. The kids knew the Babe was the greatest home run hitter of all time — that he was one of the greatest pitchers of all time — that he was an able place-hitter — that he could do more with a bat and a baseball than any player that ever lived. And the Babe could. But they also knew he was their pal.

I was present when he drove 60 miles one night before a world series game in Chicago to see a sick boy. "And if you write anything about it," he said, "I'll knock your brains out." He meant it that way.

Oddly enough, the Babe and Walter Johnson, the two stars on offense and defense, the mighty hitter and the whirlwind pitcher, died from the same cause — a tumor attached to the brain.

And once again, oddly enough, it was Babe Ruth who was Johnson's nemesis in the box and at the bat. He told me once that he had beaten Johnson six times by the scores of 1 to 0. And even the great Johnson was none too keen about facing him from the firing hill.

I've been a close friend of Babe Ruth since 1919, nearly 30 years ago when the Red Sox and Giants traveled north from spring training together.

The true story of Babe's life will never be written — the story of wrecked cars he left along the highway — the story of the night he came near dropping Miller Huggins off a train — the story of the $100,000 or more he lost in Cuba one racing winter. (The Babe told me it was $200,000.)

The story of the ribald, carefree Babe who ignored all traffic signals. I was riding home with Ruth one night after a game of golf. The Babe was late. He ignored red lights and everything else in a big car. I begged Babe to let me get out and take a taxi. The Babe only laughed.

"These cops are my pals," he said. "A funny thing happened yesterday. Maybe I'd had a shot or so too much. Anyway, my car stalled. A big cop came up and asked what the matter was.

"'It won't run,' I said.

"'You're drunk,' the cop said.

"I hit him in the nose.

"'Now I know you're drunk, you so-and-so,' the cop said.

"He shoved me out of the way and drove me home."

One day the Babe was going the wrong way on a road to some golf club.

"Hey, this is a one-way street," some traffic cop hollered.

"I'm only driving one way, you dumb — ," the Babe said.

The cop, enraged, came rushing up, "Oh, hello Babe," he said. "I didn't know it was you. Drive any way you want to."

I sat one day with Babe at St. Albans, his golf club. The Babe took out a .22 rifle, and he and a pal began shooting away the door knob at a $1 a shot. The Babe missed some guy who had just opened the door by two inches. "He should have knocked," the Babe said.

Just one day with the Babe was a big adventure. There was the time he planted a small explosive bomb in some pal's car and almost blew up the place, including the Babe and myself. "I didn't know it was that strong," was all he said.

He was a rough, rowdy, swaggering figure, more profane than anyone I ever hope to meet again, with a strong sense of decency and justice and fair play. He was a sportsman, if I ever saw one. He wanted no advantage at any start.

There was the day Miller Huggins was going to fine Ruth $5,000. He had been absent two days. The fine was to be plastered after the game. All baseball writers were notified. The Babe appeared before the game, red-eyed and dazed looking. He was in terrible shape. He hit two home runs and a triple. Huggins forgot the fine.

These are among the true stories of Babe Ruth, who had no regard for the conventions of the common or normal man, whether this included action or words. But, beyond all this, he was open-hearted, friendly, always cheerful, a great guy to be with.

I can still hear the roar of voices wherever he was. There was nothing quiet and sedate about the Babe.

He could recall few names. "I caught back of him for 10 years," Mickey Cochrane once told me. "But he never knew my name. It was 'Hello, kid.'"

Driving around, Babe always responded to those who called out, "Hey, Babe." His reply was "Hello, Mom," or "Hello, Pop."

"They can't forget my funny-looking pan," he said once. They won't forget his funny-looking pan soon. His records were terrific, but they meant little when compared to the man who was so far above all the records he ever set. I've never seen him turn a mean trick.

No game will ever see his like, his equal again. He was one in many, many lifetimes. One all alone.

1950

## Frank Graham

...........................................................................................................

# All the Way to the Grave

FROM *The New York Journal-American*

ONE OF Joe Gould's favorite stories was about the time Tex Rickard was building up Luis Firpo and wanted Italian Jack Herman as an opponent for him in Havana and Joe, who managed Herman, accepted the match and, on looking for his fighter, found him in a hospital.

"What's the matter with you?" he asked.

"I had a pain in the belly," Herman said, "and the doctor says I'm going to get appendicitis."

"Are you?" Joe asked.

"I don't think so," Herman said. "I feel great."

"Then what are you laying here for," Joe said, "when you are boxing Firpo in Havana on Wednesday?"

"I am?" Herman yelled.

And, the way Joe used to tell it, Herman jumped out of bed and pulled on his pants.

They knew the story well in the fight mob and now some of them were standing in the rain outside the Riverside Memorial Chapel. Funeral services for the little man who guided Jim Braddock to the heavyweight championship were just over and they were standing there, talking about him, and Ernie Braca said:

"He was a very game guy and he gave it a great fight but I knew he was gone when I went into Mt. Sinai to see him a couple of weeks ago. His wife, Lucille, asked me if I couldn't drop in to try and cheer him up and when I walked in, I said to him: 'What are you laying here for when you're boxing Firpo in Havana on Wednesday?'

"I thought it would get a laugh out of him but he couldn't give. He just lay there looking at me and I knew he was a goner."

One of them stood there talking with the others about Joe for a while and then he went away and he was thinking about Joe and the time when Joe and Braddock were broke and the last thing either of them could have figured was that one day Jim would be the heavyweight champion.

But in that time Joe was hustling for him, not knowing where he would be able to take him, but determined that Jim would not stay on the docks and the relief rolls because Jim was too nice a guy for that and he had a wife and children and they rated a better shake than that. Joe's own furniture was in hock and he was sleeping on the bare floor of his apartment and hoping the landlord wouldn't come around looking for the rent too soon, but he never said anything about that to anybody but kept talking Braddock and trying to get a shot for him and finally he got it from Jimmy Johnston.

It was a preliminary bout on the Baer-Carnera card in the Garden Bowl in June of 1934. Braddock was in with a fellow named Corn Griffin, out of Georgia, and knocked him out in the third round. They were on their way back to the dressing room, Joe and Jim, and Jim said to Joe:

"I did that on hash. Get me a couple of steaks and there is no telling what I will do."

A year later they were at Evans Loch Sheldrake, Jim training for the fight with Max Baer in which he was to win the championship. There was a day when Jim, having finished his work, was sitting on the veranda of the main house with Joe and Francis Albertanti. No one could have asked for a more beautiful day. A blue sky . . . a setting sun . . . trees green . . . flowers in bloom . . . birds . . . bees . . . butterflies.

Francis, who hates the country, glared through the haze of his cigar smoke at Jim.

"- - - - - - - you, Braddock," he said. "If it wasn't for you, I wouldn't be here."

Joe laughed.

"If it wasn't for Braddock," he said, "you know where we'd be, don't you?"

"On relief," Francis said.

"Right," Joe said.

Jim laughed with them and he looked at Joe and you could see he was thinking about a lot of things they had gone through together and how it was Joe who was always out there in front of him, showing him the way.

There was the night in the Garden Bowl when Jim took the champi-

onship from Max Baer . . . and the night in Chicago when he lost it to
Joe Louis.

Louis giving him a frightful beating, and at the end of the sixth
round, Joe saying to Jim:

"I'm going to stop it."

Jim, sitting in his corner, looking up at him through the haze of blood
in his eyes and saying:

"If you do, I'll never speak to you again as long as I live."

Joe, knowing Jim meant it, let the fight go on and, in the eighth
round, Louis hit him on the chin, splitting the flesh on his chin and Jim
fell on his face. And, as he lay there, his blood made little pools on the
canvas. And when the count was over, Joe helping to lift him and get
him back to his corner.

Joe wanting Jim to quit after that but Jim begging for a shot at
Tommy Farr and Joe giving in and making the match for him and, in
the Garden, Jim coming back to his corner at the end of the eighth
round of a ten-round fight and asking Joe:

"How am I doing?"

Joe saying:

"You're losing, Jim."

And Jim saying:

"Watch me do the big apple in the next two rounds."

And going out there and beating Farr in the next two rounds and
getting the decision and, in the dressing room, Joe saying:

"That was great, Jim. And that was all. You'll never fight again. But I
don't have to tell you we'll still be together, like we have been."

It was raining and the one who had been thinking about this was on
his way home and now he was thinking back, just a little while ago, to
the funeral services and Rabbi Morris Goldberg intoning in Hebrew. He
didn't know what it was then the Rabbi was saying but he knew now,
because somebody had told him:

"The Lord is my shepherd: I shall not want. He maketh me to lie
down in green pastures; He leadeth me beside the still waters. He
restoreth my soul; He leadeth me in the paths of righteousness for His
name's sake . . ."

And then he had seen the funeral cars starting for Mount Neboh
Cemetery in Brooklyn and Jim getting into one of the cars.

1947

## Red Smith

·······································································································

# Next to Godliness

FROM *The New York Herald Tribune*

THE GAME HAS been over for half an hour now, and still a knot of worshippers stands clustered, as around a shrine, out in right field adoring the spot on the wall which Cookie Lavagetto's line drive smote. It was enough to get a new contract for Happy Chandler. Things were never like this when Judge Landis was in.

Happy has just left his box. For twenty minutes crowds clamored around him, pushing, elbowing, shouting hoarsely for the autograph they snooted after the first three World Series games. Unable to get to Lavagetto, they were unwilling to depart altogether empty-handed. Being second choice to Cookie, Happy now occupies the loftiest position he has yet enjoyed in baseball. In Brooklyn, next to Lavagetto is next to godliness.

At the risk of shattering this gazette's reputation for probity, readers are asked to believe these things happened in Ebbets Field:

After 136 pitches, Floyd Bevens, of the Yankees, had the only no-hit ball game ever played in a World Series. But he threw 137 and lost, 3 to 2.

With two out in the ninth inning, a preposterously untidy box score showed one run for the Dodgers, no hits, ten bases on balls, seven men left on base, and two more aboard waiting to be left. There still are two out in the ninth.

Hugh Casey, who lost two World Series games on successive days in 1941, now is the only pitcher in the world who has won two on successive days. One pitch beat him in 1941, a third strike on Tommy Henrich, which Mickey Owen didn't catch. This time he threw only one pitch, a strike to Tommy Henrich, and this time he caught the ball himself for a double play.

Harry Taylor, who has had a sore arm half the summer, threw eleven pitches in the first inning, allowed two hits and a run, and fled with the bases filled and none out. Hal Gregg, who has had nothing at all this summer — not even so much as a sore arm — came in to throw five pitches and retired the side. Thereafter Gregg was a four-hit pitcher until nudged aside for a pinch hitter in the seventh.

In the first inning George Stirnweiss rushed behind second base and stole a hit from Pee Wee Reese. In the third Johnny Lindell caught Jackie Robinson's foul fly like Doc Blanchard hitting the Notre Dame line and came to his feet unbruised. In the fourth Joe DiMaggio caught Gene Hermanski's monstrous drive like a well-fed banquet guest picking his teeth and broke down as he did so. Seems he merely twisted an ankle, though, and wasn't damaged.

Immediately after that play — and this must be the least credible of the day's wonders — the Dodger Sym-phoney band serenaded Happy Chandler. The man who threw out the first manager for Brooklyn this year did not applaud.

In the seventh inning two Sym-phoney bandsmen dressed in motley did a tap dance on the roof of the Yankees' dugout. This amused the commissioner, who has never openly opposed clowning.

In the eighth Hermanski smashed a drive to the scoreboard. Henrich backed against the board and leaped either four or fourteen feet into the air. He stayed aloft so long he looked like an empty uniform hanging in its locker. When he came down he had the ball.

In the ninth Lindell pressed his stern against the left-field fence and caught a smash by Bruce Edwards. Jake Pitler, coaching for the Dodgers at first base, flung his hands aloft and his cap to the ground.

And finally Bucky Harris, who has managed major-league teams in Washington, Detroit, Boston, Philadelphia, and New York, violated all ten commandments of the dugout by ordering Bevens to walk Peter Reiser and put the winning run on base.

Lavagetto, who is slightly less experienced than Harris, then demonstrated why this maneuver is forbidden in the managers' guild.

Cookie hit the fence. A character named Al Gionfriddo ran home. Running, he turned and beckoned frantically to a character named Eddie Miksis. Eddie Miksis ran home.

Dodgers pummeled Lavagetto. Gionfriddo and Miksis pummeled each other. Cops pummeled Lavagetto. Ushers pummeled Lavagetto. Ushers pummeled one another. Three soda butchers in white ran onto the field and threw forward passes with their white caps. In the tangle Bevens could not be seen.

The unhappiest man in Brooklyn is sitting up here now in the far end of the press box. The *v* on his typewriter is broken. He can't write either Lavagetto or Bevens.

1951

## Red Smith

......................................................................................................................

# Miracle of Coogan's Bluff

FROM *The New York Herald Tribune*

NOW IT IS DONE. Now the story ends. And there is no way to tell it. The art of fiction is dead. Reality has strangled invention. Only the utterly impossible, the inexpressibly fantastic, can ever be plausible again.

Down on the green and white and earth-brown geometry of the playing field, a drunk tries to break through the ranks of ushers marshaled along the foul lines to keep profane feet off the diamond. The ushers thrust him back and he lunges at them, struggling in the clutch of two or three men. He breaks free, and four or five tackle him. He shakes them off, bursts through the line, runs head-on into a special park cop, who brings him down with a flying tackle.

Here comes a whole platoon of ushers. They lift the man and haul him, twisting and kicking, back across the first-base line. Again he shakes loose and crashes the line. He is through. He is away, weaving out toward center field, where cheering thousands are jammed beneath the windows of the Giants' clubhouse.

At heart, our man is a Giant, too. He never gave up.

From center field comes burst upon burst of cheering, pennants are waving, uplifted fists are brandished, hats are flying. Again and again the dark clubhouse windows blaze with the light of photographers' flash bulbs. Here comes that same drunk out of the mob, back across the green turf to the infield. Coattails flying, he runs the bases, slides into third. Nobody bothers him now.

And the story remains to be told, the story of how the Giants won the 1951 pennant in the National League. The tale of their barreling run through August and September and into October. . . . Of the final day of the season, when they won the championship and started home with it from Boston, to hear on the train how the dead, defeated Dodgers had risen from the ashes in the Philadelphia twilight. . . . Of the three-game playoff in which they won, and lost, and were losing again with one out in the ninth inning yesterday when — Oh, why bother?

Maybe this is the way to tell it: Bobby Thomson, a young Scot from Staten Island, delivered a timely hit yesterday in the ninth inning of an enjoyable game of baseball before 34,320 witnesses in the Polo Grounds. . . . Or perhaps this is better:

"Well!" said Whitey Lockman, standing on second base in the second inning of yesterday's playoff game between the Giants and Dodgers.

"Ah, there," said Bobby Thomson, pulling into the same station after hitting a ball to left field. "How've you been?"

"Fancy," Lockman said, "meeting you here!"

"Ooops!" Thomson said. "Sorry."

And the Giants' first chance for a big inning against Don Newcombe disappeared as they tagged Thomson out. Up in the press section, the voice of Willie Goodrich came over the amplifiers announcing a macabre statistic: "Thomson has now hit safely in fifteen consecutive games." Just then the floodlights were turned on, enabling the Giants to see and count their runners on each base.

It wasn't funny, though, because it seemed for so long that the Giants weren't going to get another chance like the one Thomson squandered by trying to take second base with a playmate already there. They couldn't hit Newcombe, and the Dodgers couldn't do anything wrong. Sal Maglie's most splendrous pitching would avail nothing unless New York could match the run Brooklyn had scored in the first inning.

The story was winding up, and it wasn't the happy ending that such a tale demands. Poetic justice was a phrase without meaning.

Now it was the seventh inning and Thomson was up, with runners on first and third base, none out. Pitching a shutout in Philadelphia last Saturday night, pitching again in Philadelphia on Sunday, holding the Giants scoreless this far, Newcombe had now gone twenty-one innings without allowing a run.

He threw four strikes to Thomson. Two were fouled off out of play. Then he threw a fifth. Thomson's fly scored Monte Irvin. The score was tied. It was a new ball game.

Wait a moment, though. Here's Pee Wee Reese hitting safely in the eighth. Here's Duke Snider singling Reese to third. Here's Maglie wild-pitching a run home. Here's Andy Pafko slashing a hit through Thomson for another score. Here's Billy Cox batting still another home. Where does his hit go? Where else? Through Thomson at third.

So it was the Dodgers' ball game, 4 to 1, and the Dodgers' pennant. So all right. Better get started and beat the crowd home. That stuff in the ninth inning? That didn't mean anything.

A single by Al Dark. A single by Don Mueller. Irvin's pop-up, Lockman's one-run double. Now the corniest possible sort of Hollywood schmaltz — stretcher-bearers plodding away with an injured Mueller between them, symbolic of the Giants themselves.

There went Newcombe and here came Ralph Branca. Who's at bat? Thomson again? He beat Branca with a home run the other day. Would Charley Dressen order him walked, putting the winning run on base, to pitch to the dead-end kids at the bottom of the batting order? No, Branca's first pitch was a called strike.

The second pitch — well, when Thomson reached first base he turned and looked toward the left-field stands. Then he started jumping straight up in the air, again and again. Then he trotted around the bases, taking his time.

Ralph Branca turned and started for the clubhouse. The number on his uniform looked huge. Thirteen.

1953

Red Smith

..................................................................................................................................................

# Jim and His Baubles

FROM *The New York Herald Tribune*

ONE OF THOSE voices that crowd into the living room out of the unoffending air was talking about the death of Jim Thorpe. All its owner could think of to say was that he hoped those men were satisfied now, those men who had made a career of depriving Jim of the medals he won in the Olympic Games of 1912. The inference was that by taking his baubles away from him forty years ago, the amateur athletic authorities had hastened old Jim's death.

Jim Thorpe never was happy making speeches and in recent years when he had to make a public appearance he would settle for a line that must have been fed to him by a movie press agent or some such. He would get up and say he was glad to be present and he only wished he could have his medals back. Then he would sit down.

The speech was all right. It did nobody any harm, least of all Demosthenes. Nor did it convince anybody that Jim, a burly, simple, wonderful gent in the maturity of his middle sixties, gave a whoop in a rain barrel about that long-lost hardware.

He was the greatest athlete of his time, maybe the greatest of any time in any land, and he needed no gilded geegaws to prove it. The proof is in the records and the memories of the men who knew him and watched him and played with him — especially those who tried to play football against him in a day when football was not, according to President Butler of Columbia, one of the "games decently played by decent young men."

As a matter of fact, Jim's gold medals, if he had kept them, would merely have borne false witness, testifying that in 1912 he was an amateur eligible under the rules for competition in amateur sport. He was not.

He had played two summers of professional baseball at Rocky Mount and Fayetteville in the Eastern Carolina League. Then he had returned to the Carlisle Indian School to make All-America in football in 1911 and 1912; and to win the pentathlon and decathlon in the Stockholm Olympics.

When the facts came out in 1913, Jim wrote to James F. Sullivan, secretary of the Amateur Athletic Union: "I hope I will be partly excused by the fact that I was simply an Indian schoolboy and did not know that I was doing wrong."

It was an age of innocence, indeed. Of course Jim did nothing wrong. If playing professional baseball was even a venial sin, Stan Musial's hope of heaven would be dim. But the Olympics are restricted to amateurs and Jim wasn't an amateur and wasn't entitled to the medals he won.

Amateur or professional, however, he was richly entitled to the accolade he received from King Gustav of Sweden. "Sir," said the king, heaping hardware upon him in Stockholm, "you are the greatest athlete in the world."

In the pentathlon, Jim had won the broad jump, the 200-meter hurdles, the discus throw and the 1,500-meter run. He was third in the javelin throw.

In the decathlon he was first in the high hurdles, the shotput, the high jump and the 1,500; he was third in the 100 meters, the discus, the pole vault, and the broad jump; he was fourth in the 400 meters and the javelin.

That's the sort of thing remembered by the men who knew him, rather than the nonsense about metal trinkets. Nobody who saw him on a football field could ever forget the wild glory of that indestructible Indian.

There's a man in the White House today who must retain a vivid memory of an opponent's 185-yard touchdown. Playing against a West Point team that included a cadet named Dwight Eisenhower, Jim raced ninety yards to the goal line but Carlisle was offside. On the next play he went ninety-five and this one counted.

Jim didn't need medals to assure him of his rank in any game. He understood his place clearly, and explained it clearly to Knute Rockne when the Notre Dame graduate tackled Thorpe in a professional game. "Don't do that," Jim warned. "All those people paid to see old Jim run."

When Jim played football, serious thinkers like Chancellor Day, of Syracuse University, were saying that "one human life is too big a price to pay for all the football games of the season."

That attitude puzzled Jim. As a baseball player with the Giants, he was puzzled when John McGraw said he didn't want to hear of Jim playing football after the season closed. Jim protested.

"Why not, Mac?"

"You might get hurt."

"How can you get hurt playing football?" Jim asked.

1973

## Red Smith

FROM *The New York Times*

# The Babe Was Always a Boy — One of a Kind

GRANTLAND RICE, the prince of sportswriters, used to do a weekly radio interview with some sporting figure. Frequently, in the interest of spontaneity, he would type out questions and answers in advance. One night his guest was Babe Ruth.

"Well, you know, Granny," the Babe read in response to a question, "Duke Ellington said the Battle of Waterloo was won on the playing fields of Elkton."

"Babe," Granny said after the show, "Duke Ellington for the Duke of Wellington I can understand. But how did you ever read Eton as Elkton? That's in Maryland, isn't it?"

"I married my first wife there," Babe said, "and I always hated the goddamn place." He was cheerily unruffled. In the uncomplicated world of George Herman Ruth, errors were part of the game.

Babe Ruth died twenty-five years ago but his ample ghost has been with us all summer and he seems to grow more insistently alive every time Henry Aaron hits a baseball over a fence. What, people under fifty keep asking, what was this creature of myth and legend like in real life? If he were around today, how would he react when Aaron at last broke his hallowed record of 714 home runs? The first question may be impossible to answer fully; the second is easy.

"Well, what d'you know!" he would have said when the record got away. "Baby loses another! Come on, have another beer."

To paraphrase Abraham Lincoln's remark about another deity, Ruth must have admired records because he created so many of them. Yet he was sublimely aware that he transcended records and his place in the

American scene was no mere matter of statistics. It wasn't just that he hit more home runs than anybody else, he hit them better, higher, farther, with more theatrical timing and a more flamboyant flourish. Nobody could strike out like Babe Ruth. Nobody circled the bases with the same pigeon-toed, mincing majesty.

"He was one of a kind," says Waite Hoyt, a Yankee pitcher in the years of Ruthian splendor. "If he had never played ball, if you had never heard of him and passed him on Broadway, you'd turn around and look."

Looking, you would have seen a barrel swaddled in a wrap-around camel-hair topcoat with a flat camel-hair cap on the round head. Thus arrayed he was instantly recognizable not only on Broadway in New York but also on the Ginza in Tokyo. "Baby Roos! Baby Roos!" cried excited crowds, following through the streets when he visited Japan with an all-star team in the early 1930's.

The camel-hair coat and cap are part of my last memory of the man. It must have been in the spring training season of 1948 when the Babe and everybody else knew he was dying of throat cancer. "This is the last time around," he had told Frank Stevens that winter when the head of the H. M. Stevens catering firm visited him in the French Hospital on West 30th Street, "but before I go I'm gonna get out of here and have some fun."

He did get out, but touring the Florida training camps surrounded by a gaggle of admen, hustlers and promoters, he didn't look like a man having fun. It was a hot day when he arrived in St. Petersburg, but the camel-hair collar was turned up about the wounded throat. By this time, Al Lang Stadium had replaced old Waterfront Park where he had drawn crowds when the Yankees trained in St. Pete.

"What do you remember best about this place?" asked Francis Stann of the *Washington Star.*

Babe gestured toward the West Coast Inn, an old frame building a city block beyond the right-field fence. "The day I hit the adjectival ball against that adjectival hotel." The voice was a hoarse stage whisper; the adjective was one often printed these days, but not here.

"Wow!" Francis Stann said. "Pretty good belt."

"But don't forget," Babe said, "the adjectival park was a block back this way then."

Ruth was not noted for a good memory. In fact, the inability to remember names is part of his legend. Yet he needed no record books to remind him of his own special feats. There was, for example, the time he visited Philadelphia as a "coach" with the Brooklyn Dodgers. (His coachly duties consisted of hitting home runs in batting practice.) This was in the late 1930's when National League games in Philadelphia were played in Shibe Park, the American League grounds where Babe had performed. I asked him what memories stirred on his return.

"The time I hit one into Opal Street," he said.

Now, a baseball hit over Shibe Park's right-field fence landed in 20th Street. Opal is the next street east, just a wide alley one block long. There may not be five hundred Philadelphians who know it by name, but Babe Ruth knew it.

Another time, during a chat in Hollywood, where he was an actor in the film *Pride of the Yankees,* one of us mentioned Rube Walberg, a good lefthanded pitcher with the Philadelphia Athletics through the Ruth era. To some lefthanded batters there is no dirtier word than the name of a good lefthanded pitcher, but the Babe spoke fondly:

"Rube Walberg! What a pigeon! I hit twenty-three home runs off him." Or whatever the figure was. It isn't in the record book but it was in Ruth's memory.

Obviously it is not true that he couldn't even remember the names of his teammates. It was only that the names he remembered were not always those bestowed at the baptismal font. To him Urban Shocker, a Yankee pitcher, was Rubber Belly. Pat Collins, the catcher, was Horse Nose. All redcaps at railroad stations were Stinkweed, and everybody else was Kid. One day Jim Kahn, covering the Yankees for the *New York Sun,* watched two players board a train with a porter toting the luggage.

"There go Rubber Belly, Horse Nose and Stinkweed," Jim said.

Don Heffner joined the Yankees in 1934, Ruth's last year with the team. Playing second base through spring training, Heffner was stationed directly in the line of vision of Ruth, the right fielder. Breaking camp, the Yankees stopped in Jacksonville on a night when the Baltimore Orioles of the International League were also in town. A young reporter on the *Baltimore Sun* seized the opportunity to interview Ruth.

"How is Heffner looking?" he asked, because the second baseman had been a star with the Orioles in 1933.

"Who the hell is Heffner?" the Babe demanded. The reporter should, of course, have asked about the kid at second.

Jacksonville was the first stop that year on the barnstorming trip that would last two or three weeks and take the team to Yankee Stadium by a meandering route through the American bush. There, as everywhere, Ruth moved among crowds. Whether the Yankees played in Memphis or New Orleans or Selma, Alabama, the park was almost always filled, the hotel overrun if the team used a hotel, the railroad depot thronged. In a town of 5,000, perhaps 7,500 would see the game. Crowds were to Ruth as water to a fish. Probably the only time on record when he sought to avert a mob scene was the day of his second marriage. The ceremony was scheduled for 6 A.M. on the theory that people wouldn't be abroad then, but when he arrived at St. Gregory's on West 90th Street, the church was filled and hundreds were waiting outside.

A reception followed in Babe's apartment on Riverside Drive, where the 18th Amendment did not apply. It was opening day of the baseball season but the weather intervened on behalf of the happy couple. The party went on and on, with entertainment by Peter de Rose, composer-pianist, and May Singhi Breen, who played the ukulele and sang.

Rain abated in time for a game next day. For the first time, Claire Ruth watched from a box near the Yankees' dugout, as she still does on ceremonial occasions. Naturally, the bridegroom hit a home run. Rounding the bases, he halted at second and swept off his cap in a courtly bow to his bride. This was typical of him. There are a hundred stories illustrating his sense of theater — how he opened Yankee Stadium (The House That Ruth Built) with a home run against the Red Sox, how at the age of forty he closed out his career as a player by hitting three mighty shots out of spacious Forbes Field in Pittsburgh, stories about the times he promised to hit a home run for some kid in a hospital and made good, and of course the one about calling his shot in a World Series.

That either did or did not happen in Chicago's Wrigley Field on October 1, 1932. I was there but I have never been dead sure of what I saw.

The Yankees had won the first two games and the score of the third was 4–4 when Ruth went to bat in the fifth inning with the bases empty and Charley Root pitching for the Cubs. Ruth had staked the Yankees to a three-run lead in the first inning by hitting Root for a home run with two on base. Now Root threw a strike. Ruth stepped back and lifted a finger. "One." A second strike, a second upraised finger. "Two." Then Ruth made some sort of sign with his bat. Some said, and their version has become gospel, that he aimed it like a rifle at the bleachers in right center field. That's where he hit the next pitch. That made the score 5–4. Lou Gehrig followed with a home run and the Yankees won, 7–5, ending the Series the next day.

All the Yankees, and Ruth in particular, had been riding the Cubs unmercifully through every game, deriding them as cheapskates because in cutting up their World Series money the Chicago players had voted only one-fourth of a share to Mark Koenig, the former New York shortstop who had joined them in August and batted .353 in the last month of the pennant race. With all the dialogue and pantomime that went on, there was no telling what Ruth was saying to Root. When the papers reported that he had called his shot, he did not deny it.

A person familiar with Ruth only through photographs and records could hardly be blamed for assuming that he was a blubbery freak whose ability to hit balls across county lines was all that kept him in the big leagues. The truth is that he was the complete ballplayer, certainly one of the greatest and maybe the one best of all time.

As a lefthanded pitcher with the Boston Red Sox, he won 18 games in his rookie season, 23 the next year and 24 the next before Ed Barrow assigned him to the outfield to keep him in the batting order every day. His record of pitching $29^{2}/_{3}$ consecutive scoreless innings in World Series stood 43 years before Whitey Ford broke it.

He was an accomplished outfielder with astonishing range for his bulk, a powerful arm and keen baseball sense. It was said that he never made a mental error like throwing to the wrong base.

He recognized his role as public entertainer and understood it. In the 1946 World Series the Cardinals made a radical shift in their defense against Ted Williams, packing the right side of the field and leaving the left virtually unprotected. "They did that to me in the American League one year," Ruth told the columnist, Frank Graham. "I coulda hit .600 that year slicing singles to left."

"Why didn't you?" Frank asked.

"That wasn't what the fans came out to see."

He changed the rules, the equipment and the strategy of baseball. Reasoning that if one Babe Ruth could fill a park, sixteen would fill all the parks, the owners instructed the manufacturers to produce a livelier ball that would make every man a home-run king. As a further aid to batters, trick pitching deliveries like the spitball, the emery ball, the shine ball and the mud ball were forbidden.

The home run, an occasional phenomenon when a team hit a total of twenty in a season, came to be regarded as the ultimate offensive weapon. Shortstops inclined to swoon at the sight of blood had their bats made with all the wood up in the big end, gripped the slender handle at the very hilt and swung from the heels.

None of these devices produced another Ruth, of course, because Ruth was one of a kind. He recognized this as the simple truth and conducted himself accordingly. Even before they were married and Claire began to accompany him on the road, he always occupied the drawing room on the team's Pullman; he seldom shared his revels after dark with other players, although one year he did take a fancy to a worshipful rookie named Jimmy Reese and made him a companion until management intervened; if friends were not on hand with transportation, he usually took a taxi by himself to hotel or ball park or railroad station.

Unlike other players, Ruth was never seen in the hotel dining room or sitting in the lobby waiting for some passerby to discard a newspaper.

Roistering was a way of life, yet Ruth was no boozer. Three drinks of hard liquor left him fuzzy. He could consume great quantities of beer, he was a prodigious eater and his prowess with women was legendary. Sleep was something he got when other appetites were sated. He arose when he chose and almost invariably was the last to arrive in the clubhouse, where Doc Woods, the Yankees' trainer, always had bicarbonate of soda ready. Before changing clothes, the Babe would measure out a mound of bicarb smaller than the Pyramid of Cheops, mix and gulp it down.

"Then," Jim Kahn says, "he would belch. And all the loose water in the showers would fall down."

The man was a boy, simple, artless, genuine and unabashed. This explains his rapport with children, whom he met as intellectual equals. Probably his natural liking for people communicated itself to the public to help make him an idol.

He was buried on a sweltering day in August 1948. In the pallbearers' pew, Waite Hoyt sat beside Joe Dugan, the third baseman. "I'd give a hundred dollars for a cold beer," Dugan whispered.

"So would the Babe," Hoyt said.

1974

# Red Smith

......................................................................................................................

# And All Dizzy's Yesterdays

FROM *The New York Times*

JAY HANNA DEAN, who was also known as Jerome Herman Dean but answered more readily when addressed as Dizzy, was born in Lucas, Arkansas, or maybe Bond, Mississippi, or perhaps Holdenville, Oklahoma, sometime in 1911 or thereabouts, and approximately nineteen years later pitched his first game in the major leagues. He knocked off the Pittsburgh Pirates on three hits. The following winter he showed up unannounced in the Cardinals' offices in Sportsman's Park in St. Louis and went into executive session with Branch Rickey, the vice president and general manager. Two or three hours later, aware that newspapermen were on the premises, he departed by a rear door and Rickey trudged wearily into the outer office.

The Mahatma was coatless, his collar was unbuttoned and his necktie hung loose. His hair looked as though it had been slept in. He was sweating, and over the half-glasses on the end of his nose, his eyes were glassy. "By Judas Priest!" he said. "By Judas Priest! If there were one more like him in baseball, just one, as God is my judge I'd get out of the game!"

Young Mr. Dean, it seemed, had brought up the matter of his wage for the forthcoming baseball season and had expressed a preference for a figure higher than the $3,000 then considered fair for a rookie of promise. "He told me," Rickey said, "after one game this busher told me, 'Mr. Rickey, I'll put more people in the park than anybody since Babe Ruth.'"

Within three years, editorial changes were made in the handbills Cardinals posted on railroad station platforms and similar vantage points for a hundred miles around St. Louis. Formerly they had announced: "Double-header — Cardinals vs. New York Giants, Sunday, July 8," etc.

Now the top line, set in type a mole could see at a hundred years, read simply: "DIZZY DEAN," followed in smaller type by the promise: "Will pitch Sunday, July 8 — ." The busher was putting more people in the park than anybody else, including Ruth, who had never helped the Cardinals draw a dollar.

As a ball player, Dean was a natural phenomenon, like the Grand Canyon or the Great Barrier Reef. Nobody ever taught him baseball and he never had to learn. He was just doing what came naturally when a scout named Don Curtis discovered him on a Texas sandlot and gave him his first contract. It was the fall of 1929 and the contract committed him to pitch for St. Joseph, Missouri, the following season. Diz stayed in St. Joe long enough to win seventeen games, moved up to Houston, where he won eight, and joined the Cardinals around Labor Day. Gabby Street, the manager, waited until the Cardinals had won the pennant before using him, so he had only that one start against Pittsburgh and had to settle for twenty-six victories in his first professional season.

He knew how to pitch, he was by no means helpless with a bat in his hands, and he was a fine base runner. There was a game with the Giants in 1932, Dizzy's first full season in the big leagues (he had been sent back to Houston for 1931 on the amusing theory that it would teach him humility). With the score tied and a runner on third, he went to bat in a late inning and John McGraw pulled his infielders in to cut off the run.

With the aplomb of Willie Keeler, Dean lifted a swinging bunt over the infield. The run scored easily; caught off balance, the Giants threw the ball around in a panic; Dizzy kept running until he was home, laughing fit to split.

Nobody knew where or how or when he had learned to play like this and nobody ever found out from him, for Diz was cheerfully vague about matters like the date and place of his birth, length of army service, and other details of his background. This was partly because he had no background to speak of. He and his brothers, Paul and Elmer, and their father had been itinerant farmhands, picking cotton for fifty cents a day.

On one occasion they were on the move through the Southwest with other nomads. Dizzy, Paul, and Pop found seats in one car and Elmer hitched a ride in another. Reaching a grade crossing, the first car got over ahead of a train but the one carrying Elmer had to stop. It was four years before the family was reunited.

There were things in heaven and on earth not dreamed of then in Dizzy's philosophy, things like charge accounts and bank checks, whose existence he discovered after joining the Cardinals. He found that if he signed a check, a man would give him money and later Mr. Rickey would take care of the man. If he bought something and said, "Charge it," Mr. Rickey would take care of that. He took a simple, childish pleasure in these discoveries, until he was so far overdrawn that Sam Breadon, the Cardinals' owner, put him on a cash allowance of a dollar a day to be picked up each morning from Clarence Lloyd, the traveling secretary.

One morning in Boston, Diz asked for ten dollars. Lloyd said he was sorry. Diz pleaded. Lloyd inquired why he needed the extra money. Diz only begged harder. Lloyd said that he couldn't help him without a compelling reason. Diz was still a kid, a big, gangling gawk, appealing in his ungainliness. Painfully, he stammered the explanation: it was his bride's birthday and he wanted to buy Patricia a gift. He got the saw-buck.

In time, Pat taught him about money. Just living taught him other things, including an invincible philosophy.

"Hi, Diz, how's the old arm?" Grantland Rice hailed him when Dean was winding it up with the Chicago Cubs. "It ain't what it used to be, Granny," the philosopher said, "but what the hell is?"

1947

## Stanley Woodward

·······································································································································

# One Strike Is Out

FROM *The New York Herald Tribune*

A NATIONAL League players' strike, instigated by some of the St. Louis Cardinals, against the presence in the league of Jackie Robinson, Brooklyn's Negro first baseman, has been averted temporarily and perhaps permanently quashed. In recent days Ford Frick, president of the National League, and Sam Breadon, president of the St. Louis club, have been conferring with St. Louis players in the Hotel New Yorker. Mr. Breadon flew East when he heard of the projected strike. The story that he came to consult with Eddie Dyer, manager, about the lowly state of the St. Louis club was fictitious. He came on a much more serious errand.

The strike plan, formulated by certain St. Louis players, was instigated by a member of the Brooklyn Dodgers who has since recanted. The original plan was for a St. Louis club strike on the occasion of the first game in Brooklyn, May 6, in other words last Tuesday. Subsequently the St. Louis players conceived the idea of a general strike within the National League on a certain date. That is what Frick and Breadon have been combatting in the last few days.

It is understood that Frick addressed the players, in effect, as follows:

> If you do this you will be suspended from the league. You will find that the friends you think you have in the press box will not support you, that you will be outcasts. I do not care if half the league strikes. Those who do it will encounter quick retribution. All will be suspended and I don't care if it wrecks the National League for five years. This is the United States of America and one citizen has as much right to play as another.
>
> The National League will go down the line with Robinson whatever the consequences. You will find if you go through with your intention that you have been guilty of complete madness.

Several anticipatory protests against the transfer of Robinson to the Brooklyn club were forthcoming during spring training when he was still a member of the Montreal Royals, Brooklyn farm. Prejudice has been subsequently curbed except on one occasion, when Ben Chapman, manager of the Phillies, undertook to ride Robinson from the bench in a particularly vicious manner.

It is understood that Frick took this matter up with the Philadelphia management and that Chapman has been advised to keep his bench comments above the belt.

It is understood that the players involved — and the recalcitrants are not all Cardinals — will say, if they decided to carry out their strike, that their object is to gain the right to have a say on who shall be eligible to play in the major leagues. As far as is known the move so far is confined entirely to the National League. Ringleaders apparently have not solicited the cooperation of American League players.

In view of this fact it is understood that Frick will not call the matter to the attention of Harry Chandler, the commissioner. So far, it is believed, Frick has operated with the sole aid of Breadon. Other National League club owners apparently know nothing about it.

The *New York Herald Tribune* prints this story in part as a public service. It is factual and thoroughly substantiated. The St. Louis players involved unquestionably will deny it. We doubt, however, that Frick or Breadon will go that far. A return of "No comment" from either or both will serve as confirmation. On our own authority we can say that both of them were present at long conferences with the ringleaders and that both probably now feel that the overt act has been averted.

It is not generally known that other less serious difficulties have attended the elevation of Robinson to the major leagues. Through it all, the Brooklyn first baseman, whose intelligence and degree of education are far beyond that of the average ball player, has behaved himself in an exemplary manner.

It is generally believed by baseball men that he has enough ability to play on any club in the majors. This ability has asserted itself in spite of the fact that he hasn't had anything resembling a fair chance. He has been so burdened with letters and telegrams from well-wishers and vilifiers and efforts to exploit him that he has had no chance to concentrate.

It is almost impossible to elicit comments about Robinson's presence in the National League from any one connected with baseball. Neither club owners nor players have anything to say for publication. This leads to the conclusion that the caginess of both parties, plus natural cupidity which warns against loss of salaries or a gate attraction, will keep the reactionary element under cover.

When Robinson joined the Montreal club last year, there was resentment among some Royal players. There was also a fear on the part of league officials that trouble would be forthcoming when the Royals played in Baltimore. Both the resentment and the fear were dissipated in three months. Robinson behaved like a gentleman and was cheered as wholeheartedly in Baltimore as anywhere else. Incidentally, Baltimore had its biggest attendance in 1946 and the incidence of Negroes in the crowd was not out of proportion.

Since Robinson has played with Brooklyn many difficulties have loomed, sometimes forbiddingly, but all have been circumvented. This was in part due to the sportsmanship of the fans and in part to the intelligence and planning of the Brooklyn management.

It is understood the St. Louis players recently have been talking about staging the strike on the day that Brooklyn plays its first game in St. Louis. Publicity probably will render the move abortive.

The blast of publicity which followed the *New York Herald Tribune*'s revelation that the St. Louis Cardinals were promoting a players' strike against the presence of Jackie Robinson, Brooklyn's Negro first baseman, in the National League, probably will serve to quash further strolls down Tobacco Road. In other words, it can now be honestly doubted that the boys from the Hookworm Belt will have the nerve to foist their quaint sectional folklore on the rest of the country.

The *New York Herald Tribune*'s story was essentially right and factual. The denial by Sam Breadon, St. Louis owner, that a strike was or is threatened is so spurious as to be beneath notice. The admission by Ford C. Frick, National League president, that the strike was contemplated was above and beyond the rabbitry generally adhered to by the tycoons of our national game. Such frankness, when compared with the furtiveness of other baseball barons, makes Frick the Mister Baseball of our time, whoever gets the $50,000.

From behind his iron curtain, Abie Chandler, through his front man, Walter Mulbry, denied any knowledge of the projected St. Louis players' strike. This is true. The commissioner was uninformed. Inasmuch as the projected strike did not transcend the boundaries of the National

League. Abie was told nothing about it, or at any rate, that was the reason ascribed.

When this department was investigating the story, it was discovered that almost no one except the St. Louis personnel and the astute Branch Rickey, president, had no knowledge of it, though numerous lesser Robinson impasses had badgered the Flatbush mahatma earlier in the season. Rickey declined to talk about the case even though silence had not been imposed on him. The lack of such imposition was due to the fact that the commissioner, knowing nothing about it, had not got around to placing additional gags.

Frick also kept his peace, but due to a leak similar to the one seeping from Abie's office to *The Sporting News,* we were able to discover he had knowledge of it. Knowing him to be an honest man, we decided he would not deny the story. Therefore we went ahead and printed it. If Frick had denied it, its truth might still be unestablished. As it is, whatever Mr. Breadon may conjure up, people will laugh at him.

We made no pretense of quoting Frick verbatim in the ultimatum he delivered to St. Louis. We were wrong, apparently, in stating he personally delivered it to the players. It seems he delivered it to Breadon for relay to said operatives. In view of the fact that it obviously is the most noble statement ever made by a baseball man (by proxy or otherwise) we hereby reprint it, giving Ford full credit if he wants it:

> If you do this [strike] you will be suspended from the league. You will find that the friends you think you have in the press box will not support you, that you will be outcasts. I do not care if half the league strikes. Those who do will encounter quick retribution. All will be suspended and I don't care if it wrecks the National League for five years. This is the United States of America and one citizen has as much right to play as another.
>
> The National League will go down the line with Robinson whatever the consequences. You will find if you go through with your intention that you have been guilty of complete madness.

Enough of sweetness and light. Just to supplement our story, let us say that Robinson's presence in organized baseball has been attacked by minorities ever since he joined Montreal last year. There was nothing but trouble throughout training this spring. Extravagant measures have been taken to see that untoward incidents do not occur. Most of the trouble has been caused by players from the Hookworm Belt, but at least one major league owner has openly expressed his dim view of the situation. We hesitate to name him. He is fatherly and venerable.

It is also known that another tycoon, who has expressed no open disapproval, has filed with the commissioner a secret document in which he is supposed to have stated that the presence of a Negro in baseball jeopardizes the holdings of all the major league owners.

Boy, are the clients going to run out to see Robinson when he tours the West!

1956

## Murray Kempton

........................................................................................................

# Sal Maglie . . . A Gracious Man

FROM *The New York Post*

THERE WAS the customary talk about the shadows of the years and the ravages of the law of averages when Sal Maglie went out to meet the Yankees yesterday afternoon. It was the first time, after all the years, that he had ever pitched in Yankee Stadium, the home of champions.

He threw that hump-backed let-up pitch that is last in the warm-up, and then for the first time looked at Hank Bauer. He threw the curve in; Hank Bauer made a gesture at bunting; and the strike was called.

The hitter leaned over a little; the pitch was high; Hank Bauer skittered back in haste and the ball went by the catcher's mitt and back to the wall.

"If I know Sal," the old Giant writer in the stands said, "he threw that to tell 'em off. He knows the Yankees probably think he's a little tired. He's saying to them, look fellas, I'm still around. You've got to come and get me."

"The call was for an inside pitch," said Sal Maglie later. "I threw it too high and it got away." He is a gracious man who takes no pride in the legend of special, professional venom.

He worked his arm a little and blew on his hands as though he came from a world no sun could warm. And then Bauer plunked it up to Reese; Maglie looked once at the ball and then at the fielder, and, without needing to see the catch, bent over and worked his long, brown, dealer's hand into the resin bag.

He got Joe Collins to hit on the ground to the wrong field; Mickey Mantle went all the way around; Sal Maglie heard the sound and judged it. The left fielder was still circling under it when Sal Maglie crossed the foul line on his way to the dugout. He gives very little and can afford to spend less.

He went that way through the line-up for the first three innings. It seemed a memorable incident when the first pitch to the eighth Yankee batter was a ball. The utility infield of the fifth-place team in the Westport Midget League would have eaten up anything hit by either side in those three perfect eighteen outs. "I figured," said Peewee Reese, "that both you guys weren't giving anybody anything, and we'd have to call it at midnight."

Sal Maglie ended the third for the Dodgers, walking out slowly carrying one bat, digging his spikes in as though anything is possible in this game, driving the first pitch straight to Mickey Mantle and walking over towards third base to change his cap and get his glove.

He threw the warm-up pitches; Roy Campanella was standing up and almost dancing at the plate.

Maglie got the two quick strikes on Bauer who hit to Jackie Robinson; Maglie did not look at the play; he was busy with the resin. He pushed the curve by Joe Collins; it was the third strike. Mantle was back.

The first strike was a curve and called. There were no times intruding upon the memory when he had seemed more sharp. He threw the next pitch outside, and then hit the corner again. He waited awhile, rubbing his fingers on his shirt, wiping the afternoon's first sweat off his forehead. He threw a pitch on the corner that was low by the distance of a bead of sweat from the skin; it was that close and it was called a ball.

Mantle hit a foul; Sal Maglie knew it was out of play; the left fielder was still running and he was working on a new ball. The next pitch he threw Mantle was down the middle a little inside. Roy Campanella said later that it hit his fists. Sal Maglie watched it almost curve and then stay fair in the stands; with the unseeing roar all around him, he walked back to the rubber and kicked it once.

"He'd been fouling off the outside pitches," he said later. "I thought I'd try him inside once." He stopped for a minute, naked and dry beside his locker, the skin showing through the thin hair above his forehead. "That shows what can happen when you're thinking out there and the other guy isn't." That was as close as he came to suggesting that God is too tolerant with the margin of error he assigns the very young.

Then Yogi Berra hit one hard to the wrong field; Duke Snider ran the distance of years, and tumbled up with it. Sal Maglie had no reason to know it then, but that was the inning and the run.

In the fifth Enos Slaughter was walked very fast. Billy Martin bunted. Sal Maglie came scuttling onto the grass and snatched the ball and turned around and fired it high and smoky to second just in time, a

40-year-old man throwing out a 40-year-old man and knowing he had
to hurry. He was sweating hard by this time. Harold Reese went up half
his height, met McDougald's drive and knocked it into the air, and
recovered it for the double play. Sal Maglie was watching the way the
ball went now; the sound was different; for the first time today he had to
think of the fielders.

Don Larsen went on making the rest period painfully short. Sal
Maglie took his warm-ups for the sixth; he was throwing the last one in
hard now. Andy Carey hit one over his head into center and the old
remembered tightrope walk had begun.

Larsen bunted the third strike; Maglie and Campanella scrambled off
too late to get the runner at second; they had made their mistake. Carey
went far off second; Bauer slapped the ball to left. Sal Maglie drove
himself over to back up third, but the run was in and safely in. Walter
Alston came out; the conference went on around Maglie. A man in the
stands said that if Labine was ready, it was time to bring him in. "Take
Sal out?" Campanella said later, "the way he was pitching?" Joe Collins
hit a low, hard single; Maglie went over to cover third again and came
back slamming the ball into his glove. Mantle was up.

The first pitch was out of control; then he threw two strikes, one
called, one swinging. Mantle hit the ball to the first baseman who threw
to the catcher, who threw not well to the third baseman, who fell away
and threw around Bauer to get him. After the game, Sal Maglie looked
at Jackie Robinson, sitting sombre across the dressing room; in a moment of surprise, Robinson's hair was gray. "That was a throw," he said.
"Him falling away like that." Maglie saw it, and walked to the third base
line and waited for the rundown, so as not to interfere, like a waiter at
his station, and then walked slowly back to the dugout.

He was the last to come out after the swift Dodger half of the seventh.
That appears in the boxscore to have been all it was, except that in the
bottom of the eighth, Don Larsen was the first to bat. Sal Maglie went
on with his warm-ups; alone in that great park, he and Campanella
were not looking at the hitter. He struck out Larsen; he struck out
Bauer; he struck out Joe Collins swinging. When he walked back, the
crowd noticed him and gave him a portion of its cheers. It was the last
inning of the most extraordinary season an old itinerant, never a va-
grant, ever had. "I figured," he said later, "that for me, either way, it was
the last inning, and I didn't have to save anything."

"I would like to see him," he said later, "pitch with men on bases."
Someone asked him if he had minded Larsen getting his no-hitter.

"I might have wanted him to get it," he answered, "if we hadn't had a chance all the time."

They asked him was he satisfied with the game he pitched. "How," said Sal Maglie, "am I to be satisfied? But you got to adjust yourself." To time and to ill-chance, and the way they forgot, you got to adjust yourself. Someone asked if you knew when you had a no-hitter, and he said, of course, you do. You remember who had hit, for one thing. "If you ask me two years from now," said Sal Maglie, "I'll be able to tell you every pitch I threw this year." He said it, in passing, naked, his body white except for the red from countless massages on his right arm, tearing his lunch off a long Italian sausage.

"They are pros," he said. "The way we are. You make one mistake with them and you're in trouble."

On the other side of the room, somebody asked Campanella if Maglie had made any mistakes out there. "Sal make mistakes?" said Campanella. "The only mistake he made today was pitching." He pulled on his jacket and turned to what was left of the assemblage. Maglie was going now, as losers are required to go, to get his picture taken with Don Larsen in the Yankee dressing room.

"I told you," chided Roy Campanella, as Sal Maglie went out the door, "that there would be days like this."

1957

## Dick Young

......................................................................................

# Obit on the Dodgers

FROM *The New York Daily News*

THIS IS CALLED an obit, which is short for obituary. An obit tells of a person who has died, how he lived, and of those who live after him. This is the obit on the Brooklyn Dodgers.

Preliminary diagnosis indicates that the cause of death was an acute case of greed, followed by severe political complications. Just a year ago, the Brooklyn ball club appeared extremely healthy. It had made almost a half million dollars for the fiscal period, more than any other big league club. Its president, Walter O'Malley, boasted that all debts had been cleared, and that the club was in the most solvent condition of its life, with real estate assets of about $5 million.

O'Malley contends that unhealthy environment, not greed, led to the demise of the Dodgers in Brooklyn. He points out that he became aware of this condition as long ago as 1947, when he began looking around for a new park to replace Ebbets Field, capacity 32,000.

At first, O'Malley believed the old plant could be remodeled, or at least torn down and replaced at the same site. But, after consultation with such a prominent architect as Norman Bel Geddes, and the perusal of numerous blueprints and plans, O'Malley ruled out such a possibility as unfeasible.

So O'Malley looked around for a new lot where he could build this bright, new, salubrious dwelling for his Dodgers; a dream house, complete with plastic dome so that games could be played in spite of foul weather, a plant that could be put to year-round use, for off-season sports and various attractions.

O'Malley suggested to the City of New York that the site of the new Brooklyn Civic Center, right outside the Dodger office windows in Boro

Hall, would be ideal for the inclusion of a 50,000 seat stadium — a War Memorial stadium, he proposed.

That was all very patriotic, the City Planning Commission said, but not a stadium; not there. Sorry.

So, O'Malley looked farther, and hit upon the area at Flatbush and Atlantic Avenues — virtually the heart of downtown Brooklyn, where all transit systems intersect, and where the tired Long Island Rail Road limps in at its leisure. O'Malley learned that a vast portion of the neighborhood, which included the congested Ft. Greene market, had been declared a "blighted area" by city planners who had earmarked it for rehabilitation.

Here began one of the most forceful political manipulations in the history of our politically manipulated little town. With O'Malley as the guiding spirit, plans for establishment of a Sports Authority were born. It would be the work of such an Authority to issue bonds and build a stadium with private capital — utilizing the city's condemnation powers to obtain the land.

With O'Malley pushing the issue through his lifelong political contacts, the bill was drafted in Albany, passed overwhelmingly by the City Council, squeezed through the State Legislature by one vote, and ultimately signed into law by Governor Harriman.

At that moment, April 21, 1956, the prospects for a new stadium, and a continuance of Brooklyn baseball were at their highest. Thereafter, everything went downhill. City officials, who had supported the bill originally, in the belief Albany would defeat it, went to work with their subtle sabotage. Appropriations for surveys by the Sports Center Authority were cut to the bone, and O'Malley shook his head knowingly. He was getting the works.

O'Malley, meanwhile, had been engaging in some strange movements of his own. He had leased Roosevelt Stadium, Jersey City, for three years with the announced intention of playing seven or eight games a season there. Later, he sold Ebbets Field for $3,000,000 on a lease-back deal with Marv Kratter. The lease made it possible for O'Malley to remain in Brooklyn, in a pinch, for five years. He had no intention of doing so — it was just insurance against things blowing up at both political ends.

Why was Ebbets Field sold?

Politicians claimed it was an O'Malley squeeze on them. O'Malley claimed it was a manifestation of his good intentions; that he was converting the club's assets into cash so that he might buy Sports Authority bonds and help make the new stadium a reality.

Then, O'Malley moved in a manner that indicated he didn't believe himself. At the start of '57 he visited Los Angeles. Two months later, he announced the purchase of Wrigley Field. Shortly thereafter, Los Angeles officials, headed by Mayor Paulson and County Supervisor Ken Hahn, visited O'Malley at Vero Beach, Fla.

It was there, on March 7, that serious consideration of a move to Los Angeles crystallized in the O'Malley mind. He made grandiose stipulations to the L.A.'s authorities — and was amazed to hear them say: "We will do it."

From then on, Los Angeles officials bore down hard on the project, while New York's officials quibbled, mouthed sweet nothings, and tried to place the blame elsewhere. With each passing week, it became increasingly apparent the Dodgers were headed west — and, in an election year, the politicians wanted no part of the hot potato.

Bob Moses, park commissioner, made one strong stab for New York. He offered the Dodgers park department land at Flushing Meadow — with a string or two. It wasn't a bad offer — but not as good as L.A.'s.

By now, O'Malley's every move was aimed at the coast. He brought Frisco Mayor George Christopher to dovetail the Giant move to the coast with his own. He, and Stoneham, received permission from the NL owners to transfer franchises.

That was May 28 — and since then, O'Malley has toyed with New York authorities, seeming to derive immense satisfaction from seeing them sweat unnecessarily. He was repaying them.

Right to the end, O'Malley wouldn't give a flat, "Yes, I'm moving" — as Stoneham had done. O'Malley was using New York as his saver — using it to drive a harder bargain with L.A.'s negotiator Harold McClellan, and using it in the event the L.A.'s city council were to reject the proposition at the last minute.

But L.A., with its mayor whipping the votes into line the way a mayor is expected to, passed the bill — and O'Malley graciously accepted the 300 acres of downtown Los Angeles, whereupon he will graciously build a ball park covering 12 acres.

And the Brooklyn Dodgers dies — the healthiest corpse in sports history. Surviving are millions of fans, and their memories.

The memories of a rich and rollicking history — dating back to Ned Hanlon, the first manager, and skipping delightfully through such characters as Uncle Wilbert Robinson, Casey Stengel, Burleigh Grimes, Leo

Durocher, Burt Shotten, Charley Dressen and now Walt Alston. The noisy ones, the demonstrative ones, the shrewd and cagey ones, and the confused ones. They came and they went, but always the incredible happenings remained, the retold screwy stories, the laughs, the snafued games, the laughs, the disappointments, the fights, and the laughs.

And the players: the great ones — Nap Rucker, Zack Wheat, Dazzy Vance, Babe Herman, Dolph Camilli, Whit Wyatt, Dixie Walker; the almost great ones but never quite — like Van Lingle Mungo and Pete Reiser; the modern men who made up the Dodgers' golden era — Duke Snider, Preacher Roe, Hugh Casey — and the man who made history, Jackie Robinson, and the boy who pitched Brooklyn to its only world championship in 1955, Johnny Podres.

And the brass: the conflicts of the brothers McKeever, and the trials of Charley Ebbets; the genuine sentimentality of Dearie Mulvey and the pride of her husband, Jim Mulvey; the explosive achievement of Larry MacPhail, the unpopular but undeniable success of Branch Rickey — and now, Walter O'Malley, who leaves Brooklyn a rich man and a despised man.

1979

## Jim Murray

......................................................................................................

# If You're Expecting One-Liners

FROM *The Los Angeles Times*

OK, BANG THE DRUM slowly, professor. Muffle the cymbals. Kill the laugh track. You might say that Old Blue Eye is back. But that's as funny as this is going to get.

I feel I owe my friends an explanation as to where I've been all these weeks. Believe me, I would rather have been in a press box.

I lost an old friend the other day. He was blue-eyed, impish, he cried a lot with me, laughed a lot with me, saw a great many things with me. I don't know why he left me. Boredom, perhaps.

We read a lot of books together, we did a lot of crossword puzzles together, we saw films together. He had a pretty exciting life. He saw Babe Ruth hit a home run when we were both 12 years old. He saw Willie Mays steal second base, he saw Maury Wills steal his 104th base. He saw Rocky Marciano get up. I thought he led a pretty good life.

One night a long time ago he saw this pretty lady who laughed a lot, played the piano and he couldn't look away from her. Later he looked on as I married this pretty lady. He saw her through 34 years. He loved to see her laugh, he loved to see her happy.

You see, the friend I lost was my eye. My good eye. The other eye, the right one, we've been carrying for years. We just let him tag along like Don Quixote's nag. It's been a long time since he could read the number on a halfback or tell whether a ball was fair or foul or even which fighter was down.

So, one blue eye is missing and the other misses a lot.

So my best friend left me, at least temporarily, in a twilight world where it's always 8 o'clock on a summer night.

He stole away like a thief in the night and he took a lot with him. But not everything. He left a lot of memories. He couldn't take those with him. He just took the future with him and the present. He couldn't take the past.

I don't know why he had to go. I thought we were pals. I thought the things we did together we enjoyed doing together. Sure, we cried together. There were things to cry about.

But it was a long, good relationship, a happy one. It went all the way back to the days when we arranged all the marbles in a circle in the dirt in the lots in Connecticut. We played one o'cat baseball. We saw curveballs together, trying to hit them or catch them. We looked through a catcher's mask together. We were partners in every sense of the word.

He recorded the happy moments, the miracle of children, the beauty of a Pacific sunset, snow-capped mountains, faces on Christmas morning. He allowed me to hit fly balls to young sons in uniforms two sizes too large, to see a pretty daughter march in halftime parades. He allowed me to see most of the major sports events of our time. I suppose I should be grateful that he didn't drift away when I was 12 or 15 or 29 but stuck around over 50 years until we had a vault of memories. Still, I'm only human. I'd like to see again, if possible, Rocky Marciano with his nose bleeding, behind on points and the other guy coming.

I guess I would like to see a Reggie Jackson with the count 3 and 2 and the Series on the line, guessing fastball. I guess I'd like to see Rod Carew with men on first and second and no place to put him, and the pitcher wishing he were standing in the rain someplace, reluctant to let go of the ball.

I'd like to see Stan Musial crouched around a curveball one more time. I'd like to see Don Drysdale trying not to laugh as a young hitter came up there with both feet in the bucket.

I'd like to see Sandy Koufax just once more facing Willie Mays with a no-hitter on the line. I'd like to see Maury Wills with a big lead against a pitcher with a good move. I'd like to see Roberto Clemente with the ball and a guy trying to go from first to third. I'd like to see Pete Rose sliding into home head-first.

I'd like once more to see Henry Aaron standing there with that quiet bat, a study in deadliness. I'd like to see Bob Gibson scowling at a hitter as if he had some nerve just to pick up a bat. I'd like to see Elroy Hirsch going out for a long one from Bob Waterfield, Johnny Unitas in high-cuts picking apart a zone defense. I'd like to see Casey Stengel walking to the mound on his gnarled old legs to take the pitcher out, beckoning his gnarled old finger behind his back.

I'd like to see Sugar Ray Robinson or Muhammad Ali giving a recital, a ballet, not a fight. Also, to be sure, I'd like to see a sky full of stars, moonlight on the water, and yes, the tips of a royal flush peaking out as I fan out a poker hand, and yes, a straight two-foot putt.

Come to think of it, I'm lucky. I saw all of those things. I see them yet.

1983

## Diane K. Shah

......................................................................................................................

# Oh, No! Not Another Boring
# Interview with Steve Carlton

FROM *The Los Angeles Herald Examiner*

HAVING RECENTLY PASSED a statistical benchmark, that is, having just written my 300th column, I find I am besieged by athletes begging me to interview them. I know that only 15 other sports columnists in the history of journalism have reached this plateau, but I must say this constant round of interviews does grow wearisome. Every time a new team comes to town it's the same thing. You'd think all the athletes could just get together and agree to one mass interview.

To make matters worse, I once again find myself covering the play-offs. So now the requests for interviews have intensified all the more. Yesterday morning, no sooner had I reached my office when the phone rang.

"Yeah," I said.

"Er, Miss Shah? This is Steve Carlton with the Philadelphia Phillies. I was wondering . . ."

"I haven't even had my coffee yet," I grumbled. "Don't you guys ever sleep?"

"I'm sorry," said Carlton. "It's just that I was, er, wondering if you would have time today to interview me."

"What team did you say you were from?"

"The Phillies. I'm a pitcher."

"Oh, right, I remember. But haven't I interviewed you before? When the Phillies won the 1980 World Series or after you got your 300th win? I'm sure I did."

"Actually, you didn't," Carlton said. "I was rather hoping you would, but you always walk right past me. I've even sent you notes requesting interviews, but you never reply."

"You know how many games there are in a season?" I said.

"Yes," said Carlton meekly. "But I felt I had to give it a shot."

"So what is it you want me to interview you about?" I said, trying not to sound bored.

"Well you could ask me about my tough conditioning program," he said. "The Kung Fu and pushing my arm into a tub of rice. Or how many more years I'm going to pitch. Or what I think about the play-offs."

"Same old stuff," I said, stifling a yawn. "You'd think occasionally one of you guys would come up with something new to say."

"Perhaps you could ask me about being an oenophile," Carlton suggested.

"Don't try to impress me with big words," I snapped. "I hate looking things up in the dictionary."

"Oh," said Carlton deflatedly. "Well, er, I did lead the league in strike-outs. With 275."

"Are you a Cy Young candidate then?"

"No," he said sadly. "That would be John Denny. He pitches Wednesday night."

"Don't take this personally," I said, "but readers would probably be more interested in finding out what he has to say."

"I wouldn't need much time," Carlton pleaded. "Although I usually like as much time with the writer as possible."

"I've heard that before," I sighed. "You athletes think the longer the interview the better the story. Only I'm not getting paid to shoot the breeze with you guys. I get paid to write a column. I know it's important to your line of work to get interviewed, so I try to accommodate you when I can. But it's not in my contract here at the paper to just sit around doing interviews all day."

"I'll try to be as brief as possible," said Carlton. "Perhaps we could have lunch or a cup of coffee before the game."

"Absolutely not," I screamed. "You want me to talk to you, we'll talk at the ballpark. I hate when athletes try to interfere with my private life."

"Fine," said Carlton. "What time should I meet you?"

"Well, let's see. I'll get out to Dodger Stadium about two-and-a-half hours before game time. Then I have to go up to the press box and set up my word processing machine. I have to find a plug and take the machine out of its case and make sure it works. This is a special time for me. I don't like to be rushed."

"How about after you finish word processing practice?"

"No, 'Cause then I like to stroll around the batting cage chatting with my colleagues from the other papers. It's really annoying when an athlete comes over and interrupts. Some of the best jokes I hear are said at the batting cage."

"After that?" said Carlton hopefully.

"No," I went on. "Next I have to stop in Tom Lasorda's office. I need to check out the food and which celebrities have come by. And then I have to run through the Dodger clubhouse and say hello to everyone 'cause they expect hometown writers to be friendly to them."

"Gee," said Carlton. "This is really important to me. It's the playoffs."

"Tell you what," I said. "I'll send an intermediary. I'll get Vin Scully to interview you. He'll give the tape to Steve Brener, the Dodger publicist, and he'll screen the best answers out."

"I really appreciate this," said Carlton.

"Sure," I said. "By the way, what did you say your name was?"

1985

# Ira Berkow

........................................................................................................................

# The LaMotta Nuptials

FROM *The New York Times*

NEITHER OF THE Las Vegas dailies, nor, for that matter, the *New York Times,* reported in their society news sections the wedding of Jacob (Jake) LaMotta, 63 years old, erstwhile pugilist, and Theresa Miller, younger than the bridegroom and decidedly prettier.

Perhaps it was determined in some editorial conclave that to cover one of Jake's nuptials is to cover them all, for this is the sixth time he's tied the knot. But to Jake, each, of course, is unique. His first wife divorced him, he says, "because I clashed with the drapes." Another one, Vicki, complained about not having enough clothes. "I didn't believe her," LaMotta says, "until I saw her pose nude in *Playboy* magazine."

The betrothal of LaMotta, the former world middleweight champion, to Miss Miller (this was her second trip to the altar) took place last Sunday night in Las Vegas at Maxim Hotel and Casino in a room stuffed with a wide assortment of beefy people with odd-shaped and familiar noses. They included such ex-champions as Gene Fullmer, Carmen Basilio, Willie Pep, Joey Maxim, Billy Conn, José Torres and, the best man, Sugar Ray Robinson, plus a potpourri of contenders, trainers and matchmakers, all of whom were in Las Vegas to attend the Hagler-Hearns world middleweight title fight the following night.

For LaMotta, having Robinson as the best man was a sweet and perfect touch. "I fought Sugar six times," he said. "I only beat him once. This is my sixth marriage and I ain't won one yet. So I figure I'm due."

Both the groom and the best man wore tuxedos with white corsages in their lapels. The bride was radiant in a white dress with mother-of-pearl-and-lace design, and a garland of baby's breath in her auburn hair.

The wedding party assembled under a white lattice arch in the corner of the room as District Judge Joe Pavlikowski of Clark County presided over the ceremony.

Despite the loud, happy chatter of the guests, the judge began a recital of the vows. "Quiet, please," a man shouted. "Quiet." When that didn't work, the man stuck two fingers in his mouth and whistled. That got their attention.

The judge continued. He asked Jake and Theresa if they would love and obey. They said they would, and Jake kissed the bride.

"Wait a minute," said the judge. "Not yet."

Jake looked up, and Theresa smiled. The judge coughed.

In another corner of the room, a phone rang.

Jake looked around brightly. "What round is it?" he asked.

The room broke up. Theresa, laughing, said, "I've changed my mind!" Then she hugged Jake, who smiled proudly at his bon mot.

"We've got to finish," said the judge. The room settled down somewhat. ". . . With love and affection," continued the judge, speaking quicker now. In short order, he pronounced them "Mr. and Mrs. Jake LaMotta."

Applause and cheers went up, and the couple kissed again, this time officially.

"Jake's ugly as mortal sin," observed Billy Conn. "He's a nice guy, though."

Shortly after, Jake and Carmen Basilio argued about who was uglier. The issue wasn't resolved. Steve Rossi, the comedian, who was performing at the hotel, was the master of ceremonies at the wedding. He brought the fighters onto the stage, where they talked and laughed and feinted and hit one another with friendly jabs and hooks.

When all the fighters were onstage, Rossi said, "Let's all go eat before the platform collapses."

Teddy Brenner, the matchmaker, asked Joey Maxim, "Who was the only white guy to beat Jersey Joe Walcott and Floyd Patterson?" Maxim said he didn't know. "You, ya big lug," said Brenner. They both laughed. The story gleefully made the rounds, varying a little with each telling, until finally, ". . . and so he asked Joey, 'Who was the only white guy to beat Louis and Ali?' . . ."

Someone asked Fullmer how many times he had fought Robinson.

"Three and a half," he said. "The second fight I asked my manager, 'How come they stopped it?' He said, ''Cause the referee counted to 11.'"

Basilio said he had recently retired as a physical education instructor at Le Moyne College in Syracuse. Someone asked if he had a degree.

He smiled and brushed the ashes from his cigarette off the sports jacket of the person he was talking to. "I got a degree from H.N.," he said. "The school of hard knocks."

Billy Conn, who lives in Pittsburgh, was telling about the time that his brother Jackie, a nonconformist, visited Conn on a Thanksgiving Day. "We were having the Mellons over and I told Jackie that we wanted everything to run smoothly, so here's 50 bucks and go buy a turkey for yourself. But he kept the 50 bucks and took the two turkeys we had in the stove."

What did the Conns and the Mellons eat that night?

"We didn't eat," he said, "we drank whiskey all night. Oh, Jackie was a character. Jackie's dead now."

Roger Donoghue, once a promising middleweight from Yonkers, and now a successful liquor salesman, was recalling the television-fight days of the early 1950s. Basilio came over and handed Roger a small camera and asked him to take a picture of him and his wife.

"I got hit in the head a lot," said Roger, looking at the camera, "but I'll try."

The doors of the room were opened and the clanging of slot machines was heard from the adjoining casino. People wandered in and out of the wedding party.

Jake was explaining, "You wanna go through life with someone, and she's a great kid, a great kid."

"This one," said Theresa, "is going to last until we die."

Now, Jake and his bride stepped onto the dance floor. A trio, headed by a piano player wearing a black cowboy hat, played "The Nearness of You."

Joey Maxim removed the cigar from his mouth as he watched Jake dance with his new bride. "Ain't that nice?" he said.

"Hey, buddy," said a man who walked in from the casino, "you know where a fella can get two tickets for the fight?"

## Mike Royko

....................................................................................................................

# "A Very Solid Book"

FROM *The Chicago Tribune*

A NEW YORK publishing house has sent me a copy of a new paperback book it has just brought out.

With it came a note that said: "We take pleasure in presenting you with this review copy and ask that you please send two copies of your notices to our offices."

I seldom review books in my column. The Chicago paper for which I write has a section that takes care of that. But in this case, I'm going to make an exception.

The book is called "If At First . . ." with a subtitle that says "With the exclusive inside story of the 1986 Championship Season."

The author is Keith Hernandez, who is the first baseman on the New York Mets baseball team. Actually, he didn't write it — some professional ghostwriter did. But the words and story originated with Hernandez. I will begin my review by saying that this is a very solid book. The moment I opened the package and saw what it was about, I threw it against my office wall as hard as I could.

Then I slammed it to the floor and jumped up and down on it. I beat on it with a chair for several minutes until I slumped onto my couch, emotionally and physically spent. Although slightly scuffed, the book was still intact.

It is also a book that can cause excitement. I dropped it on the desk of a friend who has had weekend season tickets at Wrigley Field for the past 10 years. It immediately stirred him to emotional heights. He shouted:

"Why are you showing me that piece of (deleted)? I say (deleted) Hernandez and (deleted) the Mets and (deleted) the whole (deleted) city of New York. And (deleted) you, too."

Then he flung it against a wall and gave it a kick. It still remained intact. I told you it was a solid book.

It's a book that can move a sensitive reader to tears, as I discovered when I showed it to a man who has been going to Cub games since 1946, a year that is known as The Beginning of Darkness.

When he looked at the cover, he choked back a sob, a tear trickled down his cheek, and he said: "Why them? Why not us? What was our sin? How can we atone for it? You know, I asked my clergyman that, and he said he wishes he knew, because he lost $50 betting against them."

And it's a powerful book. As reviewers like to say: It can hit you right in the guts. This was proven when I showed it to a confirmed bleacher-ite who said: "Excuse me. I'm going to throw up."

But enough of generalities. Let us consider the contents of this book.

On the very first page, Hernandez and his ghostwriter say: "ad made the second out on a long the Mets were through for 1986: o out, nobody on, two runs down, ox already leading the World Series en our score-board operator at"

And on page 81, Hernandez says: "round during infield practice, I draw a line man and myself and call our manager over avy? I ask. He laughs."

Moving to page 125, we find: "Oh, sweet bird of youth, however, were a different story. It's diff- quietly as I work my way out of a bad me to listen to his judgments. I wrong with my swing. I know hot to th hard-headed. Dand and I have had"

I know, it sounds kind of garbled, incomprehensible. But that's the way a story reads when you rip the pages of a book in half, one by one, as I've been doing.

Don't misunderstand me. I'm not doing that out of spite. I'm a good sport, a cheerful loser. Why, in the last two years, I don't think I've watched my video of the movie "Fail Safe," in which New York City gets nuked, more than 30 or 40 times.

The fact is, I have found this to be a useful book.

I have been tearing out the pages and crumpling them into little wads.

When I have about 30 or 40 of these wads, I put them in my fireplace under the kindling and light them. They're excellent for getting a fire started.

Then I pour myself a drink, lower the lights, sit back, and stare at the crackling flames.

And I pretend that I'm looking at Shea Stadium.

# Features
## and Longer Pieces

1932

## Ring Lardner

........................................................................................................

# Eckie

FROM *The Saturday Evening Post*

THERE WAS GREAT excitement around the Chicago Inter-Ocean office during the last two or three days of January, 1908. The prophets had declared that if we found the place still open at noon on February second, the paper would exist for six more weeks. Since the beginning of the year it had been common gossip in the town that we were on our last limbs, and the issuance of weekly pay checks was always followed by a foot race downstairs to the bank; the theory being that only the first five or six to reach the paying teller's cage would land in the money.

However, according to the best of my knowledge and belief, all the employees of the I.-O. were paid in full when publication finally ceased. I was not on hand for the funeral, because I received, on February first, an offer from Harry Shroudenbach, sporting editor of the Examiner, to join his staff immediately at the noble salary of twenty-five dollars a week, an increase of $6.50 over what I had been getting. My Inter-Ocean boss, Duke Hutchinson, advised me to grab the offer before it was withdrawn; whether from kindliness or from the fact that he was tired of seeing me around, I shall never know.

With Hugh Fullerton, star baseball writer, hibernating, the Examiner's sporting staff was numerically equal to the Inter-Ocean's. We had Shroudy, the sports editor, Duffy Cornell, his assistant, and Sam Hall and me, domestics. It was important, of course, to get the news into the paper, but more important than that, it seemed, was to write startling, pretty, perfectly fitting headlines of an intricacy which still makes me shiver in retrospect. The sport pages' first and last columns had to be crowned with what were called "Whitney heads," and I don't believe the best copy reader in the world would call them simple. They were triangular in shape, with the base on top and the vertex on the bottom; thus:

GOTCH BREAKS BEALL'S
FOOT WITH TOE HOLD
AS RECORD CROWD
AT COLISEUM
GOES STARK
MAD

Below that was a single cross line, then a double, uneven cross line —
both of them common in the heads of today — and finally a symmetri-
cal bank, in small type, that was supposed to tell everything you hadn't
told before.

These headlines were undoubtedly a delight to the eye of the reader,
but a pain in the neck to the person or persons who wrote them. One in
an evening, if you could take your time, was no trouble at all. But when
you had to tear off four or six, with a two-minute limit for each, you
were ready to spend your off day seeking oblivion.

And that reminds me of three successive off days I took — one of
them on the office and the other two on myself — during which so
much oblivion was found that it is a wonder the Examiner did not
advertise at once for another maid of all work. On Monday, my regular
day of recess, I began a preliminary reconnaissance of the South Side.
There was so much ground to cover that my explorations were far from
complete when someone told me it was Tuesday afternoon and time to
report for duty. I reported, and received a note from Shroudy stating
that he and Mr. Cornell and Mr. Hall had all left for Milwaukee to
handle the big fight. Shroudy was going to write the lead, Mr. Cornell
the detail, and Mr. Hall the notes. I can't remember what fight it was,
possibly one of the terrific battles between Billy Papke and Stanley
Ketchel.

Well, all three of them were good fight writers and any Papke-Ketchel
fight was bound to be a good fight; particularly good for a Chicago
paper because Papke's home was in Illinois and Ketchel's — whether he
ever saw it or not — in Michigan. Just the same, it seemed kind of
quaint to leave a hick like me alone in the office to take care of their
copy and all the other sport copy that would come in, while the three
experienced guys went on a junket to Milwaukee for the simple reason
that they were wild-eyed fight fans. Shroudy's instructions said I would
have to watch my step, because the stuff would arrive by wire a piece at
a time; I would have to figure out whose stuff was whose and keep it all
straightened out.

Unseen audience, I wish I had preserved the *Examiner*'s Papke-Ketchel story of that Wednesday morning. Not even a broadcaster could have got things more messed up. Lead, detail and notes were all jumbled together and Round 1 probably read something like this:

> The boys were called to the center of the ring and received instructions from William Hale Thompson, Ernest Byfield, Percy Hammond, Charles Richter, the Spring Valley Thunderbolt tore in as if he had never heard another crowd made the trip as guests of William Lydon on his yacht the Lydonia Steve cut loose with a left uppercut that nearly this makes certain another meeting between the Battling Nelson and Packey McFarland were also introduced. Steve slipped as he was about to. Seven special trains but the majority thought the round was even it was Papke's round.

That and three or four columns more of the same. The stuff had come in just in time to make the first edition; there was no chance for proofreading or rearranging. And when the edition reached the main copy desk it was greeted with such hilarity that even I woke up and took the advice of a reporter friend who told me to get out of the office before the Milwaukee train bearing my boss and his colleagues arrived back in town.

I sought a quiet spot where I knew Walter Eckersall would eventually appear. When a fellow needed a friend, there was none to be found more satisfactory than Eckie. On this occasion he convinced me that it was not my fault and escorted me in a taxi to my lodgings, leaving me, as he thought, to woo forgetfulness in sleep.

But for some reason I was still restless, and ten minutes after he had gone I was in another taxi, on another sight-seeing tour of Chicago. An account of this trip would be extremely dull, even if I were able to recall any of the details. My chauffeur and I probably called on a great many people who have moved since then. Late Wednesday afternoon it occurred to me that the sooner I knew I was fired the sooner I could start looking for a new job. I asked to be taken to the Examiner office. The meter, I was told, read $132 and this was $130.20 more than I had. The chauffeur appeared vexed at my suggestion that we meet later and talk things out, and he was searching his tool box for an instrument with which to express his mortification when who should pour forth from the office door but Shroudy himself!

"What's the matter?" he said, and was soon informed. And within the next ten minutes he saw the cashier, settled with the taxi man, assured me I was still on the staff and that he realized he had overburdened me the night before, and sent me home to sleep till six o'clock Thursday evening, "when," he added, "we'll start all over."

You will realize by this time that my bosses were pretty well supplied with the so-called milk of human kindness. This pleasant surprise, however, was a double play in which Eckie ought to be credited with an assist. I learned long afterward that the latter had pleaded my cause for hours and had even gone to his own boss, Harvey Woodruff, of the Tribune, and persuaded him to make room for me in the event I got the air from the Examiner, though the Trib already employed so many people in the sporting department that half the writers had to buy seats from the agencies or work lying on their stomachs.

Eckie would do almost anything for anybody, but his friendliness toward me was a natural — I was the only person he knew who shared his horror of going to bed. Night after night, until it was almost the next night, we would sit and just talk; nearly always on one subject — football. And I want to testify that never did I hear him brag of his own skill at that sport, skill equaled — in my opinion and that of other experts who have visited or dwelt in the wilderness west of the Hudson River — only by Jim Thorpe, of Carlisle, and George Gipp, of Notre Dame.

Thorpe and Gipp were quadruple-threat men — they could pass, run, point-kick and punt. Eckie was a triple threat; the forward pass was introduced too late for him to work on it. Nevertheless, when you consider his all-around athletic prowess and his ability as a baseball player, you must conclude that he would have been even more valuable in the modern game than in the old.

Study his equipment for a moment. As a track man at Hyde Park High School, he had done the hundred repeatedly in 10 flat. After he entered the University of Chicago, he got down to 09 4/5 in practice a couple of times and continued to do his 10 consistently in competition. Once, as a stunt, he went the route in 10 1/5 dressed in his football costume. As a quarterback he was a cool, smart director of play. Perhaps not so hard to bring down as Heston, Mahan or Grange, he was harder to catch because of his terrific speed; he played back on defense, and when an opposing team punted to him it was not punting out of danger but into it. I firmly believe Eckie was the reason for Fielding Yost's insistence that his punters learn to punt out of bounds; when a punter boots a high spiral straight down the field for fifty yards, it disheartens a coach to see the punt brought back forty of those yards in spite of faultless covering by competent ends and tackles. As safety man, he was eluded, so far as I know, just once, and that was by Willie Heston. And when Willie eluded you, you were not disgraced. You were merely grateful that you had not been killed.

Now for his kicking. In the Middle West only Pat O'Dea, of Wisconsin, not a contemporary of Eckie's, was the latter's master in drop-kicking and punting, just as he — Pat — was everybody else's superior in these two specialties. It is unnecessary to take my word for that last clause; the record books will bear me out. But Eckie's punts, well aimed and high, averaged close to forty yards, and if he failed to score on a drop kick from thirty yards out, it was almost as much of a shock to the community as seeing Jimmy Walker in a Mother Hubbard.

Seven or eight years after the close of Eckie's college career — and by this time I was a Tribune man, too — there came into the office one Saturday night a story from Harvard — or wherever Harvard had played that day — saying that Charles Brickley had kicked five goals from field in the game with Yale, breaking the world's record so far as major university competition was concerned. Well, everybody around the office knew that Eckie had done the same thing in a game against Illinois, but to make sure, Harvey Woodruff, the sporting editor, asked him.

"Why, yes," he replied, "but maybe Chicago and Illinois are just prep schools." Then, after a pause, "Listen, Woody; I didn't break a record that time any more than Brickley did this afternoon. Mr. Stagg looked it up and found that I had only tied an old record made by a fella at Purdue."

Now you mustn't ask me who the Purdue fella was. The only prominent athletes from that university whose names I can recall are G. P. Torrence, Elmer Oliphant and George Ade, and I know it was none of these.

I discovered years ago that the best way to judge an athlete's worth was by learning what his opponents, past and to come, really thought of him. It was from the people who had tried to hit, or were about to try to hit, Walter Johnson in his good years that I gleaned the knowledge that no other pitcher of our times was in his class. And the men of Yost's great, but not greatest, Michigan elevens of 1904 and 1905 were unable to hide the fact that the very name of Walter Eckersall gave them a headache.

Eckie's first start against Michigan, however, was a life-sized flop. It was on Thanksgiving Day, 1903, when freshmen were still permitted to play on the varsity. Snow had been predicted, and Marshall Field, in Chicago, was covered with hay until an hour before game time. As soon as the hay was removed, the snowfall began and in an incredibly few minutes there were six inches of it on the ground. The start of the game was delayed until it had ceased falling and the ground keeper and his crew had succeeded in removing it from the field and piling it up a yard out of bounds and behind the goal line.

During the game, which Michigan won, 28 to 0, the regular Chicago quarterback, Lee Maxwell, was hauled from a drift and taken to the locker room by relays of dog teams, to be scraped off and thawed out. Eckie replaced him, and I can still remember his *chef d'oeuvre* of the day — a pitiable attempt to punt from a pile of snow in which he was buried a couple of yards behind his own goal. The ball traveled nearly two yards and a half. It was Michigan's ball now and Michigan called Heston's signal, either through sheer venom or because it was the only signal Michigan had. You can guess what happened with half a yard to go.

In 1904, Heston's last year, the Wolverines maintained their proud record of victories which had begun with the engagement of Fielding Yost as coach three seasons before. They beat Chicago 22 to 12, I think, but Eckie's beautiful open-field running, which was responsible for his team's twelve points, had my old home state frightened to such an extent that for months afterward, children hid in the cellar if you said, "Eckersall." In the same year the late Walter Camp discovered that the United States was not bounded on the West by Pennsylvania, and honored both Eckie and Heston with positions on his All-America team. Eckie was chosen again the following season, and five years later when Mr. Camp selected his All-America Team for All Time, positions were awarded Eckie and two other Middle-Westerners, Schulz and Heston, of Michigan.

The 145-pound Chicago quarterback really came into his own in 1905. This was the season in which he kicked five goals from field against Illinois, and he added to the latter's embarrassment by running twenty-five yards for a touchdown. The battle with Wisconsin was tough, but Eckie won it with a twenty-five-yard drop kick, after dashes of fifty, forty and thirty yards had failed to subdue the battling Badgers.

But all games in my memory fade into insignificance compared with the Thanksgiving Day struggle at Marshall Field, Chicago, when Michigan, thanks to Eckie, suffered its first defeat in the reign of Yost. This game was so close and so bitterly fought, and the hostility it aroused between two formerly friendly states so marked, that the Chicago ambassador to Ann Arbor asked for his passports, and vice versa, and athletic relations were severed and stayed severed for years and years and years.

In common with everybody else from Michigan, I felt murderously inclined toward Eckie that day, and not until I got to know him would I admit to myself or anyone else that all he had done was play a great and victorious game of football against a school that had held a monopoly on football glory in the hinterlands since 1900. I could write you, from memory, whole books about that game. Instead, I shall let you off with a paragraph or two.

Chicago was badly handicapped because one of its star halfbacks, Leo De Tray, was sitting in the stand with a bandage over one damaged eye. Michigan became equally handicapped when its start tackle, Joe Curtis, was disqualified for alleged roughing of Eckie on a punt. Michigan made two or three of its familiar marches toward touchdowns, but was always stopped just short. The kicking duel between Eckie and Johnny Garrels was nearly an even thing. The Chicago line was playing over its head and Michigan's defense, led by Tom Hammond, was doing well to keep Bezdek's terrific attack from becoming fatal.

Along in the second half, Chicago had possession of the ball right up against its own goal line. Eckie dropped way back of the goal to punt, but he didn't punt. He ran the ball out nearly to midfield. This is the kind of play that is great if it works, and bone-headed if it doesn't. I have seen Thorpe and Gipp get by with similar plays, which would indicate that Lady Luck is with the stars. Chicago, with Bezdek plunging, was stopped again, and this time Eckie did punt. It was a whale of a punt and came down within inches of Michigan's goal line, where Clark, a substitute back, began to toy with it. He could not make up his mind whether to let it go for a touchback or to run it somewhere. He finally decided on the latter alternative, but it was too late. Just as he gathered the ball into his arms, he was hit, and hit hard, by Catlin and Speik, of Chicago. He was knocked, not for a goal but for a safety, and that's how the game ended, 2 to 0. And it was the first time my girl friend has ever seen me cry.

Ten years elapsed and I was doing a sport column on the Chicago Tribune. My readers had never learned to write, so I was entirely without contributions, and therefore hard up for material. On Thanksgiving morning I printed a dream story of a Michigan-Chicago game that was supposed to take place that afternoon. I wrote an introduction and followed it with a probable line-up, naming players who had been stars ten or twenty years in the past.

Now, there had been no hint of a resumption of athletic relations between Chicago and Michigan. Moreover, Thanksgiving games had been ruled out of the Middle West long, long before, because they interfered with church or turkey or something. Nevertheless, believe it or not, a crowd of more than five hundred people — this is Mr. Stagg's estimate — went to the University of Chicago's football field that day and stood around for hours, waiting for the gates or the ticket windows to open. At length they returned home mad, and many of them telephoned indignant messages to my boss.

This just goes to show that I had Chicago pretty well under my thumb when I sold it to the Sicilians. Also that the typewriter is pretty near as mighty as the rod.

1946

# Jimmy Cannon

......................................................................................................................

# Lethal Lightning

FROM *The New York Post*

ONCE, DREAMING with morphine after an operation, I believed the night climbed through the window and into my room like a second-story worker. I thought all the night had forsaken the world, and shaped like a fat man, walked through my face and up into my mind. The night had the dirty color of sickness and had no face at all as it strolled in my brain. It gradually lost the identity of a man, blowing apart the way smoke does on a windy day. It became a smelly blackness, shoving itself into the corners of my sub-consciousness like a man breaking down a door with his shoulder. It hurt me as I lay there, feeling the brightness of the room. But the filthy night stayed in my mind and I lived in it alone.

I remember that last night in Yankee Stadium when Joe Louis knocked out Billy Conn in the eighth round of a fight that had been tautly dull, the way the slow hours are for reporters sitting on a stoop and waiting for a man to die. I felt that old dream coming from a long way off and finding not me, but Billy Conn, who lay in the spurious day of the ring lights and had the aching blackness all to himself.

It ceased to be sport when Louis let the big right go, then another cobblestone of a right and then the left hook as Conn fell off the rim of the conscious and crumpled into the dark privacy of the night he alone possessed. It was like watching a friend of yours being run over by a trolley car, watching it coming and knowing what would happen but looking at it quietly, the curiosity dominating the horror and compelling you to be attentively silent. Maybe it was sudden but it was there all the time, the knockout inevitable and sure. It was there all the time like the rain in the night that never fell out of the starless sky.

All the big people waited for this plotted accident to happen and down front in the $100 seats was Bernard Baruch and close to him sat a guy who held up banks and now is a legitimate man because they don't put you in jail for selling whisky any more. Stand up and look back out of the press row and there they were, all the big people waiting for this controlled violence, licensed and sanctioned by the laws of the state.

Waiting for it to break out as the old man of the council tables where they speak as though the world were Billy Conn, and Joe Louis the atom, stopping the breathing and the living, as the world breaks into nothing. The old man sat there among the thieves and the good people and the truly talented and the Broadway trash and the black market peerage, the Cabinet member and the Hollywood people. All forgetting what they know, and some what they did, and the world rotting with the hatred of man for himself. So they were there and it was a night out for them at $100 a chair on the grass of the ball park.

So there they were at $100 a look, but back of them were empty places in the cheaper seats when Billy Conn first came into the ring. He wore a white green-bordered satin bathrobe and it gleamed under the lights where a lonely moth flew in circles as though indicating to Conn what he should do. They were there with him, those who trained him and live off him, the guy from the corner of Pitt and Dennison in East Liberty, a paid up member of the Peabody Club, which is a pool room where horse players come to shoot pool.

Johnny Ray, the manager, aimlessly moved around the ring, the name of his fighter in green-blocked letters on the black half-sleeved jersey. He was white with anxiety and seemed to be weak with nervousness as he lay his flabby white arm along the rope and looked into Conn's face as though he were trying to remember the features before they were destroyed.

Then Louis came in, big in his flashy red-edged blue robe of silk, a towel wrapped loosely around his head and moving in the wind of the night. They sat there, and the 45,266 around them on the plains of the playing field and up in the stands mumbled with impatience and expectancy and now and then a lonely shout, blurred by the distance, came down to the ringside. Now the soles of Conn's shoes were being scraped by Billy Joss, a second with an emaciated face. There was a delay because Manny Seaman was tying the laces of Louis's gloves and Conn was standing up, moving his arms slowly, the bath robe off and you noticed that there was a thick cord of fat hanging off his belly when he moved.

They came to the center in the old ritual, the microphone dropped so Eddie Joseph, the referee, could be heard telling them in a gruffly self-conscious voice what would happen if a foul were committed. Louis had a white bathrobe under the blue one and he still wore the towel and Seaman pulled that away when they went to their corners.

It was a first round of comedy, but there was no humor in it. In that round Conn flapped his left glove into Louis for the first punch of the fight and when they clinched Conn was talking to the empty-faced champion, whose mouth twitched as he pushed Conn away.

"What's your hurry, Joe?" Conn asked, muttering through the mouthpiece. "We got fifteen rounds to go."

As they moved in a polite dance of caution, looking at each other as though they were angry men about to argue instead of punch, I saw the puckers of fat where Louis's arms join his shoulders and his stomach moved when his legs did, as though it were not part of him but a slab of meat tied around his waist.

Conn danced leisurely in the first, the head cocked to the left, the legs pale and frail. Once Conn stomped at him, the way Varsity Drag dancers used to do before the Charleston ran them out of the cafes. Louis jabbed occasionally and Conn poked back at him, going backwards from side to side. Conn's fleet yet apparently unconcerned stroll caused Louis to skip, the way a marching soldier does to fall back into step. Once Conn hit to the belly but they seemed fascinated by each other and appeared to be admiring each other's style instead of going about the job they were paid to do.

As the second round started, Conn lunged out of his scampering retreat and hit Louis with a right and then a mild volley of lefts. Billy bluffed with his hands, making up and down feints as he moved his shoulders in tormenting spasms. Once Joe threw a right that couldn't locate the wet-haired head that was out of range. But his jabs were making Billy's head strain at the cords of his big neck and, at the finish, his face was blotchy and mussed with pain.

Now, in the third, Joe winced, closed his eyes and turned his head when Conn feinted at him with meaningless gestures, never getting close enough to bang at the blank-faced man who moved after him on the big feet that creaked on the pebbles of resin strewn across the canvas. Once in this round Conn flared with a harmless fury and when it was over Louis was there, waiting and harassing him with a sheep dog's harmless awareness. The jeers, which had risen timidly from the crowd in the first, were growing louder and the people insulted the fighters they had paid $1,925,564 to see.

In the fourth Louis's lance of a jab began to slam into Conn's face and once Joe ambushed Conn into a corner and slammed two powerful short lefts to the body. Billy slipped as he moved backwards and Louis politely waited for him to rise, the way a standing man takes an introduction to someone sitting at a table. They touched gloves and Conn smiled, but it was a grin of sadness. Conn, the flash and agile scientist of the ring, was moving with the panic of a sensibly fearless boxer. But Louis, who was suspected by many of being an ignoramus of the ring with nothing but strength to lick a man, was out-boxing him. In this round it became obvious that Joe was waiting and Conn was running in a fight that would end in disaster.

The fifth was the big round. It was here that Conn must have known he was scheduled for the oblivion that comes to all of them when they fight Louis. The punch was a right hand and it hit the chin. The hinges of Conn's knees bent and he started to sit down but changed his mind and moved off again after the right. Once Joe pursued him into a corner but Conn fought his way out by moving his hands with futile belligerency. Louis hit him another right and this time the smile was slow and the lips moved more in agony than anything else.

The crowd yelled at them, and it was the same in the sixth, the small man going away and the big man after him. Conn slid on his knees getting away and they touched gloves again in the friendly salute of sportsmen. The seventh was mild but when Louis jabbed it was as though he were prodding Conn with a baseball bat. Everyone in the big stockade realized the big man was coming on and the little man was going. The little man was an authority on that. Conn knew it but his legs wouldn't obey his mind and his flight was slow now and laborious.

Now Conn came to the end of the journey that started back on the street corner in Pittsburgh and ended here in tarnished glory because there was nothing in him but an arrogance that at times was wonderful but always sad. It was a bugle blown, and no one answered, and something incomplete and detached from the kid from Pittsburgh who was stricken with old age at 28 last night.

The right hand was the beginning. It cut Conn's left eye, and a brook of blood dribbled down the cheek and widened like a red stream. Louis pawed at it, and from the press rows you could see the night gathering in Conn's eyes, and the features starting to thicken with the stupidity of punishment. The finish came, unexpected because it destroyed a man, but not suddenly, because Conn was always the hunted, who escaped only temporarily from the trap. The right, the right again, and then the left, against the jaw of the falling man.

He was on his back, the blood running all over him and Joseph was counting and his voice was the timekeeper's hoarse echo. Conn's beaten body moved in his special night, the senses groping for the light and he was rising, boneless and helpless when the number 10 was reached.

There was a tumult of excited men in Louis's dressing room and he sat on a rubbing table, taking slow, small swallows out of a big bottle of mineral water.

"You finally picked the round," he said to me. "It's about time."

The flashlights were going and the reporters pressed in asking questions. Joe answered them, bending over in laughter now and then, calm and dignified and not gloating but trying to tell it the way it happened.

"I'm going out this round and fight," Louis said when someone asked him why he had closed in quickly after following Conn with a slow langour. "That's what I told my corner. I wanted to see if he could take it. He was a better fighter the first time. He didn't hurt me."

There was a cut across Conn's nose, which had been broken before, and they were working on his eye. But he was laughing and cynical with a wit that denounced himself. He did not change, Conn. Not even having Louis catch his jabs like snowballs thrown by a child could shut off his humor.

"He fixed me, didn't he?" Conn asked.

"When did he hurt you?" a reporter asked.

"When he hit me," he answered, sneering.

"What are you going to do?" a reporter said.

"He racked up my cue for me," Conn said.

"Are you going to fight again?"

"As lousy as I was," Conn said, "and you're asking that. I should re-enlist in the army I was so lousy tonight."

Over in the corner, Milton Jaffee, his co-manager, pale and trembling with confusion, stood back behind the photographers and watched the fighter talk as though relating something that was comical that had happened to someone else.

"He ain't fighting any more," Milton said. "There's an easier way to make a dollar than this. He had nothing tonight."

## W. C. Heinz

..................................................................................................

# Brownsville Bum

FROM *True*

IT'S A FUNNY THING about people. People will hate a guy all his life for what he is, but the minute he dies for it they make him out a hero and they go around saying that maybe he wasn't such a bad guy after all because he sure was willing to go the distance for whatever he believed or whatever he was.

That's the way it was with Bummy Davis. The night Bummy fought Fritzie Zivic in the Garden and Zivic started giving him the business and Bummy hit Zivic low maybe 30 times and kicked the referee, they wanted to hang him for it. The night those four guys came into Dudy's bar and tried the same thing, only with rods, Bummy went nuts again. He flattened the first one and then they shot him, and when everybody read about it, and how Bummy fought guns with only his left hook and died lying in the rain in front of the place, they all said he was really something and you sure had to give him credit at that.

"So you're Al Davis?" one of the hoods said. "Why you punch-drunk bum."

What did they expect Bummy to do? What did they expect him to do the night Zivic gave him the thumbs and the laces and walked around the referee and belted Bummy? Bummy could hook too good ever to learn how to hold himself in, if you want the truth of it.

That was really the trouble with Bummy. Bummy blew school too early, and he didn't know enough words. A lot of guys who fought Zivic used to take it or maybe beef to the referee, but Bummy didn't know how to do that. A lot of guys looking at four guns would have taken the talk and been thinking about getting the number off the car when it pulled away, but all Bummy ever had was his hook.

Bummy came out of Brownsville. In the sports pages they are always referring to Brownsville as the fistic incubator of Brooklyn, because they probably mean that a lot of fighters come out of there. Murder, Inc., came out of there, too, and if you don't believe it ask Bill O'Dwyer. If it wasn't for Brownsville maybe Bill O'Dwyer wouldn't have become the mayor of New York.

The peculiar thing about Brownsville is that it doesn't look so tough. There are trees around there and some vacant lots, and the houses don't look as bad as they do over on Second Avenue or Ninth Avenue or up in Harlem. Don't tell Charley Beecher, though, that you don't think it's so tough.

"What's the matter you sold the place?" Froike said to Charley the other day. "It ain't the same, now you sold it."

Charley Beecher used to run the poolroom with the gym behind it on the corner of Georgia and Livonia where Bummy used to train. It was a good little gym with a little dressing room and a shower, and Charley was a pretty good featherweight in the twenties, and his brother Willie, who was even a better fighter, fought Abe Attell and Johnny Dundee and Jack Britton and Leach Cross and Knockout Brown.

"For 17 years I was in business," Charley said. "Seventeen times they stuck me up."

He looked at Froike, and then he pointed with his two hands at his mouth and his ears and his eyes.

"I had guns here and here and here," he said. "All I ever saw was guns."

The worst part was that Charley knew all the guys. A week after they'd heist him they'd be back for a little contribution, maybe a C note. They'd be getting up bail for one of the boys, and they just wanted Charley to know there were no hard feelings about the heist, and that as long as he kept his dues up they'd still consider him friendly to the club. That's how tough Brownsville was.

Bummy had two brothers, and they were a big help. They were a lot older than Bummy, and the one they called Little Gangy and the other they called Duff. Right now Gangy is doing 20 to 40, just to give you an idea, and Bummy took a lot of raps for them, too, because there were some people who couldn't get back at Gangy and Duff so they took it out on the kid.

When Bummy was about seven his father used to run a candy and cigar store and did a little speaking on the side. In other words, he always had a bottle in the place, and he had Bummy hanging around in case anybody should say cop. When the signal would go up Bummy would run behind the counter and grab the bottle, and he was so small nobody could see him over the counter and he'd go out the back.

One day Bummy was going it down the street with the bottle under his coat and some real smart guy stuck out his foot. Bummy tripped and the bottle broke, and Bummy looked at the bottle and the whiskey running on the sidewalk and at the guy and his eyes got big and he started to scream. The guy just laughed and Bummy was lying right on the sidewalk in the whiskey and broken glass, hitting his head on the sidewalk and banging his fists down and screaming. A crowd came around and they watched Bummy, with the guy laughing at him, and they shook their heads and they said this youngest Davidoff kid must be crazy at that.

Davidoff was his straight name. Abraham Davidoff. In Yiddish they made Abraham into Ahvron and then Ahvron they sometimes make Bommy. All his family called him Bommy, so you can see they didn't mean it as a knock. The one who changed it to Bummy was Johnny Attell.

Johnny Attell used to run the fights at the Ridgewood Grove, a fight club in Brooklyn where some good fighters like Sid Terris and Ruby Goldstein and Tony Canzoneri learned to fight, and Johnny and a nice guy named Lew Burston managed Bummy. When Bummy turned pro and Johnny made up the show card for the fight with Frankie Reese he put the name on it as Al (Bummy) Davis, and when Bummy saw it he went right up to John's office.

"What are you doing that for?" he hollered at Johnny. "I don't want to be called Bummy."

"Take it easy," Johnny said. "You want to make money fighting, don't you? People like to come to fights to see guys they think are tough."

They sure liked to come to see Bummy all right. They sure liked to come to see him get his brains knocked out.

The first time Johnny Attell ever heard of Bummy was one day when Johnny was coming out of the Grove and Froike stopped him. Froike used to run the gym at Beecher's and handle kids in the amateurs, and he was standing there talking to Johnny under the Myrtle Avenue El.

"Also I got a real good ticket seller for you," he said to Johnny after a while.

"I could use one," Johnny said.

"Only I have to have a special for him," Froike said. "No eliminations."

"What's his name?" Johnny said.

"Giovanni Pasconi," Froike said.

"Bring him around," Johnny said.

The next week Johnny put the kid in with a tough colored boy named Johnny Williams. The kid got the hell punched out of him, but he sold $200 worth of tickets.

"He didn't do too bad," Johnny said to Froike after the fight. "I'll put him back next week."

"Only this time get him an easier opponent," Froike said.

"You get him your own opponent," Johnny said. "As long as he can sell that many tickets I don't care who he fights."

The next week Johnny put him back and he licked the guy. After the fight Johnny was walking out and he saw the kid and Froike with about 20 people around them, all of them talking Yiddish.

"Come here, Froike," Johnny said.

"What's the matter?" Froike said.

"What is this guy," Johnny said, "a Wop or a Jew?"

"He's a Jew," Froike said. "His right name's Davidoff. He's only 15, so we borrowed Pasconi's card."

"He can sure sell tickets," Johnny said.

Bummy could sell anything. That's the way Bummy learned to fight, selling. He used to sell off a pushcart on Blake Avenue. He used to sell berries in the spring and tomatoes and watermelons in the summer and apples in the fall and potatoes and onions and beans in the winter, and there are a lot of pushcarts on Blake Avenue and Bummy used to have a fight to hold his spot.

"I was the best tomato salesman in the world," Bummy was bragging once.

It was right after he knocked out Bob Montgomery in the Garden. He stiffened him in 63 seconds and he was getting $15,000, and when the sports writers came into his dressing room all he wanted to talk about was how good he could sell tomatoes.

"You go over to Jersey and get them yourself," he was telling the sports writers. "Then you don't have to pay the middle guy. You don't put them in boxes, because when you put them in boxes it looks like you're getting ready to lam. When you only got a few around it looks like you can't get rid of them so what you gotta do is pile them all up and holler: 'I gotta get rid of these. I'm gonna give 'em away!'"

The sports writers couldn't get over that. There was a lot they couldn't get over about Bummy.

When Johnny turned Bummy pro he wasn't impressed by his fighting, only his following. Every time Bummy fought for Johnny in the Grove he'd bring a couple of hundred guys with him and they'd holler for Bummy. Everybody else would holler for the other guy, because now they knew Bummy was Jewish and the Grove is in a German section of Ridgewood, and this was when Hitler was starting to go good and there was even one of those German beer halls right in the place where the waiters walked around in those short leather pants and wearing fancy vests and funny hats.

The fight that started Bummy was the Friedkin fight. Bummy was just beginning to bang guys out at the Grove and Friedkin was already a hot fighter at the Broadway Arena and they lived only blocks apart. Friedkin was a nice kid, about three years older than Bummy, kind of a studious guy they called Schoolboy Friedkin, and there was nothing between him and Bummy except that they were both coming up and the neighborhood made the match.

Like one day Bummy was standing in the candy store and a couple of guys told him Friedkin was saying he could stiffen Bummy in two heats. Then they went to Friedkin and said Bummy said Friedkin was afraid to fight. At first this didn't take, but they kept it up and one day Bummy was standing with a dame on the corner of Blake and Alabama and Friedkin came along.

"So why don't you two fight?" the dame said.

"Sure, I'll fight," Bummy said, spreading his feet.

"Right here?" Friedkin said. "Right now?"

"Sure," Bummy said.

"I'll fight whenever my manager makes the match," Friedkin said, and he walked away.

Bummy couldn't understand that, because he liked to fight just to fight. He got right in the subway and went over to see Lew Burston in Lew's office on Broadway.

"Never mind making that Friedkin match," he said to Lew.

"Why not?" Lew said.

"Because when I leave here," Bummy said, "I'm going right around to Friedkin's house and I'm gonna wait for him to come out, and we're gonna find out right away if I can lick him or he can lick me."

"Are you crazy?" Lew said.

By the time Johnny Attell made the fight outdoors for Dexter Park there was really a fire under it. They had show cards advertising it on the pushcarts on Blake Avenue and Friedkin's old man and Bummy's old man got into an argument on the street, and everybody was talking about it and betting it big. Then it was rained out five nights and Johnny sold the fight to Mike Jacobs and Mike put it into Madison Square Garden.

When Bummy started working for the fight Lew Burston came over to Beecher's to train him. When Bummy got into his ring clothes they chased everybody out of the gym, and Lew told Bummy to hit the big bag. Bummy walked up to the bag and spread his feet and pulled back his left to start his hook and Lew stopped him.

"Throw that hook away," Lew said.

"Why?" Bummy said. "What's wrong with it?"

"Nothing's wrong with it," Lew said, "only for this fight you'll have to lose that hook."

Before that Bummy was nothing but a hooker, but for weeks Lew kept him banging the big bag with rights. Then the night of the fight after Bummy was all taped and ready, Lew took him into the shower off the dressing room and he talked to Bummy.

"Now remember one thing," he said to Bummy. "I can tell you exactly how that other corner is thinking. They've got that other guy eating and sleeping with your hook for weeks. I want you to go out there and I don't want you to throw one right hand until I tell you. If you throw one right before I say so I'll walk right out on you. Do you understand?"

Bummy understood all right. He was like a kid with a new toy. He was a kid with a secret that only Bummy and Lew knew, and he went out there and did like Lew told him. Friedkin came out with his right glued along the side of his head, and for three rounds Bummy just hooked and hooked and Friedkin blocked, and a lot of people thought Friedkin was winning the fight.

"All right," Lew said, after the third round. "Now this time go right out and feint with the left, but throw the right and put everything on it."

"Don't worry," Bummy said.

Bummy walked out and they moved around for almost a minute and then Bummy feinted his hook. When he did Friedkin moved over and Bummy threw the right and Friedkin's head went back and down he went with his legs in the air in his own corner. That was all the fighting there was that night.

Now Bummy was the biggest thing in Brownsville. Al Buck and Hype Igoe and Ed Van Every and Lester Bromberg were writing about him in the New York papers, saying he was the best hooker since Charley White and could also hit with his right, and he had dough for the first time in his life.

He got $14,000 for the Friedkin fight. When he walked down the street the kids followed him, and he bought them leather jackets and baseball gloves and sodas, just to show you what money meant and how he was already looking back at his own life.

When Bummy was a kid nobody bought him anything and he belonged to a gang called the Cowboys. They used to pull small jobs, and the cops could never find them until one night. One night the cops broke into the flat where the kids used to live with some dames, and they got them all except Bummy who was with his mother that night.

Sure, Bummy was what most people call tough, but if he felt sorry for you and figured you needed him he couldn't do enough. That was the way Bummy met Barbara and fell in love.

Bummy was 19 then and one day he and Shorty were driving around and Shorty said he wanted to go to Kings County Hospital and visit a friend of his who was sick, and there was this girl about 16 years old. They sat around for a while and Shorty did all the talking and then the next time they went to see the girl Shorty was carrying some flowers and he gave them to her.

"From him," Shorty said, meaning Bummy.

When the girl left the hospital Shorty and Bummy drove her home, and then every day for a couple of weeks they used to take her for a ride and to stop off for sodas. One day the three of them were riding together in the front seat and Bummy wasn't saying anything.

"Say, Bobby," Shorty said all of a sudden, "would you like to get married?"

The girl didn't know what to say. She just looked at Shorty.

"Not to me," Shorty said. "To him."

That was the way Bummy got married. That was Bummy's big romance.

After the Friedkin fight Bummy won about three fights quick, and then they made him with Mickey Farber in the St. Nick's. Farber was out of the East Side and had a good record, and one day when Bummy finished his training at Beecher's he was sitting in the locker room soaking his left hand in a pail of ice and talking with Charley.

That was an interesting thing about Bummy's left hand. He used to bang so hard with it that after every fight and after every day he boxed in the gym it used to swell up.

"I think I'll quit fighting," Bummy said to Charley.

"You think you'll quit?" Charley said. "You're just starting to make dough."

"They're making me out a tough guy," Bummy said. "All the newspapers make me a tough guy and I don't like it and I think I'll quit."

"Forget it," Charley said.

When Charley walked out Murder, Inc., walked in. They were all there — Happy and Buggsy and Abie and Harry and the Dasher — and they were looking at Bummy soaking his hand in the ice.

"You hurt your hand?" Buggsy said.

"No," Bummy said. "It's all right."

They walked out again, and they must have gone with a bundle on Farber because the day after Bummy licked Farber he was standing under the El in front of the gym and the mob drove up. They stopped the car right in front of him and they piled out.

"What are you, some wise guy?" Buggsy said.

"What's wrong with you?" Bummy said.

"What's all this you gave us about you had a bad hand?" Buggsy said.

"I didn't say I had a bad hand," Bummy said.

"You did," Buggsy said.

"Listen," Bummy said, spreading his feet the way he used to do it, "if you guys want a fight let's start it."

Buggsy looked at the others and they looked at him. Then they all got in the car and drove off, and if you could have been there and seen that you would have gone for Bummy for it.

That was the bad part about Bummy's rap. Not enough people knew that part of Bummy until it was too late. The people who go to fights don't just go to see some guy win, but they go to see some guy get licked, too. All they knew about Bummy was some of the things they read, and he was the guy they always went to see get licked.

Even the mob that followed Bummy when he was a big name didn't mean anything to him, because he could see through that. He could see they were always grabbing at him for what they could get, and that was the thing he never got over about the time he was training in Billy West's place up in Woodstock, New York.

Bummy went up there after he came out of the Army, just to take off weight, and there are a lot of artists around there. Artists are different people, because they don't care what anybody says about a guy and they either like him or they don't like him for what they think he is. They all liked him up there, and Billy used to say that Bummy could have been Mayor of Woodstock.

Billy had a dog that Bummy never forgot, either. Bummy used to run on the roads in the mornings and Billy's dog used to run with him. Every morning, they'd go out together and one day another dog came out of a yard and went for Bummy and Billy's dog turned and went after the other dog and chased it off.

"Gee, this dog really likes me," Bummy said, when he got back to the house, and he said it like he couldn't believe it. "He's really my friend."

The fight that really started everybody hating Bummy, though, was the Canzoneri fight in the Garden. It was a bad match and never should have been made, but they made it and all Bummy did was fight it.

Canzoneri was over the hill, but he had been the featherweight champion and the lightweight champion and he had fought the best of his time and they loved him. When Bummy knocked him out it was the only time Tony was knocked out in 180 fights, and so they booed Bummy for it and they waited for him to get licked.

They didn't have to wait too long. After he knocked out Tippy Larkin in five they matched him with Lou Ambers. Just after he started training for Ambers he was in the candy store one day when an argument started between Bummy and a guy named Mersky. Nobody is going to say who started the argument but somebody called Bummy a lousy fighter and it wasn't Bummy. Somebody flipped a piece of hard candy in Bummy's face, too, and that wasn't Bummy either, and after Bummy got done bouncing Mersky up and down Mersky went to the hospital and had some pictures taken and called the cops.

The first Johnny Attell heard about it was the night after it happened. He was walking down Broadway and he met a dick he knew.

"That's too bad about your fighter," the cop said.

"What's the matter with him?" Johnny said.

"What's the matter with him?" the cop asked. "There's an eight-state alarm out for him. The newspapers are full of it. He damn near killed a guy in a candy store."

The cops couldn't find Bummy but Johnny found him. He dug up Gangy, and Gangy drove him around awhile to shake off any cops, and finally Gangy stopped the car in front of an old wooden house and they got out and went in and there was Bummy.

Bummy was sitting in a pair of pajama pants, and that was all he had on. There were four or five other guys there, and they were playing cards.

"Are you crazy?" Johnny said.

"Why?" Bummy said, playing his cards, but looking up.

"If the cops find you here they'll kill you," Johnny said. "You better come with me."

After Johnny talked awhile Bummy got dressed and he went with Johnny. Johnny took him back to New York and got him a haircut and a shave and he called Mike Jacobs. Jacobs told Johnny to take Bummy down to Police Headquarters, and when Johnny did that Sol Strauss, Mike's lawyer, showed up and he got an adjournment in night court for Bummy until after the Ambers fight.

The night Bummy fought Ambers there was Mersky right at ringside. He had on dark glasses and the photographers were all taking his picture and when Ambers beat the hell out of Bummy the crowd loved it.

The crowd, more than Ambers, hurt Bummy that night. He didn't like the licking Ambers gave him, but the hardest part was listening to the crowd and the way they enjoyed it and the things they shouted at him when he came down out of the ring.

"I quit," he said to Johnny in the dressing room. "You know what you can do with fighting?"

Johnny didn't believe him. Johnny was making matches for Jacobs in the Garden then and he matched Bummy with Tony Marteliano, but Bummy wouldn't train.

Only Johnny and Gangy knew this, and one day Johnny came out to Bummy's house and talked with Bummy. When that didn't do any good Lew Burston came out and he talked for four hours, and when he finished Bummy said the same thing.

"I don't want to be a fighter," Bummy said. "I like to fight. I'll fight Marteliano on the street right now, just for fun, but when I'm a fighter everybody picks on me. I want them to leave me alone. All I wanted was a home for my family and I got that and now I just want to hang around my mob on the street."

Johnny still didn't believe it. They put out the show cards, advertising the fight, and one day Bummy saw one of the cards in the window of a bar and he phoned Johnny in Jacobs' office.

"What are you advertising the fight for?" he said, and he was mad. "I told you I'm not gonna fight."

Before Johnny could say anything Jacobs took the phone. Johnny hadn't told him Bummy didn't want to fight.

"How are you, kid?" Jacobs said. "This is Mike."

"Listen, you toothless —— ," Bummy said. "What are you advertising me for? I'm not gonna fight."

He hung up. Mike put the phone back and turned around and when he did Bummy was suspended and Johnny was out of the Garden and back in the Ridgewood Grove.

When Bummy heard what had happened to Johnny he went over to the Grove to see him. All the time Johnny was in the Garden Bummy was a little suspicious of him, like he was a capitalist, but now he was different.

"I came over to tell you something," he said to Johnny. "I'm gonna fight."

"Forget it," Johnny said. "You can't fight."

"Who says I can't fight?" Bummy said.

"The New York Boxing Commission," Johnny said. "You're suspended."

"Let's fight out of town," Bummy said. "We'll fight where I'm not suspended."

Johnny did it better. He took Bummy back to Mike and Bummy apologized and Bummy fought Marteliano. For nine rounds they were even, and with ten seconds to go in the last round Bummy landed the hook. Marteliano went down and the referee counted nine and the bell rang and it was another big one for Bummy and he was going again.

It was Johnny's idea to get Marteliano back, but Bummy saw Fritzie Zivic lick Henry Armstrong for the welterweight title and he wanted Zivic. If you knew the two guys you knew this was a bad match for Bummy, because he just didn't know how to fight like Zivic.

There were a lot of people, you see, who called Bummy a dirty fighter, but the Zivic fight made them wrong. The Zivic fight proved that Bummy didn't know how to do it.

When he came out of the first clinch Bummy's eyes were red and he was rubbing them and the crowd started to boo Zivic. In the second clinch it was the same thing, and at the end of the round Bummy was roaring.

"He's trying to blind me," he kept saying in the corner. "He's trying to blind me."

When it started again in the second round Bummy blew. He pushed Zivic off and he dropped his hands and that crazy look came on that wide face of his and they could hear him in the crowd.

"All right, you —— ," he said, "if you want to fight dirty, okay."

He walked right into Zivic and he started belting low. There was no trying to hide anything, and the crowd started to roar and before it was over people were on their chairs throwing things and the cops were in the ring and Bummy was fined $2,500 and suspended for life.

They meant it to be for life — which wouldn't have been very long at that, when you figure Bummy lived to be all of 26 — but it didn't work out that way. About three weeks after the fight Bummy walked into Johnny's office with Shorty and Mousie, and they sat around for a time and Johnny could see Bummy was lost.

"You know what you ought to do?" Johnny said. "You ought to join the Army for a while until this blows over."

This was in December of 1940, before we got into the war. For a while Bummy sat there thinking, not saying anything.

"Could my buddies go with me?" he said.

"Sure," Johnny said.

So Johnny called up the recruiting officer and Bummy and Shorty and Mousie showed up and there were photographers there and it was a big show. Everybody was for it, and Ed Van Every wrote a story in *The Sun* in which he said this was a great move because the Army would teach Bummy discipline and get him in good physical shape.

That was a laugh. The first thing the Army did was split Bummy and Shorty and Mousie up and send them to different camps.

They sent Bummy to Camp Hulen, Texas, and their idea of discipline was to have Bummy cleaning latrines with a toothbrush.

"You got me into this," Bummy used to write Johnny. "I'm going crazy, so before I slug one of these officers you better get me out."

Johnny didn't get him out, but he got Mike Jacobs to get Bummy a leave to fight Zivic in the Polo Grounds for Army Emergency Relief. Bummy used to fight best at about 147 pounds, and when he came back from Texas he weighed close to 200.

"You look sharp in that uniform, Al," Zivic said to him when they signed for the bout.

"I'm glad you like it," Bummy said. "You put me in it."

You can imagine how Bummy was looking to get back at Zivic, but he couldn't do it. He hadn't fought for eight months, and Zivic was a real good fighter and he put lumps all over Bummy and in the tenth round the referee stopped it. They had to find Bummy to take him back to camp. They found him with his wife and they shipped him back, but then the Japs bombed Pearl Harbor and the Army decided it had enough trouble without Bummy and they turned him loose.

Bummy fought some of his best fights after that. He couldn't get his license back in New York but he fought in places like Holyoke and Bridgeport and Washington and Philadelphia and Elizabeth, New Jersey, and Boston. He didn't like it in those places, but he had to live, and so no matter where he fought he would always drive back to Brownsville after the fight and sometimes it would be four o'clock in the morning before he and Johnny would get in.

It's something when you think about Bummy and Brownsville, when you think of the money he made, almost a quarter of a million dollars, and the things he had thrown at him and the elegant places he could have gone. It was like what Lew Burston said, though, when he said the Supreme was Bummy's Opera, and the Supreme is a movie house on Livonia Street.

You have to remember, too, that Brownsville is only a subway ride from Broadway, but Bummy had never seen a real Broadway show until Chicky Bogad sent Bummy and Barbara to see *Hellza-poppin* the night before the second Farber fight.

"How long has this been going on?" Bummy said when they came out.

"How long has what been going on?" Chicky said.

"People like that on a stage," Bummy said.

"People on a stage?" Chicky said. "For years and years. For long before they had movies."

"Is that right? I'll have to see more of that," Bummy said, but he never did.

All of those fights Bummy had out of town were murders, too, because Bummy wasn't hard to hit, but the people liked to see him get hit and when the Republicans got back in power in New York, Fritzie Zivic put in a word for Bummy, saying he guessed he had egged the kid on, and Bummy got his license back. That's when they matched him with Montgomery.

"What you have to do in this one," they kept telling Bummy, "is walk right out, throw your right, and miss with it. Montgomery will grab your right arm, and that will turn you around southpaw and then you hit him with the hook."

They knew that was the only chance Bummy had, because if Montgomery got by the first round he figured to move around Bummy and cut him up. They drilled Bummy on it over and over, and they kept talking about it in the dressing room that night.

"Now what are you going to do?" Johnny Attell said to Bummy.

"I'm gonna walk right out and miss with my right," Bummy said. "He'll grab my arm and that'll turn me around southpaw and I'll throw my hook."

"Okay," Johnny said. "I guess you know it."

Bummy sat down then on one of the benches. He had his gloves on and his robe over him and he was ready to go when there was a knock on the door.

"Don't come out yet, Davis," one of the commission guys said through the door. "They're selling some War Bonds first."

When Bummy heard that he looked up from where he was sitting and you could see he was sweating, and then he keeled right over on the floor on his face. Johnny and Freddie Brown rushed over and picked him up and they stretched him on the rubbing table and Freddie brought him to, and now they weren't worried about whether Bummy would do what they told him. All they were worried about was whether they could get him in the ring.

They got him in the ring and Burston had him repeat what he was supposed to do. When the bell rang he walked right out and threw his right and missed around the head. Montgomery grabbed the arm and turned Bummy around, and when he did Bummy threw the hook and Montgomery went down. When he got up Bummy hit him again and that's all there was to it.

Montgomery was 10 to 1 over Bummy that night and they couldn't believe it. Bummy got $15,000 for that fight and he borrowed $1,500 from Jacobs and the next day when Mike paid him off he told Bummy to forget the grand and a half.

"Take it out," Bummy said, throwing the dough on the desk. "You know damn well if he kayoed me like you thought he would you were gonna take it out."

Bummy thought he'd never be broke again. He got $34,000 the night Beau Jack beat him and $15,000 when Armstrong stopped him. Then somebody sold him the idea of buying that bar and grill and somebody else sold him a couple of race horses and even after Dudy bought the bar and grill from him he was broke.

He should have been in training for Morris Reif the night he was shot. Johnny wanted him to fight Reif, just for the dough and to go as far as he could, but Bummy said that a lot of his friends would bet him and he didn't think he could beat Reif, so instead he was sitting in the back of Dudy's drinking beer and singing.

Bummy used to think he could sing like a Jewish cantor. He couldn't sing, but he was trying that night, sitting with some other guys and a cop who was off duty, when he looked through that lattice work at the bar and he saw the four guys with the guns.

"What the hell is this?" he said.

He got up and walked out and you know what happened. When Bummy stiffened the first guy one of the others fired and the bullet went into Bummy's neck. Then the three picked up the guy Bummy hit and they ran for the car. One of the guys with Bummy stuffed his handkerchief in the collar of Bummy's shirt to stop the blood, and Bummy got up and ran for the car. When he did they opened up from the car, and Bummy went flat on his face in the mud.

When the car started to pull away the cop who had been in the back ran out and fired. He hit one guy in the spine, and that guy died in Texas, and he hit another in the shoulder. The guy with the slug in his shoulder walked around with it for weeks, afraid to go to a doctor, and then one night a cop in plain clothes heard a couple of guys talking in a bar.

"You know that jerk is still walking around with the bullet in his shoulder?" the one said.

"The Bummy Davis bullet," the first said.

The cop followed them out, and when they split up he followed the first guy and got it out of him. Then the cops picked up the guy with the bullet and he sang. They picked up the other two in Kansas City and they're doing 20 to life. They were just punks, and they called themselves the Cowboys, the same as Bummy's old gang did.

It was a big funeral Bummy had. Johnny and Lew Burston paid for it. The papers had made Bummy a hero, and the newsreels took pictures outside the funeral parlor and at the cemetery. It looked like everybody in Brownsville was there.

1955

## Gerald Holland

......................................................................................................................

# Mr. Rickey and the Game

FROM *Sports Illustrated*

"I AM ASKED to speak of the game," said Branch Rickey, restating a question that had been put to him, "I am asked to reflect upon my own part in it. At the age of 73, on the eve of a new baseball season, I am importuned to muse aloud, to touch upon those things that come first to mind."

Seated in his office at Forbes Field, the home of the Pittsburgh Pirates, Branch Rickey nibbled at an unlighted cigarette and sniffed the proposition like a man suddenly come upon a beef stew simmering on a kitchen stove.

Abruptly he threw himself back in his chair and clasped his hands over his head and stared up at the ceiling. He looked 10 years younger than his actual age. Thanks to a high-protein, hamburger-for-breakfast diet, he was 30 pounds lighter than he had been three months before. His complexion was ruddy and his thick brown hair showed only a little gray at the temples. Now his great bushy eyebrows shot up and he prayed aloud:

"Lord make me humble, make me grateful . . . make me *tolerant!*"

Slowly he came down from the ceiling and put his elbows on the desk. Unconsciously, perhaps, a hand strayed across the desk to a copy of *Bartlett's Familiar Quotations*. The hand was that of an old-time catcher, big, strong and gnarled. He turned slowly in his chair and swept his eyes over the little gallery of framed photographs on the wall. Among them were George Sisler, Rickey's first great discovery, one of the greatest of the left-handed hitters, now at work down the hall as chief of Pittsburgh scouts; Rogers Hornsby, the game's greatest right-handed hitter, a betting man for whom Rickey once dared the wrath of baseball's high commissioner, Kenesaw Mountain Landis; Jackie Robinson, chosen by Rickey as the man to break down baseball's color line; Honus Wagner, the immortal Pittsburgh shortstop, now past 80, at this moment growing weaker by the day at his sister's house across town; Charley Barrett, the old Cardinal scout, Rickey's right arm in the days when St. Louis was too poor to make a Southern training trip.

Turning back to his desk, Rickey grimaced and then spoke rapidly, almost harshly:

"Of my career in baseball, let us say first of all that there have been the appearances of hypocrisy. Here we have the Sunday school mollycoddle, apparently professing a sort of public virtue in refraining from playing or watching a game of baseball on Sunday. And yet at the same time he is not above accepting money from a till replenished by Sunday baseball."

He paused and bit the unlighted cigarette in two. He dropped his voice:

"A deeply personal thing. Something not to be exploited, not to be put forward protestingly at every whisper of criticism. No, a deeply personal thing. A man's promise, a promise to his mother. Not involving a condemnation of baseball on Sunday, nor of others who might desire to play it or watch it on Sunday. Simply one man's promise — and it might as well have been a promise not to attend the theater or band concerts in the park."

His eyes went around the room and were held for a moment by the blackboard that lists the players on the 15 ball clubs in the Pittsburgh farm system. His lips moved and the words sounded like, "But is the boy *ready* for New Orleans?" Then, with a quick movement, he leaned across the desk and waggled an accusing finger.

"Hell's fire!" he exploded. "The Sunday school mollycoddle, the blue-nose, the prohibitionist has been a *liberal!* No, no, no — this has nothing to do with Jackie Robinson, I contend that there was no element of liberalism there. I will say something about that perhaps, but now the plain everyday things — the gambling, the drinking, the . . . other things. I submit that I have been a liberal about *them!*"

He was silent. He did not mention or even hint at the names of managers who won major league pennants after everyone but Branch Rickey had quit on them; nor the men who gladly acknowledge that they are still in baseball because of the confidence Rickey placed in them.

The telephone with the private number rang. Branch Rickey picked it up and traded Southpaw Paul La Palme to the St. Louis Cardinals for

Ben Wade, a relief pitcher. "You announce it," he said into the phone, "and just say La Palme for Wade and an unannounced amount of cash. We'll talk about a Class A ballplayer later. Anybody but a catcher. I don't need a catcher at that level." He put down the phone and his eyes twinkled. "Later in the day I may make a deal with Brooklyn," he said, "if I can get up the nerve." As things turned out, either he did not get up the nerve or he was unable to interest the Flatbush authorities.

He whirled around in his chair and stared out the window. He could see, if he was noticing, the end of a little street that runs down from Hotel Schenley to the ball park. It is called Pennant Place, a reminder of happier days for the Pittsburgh fans, now so ashamed of their eighth-place Pirates that only a few of them show up at the ball park — even for doubleheaders.

Rickey ran both hands furiously through his thick hair.

"A man trained for the law," he said, "devotes his entire life and all his energies to something so cosmically unimportant as a game."

He examined minutely what was left of his cigarette. Carefully, he extracted a single strand of tobacco and looked at it closely before letting it fall to the floor. Usually he chews unlighted cigars, but this day it was a cigarette.

He began to laugh.

"The law," he chuckled, "I might have stayed in the law. I do not laugh at the great profession itself. I am laughing at a case I had one time — the only case I ever had as a full-time practicing attorney. I had gone to Boise, Idaho, from Saranac to try to gain back my strength after recovering from tuberculosis. I got an office and hung out a shingle and waited for the clients. None came. Finally, I was in court one day and the judge appointed me attorney for a man who was being held on a charge the newspapers used to describe as white slavery.

"I was apprehensive, but at last I summoned enough courage to go over to the jail and see my client. Oh, he was a horrible creature. I can see him now, walking slowly up to the bars and looking me up and down with contempt. He terrified me. I began to shake like a leaf. After a minute he said, 'Who the hell are you?'

"I tried to draw myself up a little and then I said, 'Sir, my name is Branch Rickey. The court has appointed me your attorney and I would like to talk to you.' He looked me up and down again and then spat at my feet. Then he delivered what turned out to be the final words of our association. He said, 'Get the hell out of here!'"

Rickey threw back his head.

"I not only got out of there," he said, "I got out of the state of Idaho and went to St. Louis and took a job with the St. Louis Browns. I intended to stay in baseball for just one year. But when the year was up, Mr. Robert Lee Hedges, the owner, offered me a raise. There was a new baby at our house. And not much money, new or old. So I was a moral coward. I chose to stay with the game."

Rickey thought a moment.

"I might have gone into politics," he said. "As recently as 14 years ago, there was the offer of a nomination for a political office. A governorship. The governorship, in fact, of Missouri. I was tempted, flattered. But, then as I ventured a little into the political arena, I was appalled by my own ignorance of politics. But the party leaders were persuasive. They pledged me the full support of the regular party organization. They said they could not prevent any Billy Jumpup from filing, but no Billy Jumpup would have the organization's backing. It is an overwhelming thing to be offered such prospects of reaching high office. I thought it over carefully and then tentatively agreed to run, on condition that another man — a seasoned campaigner — run on the ticket with me. He said that was utterly impossible. He invited me to go with him to New York and talk to Mr. Herbert Hoover about the situation in Missouri. But afterward I still was unable to persuade my friend to run. He was Arthur Hyde, Secretary of Agriculture under Mr. Hoover. Later I learned to my sorrow the reason for Mr. Hyde's decision. He was even then mortally ill. So, regretfully, I asked that my name be withdrawn. The man who ran in my place was elected and then went on to the United States Senate.

"So, conceivably, I might have been a governor. Instead, I chose to stay with the game."

Rickey made elaborate gestures of straightening the papers on his desk.

"A life of public service," he said, peering over his glasses, "versus a life devoted to a game that boys play with a ball and bat."

He turned and picked up a baseball from a bookcase shelf.

"This ball," he said, holding it up. "This symbol. Is it worth a man's whole life?"

There was just time for another mussing of the hair before the phone rang again.

"Pooh," said Rickey into the phone after a moment. "Three poohs. Pooh-bah." He hung up.

"I was listening last night to one of the television interview programs," he said. "Senator Knowland was being interrogated. It was a discussion on a high level and the questions involved matters affecting all of us and all the world. I was listening intently and then I heard the senator say, 'Well, I think the Administration has a pretty good batting average.'"

Rickey blew out his cheeks and plucked a shred of tobacco from his lips.

"It must have been a full minute later," he went on, "and the questions had gone on to other things when I sat straight up. Suddenly I realized that to answer a somewhat difficult question this United States senator had turned naturally to the language of the game. And this language, this phrase 'a pretty good batting average,' had said exactly what he wanted to say. He had not intended to be frivolous. The reporters did not smile as though he had made a joke. They accepted the answer in the language of the game as perfectly proper. It was instantly recognizable to them. I dare say it was recognizable even in London."

He frowned, thinking hard. Then his face lit up again.

"The game invades our language!" he exclaimed. "Now, the editorial page of the New York *Times* is a serious forum, not ordinarily given to levity. Yet at the height of the controversy between the Army and Senator McCarthy, there was the line on this dignified editorial page, 'Senator McCarthy — a good fast ball, but no control.'"

Rickey slapped his thigh and leaned over the desk.

"Now, didn't that tell the whole story in a sentence?"

He waved an arm, granting himself the point.

He cherished his remnant of a cigarette.

"A man was telling me the other day," he went on, "he said he was walking through Times Square in New York one blistering day last summer. The temperature stood at 100° and the humidity made it almost unbearable. This man happened to fall in behind three postmen walking together. Their shirts were wringing wet and their mailbags were heavily laden. It struck this man that these postmen might well be irritable on such a day and, since he saw that they were talking animatedly, he drew closer so that he might hear what they were saying. He expected, of course, that they would be complaining bitterly of their dull drab jobs on this abominable day. But when he had come close enough to hear them, what were they talking about with such spirit and relish?"

He paused for effect, then with a toss of his head, he exploded:

"Leo Durocher and the New York Giants!"

Carefully, he put down his cigarette butt. Then he leaned back and rubbed his eyes with the back of his fists. He tore furiously at his hair and half swallowed a yawn.

"Mrs. Rickey and I," he said, "sat up until 2 o'clock this morning playing hearts."

He straightened the papers on his desk and said as an aside: "I contend it is the most scientific card game in the world."

He searched the ceiling for the point he was developing, found it and came down again.

"The three postmen, heavily laden on a hot, miserable day, yet able to find a happy, common ground in their discussion of this game of baseball. And in their free time, in their hours of leisure, if they had no other interest to turn to, still there was the game to bring color and excitement and good wholesome interest into their lives."

He took up the fragment of paper and tobacco that was left of the cigarette as though it were a precious jewel.

"Leisure," he said, sending his eyebrows aloft, "is a hazardous thing. Here in America we do not yet have a leisure class that knows what to do with it. Leisure can produce something fine. It may also produce something evil. Hell's fire! Leisure can produce a great symphony, a great painting, a great book."

He whirled around to the window and peered out at Pennant Place. Then, turning back like a pitcher who has just cased the situation at second base, he let go hard.

"Gee!" he cried. "Leisure can also produce a great dissipation! Leisure can be idleness and idleness can drive a man to his lowest!"

He recoiled, as from a low man standing at the side of his desk.

"Idleness is the worst thing in this world. Idleness is doing nothing and thinking of wrong things to do. Idleness is the evil that lies behind the juvenile delinquency that alarms us all. It's the most damnable thing that can happen to a kid — to have nothing to do."

He put the tattered cigarette butt in his mouth and spoke around it.

"The game that gives challenge to our youth points the way to our salvation. The competitive spirit, that's the all-important thing. The stultifying thing in this country is the down-pressure on competition, the something-for-nothing philosophy, the do-as-little-as-you-can creed — these are the most devastating influences today. This thinking is the kind that undermines a man's character and can undermine the national character as well."

He studied his shreds of cigarette with the deliberation of a diamond cutter.

"Labor and toil," he intoned, "by the sweat of thy brow shalt thou earn thy bread. Labor and toil — and something else. A joy in work, a zest. Zest, that is the word. Who are the great ballplayers of all time? The ones with zest. Ty Cobb. Willie Mays. The man down the hall, one of the very greatest, George Sisler. Dizzy Dean. Pepper Martin. We have one coming back to us this year here at Pittsburgh. Dick Groat. He has it. Highly intelligent, another Lou Boudreau, the same kind of hitter. He has it. Zest."

Rickey smiled. "Dick Groat will be one of the great ones. There will be others this year. We have 110 boys coming out of service, 475 players under contract on all our clubs. A total of $496,000 invested in player bonuses. There will be other good prospects for the Pirates among these boys. This ball club of ours will come in time. No promises for this year, but in '56, I think, yes."

He turned to look down the street to Pennant Place, then added: "A *contending* team in '56 — at least that."

(At the barbershop in Hotel Schenley it is related that Rickey's defense of his eighth-place ball club is considerably less detailed. "Patience!" he cries, anticipating the hecklers as he enters the shop.)

The door opened and Harold Roettger, Rickey's assistant, entered the room. A round-faced, studious-looking man, Roettger has been with Rickey since the old St. Louis Cardinal days. He was in the grip of a heavy cold.

"Do you remember a boy named Febbraro?" he asked, sniffling, "in the Provincial League?"

"Febbraro, Febbraro," said Rickey, frowning. "A pitcher. I saw him work in a night game."

"That's the boy," said Roettger, wiping his eyes. "He's been released."

"Aha," said Rickey, "yes, I remember the boy well. Shall we sign him?"

"We ought to talk about it," said Roettger, fighting a sneeze.

"Harold," said Rickey, "Richardson [Tommy Richardson, president of the Eastern League] is coming down for a meeting tomorrow. I wish you could be there. I devoutly wish you were not ill."

"I, too, devoutly wish I were not ill," said Roettger. "I'll go home now and maybe I'll be ready for the meeting."

"Please try not to be ill tomorrow," said Rickey. "I desperately need you at the meeting."

"I will try very hard," said Roettger, "and will you think about Feb-braro?"

"I will," said Rickey. "Go home now, Harold, and take care of yourself."

(Later, Roettger recovered from his cold and signed Febbraro for Williamsport in the Eastern League.)

As Roettger left, Rickey searched for the thread of his soliloquy.

"Hornsby," he said suddenly, "Rogers Hornsby, a man with zest for the game. And Leo, of course.

"Leo Durocher has come a long way, off the field as well as on. A quick mind, a brilliant mind, an indomitable spirit. A rugged ballplayer — and I like rugged ballplayers. But when he came to St. Louis, Leo was in trouble. No fewer than 32 creditors were breathing down his neck, suing or threatening to sue. An impossible situation. I proposed that I go to his creditors and arrange for weekly payments on his debts. This meant a modest allowance of spending money for Leo himself. But he agreed.

"There were other matters to be straightened out. Leo's associates at the time were hardly desirable ones. But he was not the kind of man to take kindly to any criticism of his friends. I thought a lot about Leo's associations, but I didn't see what I could do about them.

"Then one day during the winter I received a call from the United States Naval Academy at Annapolis. The Academy needed a baseball coach and they asked if I could recommend a man. I said I thought I could and would let them know.

"I knew my man. But I didn't dare tell him right away. Instead, I called his wife [Durocher was then married to Grace Dozier, a St. Louis fashion designer] and asked her to drop in at the office. When she arrived, I told her that I intended to recommend Leo as baseball coach at the Naval Academy.

"She looked at me a moment. Then she said, 'Would they take Leo?' I said they would if I recommended him. Then I told her I proposed to get a copy of the Naval Academy manual. I said I knew that if I handed it to Leo myself, he was quite likely to throw it back in my face. But if she were to put it in his hands, he might agree to look it over. Mrs. Durocher thought again. Then she said, 'Get the manual.'"

(Rickey has a habit of presenting ballplayers with what he considers to be worth-while reading. When Pee Wee Reese was made captain of the Dodgers, Rickey sent him Eisenhower's *Crusade in Europe*.)

"When I told Leo," Rickey continued, "he was stunned and unbelieving, then enormously but quietly pleased. I told him that I would arrange for him to report late for spring training. I made it clear that he was to decline any payment for his services. Treading softly, I mentioned that the boys he would be coaching were the finest our country had to offer. I suggested gently that any leader of such boys would, of course, have to be letter perfect in his conduct. Leo didn't blow up. He just nodded his head.

"When he reported to spring training camp, he was bursting with pride. He showed me a wrist watch the midshipmen had given him. He said, 'Mr. Rickey, I did it, I did it!'

"I said, 'You did half of it, Leo.'

"'What do you mean, half!' he demanded.

"To be a complete success in this undertaking, Leo, you must be invited back. If they ask you back for next season, then you may be sure you have done the job well."

Rickey smiled.

"They did invite him back," he said. "And this time the midshipmen gave him a silver service. He had done the job — the whole job — and I rather think that this experience was a big turning point for Leo. It lifted him into associations he had never known before and he came away with increased confidence and self-assurance and, I am quite sure, a greater measure of self-respect."

(Years later, just before Leo Durocher was suspended from baseball for a year by Commissioner A. B. Chandler, Rickey called his staff together in the Brooklyn Dodgers' offices to say of his manager: "Leo is down. But we are going to stick by Leo. We are going to stick by Leo until hell freezes over!" Now, in a manner of speaking, it was Rickey who was down — in eighth place — and Leo who was up, riding high as manager of the world champions.)

Rickey straightened his tie. He was wearing a four-in-hand. Ordinarily, he wears a bow tie, but once a month he puts on a four-in-hand as a gesture of neckwear independence.

"More than a half-century spent in the game," Rickey mused, "and now it is suggested that I give thought to some of the ideas and innovations with which I have been associated. The question arises, 'Which of these can be said to have contributed most to making baseball truly our national game?'

"First, I should say, there was the mass production of ball-players. The Cardinals were three years ahead of all the other clubs in establishing tryout camps. We looked at 4,000 boys a year. Then, of course, we had to have teams on which to place boys with varying degrees of ability and experience. That brought into being the farm system.

"There were other ideas not ordinarily remembered. With the St. Louis Browns, under Mr. Hedges, we originated the idea of Ladies Day, a very important step forward. Probably no other innovation did so much to give baseball respectability, as well as thousands of new fans.

"With the Cardinals, we developed the idea of the Knot Hole Gang. We were the first major league team to admit boys free to the ball park and again the idea was soon copied."

(In the beginning, boys joining the Cardinal Knot Hole Gang were required to sign a pledge to refrain from smoking and profanity — clearly the hand of Rickey.)

"These were ideas," Rickey went on, "and baseball was a vehicle in which such ideas might comfortably ride."

Rickey's eyes strayed to a framed motto hanging on the wall. It read: "He that will not reason is a bigot; he that cannot reason is a fool and he that does not reason is a slave."

Rickey bent down and went rummaging through the lower drawers of his desk. In a moment he came up holding a slender book. The jacket read: "*Slave and Citizen: The Negro in the Americas.* By Frank Tannenbaum."

"This book," said Rickey, "is by a Columbia University professor. Let me read now just the concluding paragraph. It says, 'Physical proximity, slow cultural intertwining, the growth of a middle group that stands in experience and equipment between the lower and upper class; and the slow process of moral identification work their way against all seemingly absolute systems of values and prejudices. Society is essentially dynamic, and while the mills of God grind slow, they grind exceeding sure. Time will draw a veil over the white and black in this hemisphere, and future generations will look back upon the record of strife as it stands revealed in the history of the people of this New World of ours with wonder and incredulity. For they will not understand the issues that the quarrel was about.'"

Rickey reached for a pencil, wrote on the flyleaf of the book and pushed it across the desk. He leaned back in his chair and thought a moment. Then he sat straight up.

"Some honors have been tendered," he said, "some honorary degrees offered because of my part in bringing Jackie Robinson into the major leagues."

He frowned and shook his head vigorously.

"No, no, no. I have declined them all. To accept honors, public applause for signing a superlative ballplayer to a contract? I would be *ashamed!*"

He turned to look out the window and turned back.

"Suppose," he demanded, "I hear that Billy Jones down the street has attained the age of 21. Suppose I go to Billy and say, 'You come with me to the polling place.' And then at the polling place I take Billy by the arm and march up to the clerks and say, 'This is Billy Jones, native American, 21 years of age,' and I demand that he be given the right to cast a ballot!"

Rickey leaned over the desk, his eyes flashing.

"Would anyone but a lunatic expect to be applauded for that?"

It immediately became clear that although Rickey deprecated his right to applause, he had never minimized the difficulties of bringing the first Negro into organized baseball.

"I talked to sociologists," he said, "and to Negro leaders. With their counsel, I worked out what I considered to be the six essential points to be considered."

He started to count on his fingers.

"Number one," he said, "the man we finally chose had to be right off the field. *Off* the field.

"Number two, he had to be right *on* the field. If he turned out to be a lemon, our efforts would fail for that reason alone.

"Number three, the reaction of his own race had to be right.

"Number four, the reaction of press and public had to be right.

"Number five, we had to have a place to put him.

"Number six, the reaction of his fellow players had to be right.

"In Jackie Robinson, we found the man to take care of points one and two. He was eminently right off and on the field. We did not settle on Robinson until after we had invested $25,000 in scouting for a man whose name we did not then know.

"Having found Robinson, we proceeded to point five. We had to have a place to put him. Luckily, in the Brooklyn organization, we had exactly the spot at Montreal where the racial issue would not be given undue emphasis.

"To take care of point three, the reaction of Robinson's own race, I went again to the Negro leaders. I explained that in order to give this boy his chance, there must be no demonstrations in his behalf, no excursions from one city to another, no presentations or testimonials. He was to be left alone to do this thing without any more hazards than were already present. For two years the men I talked to respected the reasoning behind my requests. My admiration for these men is limitless. In the best possible way, they saw to it that Jackie Robinson had his chance to make it on his own.

"Point four, the reaction of press and public, resolved itself in the course of things, and point six, the reaction of his fellow players, finally — if painfully — worked itself out."

Rickey reached across the desk and tapped the Tannenbaum book.

"Time," he said, "time."

He despaired of his cigarette now and tossed it into the wastebasket. His eyes moved around the room and he murmured half to himself: "We are not going to let anything spoil sports in this country. Some of the things I read about boxing worry me, but things that are wrong will be made right . . . in time."

He laughed.

"I don't think anyone is worried about wrestling. Isn't it a rather good-natured sort of entertainment?"

He chuckled a little more, then frowned again.

"I am asked about the minor leagues. The cry is heard, 'The minors are dying!' I don't think so. The minors are in trouble but new ways will be found to meet new situations and new problems. Up to now, I confess, the major leagues have been unable to implement any effort to protect the minor leagues from the encroachment of major league broadcasts."

(A baseball man once said that Branch Rickey is constitutionally unable to tell a falsehood. "However," this man said, "sometimes he pours over the facts of a given case such a torrent of eloquence that the truth is all but drowned.")

The door opened and Rickey jumped to his feet. His eyes lit up as he cried: "Mother!"

In the doorway stood Mrs. Rickey, carrying a box of paints the size of a brief case.

"Well, Mother!" cried Rickey, coming around from behind the desk. "How did it go? Did you get good marks?"

Mrs. Rickey, a small, smiling woman, stood looking at her husband. Childhood sweethearts in Ohio, they have been married for 49 years.

Rickey pointed dramatically to the paintbox.

"Mother has joined a painting class!" he exclaimed. "At 73 years of age, Mother has gone back to school! Well, Mother? Did you recite or what? Do they give marks? What is the teacher like?"

Mrs. Rickey walked to a chair and sat down. It was plain that she was accustomed to pursuing a policy of containment toward her husband.

"They don't give marks," she said quietly. "The teacher is very nice. He was telling us that painting opens up a whole new world. You see things and colors you never saw before."

Rickey was aghast.

"Wonderful!" he cried. "Isn't that just wonderful! Mother, we must celebrate. I'll take you to lunch!"

"All right," said Mrs. Rickey. "Where will we go?"

"The Duquesne Club," said Rickey.

"That'll be fine," said Mrs. Rickey.

(In sharply stratified Pittsburgh society, there are two standards by which to measure a man who stands at the very top: one is membership in the Duquesne Club, the other is a residence at Fox Chapel, the ultraexclusive Pittsburgh suburb. Rickey has both; the residence is an 18-room house set down on 100 acres.)

Rickey was the first to reach the sidewalk. He paced up and down waiting for Mrs. Rickey, flapping his arms against the cold, for he had forgotten to wear an overcoat that morning. Guido Roman, a tall, handsome Cuban who is Rickey's chauffeur, opened the car door.

"You want to get inside, Mr. Rickey?" he asked.

"No, Guido," said Rickey, blowing on his fingers, "I'm not cold."

A car drew up and stopped across the street. A tall, muscular young man got out.

Rickey peered sharply and ducked his head. "A thousand dollars this lad is a ballplayer," he muttered out of the side of his mouth. "But who is he, who is he?"

The young man came directly to Rickey.

"Mr. Rickey, you don't remember me," he said. "My name is George —!"

"Sure, I remember you, George!" Rickey exploded, thrusting out his hand. "You're a first baseman, right?"

"Yes, sir," said George, blushing with pleasure.

"Go right in the office and make yourself at home, George," Rickey said, beaming. "There's another first baseman in there named George — George Sisler. Say hello to him!"

"Say, thanks, Mr. Rickey," George said, hurrying to the office door.

In a moment Mrs. Rickey came out and the ride downtown in Rickey's Lincoln began. As the car pulled away from the curb, Rickey, a notorious back-seat driver, began a series of barked directions; "Right here, Guido! Left at the next corner, Guido! Red light, Guido!"

Guido, smiling and unperturbed, drove smoothly along. As the car reached the downtown business district, Rickey, peering this way and that, shouted, "Slow down, Guido!"

Guido slowed down and then Rickey whispered hoarsely: "There it is, Mother! Look!"

"What?" smiled Mrs. Rickey.

"The largest lamp store in the world! Right there! I inquired about the best place to buy a lamp and I was told that this place is the largest in the whole wide world! Right there!"

"We only want a two-way bed lamp," said Mrs. Rickey.

"I know," said Rickey. "But there's the place to get it. You could go all over the world and not find a bigger lamp store. Right turn here, Guido!"

"One way, Mr. Rickey," said Guido, cheerfully.

That was the signal for a whole comedy of errors, with Rickey directing and traffic cops vetoing a series of attempts to penetrate one-way streets and to execute left turns. Rickey grew more excited, Mrs. Rickey more calm, Guido more desperate as the Duquesne Club loomed and faded as a seemingly unattainable goal.

"Judas Priest!" Rickey finally exclaimed. "It's a perfectly simple problem! We want to go to the Duquesne Club!"

"I know how!" Guido protested, "I know the way!"

"Then turn, man, turn!"

"Get out of here!" yelled a traffic cop.

"For crying out loud!" roared Rickey. "Let's get out and walk."

"I'm not going to walk," said Mrs. Rickey, mildly. "We have a car. Let Guido go his way."

"Oh, all right," Rickey pouted. "But you'd think I'd never been downtown before!"

In a moment the car pulled up at the Duquesne Club and Rickey, serene again, jumped out and helped Mrs. Rickey from the car.

"Take the car home, Guido," he said pleasantly. "We'll call you later."

"Yes, Mr. Rickey," said Guido, mopping his brow.

A group of women came out of the Duquesne Club as the Rickeys entered. The women nodded and smiled at Mrs. Rickey. Raising his hat, Rickey bowed low, then crouched to whisper hoarsely behind his hand:

"Classmates of yours, Mother?"

He stamped his foot and slapped his thigh, choking with laughter.

"One of them is in the painting class," said Mrs. Rickey placidly. "The others are in the garden club."

At the luncheon table on the second floor, Rickey ordered whitefish for Mrs. Rickey and roast beef for himself. There were no cocktails, of course; Rickey is a teetotaler.

("I shudder to think what might have happened if Branch had taken up drinking," a former associate has said. "He does nothing in moderation and I can see him facing a bottle of whiskey and shouting: 'Men, we're going to hit that bottle and hit it *hard!*'")

The luncheon order given, Rickey excused himself and made a brief telephone call at the headwaiter's desk. Returning to the table, he sat down and began to speak of pitchers.

"The greatest pitchers I have ever seen," he said, "were Christy Mathewson and Jerome Dean."

(Rickey likes to address a man by his proper given name. He is especially fond of referring to Dizzy Dean as "Jerome.")

"Mathewson," Rickey continued, "could throw every pitch in the book. But he was economical. If he saw that he could win a game with three kinds of pitches, he would use only three. Jerome, on the other hand, had a tendency to run in the direction of experimentation. Murry Dickson has a fine assortment of pitches, but he feels an obligation to run through his entire repertory in every game."

The food had arrived and Rickey picked up knife and fork and, eying Mrs. Rickey closely, began to speak more rapidly.

"Yes," he said loudly, "Murry is the sort of pitcher who will go along splendidly until the eighth inning and then apparently say to himself: 'Oh, dear me, I have forgotten to throw my half-speed ball!' And then and there he will throw it."

Abruptly, Rickey made a lightning thrust with his fork in the direction of a pan-browned potato on the platter. Mrs. Rickey, alert for just such a stratagem, met the thrust with her own fork and they fenced for a few seconds in mid-air.

"*Jane!*" pleaded Rickey, abandoning the duel.

Mrs. Rickey deposited the potato on her own plate and passed over a small dish of broccoli.

"This will be better for you," she said quietly. "You know you're not to have potatoes."

Rickey grumbled: "I am weary of this diet. It is a cruel and inhuman thing."

"Eat the broccoli," Mrs. Rickey said.

"Jane," said Rickey, "there are times in a man's life when he wants above everything else in the world to have a potato."

"You get plenty to eat," said Mrs. Rickey. "Didn't you enjoy the meat patty at breakfast?"

Rickey shrugged his shoulders, conceding the point, and attacked his roast beef and broccoli with gusto.

"The subject of my retirement comes up from time to time," he said. "And to the direct question, 'When will you retire from baseball?' my answer is, 'Never!' But I qualify that. Now, I do foresee the day, likely next year, when I shall spend less time at my desk, at my office. I shall spend more time in the field, scouting, looking at prospects, and leave the arduous responsibilities of the general manager's position to other hands."

He looked admiringly at the baked apple before him. He put his hand on the pitcher of rich cream beside it and glanced inquiringly across the table. This time the veto was not invoked and, happily, Rickey drained the pitcher over his dessert.

After he had dropped a saccharin tablet in his coffee, he leaned back and smiled at Mrs. Rickey. Then he leaned forward again and rubbed his chin, seeming to debate something with himself. He grasped the sides of the table and spoke with the air of a conspirator.

"Here is something I intend to do," he said. "My *next* thing. A completely new idea in spring training."

He arranged the silverware to illustrate the story.

"A permanent training camp, designed and built for that purpose. Twin motels — not hotels, *motels* — with four playing fields in between as a sort of quadrangle. A public address system. Especially designed press accommodations. *Now.* One motel would be occupied by the Pittsburgh club, the other by an *American League* club. They would play a series of exhibition games and would draw better than two teams from the same league. Everything that went into the camp would be the result of our experience with training camps all through the years. It would be foolproof. And it would pay for itself because it would be operated for tourists after spring training. I *have* the land. At Fort Myers, Florida, the finest training site in the country for my money. I *have* an American League Club ready to go along with me. I *have* two thirds of the financial backing necessary."

Rickey leaned back in triumph, then came forward quickly again.

"Everybody concerned is ready to put up the cash now," he whispered, "*except me!*"

He paused for effect, then suddenly realized he had not said exactly what he intended. He burst into laughter.

"Sh-h-h," said Mrs. Rickey.

"What I mean," he said, sobering, "is that I can't go along with the plan until we have a contending ball club. But we'll get there. We'll put over this thing. It will revolutionize spring training."

It was time to get back to the office. Rickey was for sprinting down the stairs to the first floor, but Mrs. Rickey reminded him of his trick knee.

"Ah, yes, Mother," he said. "We will take the elevator."

On the street outside, Rickey remembered he had sent his car home.

"We'll get a cab down at the corner," he said. "I've got a meeting at the office. Where can I drop you, Mother?"

"Well," said Mrs. Rickey, "I thought I'd go look at some lamps."

"Oh, yes," Rickey exclaimed. "Go to that store I showed you. Mother, I understand they have the largest selection of lamps in town."

Mrs. Rickey looked at him and shook her head and smiled.

Rickey, already thinking of something else, studied the sidewalk. He raised his head and spoke firmly over the traffic.

"The game of baseball," he said, "has given me a life of joy. I would not have exchanged it for any other."

He took Mrs. Rickey by the arm. They turned and walked down the street together and vanished into the crowd.

1958

## W. C. Heinz

..................................................................................................................

# The Rocky Road of Pistol Pete

FROM *True*

"OUT IN Los Angeles," says Garry Schumacher, who was a New York baseball writer for 30 years and is now assistant to Horace Stoneham, president of the San Francisco Giants, "they think Duke Snider is the best center fielder they ever had. They forget Pete Reiser. The Yankees think Mickey Mantle is something new. They forget Reiser, too."

Maybe Pete Reiser was the purest ballplayer of all time. I don't know. There is no exact way of measuring such a thing, but when a man of incomparable skills, with full knowledge of what he is doing, destroys those skills and puts his life on the line in the pursuit of his endeavor as no other man in his game ever has, perhaps he is the truest of them all.

"Is Pete Reiser there?" I said on the phone.

This was last season, in Kokomo. Kokomo has a population of about 50,000 and a ball club, now affiliated with Los Angeles and called the Dodgers, in the Class D Midwest League. Class D is the bottom of the barrel of organized baseball, and this was the second season that Pete Reiser had managed Kokomo.

"He's not here right now," the woman's voice on the phone said. "The team played a double-header yesterday in Dubuque, and they didn't get in on the bus until 4:30 this morning. Pete just got up a few minutes ago and he had to go to the doctor's."

"Oh?" I said. "What has he done now?"

In two and a half years in the minors, three seasons of Army ball and ten years in the majors, Pete Reiser was carried off the field 11 times. Nine times he regained consciousness either in the clubhouse or in hospitals. He broke a bone in his right elbow, throwing. He broke both ankles, tore a cartilage in his left knee, ripped the muscles in his left leg, sliding.

Seven times he crashed into outfield walls, dislocating his left shoulder, breaking his right collarbone and, five times, ending up in an unconscious heap on the ground. Twice he was beaned, and the few who remember still wonder today how great he might have been.

"I didn't see the old-timers," Bob Cooke, who is sports editor of the New York *Herald Tribune,* was saying recently, "but Pete Reiser was the best ballplayer I ever saw."

"We don't know what's wrong with him," the woman's voice on the phone said now. "He has a pain in his chest and he feels tired all the time, so we sent him to the doctor. There's a game tonight, so he'll be at the ball park about 5 o'clock."

Pete Reiser is 39 years old now. The Cardinals signed him out of the St. Louis Municipal League when he was 15. For two years, because he was so young, he chauffeured for Charley Barrett, who was scouting the Midwest. They had a Cardinal uniform in the car for Pete, and he used to work out with the Class C and D clubs, and one day Branch Rickey, who was general manager of the Cardinals then, called Pete into his office in Sportsman's Park.

"Young man," he said, "you're the greatest young ballplayer I've ever seen, but there is one thing you must remember. Now that you're a professional ballplayer you're in show business. You will perform on the biggest stage in the world, the baseball diamond. Like the actors on Broadway, you'll be expected to put on a great performance every day, no matter how you feel, no matter whether it's too hot or too cold. Never forget that."

Rickey didn't know it at the time, but this was like telling Horatius that, as a professional soldier, he'd be expected someday to stand his ground. Three times Pete sneaked out of hospitals to play. Once he went back into the lineup after doctors warned him that any blow on the head would kill him. For four years he swung the bat and made the throws when it was painful for him just to shave and to comb his hair. In the 1947 World Series he stood on a broken ankle to pinch hit, and it ended with Rickey, then president of the Dodgers, begging him not to play and guaranteeing Pete his 1948 salary if he would just sit that season out.

"That might be the one mistake I made," Pete says now. "Maybe I should have rested that year."

"Pete Reiser?" Leo Durocher, who managed Pete at Brooklyn, was saying recently. "What's he doing now?"

"He's managing Kokomo," Lindsey Nelson, the TV sportcaster, said.
"Kokomo?" Leo said.

"That's right," Lindsey said. "He's riding the buses to places like La-fayette and Michigan City and Mattoon."

"On the buses," Leo said, shaking his head and then smiling at the thought of Pete.

"And some people say," Lindsey said, "that he was the greatest young ballplayer they ever saw."

"No doubt about it," Leo said. "He was the best I ever had, with the possible exception of Mays. At that, he was even faster than Willie." He paused. "So now he's on the buses."

The first time that Leo ever saw Pete on a ball field was in Clearwater that spring of '39. Pete had played one year of Class D in the Cardinal chain and one season of Class D for Brooklyn. Judge Kenesaw Mountain Landis, who was then Baseball Commissioner, had sprung Pete and 72 others from what they called the "Cardinal Chain Gang," and Pete had signed with Brooklyn for $100.

"I didn't care about money then," Pete says. "I just wanted to play."

Pete had never been in a major-league camp before, and he didn't know that at batting practice you hit in rotation. At Clearwater he was grabbing any bat that was handy and cutting in ahead of Ernie Koy or Dolph Camilli or one of the others, and Leo liked that.

One day Leo had a chest cold, so he told Pete to start at shortstop. His first time up he hit a homer off the Cards' Ken Raffensberger, and that was the beginning. He was on base his first 12 times at bat that spring, with three homers, five singles and four walks. His first time against Detroit he homered off Tommy Bridges. His first time against the Yankees he put one over the fence off Lefty Gomez.

Durocher played Pete at shortstop in 33 games that spring. The Dodgers barnstormed North with the Yankees, and one night Joe Mc-Carthy, who was managing the Yankees, sat down next to Pete on the train.

"Reiser," he said, "you're going to play for me."

"How can I play for you?" Pete said. "I'm with the Dodgers."

"We'll get you," McCarthy said. "I'll tell Ed Barrow, and you'll be a Yankee."

The Yankees offered $100,000 and five ballplayers for Pete. The Dodg-ers turned it down, and the day the season opened at Ebbets Field, Larry MacPhail, who was running things in Brooklyn, called Pete on the clubhouse phone and told him to report to Elmira.

"It was an hour before game time," Pete says, "and I started to take off my uniform and I was shaking all over. Leo came in and said: 'What's the matter? You scared?' I said: 'No. MacPhail is sending me to Elmira.' Leo got on the phone and they had a hell of a fight. Leo said he'd quit, and MacPhail said he'd fire him — and I went to Elmira.

"One day I'm making a throw and I heard something pop. Every day my arm got weaker and they sent me to Johns Hopkins and took X rays. Dr. George Bennett told me: 'Your arm's broken.' When I came to after the operation, my throat was sore and there was an ice pack on it. I said: 'What happened? Your knife slip?' They said: 'We took your tonsils out while we were operating on your arm.'"

Pete's arm was in a cast from the first of May until the end of July. His first two weeks out of the cast he still couldn't straighten the arm, but a month later he played ten games as a left-handed outfielder until Dr. Bennett stopped him.

"But I can't straighten my right arm," Pete said.

"Take up bowling," the doctor said.

When he bowled, though, Pete used first one arm and then the other. Every day that the weather allowed he went out into the back yard and practiced throwing a rubber ball left-handed against a wall. Then he went to Fairgrounds Park and worked on the long throw, left-handed, with a baseball.

"At Clearwater that next spring," he says, "Leo saw me in the outfield throwing left-handed, and he said: 'What do you think you're doin'?' I said: 'Hell, I had to be ready. Now I can throw as good with my left arm as I could with my right.' He said: 'You can do more things as a right-handed ballplayer. I can bring you into the infield. Go out there and cut loose with that right arm.' I did and it was okay, but I had that insurance."

So at 5 o'clock I took a cab from the hotel in Kokomo to the ball park on the edge of town. It seats about 2,200, 1,500 of them in the white-painted fairgrounds grandstand along the first base line, and the rest in chairs behind the screen and in bleachers along the other line.

I watched them take batting practice; trim, strong young kids with their dreams, I knew, of someday getting up there where Pete once was, and I listened to their kidding. I watched the groundskeeper open the concession booth and clean out the electric popcorn machine. I read the signs on the outfield walls, advertising the Mid-West Towel and Linen Service, Basil's Nite Club, the Hoosier Iron Works, UAW Local 292 and the Around the Clock Pizza Café. I watched the Dubuque kids climbing out of their bus, carrying their uniforms on wire coat hangers.

"Here comes Pete now," I heard the old guy setting up the ticket box at the gate say.

When Pete came through the gate he was walking like an old man. In 1941 the Dodgers trained in Havana, and one day they clocked him, in his baseball uniform and regular spikes, at 9.8 for 100 yards. Five years later the Cleveland Indians were bragging about George Case and the Washington Senators had Gil Coan. The Dodgers offered to bet $1,000 that Reiser was the fastest man in baseball, and now it was taking him forever to walk to me, his shoulders stooped, his whole body heavier now, and Pete just slowly moving one foot ahead of the other.

"Hello," he said, shaking hands but his face solemn. "How are you?"

"Fine," I said, "but what's the matter with you?"

"I guess it's my heart," he said.

"When did you first notice this?"

"About eleven days ago. I guess I was working out too hard. All of a sudden I felt this pain in my chest and I got weak. I went into the club-house and lay down on the bench, but I've had the same pain and I'm weak ever since."

"What did the doctor say?"

"He says it's lucky I stopped that day when I did. He says I should be in a hospital right now, because if I exert myself or even make a quick motion I might go — just like that."

He snapped his fingers. "He scared me," he said. "I'll admit it. I'm scared."

"What are you planning to do?"

"I'm going home to St. Louis. My wife works for a doctor there, and he'll know a good heart specialist."

"When will you leave?"

"Well, I can't just leave the ball club. I called Brooklyn, and they're sending a replacement for me, but he won't be here until tomorrow."

"How will you get to St. Louis?"

"It's about 300 miles," Pete says. "The doctor says I shouldn't fly or go by train, because if anything happens to me they can't stop and help me. I guess I'll have to drive."

"I'll drive you," I said.

Trying to get to sleep in the hotel that night I was thinking that maybe, standing there in that little ball park, Pete Reiser had admitted out loud for the first time in his life that he was scared. I was thinking of 1941, his first full year with the Dodgers. He was beaned twice and crashed his first wall and still hit .343 to be the first rookie and the youngest ballplayer to win the National League batting title. He tied Johnny Mize with 39 doubles, led in triples, runs scored, total bases and slugging average, and they were writing on the sports pages that he might be the new Ty Cobb.

"Dodgers Win On Reiser HR," the headlines used to say. "Reiser Stars As Brooklyn Lengthens Lead."

"Any manager in the National League," Arthur Patterson wrote one day in the New York *Herald Tribune*, "would give up his best man to obtain Pete Reiser. On every bench they're talking about him. Rival players watch him take his cuts during batting practice, announce when he's going to make a throw to the plate or third base during outfield drill. They just whistle their amazement when he scoots down the first base line on an infield dribbler or a well-placed bunt."

He was beaned the first time at Ebbets Field five days after the season started. A sidearm fast ball got away from Ike Pearson of the Phillies, and Pete came to at 11:30 that night in Peck Memorial Hospital.

"I was lying in bed with my uniform on," he told me once, "and I couldn't figure it out. The room was dark, with just a little night light, and then I saw a mirror and I walked over to it and lit the light and I had a black eye and a black streak down the side of my nose. I said to myself: 'What happened to me?' Then I remembered.

"I took a shower and walked around the room, and the next morning the doctor came in. He looked me over, and he said: 'We'll keep you here for five or six more days under observation.' I said: 'Why?' He said: 'You've had a serious head injury. If you tried to get out of bed right now, you'd fall down.' I said: 'If I can get up and walk around this room, can I get out?' The doc said: 'All right, but you won't be able to do it.'"

Pete got out of bed, the doctor standing ready to catch him. He walked around the room. "I've been walkin' the floor all night," Pete said.

The doctor made Pete promise that he wouldn't play ball for a week, but Pete went right to the ball park. He got a seat behind the Brooklyn dugout and Durocher spotted him.

"How do you feel?" Leo said.

"Not bad," Pete said.

"Get your uniform on," Leo said.

"I'm not supposed to play," Pete said.

"I'm not gonna play you," Leo said. "Just sit on the bench. It'll make our guys feel better to see that you're not hurt."

Pete suited up and went out and sat on the bench. In the eighth inning it was tied, 7–7. The Dodgers had the bases loaded, and there was Ike Pearson again, coming in to relieve.

"Pistol," Leo said to Pete, "get the bat."

In the press box the baseball writers watched Pete. They wanted to see if he'd stand right in there. After a beaning they are all entitled to shy, and many of them do. Pete hit the first pitch into the center-field stands, and Brooklyn won, 11 to 7.

"I could just barely trot around the bases," Pete said when I asked him about it. "I was sure dizzy."

Two weeks later they were playing the Cardinals, and Enos Slaughter hit one and Pete turned in center field and started to run. He made the catch, but he hit his head and his tail bone on that corner near the exit gate.

His head was cut, and when he came back to the bench they also saw blood coming through the seat of his pants. They took him into the clubhouse and pulled his pants down and the doctor put a metal clamp on the cut.

"Just don't slide," he told Pete. "You can get it sewed up after the game."

In August of that year big Paul Erickson was pitching for the Cubs and Pete took another one. Again he woke up in a hospital. The Dodgers were having some pretty good beanball contests with the Cubs that season, and Judge Landis came to see Pete the next day.

"Do you think that man tried to bean you?" he asked Pete.

"No sir," Pete said. "I lost the pitch."

"I was there," Landis said, "and I heard them holler: 'Stick it in his ear.'"

"That was just bench talk," Pete said. "I lost the pitch."

He left the hospital the next morning. The Dodgers were going to St. Louis after the game, and Pete didn't want to be left in Chicago.

Pete always says that the next year, 1942, was the year of his downfall, and the worst of it happened on one play. It was early July and Pete and the Dodgers were tearing the league apart. In a fourth-game series in Cincinnati he got 19 for 21. In a Sunday double-header in Chicago he went 5 for 5 in the first game, walked three times in the second game and got a hit the one time they pitched to him. He was hitting .381, and they were writing in the papers that he might end up hitting .400.

When they came into St. Louis the Dodgers were leading by ten and a half games. When they took off for Pittsburgh they left three games of that lead and Pete Reiser behind them.

"We were in the twelfth inning, no score, two outs and Slaughter hit it off Whit Wyatt," Pete says. "It was over my head and I took off. I caught it and missed that flagpole by two inches and hit the wall and dropped the ball. I had the instinct to throw it to Peewee Reese, and we just missed gettin' Slaughter at the plate, and they won, 1–0.

"I made one step to start off the field and I woke up the next morning in St. John's Hospital. My head was bandaged, and I had an awful headache."

Dr. Robert Hyland, who was Pete's personal physician, announced to the newspapers that Pete would be out for the rest of the season. "Look, Pete," Hyland told him. "I'm your personal friend. I'm advising you not to play any more baseball this year."

"I don't like hospitals, though," Pete was telling me once, "so after two days I took the bandage off and got up. The room started to spin, but I got dressed and I took off. I snuck out, and I took a train to Pittsburgh and I went to the park.

"Leo saw me and he said: 'Go get your uniform on, Pistol.' I said: 'Not tonight, Skipper.' Leo said: 'Aw, I'm not gonna let you hit. I want these guys to see you. It'll give 'em that little spark they need. Besides, it'll change the pitching plans on that other bench when they see you sittin' here in uniform.'"

In the fourteenth inning the Dodgers had a runner on second and Ken Heintzelman, the left-hander, came in for the Pirates. He walked Johnny Rizzo, and Durocher had run out of pinch hitters.

"Damn," Leo was saying, walking up and down. "I want to win this one. Who can I use? Anybody here who can hit?"

Pete walked up to the bat rack. He pulled out his stick. "You got yourself a hitter," he said to Leo.

He walked up there and hit a line drive over the second baseman's head that was good for three bases. The two runs scored, and Pete rounded first base and collapsed.

"When I woke up I was in a hospital again," he says. "I could just make out that somebody was standin' there and then I saw it was Leo. He said: 'You awake?' I said: 'Yep.' He said: 'By God, we beat 'em! How do you feel?' I said: 'How do you think I feel?' He said: 'Aw, you're better with one leg, and one eye than anybody else I've got.' I said: 'Yeah, and that's the way I'll end up — on one leg and with one eye.'

"I'd say I lost the pennant for us that year," Pete says now, although he still hit .310 for the season. "I was dizzy most of the time and I couldn't see fly balls. I mean balls I could have put in my pocket, I couldn't get near. Once in Brooklyn when Mort Cooper was pitching for the Cards I was seeing two baseballs coming up there. Babe Pinelli was umpiring behind the plate, and a couple of times he stopped the game and asked me if I was all right. So the Cards beat us out the last two days of the season."

The business office of the Kokomo ball club is the dining room of a man named Jim Deets, who sells insurance and is also the business manager of the club. His wife, in addition to keeping house, mothering six small kids, boarding Pete, an outfielder from Venezuela and a shortstop from the Dominican Republic, is also the club secretary.

"How do you feel this morning?" I asked Pete. He was sitting at the dining-room table, in a sweat shirt and a pair of light-brown slacks, typing the game report of the night before to send it to Brooklyn.

"A little better," he said.

Pete has a worn, green 1950 Chevy, and it took us eight and a half hours to get to St. Louis. I'd ask him how the pain in his chest was and he'd say that it wasn't bad or it wasn't so good, and I'd get him to talking again about Durocher or about his time in the Army. Pete played under five managers at Brooklyn, Boston, Pittsburgh and Cleveland, and Durocher is his favorite.

"He has a great mind, and not just for baseball," Pete said. "Once he sat down to play gin with Jack Benny, and after they'd played four cards Leo read Benny's whole hand to him. Benny said: 'How can you do that?' Leo said: 'If you're playin' your cards right, and I give you credit for that, you have to be holding those others.' Benny said: 'I don't want to play with this guy.'

"One spring at Clearwater there was a pool table in a room off the lobby. One night Hugh Casey and a couple of other guys and I were talking with Leo. We said: 'Gee, there's a guy in there and we've been playin' pool with him for a couple of nights, but last night he had a real hot streak.' Leo said: 'How much he take you for?' We figured it out and it was $2,000. Leo said: 'Point him out to me.'

"We went in and pointed the guy out and Leo walked up to him and said: 'Put all your money on the table. We're gonna shoot for it.' The guy said: 'I never play like that.' Leo said: 'You will tonight. Pick your own game.' Leo took him for $4,000, and then he threw him out. Then he paid us back what we'd gone for, and he said: 'Now, let that be a lesson. That guy is a hustler from New York. The next time it happens I won't bail you out.' Leo hadn't had a cue in his hands for years."

It was amazing that they took Pete into the Army. He had wanted to enlist in the Navy, but the doctors looked him over and told him none of the services could accept him. Then his draft board sent him to Jefferson Barracks in the winter of 1943, and the doctors there turned him down.

"I'm sittin' on a bench with the other guys who've been rejected," he was telling me, "and a captain comes in and says: 'Which one of you is Reiser?' I stood up and I said: 'I am.' In front of everybody he said: 'So you're trying to pull a fast one, are you? At a time like this, with a war going on, you came in here under a false name. What do you mean, giving your name as Harold Patrick Reiser? Your name's Pete Reiser, and you're the ballplayer, aren't you?' I said: 'I'm the ballplayer and they call me Pete, but my right name is Harold Patrick Reiser.' The captain says: 'I apologize. Sergeant, fingerprint him. This man is in.'"

They sent him to Fort Riley, Kansas. It was early April and raining and they were on bivouac, and Pete woke up in a hospital. "What happened?" he said.

"You've got pneumonia," the doctor said. "You've been a pretty sick boy for six days. You'll be all right, but we've been looking you over. How did you ever get into this Army?"

"When I get out of the hospital," Pete was telling me, "I'm on the board for a discharge and I'm waitin' around for about a week, and still nobody there knows who I am. All of a sudden one morning a voice comes over the bitch box in the barracks. It says: 'Private Reiser, report to headquarters immediately.' I think: 'Well, I'm out now.'

"I got over there and the colonel wants to see me. I walk in and give my good salute and he says: 'Sit down, Harold.' I sit down and he says: 'Your name really isn't Harold, is it?' I say: 'Yes, it is, sir.' He says: 'But that isn't what they call you where you're well known, is it? You're Pete Reiser the ballplayer, aren't you?' I say: 'Yes, sir.' He says: 'I thought so. Now, I've got your discharge papers right there, but we've got a pretty good ball club and we'd like you on it. We'll make a deal. You say nothing, and you won't have to do anything but play ball. How about it?' I said: 'Suppose I don't want to stay in?'

"He picked my papers up off his desk," Pete was saying, "and he tore 'em right up in my face. I can still hear that 'zip' when he tore 'em. He said: 'You see, you have no choice.'

"Then he picked up the phone and said something and in a minute a general came in. I jumped up and the colonel said: 'Don't bother to salute, Pete.' Then he said to the general: 'Major, this is Pete Reiser, the great Dodger ballplayer. He was up for a medical discharge, but he's decided to stay here and play ball for us.'

"So, the general says: 'My, what a patriotic thing for you to do, young man. That's wonderful. Wonderful.' I'm sittin' there, and when the general goes out the colonel says: 'That major, he's all right.' I said: 'But he's a general. How come you call him a major?' The colonel says: 'Well, in the regular Army he's a major and I'm a full colonel. The only reason I don't outrank him now is that I've got heart trouble. He knows it, but I never let him forget it. I always call him major.' I thought: 'What kind of an Army am I in?'"

Joe Gantenbein, the Athletics' outfielder, and George Scharein, the Phillies' infielder, were on that team with Pete, and they won the state and national semipro titles. By the time the season was over, however, the order came down to hold up all discharges.

The next season there were 17 major-league ballplayers on the Fort Riley club, and they played four nights a week for the war workers in Wichita. Pete hit a couple of walls, and the team made such a joke of the national semipro tournament that an order came down from Washington to break up the club.

"Considering what a lot of guys did in the war," Pete says, "I had no complaints, but five times I was up for discharge, and each time something happened. From Riley they sent me to Camp Livingston. From there they sent me to New York Special Services for twelve hours and I end up in Camp Lee, Virginia, in May of 1945.

"The first one I meet there is the general. He says: 'Reiser, I saw you on the list and I just couldn't pass you up.' I said: 'What about my discharge?' He says: 'That will have to wait. I have a lot of celebrities down here, but I want a good baseball team.'"

Johnny Lindell, of the Yankees, and Dave Philley, of the White Sox, were on the club and Pete played left field. Near the end of the season he went after a foul fly for the third out of the last inning, and he went right through a temporary wooden fence and rolled down a 25-foot embankment.

"I came to in the hospital, with a dislocated right shoulder," he says, "and the general came over to see me and he said: 'That was one of the greatest displays of courage I've ever seen, to ignore your future in baseball just to win a ball game for Camp Lee.' I said: 'Thanks.'

"Now it's November and the war is over, but they're still shippin' guys out, and I'm on the list to go. I report to the overseas major, and he looks at my papers and says: 'I can't send you overseas. With everything that's wrong with you, you shouldn't even be in this Army. I'll have you out in three hours.' In three hours, sure enough, I've got those papers in my hand, stamped, and I'm startin' out the door. Runnin' up to me comes a Red Cross guy. He says: 'I can get you some pretty good pension benefits for the physical and mental injuries you've sustained.' I said: 'You can?' He said: 'Yes, you're entitled to them.' I said: 'Good. You get 'em. You keep 'em. I'm goin' home.'"

When we got to St. Louis that night I drove Pete to his house and the next morning I picked him up and drove him to see the heart specialist. He was in there for two hours, and when he came out he was walking slower than ever.

"No good," he said. "I have to go to the hospital for five days for observation."

"What does he think?"

"He says I'm done puttin' on that uniform. I'll have to get a desk job."

Riding to the hospital I wondered if that heart specialist knew who he was tying to that desk job. In 1946, the year he came out of the Army, Pete led the league when he stole 34 bases, 13 more than the runner-up Johnny Hopp of the Braves. He also set a major-league record that still stands, when he stole home eight times.

"Nine times," he said once. "In Chicago I stole home and Magerkurth hollered: 'You're out!' Then he dropped his voice and he said: '_____, I missed it.' He'd already had his thumb in the air. I had nine out of nine."

I suppose somebody will beat that some day, but he'll never top the way Pete did it. That was the year he knocked himself out again trying for a diving catch, dislocated his left shoulder, ripped the muscles in his left leg and broke his left ankle.

"Whitey Kurowski hit one in the seventh inning at Ebbets Field," he was telling me. "I dove for it and woke up in the clubhouse. I was in Peck Memorial for four days. It really didn't take much to knock me out in those days. I was comin' apart all over. When I dislocated my shoulder they popped it back in, and Leo said: 'Hell, you'll be all right. You don't throw with it anyway.'"

That was the year the Dodgers tied with the Cardinals for the pennant and dropped the play-off. Pete wasn't there for those two games. He was in Peck Memorial again.

"I'd pulled a Charley horse in my left leg," Pete was saying. "It's the last two weeks of the season, and I'm out for four days. We've got the winning run on third, two outs in the ninth and Leo sends me up. He says: 'If you don't hit it good, don't run and hurt your leg.'

"The first pitch was a knockdown and, when I ducked, the ball hit the bat and went down the third base line, as beautiful a bunt as you've ever seen. Well, Ebbets Field is jammed. Leo has said: 'Don't run.' But this is a big game. I take off for first, and we win and I've ripped the muscles from my ankle to my hip. Leo says: 'You shouldn't have done it.'

"Now it's the last three days of the season and we're a game ahead of the Cards and we're playin' the Phillies in Brooklyn. Leo says to me: 'It's now or never. I don't think we can win it without you.' The first two up are outs and I single to right. There's Charley Dressen, coachin' on third, with the steal sign. I start to get my lead, and a pitcher named Charley Schanz is workin' and he throws an ordinary lob over to first. My leg is stiff and I slide and my heel spike catches the bag and I hear it snap.

"Leo comes runnin' out. He says: 'Come on. You're all right.' I said: 'I think it's broken.' He says: 'It ain't stickin' out.' They took me to Peck Memorial, and it was broken."

We went to St. Luke's Hospital in St. Louis. In the main office they told Pete to go over to a desk where a gray-haired, semistout woman was sitting at a typewriter. She started to book Pete in, typing his answer on the form. "What is your occupation, Mr. Reiser?" she said.

"Baseball," Pete said.

"Have you ever been hospitalized before?"

"Yes," Pete said.

In 1946 the Dodgers played an exhibition game in Springfield, Missouri. When the players got off the train there was a young radio announcer there, and he was grabbing them one at a time and asking them where they thought they'd finish that year.

"In first place," Reese and Casey and Dixie Walker and the rest were saying. "On top" . . . "We'll win it."

"And here comes Pistol Pete Reiser!" the announcer said. "Where do you think you'll finish this season, Pete?"

"In Peck Memorial Hospital," Pete said.

After the 1946 season Brooklyn changed the walls at Ebbets Field. They added boxes, cutting 40 feet off left field and dropping center field from 420 to 390 feet. Pete had made a real good start that season in center, and on June 5 the Dodgers were leading the Pirates by three runs in the sixth inning when Culley Rikard hit one.

"I made my turn and ran," Pete says, "and, where I thought I still had that thirty feet, I didn't."

"The crowd," Al Laney wrote the next day in the New York *Herald Tribune,* "which watched silently while Reiser was being carried away, did not know that he had held onto the ball . . . Rikard circled the bases, but Butch Henline, the umpire, who ran to Reiser, found the ball still in Reiser's glove. . . . Two outs were posted on the scoreboard after play was resumed. Then the crowd let out a tremendous roar."

In the Brooklyn clubhouse the doctor called for a priest, and the Last Rites of the Church were administered to Pete. He came to, but lapsed into unconsciousness again and woke up at 3 A.M. in Peck Memorial.

For eight days he couldn't move. After three weeks they let him out, and he made that next western trip with the Dodgers. In Pittsburgh he was working out in the outfield before the game when Clyde King, chasing a fungo, ran into him and Pete woke up in the clubhouse.

"I went back to the Hotel Schenley and lay down," he says. "After the game I got up and had dinner with Peewee. We were sittin' on the porch, and I scratched my head and I felt a lump there about as big as half a golf ball. I told Peewee to feel it and he said: 'Gosh!' I said: 'I don't think that's supposed to be like that.' He said: 'Hell, no.'"

Pete went up to Rickey's room and Rickey called his pilot and had Pete flown to Johns Hopkins in Baltimore. They operated on him for a blood clot.

"You're lucky," the doctor told him. "If it had moved just a little more you'd have been gone."

Pete was unable to hold even a pencil. He had double vision and, when he tried to take a single step, he became dizzy. He stayed for three weeks and then went home for almost a month.

"It was August," he says, "and Brooklyn was fightin' for another pennant. I thought if I could play the last two months it might make the difference, so I went back to Johns Hopkins. The doctor said: 'You've made a remarkable recovery.' I said: 'I want to play.' He said: 'I can't okay that. The slightest blow on the head can kill you.'"

Pete played. He worked out for four days, pinch hit a couple of times and then, in the Polo Grounds, made a diving catch in left field. They carried him off, and in the clubhouse he was unable to recognize anyone.

Pete was still having dizzy spells when the Dodgers went into the 1947 Series against the Yankees. In the third game he walked in the first inning, got the steal sign and, when he went into second, felt his right ankle snap. At the hospital they found it was broken.

"Just tape it, will you?" Pete said.

"I want to put a cast on it," the doctor said.

"If you do," Pete said, "they'll give me a dollar-a-year contract next season."

The next day he was back on the bench. Bill Bevens was pitching for the Yankees and, with two out in the ninth, it looked like he was going to pitch the first no-hitter in World Series history.

"Aren't you going to volunteer to hit?" Burt Shotton, who was managing Brooklyn, said to Pete.

Al Gionfriddo was on first and Bucky Harris, who was managing the Yankees, ordered Pete walked. Eddie Miksis ran for him, and when Cookie Lavagetto hit that double, the two runs scored and Brooklyn won, 3–2.

"The next day," Pete says, "the sports writers were second-guessing Harris for putting me on when I represented the winning run. Can you imagine what they'd have said if they knew I had a broken ankle?"

At the end of that season Rickey had the outfield walls at Ebbets Field padded with one-inch foam rubber for Pete, but he never hit them again. He had headaches most of the time and played little. Then he was traded to Boston, and in two seasons there he hit the wall a couple of times. Twice his left shoulder came out while he was making diving catches. Pittsburgh picked Pete up in 1951, and the next year he played into July with Cleveland and that was the end of it.

Between January and September of 1953, Pete dropped $40,000 in the used-car business in St. Louis, and then he got a job in a lumber mill for $100 a week. In the winter of 1955 he wrote Brooklyn asking for a part-time job as a scout, and on March 1, Buzzy Bavasi, the Dodger vice-president, called him on the phone.

"How would you like a manager's job?" Buzzy said.

"I'll take it," Pete said.

"I haven't even told you where it is. It's Thomasville, Georgia, in Class D."

"I don't care," Pete said. "I'll take it."

At Vero Beach that spring, Mike Gaven wrote a piece about Pete in the New York *Journal American.*

"Even in the worn gray uniform of the Class D Thomasville, Georgia, club," Mike wrote, "Pete Reiser looks, acts and talks like a big leaguer. The Dodgers pitied Pete when they saw him starting his comeback effort after not having handled a ball for two and a half years. They lowered their heads when they saw him in a chow line with a lot of other bushers, but the old Pistol held his head high. . . ."

The next spring, Sid Friedlander, of the New York *Post,* saw Pete at Vero and wrote a column about him managing Kokomo. The last thing I saw about him in the New York papers was a small item out of Tipton, Indiana, saying that the bus carrying the Kokomo team had collided with a car and Pete was in a hospital in Kokomo with a back injury.

"Managing," Pete was saying in that St. Louis hospital, "you try to find out how your players are thinking. At Thomasville one night one of my kids made a bad throw. After the game I said to him: 'What were you thinking while that ball was coming to you?' He said: 'I was saying to myself that I hoped I could make a good throw.' I said: 'Sit down.' I tried to explain to him the way you have to think. You know how I used to think?"

"Yes," I said, "but you tell me."

"I was always sayin': 'Hit it to me. Just hit it to me. I'll make the catch. I'll make the throw.' When I was on base I was always lookin' over and sayin': 'Give me the steal sign. Give me the sign. Let me go.' That's the way you have to think."

"Pete," I said, "now that it's all over, do you ever think that if you hadn't played it as hard as you did, there's no telling how great you might have been or how much money you might have made?"

"Never," Pete said. "It was my way of playin'. If I hadn't played that way I wouldn't even have been whatever I was. God gave me those legs and the speed, and when they took me into the walls that's the way it had to be. I couldn't play any other way."

A technician came in with an electrocardiograph. She was a thin, dark-haired woman and she set it up by the bed and attached one of the round metal disks to Pete's left wrist and started to attach another to his left ankle.

"Aren't you kind of young to be having pains in your chest?" she said.

"I've led a fast life," Pete said.

On the way back to New York I kept thinking how right Pete was. To tell a man who is this true that there is another way for him to do it is to speak a lie. You cannot ask him to change his way of going, because it makes him what he is.

Three days after I got home I had a message to call St. Louis. I heard the phone ring at the other end and Pete answered. "I'm out!" he said.

"Did they let you out, or did you sneak out again?" I said.

"They let me out," he said. "It's just a strained heart muscle, I guess. My heart itself is all right."

"That's wonderful."

"I can manage again. In a couple of days I can go back to Kokomo."

If his voice had been higher he would have sounded like a kid at Christmas.

"What else did they say?" I said.

"Well, they say I have to take it easy."

"Do me a favor," I said.

"What?"

"Take their advice. This time, please take it easy."

"I will," he said. "I'll take it easy."

If he does it will be the first time.

## 1958

## W. C. Heinz

......................................................................................................................

# The Ghost of the Gridiron

FROM *True*

WHEN I WAS ten years old I paid ten cents to see Red Grange run with a football. That was the year when, one afternoon a week, after school was out for the day, they used to show us movies in the auditorium, and we would all troop up there clutching our dimes, nickels or pennies in our fists.

The movies were, I suppose, carefully selected for their educational value. They must have shown us, as the weeks went by, films of the Everglades, of Yosemite, of the Gettysburg battlefield, of Washington, D.C., but I remember only the one about Grange.

I remember, in fact, only one shot. Grange, the football cradled in one arm, started down the field toward us. As we sat there in the dim, flickering light of the movie projector, he grew larger and larger. I can still see the rows and rows of us, with our thin little necks and bony heads, all looking up at the screen and Grange, enormous now, rushing right at us, and I shall never forget it. That was thirty-three years ago.

"I haven't any idea what film that might have been," Grange was saying now. "My last year at Illinois was all confusion. I had no privacy. Newsreel men were staying at the fraternity house for two or three days at a time."

He paused. The thought of it seemed to bring pain to his face, even at this late date.

"I wasn't able to study or anything," he said. "I thought and I still do, that they built me up out of all proportion."

Red Grange was the most sensational, the most publicized, and, possibly, the most gifted football player and greatest broken field runner of all time. In high school, at Wheaton, Illinois, he averaged five touchdowns a game. In twenty games for the University of Illinois, he scored thirty-one touchdowns and ran for 3,637 yards, or, as it was translated at the time, 2 miles and 117 yards. His name and his pseudonyms — The Galloping Ghost and The Wheaton Iceman — became household words, and what he was may have been summarized best by Paul Sann in his book *The Lawless Decade.*

"Red Grange, No. 77, made Jack Dempsey move over," Sann wrote. "He put college football ahead of boxing as the Golden Age picked up momentum. He also made the ball yards obsolete; they couldn't handle the crowds. He made people buy more radios: how could you wait until Sunday morning to find out what deeds Red Grange had performed on Saturday? He was 'The Galloping Ghost' and he made the sports historians torture their portables without mercy."

Grange is now 55 years old, his reddish brown hair marked with gray, but he was one with Babe Ruth, Jack Dempsey, Bobby Jones and Bill Tilden.

"I could carry a football well," Grange was saying now, "but I've met hundreds of people who could do their thing better than I. I mean engineers, and writers, scientists, doctors — whatever.

"I can't take much credit for what I did, running with a football, because I don't know what I did. Nobody ever taught me, and I can't teach anybody. You can teach a man how to block or tackle or kick or pass. The ability to run with a ball is something you have or you haven't. If you can't explain it, how can you take credit for it?"

This was last year, and we were sitting in a restaurant in Syracuse, New York. Grange was in town to do a telecast with Lindsey Nelson of the Syracuse–Penn State game. He lives now in Miami, Florida, coming out of there on weekends during the football season to handle telecasts of college games on Saturdays and the Chicago Bears' games on Sundays. He approaches this job as he has approached every job, with honesty and dedication, and, as could be expected, he is good at it. As befits a man who put the pro game on the map and made the whole nation football conscious, he has been making fans out of people who never followed the game before. Never, perhaps, has any one man done more for the game. And it, of course, has been good to him.

"Football did everything for me," he was saying now, "but what people don't understand is that it hasn't been my whole life. When I was a freshman at Illinois, I wasn't even going to go out for football. My fraternity brothers made me do it."

He was three times All-American. Once the Illinois students carried him two miles on their backs. A football jersey, with the number 77 that he made famous and that was retired after him, is enshrined at Champaign. His fellow students wanted him to run for Congress. A Senator from Illinois led him into the White House to shake hands with Calvin Coolidge. Here, in its entirety, is what was said.

"Howdy," Coolidge said. "Where do you live?"

"In Wheaton, Illinois," Grange said.

"Well, young man," Coolidge said, "I wish you luck."

Grange had his luck, but it was coming to him because he did more to popularize professional football than any other player before or since. In his first three years out of school he grossed almost $1,000,000 from football, motion pictures, vaudeville appearances and endorsements, and he could afford to turn down a Florida real estate firm that wanted to pay him $120,000 a year. Seven years ago the Associated Press, in selecting an All-Time All-American team in conjunction with the National Football Hall of Fame, polled one hundred leading sportswriters and Grange received more votes than any other player.

"They talk about the runs I made," he was saying, "but I can't tell you one thing I did on any run. That's the truth. During the depression, though, I took a licking. Finally I got into the insurance business. I almost starved to death for three years, but I never once tried to use my football reputation. I never once opened a University of Illinois year book and knowingly called on an alumnus. I think I was as good an insurance man as there was in Chicago. On the football field I had ten other men blocking for me, but I'm more proud of what I did in the insurance business, because I did it alone."

Recently I went down to Miami and visited Grange in the white colonial duplex house where he lives with his wife. They met eighteen years ago on a plane, flying between Chicago and Omaha, on which she was a stewardess, and they were married the following year.

"Without sounding like an amateur psychologist," I said, "I believe you derive more satisfaction from what you did in the insurance business, not only because you did it alone, but also because you know how you did it, and, if you had to, you could do it again. You could never find any security in what you did when you ran with a football because it was inspirational and creative, rather than calculated."

"Yes," Grange said, "you could call it that. The sportswriters used to try to explain it, and they used to ask me. I couldn't tell them anything."

I have read what many of those sportswriters wrote, and they had as much trouble trying to corner Grange on paper as his opponents had trying to tackle him on the field. . . .

Grange had blinding speed, amazing lateral mobility, and exceptional change of pace and a powerful straight-arm. He moved with high knee action, but seemed to glide, rather than run, and he was a master at using his blockers. What made him great, however, was his instinctive ability to size up a field and plot a run the way a great general can map not only a battle but a whole campaign.

"The sportswriters wrote that I had peripheral vision," Grange was saying. "I didn't even know what the word meant. I had to look it up. They asked me about my change of pace, and I didn't even know that I ran at different speeds. I had a cross-over step, but I couldn't spin. Some ball carriers can spin but if I ever tried that, I would have broken a leg."

Harold Edward Grange was born on June 13, 1903, in Forksville, Pennsylvania, the third of four children. His mother died when he was five, and his sister Norma died in her teens. The other sister, Mildred, lives in Binghamton, New York. His brother, Garland, two and a half years younger than Red, was a 165-pound freshman end at Illinois and was later with the Chicago Bears and is now a credit manager for a Florida department store chain. Their father died at the age of 86.

"My father," Grange said, "was the foreman of three lumber camps near Forksville, and if you had known him, you'd know why I could never get a swelled head. He stood six-one and weighed 210 pounds, and he was quick as a cat. He had three hundred men under him and he had to be able to lick any one of them. One day he had a fight that lasted four hours."

Grange's father, after the death of his wife, moved to Wheaton, Illinois, where he had relatives. Then he sent the two girls back to Pennsylvania to live with their maternal grandparents. With his sons, he moved into a five-room apartment over a store where they took turns cooking and keeping house.

"Can you recall," I said, "the first time you ever ran with a football?"

"I think it started," Grange said, "with a game we used to play without a football. Ten or twelve of us would line up in the street, along one curb. One guy would be in the middle of the road and the rest of us would run across the street to the curb on the other side. When the kid in the middle of the street tackled one of the runners, the one who was tackled had to stay in the middle of the street with the tackler. Finally, all of us, except one last runner, would be in the middle of the street. We only had about thirty yards to maneuver in and dodge the tackler. I got to be pretty good at that. Then somebody got a football and we played games with it on vacant lots."

In high school Grange won sixteen letters in football, basketball, track and baseball. In track he competed in the 100 and 220 yard dashes, low and high hurdles, broad jump and high jump and often won all six events. In his sophomore year on the football team, he scored 15 touchdowns, in his junior year 36 — eight in one game — and in his senior year 23. Once he was kicked in the head and was incoherent for 48 hours.

"I went to Illinois," he was saying, "because some of my friends from Wheaton went there and all the kids in the state wanted to play football for Bob Zuppke and because there weren't any athletic scholarships in those days and that was the cheapest place for me to go to. In May of my senior year in high school I was there for the Interscholastic track meet, and I just got through broad jumping when Zup came over. He said, 'Is your name Grainche?' That's the way he always pronounced my name. I said, 'Yes.' He said, 'Where are you going to college?' I said, 'I don't know.' He put his arm around my shoulders and he said, 'I hope here. You may have a chance to make the team here.' That was the greatest moment I'd known."

That September, Grange arrived at Champaign with a battered second-hand trunk, one suit, a couple of pairs of trousers and a sweater. He had been working for four summers on an ice wagon in Wheaton and saving some money, and his one luxury now that he was entering college was to pledge Zeta Phi fraternity.

"One day," he was saying, "they lined us pledges up in the living room of the fraternity house. I had wanted to go out for basketball and track — I thought there would be too much competition in football — but they started to point to each one of us and tell us what to go out for: 'You go out for cheerleader. You go out for football manager. You go out for the band.' When they came to me, they said, 'You go out for football.'

"That afternoon I went over to the gym. I looked out the window at the football practice field and they had about three hundred freshman candidates out there. I went back to the house and I said to one of the seniors, 'I can't go out for football. I'll never make that team.'

"So he lined me up near the wall, with my head down, and he hit me with this paddle. I could show you the dent in that wall where my head took a piece of plaster out — this big."

With the thumb and forefinger of his right hand, he made a circle the size of a half dollar.

"Do you remember the name of that senior?" I said.

"Johnny Hawks," Grange said. "He was from Goshen, Indiana, and I see him now and then. I say to him. 'Damn you. If it wasn't for you, I'd never have gone out for football.' He gets a great boot out of that."

"So what happened when you went out the next day?"

"We had all these athletes from Chicago I'd been reading about. What chance did I have, from a little farm town and a high school with three hundred students? I think they cut about forty that first night, but I happened to win the wind sprints and that got them at least to know my name."

It was a great freshman team. On it with Grange was Earl Britton, who blocked for Grange and did the kicking throughout their college careers, and Moon Baker and Frank Wickhorst, who transferred to Northwestern and Annapolis, respectively, where they both made All-American. After one week of practice, the freshman team played the varsity and were barely nosed out, 21–19, as Grange scored two touchdowns, one on a 60 yard punt return. From then on, the freshmen trimmed the varsity regularly and Zuppke began to give most of his time to the freshmen.

"That number 77," I said to Grange, "became the most famous number in football. Do you remember when you first got it?"

"It was just handed to me in my sophomore year," he said. "I guess anybody who has a number and does well with it gets a little superstitious about it, and I guess that began against Nebraska in my first varsity game."

That game started Grange to national fame. This was 1923, and the previous year Nebraska had beaten Notre Dame and they were to beat "The Four Horsemen" later this same season. In the first quarter Grange sprinted 35 yards for a touchdown. In the second quarter he ran 60 yards for another. In the third period he scored again on a 12 yard burst, and Illinois won, 24–7. The next day, over Walter Eckersall's story in the Chicago *Tribune*, the headline said: GRANGE SPRINTS TO FAME.

From the Nebraska game, Illinois went on to an undefeated season. Against Butler, Grange scored twice. Against Iowa, he scored the only touchdown as Illinois won, 9–6. In the first quarter against Northwestern, he intercepted a pass and ran 90 yards to score the first of his three touchdowns. He made the only touchdown in the game with the University of Chicago and the only one in the Ohio State game, this time on a 34 yard run.

"All Grange can do is run," Fielding Yost, the coach at Michigan, was quoted as saying.

"All Galli-Curci can do is sing," Zuppke said.

Grange had his greatest day in his first game against Michigan during his junior year. On that day Michigan came to the dedication of the new $1,700,000 Illinois Memorial Stadium. The Wolverines had been undefeated in twenty games and for months the nation's football fans had been waiting for this meeting. There were 67,000 spectators in the stands, then the largest crowd ever to see a football game in the Midwest.

Michigan kicked off. Grange was standing on his goal line, with Wally McIlwain, whom Zuppke was to call "the greatest open field blocker of all time" on his right, Harry Hall, the Illinois quarterback, on his left, and Earl Britton in front of him. Michigan attempted to aim the kickoff to McIlwain, but as the ball descended, Grange moved over under it.

"I've got it," he said to McIlwain.

He caught it on the 5 yard line. McIlwain turned and took out the first Michigan man to get near him. Britton cut down the next one, and Grange started underway. He ran to his left, reversed his field to avoid one would-be tackler, and, then, cutting back again to the left, ran diagonally across the field through the oncoming Michigan players. At the Michigan 40 yard line he was in the open and on the 20 yard line, Tod Rockwell, the Michigan safety man, made a futile dive for him. Grange scored standing up. Michigan never recovered.

In less than twelve minutes, Grange scored three more touchdowns on runs of 67, 56 and 44 yards. Zuppke took him out to rest him. In the third period, he re-entered the game, and circled right end for 15 yards and another touchdown. In the final quarter, he threw a pass for another score. Illinois won, 39–14. Against a powerful, seasoned and favored team, Grange had handled the ball twenty-one times, gained 402 yards running, scored five touchdowns and collaborated, as a passer, in a sixth.

"This was," Coach Amos Alonzo Stagg, the famous Chicago mentor, later wrote, "the most spectacular singlehanded performance ever made in a major game."

"Did Zuppke tell you that you should have scored another touchdown?" I asked Grange.

"That's right," Grange said. "After the fourth touchdown we called a time-out, and when Matt Bullock, our trainer, came with the water, I said to him, 'I'm dog tired. You'd better tell Zup to get me out of here.' When I got to the bench Zup said to me, 'You should have had five touchdowns. You didn't cut right on one play.' Nobody could get a swelled head around him."

"And you don't recall," I said, "one feint or cut that you made during any one of those runs?"

"I don't remember one thing I ever did on any run I made. I just remember one vision from that Michigan game. On that opening kick-off runback, as I got downfield I saw that the only man still in front of me was the safety man, Tod Rockwell. I remember thinking then, 'I'd better get by this guy, because after coming all this way, I'll sure look like a bum if he tackles me.' I can't tell you, though, how I did get by him."

When Grange started his senior year, Illinois had lost seven regulars by graduation and Harry Hall, its quarterback, who had a broken collarbone. Zuppke shifted Grange to quarterback. Illinois lost to Nebraska, Iowa and Michigan and barely beat Butler before they came to Franklin Field in Philadelphia on October 31, 1925, to play Pennsylvania.

The previous year Penn had been considered the champion of the East. They had now beaten Brown, Yale and Chicago, among others. Although Grange's exploits in the Midwest had been widely reported in Eastern papers, most of the 65,000 spectators and the Eastern sportswriters — Grantland Rice, Damon Runyon and Ford Frick among them — came to be convinced.

It had rained and snowed for 24 hours, with only straw covering the field. At the kickoff, the players stood in mud. On the third play of the game, the first time he carried the ball, Grange went 55 yards for his first touchdown. On the next kickoff he ran 55 yards again, to the Penn 25 yard line, and Illinois worked it over the goal line from there. In the second period, Grange twisted 12 yards for another score and in the third period he ran 20 yards to a touchdown. Illinois won, 24–2, with Grange carrying the ball 363 yards, and scoring three touchdowns and setting up another one, in thirty-six rushes.

Two days later when the train carrying the Illinois team arrived in Champaign, there were 20,000 students, faculty members and townspeople waiting at the station. Grange tried to sneak out of the last car but he was recognized and carried two miles to his fraternity house.

"Do you remember your feelings during those two miles?" I asked him.

"I remember that I was embarrassed," he said. "You wish people would understand that it takes eleven men to make a football team. Unless they've played it, I guess they'll never understand it, but I've never been impressed by individual performances in football, my own or anyone else's."

"Do you remember the last touchdown you scored in college?"

"To tell you the truth, I don't," he said. "It must have been against Ohio State. I can't tell you the score. I can't tell you the score of more than three or four games I ever played in."

I looked it up. Grange's last college appearance, against Ohio State, attracted 85,500 spectators at Columbus. He was held to 153 yards on the ground but threw one touchdown pass as Illinois won, 14–9. The following afternoon, in the Morrison Hotel in Chicago, he signed with Charles C. (Cash and Carry) Pyle to play professional football with the Chicago Bears, starting immediately, and he quit college. Twenty-five years later, however, he was elected to the University of Illinois Board of Trustees for a six-year term.

"I had a half year to finish when I quit," he said. "I had this chance to make a lot of money and I couldn't figure where having a sheepskin would pull any more people into football games."

"How were your marks in college?"

"I was an average student. I got B's and C's. I flunked one course, economics, and I made that up in the summer at Wheaton College. I'd leave the ice wagon at 11 o'clock in the morning and come back to it at 1 o'clock. There was so much written about my job on the ice wagon, and so many pictures of me lugging ice, that people thought it was a publicity stunt. It wasn't. I did it for eight summers, starting at 5 o'clock every morning, for two reasons. The pay was good — $37.50 a week — and I needed money. I didn't even have any decent clothes until my junior year. Also, it kept me in shape. After carrying those blocks of ice up and down stairs six days a week, my legs were always in shape when the football season started. Too many football players have to play their legs into shape in the first four or five games."

Grange played professional football from 1925 through the 1934 season, first with the Bears, then with the New York Yankees in a rival pro league that Pyle and he started, and then back with the Bears again. He was immobilized during the 1928 season with arm and knee injuries, and after that he was never able to cut sharply while carrying the ball. He did, however, score 162 touchdowns as a professional and kicked 86 conversion points, for a total of 1,058 points.

What the statistics do not show, however, is what Grange, more than any other player, did to focus public attention and approval on the professional game. In 1925, when he signed with the Bears, professional football attracted little notice on the sports pages and few paying customers. There was so little interest that the National Professional Football League did not even hold a championship playoff at the end of the season.

In ten days after he left college Grange played five games as a pro and changed all that. After only three practice sessions with the Bears, he made his pro debut against the Chicago Cardinals on Thanksgiving Day, November 26. The game ended 0–0 but 36,000 people crowded into Wrigley Field to see Grange. Three days later, on a Sunday, 28,000 defied a snowstorm to watch him perform at the same field. On the next Wednesday, freezing weather in St. Louis held the attendance down to 8,000 but on Saturday 40,000 Philadelphians watched him in the rain at Shibe Park. The next day the Bears played in the Polo Grounds against the New York Giants.

It had been raining for almost a week, and, although advance sales were almost unknown in pro football in those days, the Giants sold almost 60,000 before Sunday dawned. It turned out to be a beautiful day. Cautious fans who had not bought seats in advance stormed the ticket booths. Thousands of people were turned away but 73,651 crammed into the park. Grange did not score but the Bears won, 19–7.

That was the beginning of professional football's rise to its present popularity. At the end of those first ten days, Grange picked up a check for $50,000. He got another $50,000 when the season ended a month later.

"Can you remember," I asked him now, "the last time you ever carried a football?"

"It was in a game against the Giants in Gilmore Stadium in Hollywood in January of 1935. It was the last period, and we had a safe lead and I was sitting on the bench. George Halas said to me, 'Would you like to go in, Red?' I said, 'No, thanks.' Everybody knew this was my last year. He said, 'Go ahead. Why don't you run it just once more?'

"So I went in, and we lined up and they called a play for me. As soon as I got the ball and started to go I knew that they had it framed with the Giants to let me run. The line just opened up for me and I went through and started down the field. The farther I ran, the heavier my legs got and the farther those goal posts seemed to move away. I was thinking, 'When I make that end zone, I'm going to take off these shoes and shoulder pads for the last time.' With that something hit me from behind and down I went on about the 10 yard line. It was Cecil Irvin, a 230-pound tackle. He was so slow that, I guess, they never bothered to let him in on the plan. But when he caught me from behind, I knew I was finished."

Grange, who is 5 feet 11 and ¾ inches, weighed 180 in college and 185 in his last game with the Bears. Now he weighs 200. On December 15, 1951, he suffered a heart attack. This motivated him to give up his insurance business and to move to Florida where he and his wife own, in addition to their own home in Miami, land in Orlando and Melbourne and property at Indian Lake.

"Red," I said, "I'll bet there are some men still around whose greatest claim to fame is that they played football with you or against you. I imagine there are guys whose proudest boast is that they once tackled you. Have you ever run into a guy who thought he knew everything about football and didn't know he was talking with Red Grange?"

"Yes," he said. "Once about fifteen years ago, on my way home from work, I dropped into a tavern in Chicago for a beer. Two guys next to me and the bartender were arguing about Bronco Nagurski and Carl Brumbaugh. On the Bears, of course, I played in the backfield with both of them. One guy doesn't like Nagurski and he's talking against him. I happen to think Nagurski was the greatest football player I ever saw, and a wonderful guy. This fellow who is knocking him says to me, 'Do you know anything about football? Did you ever see Nagurski play?' I said, 'Yes, and I think he was great.' The guy gets mad and says, 'What was so great about him? What do you know about it?' I could see it was time to leave, but the guy kept at me. He said, 'Now wait a minute. What makes you think you know something about it? Who are you, anyway?' I reached into my wallet and took out my business card and handed it to him and started for the door. When I got to the door, I looked back at him. You should have seen his face."

Mrs. Grange, who had been listening to our talk, left the room and came back with a small, gold-plated medal that Grange had won in the broad jump at the Interscholastic track meet on the day when he first met Zuppke.

"A friend of mine just sent that to me," Grange said. "He wrote: 'You gave me this away back in 1921. I thought you might want it.' Just the other day I got a letter from a man in the Midwest who told me that his son just found a gold football inscribed, 'University of Illinois, 1924' with the initials H. G. on it. I was the only H. G. on that squad so it must have been mine. I guess I gave it to somebody and he lost it. I wrote the man back and said: 'If your son would like it, I'd be happy to have him keep it.'"

Mrs. Grange said, "We have a friend who can't understand why Red doesn't keep his souvenirs. He has his trophies in another friend's storage locker in Chicago. The clipping books are nailed up in a box in the garage here and Red hasn't looked at them in years."

"I don't like to look back," Grange said. "You have to look ahead."

I remembered that night when we ate in the restaurant in Syracuse. As we stood in line to get our hats and coats, Grange nudged me and showed me his hat check. In the middle of the yellow cardboard disk was the number 77.

"Has this ever happened to you before?" I said.

"Never," he said, "as far as I know."

We walked out into the cold night air. A few flakes of snow were falling.

"That jersey with the 77 on it that's preserved at Illinois," I said, "is that your last game jersey?"

"I don't know," Grange said. "It was probably a new jersey."

"Do you have any piece of equipment that you wore on the football field?"

"No," he said. "I don't have anything."

The traffic light changed, and we started across the street. "I don't even have an I-sweater," he said.

We walked about three paces.

"You know," Grange said, "I'd kind of like to have an I-sweater now."

## 1958

## Dick Schaap

## Lone Wolf of Tennis

FROM *Sport*

WHEN RICHARD ALONZO GONZALEZ stretches to the top of his toes, whips his right arm high in the air and serves a tennis ball at 112 miles an hour, he is doing more than simply powering the swiftest shot in tennis history. He is swinging at every Southern Californian who ever called a Mexican "Pancho," flailing at every tennis official who ever barred a youngster from a tournament, and whacking at every father who ever ordered his daughter to stop dating the kid from the wrong side of the tracks.

Richard Gonzalez is the greatest tennis player in the world today. He has considerable wealth and prestige, plus an incredible amount of ability — almost everything a man could want. But on his strong right shoulder sits the same chip that marks so many men who have overcome odds not of their own making. It is the chip that has made him the fiercest competitor in tennis, a relentless champion who must prove again and again that in all the world there is no one else so skillful. But it also has had a deeper, more significant effect. It has shaped Gonzalez into the lone wolf of tennis, a dark, brooding figure silhouetted against a rococo backdrop of fame, fortune and talent.

Gonzalez is a loner in the strictest sense of the word. While he was winning the most recent pro tennis tour, he did not travel with Lew Hoad, Tony Trabert and Pancho Segura in the spacious station wagons provided by promoter Jack Kramer. He drove alone in his own car, a souped-up Ford Thunderbird, picking his own routes and his own way stations. When the rest of the troupe checked in at one hotel he generally stayed at another. Usually he ate by himself, away from the bright lights and the noise. He rarely attended social functions, and when he did, he seemed to generate electric tension.

Once, the night before the tour made its annual stop in Madison Square Garden, Gonzalez went to a party on New York City's swank East End Avenue. Among the other guests was Gina Lollobrigida, the Italian movie actress who has been described as the most tempting seven syllables since "Come up and see me sometime." At the party, a press photographer suggested, quite logically, that Gina and Pancho pose for a picture together. Gina warmly agreed. Gonzalez seemed somewhat cooler. While the subjects waited, the photographer carefully adjusted his camera.

"Come on," Gonzalez snapped. "Let's get this over with."

Gina took a deep breath — and smiled.

The photographer checked his flash attachment.

"What are you waiting for?" Gonzalez demanded.

Gina smoothed her dress, wet her lips and laughed lightly.

"Stand a little closer together," the cameraman said. "Would you please smile, Pancho?"

Gonzalez scowled. "Take the damn picture," he said, and then delivered a brief lecture on the social and technological failings of press photographers. A short while later, Gina was still smiling and Gonzalez was still fuming. He left the party.

Yet the same man who verbally dissected the photographer can be genuinely pleasant and cooperative. It is one of the paradoxes of Gonzalez that he deeply wants to be friendly, but he instinctively fears anyone who might hurt or misuse him. On his most recent tour, he seems to have relaxed a little bit, but not much.

The genial, relaxed Gonzalez appears at strange times. Late one evening not long ago, he stopped in a restaurant for a light snack. It was after midnight and the match with Hoad, which had ended only 30 minutes earlier, had lasted more than two hours. He was thoroughly exhausted. Blisters seared his feet. He could easily have been curt and irascible.

As he entered the restaurant, Gonzalez spotted men seated around a table in a corner, all sipping tall glasses of white milk. "What's this," he asked, "the local milk club?" One of the men grinned. "No," he said. "We saw you play tonight and decided it was about time we got in shape."

For the first time all night, Gonzalez cracked a broad smile. He walked over to the milk table, postponing his own meal, and chatted for several minutes about tennis, conditioning and sports in general. When he was finished, he had won five lifelong fans.

His fellow professionals recognize Gonzalez' aloofness and change-ability, but, for the most part, they can neither predict nor explain his moods. Even Segura, the little Ecuadorian who is closer to Gonzalez than any other tennis player, admits that he is often puzzled by the champion. "Gorg's a funny guy," Segura says. "He's independent. He likes to be alone. I don't know why."

(The nickname of Gorg, or Gorgo, has stuck with Gonzalez since he won the 1948 U.S. Singles Championship and promptly lost half a dozen matches in a row to Ted Schroeder. Tennis writer Jim Burchard called Pancho "The Cheese Champ" which inevitably became Gorgonzalez — from Gorgonzola, an Italian cheese — and eventually Gorgo.)

Lew Hoad found Pancho's outward coolness no easier to handle than his service. "I guess," Hoad says, "that Gorg feels he can't be friendly with a fellow he has to try to beat every night. Maybe he's right. He does rather well, you know."

The only pro who advances a definite theory about Gonzalez is Tony Trabert. "He's got a persecution complex," Trabert insists. "I don't blame him for having had it originally. He was persecuted. Even his nickname was a form of persecution. In California, many prejudiced people call all persons of Mexican descent 'Pancho.' But things have changed since he was a kid. When people call him 'Pancho' now, they say it admiringly. It's time he got over his complex."

But as any psychiatrist will confirm, it is not easy to erase a feeling that has deep roots in childhood and adolescence. The first of Carmen and Manuel Gonzalez' seven children, Richard was born in Los Angeles on May 9, 1928. His father was a house painter and, although the family was never destitute, there was no extra money for luxuries. The Gonzalezes lived in a section of the south side of Los Angeles where a boy was considered an unqualified success if he grew up to become an auto mechanic.

One day, when Richard was seven years old, his father reluctantly gave him permission to cross the street alone and visit South Park, a local playground. The youngster set out on a scooter he had built from two-by-fours and roller skate wheels. When he reached the intersection, he did not stop or look or listen. He barreled into the street just as an automobile was approaching. The driver braked hard, but before the car could stop, its door handle hooked Richard's cheek. The accident left a scar several inches long. Today Pancho scarcely notices it. "Sometimes I forget which side it's on," he says.

But later there were less violent incidents that left more serious scars.

Gonzalez suffered one particularly depressing setback when he was 15. By then he was the best tennis player his age in Southern California. An above-average student, he decided his future was not in the classroom. He quit high school to spend all his spare time on the tennis court. As soon as Perry Jones, the czar of Southern California tennis, learned that Gonzalez had left school, he called the boy into his office.

"Richard," Jones began, evenly, "it isn't fair for you to play anybody who goes to school all day while you practice tennis."

"But Mr. Jones," Gonzalez said, "I don't want to go to school anymore. I want to play tennis."

Jones paused and leaned forward. "Until you return to school," he said, "I must ban you from all tournaments."

Gonzalez was crushed. He had embraced tennis, and tennis, in turn, had spurned him. Rumors spread that Jones barred Gonzalez because he was Mexican. This was not true, but by repetition, it became a popular theory. Even now, although Pancho concedes that the ban was justified, he still seems to think that somehow he should have been eligible for the junior tournaments.

Not until after four years had elapsed, including 15 months spent swabbing decks in the Navy, was Gonzalez reinstated. Then, suddenly, he received another emotional slap in the face. He had been dating an attractive blonde tennis player from the Los Angeles area. Everyone who saw them agreed that the dark, handsome Gonzalez and the pale, beautiful girl made a stunning couple. Everyone, that is, except her father. He told her to stop seeing Pancho. For a while, the girl tried deception. She took her school books, said she was going to the library and, instead, met Pancho. But, finally, the subterfuge proved too burdensome. They stopped dating.

No sensitive adolescent could experience such difficulties without absorbing considerable pain, and Richard Gonzalez was a sensitive boy. His hands were sensitive to the feel of a tennis racquet and his mind was sensitive to the sting of an antagonistic society. He reacted naturally; he withdrew into himself.

"I remember Pancho at the first tournament he ever played away from home," says Gussie Moran, the former Wimbledon sensation. "He was a quiet, shy boy who sat alone in the clubhouse. He had a forlorn look on his face and a chip on his shoulder. But when he stepped onto the tennis court, he was someone else. He was a god, patrolling his personal heaven."

Gonzalez, basically, is not much different today. He is a far better tennis player. He has sharpened his strokes to the point of perfection. Yet he still sits by himself in the locker room, his head sunk in his hands, the sweat dripping from his brow.

Until one night recently, I had seen Gonzalez play as a pro only in big cities where a sizable press corps, an army of tennis stars and the attendant fanfare always acted as a buffer against reality. The best way to understand and appreciate Richard Alonzo Gonzalez, I decided, was to see him on tour in small towns, winning most matches, living alone, traveling alone, eating alone. Late one rainy and foggy afternoon, after a quick stop at the insurance vending machine, I boarded a DC-3 and flew from Newark to join the pro tour in Corning, N.Y.

Corning is an industrial town on the southern tier of upstate New York, nestled near the Finger Lakes. It is known for producing Steuben crystal, the finest glass in the country, and Ted Atkinson, one of the finest jockeys. In Corning everything revolves around the glass works, and there, in a modern gymnasium, Pancho Gonzalez and Lew Hoad played the 67th match of their current series.

The picture of Gonzalez in action is unforgettable. For pure artistry, it rates with Musial, coiled and ready to strike; Cousy, flipping a backhanded pass; Snead, at the height of his backswing; and Arcaro, whipping a horse through the stretch. When he serves, Gonzalez strains, rears back and fires. Despite his size, he rushes catlike to the net, defying an opponent to return service. His long, light strides carry him to shots that lesser men never reach. On an overhead slam, he kicks up and follows through with frightening force. His nervous energy is never wasted. It is stacked up into a huge pile until the sheer weight of Pancho's ability falls upon an opponent, startling him at first, then bewildering him and, finally, crushing him.

For 32 games in the first set at Corning, Hoad refused to crack. Then Gonzalez broke service, held his own and won, 18–16. He also took the second set, 7–5, and stretched his series lead to five matches, 36–31. After the final point, champion and challenger shook hands perfunctorily, posed for several photographs and retired to the dressing room.

Hoad entered first, shuffled to his locker in the far corner and sat down. Gonzalez slumped onto a bench five feet away. For fully three minutes, neither said a word. The tension slowly ebbed from their faces. Then Gonzalez spoke. "Give me a towel, will you," he said to Hoad. The taut, hard lines that striped both men's brows began to disappear.

Gonzalez drained half a Coke with one swallow. "I was lucky," he said. "I hit two shots I never saw."

They changed their shirts and socks and walked back to the court for a doubles match. Just as Hoad's right arm swept up for the first serve, Gonzalez dropped his racquet loudly to the floor. "Excuse me, Lew," he said. "Did I disturb you?" The doubles served as an escape valve and, throughout the match, Gonzalez clowned openly, hitting balls behind his back and swinging vainly at shots ten feet beyond his reach. On one serve he tossed up three balls and smacked two of them. As the crowd laughed, Pancho relaxed.

Afterward, in the locker room, he stripped off his shoes and socks and poked at huge callouses beneath the large toe of each foot. "Look at this one," he said. "Full of fluid." A trace of fatigue darkened his face. "This is the toughest sport of all," he said. "Even in pro basketball, they don't play every night. Besides, when they're tired, they get a substitute. We don't. We play even when we're hurt. I've played with a sprained ankle. Lew finished a match one night after colliding with a wall and being knocked unconscious."

Gonzalez showered and put on a pair of slacks and a red polo shirt. Then he turned to me. "I'm going to get something to eat," he said. "Want to come along?" It was a stunning reversal in mood. Only six hours earlier, I had asked Gonzalez if I might ride with him. His answer had been pointed. "No," he had said. "I don't have any room."

As we walked from the locker room, a spectator shouted, "Good exhibition, Pancho." Gonzalez frowned. "It was not an exhibition," he said. "If it had been, it would not have gone on so long."

Outside, in a parking lot behind the glass works, Gonzalez unlocked his Thunderbird. Even in the dark, its yellow body and white top shimmered brightly. He switched on the electric ignition and a modified Cadillac engine roared mightily.

For Gonzalez, there is only one object more fascinating and more challenging than a tennis racket. It is a hot rod. The tennis champion of the world owns four automobiles that are constantly being tuned for drag-strip racing in California. Usually Pancho works as a mechanic, adjusting the steering, changing the gear ratio, pampering the engine. But sometimes he puts on crash helmet and goggles, settles into the driver's seat and hurtles down an old, abandoned air strip at speeds of more than 150 miles an hour.

Gonzalez let the motor idle for several minutes before he slipped into gear. Then he pulled out of the parking lot, turned right, crossed a bridge over the Chemung River and turned right again on Market Street. A few blocks down, he parked at the Athens Restaurant. He walked in and sat down on a stool by the counter. "Give me a rare hamburger steak," he told the waitress, "and a cup of coffee."

Gonzalez leaned forward, resting his elbows on the counter. "When I gain extra weight," he said, "I eat nothing but meat and liquids for a week to ten days. Then I get an awful hunger. It is something you cannot imagine. I see a piece of pie and I want it terribly."

While he ate, Gonzalez said nothing. After a second cup of coffee and a glass of milk, he smoked a cigarette and went out to the Thunderbird. By 1 A.M. he was back in his single room at the Centerway Motel. At 5, he fell asleep. "I replayed the match in my mind," he explained the next day. "I tried to figure out what I did right, why I won. Then I tried to decide how I would play the next match."

The next morning, while Hoad, Trabert and Segura toured the museum at the Corning Glass Works, Gonzalez tried to sleep. At 11:30, a steady, driving rain fell as I walked to the motel to meet Pancho. He was standing outside, conspicuous in his red polo shirt and a yellow sleeveless sweater, bent over the motor of his car. While the rain drenched him, he changed spark plugs. "You have to have two sets of spark plugs," he said, "one for the city and one for the open road."

For 15 minutes he fastened, checked and adjusted. Then he went into the motel's restaurant and ordered a bowl of Wheaties, two 3½-minute soft-boiled eggs, two cups of coffee and a glass of milk. After breakfast he returned to the car, checked it once more and packed his clothes and equipment. At 12:15, he climbed into the driver's seat and I got in beside him. We pulled away from the motel on Route 414 and started toward the next town on the tour — Clinton, N.Y., some 160 miles from Corning. Gonzalez began to relax. His hands slipped easily into the ten o'clock and four o'clock positions favored by race drivers. Two miles outside Corning, the motor suddenly sputtered, coughed and died. Despite Pancho's checks and double-checks, we were out of gas.

The road from Corning to Watkins Glen, roughly 30 miles away, is a bumpy one, but after we refueled, Gonzalez cruised along at 60 to 70 miles an hour. It was fast, but not dangerous driving. "I don't open it up," he said. "The T-Bird can do 145 miles an hour if I let it out. It'll go from zero to 115 in 15 seconds."

Then, abruptly, we headed into a sharp curve. I braked, involuntarily, where there was no brake. Gonzalez did not even take his foot off the accelerator. We whipped around the bend into a straightaway. "That's how I make up time," he said. "I don't slow down on the curves."

After we passed Watkins Glen, bounced through a long stretch of highway under construction and picked up Route 14, Lake Seneca glimmered in the rain on our right. Gonzalez ignored the scenery and concentrated on the road. "I like to travel alone," he said. "I can leave when I want. I don't have to wait for the others and they don't have to wait for me. When I want to stop and rest, I can."

Water leaked slowly through the windshield on the driver's side. "Is the feud between you and Kramer really bitter?" I asked.

"You're damn right it is," Gonzalez said. "The main reason I don't like Kramer is simple. Money."

He lit a cigarette and continued. "I'm the best player and I deserve the most money. Kramer has me over a barrel now. He's got me under contract and I can't do a thing about it. After it runs out, we'll see. Some people have suggested that I start my own tour, but that's not my idea. I'll probably stick with this. I want a better deal, though. Somebody's going to get hurt and it's not going to be me."

Under his contract, Gonzalez earns 20 per cent of the gross receipts, an income of close to $75,000 a year.

Gonzalez once dragged Kramer into court, seeking to have the contract changed. The judge threw out the case. Pancho had no legal complaint, he ruled; the contract was binding. Since then, even when they played gin rummy together at a nickel a point, Gonzalez and Kramer have not spoken. "Pancho never says a social word to me," Kramer says.

Gonzalez passed three cars easily, pulled into the right lane and began to talk about his family. "I've got three boys," he said, "Richard, Michael and Danny. Richard, the oldest, is ten and looks like he's going to be a good tennis player."

He leaned back and rubbed the scar on his left cheek. He might have been thinking about his personal troubles. He is divorced from his wife, Henrietta, and was planning to marry Madelyn Darrow, a former Miss Rheingold.

We passed Syracuse and the sun threatened to break through the heavy rain clouds. "Pro tennis is a funny game," Gonzalez said. "It's hard not to relax when you get far ahead. That's what Hoad did when he had me, 18–9. That's what I did when I had him, 32–23. He almost caught up and I had to bear down. I had to diet, practice, sleep, train. I'm training harder this year than I ever did before. I'm in the best shape of my life."

A few miles before Utica, we turned onto a side road that led into Clinton. On the outskirts of Clinton, we stopped at a service station. "Change the oil and fill it up," Gonzalez told the attendant. We ran down the road, dodging puddles, to a small restaurant. It was almost 3:30 and Pancho wanted a large meal before the night's matches. He finished off a bowl of soup, a sirloin steak, a lettuce and tomato salad, and a bottle of 7-Up. Then he hesitated. "I'll have a piece of apple pie," he said.

While he ate Gonzalez read the Utica newspaper. Next to a story announcing the arrival of the tour, there was an AP dispatch praising Jack Kramer for his work in training young Barry MacKay for the Davis Cup matches with Australia.

"Kramer's always taking the credit," Gonzalez mumbled. "I don't think he played once with the kid. We did all the work."

We hurried back to the service station and, after Pancho supervised the changing of his oil filter and bought a new set of spark plugs, we drove to the Clinton Arena, a barn-like construction that serves as home for the Clinton Comets in the Eastern Hockey League. We got out of the car, walked inside and shivered. It felt cold enough for a hockey game.

Jerry Dashe and Don Westergard, the tour's equipment managers, were installing the tour's portable canvas tennis court. "When's it going to be ready?" Gonzalez asked. "I want to get some practice."

"Not before five," Westergard called back. "You might as well go out until then."

We went back to the car and drove to a nearby hardware store. Gonzalez bought a set of wrenches, then visited the local Mercury agency. "I want some floor mats for a T-Bird," he said. "Have any?"

The owner picked out two black mats and handed them to Gonzalez. He started to fill out a sales slip. "Could you give me your name sir?" he said.

"Sure," Pancho answered. "Gonzalez."

"How do you spell that?"

"G-O-N-Z-A-L-E-Z."

"Oh," said the proprietor, "like the tennis player."

"Same guy," said Gonzalez.

"You're Pancho Gonzalez," the owner said, with considerable awe. "I've read about you."

Gonzalez turned his head away, slightly embarrassed. He didn't say a word, took his change and brought the mats out to the car. We returned to the arena, but the court still was not ready. Gonzalez stepped outside and, with his new wrenches, began working on the car. Shortly after five, he went inside, dressed and went on the court for a practice session with Segura. For half an hour, Big Pancho and Little Pancho volleyed back and forth, concentrating on lobs and backhands. Then they went into the locker room. Trabert and Hoad had just arrived. "Hey, Gorg," Trabert said, "what's that big bubble sticking out of the hood on your car?"

"That's an air filter," Gonzalez said, seriously. "I found that particles of dirt were getting into the motor and causing . . ."

"Okay, okay," said Trabert. "That's enough. You start to lose me when you get technical."

Before the preliminary match between Segura and Trabert began, Gonzalez walked outside and climbed into one of the Kramer station wagons. He tried to sleep, but had no success. Spectators, waiting in line for tickets, approached the station wagon and stared at Pancho as though he were the firing unit in a NIKE display. Children banged on the windows and asked for autographs.

Gonzalez gave up and went back into the locker room. In a few minutes, Trabert and Segura came through the door. "How'd it go, Segoo?" Gonzalez asked.

"No good, Gorg," Segura said. "He beat me again. He was really serving the ball tonight."

"How are the lights?"

"Not bad," Segura said. "Sometimes you lose the ball in them."

About 15 minutes before match time, the lines in Gonzalez' face started to harden again. By the time he ran onto the court, he was wearing his mean face, the one that he reserves for frightening opponents and reporters. But in the first set, Hoad refused to be frightened. His serve boomed across the net and skidded past Gonzalez. His passing shots and net game were superb. He easily polished off the champion, 6–2.

Then Pancho loosened up and, in 40 minutes, swept two sets, 6–3, 6–1, extending his tour lead to six matches.

When the match was finished, Gonzalez dressed quickly. The next day's match was scheduled in New Castle, Pa., almost 400 miles away.

There was a good deal of driving to be done and not much time for pleasantries. "I'll try to reach at least Buffalo tonight," he said. "Maybe I'll drive all the way." Then he climbed into the Thunderbird, switched on the ignition and, delicately, patiently, let the motor warm up. Alone in the small car, away from the crowds, the dark night enveloping him, Richard Gonzalez looked like a traveling salesman, a Willie Loman without samples. He shifted into reverse, backed out of his parking spot and started off, alone, on a 400-mile trip to a tennis match. He intended to win it.

1959

## John Lardner

······························································································

# "The Haig": *Rowdy Rebel of the Fairways*

FROM *True*

ONCE, a man named Walter Hagen had a date to play a morning round of golf in Tokyo with Prince Konoye, of the royal blood of Japan. Hagen appeared at the clubhouse at noon.

"The Prince has been waiting since ten o'clock," he was told.

"Well," said Hagen, "he wasn't going anywhere, was he?"

There you hear the voice of one who succeeded, as few members of our meekly desperate species have done, in adjusting the shape, speed and social laws of the world to his own tastes. Hagen was especially fearless of time; and, maybe for that reason, time has been respectful to Hagen. It's now more than a dozen years since the Haig quit playing even friendly golf. (It was no fun any more; the finest putting touch in the history of the game had been fatally marred by, he said, a "whisky jerk.")

That's a long while to be out of action, out of the hot news, and still to be constantly remembered. But Hagen, rusticating in a house on a hill by a lake in Michigan where the water is cold enough to chase Scotch without ice, remains a living force in sport. They still talk about him with an awe and wonder as fresh as in the days when he had the golf world in a bottle, as the old song goes, and the stopper in his hand.

"Golf never had a showman like him," Gene Sarazen said two or three years ago. "All the professionals who have a chance to go after the big money today should say a silent thanks to Walter Hagen each time they stretch a check between their fingers. It was Hagen who made professional golf what it is."

By land and sea, in airplanes and in Wall Street, the age of Walter

Hagen was the age of gorgeous individualism and golden soloists. In sports, the champions were Ruth, Dempsey, Tilden, Jones, Grange — and this fellow with sleek black hair, a full-moon face, and hooded, oddly oriental eyes, who dressed himself to shine like the Milky Way on a clear night, and who used to say, by way of explaining how life should be lived: "Don't hurry. Don't worry. You're only here on a short visit, so be sure you get a smell of the flowers."

Seemingly, Hagen lived by that rule. In earning more than a million dollars at golf, he spent money as fast as he made it and often a little faster. Once, after winning the Canadian Open, he wired ahead to a Montreal hotel, as the first step in a victory party: "Fill one bathtub with champagne." The cost of the party eventually came to $200 more than the prize money he'd won in the tournament.

But, like other things about Hagen, the gay, hedonistic code was deceptive. If he had the philosophy of a butterfly and the appetites of a Pasha, he had a brain like a pair of barber's shears.

In fact, he was full of contradictions:

1. "In swinging," said Mike King Brady, the old pro who first took him on the road in 1914, "Hagen sways like a rocking horse."

But, says Ben Hogan, in speaking of golf technique, there is a fundamental kind of rhythm which "could also be described as the *order of procedure*. Walter Hagen was probably the greatest exponent of this kind of rhythm ever to play golf."

2. Hagen was prodigal with cash, a high spender and tipper, a compulsive check-grabber, a plunger on long, bright motor cars and soft, bright clothing.

But — he took care years ago to fix things so that he lives in perfect security today, on royalties and commissions from golf equipment.

3. Hagen was a loner and an egotist at golf, a pitiless competitor. He used every trick in the book of psychology to trim his friends and fellow pros.

But — he raised the living standards and promoted the independence of all professional athletes as did no one else, even Babe Ruth. By sheer force of his own love of comfort and freedom, he carried his profession onward and upward on his back. He revolutionized the status of the golf pro — from janitor to social hero.

Hagen's first job as a club pro, in 1912, paid him $1,200 for eight months, and this was not unusual. For several years after that, few pros averaged better than $50 a week. Socially, club members treated them in a friendly but patronizing way, like a chauffeur or a valuable cook. In

1914, $75 was a pro's standard charge for an exhibition match. By 1915, Hagen was asking and getting $200 and $300 for an exhibition, and he was mixing freely with millionaires and needling them into $500 nassaus in private games. They took it and loved it. By the time he had planted his full, democratic, do-it-my-way-or-to-hell-with-you brand on golf and on society, the American pro was a big shot, with a limitless earning capacity — and the European pro had come out of the servants' entrance and knew himself to be a man, as good as his talent could make him.

4. Hagen was a party guy, a night-bird, a wrecker of training rules.

But — he was also a sure-handed, clear-eyed all-around athlete, a winner at the top level for 30 years. (He won the croquet championship of Florida in his first try at the game. And once he out-shot the whole field at a national live-bird shooting tournament.) Hagen didn't smoke or drink till he was 26. Then he became a chain-smoker, and went on winning. And when he discovered prohibition liquor, his luck stayed with him. It turned out that the man had a head like an old oaken bucket.

Take a look at him early on a hot summer morning in 1929. A golf fan stood in front of the Garden City Hotel on Long Island, admiring the dawn and thinking what a fine day it would be for the final round of the national PGA championship, when he noticed a dapper figure in a tuxedo approaching the hotel from out of the sunrise. It was Hagen — scheduled that afternoon to play Leo Diegel for the highest prize in professional golf. He had been training for the match by making a tour of Manhattan speakeasies. "Good morning," said Hagen, civilly.

"Good morning," said the startled fan. "Do you know that Diegel has been in bed since 10 o'clock?"

"No doubt he has, no doubt he has," said Hagen, as he walked on into the hotel. "But he hasn't been sleeping."

That was an accurate analysis — not only of Diegel, but of all Hagen opponents. A few hours later, Hagen won the championship by a score of 5 and 3.

The game with Diegel was one of a string of 29 PGA matches in a row that Hagen won, over a period of five years, from the best and smartest golfers in the world. In his time, he captured 11 national American and British titles, including the British Open four times and the U.S. Open twice. When he gave up the game at the age of 50, he had, in fact, proved everything.

Was he the greatest? His fellow pros said so in 1938, when they voted for him by two to one over Bobby Jones as the greatest tournament golfer they had ever seen. But "great" and "greatest" have become loose, flabby words in the sporting vocabulary. There were some who tried to describe Hagen more exactly, by calling him "the world's best bad golfer." Bob Jones himself once expressed the special, mortifying essence of Hagen even better, in something he said a few years ago, during the heyday of Ben Hogan.

In a way, Jones observed, a steady, consistent, mechanized player like Hogan makes an "easy" opponent at golf. Nothing he does surprises you; you can focus your mind on your own work. "But," Jones said, "when the other fellow misses his drive, and then misses his second shot, and then beats you out of the hole with a birdie, it gets your goat!"

He was speaking of Hagen — and Hagen had an answer to every criticism of this kind in one of his maxims: "The object of the game is to get the ball into the hole."

"Get your goat" is a gentle way of stating what Hagen did to Jones in a 72-hole match they played in Florida in 1926 for "the championship of the world" (and also, as will be noted again later, for the purpose of selling real estate). Hagen went from stump to bush to sand, and, in the end, beat Jones by the whopping margin of 12 and 11. His purse, the biggest ever paid a golfer for one match, was $7,600. Off the top of this sum, he peeled $800, and bought Jones a pair of diamond-and-platinum cufflinks.

"We must encourage the breed of amateur," Hagen explained sweetly. "They draw their share of the customers, and we take their share of the gravy."

So saying, he leaped aboard his Madame X Cadillac (a deluxe model of the period, of which Hagen owned the first specimen ever produced), and rode to his office to see how things were doing in the business (Florida golf promotion) which at that time paid him $30,000 a year and included, among other things, a blonde secretary who played the ukulele. The automobile was the latest in a line of flamboyant, Hagen-bearing vehicles that went well back into motor car history: a Chalmers, a Stephens-Duryea, a Chandler with an orange-and-black check, a red Lozier, a Pierce-Arrow, and in England, chartered Rolls-Royces and Austin-Daimlers.

This was the good life — the life toward which the Haig had begun to move a long time before, on the spring day when he climbed out the window of his seventh-grade classroom in Rochester, never to return to the field of formal education; at least, not regularly.

The schoolroom window commanded an irresistible view of the country club of Rochester. There, Hagen had first broken 80 in the year 1904, at the age of 11. As a caddie at the country club, he made 10 cents an hour, plus tips. His father, William Hagen, as a blacksmith in the railroad-car shops, made $18 a week. Once the younger Hagen had put the distractions of school behind him, he passed his father economically. A little later, he passed Andy Christy, the club pro, artistically. It cannot be said that Christy enjoyed this. In 1912, Andy went to the National Open in Buffalo with another pro, and took Hagen, who had become his assistant, along. In a practice round, Hagen shot the course in 73.

"I'm thinking," said Christy, who was shooting much higher, "that someone should be home minding the shop. You can catch a train at 5:45."

The quick trip to Buffalo was not, however, a complete blank for Hagen: a whole new world was unfolded to him there. He was struck half blind with inspiration by the sight of a golfer named Tom Anderson, who wore a white silk shirt with blue, red, black and yellow stripes, white flannel pants, a red bandanna around his neck, a loud plaid cap, and white buckskin shoes with wide laces and red soles.

By the time of the 1913 Open, at Brookline, Massachusetts, Hagen had reproduced the entire costume for his own use, except that he replaced the bandanna with an Ascot tie imported from London. This conservative touch was to be typical of his own evolving taste in clothes-horsemanship. He became a rainbow, but a smooth, sophisticated rainbow.

The 1913 U.S. Open at Brookline, which Hagen played in candy-striped shirt and red-soled shoes, was his first big tournament. It is famous today for the playoff in which a young American named Francis Ouimet beat out the British masters Vardon and Ray; few remember that Hagen finished fourth behind those three, narrowly missing the playoff. The next year, at 21, he took the title, tying the tournament record with 290.

The win was crucial — it saved Hagen from becoming a Philadelphia Phillie. The Phils had tried him out both as a right-handed pitcher and as a left-hand-hitting outfielder. Having tasted top money in golf, Hagen evaded their snares. The signs of ambidexterity, however, stayed with him for life. There was no right-hander in golf who could play the rare and occasionally vital left-handed shot better, from a tree or a wall or a water bank. Sometimes Hagen played it with a putter or the heel of a right-handed iron, sometimes with a left-handed club he carried for emergencies.

He had 85 other ways of beating you, as the pros of the old balloon-ball era discovered. The pros were, in the main, a dour, cautious, Scotsmanly lot. Once, in Florida, on the morning of a one-day $500 tournament, a group of them agreed to eliminate cabfare by accepting Hagen's invitation to drive them to the course in his new open-top car. Hagen appeared at the rendezvous a half hour late. "We must go like hell, men!" he cried, with a look at his watch. They did. It was several months before they recovered fully from the ride. Hagen won the $500.

The Al Jolson musical show "Sinbad" was playing Boston in 1919 at the time Hagen acquired his second U.S. Open title, at the Brae Burn course near there. Hagen had recently learned how to oil his metabolism with occasional "hoots." ("Hoot" was one of his favorite words for a drink of whisky. Another was "hyposonica.") He saw a good deal of the Jolson troupe, after showtime, during the tournament. A gala getaway party was arranged for the night following the last round of the Open. As things turned out, the last round left Hagen tied for first place with Mike Brady. This called for a playoff next day, but Hagen did not see his way clear to passing up the party.

In the dawn that followed the revels, he left the flower and the chivalry of "Sinbad," took a shower at his hotel, proceeded to the course by Pierce-Arrow, had two quick double Scotches in the clubhouse bar, and joined Brady at the first tee. Hagen, who did not feel entirely in the pink, decided that a dose of strategy was in order. Brady, prepared to do a man's work, had his shirt sleeves rolled well up toward the shoulders. "Listen, Mike," said Hagen, as they reached the second tee, "hadn't you better roll down those sleeves?" "What for?" Brady asked. "The gallery can see your muscles twitching," Hagen said. Brady hooked his tee shot violently, and lost the hole by two strokes. Hagen's margin at the end, as he won the championship again, was one stroke.

This, it should be noted, was medal play. Hagen's favorite style was match play, in which he could bring all the resources of his erratic long game, his murderous pitching and putting, his aggressive coolness, his concentration, and his sharp personal tactics to bear against one man. In the medal style of the open game, he was never happier than when he could reduce a tournament to man-to-man combat. The record shows — and it shows it of no one else in history — that in 30 years of big-league golf, Hagen never lost a playoff.

In private golf, in exhibitions, he tried always to introduce the personal element, the head-on gambling touch, that brought out his best. After the First World War, Hagen became the first important professional golfer to cut loose completely from the normal pro's life, a shop-and-lessons contract with a single country club. This led to endless exhibition tours. On tour, he always reached for the extra gamble.

At one strange club, he heard that the course record was 67, and offered to bet he would tie it. A member of the reception committee was wiling to stake $50 against him. "Well," Hagen said, "the sun is high, and we have lots of time. Maybe we can do better than fifty." Eventually, a pool of $3,000 was raised among members, which Hagen faded.

The membership then followed Hagen around the course in a body. On the last green, he needed to sink a 12-foot putt to tie the record. He tapped the ball, and yelled "Pay me, suckers!" before it dropped. It dropped.

A time was to arrive, and soon, when Hagen came to consider the British Open — especially on the seaside courses, lashed by wind and rain, with their shaggy rough and bony greens — as the truest test in golf, and a nagging challenge to himself personally. He was the first American-born golfer to win the British championship, at Deal in 1922. Before that, before he learned to throw away the effete book of American golf, with its high driving, pitching, and exploding, and its controllable greens, and to master the British technique of the low shot and the pitch-and-run, he was tossed back violently on the seat of his pants. On his first trip abroad, in 1920, British golf overpowered Hagen.

His playing partner on the last round was a civil old gentleman of 62, who became the only player Hagen beat in the tournament. The old gentleman finished 54th, Hagen 53rd. The American champion's golf gave the British many a dry chuckle. But Hagen startled the press by obtaining a printed retraction of one slightly nasty piece by the simple but unprecedented method of telephoning the paper's owner, Lord Northcliffe. Hagen followed this step by carrying the social revolution to France — a traditional spot for revolutions.

He traveled to the French Open at La Boulie, near Paris, with the British stars George Duncan and Abe Mitchell. The dressing room for pros was a stable, with nails for the players' clothes and stalls for the livestock. "If they don't let us use the clubhouse," Hagen told Duncan and Mitchell, appointing himself chairman of a committee of three, "we will pull out."

The British pros, limp with class consciousness, followed him into the president's office. The president finally yielded the point — though the three foreigners were the only ones to get into the clubhouse. Hagen won the tournament in a playoff with the French champion Eugene Lafitte.

Within the next few years, as the Haig made Europe and England his playground and the British Open title almost his private property, the force of his golf and his brash and gaudy independence knocked over the remaining social barriers one by one. Britain was shaken by a habit Hagen had of using first-prize money in the Open (it ran to about $300) to tip his caddy with.

The Prince of Wales, later the Duke of Windsor, followed Hagen around when he played, and automatically picked locks for him socially. (There's a story that on a green in Bermuda Hagen once said to the duke, "Hold the pin, Eddie." This is apocryphal, according to Hagen. "What I told him was, 'Hold the pin, caddie.'")

And while he removed the shackles from his fellow tradesmen, the Haig went on stealing their shirts and watches on the field of play. At La Boulie in 1920, striking a blow for liberty in France, he also ran Lafitte, his playoff opponent, dizzy. Hagen had heard that Lafitte hated to hurry his game. Hagen practically galloped around the course. At one hole, he climbed an uphill tee and drove before Lafitte had reached the top. Lafitte, panting after him, hurried his shot, and drove into the rough. The Frenchman lost the playoff by four strokes.

On the way to the playoff, Hagen used one of his favorite dodges, the wrong-club feint, to shake off Abe Mitchell. On a long hole, with his drive slightly ahead of Mitchell's, Hagen took his brassie from the bag as though to use it on the next shot. Big Abe went for the brassie too, and banged his ball into a row of trees that crossed the fairway. The Haig at once switched to his 2-iron, and hooked around the trees to a point just short of the green. The stroke he gained on this hole shut the Englishman out of the playoff.

The same ruse tricked Al Watrous out of a vital hole one day in the PGA. Hagen's tee shot fetched up against the foot of a tree. He saw where it went, but Watrous didn't. "You're away, Al," Hagen said, nonchalantly hefting his brassie. Watrous could see Hagen's club, if not Hagen's ball. He grabbed his own brassie, though what he needed was a control club for a deliberate slice. His ball bounced off a tree and into a brook. Hagen swiftly replaced the wood with a niblick, back-handed his own ball out of trouble, and won the hole and match.

It was a finesse, too, that started Bobby Jones off to disaster in their great "world championship" match in Florida in 1926. The first hole was a par 4. All its nastiness lay just beyond the green. Hagen, for his second shot, ostentatiously chose a 4-iron, and hit the ball a little softly — on purpose, critics have said. He landed short of the green. Jones, noting the shortness, used a 2-iron, overshot the carpet, had to struggle back, and lost the hole. From there on, Hagen never looked back as he marched to glory and a bag of gold and rubbed the great amateur's nose in the dirt.

It was heavily inflated dirt. The Florida land boom was on, and both Jones and Hagen had an interest in it. Hagen was president of the Pasadena Golf Club at St. Petersburg at $30,000 a year (plus a bonus of a couple of "hot lots"). Friends of the Jones family were anxious to glorify the real estate at Sarasota, down the line. The match consisted of 36 holes of golf at Jones's course, Sarasota, and 36 more a week later at Hagen's course. The region was crawling with butter-and-egg men, promoters, suckers, and other golf fans, and the air was charged with the rich flavor of gambling and excitement that Hagen loved.

The two players were clearly the world's best: Jones was American amateur and past Open champion, Hagen held the PGA and British Open titles.

Hagen took only 53 putts for the first 36 holes, and was 8 up at the end of them. On one green, after their second shots, Jones lay 40 feet from the cup and Hagen 20. Jones, using painstaking care, sank the ball — his finest putt of the match. "Whaddya know," shouted Hagen gaily, "he gets a half!" And while the meaning of these words was just coming home to his victim, he holed his own 20-footer with a quick slap. It was a gesture that Jones never forgot.

In the second half of their Florida "world series," the Hagen-Jones match went downhill in a rout. It ended at the 25th green. In one history-making stretch of 9 holes, Hagen needed only 7 putts — he got by on 7 long ones and 2 chip-ins. If the feat has ever been equalled, it was not done in the glare of the spotlight that bathed Hagen that day. The Haig agreed with other experts, as a general thing, that he always played his best golf with the 7- and 8-irons and the putter — the quick-death shots that can wipe out all past sins and break an opponent's heart. "I expect to make seven mistakes a round," Hagen used to say. "I always do. Why worry when I make them?" The short game always bailed him out.

He had an artist's passion for putting, and an engineer's skill at judging the roll and grain of a green. There was a putt in the PGA in

1925 that stopped Leo Diegel as though he had been shot with a gun. Diegel had Hagen 2 down with 2 to go in their quarter-final match. A 40-foot putt gave Diegel a 4 for the seventeenth hole; Hagen's second shot had left him 15 feet to the left of the cup on a fast downhill green with a double roll. Hagen plotted the putt with the help of a small leaf that lay uphill from the hole to the right. The ball had to stop at the leaf, catch the momentum of the green there, and roll downhill at an angle to find the cup. It did all of that. As it dropped, Diegel fell flat on his face on the green. Hagen won the next hole easily, squaring the match, and ended it on the fourth extra hole. Or, it might be said, he won it on the third extra hole. There, an intricate putt put Hagen down in 4. Diegel had a curving 30-inch putt to tie. It was a tricky one, as both men knew in their hearts. Suddenly, Hagen knocked Diegel's ball aside. "I'll give you that one, Leo," he said. "Let's play another hole." The surprise of the gesture wrecked what was left of Diegel's nerves. Overwrought, he blooped his next drive into a hayfield, and Hagen marched grandly on to the title.

Though he gave up normal pro-shop duties when he was 26, Hagen was a master club-maker and club-valet. Back in his early days, to earn a few extra dollars, he had worked as a mandolin-maker, and as a wood finisher in a piano factory. However, he had never made mandolins or finished pianos in the deep south, where conditions are a little different. In Florida, in the 1920's, the Haig launched a golf club factory that he figured would make him rich for life. In a roundabout way, it did. The clubs he produced were like poems by Keats — in Florida. When they were shipped north, however, the colder weather warped and shrank their shafts till they rattled like a spoon in a cup of coffee.

Hagen was in the red for $200,000 at the point where another rich friend, L. A. Young, Detroit's leading auto spring tycoon, put up his bail. The plant was shifted to Michigan. Under Young's management, and later under the Wilson Co.'s, it has provided the royalties that have kept Hagen in comfort, bright plumage, fast cars, and "hoots" for the rest of his life.

The adventure proved what every golf pro in the world came to be convinced of in time: that you cannot top a man who has God and the angels on his side. At the Inwood course, where he won his first PGA title in 1921, Hagen liked to play the seventeenth hole by driving down the eighteenth fairway — it gave him a more open shot at the green. During the night after the first round of the PGA, Jock Mackie, the home pro, with the backing of a group of local comedians, set up a big willow tree between the two fairways in such a position as to block Hagen's drive. The sudden sight of the tree, as he teed up his ball, gave the Haig a start. At almost the same moment, a gust of wind shook loose the tree's wiring and knocked the willow over on its side. "Excellent timing," said Hagen smugly, and made his usual drive.

Even the spectators, as time went on, became infected by a sense of the fellow's omnipotence. There was a one-day tournament at Catalina Island, in the 1920's, for which Hagen showed up late — he had been shooting goats in the mountains all morning with William Wrigley, the island's owner. Hagen raced around the course to finish before dark. With three holes to go, he learned of a low score by Horton Smith which led the field at the moment, with everyone in but Hagen. Seeing Smith in the gallery, Hagen called out genially, "Well, kid, I can tie you with a 3–2–1!" He got the 3, then got the 2, and then announced to the crowd, winking one inscrutable eye, "Now for the hole-in-one!" The hole was 190 yards. Hagen's tee shot hit the flag gently and stopped a foot from the cup.

Few mortal men can call a hole-in-one. And yet, Hagen once bet $10 even money at a short hole, in an exhibition match, that he would sink his tee shot, and then sank it. "The idea, when betting even money on a 100,000-to-1 shot," Hagen said mysteriously, as he pocketed the sawbuck, "is to recognize the one time when it comes along. It is done by clean living."

As noted, the U.S. PGA tournament was Hagen's special oyster for five straight years. It had to be. A cup went to the winner — and Hagen, unknown to everyone, had mislaid the cup. The name of this object was the Rodman Wanamaker Trophy, valued at $1,500. One day in 1925, Hagen, the temporary owner, left it in a taxicab in New York. He was always careless with silver. In 1926, he won the championship again. "You already have the Cup, Walter," the officials told him, "so keep it."

The same thing happened in 1927. In 1928, however, the patient Leo Diegel broke through and won the title. Hagen was asked to turn over the cup. "Well, I would like to," he said, "but I haven't got the slightest idea where it is." The pros themselves saved the situation by chipping in for another cup for Diegel.

Hazy or not as to certain kinds of detail, the old brain continued to perform like a shears, in one way, and like an oaken bucket, in another, as the Haig's golfing years drew to an end. They tell of a day in Belleair, Florida, in the West Coast Open, which followed a long, hard night. Hagen groped his way to the course, and took three practice shots. He topped a spoon shot, which traveled 40 feet. He topped a 2-iron shot, which traveled 20 feet. He topped a 5-iron shot, which traveled 6 feet. "Okay, I'm ready to play," Hagen said. He toured the course in 62.

And the Haig himself tells in his breezy book, *The Walter Hagen Story,* of another morning-after when his practice shots did the same kind of tricks, and the bright sun cut into his eyeballs like a knife. It was in Tampa, in 1935, when Hagen was 42. With a final hooker of corn liquor in him, he moved out from the soothing shadows of the locker room into the shimmering heat of the morning. Near the first tee, he saw three old friends from the Philadelphia Athletics ball club, Jimmy Foxx, Mickey Cochrane and Cy Perkins, waiting with the gallery to watch him tee off in the tournament. Hagen tottered over to them and shook their hands with loving enthusiasm. "Hiya, Jimmy. Hiya, Mike. Hiya, Cy," he said. "Haven't seen you in a hell of a long time." "Good luck, Haig," said Mr. Foxx, Mr. Cochrane and Mr. Perkins.

Hagen played the first nine holes more or less by instinct — and on the ninth green found himself needing a short putt for a 30. Looking up at the gallery, he noted with surprise and pleasure the presence of three old friends, Jimmy Foxx, Mickey Cochrane, and Cy Perkins. The Haig beamed, and walked over to shake hands. "Hiya, Jimmy. Hiya, Mike. Hiya, Cy," he yelled. "Haven't seen you in a hell of a long time."

The three Athletics were convulsed by this second ceremony. Their laughter faded into awe when they heard Hagen's score. He sank the putt, took a 64 for the day, and won the tournament with 280. It was to be Hagen's last win in any big tournament.

But once in a while, in the few golfing years that were left to him, the magic of his bold, sudden-death touch came back again. Hagen was in his forties when he broke the course record at Inverness, Scotland, with a 64. In 1943, at the age of 50 he captained a pickup team against the American Ryder Cup team, and shot a 71 in his first match. Thus, his career overlapped to a degree those of the stars of the next generation. He saw them all — and, with the cheerful arrogance of a giant of the days when men were men, he gave them nothing. If they were brought together in their respective primes, he says, he, Jones and Sarazen could beat Snead, Hogan and Middlecoff, match or medal, for money, chalk or marbles. Modern equipment and golf-course engineering have lowered scores. But the fewer, cruder clubs of the old days increased the skill of the players. And by playing in all weathers, dirty and clean, they acquired a strength and wisdom, down to the marrows of their bones, that the new men cannot equal.

Until he settled in the house he lives in today — on Long Lake, near Traverse City, Michigan, with big fish to the right of him and tall highballs to the left and a sleek paunch like a Mongol chieftain's — the Haig never had a permanent home. The need of crowds, new crowds, with new faces and tastes (and new money), kept him tramping about the world for years, to England, Ireland, France, Scotland, Germany, Africa, Hawaii, Australia, New Zealand, China, the Philippines, Japan.

Even when he wasn't playing, the crowds still came to him. Johnny Farrell, himself a U.S. Open champion of the 1920's, was playing a major tournament one day, and burning up the course. Al Watrous walked over from a nearby tee to pass the time of day. "How's it going, Johnny?" he asked. "Terrific!" Farrell said. "I can't miss. Looks like I may break the course record."

"That's fine," Watrous said. He looked around. "Where's your gallery?" Farrell smiled philosophically. "Over behind the caddie house," he said, "watching Hagen play mumblety-peg."

The new men cannot hope to equal Hagen as a showman — but they play for big money today chiefly because Hagen boosted the price scale, by his showmanship. The Haig used to say: "Make the hard ones look easy, and the easy ones look hard." He did, and for 30 years, hard and easy, he made them all.

## Jimmy Breslin

······································································································

# Racing's Angriest Young Man

FROM *True*

THE SHACK was on stilts so the floor wouldn't be against the ground in wintertime. But it didn't matter because when you went out to the creek for drinking water and brought it back in a basin, the way Bill Hartack had to before dinner every night, any of it that would drip on the floor quickly turned to ice. A pot-bellied stove was the only warm thing in shack number 371 and this does not constitute a heating system, even for a tiny three-room shack. But it was all they had because Hartack's father worked at soft coal in the mines around Colver, Pennsylvania, and there was no money in this. Nor was there much of a life in the shack. Hartack's mother had been killed when he was 7 and he had to raise his two sisters while his father dug coal.

You always remember this when you tell about Bill Hartack, the talented jockey who is one of the most controversial people in sports. It might make him easier to understand, you think.

But then Hartack will be at a race track, acting the way he did at Churchill Downs last May 7, and you forget everything because there is only one way to describe him. You say, simply, that his attitude is *to hell with everybody* and you have captured Hartack.

At 4:30 that afternoon, a guy in khaki work shirt and pants who is an assistant starter at Churchill Downs came up to Hartack's horse, a blaze-faced colt named Venetian Way. The guy took the horse by the bit, let him prance for a moment, then led him into stall number nine of the starting gate so they could begin the Kentucky Derby.

When the 14 horses all were locked into the gate, they slammed nervously into the tin sides and fronts of the stalls and the jockeys were calling "Not yet" and "No chance, boss" to the starter and there was a lot of noise and tension. Then the bell rang and the gate clacked open and, with riders yelping, the horses came out. Each made a leap first, because a race horse always is surprised to see the ground when the gate opens and he jumps at it. Then the horses started to run with the long, beautiful stride of a thoroughbred and there was a roar from the big crowd.

Hartack pushed Venetian Way into fourth, then took a snug hold on the reins. His horse was full of run, but Hartack wanted to keep him fourth, just off the leaders, and he stayed there until they were running down the backstretch. Then it turned into no contest. Bally Ache, one of the favorites, was leading. But not by enough. Tompion, the top choice, was in third position but he was creaking. On the final turn, Hartack let his horse out. Venetian Way made a big move and simply ran past Bally Ache as they swung by the five-sixteenth pole and headed into the long stretch.

With the thousands of people screaming from the three-decked stands, Venetian Way began widening the space. Hartack seemed to become frantic as his horse took over the race. He was whipping with his left hand and rolling from side to side in the saddle, the way the book says a jockey should not ride but the way Hartack always does. At the eight-pole Venetian Way had four lengths and Hartack was a wild, all-out jock giving the horse the kind of ride you must have when the purse is $160,000. Venetian Way won big.

After the winner's circle ceremonies, Hartack came into the crowded jockeys' room. At Churchill Downs, everything is a rotting, soot-covered mess and the jocks' room isn't much better. It is cluttered and steamy and, at this moment, was mobbed with reporters. It didn't look like much of a place, but it always has been one of the great sights in a jockey's life. You love everything when you win a Derby and it is all one big thrill of money.

But Hartack came into the room with that quick, long stride of his and his brown eyes flashed. He gave the reporters a dark look and said nothing as he went to his locker. He was obviously about to make a scene. There was no sense trying to relate him to a shack in Pennsylvania now.

The explosion came the moment the first newsman opened his mouth. "Willie," he began, "when did you think you had the race won?"

"Jeeez!" Hartack snapped. "Don't call me Willie. That's disrespectful. The name is Bill. And *that* is a stupid question. I stopped answering that one forty years ago. When you ask me an intelligent question I'll answer you."

People are encountered in all walks of life with a chip on their shoulder because of harsh backgrounds. But you would have to be born of Murder, Inc. to be this angry after winning a Kentucky Derby.

For those who did not walk out on this blast, Hartack had a short description of the race, along with his usual course in journalism for those present. Reporters, he said, misquote him. And, he made it clear, newspapermen bother him. In fact, he didn't want to be bothered by anything except riding. Then he left to ride a horse in the eighth race. He finished second and was even madder after that. *To hell with everything, Hartack says, except getting home first on a horse.*

Winning horse races is something he can do. He has had two winners and a second in four Kentucky Derby rides. He won a Belmont Stakes, a Preakness, two Florida Derbys, the Flamingo, the Woodward, Arlington Classic. He has won virtually every major race the sport has and you can tap out that this is going to be the story for years to come. Just as big as the story they will go on making out of Hartack's behavior. For this is a kid who simply will not bend. It is either his way or you can go home, and most people don't like his way.

Two days after the Kentucky Derby, Hartack was sitting in the coffee shop of the Bo-Bet Motel, which is a short distance away from the Garden State Race Track in Camden, New Jersey. He had on a black sports jacket and gray slacks and a crisp white shirt which was open at the collar. He is 27, but he looks younger because he is only 5 feet, 4 inches and weighs 114 pounds. But when he toyed with the cup of coffee in front of him and started to talk you could see this was no little kid who could be moved around easily. And the guys at the table with him — Felix Bocchicchio, the old fight manager who owns the motel, Scratch Sheet Pestano, the jockey's agent, and a couple of newspapermen — did all the listening.

"There's only one thing that counts," Hartack was saying. "Words don't mean anything. They can misquote me all they want or write something bad about me, but the only thing that counts is the chart of last Saturday's race. It says Venetian Way, number one. It don't say nothing else. And nobody can change it. Everything else, they can have. The only thing I'm accountable for in this business is the race I ride. I have to stand up for the owner of the horse, the trainer and the people who bet on him. And I have to see another jock doesn't get hurt because of me. I don't have to worry about anything else. And I wish they wouldn't worry about me. Everybody is trying to run my life so hard they haven't got time to run their own."

He jammed a filter-tip cigarette between his teeth and started to light it. His speech was over. And he had left very little room for rebuttal. No matter what he was like, he had just brought home a 6–1 shot in the biggest race in America, and you had no argument.

You rarely do. Six weeks later, he came out of the gate in the Belmont Stakes aboard an 8–1 shot named Celtic Ash and for a half mile he held Celtic Ash back 10 lengths off the leaders. That was how he had been told to ride the late-running horse and Hartack followed instructions to the stride. First money was $96,785 and Hartack would get 10 per cent of it, but this didn't cause him to get jumpy and move up his horse too early, as nearly all of them do. He just sat there, way out of it. It took strong nerves. At the half-mile pole he moved to the outside to get a clear path in front of him. Going into the last big turn, he finally let Celtic Ash out. Then he started to slam and kick and push at the horse and it all worked out. Hartack came into the stretch with a live horse under him and won by five and a half lengths over Venetian Way — with whom Hartack had parted company after the Preakness because of a disagreement with the trainer. It's hard to argue against winners that pay 8–1.

Vic Sovinski, Venetian Way's trainer, found this out. He is a big ex-baker from Kankakee, Illinois, who has been accused of training a horse as if he were slapping together a tray of prune Danish. At Louisville, before the Derby, Sovinski was around knocking Hartack's brains out over the way Bill had ridden the horse in a warmup race the week before. Sovinski wanted the horse worked out an extra two furlongs after the finish. Hartack, who found the muddy going was bothering his horse, didn't push Venetian Way during the work. Sovinski said he loafed. Hartack thought he had saved the horse from being senselessly worn out. The press, always receptive to knocks on Hartack, trumpeted Sovinski's views. The Derby, of course, took care of that argument.

But after Venetian Way ran a poor fifth in the Preakness, Sovinski blew up again and yanked Hartack off him. The jockey promptly jumped on Celtic Ash. Then he explained the case of Venetian Way.

"Horses reach a peak, then they need a layoff," he said after the Preakness. "Venetian Way needed a freshener. He didn't get it. So he ran two races back in the pack. Then he was up again and ran second in the Belmont. Was I glad to beat him in the Belmont? What do I care? I don't have time to worry about particular horses I beat. I just want to beat them all."

In the Venetian Way case, Hartack was mostly silent for one of the few times in his career. This was because there was a steady stream of talk around the tracks that Venetian Way had been a sore-footed horse and only an analgesic called butazolidin had soothed him at Churchill Downs. It was ruled illegal at the Preakness and elsewhere. Hartack did not care to get into any discussion of this.

But in just about every other storm to come up during his career, he has been in there saying exactly what was on his mind. Because of this, people constantly compare him to baseball's Ted Williams. This is an untrue comparison. Williams is nasty, in general, only to sportswriters and spectators. When stacked against Hartack's style, this is like hating Russia. Anybody can do it.

Hartack goes all the way. He takes on anybody, from a groom to a steward or an owner of horses or a track itself and if he thinks he is right you can throw in Eisenhower, too, because while he can be tough and unmannerly and anything else they say about him he is not afraid.

He is a little package of nerves who has been suspended for using abusive language to stewards, for fighting with another jockey, for leaving the track and not finishing his day's riding because he lost a photo finish. He snaps at writers, agents, owners or anybody else in sight. The people who have anything good to say about him are few.

But nobody ever can say Hartack doesn't try. When he rides a race horse, he is going to do one thing. He is going to get down flat on his belly and slash whip streaks into the horse's side and try to get home first. Which is all anybody could want from a jockey.

But even those few people who have a good relationship with him will tell you that he is no fun when he loses. He is unbearable, no matter who is around. Since jockeys lose more often than they win, meetings with Hartack are on a catch-it-right basis. Most people don't like him because of this. But if there is anybody in sports who can afford to act this way, it is Hartack. He comes honest.

"Bill can walk on any part of a race track," Chick Lang, who used to be his agent, said one day last summer, "and he doesn't have to duck anybody. He can look everybody in the eye. There is nobody, no place, who can come up with a story on him about larceny or betting or something like that. How many can you say that about?"

Lang was extolling the rider while having a drink at a bar near Pimlico Race Track, where he now is employed. After six years of doing business with Hartack and taking down $50,000 a year for it, Lang found even the money couldn't soothe his nerves any more.

"It became just one big squabble," Lang said. "Bill would be fighting with me, then with an owner or a newspaperman or a trainer and it just got to be too much for both of us. He acts unhappy all the time. He acts as if he hates everything about what he's doing. I don't know what it is."

This drive, which makes Hartack a person who wants to win so badly he upsets you, comes from classic reasons. A boyhood in a Pennsylvania coal town during the depression does not make you easy going and philosophical about life. For a year and a half the family lived on the 50 cents a day credit at the company store which Bill's father earned by digging soft coal. For 50 cents a day, you lived on potatoes.

On December 13, 1940, Hartack's mother, father and year-old sister Maxine got into a battered car his father had borrowed so he could make the 30-mile drive to the mine company office where he was to be paid. By this time, miners were being paid money instead of potatoes. On the way, a trailer truck slammed into the car, throwing it down a hill. Bill's father was in the hospital for 10 weeks. Maxine, the baby, had to stay for a year. Bill's mother died on Christmas morning. He and his sister Florence, who was 6 then, were taken care of by neighbors. It was not a good day for a kid.

"I barely remember it," Hartack says. But you figure he carries it with him someplace, whether he knows it or not.

A year later, the Hartack's shack caught fire and the four of them barely escaped the flames. They moved in with some other people while his father built a new house.

With his father working the long hours of a miner, Hartack took over the job of raising his two sisters. He saw they were up in the morning and had breakfast and made school. At night he cooked dinner for the family. As for himself, school in Black Lick Township was rough; Bill was small and the other kids, big-necked sons of miners, beat hell out of him.

So Hartack took it out on schoolbooks. He was valedictorian of his high school class.

When he graduated, at 18, Bill was thinking about an office job in Johnstown. Anything but the mines. When the office job didn't materialize, Hartack's father spoke to Andy Bruno, a friend who was a jockeys' agent. Bruno agreed to get Bill a job with horses. Hartack gave his son a dollar and let him drive away with Bruno to the Charlestown, West Virginia, track. Hartack picked up horses quickly. After he rode that first winner, he never stopped.

With this background, you'd think, it would be impossible for Hartack to miss. He had all the hunger and sorrow and hardness a kid ever would need to drive him to the top. It is the standard formula for successful athletes. But there have been fighters who have come out of the slums and they quit when you come into them and there are jockeys who had hunger and should be all out, but when it gets tough they shy away from the rail and take the easy way home.

Hartack, when he first came to the track, brought more than hunger with him. You can find that out by talking to his father. Bill Hartack, Sr., is a slight man with close cropped brown hair which has only a little gray in it, a thin mustache and a slight European accent. He was asked if Bill's early years were what made him so tough when he loses.

"Part of it," his father said, "but not all. I see him today how he acts and I don't say anything because he's just the same as I was. When I worked it was piece work. You got paid for the amount of coal you loaded. I set a record for soft coal that lasted until they brought in machines. I worked from when the sun came up to when the sun came down. And even when I was getting only that 50 cents a day for food I worked like that. I'd come to work with only some water in my lunch pail, not even a piece of bread, but I couldn't let anybody dig more coal than me. Once, another fella dug more than me during a week. I was so mad that when I went home I couldn't sleep nights. I couldn't wait to get back and dig more coal than him. It had me crazy. You couldn't talk to me."

"The boy is just like him," Bocchicchio said. "When he first came to stay with me here, I'm looking for him one day. It's a Sunday. He ain't been out of his room for dinner the night before and now breakfast and lunch has gone by and I don't see him. It's getting dark and I'm worried. I go over to his room and knock on the door and he let me in. He was still in bed. He don't want to talk. So I leave him alone. But I get right on the phone with Bill here and I ask him what he wants me to do. He says, 'Did he have any winners yesterday?' I says no. So he laughs. 'He'll be all right in time for the track,' he tells me. That's what this kid is like. If he don't win, you can't talk to him."

"When I was young," Mr. Hartack said, "I had a terrible temper. I fight. In the mines I argue with anybody. But you find when you get older, you mellow and you're not so mad any more. Bill will be like that. It will take a little while, but he'll mellow. But he'll still want to win. That he'll never get over."

This win-or-shoot-yourself attitude of Hartack's comes out, during a race, in the form of a rail-brushing, whip-slamming kid who will take any chance on a horse to win. Regarded on form alone, Hartack seems to be a poor rider. The secret of being a jockey is to keep a good-looking seat on a horse. Hartack, on the other hand, does it all wrong. He rolls from side to side in such a pronounced manner that even an amateur from the stands can see it.

"The form doesn't look classic," Jimmy Jones of Calumet tells you, "but it really doesn't matter none, because he has a way of making horses run for him. And that's what the business is."

Horses ran for Hartack from the start. When Bill came to Charlestown, Bruno, the agent friend of his father's, turned him over to trainer Junie Corbin, a veteran trainer on the small, half-mile track circuit. Hartack had no particular interest in becoming a jockey when he arrived, but under Corbin he learned the business.

On October 10, 1952, with just two races behind him, he held onto a horse named Nickleby for dear life and came home on top to pay $18.40 at Waterford Park, West Virginia. Since then, he has never stopped. By 1954 he was one of the top jockeys on the half-mile circuit. A year later Corbin ran into trouble with his stable — a groom had given caffeine to a horse. When Corbin was suspended for this, his bankroll couldn't take the layover. So he sold Hartack's contract for $15,000 to the big Ada L. Rice Stable. Chick Lang was in the picture as agent now and at the first opportunity, a year and a half later, he and Hartack went free lance, meaning they could take whatever mounts were open. Calumet Farm asked for a first call on Hartack — and got it because of the horseflesh they were putting under Bill's rear end each day.

From then on he made it big. In 1957 his horses won a total of $3,331,257 in purses. This is a record for a jockey. He also won 43 stakes, which topped a mark set by Eddie Arcaro. As a rider he is in a special little class with Arcaro and Willie Shoemaker. And in three of the last six years Hartack has been off by himself as national riding champion.

He has taken his father out of the mines and put him on a farm he bought at Charlestown, West Virginia. He has his younger sister in college. And life for him has become a series of new hi-fi sets, a different date whenever he picks up a phone, plenty of money — and live horses.

Hartack, like most people who don't have to live with women, is not against them. "There must be 150 girls around Miami I can call up for dates," he says. The situation is similar in Louisville or Oceanport, New Jersey, or wherever else he rides for a living. But it is strictly on a spur-of-the-moment basis. Riding horses and winning on them is basically his whole life.

Money or acclaim never will change his attitude. A look at him in his own surroundings shows this. One warm Tuesday morning last February, for example, Hartack stepped out of his $50,000 brick-and-redwood ranch house in Miami Springs and walked across the lawn to a beige, spoke-wheeled Cadillac which was in the driveway. He keeps the car outside because the big garage has been turned into a closet to hold his 150 suits.

It was 11:45 A.M. when Hartack pulled away from the house and started for Hialeah. The street was lined with palm trees and expensive houses. Sprinklers played on the lawns and the sun glinted on the wet grass. Hartack was fresh-eyed. He had slept for 11 hours and when Paul Foley, a guy who stays with him, woke him up, Bill took a shower, swallowed orange juice and coffee and left for the job of riding horses. For the last five years he has been going to his business like this and making anywhere from $150,000 to $200,000 a year. For anybody who ever has had to go to work hours earlier each morning, packed into a train with nervous, bleak-faced commuters who spend most of their time at home two-stepping with bill collectors, Hartack's way of life is the kind of thing you would steal for.

Hartack didn't talk as he drove to the track. He was thinking about the horses he would ride that day. At night, he reads the *Racing Form* and carefully goes over every horse in each race and as he does this he tries to remember their habits. One will swing wide on a turn, he will tell himself, so if he gets a chance he will stay behind that one and then move inside him on the turn. This reading and remembering is something a jockey must do or he isn't worth a quarter. Hartack, as he drove to the track, ran over the horses in his mind. He was mute as he pulled the car into the officials' lot at the track. His face was solemn as he walked through the gate and into the jockeys' room. Inside, he undressed, put on a white T-shirt and whipcord riding pants, then sat quietly while a valet tugged on his riding boots. The other jockeys paid no attention to him except for a nod here and there and Hartack returned it. Then he took out the program and the *Racing Form* and began to look at them again.

"How do you feel," a guy asked him.

"Terrible," he said. "My stomach bothers me. It always bothers me." He kept reading the paper. It was the best you ever will get in the way of conversation when Hartack is on a track.

Outside, Chick Lang was standing on the gravel walk in front of the racing secretary's office. He was shaking his head. Lang is a heavy, round-faced, blond-haired guy of 32. He had been at the barns at 5:45

A.M. talking to trainers and owners and making deals with them for Hartack to ride their mounts.

"I don't know whether life is worth all this," Lang was saying. "You saw how he was today? Concentrating, serious. Nobody allowed to talk. That's fine. It's the way he wants it and that's the way it should be. But what about other people? Don't you think he should give them something, too? Last week, on Wednesday, he went to the coast to ride Amerigo in the San Juan Capistrano Handicap.

"Before he left we talked and decided that he wouldn't take any mounts here until Monday. That was yesterday. So I went out and booked him on seven horses. What happens? Sunday night he calls me from Las Vegas. 'I can't get a plane out of here,' he said.

"Well, you've been to Vegas. They run planes out of there like they were streetcars. But that's what he tells me. Now I've got to get on the phone and start trying to find trainers and tell them Hartack can't ride the next day. It embarrasses hell out of me. Here I make commitments and then I have to break them. It's terrible."

Trouble is something Hartack will take — or he will make — and he doesn't care about it. And while carrying around this winning-is-all-that-matters attitude he has had plenty of jams.

The business of newspapermen, for example. Hartack has one of the worst relationships any athlete ever has had with newspapers and he is not about to improve it.

Now many people do not like sportswriters, particularly the wives of sportswriters, and in many athletic circles it is considered a common, decent hatred for a person to have. But most sportswriters whom Hartack dislikes couldn't care less. And, the notion is, neither does the reading public. Ofttimes, the public is having enough trouble deciphering what sportswriters write without having to take on the additional burden of remembering that there is a feud between Hartack and the press box. But it is important to Hartack that he does not like the writers. And they put in the papers that his name is "Willie" and he blows up at them.

Hartack has troubles with officials, too, and these cost him. Suspensions dot his career. Last year, for example, he snarled at Garden State stewards — they insisted he cursed — and was set down for the remainder of the meeting. In 1958 he was set down for 15 days by Atlantic City stewards when he was first under the wire on a horse called Nitrophy. But Jimmy Johnson, who finished second on Tote All, lodged a foul claim against Hartack, saying his horse had been interfered with.

The stewards allowed the claim and took down Hartack's horse. Hartack tried to take down Johnson with a left hand in the jocks' room. For his troubles both on the track and off it, Bill was given 15 days. In the last two years, Bill has been set down a total of 61 days. And he has been fined and reprimanded several times. At Hialeah in February he lost a photo with a horse called Cozy Ada and after it he was in a rage. "What do I have to do to get a shake here?" he snapped, walking out on the rest of his riding commitments. He was fined $100 for this. This is a kid who simply cannot stand losing, even to a camera.

His temperament does not make him a hero with other jockeys. There was a night last summer in the bar of the International Hotel, which is at New York's Idlewild Airport, and Willie Shoemaker and Sammy Boulmetis and some other horse guys were sitting around over a drink and Hartack's name was mentioned.

"I can't figure him out," Boulmetis was saying. "One day he seems nice to you. Next day he won't even talk to you."

Walter Blum, another rider, had an opinion, too. "You know," he said, "you can't live with him. He just wants to make you hate him. I mean, he really works at it."

Through all this, Hartack's outlook has been the same. "I do my job," he says. "I do what I think best. If I make a mistake, that's that. But the only place a mistake shows is the official chart of a race. If I don't win, that's a mistake. Nothing else counts. Not you or anybody else. Only that result."

To get down and wrestle with the truth, Hartack's attitude is, on many occasions, the only right one in racing.

Take, for example, the warm afternoon in February of 1959 at Hialeah when Hartack started jogging a horse called Greek Circle to the starting gate. To Hartack, the parade to the post is all important. He gets the feel of his mount by tugging on one rein, then the other and watching the horse's reaction. He tries to find out if the horse is favoring one foot or another or likes to be held tightly or with a normal pressure on the bit. Greek Circle responded to nothing. The horse seemed to have no coordination at all and that was enough for Hartack.

"My horse isn't right," he yelled to the starter. "He can't coordinate himself. He's almost falling down right now. I'm getting off him."

The starter called for a veterinarian and Hartack jogged the horse for the vet, Dr. George Barksdale.

"The horse is fine," Dr. Barksdale said. "Take him into the gate. He'll run fine."

Hartack's answer was simple. He stopped the horse and swung his fanny off him and dropped to the ground. The veterinarian shrugged. Across the way, in the stands, they were adding up figures and a neat little sum of $5,443.56 had been set aside as the track's share of the $136,089 bet on Greek Circle. Because the next race, the Widener, was on television and time was a problem now, the track stewards had to order the horse scratched and the money bet on him returned.

They knocked Hartack's brains out on this one. He was in headlines across the nation the next day as a little grandstander who should have been suspended for his actions.

But when the smoke cleared and you could think about it objectively, you could see who was wrong. Eddie Arcaro, over many glasses of a thing called Blue Sunoco in the Miami Airport bar a week later, talked about it. "Nobody in his right mind, the vet included, could knock Hartack for that. Do you know how many jocks have been killed because they were on broken down horses? And they tell me this horse has been sore all year. Bad sore, too. Hartack was right. It took a little guts, too."

Then on May 16, 1959, Hartack was aboard Vegeo at Garden State and as he got into the gate, the horse was nervous and reared up and Bill yelled to Cecil Phillips, the starter, that he wasn't ready to go. Phillips' answer was to press the sticks of wood in his hand together and they completed the electric circuit which made the gate open and the race start. Hartack's horse was rearing in the air and by the time he got him straightened out the field was up the track and the race was lost.

Hartack went to the track stewards with this complaint. Now Hartack coming off a loser is bad enough. But a Hartack coming off a loser that he felt is somebody else's fault is really something. This is a Khrushchev who rides horses. He called the stewards and snapped at them. Their version was that he cursed. They set him down for the remainder of the meeting.

"I get in trouble because of these things," Hartack tells you. "But I'm never going to stop because I'm right. I'm doing it honestly. The only reason I get my name around is that I'm the only one who does it. When I have a horse under me that's broken down, I won't ride him. And if the starter blows my chances in a race, I yell about it. It doesn't just happen to me. It happens to everybody else. But the rest of these riders are afraid to say anything about it. They get on a horse that's broken down and they keep quiet. Then they give him an easy ride, so they won't take any chances of getting hurt, and when they come back they give some ridiculous excuse to satisfy the trainer. You know, 'The horse lugged in' or 'he propped on me' or 'he tried to get out on me.' In the meantime, the public has bet its money on the horse and they didn't get a fair shake. But the jocks feel you don't have to make an excuse to them. They don't count. Well, I look on it differently. I owe loyalty to anybody who bets on my horse. The person who does that is going to get the best I can give him. Nothing is going to stop me from doing that."

If you have been around Hartack on race tracks, and watched him as he tries to win, you would know how far he is willing to carry his fight. Like the dark, rain-flecked Saturday in Louisville in 1958.

The driver moved his ambulance slowly through the filth of Churchill Downs' grandstand betting area and he had his hand on the horn to make people get out of the way as he headed for the gate.

Hartack was on a stretcher in the back of the ambulance. He had a wooden ice cream spoon stuck between his teeth so when the pain hit him he could bite into it. The stick doesn't help take pain away, but you do not bite your lip when pain comes if you have a stick between your teeth, so Hartack could grimace and tighten his teeth on the wood each time the ambulance hit a bump.

His body was covered with mud and his left leg was propped on a pillow. He looked tiny and helpless, the way jockeys always do when they are hurt. A few minutes before, a 2-year-old filly named Quail Egg had become frightened in the starting gate and she flipped Hartack. As he rolled around in the mud under the horse, Quail Egg started to thrash at the ground with her hooves. Then the horse fell heavily on Hartack and a bone in his leg snapped.

As the ambulance moved into a main street, where it was smoother riding, Hartack put the stick to the side of his mouth and muttered some words to Chick Lang.

"Nothing heavy on this leg," he said. "Don't let them put a heavy cast on this leg, Chick. We got to ride that horse next week."

The Kentucky Derby was to be run on the next Saturday and Hartack was contracted to ride Tim Tam. Now he was flattened out on a stretcher in an ambulance and his leg was broken, but he still was talking about riding the horse.

Then he called a company in Chicago which makes special braces. "I want a real light one. Aluminum," he told them. "Make it special. It has to go inside a riding boot. I need it by Wednesday."

"He won't listen to me," the staff doctor from the hospital in Louis-ville said quietly. "The fibula is snapped and there are some ripped ligaments around it. That leg will need a long time."

It did. Hartack was out for six weeks. But if you had seen him with a stick in his mouth and pain waving through his body and heard him talking about trying to ride a horse, then you had to say that he is a kid with something to him.

Every time Hartack has been hurt he has been like this. On July 10, 1957, he was moving around the last turn at Arlington Park on a horse called Smoke-Me-Now. The one in front, Spy Boss, had been running steadily, but he became tired and started to fall apart all at once and Smoke-Me-Now ran up his heels. With a thoroughbred horse in full motion, it only takes the slightest flick against his ankles to cause a spill. This time Smoke-Me-Now caught it good and he went down in a crash. Hartack was tossed into the air. His little body flipped in a somersault and he landed on his back. Nobody would pick him up until an ambu-lance came.

They took him to a hospital in Elgin, Illinois, and the doctors said Hartack had a badly sprained back and muscles were torn and he'd be out for a couple of weeks at a minimum. This was on a Thursday. On Saturday, Hartack was scheduled to ride Iron Liege, for the Calumet Farm, in the $100,000 Arlington Classic. Hartack likes $100,000 races.

At 8 o'clock on Friday night, Dogwagon, who is an exercise boy for Calumet, was sitting in a camp chair in front of the barn at Arlington Park and a guy came over and asked who was riding a stable pony around the area at this time of night.

"That is Mr. Bill Hartack," Dogwagon said. "Mr. Bill Hartack has a fine feeling for money and right now he is teaching his back to feel the same ways. He strapped up like he was a fat ole woman trying to keep the rolls in. But he goin' be ridin' Iron Liege tomorrow and he'll be therebouts when they pass out the money, too."

Hartack was jogging back and forth across the stable area on a painted pony. He came back to the barn, after 45 minutes of this. He hopped off and went to a phone to tell Calumet's Jimmy Jones that he could ride the next day. He was beat a nose on Iron Liege and he went into a rage because he lost the race.

In the tack room, somebody passed by and said, "You did a wonder-ful job getting second. I mean, you're lucky you can walk, much less ride."

"I don't care if I have one leg," Hartack snapped. "That's no excuse. I wanted to win the race."

Which is the whole game with Hartack. There isn't a thing in the world you can say is wrong with him except he cannot stand to lose. And he does not think anything else in the world matters except not losing.

Last June, for example, Hartack was at Monmouth Park and was due in New York to see Floyd Patterson fight Ingemar Johansson. Scratch Sheet Pestano, his agent, was at the bar in Jack Dempsey's Restaurant on Broadway, Hartack's ringside seats in his pocket.

"You meeting Hartack?" somebody asked him.

"When I get the race results, I'll let you know," Pestano said.

He went into a phone booth and called a newspaper office for the day's results at Monmouth. Hartack was on seven horses. As Pestano listened to the guy on the other end, his face became longer. He came out of the phone booth with the tickets in his hand.

"You meet him and give them to him," he told somebody with him. "He lost on seven horses today. Every one of them should have been up there. He won't be fit to live with tonight. I'm going home. I don't want to be anywhere near him. He just can't stand losing."

Mr. Harry (Champ) Segal, dean of Broadway horse players, was listening to the conversation.

"If all them jockeys was like that maybe you could cash a bet now and then," the Champ said.

Which is what everybody has to say about Hartack, whether they care for him or not.

1960

John Updike

·····································································································

# Hub Fans Bid Kid Adieu

FROM *The New Yorker*

FENWAY PARK, in Boston, is a lyric little bandbox of a ball park. Everything is painted green and seems in curiously sharp focus, like the inside of an old-fashioned peeping-type Easter egg. It was built in 1912 and rebuilt in 1934, and offers, as do most Boston artifacts, a compromise between Man's Euclidean determinations and Nature's beguiling irregularities. Its right field is one of the deepest in the American League, while its left field is the shortest; the high left-field wall, three hundred and fifteen feet from home plate along the foul line, virtually thrusts its surface at right-handed hitters. On the afternoon of Wednesday, September 28, as I took a seat behind third base, a uniformed groundkeeper was treading the top of this wall, picking batting-practice home runs out of the screen, like a mushroom gatherer seen in Wordsworthian perspective on the verge of a cliff. The day was overcast, chill, and uninspirational. The Boston team was the worst in twenty-seven seasons. A jangling medley of incompetent youth and aging competence, the Red Sox were finishing in seventh place only because the Kansas City Athletics had locked them out of the cellar. They were scheduled to play the Baltimore Orioles, a much nimbler blend of May and December, who had been dumped from pennant contention a week before by the insatiable Yankees. I, and 10,453 others, had shown up primarily because this was the Red Sox's last home game of the season, and therefore the last time in all eternity that their regular left fielder, known to the headlines as TED, KID, SPLINTER, THUMPER, TW, and, most cloyingly, MISTER WONDERFUL, would play in Boston. "WHAT WILL WE DO WITHOUT TED? HUB FANS ASK" ran the headline on a newspaper being read by a bulb-nosed cigar smoker a few rows away. Williams's retirement had been announced, doubted (he had been threatening retirement for years), confirmed by Tom Yawkey, the Red Sox owner, and at last widely accepted as the sad but probable truth. He was forty-two and had redeemed his abysmal season of 1959 with a — considering his advanced age — fine one. He had been giving away his gloves and bats and had grudgingly consented to a sentimental ceremony today. This was not necessarily his last game; the Red Sox were scheduled to travel to New York and wind up the season with three games there.

I arrived early. The Orioles were hitting fungos on the field. The day before, they had spitefully smothered the Red Sox, 17–4, and neither their faces nor their drab gray visiting-team uniforms seemed very gracious. I wondered who had invited them to the party. Between our heads and the lowering clouds a frenzied organ was thundering through, with an appositeness perhaps accidental, "You *maaaade* me love you, I didn't wanna do it, I didn't wanna do it . . ."

The affair between Boston and Ted Williams has been no mere summer romance; it has been a marriage, composed of spats, mutual disappointments, and, toward the end, a mellowing hoard of shared memories. It falls into three stages, which may be termed Youth, Maturity, and Age; or Thesis, Antithesis, and Synthesis; or Jason, Achilles, and Nestor.

First, there was the by now legendary epoch when the young bridegroom came out of the West, announced "All I want out of life is that when I walk down the street folks will say 'There goes the greatest hitter who ever lived.'" The dowagers of local journalism attempted to give elementary deportment lessons to this child who spake as a god, and to their horror were themselves rebuked. Thus began the long exchange of backbiting, hat-flipping, booing, and spitting that has distinguished Williams's public relations. The spitting incidents of 1957 and 1958 and the similar dockside courtesies that Williams has now and then extended to the grandstand should be judged against this background: The left-field stands at Fenway for twenty years have held a large number of customers who have bought their way in primarily for the privilege of showering abuse on Williams. Greatness necessarily attracts debunkers but in Williams's case the hostility has been systematic and unappeasable. His basic offense against the fans has been to wish that they weren't there. Seeking a perfectionist's vacuum, he has quixotically desired to sever the game from the ground of paid spectatorship and publicity that supports it. Hence his refusal to tip his cap to the crowd or turn the other cheek to newsmen. It has been a costly theory — it has probably cost him, among other evidences of goodwill, two Most Valuable Player awards, which are voted by reporters — but he has held to it from his rookie year on. While his critics, oral and literary, remained beyond the reach of his discipline, the opposing pitchers were accessible, and he spanked them to the tune of .406 in 1941. He slumped to .356 in 1942 and went off to war.

In 1946, Williams returned from three years as a marine pilot to the second of his baseball avatars, that of Achilles, the hero of incomparable prowess and beauty who nevertheless was to be found sulking in his tent while the Trojans (mostly Yankees) fought through to the ships. Yawkey, a timber and mining maharajah, had surrounded his central jewel with many gems of slightly lesser water, such as Bobby Doerr, Dom DiMaggio, Rudy York, Birdie Tebbetts, and Johnny Pesky. Throughout the late forties, the Red Sox were the best paper team in baseball, yet they had little three-dimensional to show for it, and if this was a tragedy, Williams was Hamlet. A succinct review of the indictment — and a fair sample of appreciative sports-page prose — appeared the very day of Williams's valedictory, in a column by Huck Finnegan in the *Boston American* (no sentimentalist, Huck):

> Williams's career, in contrast [to Babe Ruth's], has been a series of failures except for his averages. He flopped in the only World Series he ever played in (1946) when he batted only .200. He flopped in the playoff game with Cleveland in 1948. He flopped in the final game of the 1949 season with the pennant hinging on the outcome (Yanks 5, Sox 3). He flopped in 1950 when he returned to the lineup after a two-month absence and ruined the morale of a club that seemed pennant-bound under Steve O'Neill. It has always been Williams's records first, the team second, and the Sox non-winning record is proof enough of that.

There are answers to all this, of course. The fatal weakness of the great Sox slugging teams was not-quite-good-enough pitching rather than Williams's failure to hit a home run every time he came to bat. Again, Williams's depressing effect on his teammates has never been proved. Despite ample coaching to the contrary, most insisted that they *liked* him. He has been generous with advice to any player who asked for it. In an increasingly combative baseball atmosphere, he continued to duck beanballs docilely. With umpires he was gracious to a fault. This courtesy itself annoyed his critics, whom there was no pleasing. And against the ten crucial games (the seven World Series games with the St. Louis Cardinals, the 1948 play-off with the Cleveland Indians, and the two-game series with the Yankees at the end of the 1949 season, winning either one of which would have given the Red Sox the pennant) that make up the Achilles' heel of Williams's record, a mass of statistics can be set showing that day in and day out he was no slouch in the clutch. The correspondence columns of the Boston papers now and then suffer a sharp flurry of arithmetic on this score; indeed, for Williams to have distributed all his hits so they did nobody else any good would constitute a feat of placement unparalleled in the annals of selfishness.

Whatever residue of truth remains of the Finnegan charge those of us who love Williams must transmute as best we can, in our own personal crucibles. My personal memories of Williams begin when I was a boy in Pennsylvania, with two last-place teams in Philadelphia to keep me company. For me, "W'ms, if" was a figment of the box scores who always seemed to be going 3-for-5. He radiated, from afar, the hard blue glow of high purpose. I remember listening over the radio to the All-Star Game of 1946, in which Williams hit two singles and two home runs, the second one off a Rip Sewell "blooper" pitch; it was like hitting a balloon out of the park. I remember watching one of his home runs from the bleachers of Shibe Park; it went over the first baseman's head and rose meticulously along a straight line and was still rising when it cleared the fence. The trajectory seemed qualitatively different from anything anyone else might hit. For me, Williams is the classic ballplayer of the game on a hot August weekday, before a small crowd, when the only thing at stake is the tissue-thin difference between a thing done well and a thing done ill. Baseball is a game of the long season, of relentless and gradual averaging-out. Irrelevance — since the reference point of most individual games is remote and statistical — always threatens its interest, which can be maintained not by the occasional heroics that sportswriters feed upon but by players who always *care;* who care, that is to say, about themselves and their art. Insofar as the clutch hitter is not a sportswriter's myth, he is a vulgarity, like a writer who writes only for money. It may be that, compared to managers' dreams such as Joe DiMaggio and the always helpful Stan Musial, Williams is an icy star. But of all team sports, baseball, with its graceful intermittences of action, its immense and tranquil field sparsely settled with poised men in white, its dispassionate mathematics, seems to me, best suited to accommodate, and be ornamented by, a loner. It is an essentially lonely game. No other player visible to my generation has concentrated within himself so much of the sport's poignance, has so assiduously refined his natural skills, has so constantly brought to the plate that intensity of competence that crowds the throat with joy.

By the time I went to college, near Boston, the lesser stars Yawkey had assembled around Williams had faded, and his craftsmanship, his rigorous pride, had become itself a kind of heroism. This brittle and temperamental player developed an unexpected quality of persistence. He was always coming back — back from Korea, back from a broken collarbone, a shattered elbow, a bruised heel, back from drastic bouts of flu and ptomaine poisoning. Hardly a season went by without some enfeebling mishap, yet he always came back, and always looked like himself. The delicate mechanism of timing and power seemed locked, shockproof, in some case outside his body. In addition to injuries, there were a heavily publicized divorce, and the usual storms with the press, and the Williams Shift — the maneuver, custom-built by Lou Boudreau, of the Cleveland Indians, whereby three infielders were concentrated on the right side of the infield, where a left-handed pull hitter like Williams generally hits the ball. Williams could easily have learned to punch singles through the vacancy on his left and fattened his average hugely. This was what Ty Cobb, the Einstein of average, told him to do. But the game had changed since Cobb; Williams believed that his value to the club and to the game was as a slugger, so he went on pulling the ball, trying to blast it through three men, and paid the price of perhaps fifteen points of lifetime average. Like Ruth before him, he bought the occasional home run at the cost of many directed singles — a calculated sacrifice certainly not, in the case of a hitter as average-minded as Williams, entirely selfish.

After a prime so harassed and hobbled, Williams was granted by the relenting fates a golden twilight. He became at the end of his career perhaps the best *old* hitter of the century. The dividing line came between the 1956 and the 1957 seasons. In September of the first year, he and Mickey Mantle were contending for the batting championship. Both were hitting around .350, and there was no one else near them. The season ended with a three-game series between the Yankees and the Sox, and living in New York then, I went up to the Stadium. Williams was slightly shy of the four hundred at-bats needed to qualify; the fear was expressed that the Yankee pitchers would walk him to protect Mantle. Instead, they pitched to him — a wise decision. He looked terrible at the plate, tired and discouraged and unconvincing. He never looked very good to me in the Stadium. (Last week, in *Life*, Williams, a sportswriter himself now, wrote gloomily of the Stadium, "There's the bigness of it. There are those high stands and all those people smoking — and, of course, the shadows. . . . It takes at least one series to get accustomed to the Stadium and even then you're not sure.") The final outcome in 1956 was Mantle .353, Williams .345.

The next year, I moved from New York to New England, and it made all the difference. For in September of 1957, in the same situation, the story was reversed. Mantle finally hit .365; it was the best season of his career. But Williams, though sick and old, had run away from him. A bout of flu had laid him low in September. He emerged from his cave in the Hotel Somerset haggard but irresistible; he hit four successive pinch-hit home runs. "I feel terrible," he confessed, "but every time I take a swing at the ball it goes out of the park." He ended the season with thirty-eight home runs and an average of .388, the highest in either league since his own .406, and, coming from a decrepit man of thirty-nine, an even more supernal figure. With eight or so of the "leg hits" that a younger man would have beaten out, it would have been .400. And the next year, Williams, who in 1949 and 1953 had lost batting championships by decimal whiskers to George Kell and Mickey Vernon, sneaked in behind his teammate Pete Runnels and filched his sixth title, a bargain at .328.

In 1959, it seemed all over. The dinosaur thrashed around in the .200 swamp for the first half of the season, and was even benched ("rested," Manager Mike Higgins tactfully said). Old foes like the late Bill Cunningham began to offer batting tips. Cunningham thought Williams was jiggling his elbows; in truth, Williams's neck was so stiff he could hardly turn his head to look at the pitcher. When he swung, it looked like a Calder mobile with one thread cut; it reminded you that since 1953 Williams's shoulders had been wired together. A solicitous pall settled over the sports pages. In the two decades since Williams had come to Boston, his status had imperceptibly shifted from that of a naughty prodigy to that of a municipal monument. As his shadow in the record books lengthened, the Red Sox teams around him declined, and the entire American League seemed to be losing life and color to the National. The inconsistency of the new superstars — Mantle, Colavito, and Kaline — served to make Williams appear all the more singular. And off the field, his private philanthropy — in particular his zealous chairmanship of the Jimmy Fund, a charity for children with cancer — gave him a civic presence somewhat like that of Richard Cardinal Cushing. In religion, Williams appears to be a humanist, and a selective one at that, but he and the cardinal, when their good works intersect and they appear in the public eye together, make a handsome and heartening pair.

Humiliated by his 1959 season, Williams determined, once more, to come back. I, as a specimen Williams partisan, was both glad and fearful. All baseball fans believe in miracles; the question is, how *many* do you believe in? He looked like a ghost in spring training. Manager Jurges warned us ahead of time that if Williams didn't come through he would be benched, just like anybody else. As it turned out, it was Jurges who was benched. Williams entered the 1960 season needing eight home runs to have a lifetime total of 500; after one time at bat in Washington, he needed seven. For a stretch, he was hitting a home run every second game that he played. He passed Lou Gehrig's lifetime total, then the number 500, then Mel Ott's total, and finished with 521, thirteen behind Jimmy Foxx, who alone stands between Williams and Babe Ruth's unapproachable 714. The summer was a statistician's picnic. His two-thousandth walk came and went, his eighteen-hundredth run batted in, his sixteenth All-Star Game. At one point, he hit a home run off a pitcher, Don Lee, off whose father, Thornton Lee, he had hit a home run a generation before. The only comparable season for a forty-two-year-old man was Ty Cobb's in 1928. Cobb batted .323 and hit one homer. Williams batted .316 but hit twenty-nine homers.

In sum, though generally conceded to be the greatest hitter of his era, he did not establish himself as "the greatest hitter who ever lived." Cobb, for average, and Ruth, for power, remain supreme. Cobb, Rogers, Hornsby, Joe Jackson, and Lefty O'Doul, among players since 1900, have higher lifetime averages than Williams's .344. Unlike Foxx, Gehrig, Hack Wilson, Hank Greenberg, and Ralph Kiner, Williams never came close to matching Babe Ruth's season home-run total of sixty. In the list of major league batting records, not one is held by Williams. He is second in walks drawn, third in home runs, fifth in lifetime averages, sixth in runs batted in, eighth in runs scored and in total bases, fourteenth in doubles, and thirtieth in hits. But if we allow him merely average seasons for the four-plus seasons he lost to two wars, and add another season for the months he lost to injuries, we get a man who in all the power totals would be second, and not a very distant second, to Ruth. And if we further allow that these years would have been not merely average but prime years, if we allow for all the months when Williams was playing in sub-par condition, if we permit his early and later years in baseball to be some sort of index of what the middle years could have been, if we give him a right-field fence that is not, like Fenway's, one of the most distant in the league, and if — the least excusable "if" — we imagine him condescending to outsmart the Williams Shift, we can defensibly assemble, like a colossus induced from the sizable fragments that do remain, a statistical figure not incommensurate with his grandiose ambition. From the statistics that are on the books, a good case can be made that in the *combination* of power and average Williams is first; nobody else ranks so high in both categories. Finally, there is the witness of the eyes; men whose memories go back to Shoeless Joe Jackson — another unlucky natural — rank him and Williams together as the best-looking hitters they have seen. It was for our last look that ten thousand of us had come.

Two girls, one of them with pert buckteeth and eyes as black as vest buttons, the other with white skin and flesh-colored hair, like an underdeveloped photograph of a redhead, came and sat on my right. On my other side was one of those frowning, chestless young-old men who can frequently be seen, often wearing sailor hats, attending ball games alone. He did not once open his program but instead tapped it, rolled up, on his knee as he gave the game his disconsolate attention. A young lady, with freckles and a depressed, dainty nose that by an optical illusion seemed to thrust her lips forward for a kiss, sauntered down into the box seats and with striking aplomb took a seat right behind the roof of the Oriole dugout. She wore a blue coat with a Northeastern University emblem sewed to it. The girls beside me took it into their heads that this was Williams's daughter. She looked too old to me, and why would she be sitting behind the visitors' dugout. On the other hand, from the way she sat there, staring at the sky and French-inhaling, she clearly was *some*body. Other fans came and eclipsed her from view. The crowd looked less like a weekday ball park crowd than like the folks you might find in Yellowstone National Park, or emerging from automobiles at the top of scenic Mount Mansfield. There were a lot of competitively well-dressed couples of tourist age, and not a few babes in arms. A row of five seats in front of me was abruptly filled with a woman and four children, the youngest of them two years old, if that. Someday, presumably, he could tell his grandchildren that he saw Williams play. Along with these tots and second-honeymooners, there were Harvard freshmen, giving off that peculiar nervous glow created when a quantity of insouciance is saturated with insecurity; thick-necked army officers with brass on their shoulders and lead in their voices; pepper-

ings of priests; perfumed bouquets of Roxbury Fabian fans; shiny salesmen from Albany and Fall River; and those gray, hoarse men —
taxidrivers, slaughterers, and bartenders — who will continue to click
through the turnstiles long after everyone else has deserted to television and tramporamas. Behind me, two young male voices blossomed,
cracking a joke about God's five proofs that Thomas Aquinas exists —
typical Boston College levity.

The batting cage was trundled away. The Orioles fluttered to the
sidelines. Diagonally across the field, by the Red Sox dugout, a cluster of
men in overcoats were festering like maggots. I could see a splinter of
white uniform, and Williams's head, held at a self-deprecating and
evasive tilt. Williams's conversational stance is that of a six-foot-three-
inch man under a six-foot ceiling. He moved away to the patter of flash
bulbs, and began playing catch with a young Negro outfielder named
Willie Tasby. His arm, never very powerful, had grown lax with the
years, and his throwing motion was a kind of muscular drawl. To catch
the ball, he flicked his glove hand onto his left shoulder (he batted left
but threw right, as every schoolboy ought to know) and let the ball plop
into it comically. This catch session with Tasby was the only time all
afternoon I saw him grin.

A tight little flock of human sparrows who, from the lambient and
pampered pink of their faces, could only have been Boston politicians moved toward the plate. The loudspeakers mammothly coughed
as someone huffed on the microphone. The ceremonies began. Curt
Gowdy, the Red Sox radio and television announcer, who sounds like
everybody's brother-in-law, delivered a brief sermon, taking the two
words "pride" and "champion" as his text. It began, "Twenty-one years
ago, a skinny kid from San Diego, California . . ." and ended, "I don't
think we'll ever see another like him." Robert Tibolt, chairman of the
board of the Greater Boston Chamber of Commerce, presented Williams with a big Paul Revere silver bowl. Harry Carlson, a member of
the sports committee of the Boston Chamber, gave him a plaque, whose
inscription he did not read in its entirety, out of deference to Williams's
distaste for this sort of fuss. Mayor Collins presented the Jimmy Fund
with a thousand-dollar check.

Then the occasion himself stooped to the microphone, and his voice
sounded, after the others, very Californian; it seemed to be coming,
excellently amplified, from a great distance, adolescently young and as
smooth as a butternut. His thanks for the gifts had not died from our
ears before he glided, as if helplessly, into "In spite of all the terrible

things that have been said about me by the maestros of the keyboard up there . . ." He glanced up at the press rows suspended above home plate. (All the Boston reporters, incidentally, reported the phrase as "knights of the keyboard," but I heard it as "maestros" and prefer it that way.) The crowd tittered, appalled. A frightful vision flashed upon me, of the press gallery pelting Williams with erasers, of Williams clambering up the foul screen to slug journalists, of a riot, of Mayor Collins being crushed. ". . . And they *were* terrible things," Williams insisted, with level melancholy, into the mike. "I'd like to forget them, but I can't." He paused, swallowing his memories, and went on. "I want to say that my years in Boston have been the greatest thing in my life." The crowd, like an immense sail going limp in a change of wind, sighed with relief. Taking all the parts himself, Williams then acted out a vivacious little morality drama in which an imaginary tempter came to him at the beginning of his career and said, "Ted, you can play anywhere you like." Leaping nimbly into the role of his younger self (who in biographical actuality had yearned to be a Yankee), Williams gallantly chose Boston over all the other cities, and told us that Tom Yawkey was the greatest owner in baseball and we were the greatest fans. We applauded ourselves heartily. The umpire came out and dusted the plate. The voice of doom announced over the loudspeakers that after Williams's retirement his uniform number, 9, would be permanently retired — the first time the Red Sox had so honored a player. We cheered. The national anthem was played. We cheered. The game began.

Williams was third in the batting order, so he came up in the bottom of the first inning, and Steve Barber, a young pitcher who was not yet born when Williams began playing for the Red Sox, offered him four pitches, at all of which he disdained to swing, since none of them were within the strike zone. This demonstrated simultaneously that Williams's eyes were razor-sharp and that Barber's control wasn't. Shortly, the bases were full, with Williams on second. "Oh, I hope he gets held up at third! That would be wonderful," the girl beside me moaned, and, sure enough, the man at bat walked and Williams was delivered into our foreground. He struck the pose of Donatello's David, the third-base bag being Goliath's head. Fiddling with his cap, swapping small talk with the Oriole third baseman (who seemed delighted to have him drop in), swinging his arms with a sort of prancing nervousness, he looked fine — flexible, hard, and not unbecomingly substantial through the middle. The long neck, the small head, the knickers whose cuffs were worn down near his ankles — all these points, often observed by caricaturists, were visible in the flesh.

One of the collegiate voices behind me said, "He looks old, doesn't he, old; big deep wrinkles in his face . . ."

"Yeah," the other voice said, "but he looks like an old hawk, doesn't he?"

With each pitch, Williams danced down the baseline, waving his arms and stirring dust, ponderous but menacing, like an attacking goose. It occurred to about a dozen humorists at once to shout "Steal home! Go, go!" Williams's speed afoot was never legendary. Lou Clinton, a young Sox outfielder, hit a fairly deep fly to center field. Williams tagged up and ran home. As he slid across the plate, the ball, thrown with unusual heft by Jackie Brandt, the Oriole center fielder, hit him on the back.

"Boy, he was really loafing, wasn't he?" one of the boys behind me said.

"It's cold," the other explained. "He doesn't play well when it's cold. He likes heat. He's a hedonist."

The run that Williams scored was the second and last of the inning. Gus Triandos, of the Orioles, quickly evened the score by plunking a home run over the handy left-field wall. Williams, who had had this wall at his back for twenty years, played the ball flawlessly. He didn't budge. He just stood there, in the center of the little patch of grass that his patient footsteps had worn brown, and, limp with lack of interest, watched the ball pass overhead. It was not a very interesting game. Mike Higgins, the Red Sox manager, with nothing to lose, had restricted his major league players to the left-field line — along with Williams, Frank Malzone, a first-rate third baseman, played the game — and had peopled the rest of the terrain with unpredictable youngsters fresh, or not so fresh, off the farms. Other than Williams's recurrent appearances at the plate, the *maladresse* of the Sox infield was the sole focus of suspense; the second baseman turned every grounder into a juggling act, while the shortstop did a breathtaking impersonation of an open window. With this sort of assistance, the Orioles wheedled their way into a 4–2 lead. They had early replaced Barber with another young pitcher, Jack Fisher. Fortunately (as it turned out), Fisher is no cutie; he is willing to burn the ball through the strike zone, and inning after inning this tactic punctured Higgins's string of test balloons.

Whenever Williams appeared at the Plate — pounding the dirt from his cleats, gouging a pit in the batter's box with his left foot, wringing resin out of the bat handle with his vehement grip, switching the stick at the pitcher with an electric ferocity — it was like having a familiar Leonardo appear in a shuffle of *Saturday Evening Post* covers. This man, you realized — and here, perhaps, was the difference, greater than the difference in gifts — really intended to hit the ball. In the third inning, he hoisted a high fly to deep center. In the fifth, we thought he had it; he smacked the ball hard and high into the heart of his power zone, but the deep right field in Fenway and the heavy air and a casual east wind defeated him. The ball died. Al Pilarcik leaned his back against the big "380" painted on the right-field wall and caught it. On another day, in another park, it would have been gone. (After the game, Williams said, "I didn't think I could hit one any harder than that. The conditions weren't good.")

The afternoon grew so glowering that in the sixth inning the arc lights were turned on — always a wan sight in the daytime, like the burning headlights of a funeral procession. Aided by the gloom, Fisher was slicing through the Sox rookies, and Williams did not come to bat in the seventh. He was second up in the eighth. This was almost certainly his last time to come to the plate in Fenway Park, and instead of merely cheering, as we had at his three previous appearances, we stood, all of us — stood and applauded. Have you ever heard applause in a ball park? Just applause — no calling, no whistling, just an ocean of hand-claps, minute after minute, burst after burst, crowding and running together in continuous succession like the pushes of surf at the edge of the sand. It was a somber and considered tumult. There was not a boo in it. It seemed to renew itself out of a shifting set of memories as the kid, the marine, the veteran of feuds and failures and injuries, the friend of children, and the enduring old pro evolved down the bright tunnel of twenty-one summers toward this moment. At last, the umpire signaled for Fisher to pitch; with the other players, he had been frozen in position. Only Williams had moved during the ovation, switching his bat impatiently, ignoring everything except his cherished task. Fisher wound up, and the applause sank into a hush.

Understand that we were a crowd of rational people. We knew that a home run cannot be produced at will; the right pitch must be perfectly met and luck must ride with the ball. Three innings before, we had seen a brave effort fail. The air was soggy; the season was exhausted. Nevertheless, there will always lurk, around a corner in a pocket of our knowledge of the odds, an indefensible hope, and this was one of the times, which you now and then find in sports, when a density of expectation hangs in the air and plucks an event out of the future.

Fisher, after his unsettling wait, was wide with the first pitch. He put the second one over, and Williams swung mightily and missed. The crowd grunted, seeing that classic swing, so long and smooth and quick, exposed, naked in its failure. Fisher threw the third time, Williams swung again, and there it was. The ball climbed on a diagonal line into the vast volume of air over center field. From my angle, behind third base, the ball seemed less an object in flight than the tip of a towering, motionless construct, like the Eiffel Tower or the Tappan Zee Bridge. It was in the books while it was still in the sky. Brandt ran back to the deepest corner of the outfield grass; the ball descended beyond his reach and struck in the crotch where the bullpen met the wall, bounced chunkily, and, as far as I could see, vanished.

Like a feather caught in a vortex, Williams ran around the square of bases at the center of our beseeching screaming. He ran as he always ran out home runs — hurriedly, unsmiling, head down, as if our praise were a storm of rain to get out of. He didn't tip his cap. Though we thumped, wept, and chanted "We want Ted" for minutes after he hid in the dugout, he did not come back. Our noise for some seconds passed beyond excitement into a kind of immense open anguish, a wailing, a cry to be saved. But immortality is nontransferable. The papers said that the other players, and even the umpires on the field, begged him to come out and acknowledge us in some way, but he never had and did not now. Gods do not answer letters.

Every true story has an anticlimax. The men on the field refused to disappear, as would have seemed decent, in the smoke of Williams's miracle. Fisher continued to pitch, and escaped further harm. At the end of the inning, Higgins sent Williams out to his left-field position, then instantly replaced him with Carrol Hardy, so we had a long last look at Williams as he ran out there and then back, his uniform jogging, his eyes steadfast on the ground. It was nice, and we were grateful, but it left a funny taste.

One of the scholasticists behind me said, "Let's go. We've seen everything. I don't want to spoil it." This seemed a sound aesthetic decision. Williams's last word had been so exquisitely chosen, such a perfect fusion of expectation, intention, and execution, that already it felt a little unreal in my head, and I wanted to get out before the castle collapsed. But the game, though played by clumsy midgets under the feeble glow of the arc lights, began to tug at my attention, and I loitered in the runway until it was over. Williams's homer had, quite incidentally, made the score 4–3. In the bottom of the ninth inning, with one out, Marlin Coughtry, the second-base juggler, singled. Vic Wertz, pinch-hitting, doubled off the left-field wall, Coughtry advancing to third. Pumpsie Green walked, to load the bases. Willie Tasby hit a double-play ball to the third baseman, but in making the pivot throw Billy Klaus, an ex-Red Sox infielder, reverted to form and threw the ball past the first baseman and into the Red Sox dugout. The Sox won, 5–4. On the car radio as I drove home I heard that Williams had decided not to accompany the team to New York. So he knew how to do even that, the hardest thing. Quit.

1961

## Al Stump

.................................................................................................

# The Fight to Live

FROM *True*

EVER SINCE SUNDOWN the Nevada intermountain radio had been crackling warnings: "Route 50 now highly dangerous. Motorists stay off. Repeat: AVOID ROUTE 50."

By one in the morning the 21-mile, steep-pitched passage from Lake Tahoe's 7,000 feet in Carson City, a snaky grade most of the way, was snow-struck, ice-sheeted, thick with rock slides, and declared unfit for all transport vehicles by the State Highway Patrol.

Such news was right down Ty Cobb's alley. Anything that smacked of the impossible brought an unholy gleam to his eye. The gleam had been there in 1959 when a series of lawyers advised Cobb that he stood no chance against the Sovereign State of California in a dispute over income taxes, whereupon he bellowed defiance and sued the commonwealth for $60,000 and damages. It had been there more recently when doctors warned that liquor would kill him. From a pint of whiskey per day he upped his consumption to a quart and more.

Sticking out his chin, he told me, "I think we'll take a little run into town tonight."

A blizzard rattled the windows of Cobb's luxurious hunting lodge on the crest of Lake Tahoe, but to forbid him anything — even at the age of 73 — was to tell an ancient tiger not to snarl. Cobb was both the greatest of all ball players and a multimillionaire whose monthly income from stock dividends, rents, and interests ran to $12,000. And he was a man contemptuous, all his life, of any law other than his own.

"We'll drive in," he announced, "and shoot some craps, see a show and say hello to Joe DiMaggio — he's in Reno at the Riverside Hotel."

I looked at him and felt a chill. Cobb, sitting there haggard and unshaven in his pajamas and a fuzzy old green bathrobe at one o'clock in the morning, wasn't fooling.

"Let's not," I said. "You shouldn't be anywhere tonight but in bed."

"Don't argue with me!" he barked. "There are fee-simple sonof-bitches all over the country who've tried it and wish they hadn't." He glared at me, flaring the whites of his eyes the way he'd done for 24 years to quaking pitchers, basemen, umpires, and fans.

"If you and I are going to get along," he went on ominously, *"don't increase my tension."*

We were alone in his isolated ten-room $75,000 lodge, having arrived six days earlier, loaded with a large smoked ham, a 20-pound turkey, a case of Scotch and another of champagne, for purposes of collaborating on Ty's book-length autobiography — a book which he'd refused to write for 30 years, but then suddenly decided to place on record before he died. In almost a week's time we hadn't accomplished 30 minutes of work.

The reason: Cobb didn't need a risky auto trip into Reno, but immediate hospitalization, and by the emergency-door entrance. He was desperately ill and had been even before we'd left California.

We had traveled 250 miles to Tahoe in Cobb's black Imperial limousine, carrying with us a virtual drugstore of medicines. These included Digoxin (for his leaky heart), Darvon (for his aching back), Tace (for a recently operated-upon malignancy of the pelvic area), Fleet's compound (for his infected bowels), Librium (for his "tension" — that is, his violent rages), codeine (for his pain), and an insulin needle-and-syringe kit (for his diabetes), among a dozen other panaceas which he'd substituted for doctors. Cobb despised the medical profession.

At the same time, his sense of balance was almost gone. He tottered about the lodge, moving from place to place by grasping the furniture. On any public street, he couldn't navigate 20 feet without clutching my shoulder, leaning most of his 208 pounds upon me and shuffling along at a spraddle-legged gait. His bowels wouldn't work: they impacted, repeatedly, an almost total stoppage which brought moans of agony from Cobb when he sought relief. He was feverish, with no one at his Tahoe hideaway but the two of us to treat this dangerous condition.

Everything that hurts had caught up with his big, gaunt body at once and he stuffed himself with pink, green, orange, yellow, and purple pills — guessing at the amounts, often, since labels had peeled off many of the bottles. But he wouldn't hear of hospitalizing himself.

"The hacksaw artists have taken $50,000 from me," he said, "and they'll get no more." He spoke of "a quack" who'd treated him a few years earlier. "The joker got funny and said he found urine in my whiskey. I fired him."

His diabetes required a precise food-insulin balance. Cobb's needle wouldn't work. He'd misplaced the directions for the needed daily insulin dosage and his hands shook uncontrollably when he went to plunge the needle into a stomach vein. He spilled more of the stuff than he injected.

He'd been warned by experts — from Johns Hopkins to California's Scripps Clinic — that liquor was deadly. Tyrus snorted and began each day with several gin-and-orange-juices, then switched to Old Rarity Scotch, which held him until night hours, when sleep was impossible, and he tossed down cognac, champagne, or "Cobb Cocktails" — Southern Comfort stirred into hot water and honey.

A careful diet was essential. Cobb wouldn't eat. The lodge was without a cook or manservant — since, in the previous six months, he had fired two cooks, a male nurse, and a handyman in fits of anger — and any food I prepared for him he pushed away. As of the night of the blizzard, the failing, splenetic old king of ball players hadn't touched food in three days, existing solely on quarts of booze and booze mixtures.

My reluctance to prepare the car for the Reno trip burned him up. He beat his fists on the arms of his easy chair. "I'll go alone!" he threatened.

It was certain he'd try it. The storm had worsened, but once Cobb set his mind on an idea, nothing could change it. Beyond that, I'd already found that to oppose or annoy him was to risk a violent explosion. An event of a week earlier had proved *that* point. It was then I discovered that he carried a loaded Luger wherever he went and looked for opportunities to use it.

En route to Lake Tahoe, we'd stopped overnight at a motel near Hangtown, California. During the night a party of drunks made a loud commotion in the parking lot. In my room next to Cobb's, I heard him cursing and then his voice, booming out the window.

"Get out of here, you — heads!"

The drunks replied in kind. Then everyone in the motel had his teeth jolted.

Groping his way to the door, Tyrus the Terrible fired three shots into the dark that resounded like cannon claps. There were screams and yells. Reaching my door, I saw the drunks climbing each other's backs in their rush to flee. Before anyone could think of calling the police, the manager was cut down by the most caustic tongue ever heard in a baseball clubhouse.

"What kind of a pest house is this?" roared Cobb. "Who gave you a license, you mugwump? Get the hell out of here and see that I'm not disturbed! I'm a sick man and I want it quiet!"

"B-b-beg your pardon, Mr. Cobb," the manager said feebly. He apparently felt so honored to have baseball's greatest figure as a customer that no police were called. When we drove away the next morning, a crowd gathered and stood gawking with open mouths.

Down the highway, with me driving, Cobb checked the Luger and reloaded its nine-shell clip. "Two of those shots were in the air," he remarked. "The *third* kicked up gravel. I've got permits for this gun from governors of three states. I'm an honorary deputy sheriff of California and a Texas Ranger. So we won't be getting any complaints."

He saw nothing strange in his behavior. Ty Cobb's rest had been disturbed — therefore he had every right to shoot up the neighborhood.

About then I began to develop a twitch of the nerves, which grew worse with time. In past years, I'd heard reports of Cobb's weird and violent ways, without giving them much credence. But until early 1960 my own experience with the legendary Georgian had been slight, amounting only to meetings in Scottsdale, Arizona, and New York to discuss book-writing arrangements and to sign the contract.

Locker-room stories of Ty's eccentricities, wild temper, ego, and miserliness sounded like the usual scandalmongering you get in sports. I'd heard that Cobb had flattened a heckler in San Francisco's Domino Club with one punch; had been sued by Elbie Felts, an ex-Coast League player, after assaulting Felts; that he booby-trapped his Spanish villa at Atherton, California, with high-voltage wires; that he'd walloped one of his ex-wives; that he'd been jailed in Placerville, California, at the age of 68 for speeding, abusing a traffic cop, and even inviting the judge to return to law school at his, Cobb's, expense.

I passed these things off. The one and only Ty Cobb was to write his memoirs and I felt highly honored to be named his collaborator.

As the poet Cowper reflected, "The innocents are gay." I was eager to start. Then — a few weeks before book work began — I was taken aside and tipped off by an in-law of Cobb's and one of Cobb's former teammates with the Detroit Tigers that I hadn't heard the half of it. "Back out of this book deal," they urged. "You'll never finish it and you might get hurt."

They went on: "Nobody can live with Ty. Nobody ever has. That includes two wives, who left him, butlers, housekeepers, chauffeurs, nurses, and a few mistresses. He drove off all his friends long ago. Max Fleischmann, the yeast-cake heir, was a pal of Ty's until the night a house guest of Fleischmann's made a remark about Cobb spiking other players when he ran the bases. The man only asked if it was true. Cobb knocked the guy into a fish pond and after that Max never spoke to him again. Another time, a member of Cobb's family crossed him — a woman, mind you. He broke her nose with a ball bat.

"Do you know about the butcher? Ty didn't like some meat he bought. In the fight, he broke up the butcher shop. Had to settle $1,500 on the butcher out of court."

"But I'm dealing with him strictly on business," I said.

"So was the butcher," replied my informants. "In baseball, a few of us who really knew him well realized that he was wrong in the head — unbalanced. He played like a demon and had everybody hating him because he *was* a demon. That's how he set all those records that nobody has come close to since 1928. It's why he was always in a brawl, on the field, in the clubhouse, behind the stands and in the stands. The public's never known it, but Cobb's always been off the beam where other people are concerned. Sure, he made millions in the stock market — but that's only cold business. He carried a gun in the big league and scared hell out of us. He's mean, tricky, and dangerous. Look out he doesn't blow up some night and clip you with a bottle. He specializes in throwing bottles.

"Now that he's sick he's worse than ever. And you've signed up to stay with him for months. You poor sap."

Taken aback, but still skeptical, I launched the job — with my first task to drive Cobb to his Lake Tahoe retreat, where, he declared, we could work uninterrupted.

As indicated, nothing went right from the start. The Hangtown gunplay incident was an eye-opener. Next came a series of events, such as Cobb's determination to set forth in a blizzard to Reno, which were too strange to explain away. Everything had to suit his pleasure or he had a tantrum. He prowled about the lodge at night, suspecting trespassers, with the Luger in hand. I slept with one eye open, ready to move fast if necessary.

At one o'clock in the morning of the storm, full of pain and 90-proof, he took out the Luger, letting it rest casually between his knees. I had continued to object to a Reno excursion in such weather.

He looked at me with tight fury and said, biting out the words:

"In 1912 — and you can write this down — I killed a man in Detroit. He and two other hoodlums jumped me on the street early one morning with a knife. I was carrying something that came in handy in my early days — a Belgian-made pistol with a heavy raised sight at the barrel end.

"Well, the damned gun wouldn't fire and they cut me up the back."

Making notes as fast as he talked, I asked, "Where in the back?"

"Well, DAMMIT ALL TO HELL, IF YOU DON'T BELIEVE ME, COME AND LOOK!" Cobb flared, jerking up his shirt. When I protested that I believed him implicitly, only wanted a story detail, he picked up a half-full whiskey glass and smashed it against the brick fireplace. So I gingerly took a look. A faint whitish scar ran about five inches up the lower left back.

"Satisfied?" jeered Cobb.

He described how, after a battle, the men fled before his fists.

"What with you wounded and the odds 3-1," I said, "that must have been a relief."

"Relief? Do you think they could pull that on *me*? I WENT AFTER THEM!"

Where anyone else would have felt lucky to be out of it, Cobb chased one of the mugs into a dead-end alley. "I used that gunsight to rip and slash and tear him for about ten minutes until he had no face left," related Ty, with relish. "Left him there, not breathing, in his own rotten blood."

"What was the situation — where were you going when it happened?"

"To catch a train to a ball game."

"You saw a doctor, instead?"

"I DID NOTHING OF THE SORT, DAMMIT! I PLAYED THE NEXT DAY AND GOT TWO HITS IN THREE TIMES UP!"

Records I later inspected bore out every word of it: on June 3, 1912, in a blood-soaked, makeshift bandage, Ty Cobb hit a double and triple for Detroit, and only then was treated for the knife wound. He was that kind of ball player through a record 3,033 games. No other player burned with Cobb's flame. Boze Bulger, a great old-time baseball critic, said, "He was possessed by the Furies."

Finishing his tale, Cobb looked me straight in the eye.

*"You're driving me to Reno tonight,"* he said softly. The Luger was in his hand.

Even before I opened my mouth, Cobb knew he'd won. He had a sixth sense about the emotions he produced in others: in this case, fear. As far as I could see (lacking expert diagnosis and as a layman understands the symptoms), he wasn't merely erratic and trigger-tempered, but suffering from megalomania, or acute self-worship; delusions of persecution; and more than a touch of dipsomania.

Although I'm not proud of it, he scared hell out of me most of the time I was around him.

And now he gave me the first smile of our association. "As long as you don't aggravate my tension," he said, "we'll get along."

Before describing the Reno expedition, I would like to say in this frank view of a mighty man that the greatest, and strangest, of all American sport figures had his good side, which he tried to conceal. During the final ten months of his life I was his one constant companion. Eventually, I put him to bed, prepared his insulin, picked him up when he fell down, warded off irate taxi drivers, bartenders, waiters, clerks, and private citizens whom Cobb was inclined to punch, cooked what food he could digest, drew his bath, got drunk with him, and knelt with him in prayer on black nights when he knew death was near. I ducked a few bottles he threw, too.

I think, because he forced upon me a confession of his most private thoughts, that I know the answer to the central, overriding secret of his life: was Ty Cobb psychotic throughout his baseball career?

Kids, dogs, and sick people flocked to him and he returned their instinctive liking. Money was his idol, but from his $4 million fortune he assigned large sums to create the Cobb Educational Foundation, which financed hundreds of needy youngsters through college. He built and endowed a first-class hospital for the poor of his backwater home town, Royston, Georgia. When Ty's spinster sister, Florence, was crippled, he tenderly cared for her until her last days. The widow of a onetime American League batting champion would have lived in want but for Ty's steady money support. A Hall of Fame member, beaned by a pitched ball and enfeebled, came under Cobb's wing for years. Regularly he mailed dozens of anonymous checks to indigent old ball players (relayed by a third party) — a rare act among retired tycoons in other lines of business.

If you believe such acts didn't come hard for Cobb, guess again: he was the world's champion pinchpenny.

Some 150 fan letters reached him each month, requesting his autograph. Many letters enclosed return-mail stamps. Cobb used the stamps for his own outgoing mail. The fan letters he burned.

"Saves on firewood," he'd mutter.

In December of 1960, Ty hired a one-armed "gentleman's gentleman" named Brownie. Although constantly criticized, poor Brownie worked hard as cook and butler. But when he mixed up the grocery order one day, he was fired with a check for a week's pay — $45 — and sent packing.

Came the middle of that night and Cobb awakened me.

"We're driving into town *right now*," he stated, "to stop payment on Brownie's check. The bastard talked back to me when I discharged him. He'll get no more of my money."

All remonstrations were futile. There was no phone, so we had to drive 20 miles from Cobb's Tahoe lodge into Carson City, where he woke up the president of the First National Bank of Nevada and arranged for a stop-pay on the piddling check. The president tried to conceal his anger — Cobb was a big depositor in his bank.

"Yes sir, Ty," he said. "I'll take care of it first thing in the morning."

"You goddamn well better," snorted Cobb. And then we drove through the 3 A.M. darkness back to the lake.

But this trip was a light workout compared to that Reno trip.

Two cars were available at the lodge. Cobb's 1956 Imperial had no tire chains, but the other car did.

"We'll need both for this operation," he ordered. "One car might get stuck or break down. I'll drive mine and you take the one with chains. You go first. I'll follow your chain marks."

For Cobb to tackle precipitous Route 50 was unthinkable in every way. The Tahoe road, with 200 foot drop-offs, has killed a recorded 80 motorists. Along with his illness, his drunkenness, and no chains, he had bad eyes and was without a driver's license. California had turned him down at his last test; he hadn't bothered to apply in Nevada.

Urging him to ride with me was a waste of breath.

A howling wind hit my car a solid blow as we shoved off. Sleet stuck to the windshield faster than the wipers could work. For the first three miles, snowplows had been active, and at 15 mph, in second gear, I managed to hold the road. But then came Spooner's Summit, 7,000 feet high, and then a steep descent of nine miles. Behind me, headlamps blinking, Cobb honked his horn, demanding more speed. Chainless, he wasn't getting traction. *The hell with him,* I thought. Slowing to third gear, fighting to hold a roadbed I couldn't see even with my head stuck out the window, I skidded along. No other traffic moved as we did our crazy tandem around icy curves, at times brushing the guard rails. Cobb was blaring his horn steadily now.

*And then here came Cobb.*

Tiring of my creeping pace, he gunned the Imperial around me in one big skid. I caught a glimpse of an angry face under a big Stetson hat and a waving fist. He was doing a good 3 mph when he'd gained 25 yards on me, fishtailing right and left, but straightening as he slid out of sight in the thick sleet.

I let him go. Suicide wasn't in my contract.

The next six miles was a matter of feeling my way and praying. Near a curve, I saw tail lights to the left. Pulling up, I found Ty swung sideways and buried, nose down, in a snow bank, his hind wheels two feet in the air. Twenty yards away was a sheer drop-off into a canyon.

"You hurt?" I asked.

"Bumped my — head," he muttered. He lit a cigar and gave four-letter regards to the Highway Department for not illuminating the "danger" spot. His forehead was bruised and he'd broken his glasses.

In my car, we groped our way down-mountain, a nightmare ride, with Cobb alternately taking in Scotch from a thermos jug and telling me to step on it. At 3 A.M. in Carson City, an all-night garage man used a broom to clean the car of snow and agreed to pick up the Imperial — "when the road's passable." With dawn breaking, we reached Reno. All I wanted was a bed and all Cobb wanted was a craps table.

He was rolling now, pretending he wasn't ill, and with the Scotch bracing him. Ty was able to walk into the Riverside Hotel casino with a hand on my shoulder and without staggering so obviously as usual. Everybody present wanted to meet him. Starlets from a film unit on location in Reno flocked around and comedian Joe E. Lewis had the band play "Sweet Georgia Brown" — Ty's favorite tune.

"Hope your dice are still honest," he told Riverside co-owner Bill Miller. "Last time I was here I won $12,000 in three hours."

"How I remember, Ty," said Miller. "How I remember."

A scientific craps player who'd won and lost huge sums in Nevada in the past, Cobb bet $100 chips, his eyes alert, not missing a play around the board. He soon decided that the table was "cold" and we moved to another casino, then a third. At this last stop, Cobb's legs began to grow shaky. Holding himself up by leaning on the table edge with forearms, he dropped $300, then had a hot streak in which he won over $800. His voice was a croak as he told the other players, "Watch 'em and weep."

But then suddenly his voice came back. When the stickman raked the dice his way, Cobb loudly said, "You touched the dice with your hand."

"No, sir," said the stickman. "I did *not*."

"I don't lie!" snarled Cobb.

"I don't lie either," insisted the stickman.

"Nobody touches my dice!" Cobb, swaying on his feet, eyes blazing, worked his way around the table toward the croupier. It was a weird tableau. In his crumpled Stetson and expensive camel's-hair coat, stained and charred with cigarette burns, a three-day beard grizzling his face, the gaunt old giant of baseball towered over the dapper gambler.

"You fouled the dice. I saw you," growled Cobb, and then he swung.

The blow missed, as the stickman dodged, but, cursing and almost falling, Cobb seized the wooden rake and smashed it over the table. I jumped in and caught him under the arms as he sagged.

And then, as quickly as possible, we were put into the street by two large uniformed guards. "Sorry, Mr. Cobb," they said, unhappily, "but we can't have this."

A crowd had gathered and as we started down the street, Cobb swearing and stumbling and clinging to me, I couldn't have felt more conspicuous if I'd been strung naked from the neon arch across Reno's main drag, Virginia Street. At the street corner, Ty was struck by an attack of breathlessness. "Got to stop," he gasped. Feeling him going limp on me, I turned his six-foot body against a lamppost, braced my legs, and with an underarm grip held him there until he caught his breath. He panted and gulped for air.

His face gray, he murmured, "Reach into my left-hand coat pocket." Thinking he wanted his bottle of heart pills, I did. But instead pulled out a six-inch-thick wad of currency, secured by a rubber band. "Couple of thousand there," he said weakly. "Don't let it out of sight."

At the nearest motel, where I hired a single, twin-bed room, he collapsed on the bed in his coat and hat and slept. After finding myself some breakfast, I turned in. Hours later I heard him stirring. "What's this place?" he muttered.

I told him the name of the motel — Travelodge.

"Where's the bankroll?"

"In your coat. You're wearing it."

Then he was quiet.

After a night's sleep, Cobb felt well enough to resume his gambling. In the next few days, he won more than $3,000 at the tables, and then we went sight-seeing in historic Virginia City. There as in all places, he stopped traffic. And had the usual altercation. This one was at the Bucket of Blood, where Cobb accused the bartender of serving watered Scotch. The bartender denied it. Crash! Another drink went flying.

Back at the lodge a week later, looking like the wrath of John Barleycorn and having refused medical aid in Reno, he began to suffer new and excruciating pains — in his hips and lower back. But between groans he forced himself to work an hour a day on his autobiography. He told inside baseball tales never published:

". . . Frank Navin, who owned the Detroit club for years, faked his turnstile count to cheat the visiting team and Uncle Sam. So did Big Bill Devery and Frank Farrell, who owned the New York Highlanders — later called the Yankees.

". . . Walter Johnson, the Big Train, tried to kill himself when his wife died.

". . . Grover Cleveland Alexander wasn't drunk out there on the mound, the way people thought — he was an epileptic. Old Pete would fall down with a seizure between innings, then go back and pitch another shutout.

". . . John McGraw hated me because I tweaked his nose in broad daylight in the lobby of the Oriental Hotel, in Dallas, after earlier beating the hell out of his second baseman, Buck Herzog, upstairs in my room."

But before we were well started, Cobb suddenly announced we'd go riding in his 23-foot Chris-Craft speedboat tied up in a boathouse below the lodge. When I went down to warm it up, I found the boat sunk to the bottom of Lake Tahoe in 15 feet of water.

My host broke all records for blowing his stack when he heard the news. He saw in this a sinister plot. "I told you I've got enemies all around here! It's sabotage as sure as I'm alive!"

A sheriff's investigation turned up no clues. Cobb sat up all night for three nights with his Luger. "I'll salivate the first dirty skunk who steps foot around here after dark," he swore.

Parenthetically, Cobb had a vocabulary all his own. To "salivate" something meant to destroy it. Anything easy was "soft-boiled," to outsmart someone was to "slip him the oskafagus," and all doctors were "truss-fixers." People who displeased him — and this included almost everyone he met — were "fee-simple sonsofbitches," "mugwumps," or (if female) "lousy slits."

Lake Tahoe friends of Cobb's had stopped visiting him long before, but one morning an attractive blonde of about 50 came calling. She was an old chum — in a romantic way, I was given to understand, of bygone years — but Ty greeted her coldly. "Lost my sexual powers when I was 69," he said, when she was out of the room. "What the hell use to me is a woman?"

The lady had brought along a three-section electric vibrator bed, which she claimed would relieve Ty's back pains. We helped him mount it. He took a 20-minute treatment. Attempting to dismount, he lost balance, fell backward, the contraption jackknifed, and Cobb was pinned, yelling and swearing, under a pile of machinery.

When I freed him and helped him to a chair, he told the lady — in the choicest gutter language — where she could put her bed. She left, sobbing.

"That's no way to talk to an old friend, Ty," I said. "She was trying to do you a favor."

"And you're a hell of a poor guest around here, too!" he thundered. "You can leave any old time!" He quickly grabbed a bottle and heaved it in my direction.

"Thought you could throw straighter than that!" I yelled back. Cobb broke out a bottle of vintage Scotch, said I was "damned sensitive," half-apologized, and the matter was forgotten.

While working one morning on an outside observation deck, I heard a thud inside. On his bedroom floor, sprawled on his back, lay Ty. He was unconscious, his eyes rolled back, breathing shallowly. I thought he was dying.

There was no telephone. "Eavesdropping on the line," Cobb had told me. "I had it cut off." I ran down the road to a neighboring lodge and phoned a Carson City doctor, who promised to come immediately.

Back at the lodge, Ty remained stiff and stark on the floor, little bubbles escaping his lips. His face was bluish-white. With much straining, I lifted him halfway to the bed and by shifting holds finally rolled him onto it, and covered him with a blanket. Twenty minutes passed. No doctor.

Ten minutes later, I was at the front door, watching for the doctor's car, when I heard a sound. There stood Ty, swaying on his feet. "You want to do some work on the book?" he said.

His recovery didn't seem possible. "But you were out cold a minute ago," I said.

"Just a dizzy spell. Have 'em all the time. Must have hit my head on the bedpost when I fell."

The doctor, arriving, found Cobb's blood pressure standing at a grim 210 on the gauge. His temperature was 101 degrees and, from gross neglect of his diabetes, he was in a state of insulin shock, often fatal if not quickly treated. "I'll have to hospitalize you, Mr. Cobb," said the doctor.

Weaving his way to a chair, Cobb angrily waved him away. "Just send me your bill," he grunted. "I'm going home."

"Home" was the multimillionaire's main residence at Atherton, California, on the San Francisco Peninsula, 250 miles away, and it was there he headed later that night. With some hot soup and insulin in him, Cobb recovered with the same unbelievable speed he'd shown in baseball. In his heyday, trainers often sewed up deep spike cuts in his knees, shins, and thighs, on a clubhouse bench, without anesthetic, and he didn't lose an inning. Grantland Rice one 1920 day sat beside a bedridden, feverish Cobb, whose thighs, from sliding, were a mass of raw flesh. Sixteen hours later, he hit a triple, double, three singles, and stole two bases to beat the Yankees. On the Atherton ride, he yelled insults at several motorists who moved too slowly to suit him. Reaching Atherton, Ty said he felt ready for another drink.

My latest surprise was Cobb's 18-room, two-story, richly landscaped Spanish-California villa at 48 Spencer Lane, an exclusive neighborhood. You could have held a ball game on the grounds.

But the $90,000 mansion had no lights, no heat, no hot water.

"I'm suing the Pacific Gas & Electric Company," he explained, "for overcharging me on the service. Those rinky-dinks tacked an extra $16 on my bill. Bunch of crooks. When I wouldn't pay, they cut off my utilities. Okay — I'll see them in court."

For months previously, Ty Cobb had lived in a totally dark house. The only illumination was candlelight. The only cooking facility was a portable Coleman stove, such as campers use. Bathing was impossible, unless you could take it cold. The electric refrigerator, stove, deep-freeze, radio and television, of course, didn't work. Cobb had vowed to "hold the fort" until his trial of the P. G. & E. was settled. Simultaneously, he had filed a $60,000 suit in San Francisco Superior Court against the State of California to recover state income taxes already collected — on the argument that he wasn't a permanent resident of

California, but of Nevada, Georgia, Arizona, and other waypoints. State's attorneys claimed he spent at least six months per year in Atherton, thus had no case.

"I'm gone so much from here," he claimed, "that I'll win hands-down." All legal opinion, I later learned, held just the opposite view, but Cobb ignored their advice.

Next morning, I arranged with Ty's gardener, Hank, to turn on the lawn sprinklers. In the outdoor sunshine, a cold-water shower was easier to take. From then on, the back yard became my regular washroom.

The problem of lighting a desk so that we could work on the book was solved by stringing 200 feet of cord, plugged into an outlet of a neighboring house, through hedges and flower gardens and into the window of Cobb's study, where a single naked bulb, hung over the chandelier, provided illumination.

The flickering shadows cast by the single light made the vast old house seem haunted. No "ghost" writer ever had more ironical surroundings.

At various points around the premises, Ty showed me where he'd once installed high-voltage wires to stop trespassers. "Curiosity-seekers?" I asked. "Hell, no," he said. "Detectives broke in here once looking for evidence against me in a divorce suit. After a couple of them got burned, they stopped coming."

To reach our bedrooms, Cobb and I groped our way down long, black corridors. Twice he fell in the dark. And then, collapsing completely, he became so ill that he was forced to check in at Stanford Hospital in nearby Palo Alto. Here another shock was in store.

One of the physicians treating Ty's case, a Dr. E. R. Brown, said, "Do you mean to say that this man has traveled 700 miles in the last month without medical care?"

"Doctor," I said, "I've hauled him in and out of saloons, motels, gambling joints, steam baths, and snow banks. There's no holding him."

"It's a miracle he's alive. He has almost every major ailment I know about."

Dr. Brown didn't reveal to me Ty's main ailment, which news Cobb, himself, broke late one night from his hospital bed. "It's cancer," he said, bluntly. "About a year ago I had most of my prostate gland removed when they found it was malignant. Now it's spread up into the backbones. These pill-peddlers here won't admit it, but I haven't got a chance."

Cobb made me swear I'd never divulge the fact before he died. "If it gets in the papers, the sob sisters will have a field day. I don't want sympathy from anybody."

At Stanford, where he absorbed seven massive doses of cobalt radiation, the ultimate cancer treatment, he didn't act like a man on his last legs. Even before his strength returned, he was in the usual form.

"They won't let me have a drink," he said, indignantly. "I want you to get me a bottle. Smuggle it in in your tape-recorder case."

I tried, telling myself that no man with terminal cancer deserves to be dried up, but sharp-eyed nurses and orderlies were watching. They searched Ty's closet, found the bottle, and over his roars of protest appropriated it.

"We'll have to slip them the oskefagus," said Ty.

Thereafter, a drink of Scotch-and-water sat in plain view in his room, on the bedside table, under the very noses of his physicians — and nobody suspected a thing. The whiskey was in an ordinary water glass, and in the liquid reposed Ty's false teeth.

There were no dull moments while Cobb was at the hospital. He was critical of everything. He told one doctor that he was not even qualified to be an intern, and told the hospital dietician — at the top of his voice — that she and the kitchen workers were in a conspiracy to poison him with their "foul" dishes. To a nurse he snapped, "If Florence Nightingale knew about you, she'd spin in her grave."

(Stanford Hospital, incidentally, is one of the largest and top-rated medical plants in the United States.)

But between blasts he did manage to buckle down to work on the book, dictating long into the night into a microphone suspended over his bed. Slowly the stormy details of his professional life came out. He spoke often of having "forgiven" his many baseball enemies, then lashed out at them with such passionate phrases that it was clear he'd done no such thing. High on his "hate" list were McGraw; New York sports writers; Hub Leonard, a pitcher who in 1926 accused Cobb and Tris speaker of "fixing" a Detroit-Cleveland game; American League President Ban Johnson; one-time Detroit owner Frank Navin; former Baseball Commissioner Kenesaw Mountain Landis; and all those who intimated that Cobb ever used his spikes on another player without justification.

After a night when he slipped out of the hospital, against all orders, and we drove to a San Francisco Giants-Cincinnati Reds game at Candlestick Park, 30 miles away, Stanford Hospital decided it couldn't help Tyrus R. Cobb, and he was discharged. For extensive treatment his bill ran to more than $1,200.

"That's a nice racket you boys have here," he told the discharging doctors. "You clip the customers and then every time you pass an undertaker, you wink at him."

"Good-by, Mr. Cobb," snapped the medical men.

Soon after this Ty caught a plane to his native Georgia and I went along. "I want to see some of the old places again before I die," he said.

It now was Christmas eve of 1960 and I'd been with him for three months and completed but four chapters. The project had begun to look hopeless. In Royston, a village of 1,200, Cobb headed for the town cemetery. I drove him there, we parked, and I helped him climb a windswept hill through the growing dusk. Light snow fell. Faintly, yule chimes could be heard.

Amongst the many headstones, Ty looked for the plot he'd reserved for himself while in California and couldn't locate it. His temper began to boil. "Dammit, I ordered the biggest damn mausoleum in the grave-yard! I know it's around here somewhere." On the next hill, we found it: a large marble, walk-in-size structure with "Cobb" engraved over the entrance.

"You want to pray with me?" he said, gruffly. We knelt and tears came to his eyes.

Within the tomb, he pointed to crypts occupied by the bodies of his father, Professor William Herschel Cobb, his mother, Amanda (Chit-wood) Cobb, and his sister, Florence, whom he'd had disinterred and placed here. "My father," he said reverently, "was the greatest man I ever knew. He was a scholar, state senator, editor, and philosopher. I wor-shipped him. So did all the people around here. He was the only man who ever made me do his bidding."

Arising painfully, Ty braced himself against the marble crypt that soon would hold his body. There was an eerie silence in the tomb. He said deliberately:

"My father had his head blown off with a shotgun when I was 18 years old — *by a member of my own family.* I didn't get over that. I've never gotten over it."

We went back down the hill to the car. I asked no questions that day.

Later, from family sources and old Georgia friends of the baseball idol, I learned about the killing. One night in August of 1905, they related, Professor Cobb announced that he was driving from Royston to a neighboring village and left home by buggy. But, later that night, he doubled back and crept into his wife's bedroom by the way of the window. "He suspected her of being unfaithful to him," said these sources. "He thought he'd catch her in the act. But Amanda Cobb was a good woman. She was all alone when she saw a menacing figure climb through her window and approach her bed. In the dark, she assumed it to be a robber. She kept a shotgun handy by her bed and she used it. Everybody around here knows the story, but it was hushed up when Ty became famous."

News of the killing reached Ty in Augusta, where he was playing minor-league ball, on August 9. A few days later he was told that he'd been purchased by the Detroit Tigers, and was to report immediately. "In my grief," Cobb says in the book, "it didn't matter much. . . ."

Came March of 1961 and I remained stuck to the Georgia Peach like court plaster. He'd decided that we were born pals, meant for each other, that we'd complete a baseball book beating anything ever published. He had astonished doctors by rallying from the spreading cancer and, between bouts of transmitting his life and times to a tape recorder, was raising more whoopee than he had at Lake Tahoe and Reno.

Spring-training time for the big leagues had arrived and we were ensconced in a $30-a-day suite at the Ramada Inn at Scottsdale, Arizona, close by the practice parks of the Red Sox, Indians, Giants, and Cubs. Here, each year, Cobb held court. He didn't go to see anybody; Ford Frick, Joe Cronin, Ted Williams, and other diamond notables came to him. While explaining to sports writers why modern stars couldn't compare to the Wagners, Lajoies, Speakers, Jacksons, Mathewsons, and Planks of his day, Ty did other things.

For one, he commissioned a noted Arizona artist to paint him in oils. He was emaciated, having dropped from 208 pounds to 176. The preliminary sketches showed up his sagging cheeks and thin neck.

"I wouldn't let you kalsomine my toilet," ripped out Ty, and fired the artist.

But at analyzing the Dow-Jones averages and playing the stock market, he was anything but eccentric. Twice a week he phoned experts around the country, determined good buys, and bought in blocks of 500 to 1,500 shares. He made money consistently, even when bedridden, with a mind that read behind the fluctuations of a dozen different issues. "The State of Georgia," Ty remarked, "will realize about one million dollars from inheritance taxes when I'm dead. But there isn't a man alive who knows what I'm worth." According to the *Sporting News*, there was evidence upon Cobb's death that his worth approximated $12 million. Whatever the true figure, he did not confide the amount to me — or, most probably, to anyone except attorneys who drafted his last will and testament. And Cobb fought off making his will until the last moment.

His fortune began in 1908, when he bought into United (later General) Motors; as of 1961, he was "Mr. Coca-Cola," holding more than 20,000 shares of stock, valued at $85 per share. Wherever we traveled, he carried with him, stuffed into an old brown bag, more than $1 million in stock certificates and negotiable government bonds. The bag never was locked up. Cobb assumed nobody would dare rob him. He tossed the bag into any handy corner of a room, inviting theft. And in Scottsdale it turned up missing.

Playing Sherlock, he narrowed the suspects to a room maid and a man he'd hired to cook meals. When questioned, the maid broke into tears and the cook quit (fired, said Cobb). Hours later, I discovered the bag under a pile of dirty laundry.

Major-league owners and league officials hated to see him coming, for he thought their product was putrid and said so, incessantly. "Today they hit for ridiculous averages, can't bunt, can't steal, can't hit-and-run, can't place-hit to the opposite field, and you can't call them ball players." He told sports writers, "I blame Frick, Cronin, Bill Harridge, Horace Stoneham, Dan Topping, and others for wrecking baseball's traditional league lines. These days, any tax-dodging mugwump with a bankroll can buy a franchise, field some semi-pros, and get away with it. Where's our integrity? Where's *baseball?*"

No one could quiet Cobb. Who else had a lifetime average of .367, made 4,191 hits, scored 2,244 runs, won 12 batting titles, stole 892 bases, repeatedly beat whole teams single-handedly? Who was first into the Hall of Fame? Not Babe Ruth — but Cobb, by a landslide vote.

By early April, he could barely make it up the ramp of the Scottsdale Stadium, even hanging onto me. He had to stop, gasping for breath, every few steps. But he kept coming to games — loving the sounds of the ball park. His courage was tremendous. "Always be ready to catch me if I start to fall," he said. "I'd hate to go down in front of the fans."

People of all ages were overcome with emotion upon meeting him; no sports figure I've known produced such an effect upon the public.

We went to buy a cane. At a surgical supply house, Cobb inspected a dozen $25 malacca sticks, bought the cheapest, $4, white-ash cane they had. "I'm a plain man," he informed the clerk, the $7,500 diamond ring on his finger glittering.

But pride kept the old tiger from ever using the cane, any more than he'd wear the $600 hearing aid built into the bow of his glasses.

One day a Mexican taxi driver aggravated Cobb with his driving. Throwing the fare on the ground, he waited until the cabbie had bent to retrieve it, then tried to punt him like a football.

"What's your sideline," he inquired, "selling opium?"

It was all I could do to keep the driver from swinging on him. Later, a lawyer called on Cobb, threatening a damage suit. "Get in line, there's 500 ahead of you," said Tyrus, waving him away.

Every day was a new adventure. He was fighting back against the pain that engulfed him again — cobalt treatments no longer helped — and I could count on trouble anywhere we went. He threw a salt shaker at a Phoenix waiter, narrowly missing. One of his most treasured friendships — with Ted Williams — came to an end.

From the early 1940's, Williams had sat at Ty Cobb's feet. They often met, exchanged long letters on the art of batting. At Scottsdale one day, Williams dropped by Ty's rooms. He hugged Ty, fondly rumpled his hair, and accepted a drink. Presently the two greatest hitters of past and present fell into an argument over what players should comprise the all-time, all-star team. Williams declared, "I want DiMaggio and Hornsby on my team over anybody you can mention."

Cobb's face grew dark. "Don't give me that! Hornsby couldn't go back for a pop fly and he lacked smartness. DiMaggio couldn't hit with Speaker or Joe Jackson."

"The hell you say!" came back Williams, jauntily. "Hornsby out-hit *you* a couple of years."

Almost leaping from his chair, Cobb shook a fist. He'd been given the insult supreme — for Cobb always resented, and finally hated, Rogers Hornsby. Not until Cobb was in his sixteenth season did Hornsby top him in the batting averages. "Get . . . away from me!" choked Cobb. "Don't come back!"

Williams left with a quizzical expression, not sure how much Cobb meant it. The old man meant it all the way. He never invited Williams back, nor talked to him, nor spoke his name again. "I cross him off," he told me.

We left Arizona shortly thereafter for my home in Santa Barbara, California. Now failing fast, Tyrus had accepted my invitation to be my guest. Two doctors inspected him at my beach house by the Pacific and gave their opinions: he had a few months of life left, no more. The cancer had invaded the bones of his skull. His pain was intense, unrelenting — requiring heavy sedation — yet with teeth bared and sweat pouring down his face, he fought off medical science. "They'll never get me on their damn hypnotics," he swore. "I'll never die an addict . . . an idiot. . . ."

He shouted, "Where's anybody who cares about me? Where are they? The world's lousy . . . no good."

One night later, on May 1, Cobb sat propped up in bed, overlooking a starlit ocean. He had a habit, each night, of rolling up his trousers and placing them under his pillows — an early-century ball player's trick, dating from the time when Ty slept in strange places and might be robbed. I knew that his ever-present Luger was tucked into that pants-roll.

I'd never seen him so sunk in despair. At last the fire was going out. "Do we die a little at a time, or all at once?" he wondered aloud. "I think Max had the right idea."

The reference was to his onetime friend, multimillionaire Max Fleischmann, who'd cheated lingering death by cancer some years earlier by putting a bullet through his brain. Ty spoke of Babe Ruth, another cancer victim. "If Babe had been told what he had in time, he could've got it over with."

Had I left Ty that night, I believe he would have pulled the trigger. His three living children (two were dead) had withdrawn from him. In the wide world that had sung his fame, he had not one intimate friend remaining.

But we talked, and prayed, until dawn, and then sleep came; in the morning, aided by friends, I put him into a car and drove him home, to the big, gloomy house in Atherton. He spoke only twice during the six-hour ride.

"Have you got enough to finish the book?" he asked.

"More than enough."

"Give 'em the word then. I had to fight all my life to survive. They all were against me . . . tried every dirty trick to cut me down. But I beat the bastards and left them in the ditch. Make sure the book says that. . . ."

I was leaving him now, permanently, and I had to ask one question I'd never put to him before.

"Why did you fight so hard in baseball, Ty?"

He'd never looked fiercer than then, when he answered. "I did it for my father, who was an exalted man. They killed him when he was still young. They blew his head off the same week I became a major leaguer.

He never got to see me play. But I knew he was watching me and I never let him down."

You can make what you want of that. Keep in mind what Casey Stengel said, later: "I never saw anyone like Cobb. No one even close to him. When he wiggled those wild eyes at a pitcher, you knew you were looking at the one bird nobody could beat. It was like he was superhuman."

To me it seems that the violent death of a father whom a sensitive, highly talented boy loved deeply, and feared, engendered, through some strangely supreme desire to vindicate that father, the most violent, successful, thoroughly maladjusted personality ever to pass across American sports. The shock tipped the 18-year-old mind, making him capable of incredible feats.

Off the field, he was still at war with the world. For the emotionally disturbed individual, in most cases, does not change his pattern. To reinforce that pattern, he was viciously hazed by Detroit Tiger veterans when he was a rookie. He was bullied, ostracized, and beaten up — in one instance, a 210-pound catcher named Charlie Schmidt broke the 165-pound Ty Cobb's nose. It was persecution immediately heaped upon the deepest desolation a young man can experience.

Yes, Ty Cobb was a badly disturbed personality. It is not hard to understand why he spent his entire life in deep conflict. Nor why a member of his family, in the winter of 1960, told me, "I've spent a lot of time terrified of him . . . I think he was psychotic from the time that he left Georgia to play in the big league."

"Psychotic" is not a word I'd care to use. I believe that he was far more than the fiercest of all competitors. He was a vindicator who believed that "father was watching" and who could not put that father's terrible fate out of his mind. The memory of it threatened his sanity.

The fact that he recognized and feared this is revealed in a tape recording he made, in which he describes his own view of himself: "I was like a steel spring with a growing and dangerous flaw in it. If it is wound too tight or has the slightest weak point, the spring will fly apart and then it is done for. . . ."

The last time I saw him, he was sitting in his armchair in the Atherton mansion. The place still was without lights or heat. I shook his hand in farewell, and he held it a moment longer.

"What about it? Do you think they'll remember me?" He tried to say it as if it didn't matter.

"They'll always remember you," I said.

On July 8, I received in the mail a photograph of Ty's mausoleum on the hillside in the Royston cemetery with the words scribbled on the back: *"Any time now."* Nine days later he died in an Atlanta hospital. Before going, he opened the brown bag, piled $1 million in negotiable securities beside his bed, and placed the Luger atop them.

From all of major-league baseball, three men and three only appeared for his funeral.

1964

## Stan Fischler

........................................................................................................

# A Rough Time on the Road

FROM *Sports Illustrated*

ON JANUARY 2, 1929, the Boston Bruins boarded a night train to Montreal for a National Hockey League game there the following evening against the Montreal Maroons. As the train was pulling out of the North Station, Art Ross, the Bruins' manager, walked through the Pullman sleeping car, counting the players. When Ross reached the last berth, he realized that one of them, Eddie Shore, was missing.

"Ross didn't know it," Shore said recently, "but I was then running down the platform trying to jump on the last car of the train. I didn't make it. I just missed the train because my taxi got tied up in a traffic accident coming across town."

Shore was determined to get to Montreal in time for the game. The Bruins were already shorthanded because of injuries, and Shore was well aware that Ross levied a $500 fine on any player who missed a road trip. Shore checked the train schedule and found that the next express to Montreal in the morning would not reach there until after the game had started. He learned that all of the airline planes were grounded because of stormy weather. He was about to rent an automobile when a wealthy Boston friend offered to lend him a limousine with a chauffeur. At 11:30 that night Shore and the chauffeur started the 350-mile drive north over iced and snow-blocked New England mountain roads. It was sleeting, and in those days there were no paved express highways, no sanding trucks and no road patrols. The chauffeur drove very slowly through the storm. "I was not happy about the way he was driving," Shore said, "and I told him so. He apologized and said he didn't have chains and didn't like driving in the winter. The poor fellow urged me to turn back to Boston."

At that point the car skidded to the lip of a ditch. Shore took over at the wheel and drove to an all-night service station where he had tire chains put on. By then the sleet storm had thickened into a blizzard. Snow caked either side of the lone windshield wiper, and within minutes the wiper blade froze solid to the glass. "I couldn't see out the window," says Shore, "so I removed the top half of the windshield."

His face was exposed to the blasts of the icy wind and snow but he managed to see the road. At about 5 A.M., in the mountains of New Hampshire, "we began losing traction. The tire chains had worn out."

Slowly, Shore eased the car around a bend in the road where he could see the lights of a construction camp flickering. He awakened a gas station attendant there, installed a new set of chains and weaved on. "We skidded off the road four times," he says, "but each time we managed to get the car back on the highway again."

The second pair of chains fell off at three the next afternoon. This time Shore stopped the car and ordered the chauffeur to take over the wheel. "I felt that a short nap would put me in good shape," he says. "All I asked of the driver was that he go at least twelve miles an hour and stay in the middle of the road."

But the moment Shore dozed off, the chauffeur lost control of the big car and it crashed into a deep ditch. Neither Shore nor the chauffeur nor the car suffered any damage so Shore hiked a mile to a farmhouse for help. "I paid $8 for a team of horses," says Shore, "harnessed the horses and pulled the car out of the ditch. We weren't too far from Montreal and I thought we'd make it in time if I could keep the car on the road."

He did and at 5:30 P.M. Shore drove up to the Windsor Hotel, the Bruins' headquarters. He staggered into the lobby and nearly collapsed. "He was in no condition for hockey," says Ross. "His eyes were bloodshot, his face frostbitten and windburned, his fingers bent and set like claws after gripping the steering wheel so long. And he couldn't walk straight. I figured his legs were almost paralyzed from hitting the brake and clutch."

Nevertheless Shore ate a steak dinner, his first real meal in twenty-four hours, and refused the coach's orders to go to sleep. "I was tired all right," Shore says, "but I thought a twenty- or thirty-minute nap would be enough, then I'd be set to play."

An hour later Dit Clapper and Cooney Weiland of the Bruins entered Shore's room and shook him gently. Nothing happened. They rolled him over the bed and onto the floor. Still nothing happened. Weiland filled several glasses with water and poured them over Shore's face. This time he woke up and immediately insisted on playing.

Ross didn't want him to play. "I knew how durable he was," the coach says, "but there's a limit to human endurance. I finally decided to let him get on the ice, but at the first sign of weakness or sleepwalking I'd send him to the dressing room. I had to worry about him being groggy. What if he got hit hard and wound up badly hurt?"

The game was rough and fast. The powerful Maroons penetrated Boston's defense often, but Shore always helped repulse them. He smashed Hooley Smith to the ice with a vicious body check and drew the game's first penalty. Ross considered benching him at this point, but changed his mind. When the penalty had elapsed, Shore jumped on the ice and appeared stronger than ever. Shortly before the halfway point in the second period he skated behind his net to retrieve the puck. He faked one Montreal player, picked up speed at center ice and swerved to the left when he reached the Maroons' blue line. He sped around the last defenseman and shot. "I would say I was fifteen feet out to the left," he says. "I can remember exactly how my shot went. It was low, about six inches off the ice, and went hard into the right corner of the net." The time of the goal was 8:20 of the second period. The Bruins led 1–0.

Shore still showed no signs of his ordeal during the third period (he had another two-minute penalty), and almost twenty-four hours after he had chased the train down the North Station platform in Boston the final buzzer sounded. Apart from the two penalties, Shore had played the entire game without relief and, what's more, had scored the only goal of the game. Coach Ross never fined him for missing the train.

1969

## Thomas McGuane

·····································································································

# The Longest Silence

FROM *Sports Illustrated*

WHAT IS EMPHATIC in angling is made so by the long silences — the unproductive periods. For the ardent fisherman, progress is toward the kinds of fishing that are never productive in the sense of the blood riots of the hunting-and-fishing periodicals. Their illusions of continuous action evoke for him, finally, a condition of utter, mortuary boredom. Such an angler will always be inclined to find the gunnysack artists of the heavy kill rather cretinoid, their stringerloads of gaping fish appalling.

No form of fishing offers such elaborate silences as fly-fishing for permit. The most successful permit fly-fisherman in the world has very few catches to describe to you. Yet there is considerable agreement that taking a permit on a fly is the extreme experience of the sport. Even the guides allow enthusiasm to shine through their cool, professiona personas. I once asked one who specialized in permit if he liked fishing for them. "Yes, I do," he said reservedly, "but about the third time the customer asks, 'Is they good to eat?' I begin losing interest."

The recognition factor is low when you catch a permit. If you wake up your neighbor in the middle of the night to tell him of your success, shaking him by the lapels of his Dr. Dentons and shouting to be heard over his million-BTU air conditioner, he may well ask you what a permit is, and you will tell him it is like a pompano, and rolling over, he will tell you he cherishes pompano like he had it at Joe's Stone Crab in Miami Beach, with key lime pie afterward. If you have one mounted, you'll always be explaining what it is to people who thought you were talking about your fishing license in the first place. In the end you take the fish off the conspicuous wall and put it upstairs, where you can see it when Mom sends you to your room. It's private.

I came to it through bonefishing. The two fish share the same marine habitat, the negotiation of which in a skiff can be somewhat hazardous. It takes getting used to, to run wide open at 30 knots over a close bottom, with sponges, sea fans, crawfish traps, conchs, and starfish racing under the hull with awful clarity. The backcountry of the Florida Keys is full of hummocks, narrow, winding waterways and channels that open with complete arbitrariness to basins, and, on every side, the flats that preoccupy the fisherman. The process of learning to fish this region is one of learning the particularities of each of these flats. The channel flats with crunchy staghorn-coral bottoms, the bare sand flats, and the turtle-grass flats are all of varying utility to the fisherman, and depending upon tide, these values are in a constant condition of change. The principal boat wreckers are the yellow cap-rock flats and the more mysterious coral heads. I was personally plagued by a picture of one of these enormities coming through the hull of my skiff and catching me on the point of the jaw. I had the usual Coast Guard safety equipment, not excluding floating cushions emblazoned FROST-FREE KEY WEST and a futile plastic whistle. I added a navy flare gun. As I learned the country, guides would run by me in their big skiffs and 100-horse engines. I knew they never hit coral heads and had, besides, CB radios with which they might call for help. I dwelled on that and sent for radio catalogues.

One day when I was running to Content Pass on the edge of the Gulf of Mexico, I ran aground wide open in the backcountry. Unable for the moment to examine the lower unit of my engine, I got out of the boat, waiting for the tide to float it, and strolled around in four inches of water. It was an absolutely windless day. The mangrove islands stood elliptically in their perfect reflections. The birds were everywhere — terns, gulls, wintering ducks, skimmers, all the wading birds, and, crying down from their tall shafts of air, more ospreys than I had ever seen. The gloomy bonanza of the Overseas Highway with its idiot billboard montages seemed very far away.

On the western edge of that flat I saw my first permit, tailing in two feet of water. I had heard all about permit but had been convinced I'd never see one. So, looking at what was plainly a permit, I did not know what it was. That evening, talking to my friend Woody Sexton, a permit expert, I reconstructed the fish and had it identified for me. I grew retroactively excited, and Woody apprised me of some of the difficulties associated with catching one of them on a fly. A prompt, immobilizing humility came over me forthwith.

After that, over a long period of time, I saw a good number of them. Always, full of hope, I would cast. The fly was anathema to them. One look and they were gone. I cast to a few hundred. It seemed futile, all wrong, like trying to bait a tiger with watermelons. The fish would see the fly, light out or ignore it, sometimes flare at it, but never, never touch it. I went to my tying vise and made flies that looked like whatever you could name, flies that were praiseworthy from anything but a practical point of view. The permit weren't interested, and I no longer even caught bonefish. I went back to my old fly, a rather ordinary bucktail, and was relieved to be catching bonefish again. I thought I had lost what there was of my touch.

One Sunday morning I decided to conduct services in the skiff, taking the usual battery of rods for the permit pursuit. More and more the fish had become a simple abstraction, even though they had made one ghostly midwater appearance, poised silver as moons near my skiff, and had departed without movement, like a light going out. But I wondered if I had actually seen them. I must have. The outline and movement remained in my head — the dark fins, the pale gold of the ventral surface, and the steep, oversized scimitar tails. I dreamed about them.

This fell during the first set of April's spring tides — exaggerated tides associated with the full moon. I had haunted a long, elbow-shaped flat on the Atlantic side of the keys, and by Sunday there was a large movement of tide and reciprocal tide. A 20-knot wind complicated my still unsophisticated poling, and I went down the upper end of the flat yawing from one edge to the other and at times raging as the boat tried to swap ends against my will. I looked around, furtively concerned with whether I could be seen by any of the professionals. At the corner of the flat I turned downwind and proceeded less than 40 yards when I spotted, on the southern perimeter of the flat, a large stingray making a strenuous mud. When I looked closely it seemed there was something else swimming in the disturbance. I poled toward it for a better look. The other fish was a very large permit. The ray had evidently stirred up a crab and was trying to cover it to prevent the permit from getting it. The permit, meanwhile, was whirling around the ray, nipping its fins to make it move off the crab.

Now my problem was to set the skiff up above the fish, get rid of the push pole, drift down, and make a cast. I quietly poled upwind, wondering why I had not been spotted. I was losing my breath with excitement; the little expanse of skin beneath my sternum throbbed like a frog's throat. I acquired a fantastic lack of coordination. Turning in the wind, I beat the boat with the push pole, like a gong. I conducted what a friend has described as a Chinese fire drill. After five minutes of the direst possible clownage I got into position and could still see the permit's fins breaking the surface of the ray's mud. I laid the push pole down, picked up my fly rod, and, to my intense irritation, saw that the ray had given up and was swimming, not seeing me, straight to the skiff. The closing rate was ruinous. I couldn't get a cast off in time to do anything. About 20 feet from the boat the ray sensed my presence and veered 15 feet off my starboard gunwale, leaving the permit swimming close to the ray but on my side. As soon as I could see the permit perfectly, it started to flush, but instead just crossed to the opposite side of the ray. Taking the only chance offered me, I cast over the ray, hoping my line would not spook it and, in turn, the permit. The fly fell with lucky, agonizing perfection, three feet in front of the permit on its exact line of travel. There was no hesitation; the fish darted forward and took — the one-in-a-thousand shot. I lifted the rod, feeling the rigid bulk of the still unalarmed fish, and set the hook. He shimmered away, my loose line jumping off the deck. And then the rod suddenly doubled and my leader broke. A loop of line had tightened itself around the handle of the reel.

I was ready for the rubber room. I had been encouraged to feel it might be five years before I hooked another. I tried to see all that was good in other kinds of fishing. I thought of various life-enhancing things I could do at home. I could turn to the ennobling volumes of world literature on my shelves. I might do some oils, slap out a gouache or two. But I could not distract myself from the mental image of my lovingly assembled fly rushing from my hands on the lip of a big permit.

I had to work out a routine that would not depend on such exceptional events for success. One technique, finally, almost guaranteed me shots at permit, and that was to stake out my skiff on the narrow channel flats that are covered with a crunchy layer of blue-green staghorn coral. Permit visit these in succession, according to tide and a hierarchy of flat values known mainly to them but intuited by certain strenuous fishermen. I liked to be on these flats at the early incoming tide — the young flood, as it is called — and fish to the middle incoming or, often, to the slack high. The key was to be able to stand for six hours and watch an acre of bottom for any sign of life at all. The body would give out in the following sequence: arches, back, hips. Various dehydration problems developed. I carried ice and drank quinine water until my ears rang. Pushups and deep knee bends on the casting deck helped. And, like anyone else who uses this method, I became an active fantasizer. The time was punctuated by the appearances of oceanic wildlife, fish and turtles that frequented the area as well as many that did not. With any luck at all the permit came, sometimes in a squadron and in a hurry, sometimes alone with their tails in the air, rooting along the hard edge of the flat. The cast would be made, the line and leader would straighten and the fly fall. On a normal day the fly only made the permit uncomfortable, and it would turn and gravely depart. On another the fly so horrified the fish that it turned tail and bolted. On very few days it sprinted at the fly, stopped a few inches short, ran in a circle when the fly was gently worked, returned and flared at it, flashed at it, saw the boat and flushed.

On very hot days when the cumulus clouds stacked in a circle around the horizon, a silky sheen of light lay on the water, so that the vision had to be forced through until the head ached. Patience was strained from the first, and water seemed to stream from the skin. At such times I was counting on an early sighting of fish to keep my attention. And when this did not happen I succumbed to an inviting delusion. I imagined the best place to fish was somewhere very far away, and it would be necessary to run the country.

I reeled up my line and put the rod in its holder. I took the push pole out of the bottom and secured it in its chocks on the gunwale. Then I let the wind carry me off the flat. I started the engine and put it in forward, suffering exquisitely a moment more, then ran the throttle as far as it would go. The bow lifted, then lowered on plane, the stern came up, and the engine whined satisfactorily. Already the perspiration was drying, and I felt cool and slaked by the spray. Once on top, standing and steering, running wide open, I projected on my mind what was remembered of a suitable chart to get to this imaginary place where the fish were thick enough to walk on. I looked up and was reproved by the vapor trail of a Navy Phantom interceptor. I ran up the channels, under the bridge, using all the cheap tricks I though I could get away with, short-cutting flats when I thought I had enough water, looking back to see if I had made a mud trail, running the banks to get around basins because the coral heads wouldn't grow along a bank, running tight to the keys in a foot and a half of water when I was trying to beat the wind, and finally shutting down on some bank or flat or along some tidal pass not unlike the one I just ran from. It was still as hot as it could be, and I still could not see. The sweat was running onto my Polaroids, and I was hungry and thinking I'd call it a day. When I got home I rather abashedly noted that I had burned a lot of fuel and hadn't made a cast.

The engine hadn't been running right for a week, and I was afraid of getting stranded or having to sleep out on some buggy flat or, worse, being swept to Galveston on an offshore wind. I tore the engine down and found the main bearing seal shot and in need of replacement. I drove to Big Pine to get parts and arrived about the time the guides, who center there, were coming in for the day. I walked to the dock, where the big skiffs with their excessive engines were nosed to the breakwater. Guides mopped decks and needled each other. Customers, happy and not, debarked with armloads of tackle, sun hats, oil, thermoses, and picnic baskets. A few of these sporty dogs were plastered. One fragile lady, owlish with sunburn, tottered from the casting deck of a guide's skiff and drew herself up on the dock. "Do you know what the whole trouble was?" she inquired of her companion, perhaps her husband, a man very much younger than herself.

"No, what?" he said. She smiled and pitied him.

"Well, *think* about it." The two put their belongings into the trunk of some kind of minicar and drove off too fast down the Overseas Highway. Four hours would put them in Miami.

It seemed to have been a good day. A number of men went up the dock with fish to be mounted. One man went by with a bonefish that might have gone 10 pounds. Woody Sexton was on the dock. I wanted to ask how he had done but knew that ground rules forbid the asking of this question around the boats. It embarrasses guides who have had bad days, on the one hand, and on the other, it risks passing good fishing information promiscuously. Meanwhile, as we talked, the mopping and needling continued along the dock. The larger hostilities are reserved for the fishing grounds themselves, where various complex snubbings may be performed from the semi-anonymity of the powerful skiffs. The air can be electric with accounts of who cut off who, who ran the bank on who, and so on. The antagonism among the skiff guides, the offshore guides, the pompano fishermen, the crawfishermen, the shrimpers, produces tales of shootings, of disputes settled with gaffs, of barbed wire strung in guts and channels to wreck prop and drive shafts. Some of the tales are true. Woody and I made a plan to fish when he got a day off. I found my engine parts and went home.

I worked out two or three bonefish patterns for the inside bank of Loggerhead Key. The best of these was a turn-off point where the bonefish which were contouring the bank hit a small ridge and turned up onto the flat itself. By positioning myself at this turning point, I would be able to get casts off to passing fish and be able to see a good piece of the bank, down light, until noon.

One day I went out and staked the boat during the middle-incoming water of another set of new moon tides. I caught one bonefish early in the tide, a lively fish that went 100 yards on his first run and doggedly resisted me for a length of time that was all out of proportion to his weight. I released him after giving him a short revival session and then just sat and looked at the water. I could see Woody fishing with a customer, working the outside of the bank for tarpon.

It was a queer day to begin with. The vital light flashed on and off around the scudding clouds, and there were slight foam lines on the water from the wind. The basin that shelved off from my bank was active with diving birds, particularly great brown pelicans, whose wings sounded like luffing sails and who ate with submerged heads while blackheaded gulls tried to rob them. The birds were drawn to the basin by a school of mullet that was making an immense mud slick hundreds of yards across. In the sun the slick glowed a quarter of a mile to the south. I didn't pay it much attention until it began by collective will or chemical sensors to move onto my bank. Inexorably, the huge disturbance progressed and flowed toward me. In the thinner water the mullet school was compressed, and the individual fish became easier targets for predators. Big oceanic barracuda were with them and began slashing and streaking through the school like bolts of lightning. Simultaneously, silver sheets of mullet, sometimes an acre in extent, burst out of the water and rained down again. In time my skiff was in the middle of it, and I could see the opaque water was inch by inch alive.

Some moments later, not far astern of me, perhaps 70 feet, a large blacktip shark swam up onto the bank and began traveling with grave sweeps of its tail through the fish, not as yet making a move for them. Mullet and smaller fish nevertheless showered out in front of the shark as it coursed through. Behind the shark I could see another fish flashing unclearly. I supposed it was a jack crevalle, a pelagic fish, strong for its size, that often follows sharks. I decided to cast. The distance was all

I could manage. I got off one of my better shots, which nevertheless fell slightly behind target. I was surprised to see the fish drop back to the fly, turn and elevate high in the water, then take. It was a permit.

I set the hook sharply, and the fish started down the flat. Remembering my last episode, I kept the loose, racing line well away from the reel handle for the instant the fish took to consume it. Then the fish was on the reel. I lowered the rod tip and cinched the hook, and the fish began to accelerate, staying on top of the flat, so that I could see its wildly extending wake. Everything was holding together: the hookup was good, the knots were good. At 150 yards the fish stopped, and I got back line. I kept at it and got the fish within 80 yards of the boat. Then suddenly it made a wild, undirected run, not permitlike at all, and I could see that the blacktip shark was chasing it. The blacktip struck and missed the permit three or four times, making explosions in the water that sickened me. I released the drag, untied the boat, and started the engine. Woody was poling toward me at the sound of my engine. His mystified client dragged a line astern.

There was hardly enough water to move in. The prop was half buried, and at full throttle I could not get up on plane. The explosions continued, and I could only guess whether or not I was still connected to the fish. I ran toward the fish, a vast loop of line trailing, saw the shark once, and ran over him. I threw the engine into neutral and waited to see what happened and tried to regain line. Once more I was tight to the permit. Then the shark reappeared. He hit the permit once, killed it, and ate the fish, worrying it like a dog and bloodying the water.

Then an instant later I had the shark on my line and running. I fought him with irrational care: I now planned to gaff the blacktip and retrieve my permit piece by piece. When the inevitable cutoff came I dropped the rod in the boat and, empty-handed, wondered what I had done to deserve this.

I heard Woody's skiff and looked around. He swung about and coasted alongside. I told him it was a permit, as he had guessed from my starting up on the flat. Woody began to say something when, at that not unceremonial moment, his client broke in to say that it was hooking them that was the main thing. We stared at him until he added, "Or is it?"

Often afterward we went over the affair and talked about what might have been done differently, as we had with the first permit. One friend carries a carbine on clips under the gunwale to take care of sharks. But I felt that with a gun in the skiff during the excitement of a running fish,

I would plug myself or deep-six the boat. Woody knew better than to assure me there would be other chances. Knowing that there might very well not be was one of our conversational assumptions.

One morning we went to look for tarpon. Woody had had a bad night of it. He had awakened in the darkness of his room about three in the morning and watched the shadowy figure of a huge land crab walk across his chest. Endlessly it crept to the wall and then up it. Carefully silhouetting the monster, Woody blasted it with a karate chop. At breakfast he was nursing a bruise on the side of his hand. We were, at 6 A.M., having grits and eggs at the Chat and Chew restaurant. A trucker who claimed to have driven from Loxahatchee in three hours flat was yelling for "oss tie." And when the girl asked if he really wanted iced tea this early in the morning he replied, "Dash rat. Oss tie." My breakfast came and I stared at it listlessly. I couldn't wake up in the heat. I was half dreaming and imagined the land crab performing some morbid cadenza on my pile of grits.

We laid out the rods in the skiff. The wind was coming out of the east, that is, over one's casting hand from the point we planned to fish, and it was blowing fairly stiff. But the light was good, and that was more important. We headed out of Big Pine, getting into the calm water along Ramrod Key. We ran in behind Pye Key, through the hole behind Little Money, and out to Southeast Point. The sun was already huge, out of hand, like Shakespeare's "glistening Phaethon." I had whitened my nose and mouth with zinc oxide, and felt, handling the mysterious rods and flies, like a shaman. I still had to rig the leader of my own rod; and as Woody jockeyed the skiff with the pole, I put my leader together. I retained enough of my trout-fishing sensibilities to continue to be intrigued by tarpon leaders with their array of arcane knots: the butt of the leader is nail knotted to the line, blood knotted to monofilament of lighter test; the shock tippet that protects the leader from the rough jaws of tarpon is tied to the leader with a combination Albright Special and Bimini Bend; the shock tippet is attached to the fly either by a perfection loop, a clinch, or a Homer Rhodes Loop; and to choose one is to make a moral choice. You are made to understand that it would not be impossible to fight about it or, at the very least, quibble darkly.

We set up on a tarpon pass point. We had sand spots around us that would help us pick out the dark shapes of traveling tarpon. And we expected tarpon on the falling water, from left to right. I got up on the bow with 50 feet of line coiled on the deck. I was barefoot so I could feel if I stepped on a loop. I made a couple of practice casts — harsh, indecorous, tarpon-style, the opposite of the otherwise appealing dry-fly caper — and scanned for fish.

The first we saw were, from my point of view, spotted from too great a distance. That is, there was a long period of time before they actually broke the circle of my casting range, during which time I could go, quite secretly but completely, to pieces. The sensation for me, in the face of these advancing forms, was as of a gradual ossification of the joints. Moviegoers will recall the early appearances of Frankenstein's monster, his ambulatory motions accompanied by great rigidity of the limbs, almost as though he could stand a good oiling. I was hard put to see how I would manage anything beyond a perfunctory flapping of the rod. I once laughed at Woody's stories of customers who sat down and held their feet slightly aloft, treading the air or wobbling their hands from the wrists. I giggled at the story of a Boston chiropractor who fell over on his back and barked like a seal.

"Let them come in now," Woody said.

"I want to nail one, Woody."

"You will. Let them come."

The fish, six of them, were surging toward us in a wedge. They ran from 80 to 110 pounds. "All right, the lead fish, get on him," Woody said. I managed the throw. The fly fell in front of the fish. I let them overtake it before starting my retrieve. The lead fish, big, pulled up behind the fly, trailed, and then made the shoveling, open-jawed uplift of a strike that is not forgotten. When he turned down I set the hook, and he started his run. The critical stage, that of getting rid of loose line piled around one's feet, ensued. You imagine that if you are standing on a coil, you will go to the moon when that coil must follow its predecessors out of the rod. This one went off without a hitch, and it was only my certainty that someone had done it before that kept me from deciding that we had made a big mistake.

The sudden pressure of the line and the direction of its resistance apparently confused the tarpon, and it raced in close-coupled arcs around the boat. Then, when it had seen the boat, felt the line, and isolated a single point of resistance, it cleared out at a perfectly insane rate of acceleration that made water run three feet up my line as it sliced through. The jumps — wild, greyhounding, end over end, rattling — were all crazily blurred as they happened, while I pictured my reel exploding like a racing clutch and filling me with shrapnel.

This fish, the first of six that day, broke off. So did the others, destroying various aspects of my tackle. Of the performances, it is not simple to generalize. The closest thing to a tarpon in the material world is the Steinway piano. The tarpon, of course, is a game fish that runs to extreme sizes, while the Steinway piano is merely an enormous musical instrument, largely wooden and manipulated by a series of keys. However, the tarpon when hooked and running reminds the angler of a piano sliding down a precipitous incline and while jumping makes cavities and explosions in the water not unlike a series of pianos falling from a great height. If the reader, then, can speculate in terms of pianos that herd and pursue mullet and are themselves shaped like exaggerated herrings, he will be a very long way toward seeing what kind of thing a tarpon is. Those who appreciate nature as we find her may rest in the knowledge that no amount of modification can substitute the man-made piano for the real thing — the tarpon. Where was I?

As the sun moved through the day the blind side continually changed, forcing us to adjust position until, by afternoon, we were watching to the north. Somehow, looking up light. Woody saw four permit coming right in toward us, head-on. I cast my tarpon fly at them, out of my accustomed long-shot routine, and was surprised when one fish moved forward of the pack and followed up the fly rather aggressively. About then they all sensed the skiff and swerved to cross the bow about 30 feet out. They were down close to the bottom now, slightly spooked. I picked up, changed direction, and cast a fairly long interception. When the fly lit, well out ahead, two fish elevated from the group, sprinted forward, and the inside fish took the fly in plain view.

The certainty, the positiveness of the take in the face of an ungodly number of refusals and the long, unproductive time put in, produced immediate tension and pessimism. I waited for something to go haywire.

I hooked the fish quickly and threw slack. It was only slightly startled and returned to the pack, which by this time had veered away from the shallow flat edge and swung back toward deep water. The critical time of loose line passed slowly. Woody unstaked the skiff and was poised to see which way the runs would take us. When the permit was tight to the reel I cinched him once, and he began running. The deep water kept the fish from making the long, sustained sprints permit make on the flats. This fight was a series of assured jabs at various clean angles from the skiff. We followed, alternately gaining and losing line. Then, in some way, at the end of this blurred episode, the permit was flashing beside the boat, looking nearly circular, and the only visual contradiction to his perfect poise was the intersecting leader seemingly inscribed from the tip of my arcing rod to the precise corner of his jaw.

Then we learned that there was no net in the boat. The fish would have to be tailed. I forgave Woody in advance for the permit's escape. Woody was kneeling in the skiff, my line disappearing over his shoulder, the permit no longer in my sight, Woody leaning deep from the gunwale. Then, unbelievably, his arm was up, the black symmetry of tail above his fist, the permit perpendicular to the earth, then horizontal on the floorboards. A pile of loose fly line was strewn in curves that wandered around the bottom of the boat to a gray-and-orange fly that was secured in the permit's mouth. I sat down numb and soaring.

I don't know what this kind of thing indicates beyond the necessary, ecstatic resignation to the moment. With the beginning over and, possibly, nothing learned, I was persuaded that once was not enough.

1970

## Hunter S. Thompson

......................................................................................................

# The Kentucky Derby
# Is Decadent and Depraved

FROM *Scanlan's*

*Welcome to Derbytown*

I GOT OFF the plane around midnight and no one spoke as I crossed the dark runway to the terminal. The air was thick and hot, like wandering into a steam bath. Inside, people hugged each other and shook hands . . . big grins and a whoop here and there: "By God! You old *bastard! Good* to see you, boy! *Damn* good . . . and I *mean* it!"

In the air-conditioned lounge I met a man from Houston who said his name was something or other — "but just call me Jimbo" — and he was here to get it on. "I'm ready for *anything,* by God! Anything at all. Yeah, what are you drinkin?" I ordered a Margarita with ice, but he wouldn't hear of it: "Naw, naw . . . what the hell kind of drink is that for Kentucky Derby time? What's *wrong* with you, boy?" He grinned and winked at the bartender. "Goddam, we gotta educate this boy. Get him some good *whiskey. . . ."*

I shrugged. "Okay, a double Old Fitz on ice." Jimbo nodded his approval.

"Look." He tapped me on the arm to make sure I was listening. "I know this Derby crowd, I come here every year, and let me tell you one thing I've learned — this is no town to be giving people the impression you're some kind of faggot. Not in public, anyway. Shit, they'll roll you in a minute, knock you in the head and take every goddam cent you have."

I thanked him and fitted a Marlboro into my cigarette holder. "Say," he said, "you look like you might be in the horse business . . . am I right?"

"No," I said. "I'm a photographer."

"Oh yeah?" He eyed my ragged leather bag with new interest. "Is that what you got there — cameras? Who you work for?"

"*Playboy*," I said.

He laughed. "Well goddam! What are you gonna take pictures of — nekkid horses? Haw! I guess you'll be workin' pretty hard when they run the Kentucky Oaks. That's a race just for fillies." He was laughing wildly. "Hell yes! And they'll all be nekkid too!"

I shook my head and said nothing; just stared at him for a moment, trying to look grim. "There's going to be trouble," I said. "My assignment is to take pictures of the riot."

"What riot?"

I hesitated, twirling the ice in my drink. "At the track. On Derby Day. The Black Panthers." I stared at him again. "Don't you read the newspapers?"

The grin on his face had collapsed. "What the *hell* are you talkin about?"

"Well . . . maybe I shouldn't be telling you. . . ." I shrugged. "But hell, everybody else seems to know. The cops and the National Guard have been getting ready for six weeks. They have 20,000 troops on alert at Fort Knox. They've warned us — all the press and photographers — to wear helmets and special vests like flak jackets. We were told to expect shooting. . . ."

"No!" he shouted; his hands flew up and hovered momentarily between us, as if to ward off the words he was hearing. Then he hacked his fist on the bar. "Those sons of bitches! God Almighty! The Kentucky Derby!" He kept shaking his head. "No! *Jesus!* That's almost too bad to believe!" Now he seemed to be jagging on the stool, and when he looked up his eyes were misty. "Why? Why *here*? Don't they respect *anything*?"

I shrugged again. "It's not just the Panthers. The FBI says busloads of white crazies are coming in from all over the country — to mix with the crowd and attack all at once, from every direction. They'll be dressed like everybody else. You know — coats and ties and all that. But when the trouble starts . . . well, that's why the cops are so worried."

He sat for a moment, looking hurt and confused and not quite able to digest all this terrible news. Then he cried out: "Oh . . . Jesus! What in the name of God is happening in this country? Where can you get away from it?"

"Not here," I said, picking up my bag. "Thanks for the drink . . . and good luck."

He grabbed my arm, urging me to have another, but I said I was overdue at the Press Club and hustled off to get my act together for the awful spectacle. At the airport newsstand I picked up a *Courier-Journal* and scanned the front page headlines: "Nixon Sends GI's into Cambodia to Hit Reds" . . . "B-52's Raid, then 2,000 GI's Advance 20 Miles" . . . "4,000 U.S. Troops Deployed Near Yale as Tension Grows Over Panther Protest." At the bottom of the page was a photo of Diane Crump, soon to become the first woman jockey ever to ride in the Kentucky Derby. The photographer had snapped her "stopping in the barn area to fondle her mount, Fathom." The rest of the paper was spotted with ugly war news and stories of "student unrest." There was no mention of any protest action at a small Ohio school called Kent State.

I went to the Hertz desk to pick up my car, but the moon-faced young swinger in charge said they didn't have any. "You can't rent one anywhere," he assured me. "Our Derby reservations have been booked for six weeks." I explained that my agent had confirmed a white Chrysler convertible for me that very afternoon but he shook his head. "Maybe we'll have a cancellation. Where are you staying?"

I shrugged. "Where's the Texas crowd staying? I want to be with my people."

He sighed. "My friend, you're in trouble. This town is flat *full.* Always is, for the Derby."

I leaned closer to him, half-whispering: "Look, I'm from Playboy. How would you like a job?"

He backed off quickly. "What? Come on, now. What kind of a job?"

"Never mind," I said. "You just blew it." I swept my bag off the counter and went to find a cab. The bag is a valuable prop in this kind of work; mine has a lot of baggage tags on it — SF, LA, NY, Lima, Rome, Bangkok, that sort of thing — and the most prominent tag of all is a very official, plastic-coated thing that says "Photog. Playboy Mag." I bought it from a pimp in Vail, Colorado, and he told me how to use it. "Never mention Playboy until you're sure they've seen this thing first," he said. "Then, when you see them notice it, that's the time to strike. They'll go belly up every time. This thing is magic, I tell you. Pure magic."

Well . . . maybe so. I'd used it on the poor geek in the bar, and now, humming along in a Yellow Cab toward town, I felt a little guilty about jangling the poor bugger's brains with that evil fantasy. But what the hell? Anybody who wanders around the world saying, "Yes, I'm from Texas," deserves whatever happens to him. And he had, after all, come

here once again to make a 19th century ass of himself in the midst of
some jaded, atavistic freakout with nothing to recommend it except a
very saleable "tradition." Early in our chat, Jimbo had told me that he
hasn't missed a Derby since 1954. "The little lady won't come anymore,"
he said. "She just grits her teeth and turns me loose for this one. And
when I say 'loose' I do mean *loose!* I toss ten-dollar bills around like they
were goin' outa style! Horses, whiskey, women . . . shit, there's women in
this town that'll do *anything* for money."

Why not? Money is a good thing to have in these twisted times. Even
Richard Nixon is hungry for it. Only a few days before the Derby he
said, "If I had any money I'd invest it in the stock market." And the
market, meanwhile, continued its grim slide.

## Waiting for Steadman

The next day was heavy. With 30 hours to post time I had no press
credentials and — according to the sports editor of the Louisville Courier-Journal — no hope at all of getting any. Worse, I needed two sets;
one for myself and another for Ralph Steadman, the English illustrator
who was coming from London to do some Derby drawings. All I knew
about him was that this was his first visit to the United States. And the
more I pondered that fact, the more it gave me fear. Would he bear up
under the heinous culture shock of being lifted out of London and
plunged into a drunken mob scene at the Kentucky Derby? There was
no way of knowing. Hopefully, he would arrive at least a day or so
ahead, and give himself time to get acclimated. Maybe a few hours of
peaceful sightseeing in the Bluegrass country around Lexington. My
plan was to pick him up at the airport in the huge Pontiac Ballbuster I'd
rented from a used car salesman named Colonel Quick, then whisk him
off to some peaceful setting to remind him of England.

Colonel Quick had solved the car problem, and money (four times
the normal rate) had bought two rooms in a scumbox on the outskirts
of town. The only other kink was the task of convincing the moguls at
Churchill Downs that *Scanlan's* was such a prestigious sporting journal
that common sense compelled them to give us two sets of the best press
tickets. This was not easily done. My first call to the publicity office
resulted in total failure. The press handler was shocked at the idea that
anyone would be stupid enough to apply for press credentials two days
before the Derby. "Hell, you can't be serious," he said. "The deadline
was two months ago. The press box is full; there's no more room . . . and
what the hell is *Scanlan's Monthly* anyway?"

I uttered a painful groan. "Didn't the London office call you? They're flying an artist over to do the paintings. Steadman. He's Irish, I think. Very famous over there. I just got in from the Coast. The San Francisco office told me we were all set."

He seemed interested, and even sympathetic, but there was nothing he could do. I flattered him with more gibberish, and finally he offered a compromise: he could get us two passes to the clubhouse grounds.

"That sounds a little weird," I said. "It's unacceptable. We *must* have access to everything. *All* of it. The spectacle, the people, the pageantry and certainly the race. You don't think we came all this way to watch the damn thing on television, do you? One way or another we'll get inside. Maybe we'll have to bribe a guard — or even Mace somebody." (I had picked up a spray can of Mace in a downtown drugstore for $5.98 and suddenly, in the midst of that phone talk, I was struck by the hideous possibilities of using it out at the track. Macing ushers at the narrow gates to the clubhouse inner sanctum, then slipping quickly inside, firing a huge load of Mace into the governor's box, just as the race starts. Or Macing helpless drunks in the clubhouse restroom, for their own good. . . .)

By noon on Friday I was still without credentials and still unable to locate Steadman. For all I knew he'd changed his mind and gone back to London. Finally, after giving up on Steadman and trying unsuccessfully to reach my man in the press office, I decided my only hope for credentials was to go out to the track and confront the man in person, with no warning — demanding only one pass now, instead of two, and talking very fast with a strange lilt in my voice, like a man trying hard to control some inner frenzy. On the way out, I stopped at the motel desk to cash a check. Then, as a useless afterthought, I asked if by any wild chance Mr. Steadman had checked in.

The lady on the desk was about fifty years old and very peculiar-looking; when I mentioned Steadman's name she nodded, without looking up from whatever she was writing, and said in a low voice, "You bet he did." Then she favored me with a big smile. "Yes, indeed. Mr. Steadman just left for the racetrack. Is he a friend of yours?"

I shook my head. "I'm supposed to be working with him, but I don't even know what he looks like. Now, goddammit, I'll have to find him in that mob at the track."

She chuckled. "You won't have any trouble finding him. You could pick that man out of any crowd."

"Why?" I asked. "What's wrong with him? What does he look like?"

"Well . . ." she said, still grinning, "he's the funniest looking thing I've seen in a long time. He has this . . . ah . . . this *growth* all over his face. As a matter of fact it's all over his *head*." She nodded. "You'll know him when you see him; don't worry about that."

Great creeping Jesus, I thought. That screws the press credentials. I had a vision of some nerve-rattling geek all covered with matted hair and string-warts showing up in the press office and demanding *Scanlan's* press packet. Well . . . what the hell? We could always load up on acid and spend the day roaming around the grounds with big sketch pads, laughing hysterically at the natives and swilling mint juleps so the cops wouldn't think we're abnormal. Perhaps even make the act pay up: set up an easel with a big sign saying, "Let a Foreign Artist Paint Your Portrait, $10 Each. Do It NOW!"

*A Huge Outdoor Loony Bin*

I took the expressway out to the track, driving very fast and jumping the monster car back and forth between lanes, driving with a beer in one hand and my mind so muddled that I almost crushed a Volkswagen full of nuns when I swerved to catch the right exit. There was a slim chance, I thought, that I might be able to catch the ugly Britisher before he checked in.

But Steadman was already in the press box when I got there, a bearded young Englishman wearing a tweed coat and HAF sunglasses. There was nothing particularly odd about him. No facial veins or clumps of bristly warts. I told him about the model woman's description and he seemed puzzled. "Don't let it bother you," I said. "Just keep in mind for the next few days that we're in Louisville, Kentucky. Not London. Not even New York. This is a weird place. You're lucky that mental defective at the motel didn't jerk a pistol out of the cash register and blow a big hole in you." I laughed, but he looked worried.

"Just pretend you're visiting a huge outdoor loony bin," I said. "If the inmates get out of control we'll soak them down with Mace." I showed him the can of "Chemical Billy," resisting the urge to fire it across the room at a rat-faced man typing diligently in the Associated Press section. We were standing at the bar, sipping the management's scotch and congratulating each other on our sudden, unexplained luck in picking up two sets of fine press credentials. The lady at the desk had been very friendly to him, he said. "I just told her my name and she gave me the whole works."

By midafternoon we had everything under control. We had seats looking down on the finish line, color TV and a free bar in the press room, and a selection of passes that would take us anywhere from the clubhouse roof to the jockey room. The only thing we lacked was unlimited access to the clubhouse inner sanctum in sections "F&G" . . . and I felt we needed that, to see the whiskey gentry in action. The governor would be in "G." Barry Goldwater would be in a box in "G" where we could rest and sip juleps, soak up a bit of atmosphere and the Derby's special vibrations.

The bars and dining rooms are also in "F&G," and the clubhouse bars on Derby Day are a very special kind of scene. Along with the politicians, society belles and local captains of commerce, every half-mad dingbat who ever had any pretensions to anything within 500 miles of Louisville will show up there to get strutting drunk and slap a lot of backs and generally make himself obvious. The Paddock bar is probably the best place in the track to sit and watch faces. Nobody minds being stared at; that's what they're in there for. Some people spend most of their time in the Paddock; they can hunker down at one of the many wooden tables, lean back in a comfortable chair and watch the ever-changing odds flash up and down on the big tote board outside the window. Black waiters in white serving jackets move through the crowd with trays of drinks, while the experts ponder their racing forms and the hunch bettors pick lucky numbers or scan the lineup for right-sounding names. There is a constant flow of traffic to and from the pari-mutuel windows outside in the wooden corridors. Then, as post time nears, the crowd thins out as people go back to their boxes.

Clearly, we were going to have to figure out some way to spend more time in the clubhouse tomorrow. But the "walkaround" press passes to F&G were only good for 30 minutes at a time, presumably to allow the newspaper types to rush in and out for photos or quick interviews, but to prevent drifters like Steadman and me from spending all day in the clubhouse, harassing the gentry and rifling an odd handbag or two while cruising around the boxes. Or macing the governor. The time limit was no problem on Friday, but on Derby Day the walkaround passes would be in heavy demand. And since it took about 10 minutes to get from the press box to the Paddock, and 10 more minutes to get back, that didn't leave much time for serious people-watching. And unlike most of the others in the press box, we didn't give a hoot in hell what was happening on the track. We had come there to watch the *real* beasts perform.

*View from Thompson's Head*

Later Friday afternoon, we went out on the balcony of the press box and I tried to describe the difference between what we had seen today and what would be happening tomorrow. This was the first time I'd been to a Derby in 10 years, but before that, when I lived in Louisville, I used to go every year. Now, looking down from the press box, I pointed to the huge grassy meadow enclosed by the track. "That whole thing," I said, "will be jammed with people; fifty thousand or so, and most of them staggering drunk. It's a fantastic scene — thousands of people fainting, crying, copulating, trampling each other and fighting with broken whiskey bottles. We'll have to spend some time out there, but it's hard to move around, too many bodies."

"Is it safe out there? Will we *ever* come back?"

"Sure," I said. "We'll just have to be careful not to step on anybody's stomach and start a fight." I shrugged. "Hell, this clubhouse scene right below us will be almost as bad as the infield. Thousands of raving, stumbling drunks, getting angrier and angrier as they lose more and more money. By midafternoon they'll be guzzling mint juleps with both hands and vomiting on each other between races. The whole place will be jammed with bodies, shoulder to shoulder. It's hard to move around. The aisles will be slick with vomit; people falling down and grabbing at your legs to keep from being stomped. Drunks pissing on themselves in the betting lines. Dropping handfuls of money and fighting to stoop over and pick it up."

He looked so nervous that I laughed. "I'm just kidding," I said. "Don't worry. At the first hint of trouble I'll start Macing everybody I can reach."

He had done a few good sketches but so far we hadn't seen that special kind of face that I felt we would need for the lead drawing. It was a face I'd seen a thousand times at every Derby I'd ever been to. I saw it, in my head, as the mask of the whiskey gentry — a pretentious mix of booze, failed dreams and a terminal identity crisis; the inevitable result of too much inbreeding in a closed and ignorant culture. One of the key genetic rules in breeding dogs, horses or any other kind of thoroughbred is that close inbreeding tends to magnify the weak points in a bloodline as well as the strong points. In horse breeding, for instance, there is a definite risk in breeding two fast horses who are both a little crazy. The offspring will likely be very fast and also very crazy. So the trick in breeding thoroughbreds is to retain the good traits and filter out the bad. But the breeding of humans is not so wisely supervised, particularly in a narrow Southern society where the closest kind of inbreeding is not only stylish and acceptable, but far more convenient — to the parents — than setting their offspring free to find their own mates, for their own reasons and their own ways. ("Goddam, did you hear about Smitty's daughter? She went crazy in Boston last week and married a nigger!")

So the face I was trying to find in Churchill Downs that weekend was a symbol, in my own mind, of the whole doomed atavistic culture that makes the Kentucky Derby what it is.

On our way back to the motel after Friday's races I warned Steadman about some of the other problems we'd have to cope with. Neither of us had brought any strange illegal drugs, so we would have to get by on booze. "You should keep in mind," I said, "that almost everybody you talk to from now on will be drunk. People who seem very pleasant at first might suddenly swing at you for no reason at all." He nodded, staring straight ahead. He seemed to be getting a little numb and I tried to cheer him up by inviting him to dinner that night, with my brother.

## *"What Mace?"*

Back at the motel we talked for a while about America, the South, England, just relaxing a bit before dinner. There was no way either of us could have known, at the time, that it would be the last normal conversation we would have. From that point on, the weekend became a vicious, drunken nightmare. We both went completely to pieces. The main problem was my prior attachment to Louisville, which naturally led to meetings with old friends, relatives, etc., many of whom were in the process of falling apart, going mad, plotting divorces, cracking up under the strain of terrible debts or recovering from bad accidents. Right in the middle of the whole frenzied Derby action, a member of my own family had to be institutionalized. This added a certain amount of strain to the situation, and since poor Steadman had no choice but to take whatever came his way, he was subjected to shock after shock.

Another problem was his habit of sketching people he met in the various social situations I dragged him into, then giving them the sketches. The results were always unfortunate. I warned him several times about letting the subjects see his foul renderings, but for some perverse reason he kept doing it. Consequently, he was regarded with fear and loathing by nearly everyone who'd seen or even heard about his work. He couldn't understand it. "It's sort of a joke," he kept saying.

"Why, in England it's quite normal. People don't take offense. They understand that I'm just putting them on a bit."

"Fuck England," I said. "This is Middle America. These people regard what you're doing to them as a brutal, bilious insult. Look what happened last night. I thought my brother was going to tear your head off."

Steadman shook his head sadly. "But I liked him. He struck me as a very decent, straightforward sort."

"Look, Ralph," I said. "Let's not kid ourselves. That was a very horrible drawing you gave him. It was the face of a monster. It got on his nerves very badly." I shrugged. "Why in hell do you think we left the restaurant so fast?"

"I thought it was because of the Mace," he said.

"What Mace?"

He grinned. "When you shot it at the headwaiter, don't you remember?"

"Hell, that was nothing," I said. "I missed him . . . and we were leaving, anyway."

"But it got all over us," he said. "The room was full of that damn gas. Your brother was sneezing and his wife was crying. My eyes hurt for two hours. I couldn't see to draw when we got back to the motel."

"That's right," I said. "The stuff got on her leg, didn't it?"

"She was angry," he said.

"Yah . . . well, okay . . . let's just figure we fucked up about equally on that one," I said. "But from now on let's try to be careful when we're around people I know. You won't sketch them and I won't Mace them. We'll just try to relax and get drunk."

"Right," he said. "We'll go native."

*Derby Morning*

It was Saturday morning, the day of the Big Race, and we were having breakfast in a plastic hamburger palace called the Ptomaine Village. Our rooms were just across the road in a foul scumbox of a place called the Horn Suburban Hotel. They had a dining room, but the food was so bad that we couldn't handle it anymore. The waitresses seemed to be suffering from shin splints; they moved around very slowly, moaning and cursing the "darkies" in the kitchen.

Steadman liked the Ptomaine Village because it had fish and chips. I preferred the "french toast," which was really pancake batter, fried to the proper thickness and then chopped out with a sort of cookie cutter to resemble pieces of toast.

Beyond drink and lack of sleep, our only real problem at that point was the question of access to the clubhouse. Finally we decided just to go ahead and steal two passes, if necessary, rather than miss that part of the action. This was the last coherent decision we were able to make for the next 48 hours. From that point on — almost from the very moment we started out to the track — we lost all control of events and spent the rest of the weekend just churning around in a sea of drunken horrors. My notes and recollections from Derby Day are somewhat scrambled.

But now, looking at the big red notebook I carried all through that scene, I see more or less what happened. The book itself is somewhat mangled and bent; some of the pages are torn, others are shriveled and stained by what appears to be whiskey, but taken as a whole, with sporadic memory flashes, the notes seem to tell the story. To wit:

## Unscrambling Derby Day — I

*Steadman Is Worried About Fire*

Rain all nite until dawn. No sleep. Christ, here we go, a nightmare of mud and madness. . . . Drunks in the mud. Drowning, fighting for shelter. . . . But no. By noon the sun burns, perfect day, not even humid.

Steadman is now worried about Fire. Somebody told him about the clubhouse catching on fire two years ago. Could it happen again? Horrible. Trapped in the press box. Holocaust. A hundred thousand people fighting to get out. Drunks screaming in the flames and the mud, crazed horses running wild. Blind in the smoke. Grandstand collapsing into the flames with us on the roof. Poor Ralph is about to crack. Drinking heavily, into the Haig.

Out to the track in a cab, avoid that terrible parking in people's front yards, $25 each, toothless old men on the street with big signs: Park Here, flagging cars in the yard. "That's fine, boy, never mind the tulips." Wild hair on his head, straight up like a clump of reeds.

Sidewalks full of people all moving in the same direction, towards Churchill Downs. Kids hauling coolers and blankets, teenyboppers in tight pink shorts, many blacks . . . black dudes in white felt hats with leopard-skin bands, cops waving traffic along.

The mob was thick for many blocks around the track; very slow going in the crowd, very hot. On the way to the press box elevator, just inside the clubhouse, we came on a row of soldiers all carrying long white riot sticks. About two platoons, with helmets. A man walking next to us said they were waiting for the governor and his party. Steadman eyed them nervously. "Why do they have those clubs?"

"Black Panthers," I said. Then I remembered good old "Jimbo" at the airport and I wondered what he was thinking right now. Probably very nervous; the place was teeming with cops and soldiers. We pressed on through the crowd, through many gates, past the paddock where the jockeys bring the horses out and parade around for a while before each race so the bettors can get a good look. Five million dollars will be bet today. Many winners, more losers. What the hell. The press gate was jammed up with people trying to get in, shouting at the guards, waving strange press badges: Chicago Sporting Times, Pittsburgh Police Athletic League . . . they were all turned away. "Move on, fella, make way for the working press." We shoved through the crowd and into the elevator, then quickly up to the free bar. Why not? Get it on. Very hot today, not feeling well, must be this rotten climate. The press box was cool and airy, plenty of room to walk around and balcony seats for watching the race or looking down at the crowd. We got a betting sheet and went outside.

## Unscrambling D-day II

*Clubhouse/Paddock Bar*

Pink faces with a stylish Southern sag, old Ivy styles, seersucker coats and buttondown collars. "Mayblossom Senility" (Steadman's phrase) . . . burnt out early or maybe just not much to burn in the first place. Not much energy in these faces, not much *curiosity*. Suffering in silence, nowhere to go after thirty in this life, just hang on and humor the children. Let the young enjoy themselves while they can. Why not? The grim reaper comes early in this league . . . banshees on the lawn at night, screaming out there beside that little iron nigger in jockey clothes. Maybe he's the one who's screaming. Bad DT's and too many snarls at the bridge club. Going down with the stock market. Oh Jesus, the kid has wrecked the new car, wrapped it around that big stone pillar at the bottom of the driveway. Broken leg? Twisted eye? Send him off to Yale, they can cure anything up there.

Yale? Did you see today's paper? New Haven is under siege. Yale is swarming with Black Panthers. . . . I tell you, Colonel, the world has gone mad, stone mad. Why they tell me a goddam woman jockey might ride in the Derby today.

I left Steadman sketching in the Paddock bar and went off to place our bets on the sixth race. When I came back he was staring intently at a group of young men around a table not far away. "Jesus, look at the corruption in that face!" he whispered. "Look at the madness, the fear, the greed!" I looked, then quickly turned my back on the table he was drawing. The face he'd picked out to draw was the face of an old friend of mine, a prep school football star in the good old days with a sleek red Chevy convertible and a very quick hand, it was said, with the snaps of a 32 B brassiere. They called him "Cat Man."

But now, a dozen years later, I wouldn't have recognized him anywhere but here, where I should have expected to find him, in the Paddock bar on Derby Day . . . fat slanted eyes and a pimp's smile, blue silk suit and his friends looking like crooked bank tellers on a binge. . . .

Steadman wanted to see some Kentucky Colonels, but he wasn't sure what they looked like. I told him to go back to the clubhouse men's rooms and look for men in white linen suits vomiting in the urinals. "They'll usually have large brown whiskey stains on the fronts of their suits," I said. "But watch the shoes, that's the tip-off. Most of them manage to avoid vomiting on their own clothes, but they never miss their shoes."

In a box not far from ours was Colonel Anna Friedman Goldman, *Chairman and Keeper of the Great Seal of the Honorable Order of Kentucky Colonels.* Not all the 76 million or so Kentucky Colonels could make it to the Derby this year, but many had kept the faith and several days prior to the Derby they gathered for their annual dinner at the Seelbach Hotel.

The Derby, the actual race, was scheduled for late afternoon, and as the magic hour approached I suggested to Steadman that we should probably spend some time in the infield, that boiling sea of people across the track from the clubhouse. He seemed a little nervous about it, but since none of the awful things I'd warned him about had happened so far — no race riots, firestorms, or savage drunken attacks — he shrugged and said, "Right, let's do it."

To get there we had to pass through many gates, each one a step down in status, then through a tunnel under the track. Emerging from the tunnel was such a culture shock that it took us a while to adjust.

"Cool almighty!" Steadman muttered. "This is a . . . Jesus!" He plunged ahead with his tiny camera, stepping over bodies, and I followed, trying to take notes.

### Unscrambling D-day III

*The Infield*

Total chaos, no way to see the race, not even the track . . . nobody cares. Big lines at the outdoor betting windows, then stand back to watch winning numbers flash on the big board, like a giant bingo game.

Old blacks arguing about bets; "Hold on there, I'll handle this" (waving pint of whiskey, fistful of dollar bills); girl riding piggyback, T-shirt says, "Stolen from Fort Lauderdale Jail." Thousands of teenagers, group singing "Let the Sun Shine In," ten soldiers guarding the American flag and a huge fat drunk wearing a blue football jersey (No. 80) reeling around with quart of beer in hand.

No booze sold out here, too dangerous . . . no bathrooms either. Muscle Beach. . . . Woodstock . . . many cops with riot sticks, but no sign of riot. Far across the track the clubhouse looks like a postcard from the Kentucky Derby.

### Unscrambling D-day IV

*"My Old Kentucky Home"*

We went back to the clubhouse to watch the big race. When the crowd stood to face the flag and sing "My Old Kentucky Home," Steadman faced the crowd and sketched frantically. Somewhere up in the boxes a voice screeched, "Turn around, you hairy freak!" The race itself was only two minutes long, and even from our super-status seats and using 12-power glasses, there was no way to see what was really happening. Later, watching a TV rerun in the press box, we saw what happened to our horses. Holy Land, Ralph's choice, stumbled and lost his jockey in the final turn. Mine, Silent Screen, had the lead coming into the stretch, but faded to fifth at the finish. The winner was a 16–1 shot named Dust Commander.

Moments after the race was over, the crowd surged wildly for the exits, rushing for cabs and busses. The next day's *Courier* told of violence in the parking lot; people were punched and trampled, pockets were picked, children lost, bottles hurled. But we missed all this, having retired to the press box for a bit of post-race drinking. By this time we were both half-crazy from too much whiskey, sun fatigue, culture shock, lack of sleep and general dissolution. We hung around the press box long enough to watch a mass interview with the winning owner, a dapper little man named Lehmann who said he had just flown into Louisville that morning from Nepal, where he'd "bagged a record tiger." The sportswriters murmured their admiration and a waiter filled Lehmann's glass with Chivas Regal. He had just won $127,000 with a horse that cost him $6,500 two years ago. His occupation, he said, was "retired contractor." And then he added, with a big grin, "I just retired."

The rest of that day blurs into madness. The rest of that night too. And all the next day and night. Such horrible things occurred that I can't bring myself even to think about them now, much less put them down in print. Steadman was lucky to get out of Louisville without serious injuries, and I was lucky to get out at all. One of my clearest memories of that vicious time is Ralph being attacked by one of my old friends in the billiard room of the Pendennis Club in downtown Louisville on Saturday night. The man had ripped his own shirt open to the waist before deciding that Ralph wasn't after his wife. No blows were struck, but the emotional effects were massive. Then, as a sort of final horror, Steadman put his fiendish pen to work and tried to patch things up by doing a little sketch of the girl he'd been accused of hustling. That finished us in the Pendennis.

## Getting Out of Town

Sometime around 10:30 Monday morning I was awakened by a scratching sound at my door. I leaned out of bed and pulled the curtain back just far enough to see Steadman outside. "What the fuck do you want?" I shouted.

"What about having breakfast?" he said.

I lunged out of bed and tried to open the door, but it caught on the night-chain and banged shut again. I couldn't cope with the chain! The thing wouldn't come out of the track — so I ripped it out of the wall with a vicious jerk on the door. Ralph didn't blink. "Bad luck," he muttered.

I could barely see him. My eyes were swollen almost shut and the sudden burst of sunlight through the door left me stunned and helpless like a sick mole. Steadman was mumbling about sickness and terrible heat; I fell back on the bed and tried to focus on him as he moved around the room in a very distracted way for a few moments, then suddenly darted over to the beer bucket and seized a Colt .45. "Christ," I said. "You're getting out of control."

He nodded and ripped the cap off, taking a long drink. "You know, this is really awful," he said finally. "I must get out of this place . . ." he shook his head nervously. "The plane leaves at 3:30, but I don't know if I'll make it."

I barely heard him. My eyes had finally opened enough for me to focus on the mirror across the room and I was stunned at the shock of recognition. For a confused instant I thought that Ralph had brought somebody with him — a model for that one special face we'd been looking for. There he was, by God — a puffy, drink-ravaged, disease-ridden caricature . . . like an awful cartoon version of an old snapshot in some once-proud mother's family photo album. It was the face we'd been looking for — and it was, of course, my own. Horrible, horrible. . . .

"Maybe I should sleep a while longer," I said. "Why don't you go on over to the Ptomaine Village and eat some of those rotten fish and chips? Then come back and get me around noon. I feel too near death to hit the streets at this hour."

He shook his head. "No . . . no . . . I think I'll go back upstairs and work on those drawings for a while." He leaned down to fetch two more cans out of the beer bucket. "I tried to work earlier," he said, "but my hands keep trembling . . . It's teddible, teddible."

"You've got to stop this drinking," I said.

He nodded. "I know. This is no good, no good at all. But for some reason I think it makes me feel better. . . ."

"Not for long," I said. "You'll probably collapse into some kind of hysterical DT's tonight — probably just about the time you get off the plane at Kennedy. They'll zip you up in a straitjacket and drag you down to the Tombs, then beat you on the kidneys with big sticks until you straighten out."

He shrugged and wandered out, pulling the door shut behind him. I went back to bed for another hour or so, and later — after the daily grapefruit juice run to the Nite Owl Food Mart — we drove once again to the Ptomaine Village for a fine lunch of dough and butcher's offal, fried in heavy grease.

By this time Ralph wouldn't even order coffee; he kept asking for more water. "It's the only thing they have that's fit for human consumption," he explained. Then, with an hour or so to kill before he had to catch the plane, we spread his drawings out on the table and pondered

them for a while, wondering if he'd caught the proper spirit of the thing
. . . but we couldn't make up our minds. His hands were shaking so
badly that he had trouble holding the paper, and my vision was so
blurred that I could barely see what he'd drawn. "Shit," I said. "We both
look worse than anything you've drawn here."

He smiled. "You know — I've been thinking about that," he said. "We
came down here to see this teddible scene: people all pissed out of their
minds and vomiting on themselves and all that . . . and now, you know
what? It's us. . . ."

Huge Pontiac Ballbuster blowing through traffic on the expressway. The
journalist is driving, ignoring his passenger who is now nearly naked
after taking off most of his clothing, which he holds out the window,
trying to wind-wash the Mace out of it. His eyes are bright red and his
face and chest are soaked with the beer he's been using to rinse the awful
chemical off his flesh. The front of his woolen trousers is soaked with
vomit; his body is racked with fits of coughing and wild choking sobs.
The journalist rams the big car through traffic and into a spot in front
of the terminal, then he reaches over to open the door on the passenger's side and shoves the Englishman out, snarling: "Bug off, you worthless faggot! You twisted pigfucker! [Crazed laughter.] If I weren't sick I'd
kick your ass all the way to Bowling Green — you scumsucking foreign
geek. Mace is too good for you. . . . We can do without your kind in
Kentucky."

1971

## John McPhee

# Centre Court

FROM *Playboy*

HOAD ON COURT 5, weathered and leonine, has come from Spain, where he lives on his tennis ranch in the plains of Andalusia. Technically, he is an old hero trying a comeback but, win or lose, with this crowd it is enough of a comeback that Hoad is here. There is tempestuous majesty in him, and people have congregated seven deep around his court just to feel the atmosphere there and to see him again. Hoad serves explosively, and the ball hits the fence behind his opponent without first intersecting the ground. His precision is off. The dead always rise slowly. His next serve splits the service line. Hoad is blasting some hapless Swiss into submission. As he tosses the ball up to serve again, all eyes lift above the court and the surrounding hedges, the green canvas fences, the beds of climbing roses, the ivy-covered walls — and at the top of the ball's parabola, it hangs for an instant in the sky against a background of half-timbered houses among plane trees and poplars on suburban hills. Rising from the highest hill is the steeple of St. Mary's Church, Wimbledon, where Hoad was married sixteen years ago. He swings through the ball and hits it very deep. "Fault." Hoad's wife, Jenny, and their several children are at the front of the crowd beside the court, watching with no apparent dismay as Hoad detonates his spectacularly horizontal serves.

Smith, in a remote part of the grounds, is slowly extinguishing Jaime Fillol. Tall, straightforward, All-American, Stan Smith is ranked number one in the United States. He grew up in Pasadena, where his father sold real estate. A fine basketball player, Smith gave it up for tennis. He is a big hitter who thinks with caution. Under the umpire's chair is his wallet. The locker rooms of Wimbledon are only slightly less secure than the vaults of Zurich, but Smith always takes his wallet with him to the court. Fillol, a *Chileno*, supple and blue-eyed, says "Good shot" when Smith drives one by him. Such remarks are rare at Wimbledon, where Alphonse would have a difficult time finding Gaston. The players are not, for the most part, impolite, but they go about their business silently. When they show appreciation of another player's shot, it is genuine. There is no structure to Fillol's game. Now he dominates, now he crumbles. Always he faces the big, controlled, relentless power of the all but unwavering Smith. Smith does not like to play on these distant courts close to the walls of the Wimbledon compound. The wind rattles the ivy and the ivy sometimes rattles Smith — but hardly enough to save Fillol.

John Alexander has brown hair that shines from washing. It hangs straight and touches the collar of his shirt in a trimmed horizontal line. The wind gusts, and the hair flows behind him. Not yet twenty, he is tall, good-looking, has bright clear eyes and could be a Shakespearean page. In his right hand is a Dunlop. He drives a forehand deep cross-court. There is little time for him to get position before the ball comes back — fast, heavy, fizzing with topspin.

In Alexander's mind there is no doubt that the man on the other side of the net is the best tennis player on earth. He hit with him once, in Sydney, when Laver needed someone to warm him up for a match with Newcombe. But that was all. He has never played against him before, and now, on the Number One Court, Alexander feels less the hopeless odds against him than a sense of being honored to be here at all, matched against Laver in the preeminent tournament of lawn tennis. The Number One Court is one of Wimbledon's two stadiums, and it is a separate closed world, where two players are watched in proximity by seven thousand pairs of eyes. Laver is even quicker and hits harder than Alexander had imagined, and Alexander, in his nervousness, is overhitting. He lunges, swings hard, and hits wide.

Laver is so far ahead that the match has long since become an exhibition. Nonetheless, he plays every point as if it were vital. He digs for gets. He sends up topspin lobs. He sprints and dives for Alexander's smashes. He punches volleys toward the corners and, when they miss, he winces. He is not playing against Alexander. He is playing against perfection. This year, unlike other years, he does not find himself scratching for form. He feels good in general, and he feels good to be here. He would rather play at Wimbledon than anywhere else at all, because, as he explains, "It's what the atmosphere instills here. At Wimbledon things come to a pitch. The best grass. The best crowd. The royalty. You all of a sudden feel the whole thing is important. You play your best tennis."

Laver, playing Alexander in the second round, is in the process of defending the Wimbledon title. In the history of this sport, no player has built a record like Laver's. There have been only three grand slams — one by Budge, two by Laver. Wimbledon is the tournament the players most want to win. It is the annual world championship. Budge won Wimbledon twice. Perry won it three times. Tilden won it three times. Laver has won Wimbledon four times, and no one at Wimbledon this afternoon has much doubt that he is on his way to his fifth championship. There are a hundred and twenty-eight men in this tournament, and a hundred and twenty-seven of them are crowded into the shadow of this one small Australian. Winning is everything to tennis players, although more than ninety-nine per cent of them are certain losers — and they expect to lose to him. Laver, who has a narrow and delicate face, freckles, a hawk's nose, thinning red hair, and the forearm of a Dungeness crab, is known to all of them as Rocket. Alexander, who is also Australian and uses a Dunlop no doubt because Laver does, has just aced the Rocket twice and leads him forty–love. To prepare for this match, Alexander hit with Roger Taylor, who is left-handed, and practiced principally serving to Taylor's backhand. Alexander serves again, to Laver's backhand. When Laver is in trouble, fury comes into his game. He lashes out now and passes Alexander on the right. He passes Alexander on the left. He carries him backward from forty–love to advantage out. Alexander runs to the net under a big serve. A crosscourt backhand goes by him so fast that his racquet does not move. In the press section, Roy McKelvie, dean of English tennis writers, notifies all the other tennis writers that beating Laver would be a feat comparable to the running of the first four-minute mile. The match is over. "Thank you," Laver says to Alexander at the net. "I played well." A person who has won two grand slams and four Wimbledons can say that becomingly. The remark is honest and therefore graceful. Alexander took four games in three sets. "I've improved. I've learned more possibilities," he says afterward. "It should help me. The improvement won't show for a while, but it is there."

Roger Taylor leans against the guardrail on the sun-deck roof of the Players' Tea Room. He is twenty-five feet above the ground — the Players' Tea Room is raised on concrete stilts — and from that high perspective he can see almost all the lawns of Wimbledon. There are sixteen grass courts altogether, and those that are not attended with grandstands are separated by paved walkways ten feet wide. Benches line the edges of the walkways. Wimbledon is well designed. Twenty-five thousand people can move about in its confined spaces without feeling particularly crowded. Each court stands alone and the tennis can be watched at point-blank range. The whole compound is somehow ordered within ten acres and all paths eventually lead to the high front façade of the Centre Court, the name of which, like the name Wimbledon itself, is synecdochical. "Centre Court" refers not only to the *ne plus ultra* tennis lawn but also to the entire stadium that surrounds it. A three-story dodecagon with a roof that shelters most of its seats, it resembles an Elizabethan theater. Its exterior walls are alive with ivy and in planter boxes on a balcony above its principal doorway are rows of pink and blue hydrangeas. Hydrangeas are the hallmark of Wimbledon. They are not only displayed on high but also appear in flower beds among the outer courts. In their pastel efflorescence, the hydrangeas appear to be geraniums that have escalated socially. When the Wimbledon fortnight begins each year, London newspapers are always full of purple language about the green velvet lawns and the pink and blue hydrangeas. The lawns are tough and hard and frequently somewhat brown. Their color means nothing to the players or to the ground staff, and this is one clue to the superiority of Wimbledon courts over the more lumpy but cosmetic sods of tennis lawns elsewhere. The hydrangeas, on the other hand, are strictly show business. They are purchased for the tournament.

Taylor is watching a festival of tennis from the roof of the Tea Room. Szorenyi against Morozova, Roche against Ruffels, Brummer against O'Hara, Drysdale against Spear — he can see fourteen matches going on at the same time, and the cork-popping sound of the tennis balls fills the air. "This is the greatest tournament in the world," he says. "It is a tremendous thrill to play in it. You try to tune yourself up for it all year." Taylor is somewhat unusual among the people milling around him on the sun deck. For the most part, of course, they are aliens, and their chatter is polyglot. Hungarians, Japanese, Finns, Colombians, Greeks — they come from forty nations, while home to Taylor is a three-room flat in Putney, just up the road from Wimbledon. Taylor is a heavy-set man with dark hair and a strong, quiet manner. His father is a Sheffield steelworker. His mother taught him his tennis. And now he is seeded sixteenth at Wimbledon. It took him five sets to get out of the first round, but that does not seem to have shaken his composure. His trouble would appear to be in front of him. In the pattern of the draw, the sixteenth seed is the nearest seeded player to the number-one seed, which is tantamount to saying that Taylor's outlook is pale.

On the promenade below, a Rolls-Royce moves slowly through the crowd. It contains Charlie Pasarell, making his appearance to compete in singles. Is Pasarell so staggeringly rich that he can afford to ride to his matches in a Rolls-Royce? Yes — as it happens — but the Rolls in this case is not his. It is Wimbledon's and it has been sent by the tennis club to fetch him. Wimbledon is uniquely considerate toward players, going to great lengths to treat them as if they were plenipotentiaries from their respective nations and not gifted gibbons, which is at times their status elsewhere. Wimbledon has a whole fleet of Rolls-Royces — and Mercedes, Humbers, and Austin Princesses — that deploy to all parts of London, to wherever the players happen to be staying, to collect them for their matches. Each car flies from its bonnet a small pennon in the colors of Wimbledon — mauve and green. Throughout the afternoons, these limousines enter the gates and murmur through the crowd to deliver to the locker rooms not only the Emersons, the Ashes, the Ralstons, and the Roches but also the Dowdeswelles, the Montrenauds, the Dibleys, and the Phillips-Moores.

In the Players' Tea Room, the players sit on pale-blue wicker chairs at pale-blue wicker tables eating strawberries in Devonshire cream. The tearoom is glassed-in on three sides, overlooking the courts. Hot meals are served there, to players only — a consideration absent in all other places where they play. Wimbledon is, among other things, the business convention of the tennis industry, and the tearoom is the site of a thousand deals — minor endorsements, major endorsements, commitments to tournaments over the coming year. The Players' Tea Room is the meat market of international tennis. Like bullfight impresarios converging on Madrid from all parts of Spain at the *Feria* of San Isidro, tournament directors from all parts of the world come to the Players' Tea Room at Wimbledon to bargain for — as they put it — "the horse-flesh." The Tea Room also has a first-rate bar, where, frequently enough, one may encounter a first-rate bookie. His name is Jeff Guntrip. He is a trim and modest-appearing man from Kent. His credentials go far deeper than the mere fact that he is everybody's favorite bookie. Years ago, Guntrip was a tennis player. He competed at Wimbledon.

In the Members' Enclosure, on the Members' Lawn, members and their guests are sitting under white parasols, consuming best-end-of-lamb salad and strawberries in Devonshire cream. Around them are pools of goldfish. The goldfish are rented from Harrods. The members are rented from the uppermost upper middle class. Wimbledon is the annual convention of this stratum of English society, starboard out, starboard home. The middle middle class must have its strawberries and cream, too, and — in just the way that hot dogs are sold at American sporting events — strawberries and thick Devonshire cream are sold for five shillings the dish from stalls on the Tea Lawn and in the Court Buffet. County representatives, whoever they are, eat strawberries and cream in the County Representatives' Enclosure. In the Officials' Buttery, officials, between matches, eat strawberries and cream. An occasional strawberry even makes its way into the players' locker rooms, while almost anything else except an authentic player would be squashed en route. The doors are guarded by bobbies eight feet tall with nightsticks by Hillerich & Bradsby. The ladies' dressing room at Wimbledon is so secure that only two men have ever entered it in the history of the tournament — a Frenchman and a blind masseur. The Frenchman was the great Jean Borotra, who in 1925 effected his entry into the women's locker room and subsequently lost his Wimbledon crown.

The gentlemen's dressing room is *sui generis* in the sportive world, with five trainer-masseurs in full-time attendance. Around the periphery of the locker areas are half a dozen completely private tub rooms. When players come off the courts of Wimbledon, they take baths. Huge spigots deliver hot waterfalls into pond-sized tubs, and on shelves beside the tubs are long-handled scrub brushes and sponges as big as footballs. The exhausted athletes dive in, lie on their backs, stare at the ceiling, and float with victory or marinate in defeat. The tubs are the one place in Wimbledon where they can get away from one another. When they are finally ready to arrange themselves for their return to society, they find on a shelf beneath a mirror a bottle of pomade called Extract of Honey and Flowers.

Smith comes into the locker room, slowly removes his whites, and retreats to the privacy of a tub closet, where, submerged for twenty-five minutes, he contemplates the loss of one set in the course of his match with Fillol. He concludes that his trouble was the rustling ivy. Scott comes in after a 14–12 finish in a straight-set victory over Krog. Scott opens his locker. Golf balls fall out. Scott runs four miles a day through the roughs of the golf course that is just across Church Road from the tennis club — the All-England Lawn Tennis and Croquet Club, Wimbledon. Other players — Graebner, Kalogeropoulos, Diepraam, Tiriac — are dressing for other matches. Upwards of sixty matches a day are played on the lawns of Wimbledon, from two in the afternoon until sundown. The sun in the English summer takes a long time going down. Play usually stops around 8 P.M.

Leaving the locker room dressed for action, a tennis player goes in one of two directions. To the right, a wide portal with attending bobbies leads to the outer courts. To the left is a pair of frosted-glass doors that resemble the entry to an operating amphitheater in a teaching hospital. Players going through those doors often enough feel just as they would if they were being wheeled in on rolling tables. Beyond the frosted glass is the Centre Court — with the B.B.C., the Royal Box, and fourteen thousand live spectators in close propinquity to the hallowed patch of ground on which players have to hit their way through their nerves or fall if they cannot. There is an archway between the locker room and the glass doors, and over this arch the celebrated phrase of Kipling has been painted: "IF YOU CAN MEET WITH TRIUMPH AND DISASTER AND TREAT THOSE TWO IMPOSTORS JUST THE SAME."

Rosewall is on the Number Eight Court, anesthetizing Addison. Rosewall wears on his shirt the monogram BP. What is this for? Has he changed his name? Not precisely. Here in this most august of all the milieus of tennis, here in what was once the bastion of all that was noblest and most amateur in sport, Rosewall is representing British Petroleum. Rosewall represents the oil company so thoroughly, in fact, that on the buff blazer he wears to the grounds each day, the breast pocket is also monogrammed BP. There is nothing unusual in this respect about Rosewall. All the tennis players are walking billboards. They are extensions of the outdoor-advertising industry. Almost every-thing they drink, wear, and carry is an ad for some company. Laver won his grand slams with a Dunlop. He has used a Dunlop most of his life. His first job after he left his family's farm in Queensland was in a Dun-lop factory in Sydney, making racquets. Recently, though, he has agreed to use Donnay racquets in certain parts of the world, and Chemold (gold-colored metal) racquets elsewhere, for an aggregate of about thirty thousand dollars a year. In the United States he still uses his Dunlops. Donnay has him under contract at Wimbledon; however, the word among the players is that the Rocket is still using his Dunlops but has had them repainted to look like Donnays. Roche and Emerson are under contract to Chemold. They also have golden racquets. All things together, Ashe makes about a hundred and twenty-five thousand dollars a year through such deals. He gets fifty-thousand for using the Head Competition, the racquet that looks like a rug beater. He gets twenty-five thousand from Coca-Cola for personal appearances arranged by the company and for drinking Coke in public as frequently as he can, particularly when photographers happen to be shooting him. Lutz and Smith are under contract to consume Pepsi-Cola — in like volume but for less pay. Ask Pasarell if he likes Adidas shoes. "I do, in Europe," he enthuses. He is paid to wear Adidas in Europe, but in the United States he has a different deal, the same one Lutz, Graebner, Smith, and King have, with Uniroyal Pro Keds.

Players endorse nets, gut, artificial court surfaces, and every item of clothing from the jock on out. Some players lately have begun to drink — under contract — a mysterious brown fluid called Biostrath Elixir. Made in a Swiss laboratory, it comes in small vials and contains honey, malt, orange juice, and the essences of ninety kinds of medicinal herbs. Others have signed contracts to wear copper bracelets that are said to counteract voodoo, rheumatism, and arthritis. Nearly everyone's clothing contract is with one or the other of the two giants of tennis haberdashery — Fred Perry and René Lacoste. When Pilic appears in a Perry shirt and Ashe in a Lacoste shirt, they are not so much wearing these garments as advertising them. Tennis is a closed world. Its wheeler-dealers are bygone players (Kramer, Dell). Its outstanding bookie is a former player. Even its tailors, apparently, must first qualify as Wimbledon champions — Lacoste, 1925, 1928; Perry, 1934, 1935, 1936. Rosewall has somehow escaped these two. He wears neither the alligator emblem of Lacoste nor the triumphal garland of Perry. However, he is hardly in his shirt for nothing. In addition to the BP, Rosewall's shirt displays a springing panther — symbol of Slazenger. All this heraldry makes him rich before he steps onto the court, but it doesn't seem to slow him up. He is the most graceful tennis player now playing the game, and gracefully he sutures Addison, two, four and zero.

The Russians advance in mixed doubles. Keldie and Miss Harris have taken a set from the Russians, but that is all the Russians will yield. Keldie is a devastatingly handsome tall fellow who wears tinted wraparound glasses and has trouble returning serve. Miss Harris has no difficulty with returns. In mixed doubles, the men hit just as hard at the women as they do at each other. Miss Harris is blond, with her part in the middle and pigtails of the type that suggests windmills and canals. She is quite pretty and her body is lissome all the way to her ankles, at which point she turns masculine in Adidas shoes with three black bands. The Russians show no expressions on their faces, which are young and attractive, dark-eyed. The Soviet Union decided to go in for tennis some years ago. A program was set up. Eight Russians are now at

Wimbledon, and these — Metreveli and Miss Morozova — are the outstanding two. Both use Dunlops. They play with balletic grace — remarkable, or so it seems, in people to whose part of the world the sport
is so alien. Miss Morozova, a severely beautiful young woman, has high
cheekbones and almond eyes that suggest remote places to the east —
Novosibirsk, Semipalatinsk. The Russians, like so many players from
other odd parts of the earth, are camouflaged in their playing clothes.
They are haberdashed by Fred Perry, so they appear more to come from
Tennis than from Russia. Think how bad but how distinctive they would
look if their clothes had come from GUM. Think what the Indians
would look like, the Brazilians, the Peruvians, the Japanese, if they
brought their clothes from home. Instead, they all go to Fred Perry's
stock room on Vigo Street in London and load up for the year. The
Russians are not permitted to take cash back to Russia, so they take
clothing instead and sell it when they get home. Perry has a line of
colored garments as well as white ones, and the Russians take all that is
red. Not a red shirt remains in stock once the Russians have been to
Vigo Street. Miss Morozova fluidly hits a backhand to Keldie's feet. He
picks it up with a half volley. Metreveli puts it away. Game, set, and
match to Metreveli and Miss Morozova. No expression.

Graebner and Tiriac, on Court 3, are a vaudeville act. The draw has
put it together. Graebner, the paper salesman from Upper Middle Manhattan, has recently changed his image. He has replaced his horn-
rimmed glasses with contact lenses, and he has grown his soft and
naturally undulant dark-brown hair to the point where he is no longer
an exact replica of Clark Kent but is instead a living simulacrum of
Prince Valiant. Tiriac hates Wimbledon. Tiriac, who is Rumanian, feels
that he and his doubles partner, Nastase, are the best doubles team in
the world. Wimbledon disagrees. Tiriac and Nastase are not seeded in
doubles, and Tiriac is mad as hell. He hates Wimbledon and, by exten-
sion he hates Graebner. So he is killing Graebner. He has taken a set
from him, now leads him in the second, and Graebner is fighting for his
life. Tiriac is of middle height. His legs are unprepossessing. He has a
barrel chest. His body is encased in a rug of hair. Off court, he wears
cargo-net shirts. His head is covered with medusan wires. Above his
mouth is a mustache that somehow suggests that this man has been to
places most people do not imagine exist. By turns, he glowers at the
crowd, glares at the officials, glares at God in the sky. As he waits for
Graebner to serve, he leans forward, swaying. It is the nature of Tiriac's
posture that he bends forward all the time, so now he appears to be

getting ready to dive into the ground. Graebner hits one of his big crunch serves, and Tiriac slams it back, down the line, so fast that Graebner cannot reach it. Graebner throws his racquet after the ball. Tiriac shrugs. All the merchants of Mesopotamia could not equal Tiriac's shrug. Graebner serves again. Tiriac returns, and stays on the base line. Graebner hits a backhand that lands on the chalk beside Tiriac. "Out!" shouts the linesman. Graebner drops his racquet, puts his hands on his hips, and examines the linesman with hatred. The linesman is seventy-two years old and has worked his way to Wimbledon through a lifetime of similar decisions in Somerset, Cornwall, and Kent. But if Graebner lives to be ninety, he will never forget that call, or that face. Tiriac watches, inscrutably. Even in his Adidas shoes and his Fred Perry shirt, Tiriac does not in any way resemble a tennis player. He appears to be a panatela ad, a triple agent from Alexandria, a used-car salesman from central Marrakesh. The set intensifies. Eleven all. Twelve all. Graebner begins to chop the turf with his racquet. Rain falls. "Nothing serious," says Mike Gibson, the referee. "Play on." Nothing is serious with Gibson until the balls float. Wimbledon sometimes has six or eight showers in an afternoon. This storm lasts one minute and twenty-two seconds. The sun comes out. Tiriac snaps a backhand past Graebner, down the line. "Goddamn it!" Graebner shouts at him. "You're so lucky! My God!" Tiriac has the air of a man who is about to close a deal in a back room behind a back room. But Graebner, with a Wagnerian forehand, sends him spinning. Graebner, whose power is as great as ever, has continually improved as a competitor in tight places. The forehands now come in chords. The set ends 14–12, Graebner; and Graebner is still alive at Wimbledon.

When the day is over and the Rolls-Royces move off toward central London, Graebner is not in one. Graebner and his attorney waive the privilege of the Wimbledon limousines. They have something of their own — a black Daimler, so long and impressive that it appears to stop for two traffic lights at once. Graebner's attorney is Scott, who is also his doubles partner. They have just polished Nowicki and Rybarczyk off the court, 6–3, 10–12, 6–3, 6–3, and the Daimler's chauffeur takes them the fifteen miles to the Westbury, a hotel in Mayfair that is heavy with tennis players. Emerson is there, and Ashe, Ralston, Pasarell, Smith, Lutz, van Dillen. Dell and Kramer are both there. Dell, lately captain of the American Davis Cup Team, has created a principality within the anarchy of tennis. He is the attorney-manager of Ashe, Lutz, Pasarell, Smith, Kodes, and others. Dell and Kramer sit up until 3 A.M. every night

picking lint off the shoulders of chaos. Their sport has no head anymore, no effective organization, and is still in the flux of transition from
devious to straightforward professionalism. Kramer, who is, among
other things, the most successful impresario the game has ever known,
once had all the power in his pocket. Dell, who is only thirty-two,
nightly tries to pick the pocket, although he knows the power is no
longer there. Every so often they shout at each other. Kramer is an
almost infinitely congenial man. He seems to enjoy Dell in the way that
a big mother cat might regard the most aggressive of the litter — with
nostalgic amusement and, now and again, a paw in the chops.

Ashe goes off to Trader Vic's for dinner dressed in a sunburst dashiki,
and he takes with him two dates. Ralston joins them, and raises an
eyebrow. "There is no conflict here," Ashe says, calmly spreading his
hands toward the two women. Later in the evening, Ashe will have still
another date, and she will go with him to a casino, where they will shoot
craps and play blackjack until around 1 A.M., when Ashe will turn into a
tennis player and hurry back to the hotel to get his sleep.

In his flat in Dolphin Square, Laver spends the evening, as he does
most evenings, watching Western films on television. Many players take
flats while they are in England, particularly if they are married. They
prefer familial cooking to the tedium of room service. Some stay in
boardinghouses. John Alexander and fifteen other Australians are in a
boardinghouse in Putney. Dolphin Square is a vast block of flats, made
of red brick, on the Embankment overlooking the Thames. Laver sits
there in the evening in front of the television set, working the grips of
his racquets. He wraps and rewraps the grips, trying for just the right
feel in his hand. If the movie finishes and some commentator comes on
and talks tennis, Laver turns him off and rotates the selector in quest of
additional hoofbeats. He unwraps a new grip for the third or fourth
time and begins to shave the handle with a kitchen knife. He wraps the
grip again, feels it, moves the racquet through the arc of a backhand,
then unwraps the grip and shaves off a little more wood.

Gonzales sometimes drills extremely small holes in his racquets, to
change the weight. Gonzales, who is not always consistent in his approach to things, sometimes puts lead tape on his racquets to increase
the weight. Beppe Merlo, the Italian tennis player, strings his own
racquets, and if a string breaks while he is playing, he pulls gut out of
his cover and repairs the damage right there on the court. Merlo likes
to string his racquets at thirty pounds of tension — each string as tight
as it would be if it were tied to a rafter and had a thirty-pound weight

hanging on it. Since most players like their racquets at sixty pounds minimum, Merlo is extremely eccentric. He might as well be stringing snowshoes. When someone serves to him, the ball disappears into his racquet. Eventually, it comes out, and it floats back toward his opponent like a milkweed seed. Merlo's game does not work at all well on grass. He is fantastic on clay.

Many players carry their own sets of gut with them. Professional stringers do the actual work, of course, using machines that measure the tension. Emerson likes his racquets at sixty-three pounds, very tight, and so does Smith. Since the frame weight of "medium" tennis racquets varies from thirteen to thirteen and three-quarters ounces, Smith goes to the Wilson factory whenever he can and weighs and feels racquets until he has selected a stack of them. He kills a racquet in six weeks. The thing doesn't break. It just becomes flaccid and dies. Strings go dead, too. They last anywhere from ten to twenty-eight days. Smith likes a huge grip — four and seven-eighths inches around. Some Americans wrap tape around their handles to build them up, and then they put new leather grips on. Australians generally like them smaller, four and five-eighths, four and a half. As Laver whittles away beside the television, he is progressing toward four and a half. When he is ready to go to bed, he switches off the television and, beside it, leaves a little pile of wood chips and sawdust on the floor.

Dennis Ralston carries his own pharmacy with him wherever he goes — Achromycin, Butazolidin, Oxazepam, Robaxin, Sodium Butabarbital. He is ready for anything except sleep. The night before a match, he lies with a pillow over his head and fights total awareness. At 3 A.M., he complains bitterly about the traffic on New Bond Street, outside the Westbury. There is no traffic on New Bond Street outside the Westbury. Mayfair is tranquil in the dead of night, even if the tennis players are not. All over London, tennis players are staring open-eyed at dark ceilings. Some of them get up in the night and walk around talking to themselves — while Laver sleeps in Dolphin Square. Laver can sleep anywhere — in cars, trains, planes. He goes to bed around 1 A.M., and always sets an alarm clock or he would oversleep, even before a final.

Laver becomes quieter before a match. He and his wife, Mary, ordinarily laugh and joke and kid around a lot together, but he becomes silent as a match draws near. "The faster the pace, the more demands there are upon him, the better," she says. So Laver goes out in the morning and does the shopping. He drops off the laundry. Sometimes he washes clothes in the bathtub. He goes to his favorite butcher and

buys a steak. He also buys eggs and greens. Back in the flat, two and a
half hours before the match, he cooks his training meal. It is always the
same — steak, eggs, and greens. He likes to cook, and prefers to do it
himself. It keeps him busy. Then he gets into his car — a hired English
Ford — and drives to Wimbledon. He ignores the club limousines. He
wants to drive. "If he weren't a tennis player, he'd be a road racer," Mary
says. "He has a quick, alert mind. He's fast. He's fast of body, and his
mind works that way as well. The faster the pace of things, the faster he
moves." He particularly likes driving on the left-hand side of the road. It
reminds him of Australia, of which he sees very little anymore. His
home is in California. Each day, he plots a different route through
Greater South London to Wimbledon. This is his private rally. It is a
rule of the tournament that if a player is so much as ten minutes late his
opponent wins by a walkover. Laver knows his labyrinth — every route
alternative, every mews and byway, between the Embankment and the
tennis club, and all the traffic of London has yet to stop him. He turns
off Church Road into the parking lot. His mind for many hours has
been preoccupied with things other than tennis, with cowboys and sleep
and shopping lists and cooking and driving. He never ponders a draw
or thinks about an opponent. But now he is ready to concentrate his
interest on the game — for example, on Wimbledon's opening day,
when the defending champion starts the tournament with a match in
the Centre Court.

Laver walks under the Kipling line and through the glass doors, and
fourteen thousand people stand up and applaud him, for he is the most
emphatic and enduring champion who has ever played on this court.
He stacks his extra racquets against the umpire's chair, where the tournament staff has placed bottles of orange squash and of Robinson's
Lemon Barley Water should he or his opponent require them during
change-overs. There is plain water as well, in a jug called the Bartlett
Multipot. Behind the umpire's chair is a green refrigerator, where tennis
balls are kept until they are put into play. A ball boy hands him two and
Laver takes the court. He swings easily through the knockup. The
umpire says, "Play." Laver lifts his right hand, sending the first ball up
into the air, and the tournament is under way. He swings, hits. His
opponent can barely touch the ball with his racquet. It is a near ace, an
unplayable serve, fifteen–love. Laver's next serve scythes into the backhand court. It is also unplayable. Thirty–love.

The man across the net is extremely nervous. His name is George
Seewagen. He comes from Bayside, New York. This is his first Wimble-

don and his friends have told him that if you don't get a game in the first round, you never get invited back. Seewagen would like to get two games. At Forest Hills thirty-four years ago, Seewagen's father played J. Donald Budge in the opening round. The score was 6–0, 6–1, 6–0. When Seewagen, Jr., arrived in London, he was, like nearly everyone else, tense about the luck of the coming draw, and before it was published he told his doubles partner, "Watch me. I'll have to play Laver in the Centre Court in the first round." The odds were 111 to 1 that this would not happen, but Seewagen had read the right tea leaf, as he soon learned.

"It was hard to believe. I sort of felt a little bit upset. Moneywise, London's pretty expensive. First-round losers get a hundred pounds and that's not much. I figured I needed to win at least one match in order to meet my expenses, but now I'd had it. Then I thought of the instant recognition. People would say, 'There's the guy that's opening up Wimbledon with Laver.' At least, my name would become known. But then, on the other hand, I thought, What if I don't get a game? Think of it. What if I don't win even one game?"

Seewagen is an extremely slender — in fact, thin — young man with freckles, a toothy grin, tousled short hair. He could be Huckleberry Finn. He looks nineteen and is actually twenty-three. His credentials are that he played for Rice University, that he beat someone named Zan Guerry in the final of the 1969 amateur championship in Rochester, and that he is the varsity tennis coach at Columbia University. There were, in other words, grounds for his gnawing fears. By the eve of Wimbledon, Seewagen's appearance was gaunt.

Everyone goes to Hurlingham on that ultimate Sunday afternoon. All through the previous fortnight, the tennis players of the world have gradually come to London, and by tradition they first convene at Hurlingham. Hurlingham is a Victorian sporting club with floor-to-ceiling windows, sixteen chimney pots, and wide surrounding lawns — bowling lawns, tennis lawns, croquet lawns, putting lawns — under giant copper beeches, beside the Thames. Some players play informal sets of doubles. Others merely sit on the lawns, sip Pimm's Cups under the sun, and watch women in pastel dresses walking by on maroon pathways. In the background are people in their seventies, dressed in pure white, tapping croquet balls with deadly skill across textured grasses smooth as broadloom. A uniformed band, with folding chairs and music stands, plays "Bow, Bow, Ye Lower Middle Classes" while tea is served beneath the trees — a strawberry tart, sandwiches, petits fours, fruitcake, and a not-so-bitter macaroon. Arthur Ashe, eating his tea, drinking the at-

mosphere, says, "This is my idea of England." On a slope a short
distance away, Graham Stillwell, Ashe's first-round opponent, sits with
his wife and his five-year-old daughter, Tiffany. This is the second
straight year that Ashe has drawn Stillwell in the first round at Wimbledon, and last year Stillwell had Ashe down and almost out — twice
Stillwell was serving for the match — before Ashe won the fifth set,
12–10. Reporters from the *Daily Mirror* and the *Daily Sketch* now come
up to Ashe and ask him if he has been contacted by certain people who
plan to demonstrate against the South African players at Wimbledon.
"Why should they contact me?" Ashe says. "I'm not a South African."
Mrs. Stillwell rises from the sloping lawn and stretches her arms. "My
God! She's pregnant again," Ashe observes. Jean Borotra, now seventy-
two, is hitting beautiful ground strokes with Gardnar Mulloy. Borotra
wears long white trousers. Two basset hounds walk by, leashed to a man
in a shirt of broad pink and white stripes. The band is playing the music
of Albéniz. The lady tennis players drift about, dressed, for some reason,
in multicolored Victorian gowns. Laver, in dark slacks and a sport shirt
of motley dark colors, stands near the clubhouse, watching it all with his
arms folded. He seems uncomfortable. He looks incongruous — small,
undynamic, unprepossessing, vulnerable — but every eye at Hurlingham, sooner or later in the afternoon, watches him in contemplation.
He stands out no more than a single blade of grass, but no one fails to
see him, least of all Seewagen, who stands at the edge of the party like a
figure emerging from a haunted forest. He wears an old worn-out pair
of lightweight sneakers, of the type that tennis players do not use and
sailors do, and a baggy gray sweater with the sleeves shoved far up his
thin brown arms. Veins stand out on the backs of his hands and across
his forearms. He grins a little, but his eyes are sober. His look is profoundly philosophical. Gene Scott informs him that players scheduled
for the Centre Court are entitled to a special fifteen minutes of practice
on an outside court beforehand. "Good, I'll take McManus," Seewagen
says. McManus, from Berkeley and ranked tenth in the United States, is
left-handed. He is also short and redheaded. He has the same build
Laver has, much the same nose and similar freckles as well. Players
practicing with McManus easily fantasize that they are hitting with the
Rocket himself, and thus they inflate their confidence. McManus is the
favorite dummy of everyone who has to play against Laver. Ashe speaks
quietly to Seewagen and tells him not to worry. "You'll never play
better," Ashe says. "You'll get in there, in the Centre Court, and you'll get

inspired, and then when the crowd roars for your first great shot, you'll want to run into the locker room and call it a day."

"I hope it isn't a wood shot," says Seewagen, looking straight ahead.

Game to Laver. He leads, one game to love, first set. Laver and Seewagen change ends of the court. Laver went out to the Pontevecchio last night, on the Old Brompton Road. He ate lasagna and a steak *filet* with tomato sauce. He drank Australian beer. Then he went home and whittled a bit before retiring. At Chesham House, in Victoria, Seewagen fell asleep in his bed reading *Psycho Cybernetics,* by Maxwell Maltz. After one game Seewagen has decided that Laver is even better than he thought he was. Laver is, for one thing, the fastest of all tennis players. He moves through more square yards per second than anyone else, covering ground like a sonic boom. In his tennis clothes, he is not un-prepossessing. His legs are powerfully muscled. His left forearm looks as if it could bring down a tree. He is a great shotmaker, in part because he moves so well. He has every shot from everywhere. He can hurt his opponent from any position. He has extraordinary racquet-handling ability because his wrist is both strong and flexible. He can come over his backhand or slice it. He hits big shots, flick shots, spin shots, and rifle shots on the dead run. He lobs well. He serves well. His forehand is the best in tennis. He has one weakness. According to Gonzales, that is, Laver has one weakness — his bouncing overhead. The bouncing over-head is the shot a tennis player hits when a bad lob bounces at his feet and he cannon-balls his helpless opponent. Gonzales is saying that Laver has no weaknesses at all. Seewagen walks to the base line, visibly nervous, and prepares to serve. He is not pathetic. There is something tingling about a seven-hundred-to-one shot who merely shows up at the gate. In the end, at the net, Laver, shaking hands, will say to him gently, "You looked nervous. It's very difficult playing in here the first time over." Seewagen begins with a double fault. Love–fifteen. Now, however, a deep atavistic athleticism rises in him and defeats his nerves. He serves, rushes, and punches two volleys past Laver, following them with an unplayable serve. Forty–fifteen. Serve, rush, volley — game to Mr. Seewagen. Games are one all, first set.

"His topspin is disguised," Seewagen notes, and he prepares, with a touch of unexpected confidence, for Laver's next service assault. Game to Mr. Laver. He leads, two games to one, first set. Seewagen now rises again, all the way to forty–fifteen, from which level he is shoved back to deuce. Tossing up the ball, he cracks a serve past Laver that Laver can barely touch, let alone return. Advantage Seewagen. The source of all this power is not apparent, but it is coming from somewhere. He lifts the ball. He blasts. Service ace. Right through the corner. The crowd roars. It is Seewagen's first great shot. He looks at the scoreboard — two all — and it gives him what he will describe later as a charge. ("At that moment, I should have walked off.") 6–2, 6–0, 6–2.

Hewitt, in anger, hits one into the grandstand and it goes straight toward an elderly lady. She makes a stabbing catch with one hand and flips the ball to a ball boy. There is nothing lightweight about this English crowd. Ted Heath, Margaret, Anne, Charles, Lady Churchill, and the odd duke or baron might turn up — diverting attention to the Royal Box — but withal one gets the impression that there is a high percentage of people here who particularly know where they are and what they are looking at. They queue for hours for standing room in the Centre Court. They miss nothing and they are polite. The crowd at Forest Hills likes dramaturgy and emotion — players thanking God after chalk-line shots or falling to their knees in total despair — and the crowd in the Foro Italico throws cushions. But the British do not actually approve of that sort of thing, and when one of the rogue tennis players exhibits conduct they do not like, they cry, "Shame!"

"You bloody fools!" Hewitt shouts at them.

Hewitt has the temper of a grenade. He hits another ball in anger. This time it goes over the roof and out of sight. "Shame, Hewitt, shame!"

Rain falls. Umbrellas bloom. Mike Gibson's mustache is drooping from the wet, but he says, "Play on. It's not much." All matches continue. The umbrellas are black, red, green, yellow, orange, pink, paisley, and transparent. It is cold at Wimbledon. It often is — shirt sleeves one day, two pullovers and a mac the next. Now the players are leaving water tracks on the courts, and Gibson at last suspends play. Groundsmen take down the nets and cover the lawns with canvas. The standees do not give up their places, in the cold rain. The groundsmen go in under the grandstand to the Groundsmen's Bar, where they drink lager and offer one another cigarettes. "Will you have a smoke, Jack, or would you rather have the money?" The sun comes out for exactly three minutes. Then more rain falls. Half an hour later, play resumes.

Dell is supposed to be on Court 14, playing mixed doubles, but he is still in a phone booth talking to the office of Guntrip, the bookie. Dell bets heavily on his own players — a hundred pounds here, two hundred there — and even more heavily against Laver. Dell is a talented gambler and he views the odds as attractive. Besides, Dell and Laver are the same age, and Dell can remember beating Laver when they were boys. Shrewd and realistic, Dell reasons that anyone who ever lost to Donald Dell cannot be invincible. In the end, he repeats his name to the clerk at Guntrip's, to be sure the clerk has it right. "Dell," he says. "D as in David, E as in Edward, L as in loser, L as in loser."

The field of women players is so thin that even some of the women themselves are complaining. Chubby little girls with orange ribbons in their hair hit parabolic ground strokes back and forth and seem incongruous on courts adjacent to an Emerson, a Lutz, or a Pasarell, whose ground strokes sound like gunfire. Billie Jean King slaps a serve into the net and cries out, "That stinks!" Billie Jean is trimmer, lighter, more feminine than she was in earlier years, and somehow less convincing as a challenger to Margaret Court. Yet everyone else seems far below these two. Miss Goolagong is still a few years away. "Have you seen the abo, Jack?" says Robert Twynam, head groundsman, to his assistant, John Yardley. The interesting new players are the ones the groundsmen find interesting. They go to watch Miss Goolagong and they notice that her forehand has a tendency to go up and then keep going up. When it starts coming down, they predict, she will be ready for anybody, for her general game is smooth and quite strong and unflinchingly Australian. Australians never give up, and this one is an aborigine, a striking figure with orange-brown hair and orange-brown skin, in a Teddy Tinling dress and Adidas shoes, with a Dunlop in her hand. Margaret Court is breaking everything but the cool reserve of Helga Niessen, the Berlin model. Between points, Miss Niessen stands with her feet crossed at the ankles. The ankles are observed by a Chinese medical student who is working the tournament with the ground staff. "Look at those ankles. Look at those legs," he says. "She is a woman." He diverts his attention to Margaret Court, who is five feet eight, has big strong hands, and, most notably, the ripple-muscled legs of a runner. "Look at those legs," says the Chinese medical student. "The lady is a man."

Hoad, in the Centre Court, is moving so slowly that a serve bounces toward him and hits him in the chest. The server is El Shafei, the chocolate-eyed Egyptian. Hoad is in here because all Britain wants to see him on television. Stiffened by time and injury, he loses two sets before his cartilage begins to bend. In the third set, his power comes, and he breaks the Egyptian. The Egyptian is a heavy-framed man, like Hoad, and in the fourth set, they pound each other, drive for drive — wild bulls of the tennis court. Hoad thinks he is getting bad calls and enormous anger is rising within him. The score is three all. Shafei is serving, at deuce. He lifts the ball and blows one past Hoad for a service ace. Hoad looks toward the net-cord judge with expanding disbelief. He looks toward Shafei, who has not moved from the position from which he hit the serve — indicating to Hoad that Shafei expected to hit a second one. Slowly, Hoad walks forward, toward the officials, toward Shafei, toward the center of the court. The crowd is silent. Hoad speaks. A microphone in Scotland could pick up what he says. "That god-damned ball was a let!" The net-cord judge is impassive. The umpire says, "May I remind you that play is continuous." Hoad replies, repeats, "That god-damned ball was a let!" He turns to the Egyptian. Unstirring silence is still the response of the crowd, for one does not throw hammers back at Thor. "The serve was a let. You know that. Did you hear it hit the tape?" Hoad asks, and Shafei says, "No." Hoad lifts his right arm, extends it full length, and points steadily at the Egyptian's eyes. "You lie!" he says slowly, delivering each syllable to the roof. A gulf of quiet follows, and Hoad does not lower his arm. He draws a breath slowly, then says again, even more slowly, "You lie." Only Garrick could have played that one. It must have stirred bones in the Abbey, and deep in the churchyards of Wimbledon, for duels of great moment here have reached levels more serious than sport. This is where Canning fought Castlereagh, where Pitt fought Tierney, where Lord Winchelsea fought the Duke of Wellington. Ceawlin of the West Saxons fought Ethelbert of Kent here, when the terrain was known as Wibbas dune — home of the Saxon, Wibba (Wibbas dune, Wipandune, Wilbaldowne, Wymblyton). Hoad returns to the base line, and when the Egyptian serves again, Hoad breaks him into pieces. Game and fourth set to Hoad. Sets are two all. In his effort, though, Hoad has given up the last of his power. Time has defeated him. Twice the champion, he has failed his comeback. His energy drains away in the fifth set — his last, in all likelihood, at Wimbledon.

Ralston, at the umpire's chair, pries the cap off a vial of Biostrath and sucks out the essences of the ninety medicinal herbs. Dennis has no contract with Biostrath. He is not drinking the stuff for money. He is drinking it for his life. Beside him stands his opponent, John Newcombe, the second-best forehand, the second-best volley, the second-best tennis player in the world. Dennis follows the elixir with a Pepsi-Cola, also without benefit of a contract. The score is 4–5, first set. Ralston and Newcombe return to the base lines, and Ralston tosses up a ball to serve. The crowd is chattering, gurgling like a mountain stream.

Prince Charles has just come in and is settling into his seat. "Quiet, please," says the umpire, and the stream subsides. Ralston serves, wins — six all. Seven all. Eight all. Nine all. Ten all. There is a lot of grinning back and forth across the net. Newcombe drives a backhand down the line. Ralston leaps, intercepts it, and drops the ball into Newcombe's court for a winner. Newcombe looks at Ralston. Ralston grins. Newcombe smiles back. It is an attractive match, between two complete professionals. Newcombe passes Ralston with a forehand down the line. "Yep," says Ralston. Ralston finds a winner in a drop shot overhead. "Good shot," calls Newcombe. Eleven all. When they shout, it is at themselves. Newcombe moves to the net behind a fragile approach shot, runs back under a humiliatingly good lob, and drives an off-balance forehand into the net. "John!" he calls out. "Idiotic!" Ralston tosses a ball up to serve, but catches it instead of hitting it. He is having a problem with the sun, and he pauses to apologize to Newcombe for the inconvenience the delay might be causing him. Small wonder they can't beat each other. Grace of this kind has not always been a characteristic of Ralston — of Newcombe, yes, but Ralston grew up tightly strung in California, and in his youth his tantrums were a matter of national report. He is twenty-seven now and has changed. Quiet, serious, introspective, coach of the U.S. Davis Cup Team, he has become a professional beyond the imagination of most people who only knew him long ago. He plans his matches almost on a drawing board. Last night, he spent hours studying a chart he has made of every shot Newcombe has hit in this tournament. 13–12. Dennis opens another Biostrath and another Pepsi-Cola. He knows what the odds have become. The winner of this set, since it has gone so far, will in all likelihood be the winner of the match. Ralston has been a finalist at Wimbledon. But he has never won a major international tournament. In such tournaments, curiously enough, he has played Newcombe ten times and has won seven, but never for the biggest prize. Newcombe has a faculty for going all the way. Ralston, meanwhile, has pointed his life toward doing so at least once, and, who knows, he tells himself, this could be the time. He toes the line and tosses up the ball. He catches it, and tosses it up again. The serve is bad. The return is a winner. Love–fifteen. He has more trouble with the sun. Love–thirty. Catastrophe is falling from nowhere. Love–forty. Serve, return, volley. Fifteen–forty. He serves. Fault. He serves again. Double fault. Game and first set to Newcombe, 14–12. Ralston looks up, over the trigger of a thousand old explosions, and he forces a smile. 14–12, 9–7, 6–2. When it is over, the ball boys carry out seven empty bottles of Pepsi-Cola and four empty vials of the ninety medicinal herbs.

Kramer is in a glassed-in booth at one corner of the court, commenting on the action for the BBC. For an American to be engaged to broadcast to the English, extraordinary credentials, of one kind or another, are required. Just after the Second World War, Kramer first displayed his. Upwards of fifty American players now come to Wimbledon annually, but Kramer, in 1946, was one of three to cross the ocean. "Now it's a sort of funsy, 'insy' thing to do," he has said. "But in my time, if you didn't think you had a top-notch chance, you didn't come over. To make big money out of tennis, you had to have the Wimbledon title as part of your credits. I sold my car, a 1941 Chevrolet, so I could afford to bring my wife, Gloria, with me." That was long before the era of the Perry-Lacoste-Adidas bazaar, and Kramer, at Wimbledon, wore his own clothes — shorts that he bought at Simpson's and T-shirts that had been issued to him during the war, when he was a sailor in the United States Coast Guard. Now, as he watches the players before him and predicts in his expert way how one or the other will come slowly unstuck, he looks past them across the court and up behind the Royal Box into an entire segment of the stadium that was gone when he first played here. At some point between 1939 and 1945, a bomb hit the All-England tennis club, and with just a little more wind drift it would have landed in the center of the Centre Court. Instead, it hit the roof over the North East Entrance Hall. Kramer remembers looking up from the base line, ready to serve, into a background of avalanched rubble and twisted girders against the sky. He slept in the Rembrandt, which he remembers as "an old hotel in South Kensington," and he ate steak that he had brought with him from the United States, thirty pounds or so of whole tenderloins. Needless to say, there was no Rolls-Royce flying Wimbledon colors to pick him up at the Rembrandt. Kramer went to Wimbledon, with nearly everyone else, on the underground — Gloucester Road, Earl's Court, Fulham Broadway, Parsons Green, Putney Bridge, East Putney, Southfields, Wimbledon. He lost the first time over. A year later, he returned with his friend Tom Brown, and together they hit their way down opposite sides of the draw and into the Wimbledon final. A few hours before the match, Kramer took what remained of his current supply of *filet mignon*, cut it in half, and shared it with Tom Brown. Kramer was twenty-five and his game had come to full size — the Big Game, as it was called, the serve, the rush, the jugular volley. When Kramer proved what he could do, at Wimbledon, he changed for all foreseeable time the patterns of the game. He destroyed Brown in forty-seven minutes, still the fastest final in Wimbledon's history, and then — slender, crewcut, big in the ears — he was led to the Royal Box for a word or two with the King and Queen. The Queen said to him, "Whatever happened to that redheaded young man?" And Kramer told her that Donald Budge was alive and doing O.K. The King handed Kramer the Wimbledon trophy. "Did the court play well?" the King asked him. "Yes, it did, sir," Kramer answered. It was a tennis player's question. In 1926, the King himself had competed in this same tournament and had played in the Centre Court. A faraway smile rests on Kramer's face as he remembers all this. "Me in my T-shirt," he says, with a slight shake of his head.

Frew McMillan, on Court 2, wears a golfer's billowing white visored cap, and he looks very much like a golfer in his style of play, for he swings with both hands and when he completes a stroke, his arms follow the racquet across one shoulder and his eyes seem to be squinting down a fairway. Court 2 has grandstands on either side and they are packed with people. McMillan is a low-handicap tennis player who can dig some incredible ground strokes out of the rough. A ball comes up on his right side and he drives it whistling down the line, with a fading hook on the end. The ball comes back on his left side, and, still with both hands, overlapping grip, he hits a cross-court controlled-slice return for a winner. The gallery applauds voluminously. McMillan volleys with two hands. The only strokes he hits with one hand are the serve and the overhead. He has an excellent chip shot and a lofty topspin wedge. He putts well. He is a lithe, dark, attractive, quiet South African. In the South African Open, he played Laver in the final. Before Laver had quite figured out what sort of a match it was, McMillan had him down one set to nought. Then Laver got out his mashie and that was the end of McMillan in the South African Open. When McMillan arrived in London and saw the Wimbledon draw, he felt, in his words, a cruel blow, because his name and Laver's were in the same pocket of the draw, and almost inevitably they would play in the third round. "But maybe I have a better chance against him earlier than later," he finally decided. "You feel you have a chance. You have to — even if it is a hundred to one." Now the grandstands are jammed in Court 2, and, high above, the railing is crowded on the Tea Room roof, for McMillan, after losing the first set, has broken Laver and leads him 5–3 in the second.

"I got the feeling during the match that I had more of a chance beating him on the court than thinking about it beforehand. You realize the chap isn't infallible. It's almost as if I detected a chip in his armor."

Laver has netted many shots and has hit countless others wide or deep. He cannot find the lines. He is preoccupied with his serves, which are not under control. He spins one in too close to the center of the service box. McMillan blasts it back. Advantage McMillan. Laver lifts the ball to serve again. Fault. He serves again. Double fault. Game and set to McMillan, 6–3.

When this sort of thing happens, Laver's opponent seldom lives to tell the tale. One consistent pattern in all the compiled scores in his long record is that when someone takes a set from him, the score of the next set is 6–0, Laver, or something very near it. Affronted, he strikes twice as hard. "He has the physical strength to hit his way through nervousness," McMillan says. "That's why I believe he's a great player."

Laver breaks McMillan in the opening game of the third set. He breaks him again in the third game. His volleys hit the corners. His drives hit the lines. McMillan's most powerful blasts come back at him faster than they left his racquet. McMillan hits a perfect drop shot. Laver is on it like the light. He snaps it unreachably down the line. Advantage Laver. McMillan hits one deep to Laver's backhand corner, and Laver, diving as he hits it, falls. McMillan sends the ball to the opposite corner. Laver gets up and sprints down the base line. He not only gets to the ball — with a running forehand rifle shot, he puts it away. It is not long before he is shaking McMillan's hand at the net. "Well played," McMillan says to him (6–2, 3–6, 6–0, 6–2). "Yes, I thought I played pretty well," Laver tells him. And they make their way together through the milling crowd. McMillan will frequently say what a gentle and modest man he finds Laver to be. "It may be why he is what he is," McMillan suggests, "You can see it in his eyes."

B. M. L. de Roy van Zuydewijn is a loser in the Veterans' Event — gentlemen's doubles. So is the seventy-two-year-old Borotra. Riggs and Drobny, on Court 5, persevere. Over the years, Riggs and Drobny have eaten well. Each is twice the shadow of his former self. The Hungarians Bujtor and Stolpa are concentrating on Riggs as the weaker of the two.

Game to Seewagen and Miss Overton, the honey-blond Miss Overton. They lead Dell and Miss Johnson five games to four, second set. Dell is not exactly crumbling under the strain. These peripheral matches are fairly informal. Players talk to one another or to their friends on the side lines, catching up on the news. Seewagen and Miss Overton appear to be playing more than tennis. Dell is tired — up half the night making deals and arguing with Kramer, up early in the morning to do business over breakfast with bewildered Europeans, who find him in his hotel room in a Turkish-towel robe, stringy-haired and wan, a deceptive glaze in his eyes, offering them contracts written on fly-paper.

The Russians enter the Centre Court to play mixed doubles. Princess Anne is in the Royal Box. The Russians hesitate, and look at each other in their ceramic way, and then they grin, they shrug, and they turn toward the Royal Box and bend their heads. The people applaud.

Nastase is Nijinsky — leaping, flying, hitting jump-shot overheads, sweeping forehands down the line. Tiriac is in deep disgrace. Together they have proved their point. They have outlasted most of the seeded pairs in the gentlemen's doubles. But now they are faltering against Rosewall and Stolle, largely because Tiriac is playing badly. Stolle hits an overhead. Tiriac tries to intercept it near the ground. He smothers it into the court. Nastase, behind him, could have put the ball away after it had bounced. Tiriac covers his face with one hand and rubs his eyes. He slinks back to the base line like someone caught red-handed. But now he redeems himself. The four players close in for a twelve-shot volley, while the ball never touches the ground. It is Tiriac who hits number twelve, picking it off at the hip and firing it back through Stolle.

Lutz crashes, and the injury appears to be serious. Playing doubles in the Centre Court with his partner, Smith, he chases an angled overhead, and he crashes into the low wall at the front of the grandstand. He makes no effort to get up. He quivers. He is unconscious. "Get a doctor, please," says the umpire. A nurse in a white cap and a gray uniform that nearly reaches her ankles hurries across the lawn. The crowd roars with laughter. There is something wondrous in the English sense of humor that surfaces in the presence of accidents, particularly if they appear to be fatal. The laughter revives Lutz. He comes to, gets up, returns to the court, shakes his head a few times, resumes play, and drives a put-away into the corner after an eight-shot ricochet volley. Lutz is tough. He was a high-school football player in California and he once promised himself that he would quit tennis and concentrate on football unless he should happen to win the national junior championship. He won, and gave up football. Additional medical aid comes from outside the stadium. Another nurse has appeared. She hovers on the edge of play. When she sees an opportunity, she hurries up to Smith and gives him an aspirin.

If Lutz had broken three ribs, he would not have mentioned it as long as he continued to play, and in this respect he is like the Australians. There is an Australian code on the matter of injuries, and it is one of the things that give the Australians a stature that is not widely shared by the hypochondriac Americans and the broken-wing set from mainland Europe. The Australian code is that you do not talk about injuries, you hide them. If you are injured, you stay out, and if you play, you are not injured. The Australians feel contempt for players who put their best injury forward. An Australian will say of such a man, "I have never beaten him when he was healthy." Laver developed a bad wrist a year or so ago at Wimbledon, and he and his wife got into a telephone kiosk so that she could tape the wrist in secrecy. If he had taped it himself, no one would ever have known the story. His wife would rather praise him than waltz with the Australian code. His wife is an American.

"Bad luck, Roger." This is what Roger Taylor's friends are saying to him, because he has to play Laver, in the fourth round, in the Centre Court tomorrow. The champion always plays in one of the two stadiums or on the Number Two Court, the only places that can take in all the people who want to see him. "Don't worry, though, Roger. It's no disgrace if Rocket is the man who puts you out. You've got nothing to lose."

"I've got everything to lose," Taylor tells them. "To lose at Wimbledon is to lose. This is what competition is all about. You've got to think you have a chance. You might hope for twenty-five let cords or something, but you always think there's a chance you'll get through."

"Bad luck, Roger."

Roger takes a deep hot bath, goes home to his two-bedroom flat on Putney Hill, and continues to work himself up, talking to his mother, his father, and his wife, over a glass of beer.

"That's enough beer, Roger."

"I don't live like a monk. I want to loosen up." He eats a slice of fried liver and opens another beer. "All my chances will hinge on how well I serve. I'll have to serve well to him, to keep him a little off balance on his returns. If I can't do that, I'll be in dire trouble. If you hit the ball a million miles an hour, he hits it back harder. You can't beat a player like that with sheer speed — unless he's looking the other way. I plan to float back as many service returns as I can. The idea is not to let it get on top of you that you're going to play these people. There's a tendency to sort of lie down and roll over."

Games are three all, first set. Taylor feels weak from tension. Laver is at ease. "We'd played often enough," Laver will say later. "I knew his game — left-handed, slice serve, better forehand than backhand, a good lob. He's very strong. He moves well for a big man. There was no special excitement. My heart wasn't pounding quite as hard as it sometimes does."

Taylor floats back a service return, according to plan. Laver reaches high, hits a semi-overhead volley, and the ball lands in the exact corner of the court. It bounces into the stadium wall. The crowd roars for him, but he is also hitting bad shots. There is a lack of finish on his game. He wins the first set, 6–4.

"My concentration lapsed continually. I was aware of too many things — the troublesome wind, the court being dry and powdery. I magnified the conditions. I played scratchy in the first set. I felt I'd get better in the next set."

A break point rises against Laver in the first game of the second set. He lifts the ball to serve. He hits it into the net. "Fault." He spins the next one — into the net. "Double fault." "Oh, just throw it up and hit it," he says aloud to himself, thumping his fist into the strings of his racquet.

"When you lose your rhythm, serving, it's because of lack of concentration. I found myself thinking too much where the ball should be going. You don't think about your serve, you think about your first volley. If you think about getting your serve in, you make errors. I didn't know where my volleys were going. I missed easy smashes."

Taylor is floating back his returns. He is keeping Laver off balance. With his ground strokes, he is hitting through the wind. There is an explosion of applause for him when he wins the second set, 6–4. No one imagines that he will do more, but it is enough that Taylor, like McMillan, has won a set from Laver — and more than enough that he is English.

"Roger was playing some good tennis. When I played fairly well, he played better."

First game, third set — love–forty — Laver serving. There is chatter in the crowd, the sound of the mountain stream. "Quiet, please!" Laver hits his way back to thirty–forty. He serves, rushes, and punches a volley down the line — out. Game and another service break to Taylor. Five times, Laver has hit his running rifle-shot forehand into the net. He has repeatedly double-faulted. His dinks fall short. His volleys jump the base line. Taylor, meanwhile, is hitting with touch and power. He is digging for everything. Laver is not covering the court. Both feet off the ground, Laver tries a desperation shot from the hip, and he nets it.

Advantage Taylor. Taylor serves — a near ace, unplayable. Game and third set to Taylor, 6–2. He leads two sets to one. Unbelievable. Now the time has certainly come for Laver to react, as he so often does, with vengeance.

"When your confidence is drained, you tend to do desperation shots. My desperation shots, a lot of times, turn matches. I felt something was gone. I didn't have strength to get to the net quickly. I can't explain what it was. If you're not confident, you have no weight on the ball. You chase the ball. You look like a cat on a hot tin roof."

Laver serves, moves up, and flips the volley over the base line. "Get it down!" he shouts to himself. His next volley goes over the base line. Now he double-faults. Now he moves under a high, soft return. He punches it into a corner. Taylor moves to the ball and sends it back, crosscourt. Laver, running, hits a rolling top-spin backhand — over the base line. Advantage Taylor. Break point. The whispering of the crowd has become the buzz of scandal.

His red hair blowing in the wind, Laver lifts the ball to serve against the break. Suddenly, he looks as fragile as he did at Hurlingham and the incongruity is gone. The spectators on whom this moment is making the deepest impression are the other tennis players — forty or so in the grandstands, dozens more by the television in the Players' Tea Room. Something in them is coming free. The man is believable. He is vulnerable. He has never looked more human. He is not invincible.

"The serve is so much of the game. If you serve well, you play well. If not, you are vulnerable. If you play against someone who is capable of hitting the ball as hard as Roger can, you are looking up the barrel."

Laver serves. "Fault." He serves again. "Double fault." Game and service break to Taylor, fourth set. Laver, without apparent emotion, moves into the corner, and the shadow that until moments ago seemed to reach in a hundred directions now follows him alone. The standard he has set may be all but induplicable, but he himself has returned to earth. He will remain the best, and he will go on beating the others. The epic difference will be that, from now on, they will think that they can beat him.

Taylor lobs. Laver runs back, gets under the bouncing ball, kneels, and drives it into the net. He is now down 1–5. He is serving. He wins three points, but then he volleys into the net, again he volleys into the net, and again he volleys into the net — deuce. He serves. He moves forward. He volleys into the net. Advantage Taylor — match point. The sound of the crowd is cruel. "Quiet, please!" the umpire says. Laver serves, into the net. He appears to be trembling. He serves again. The ball does not touch the ground until it is out of the court beyond the base line.

Photographers swarm around him and around Taylor. "Well done, Roger. Nice," Laver says, shaking Taylor's hand. His eyes are dry. He walks patiently through the photographers, toward the glass doors. In the locker room, he draws a cover over his racquet and gently sets it down. On the cover are the words ROD LAVER — GRAND SLAM.

"I feel a little sad at having lost. I played well early in the tournament. I felt good, but I guess deep down something wasn't driving me hard enough. When I had somewhere to aim my hope, I always played better. Deep down in, you wonder, 'How many times do you have to win it?'"

## Arthur Kretchmer

........................................................................................................................

# Butkus

FROM *Playboy*

DICK BUTKUS slowly unraveled his mass from the confines of a white Toronado and walked into the Golden Ox Restaurant on Chicago's North Side. He is built large and hard, big enough to make John Wayne look like his loyal sidekick. When he walks, he leads with his shoulders, and the slight forward hunch gives him an aura of barely restrained power. He always seems to be ready.

As he walked through the restaurant, he was recognized by most of the men sitting at lunch. But the expression on their faces was not the one of childlike surprise usually produced by celebrities. It was of frightened awe. It read: "Holy Christ! He really *is* an ape. He could tear me apart and he might *love* it."

Ten rolling steps into the restaurant, with all eyes fixed on him, he was stopped by an ebullient lady with a thick German accent, a member of the staff. "Mr. Boot-kuss!" she scolded him. "What have you done to yourself? You look so thin."

He smiled shyly. Not even the ferocious Dick Butkus can handle a rampant maternal instinct. "Aw," he said. "I'm just down to my playing weight."

Butkus chose a table in a far corner of the restaurant. It was a Friday afternoon, two days before the Chicago Bears were to meet the Minnesota Vikings in the first of two games the teams would play in 1970. The Vikings had won the NFL championship the year before and seemed likely to repeat. The Bears were presenting their usual combination of erratic offense and brutal defense and appeared to be on the verge of another undistinguished season. Butkus was joined at the table by a business associate and a journalist. He ordered a sandwich and a liter of dark beer. He doesn't like journalists and is cautious to the point of hostility with them. But he fields the questions, because it's part of his business.

"Do you think you can beat the Vikings?"

Butkus answers, "Yeah, the defense can beat them. I don't know if the offense can score any points. But we can take it to those guys."

"Have you ever been scared on a football field?"

"Scared?" he repeats, puzzled. "Of what?"

Then he smiles, knowing the effect he's had on his questioner. "Just injuries," he says. "That's the only thing to be afraid of. I'm always hurt, never been healthy. If I ever felt really great and could play a hundred percent, shit, nobody'd know what was going on, it would be so amazing."

"Does anybody play to intentionally hurt other guys?"

"Some assholes do. The really good ones don't."

"Dave Meggyesy, the ex-Cardinal, says that football is so brutal he was taught to use his hands to force a man's cleats into the turf and then drive his shoulder into the man's knee to rip his leg apart. That ever happen to you?"

"Hell, no! All you'd have to do is roll with the block and step on the guy's face."

That's my man. Richard Marvin Butkus, 28 years old, 245 pounds, six feet, three inches tall, middle linebacker for the Chicago Bears football team, possibly the best man to ever play the position. To a fan, the story on Butkus is very simple. He's the meanest, angriest, toughest, dirtiest son of a bitch in football. An animal, a savage, subhuman. But as good at his game as Ty Cobb was at his, or Don Budge at his, or Joe Louis at his.

As one of the Bear linemen said to me, "When you try to pick the best offensive guard, there are about five guys who are really close; it's hard to pick one. The same thing's true about most positions. But Butkus *is* the best. He's superman. He's the greatest thing since popcorn."

The Minnesota game is being played on a warm, sunny autumn day at Chicago's Wrigley Field before a capacity crowd. Both teams have come out to warm up, but Butkus is late, because his right knee is being shot up with cortisone. It was injured three weeks before in a game with the New York Giants. Butkus was caught from the blind side while moving sideways and the knee collapsed. Until then, the Giants had been play-ing away from him. When they realized he was hurt, they tried to play at him and he simply stuffed them. Giant quarterback Fran Tarkenton said afterward, "Butkus has the most concentration of any man in the game. He's fantastic. And after he was hurt, he dragged that leg around the whole field. He was better after the injury than before — better on that one damn leg than with two."

When Butkus finally comes out, his steps are hesitant, like he is trying to walk off a cramp. You notice immediately that he looks even bigger in pads and helmet — bigger than anyone else on the field, bigger than players listed in the program as outweighing him. He has the widest shoulders on earth. His name seems too small for him; the entire alpha-bet could be printed on the back of his uniform and there'd be room left over.

Both teams withdraw after warm-ups and the stadium announcer reads the line-ups. The biggest hand from the restless fans comes when Butkus' name is announced. In the quiet that follows the applause, a raucous voice from high in the stands shouts, "Get Butkus' ass."

The players return to the field and string out along the side line. Both team benches at Wrigley Field are on the same side of the field, the Bears to the north and the Vikings to the south. Near midfield, opposing players and coaches stand quite close to each other, but there is almost no conversation between them, abusive or otherwise. As the Vikings ar-range themselves for the national anthem, linebacker Wally Hilgenberg roars in on tight end John Beasley, a teammate, and delivers a series of resounding two-fisted hammer blows to Beasley's shoulder pads, exhal-ing loud whoops as his fists land. Beasley then smashes Hilgenberg. Everyone is snarling and hissing as the seconds tick away before the kickoff. Butkus is one of the few who show no signs of nervousness. That is true off the field and on. He does not fidget nor pace. Mostly, he just stands rather loosely and stares.

After the anthem, the tempo on the side line increases. The Bears will be kicking off. Howard Mudd, an offensive guard who was all-pro when the Bears obtained him in a trade from San Francisco, is screaming, "KICKOFF KICKOFF KICKOFF," trying to get everyone else up as well as discharge some of his own energy. Mudd is a gap-toothed, blue-eyed 29-year-old with a bald spot at his crown who arrives at the field about 8:30 A.M. — fully four and a half hours before the game. He spends a lot of that time throwing up.

As I watch the Vikings' first offensive series from the side line, the sense of space and precision that the fan gets, either up in the stadium or at home on television, is destroyed. The careful delineation of plays done by the TV experts becomes absurd. At ground level, all is mayhem; sophistication and artistry are destroyed by the sheer velocity of the game. Each snap of the ball sets off 21 crazed men dueling with one another for some kind of edge — the 22nd, the quarterback, is the only one trying to maintain calm and seek some sense of order in the asylum.

It's the sudden, isolated noise that gets you. There is little sound just before each play begins — the crowd is usually quiet. At the snap, the tense vacuum is broken by sharp grunts and curses from the linemen as they slam into one another. The sudden smash of a forearm is sickening; and then there is the most chilling sound of all: the hollow thud as a launched, reckless body drives a shoulder pad into a ball carrier's head — a sound more lonely and terrifying than a gunshot.

After receiving the kickoff, the Vikings are forced to punt when a third-down pass from Gary Cuozzo, the Viking quarterback, to Gene Washington falls incomplete. As the Bears come off the field, Butkus is screaming at left linebacker Doug Buffone and cornerback Joe Taylor, because Washington was open for the throw. Luckily, he dropped it. They are having a problem with the signals. There is something comical about Butkus screaming with his helmet on. His face is so large that it seems to be trying to get *around* the helmet, as if the face were stuffed into it against its will.

That third-down play was marked by a lapse in execution by both offense and defense. It was one of those plays where all the neatly drawn lines in the playbook are meaningless. The truth about football is that, rather than being a game of incredible precision, it is a game of breakdowns, of entropy. If all plays happened as conceived, it would be too easy a sport. But the reality is that the timing is usually destroyed by a mental error, by a misstep, by a defenseman getting a bigger piece of a man than he was expected to, by the mere pace of the action being beyond a man's ability to think clearly when he's under pressure. Or by his being belted in the neck and knee simultaneously while he's supposed to be running nine steps down and four steps in.

The Bears don't get anywhere against the Viking defense and Butkus is back out quickly. On the field, his presence is commanding. He doesn't take a stance so much as install himself a few feet from the offensive center, screwing his heels down and hunching forward, hands on knees. His aura is total belligerence. As Cuozzo calls the signals, all of

Butkus goes into motion. His mouth is usually calling signals of his own, his hands come off his knees, making preliminary pawing motions, and his legs begin to drive in place. No one in football has a better sense of where the ball will go, and Butkus moves instantly with the snap.

Two Cuozzo passes under pressure set up a Viking touchdown. On the Bears next set of offensive plays, they can't get anything going, and the defense is back out. On the second play from scrimmage, the Vikings set up a perfect sweep, a play that looks great each time you put it on the blackboard but works right one time in ten. This is one of those times. Guards Milt Sunde and Ed White lead Clint Jones around the left side with no one in front of them except Butkus, who is moving over from his position in the middle. All four bodies are accelerating rapidly. The play happens right in front of me and Butkus launches himself around Sunde and smashes both forearms into White, clawing his way over the guard to bring Jones down for no gain. He has beaten three men.

The Vikings are forced to punt after that and the Bears get their first first down. Then, on first and ten, Bear quarterback Jack Concannon lobs a perfect pass to halfback Craig Baynham; who is open in the Viking secondary. Baynham drops it. And that is about as much as the Bear offense will show this day.

With 56 seconds left in the half, the Vikings have the ball again. Cuozzo is trapped in the backfield trying to pass; and as he sets to throw, the ball falls to the ground and the Bears pick it up. The officials rule that Cuozzo was in the act of throwing and therefore the Vikings maintain possession on an incomplete pass. The Bears and all of Wrigley Field think it's a fumble and are expressing themselves accordingly. Butkus is enraged and is ranting at all the officials at once. But the Vikings keep the ball and a few seconds later try a field goal from the Bear 15. Butkus is stunting in the line, looking for a place to get through to block the kick. At the snap, he charges over tackle Ron Yary but is savagely triple-teamed and stopped. The field goal is good. When Yary comes off the field, he is bleeding heavily from the bridge of his nose but doesn't seem to notice it.

As the half ends, a ruddy-looking gray-haired man who had been enthusiastically jeering the officials on the Cuozzo call slumps forward in his seat. Oxygen and a stretcher are dispatched immediately and the early diagnosis is a heart attack. He is rushed from the stadium, but the betting among the side-line spectators — an elite group of photographers, friends of the athletes and hangers-on — is that he won't make it. They are right; the man is taken to a hospital and pronounced dead on arrival. A spectator, watching the game from behind a ground-level barricade, says, "If he had a season ticket, I'd like to buy it."

The second half is more of the same for the Bears' offense. Concannon throws another perfect touchdown pass, but it's dropped; and the Vikings maintain their edge. The surprising thing is that the Bears never give up. With the score 24–0, the Bear offensive line is still hitting and, God knows, so is the defense. The Bears have a reputation as a physical team, and it's justified. They have often given the impression, especially in the days when George Halas was coaching them, of being a bunch of guys who thought the best thing you could do on a Sunday afternoon was go out and kick a little ass. Winning was a possible but not necessary adjunct to playing football.

As Butkus comes off the field at the end of the third quarter, he's limping noticeably, but it hasn't affected his play. Cuozzo has had most of his success throwing short passes to the outside, but he continues to run plays in Butkus' area. The plays begin to take on a hypnotic pattern for me. Every three downs or so, there is this paradigm running play: Tingelhoff, the center, charges at Butkus, who fends him off with his forearms. Then Butkus moves to the hole that Osborn or Brown has committed himself to. Butkus, legs driving, arms outstretched, seems to simply step forward and embrace the largest amount of space he can. And he smothers everything in it — an offensive lineman, possibly one of his own defensive linemen and the ball carrier. Then he simply hangs on and bulls it all to the ground.

Finally, the game ends with a sense of stupefying boredom, because everyone seems to realize at once that there was never any hope. As the fans file out, one leans over a guardrail and screams at Bear head coach Jim Dooley. "Hey, Dooley! Whydoncha give Butkus a break? Trade him!" This is met with approval from his friends.

A few days after the Viking game, Butkus is in another North Side German restaurant. He is quiet, reserved and unhappy, because he feels that the Vikings didn't show the Bears much, didn't beat them physically nor with any great show of proficiency. I can't help thinking that a man of his talent would get tired of this kind of second-rate football.

"Don't you ever get bored? Don't you think of retiring from this grind?"

"No way!"

"But what do you get from it? It's got to be very frustrating. Why do you play?"

"Hell. That's like asking a guy why he fucks."

The following Sunday, the Bears are flat and lose badly to an amazing passing display from the San Diego Chargers. But they have been pointing toward their next big game — a rematch with an old and hated rival, the Detroit Lions. Earlier in the year, on national television, the Bears led the Lions for a half but ended up losing. After that game, Lion head coach Joe Schmidt said that his middle linebacker, Mike Lucci, was the best in football and that Butkus was overrated. The Lions generally said that Butkus was dirty rather than good. It added a little spice to a game that didn't need any.

The question of linebacking is an interesting one to consider. To play that position, a man must be strong enough in the arms and shoulders to fight off offensive linemen who often outweigh him, fast enough to cover receivers coming out of the backfield and rangy enough to move laterally with speed. But the real key to the position is an instantaneous ferocity — the ability to burst rather than run. And the man must function in the face of offenses that have been specifically designed to influence his actions away from the ball. Butkus is regarded as the strongest of middle linebackers, the very best at stopping running plays.

I once asked Howard Mudd if the 49ers, his previous team, had a special game plan for Butkus. "Sure," he said. "The plan was to not run between the tackles; always ensure that you block Dick. Once the game started, the plan changed, though. It became. 'Don't run. Just pass.'"

Mudd also pointed out something that belies Butkus' reputation for viciousness. "He doesn't try to punish the blockers," Mudd said. "He doesn't hit you in the head, like a lot of guys. The first time I played against him, I was — well — almost disappointed. It wasn't like hitting a wall or anything. He didn't mess with me, he went *by* me. All he wants is the ball. When he gets to the ball carrier, he really rings that man's bell."

In the Bear defense, Butkus is responsible for calling the signals and for smelling out the ball. If he has a weakness, it's that he sometimes seems to wallow a bit on his pass drops, allowing a man to catch a pass in front of him and assuming that the force of his tackle will have an effect on the man's confidence. It often does.

*   *   *

The night before the Lions game, Butkus was at his home in a suburb about 40 minutes' drive from Wrigley Field. It's an attractive ranch-style brick house. In front of the garage is a white pickup truck with the initials D. B. unobtrusively hand-lettered on the door. Inside the garage is a motorcycle. These are Butkus' toys. The main floor of the house is charmingly furnished and reflects the taste of his wife, Helen, an attractive auburn-haired woman who is expecting their third child early in 1971. She is a lively but reserved woman who runs the domestic side of their lives and attempts to keep track of Nikki, a four-year-old girl, and Ricky, a three-year-old boy — two golden-haired and rugged children.

The basement of the house belongs mostly to Butkus. Its finished, paneled area contains a covered pool table — he doesn't enjoy the game very much nor play it well — and a bar. Along the walls are as many trophies and glory photos as a man could ever hope for. The only photograph he calls to a visitor's attention is an evocative one from *Sports Illustrated* that shows him in profile, looking grimy and tired, draining the contents of a soft-drink cup.

At the far end of the basement is Butkus' workroom. The area is dominated by a large apparatus of steel posts and appendages that looks like some futuristic torture chamber. It's called a Universal Gym and its various protrusions allow him to exercise every part of his body. There is other exercise equipment about and in a far corner is a sauna. Butkus works out regularly but not to build strength. His objective is to keep his weight down and his muscles loose.

After an early dinner with the family, Butkus secluded himself in the bedroom with his playbooks and .16mm projector for a last look at the Lions' offense in its shadowy screen incarnation. Just after ten o'clock, he went to sleep. He woke early the next morning and went to early Mass, at 6:30, so that he didn't have to dress up. He and the priest were the only ones there. He returned home to eat a big steak and, after breakfast, he spent some more time with the playbooks. About ten o'clock he left the house for the drive to the ball park.

"He's real quiet before a game," Mrs. Butkus says, "but he's usually quiet. When he was dating me, my mother used to ask, 'Can't he talk?' I don't think he gets nervous before a game. I think it's just anticipation. He really wants to get at them."

She is remarkably cheerful about football and likes to talk about her husband's prowess. Her favorite story is one that she learned when she met Fuzzy Thurston, one of the great offensive linemen from Vince Lombardi's years at Green Bay. "Fuzzy told me," she says, "that when

Dick played against the Packers the first time, Lombardi growled, 'Let's smear this kid's face.' But Fuzzy says they just couldn't touch him. After the game, Lombardi said, 'He's the best who ever played the position.'"

The day of the Lions game is cool and clear. When Butkus comes out, his expression is blank. The Bears are quieter and more fidgety than before the Viking game. It's immediately apparent that this game will be played at a higher pitch than the previous ones, nearly off the scale that measures human rage. People who play football and who write about it like to talk about finesse, about a lineman's "moves." But when the game is really on, the finesse gets very basic. The shoulder dip and slip is replaced by the clenched fist to the head, the forearm chop to the knee and the helmet in the face.

From the opening play, the fans show they are in a wild mood. They have begun to call Mike Lucci (pronounced Loo*chee*) Lucy. And when Lucci is on the field, they taunt him mercilessly. "Hey, Lucy! You're not big enough to carry Butkus' shoes."

The Lions are stopped on their first offensive series, and punt. As the ball sails downfield, Butkus and Ed Flanagan, the Detroit center, trade punches at midfield. They are both completely out of the play.

Soon enough, the Bear defense is back out. Butkus seems to be in a frenzy. He stunts constantly, pointing, shouting, trying to rattle Lion quarterback Bill Munson. On first down at the Lions' 20, he stuns Flanagan, who is trying to block him, with his forearm and knifes through on the left side to bring down Mel Farr for a five-yard loss.

On second down, Munson hands off to Farr going to his left. The left tackle, Roger Shoals, has gotten position on defensive end Ed O'Bradovich, as Farr cuts to the side line. Butkus, coming from the middle, lunges around the upright Shoals-O'Bradovich combination like a snake slithering around a tree and slashes at the runner's knees with his outstretched forearm. Farr crumbles.

On third down, Munson tries to pass to Altie Taylor in front of right linebacker Lee Roy Caffey. Caffey cocks his arm to ram it down Taylor's throat as he catches the ball, but Taylor drops the pass and Caffey relaxes the arm and pats him on the helmet.

The Lions set to punt and Butkus lurches up and down the line, looking for a gap. He finds one and gets a piece of the ball with his hand. The punt is short and the Bears have good position at midfield. On the first play from scrimmage, Concannon drops back and drills a pass to Dick Gordon, who has gotten behind two defenders. Gordon goes in standing up for a touchdown and pandemonium takes over Wrigley Field.

The game settles down a bit after that and the only other score for a while is a Lion field goal. Munson is trying to get a running game going to the outside, but Butkus is having an incredible day. He is getting outside as fast as Farr and Taylor. The runner and Butkus are in some strange *pas de deux*. Both seem to move to the same place at the same time, the runner driving fiercely with his legs, trying to set his blocks and find daylight. Butkus seems, by comparison, oddly graceful, his legs taking long lateral strides, his arms outstretched, fending off would-be blockers. But it's all happening at dervish speed and each impact has a jarring effect on the runner. Lucci, when he's on the field, just doesn't dominate the action and is taking abuse from the fans. He's neither as strong nor as quick. He's good on the pass drops, possibly better than Butkus, but he's not the same kind of destructive tackler.

Midway in the second quarter, Detroit cornerback Dick LeBeau intercepts a Concannon pass intended for Gordon. Gordon had gone inside and Concannon had thrown outside. Entropy again. The half ends with the score 7–3, Bears. On the side line after the half-time break, the Bears are back at high pitch. Concannon is yelling, "Go, defense," and Abe Gibron, the Bears' defensive coach, is offering, "Hit 'em to hurt 'em!" A wide man of medium height, Gibron was an all-pro tackle for many years in pro football's earlier era. He is a coach in the Lombardi mold, full of venom and fire — abusive to foe and friend. He is sometimes comical to watch as he walks the side line hurling imprecations for the entire football game: but his defenses are solid and brutal.

The intensity of the hitting seems to be increasing. Butkus makes successive resounding tackles, once on Farr and once on Taylor. He does not tackle so much as explode his shoulder into a man, as if he were trying to drive him under the ground. The effect is enhanced by his preference for hitting high, for getting as big a piece as he can. Butkus once told a television sports announcer, "I sometimes have a dream where I hit a man so hard his head pops off and rolls downfield." On a third-down play, Munson passes deep and Butkus, far downfield, breaks up the pass with his hand. The fans are overjoyed and have a few choice things to say about Lucci's parentage.

The Bears get the ball, but Concannon is intercepted again and the defense gets ready to go back in. As Butkus and the others stand tensely on the side line, it's clear to everyone that they are Chicago's only chance to win; the offense is just too sluggish. The "Ds," as they are called, have all the charisma on this team, and as they prepare to guts it out some more, I am overcome by a strange emotion. Stoop-shouldered and sunken-chested, weighing all of 177 pounds rather meagerly spread over a six-foot, three-inch frame, I want to join them. Not merely want but feel compelled to go out there and get my shoulder in — smash my body against the invaders. At this moment, those 11 men — frustrated, mean and near exhaustion — are the only possibility for gallantry and heroism that I know. The urge to be out there wells up in me the way it does in a kid reacting to a field sergeant who asks for the impossible — because to not volunteer involves a potential loss of manhood that is too great to face.

The defenses dominate the game for a while, but a short Bear punt gives the Lions good position and they get a field goal. A bit later, Munson passes for a touchdown and the Lions take the lead, 13–7. The Lions were favored in the betting before the game by as much as 16 points, and after the touchdown, the side-liners are murmuring things like, "I'm still all right, I got thirteen and a half."

With four minutes left in the game and the score 16–10 after each team has added a field goal, coach Dooley pulls Concannon in favor of the younger, less experienced but strong-armed Bobby Douglass, his second-string quarterback. A clumsy hand-off on a fourth and one convinced Dooley that Concannon was tired, although Concannon will indicate afterward that he wasn't. Pulling him at this point in the game, when the Bears obviously have only one chance to score and when a touchdown and point after would win, is an unusual thing to do, and Concannon is upset. He is a dark, scraggly-haired Irishman, very high strung, a ballplayer who stares at the fans when they're abusing him. He never feigns indifference. Now he is standing on the side line, head slightly bowed, pawing the ground with his cleats while someone else runs his team. His hands are firmly thrust into his warm-up jacket and all the time he stands there, intently watching the game, he repeats venomously over and over, "Stuff 'em! Stuff 'em! Fuck you, Lions! Goddamn it! Goddamn it! Fuck you, Lions!"

Douglass doesn't move the team and the Lions take over. Gibron is screaming that there's plenty of time. There is one minute, 36 seconds on the clock. Altie Taylor gets a crucial, time-consuming first down. Butkus tackles him viciously from behind, nearly bisecting him with his helmet; but the Bears are losers again.

The Bear defense had played tough football, and Butkus had played a great game. I said as much to him and he replied, "Hell, we're just losin' games again. It don't matter what else happened." But he didn't deny the ferocity of the Bear defense: "You didn't see a lot of that second effort out there," he said, referring to the Lion backs. "They weren't running as hard as they might."

"Do you think you intimidated them?"

"They knew they were getting hit. And when you know you're getting in there, then you really lay it on them."

"What was the reason for the punches with Flanagan?"

"I wanted to let him know he was going to be in a game."

Butkus seemed to talk all the time on the field. Was he calling signals to his own players or yelling at Detroit?

"Mostly it's signals for our side, but every once in a while, I'll say something to jag them a little."

"Like what?"

"Oh, you know. Call them a bunch of faggots or somethin'. Or I told sixty-three after a play when I got around him that he threw a horseshit block."

Butkus says these things in an emotionless voice — almost shrugging the words out rather than speaking them. His speech is filled with the nasal sounds of Chicago's Far South Side, and he is very much a neighborhood kid grown up. His tastes are simple — in food, in entertainment, in people. He doesn't run with a fast crowd. If you ask him what he does for kicks, he shrugs, "I don't know, just goof around, I guess." He has wanted to play football all his life, and one of his most disarming and embarrassing statements when he was graduated from college was, "I came here to play football. I knew they weren't going to make a genius out of me."

As a kid, Butkus loved to play baseball. Surprisingly, he couldn't hit but had all the other skills. He pitched, caught and played the infield. He had the grace of a "good little man," and that may be one key to his success. Unlike most big football players, who find it hard to walk and whistle at the same time, and have to be taught how to get around the field, Butkus has the moves of a quick, slippery small man who happens to have grown to 245 pounds.

By the time he got to high school, Butkus was committed to football. His high school coach wouldn't let him scrimmage in practice for fear that the overenthusiastic Butkus would hurt some of the kids on his own team.

He distrusts worldliness in most forms, except that he knows that his stardom can make money and he works at it. He has changed his hair style from the crewcut he wore in his early years to something a bit longer, but he's far from shaggy. His clothes are without style. He wears open-collar shirts, shapeless slacks and button-front cardigan sweaters that he never buttons. A floppy, unlined tan raincoat is his one concession to Chicago winters.

He is genuinely shy and deferential on all matters except football, and his façade is quiet cynicism. He especially dislikes bravado and gunghoism when he has reason to believe they're false, as he does with many of the Bear offensive players. Although he has a reputation for grimness, he smiles rather easily. And his laugh is a genuine surprise; it's a small boy's giggle, thoroughly disconcerting in his huge frame.

His shyness comes out in odd ways. When asked if, as defensive captain, he ever chews out another player for a missed assignment, he says, "Nah. Who am I to tell somebody else that he isn't doing the job? After all, maybe I'm not doing my job so good." Butkus is serious.

That sort of resignation makes him an ideal employee — sometimes to his own detriment. Butkus thinks, for example, that his original contract with the Bears was for too little money — and he's been suffering financially ever since. But he refuses to consider holding out for a renegotiation or playing out his contract option in order to get a better deal with a new team. "I made my mistake," he says. "Now I gotta live with it." And, although you probably couldn't find a coach in the world who wouldn't trade his next dozen draft choices for him, Butkus thinks that if he did something so downright daring as leave the Bears, no other team would take him, because he'd have marked himself a renegade.

This is not so much naïveté on Butkus' part as it is a deeply conservative strain in the man. When he saw a quote from Alex Johnson, the troubled California Angels baseball player, suggesting that he wanted to be treated like a human being, not like an athlete, Butkus said, "Hell, if he doesn't want to be treated like an athlete, let him go work the line in a steel mill. Ask those guys if they're treated like human beings."

Yet Butkus is not a company man. If anything, he is brutally cynical about established authorities — especially the management of the Chicago Bears football club — but he abhors being in a position where he finds himself personally exposed, and distrusts anyone who would willingly place himself in that position.

He especially dislikes personal contact with the fans. He complains about being stared at and being interrupted in restaurants. He is also inclined to moan about the ephemeral nature of his career. "It could be over any time," he says. "An injury could do it tomorrow. And even if I stay healthy, hell, it's all gonna be over in ten years." I ask if he has any plans for the future. "Not as a hanger-on, trying to live off my name. When it's over, I'm gonna hang up the fifty-one and get out. I'm not gonna fool around as some comedian or public speaker."

For the present, Butkus determinedly, but with no joy, does as much off-field promotional activity as he can get. He attends awards dinners and other ceremonial functions and will appear at just about any sports-related event that comes along. He's done some television appearances and made one delightful commercial for Rise shaving cream. This year, International Merchandising Corporation (the president of IMC, Mark McCormack, is the man who merchandised Arnold Palmer, among others) contacted Butkus and now manages his finances. His name has begun to appear on an assortment of sports gear and may yet make its way to hair dressings and other such men's items. When I told Butkus that he had taken his place in the pantheon of great middle linebackers, along with Sam Huff and Ray Nitschke, he said, "Hell, I'm going to make more money this year than those guys ever thought about."

Over the following six weeks, the Bears played a lot of mediocre football; they won two, lost four — although two of those were very close.

The next time I saw Butkus was on a cold, damp Thursday — a practice day for the Bears' return match with the Packers. The numbing grayness of the Chicago winter day was matched only by the Bears' mood at practice. They were sluggish and disconnected and seemed to be going through motions to run out the string. The Packer game was the next-to-last one of the season. Butkus was working with the defense under coaches Gibron and Don Shinnick. Shinnick is the Bears' linebacker coach and a veteran of 13 years with the Baltimore Colts. He is an enthusiastic, straightforward man who doesn't hassle his players. He is Butkus' favorite coach, and the impression you get from talking to either of them is that they both think that Don Shinnick and Dick Butkus are the only two men in the world qualified to talk about football.

The defense was working on its pass coverage against some second-string receivers. Doug Buffone was bitching to Shinnick because they weren't practicing against the first string and couldn't get their timing right. They had practiced with the first string before their Baltimore

game and Buffone said that it was directly responsible for five intercep-
tions in the game. Shinnick agreed but gave Buffone an "I don't make
the rules" look and they both went back to the drill.

Gibron was installing some new formations to defend against Green
Bay. One was called Duck and the other Cora. They tried out some plays
to see if everyone could pick up Butkus' signal. Butkus called "Duck" if
he wanted one formation in the backfield and "Cora" for another and
they relayed it to one another. Gibron was unhappy with the rhythm
and said, "Listen. Don't say 'Duck.' It could be 'fuck' or 'suck' or anything. Say 'Quack quack' instead, OK?" For the next few minutes, the
Bears shouted "Quack quack" as loud as they could. Butkus just stared
at Gibron. Then they ran some patterns.

Shortly, the defense left the field so Concannon and the first-string
receivers could work out without interference. Butkus stood morosely
on the side line with Ed O'Bradovich, the only team member he is really
close to.

O.B., as he is called, is a huge curly-haired man endowed with a nonchalant grace and good humor. He looks like he's never shown concern
for anything, especially his own safety.

A visitor at the practice says to Butkus, "That quack-quack stuff
sounds pretty good."

"It's not quack, quack," says Butkus, glowering. "It's Duck."

Butkus is about two weeks into a mustache. "It's for one of those
Mexican cowboy movies," he says.

O'Bradovich says, "You're gonna look like an overgrown Mexican
faggot."

"Yeah, who's gonna tell me?" At that minute, a burst of sharp, raucous
howling rises up where the offensive linemen are working on their pass
blocking. "Look at 'em," Butkus says. "Let's see how much noise they
make against Green Bay on Sunday."

As I look around the practice field, there seems to be chaos among
the players. If I were a betting man, I'd go very heavy against the Bears.
They seem totally dispirited. "It's all horseshit," Butkus says. "Everybody
wants it to be over."

Just before the practice breaks up, coach Dooley calls everyone together and says, "All right! Now, we've had these three good practices
this week. And we're ready. Let's do a big job out here Sunday." All the
players leave after a muffled shout — except for Concannon, who runs
some laps, and Mac Percival, the place kicker, who has been waiting for
a clear field to practice on. One of the coaches holds for Percival, and as

I head for the stands, Percival makes nine field goals in a row from the 36-yard line before missing one.

Sunday is sunny, but three previous days of rain have left the side lines muddy, although the field itself is in good shape. The air is damp and cold; it's a day when the fingers and toes go numb quickly and the rest of the body follows. Bear-Packer games are usually brutal affairs, but this game is meaningless in terms of divisional standings: both teams are out of contention. There is speculation, however, that each head coach — Phil Bengtson of the Packers and Dooley of the Bears — has his job on the line and that the one who loses the game will also lose his job.

When the line-ups for the game are announced, the biggest hand is not for Butkus but for Bart Starr, Green Bay's legendary quarterback. If Butkus is the symbol of the game's ferocity, then Starr is the symbol of its potential for innocence and glory. He is the third-string quarterback who made good — Lombardi's quarterback — an uncanny incarnation of skill, resourcefulness, dedication and humility. He is the Decent American, a man of restraint and self-discipline who would be tough only in the face of a tough job. But he is so much in awe of the game he plays that he wept unashamedly after scoring the *winning* touchdown in Green Bay's last-second victory over Dallas in minus-13-degree weather for the NFL championship in 1967.

The Packers receive and on the first two plays from scrimmage, But-kus bangs first Donny Anderson, then Dave Hampton to the ground. He has come out ferocious. A third-down play fails and the Packers punt. On the Bears' first play from scrimmage, Concannon throws a screen pass to running back Don Shy, who scampers 64 yards to the Packer 15. Concannon completes a pass to George Farmer and then throws a short touchdown pass to Dick Gordon. Bears lead, 7–0.

Green Bay's ball: Starr hands off to Hampton, who slips before he gets to the line of scrimmage. On second and ten, Butkus stunts a bit, then gets an angle inside as Starr goes back to pass. Butkus gets through untouched and slams Starr for an eight-yard loss. The Packers are stopped again, and punt. As Starr comes off the field, he heads for the man with the headset on to find out from the rooftop spotters just what the hell is going on.

On the Bears' next offensive play, Concannon drops back and arcs a pass to Farmer, who has gotten behind Bob Jeter. Touchdown, Bears lead, 14–0, and there is ecstasy in the air. It is a complete turnaround and my shock at the Bears today — after watching them on Thursday — is testimony to how difficult sports clichés are to overcome. I am obsessed with whether the team is up or down, as if that were the essence of the game. Actually, for all anyone knows, the Packers might have come to Wrigley Field "up" out of their minds. It doesn't matter. The Bears are just good this day; they are at a peak of physical skill as well as emotional drive. Concannon is very close to his finest potential and, for all it matters, might be depressed emotionally. What counts is that his passes are perhaps an eighth of an inch truer as he loops his arm, and that is enough to touch greatness.

All the Bears are teeing off from their heels. When the game began, Bob Brown, the Packers' best pass rusher, sneered at Jim Cadile, Bear guard, the man across the line from him, "I'm gonna kill you."

Cadile drawled, "I'll be here all day."

The Packers now have the ball, third down, on their own 19. Starr drops back to pass and, with no open receiver, starts to run the ball himself. As he gets to the line of scrimmage, he is tripped up with four Bears closing in on him, one of whom is Butkus. I'm watching the play from the side line right behind Starr. From that vantage point Butkus, looking for a piece of Starr, is all helmet and shoulders brutally launched. The piece of Starr that Butkus gets is his head. Starr lies on the ground as the Packer trainer comes to his aid. The crowd noise is deafening.

Starr is helped from the field and immediately examined by the team physician, who checks his eyes to see if there are signs of concussion. The doctor leaves him and Starr, who looks frail at six feet, one inch, 190 pounds in the land of giants, puts his helmet on and says that he's all right. When the Bears are stopped on a drive and punt, he returns and immediately goes to work completing some short, perfectly timed passes. He moves the Packers to the Bear 15. Then, on second down, he is smashed trying to pass and comes off the field again. He is replaced by a rookie named Frank Patrick, who can't get anything going, and the Packers kick a field goal. Starr is now seated on the bench, head in hands, sniffing smelling salts. He's out for the day.

The game turns into a blood-lust orgy for the Bears. O'Bradovich is playing across from offensive tackle Francis Peay. Vince Lombardi had obtained Peay from the New York Giants, predicting that the tackle was going to be one of the greats, and he is good, indeed. But on this day, O'Bradovich is looming very large in Peay's life. In fact, he is kicking the shit out of him, actually hurling Peay's body out of his way each time

Patrick tries to set up to pass. The Packer rookie is in the worst possible position for an inexperienced quarterback. He has to pass and the defense knows it. The linemen don't have to protect against the running game and just keep on coming.

Lee Roy Caffey had been traded to Chicago by the Packers. After each set of violent exhibitions by the Bear defense, he comes off the field right in front of Packer coach Bengtson, screaming, "You motherfucker. You traded me! And we're gonna kill you!"

One of the most impressive pass plays of the game comes in the second quarter, with the score 14–3 and the Bears driving. Concannon throws a short high pass down the side line that George Farmer has to go high in the air to catch. Farmer seems to hang for a moment, as if the football has been nailed in place and his body were suspended from it. In that vulnerable position, Ray Nitschke, the Packers' middle linebacker, crashes him with a rolling tackle that swings Farmer's body like a pendulum. As Farmer turns horizontal, still in the air, Willie Wood, the safety, crushes him and Farmer bounces on the ground. But he holds onto the football.

A few plays later, Concannon, looking for a receiver at the Packer 25-yard line, finds no one open and runs in for a touchdown. It is a day when he can do no wrong.

The hysteria on the field even works its way up to the usually cool stadium announcer. In the third quarter, when Dick Gordon beats Doug Hart for another touchdown pass from Concannon, the announcer, with his mike behind his back, screams in livid rage at the Packer defender, "You're shit, Hart! You're shit!" Then he puts the instrument to his mouth and announces to the fans in his best oratorical voice, "Concannon's pass complete to Gordon. Touchdown Bears."

At the Packer bench, Bart Starr is spending the day with his head bowed, pawing the turf with his cleats. It occurs to me that every quarterback I have watched this year has spent a lot of his time in that position: Concannon, Munson, Unitas when the Bears were leading Baltimore, and now Starr.

Behind Starr, Ray Nitschke has just come off the field after the Bear touchdown. Nitschke is one of the great figures from Green Bay's irrepressible teams of the Sixties, and his face looks like he gave up any claims on the sanctity of his body when he decided to play football. He is gnarled, bald and has lost his front teeth. He constantly flexes his face muscles, opening and clamping his jaw in a set of grotesque expressions. He has put on a long Packer cape and is prowling the side line, exhaling plumes of vapor from his nostrils, the cape flowing gracefully behind him. There is something sublime in the image. Nitschke is the caped crusader; had there ever really been a Batman, he could not have been a pretty-boy millionaire — he'd have been this gnarled avenger.

As the game progresses further in the third quarter, the hysteria increases and it's hard to follow the play sequences or the score, and little details intrude on my mind:

• Little Cecil Turner, the swift black return specialist, running back a kickoff after the Packers score a touchdown, is finding daylight. As he works his way upfield, a black Packer screams to his teammates on the field, "Kill that dude!"

• O'Bradovich, coming off the field after hurling Peay around some more, sits down with his sleeves rolled up in a spot where he can avoid the heat from the side-line blowers — on a day when it's so cold that a man standing next to me is warming his hands over the open flame of his cigarette lighter.

• Willie Holman, Bear defensive tackle, barrels into Patrick as he tries to pass. The ball has no speed and is intercepted. Holman's shot actually rings in the ears for a moment. That night on the TV returns, you can't even tell that Holman caused the interception, because there is no sound, no sense of the brutality of the play.

• Butkus is dumped on his ass by Gale Gillingham as he tries to blitz Patrick. Gillingham is one of the very good offensive guards around and it's an incredible shot. The only time I've seen Butkus go backward all year.

• Jim Ringo, the nine-year all-pro center who now coaches the Bear offensive line, winces with pain each time a Bear defensive lineman wipes out one of Green Bay's offensive linemen. It's obvious that Ringo simply hates all defensive players, even his own.

Late in the fourth quarter, with the game safely out of reach, 35–10, Butkus comes out and is replaced by John Neidert. Gibron and the defense are now very much interested in the game again. The Packers get a little drive going and are at the Bear 13. Neidert is getting a lot of information from the Bear bench, especially from Gibron. To show some respect for the rule that prohibits coaching from the side line while the clock is running, Gibron wants to call his signals discreetly. He is trying to whisper "Double-zone ax" across a distance of some 25 yards.

Double zone means that the cornerbacks will play the wide receivers tight, one on one. Ax means that the middle linebacker will take the tight end alone on the short drop. On the next play, Patrick completes a pass to the tight end for the score. As Neidert comes off the field, he is heartbroken and Gibron is screaming, "Neidert, whatsamatta witchoo? If you don't know it, say so. Did you have the ax in?" Neidert, who looks too confused to think, only nods and kneels down, looking as if he is close to tears. It's possible that at the end of this already decided football game, on a meaningless score, his football career might be over. It's the one upsetting thought in an otherwise brilliant day for the Bears.

Two months after the Packer game, after a trip to Los Angeles to play in the Pro Bowl, Butkus goes into the hospital to have his knee operated on. He leaves the hospital afterward but suffers great pain for days and finally returns to see if anything can be done about it. Butkus thinks a muscle was strained when the cast was put on; the doctor doesn't agree and can't understand why he is having so much pain. I went to visit Butkus at Illinois Masonic Hospital, a typically ugly yellow-walled institution. When I get to his room, he is playing gin rummy with a friend and is in a very scowly mood.

He doesn't look like a typical patient. He isn't wearing a hospital gown, just a pair of shorts, and his upper body is almost wider than the bed. The impression is that any moment he may get out of bed, pick it up as if it were an attaché case and walk out. He offers me a beer from a large container filled with ice and cans.

He gets bored with the rummy game very quickly and his guest departs.

"How do you feel?"

"Horseshit."

Butkus describes the pain he's been having in the side of his knee and tells me the doctor just keeps saying that Gale Sayers was up and around the day after his knee was operated on. He isn't happy with the doctor. His wife, who is nine months pregnant, enters. We all discuss the pain for a minute and she makes it clear that she thinks it may be partly psychosomatic.

Butkus talks about a condominium he's bought on Marco Island in Florida and a big Kawasaki bike that he hasn't been able to ride because of the operation. He is very uncomfortable and we get into some more beers.

I ask if he was trying to hurt Starr in the Green Bay game. "Nah," he says. "I just went in there with everybody else. That's what you gotta do. But you should see the mail from Wisconsin. I got a letter that said, 'You shouldn't hit old people.' Another one said, 'I hope you get yours.'"

Butkus continually reaches down to massage his leg, which is wrapped from hip to toe in a bandage. A nurse comes in with a paper cup containing an assortment of brightly colored capsules. He asks which one is the painkiller, but the nurse refuses to tell him. She explains that he has been taking a number of sedatives since his arrival in the hospital and Butkus is disturbed that he's been swallowing a lot of stuff that hasn't done any good. "We didn't want to give you anything too strong," she tells him archly. "We thought you were taking care of yourself with the beer." It is apparent that a lot of people are enjoying the fact that the big mean Butkus is acting like a six-year-old. He looks at the nurse with puzzlement and annoyance. He doesn't think that any of this is the least bit funny and goes back to rubbing his knee.

"Do you think the operation is going to make you cautious?"

"No. But nobody's going to hit this knee again. No way."

During the next few weeks, the knee continued to trouble him. He had an unusual reaction to the catgut that had been used to rebuild the joint and his body was trying to reject it. He was often in pain and became adept at squeezing pus and sometimes chunks of catgut from the suppurating incision. At the end of March, the doctor opened the knee again and cleaned it out. This time, the doctor and Butkus were satisfied and a second operation, planned to rebuild the other side of the knee, was canceled because the joint seemed sound again.

Early in April, Butkus went to Florida to relax. He returned to Chicago after a brief stay and fell into an off-season pattern. Fool with the Kawasaki, have beers with O'Bradovich, spend Sundays with his family. In late May, he started to tune his body on the Universal Gym.

On a hot, rainy morning last June, I arrived at Butkus' house to find him sitting in the kitchen jouncing Matthew Butkus, who had been born in late February (8 pounds, 13 ounces), on his knee. The father was cooing and the son was grinning, as well he should, considering that he was spending much of his first few months surrounded by the protective comfort of those huge hands.

Butkus was still unsure of the knee. "I think I'll really be able to go on it around December first," he said. That would mean missing three months of the season. I didn't know if he was serious, and it occurred to me that he didn't either. He was to see the doctor that afternoon. I had an appointment to visit his parents, who live nearby, and as I left, his wife said, "If that knee isn't OK, I'm moving South. He'll be impossible to live with."

Butkus' parents are Lithuanian. They have seven children (Dick is the youngest and smallest of five boys) and 22 grandchildren; the family is loyal and gathers frequently.

When I got to the house, Mr. Butkus, 80 years old, a bushy-browed, weathered man of medium height, was working with a spade on the grounds. The rain had stopped and the day had turned sunny and hot. He was calmly digging out weeds in a small thicket bordering an expansive lawn that fronted the house. A white-plaster statue sat in the middle of the lawn. Mr. Butkus is a friendly man of few words who has little to say about his youngest son's success. It's simply not something that he relates to easily. The senior Mrs. Butkus is quite another story. She's a big woman who clearly supplied her sons' breadth of shoulder and chest. She is a bit immobilized now from a recent fall and thoroughly fills the armchair she is seated in. Butkus bought the house for his parents a few years ago. The living room is filled with the furniture and remnants of other places and times, and the harsh early-afternoon light seems to be cooled by its journey around the knickknacks to the corner of the room, where she is sitting. His mother says of Dick: "He didn't make any special trouble. He liked practical jokes a lot but never got into any real trouble. He was full of mischief and energy — like any other boy." There is something hard in her attitude, something that comes from raising a lot of children. Life is not wonderful, nor too simple, but it's not too bad, either. It's to be endured — and sometimes bullied. As she stares out the window, thinking about Dick, she says, "When he was a kid, his brothers would take him to the College All-Star game. He'd sit there and say, 'I'm going to play here. This is where I'm going.'" She pauses, and then continues: "You know, his brother Ronnie played for a while with the old Chicago Cardinals. He had to stop because of a knee injury." Then she turns to me and says, "I hope Dick gets well. It's his life."

## 1975

## Roger Angell

....................................................................................................................................

# Gone for Good

FROM *The New Yorker*

THE PHOTOGRAPH shows a perfectly arrested moment of joy. On one side — the left, as you look at the picture — the catcher is running toward the camera at full speed, with his upraised arms spread wide. His body is tilting toward the center of the picture, his mask is held in his right hand, his big glove is still on his left hand, and his mouth is open in a gigantic shout of pleasure. Over on the right, another player, the pitcher, is just past the apex of an astonishing leap that has brought his knees up to his chest and his feet well up off the ground. Both of *his* arms are flung wide, and he, too, is shouting. His hunched, airborne posture makes him look like a man who just made a running jump over a sizable object — a kitchen table, say. By luck, two of the outstretching hands have overlapped exactly in the middle of the photograph, so that the pitcher's bare right palm and fingers are silhouetted against the catcher's glove, and as a result the two men are linked and seem to be executing a figure in a manic and difficult dance. There is a further marvel — a touch of pure fortune — in the background, where a spectator in dark glasses, wearing a dark suit, has risen from his seat in the grandstand and is lifting his arms in triumph. This, the third and central Y in the picture, is immobile. It is directly behind the overlapping hand and glove of the dancers, and it binds and recapitulates the lines of force and the movements and the theme of the work, creating a composition as serene and well ordered as a Giotto. The subject of the picture, of course, is classical — the celebration of the last out of the seventh game of the World Series.

This famous photograph (by Rusty Kennedy, of the Associated Press) does not require captioning for most baseball fans or for almost anyone within the Greater Pittsburgh area, where it is still prominently featured in the art collections of several hundred taverns. It may also be seen, in a much enlarged version, on one wall of the office of Joe L. Brown, the general manager of the Pittsburgh Pirates, in Three Rivers Stadium. The date of the photograph is October 17, 1971; the place is Memorial Stadium, in Baltimore. The catcher is Manny Sanguillen, of the Pirates, and his leaping teammate is pitcher Steve Blass, who has just defeated the defending (and suddenly former) World Champion Baltimore Orioles by a score of 2–1, giving up four hits.

I am not a Pittsburgher, but looking at this photograph never fails to give me pleasure, not just because of its aesthetic qualities but because its high-bounding happiness so perfectly brings back that eventful World Series and that particular gray autumn afternoon in Baltimore and the wonderful and inexpungible expression of joy that remained on Steve Blass's face after the game ended. His was, to be sure, a famous victory — a close and bitterly fought pitchers' battle against the Orioles' Mike Cuellar, in which the only score for seven innings had been a solo home run by the celebrated Pirate outfielder Roberto Clemente. The Pirates had scored again in the eighth, but the Orioles had responded with a run of their own and had brought the tying run around to third base before Blass shut them off once and for all. The win was the culmination of a stirring uphill fight by the Pirates, who had fallen into difficulties by losing the first two games to the Orioles; Steve Blass had begun their comeback with a wonderfully pitched three-hit, 5–1 victory in the third game. It was an outstanding Series, made memorable above all by the play of Roberto Clemente, who batted .414 over the seven games and fielded his position with extraordinary zeal. He was awarded the sports car as the most valuable player of the Series, but Steve Blass was not far out of the running for the prize. After that last game, Baltimore manager Earl Weaver said, "Clemente was great, all right, but if it hadn't been for Mr. Blass, *we* might be popping the corks right now."

I remember the vivid contrast in styles between the two stars in the noisy, floodlit, champagne-drenched Pirate clubhouse that afternoon. Clemente, at last the recipient of the kind of national attention he had always deserved but had rarely been given for his years of brilliant play, remained erect and removed, regarding the swarming photographers with a haughty, incandescent pride. Blass was a less obvious hero — a competent but far from overpowering right-hander who had won fifteen games for the Pirates that year, with a most respectable 2.85 earned-run average, but who had absorbed a terrible pounding by the San

Francisco Giants in the two games he pitched in the National League playoffs, just before the Series. His two Series victories, by contrast, were momentous by any standard — and, indeed, were among the very best pitching performances of his entire seven years in the majors. Blass, in any case, celebrated the Pirates' championship more exuberantly than Clemente, exchanging hugs and shouts with his teammates, alternately smoking a cigar and swigging from a champagne bottle. Later, I saw him in front of his locker with his arm around his father, Bob Blass, a plumber from Falls Village, Connecticut, who had once been a semipro pitcher; the two Blasses, I saw, were wearing identical delighted, non-stop smiles.

Near the end of an article I wrote about that 1971 World Series, I mentioned watching Steve Blass in batting practice just before the all-important seventh game and suddenly noticing that, in spite of his impending responsibilities, he was amusing himself with a comical parody of Clemente at the plate: "Blass . . . then arched his back, cricked his neck oddly, rolled his head a few times, took up a stance in the back corner of the batter's box, with his bat held high, and glared out at the pitcher imperiously — Clemente, to the life." I had never seen such a spirited gesture in a serious baseball setting, and since then I have come to realize that Steve Blass's informality and boyish play constituted an essential private style, as original and as significant as Clemente's eagle-like pride, and that each of them was merely responding in his own way to the challenges of an extremely difficult public profession. Which of the two, I keep wondering, was happier that afternoon about the Pirates' championship and his part in it? Roberto Clemente, of course, is dead; he was killed on December 31, 1972, in Puerto Rico, in the crash of a plane he had chartered to carry emergency relief supplies to the victims of an earthquake in Nicaragua. Steve Blass, who is now thirty-three, is out of baseball, having been recently driven into retirement by two years of pitching wildness — a sudden, near-total inability to throw strikes. No one, including Blass himself, can cure or explain it.

The summer of 1972, the year after his splendid World Series, was in most respects the best season that Steve Blass ever had. He won nineteen games for the Pirates and lost only eight, posting an earned-run average of 2.48 — sixth-best in the National League — and being selected for the NL All-Star team. What pleased him most that year was his consistency. He went the full distance in eleven of the thirty-two games he started, and averaged better than seven and a half innings per start —

not dazzling figures (Steve Carlton, of the Phillies, had thirty complete games that year, and Bob Gibson, of the Cards, had twenty-three) but satisfying ones for a man who had once had inordinate difficulty in finishing games. Blass, it should be understood, was not the same kind of pitcher as a Carlton or a Gibson. He was never a blazer. When standing on the mound, he somehow looked more like a journeyman pitcher left over from the nineteen thirties or forties than like one of the hulking, hairy young flingers of today. (He is six feet tall, and weighs about one hundred and eighty pounds.) Watching him work, you sometimes wondered how he was getting all those batters out. The word on him among the other clubs in his league was something like: Good but not overpowering stuff, excellent slider, good curve, good change-up curve. A pattern pitcher, whose slider works because of its location. No control problems. Intelligent, knows how to win.

I'm not certain that I saw Blass work in the regular season of 1972, but I did see him pitch the opening game of the National League playoffs that fall against the Cincinnati Reds, in Pittsburgh. After giving up a home run to the Reds' second batter of the day, Joe Morgan, which was hit off a first-pitch fastball, Blass readjusted his plans and went mostly to a big, slow curve, causing the Reds to hit innumerable rainmaking outfield flies, and won by 5–1. I can still recall how Blass looked that afternoon — his characteristic, feet-together stance at the outermost, first-base edge of the pitching rubber, and then the pitch, delivered with a swastikalike scattering of arms and legs and a final lurch to the left — and I also remember how I kept thinking that at any moment the sluggers of the Big Red Machine would stop overstriding and overswinging against such unintimidating deliveries and drive Blass to cover. But it never happened — Blass saw to it that it didn't. Then, in the fifth and deciding game, he returned and threw seven and one-third more innings of thoughtful and precise patterns, allowing only four hits, and departed with his team ahead by 3–2 — a pennant-winning outing, except for the fact that the Pirate bullpen gave up the ghost in the bottom of the ninth, when a homer, two singles, and a wild pitch entitled the Reds to meet the Oakland A's in the 1972 World Series. It was a horrendous disappointment for the Pittsburgh Pirates and their fans, for which no blame at all could be attached to Blass.

My next view of Steve Blass on a baseball diamond came on a cool afternoon at the end of April this year. The game — the White Sox vs. the Orioles — was a close, 3–1 affair, in which the winning White Sox pitcher, John McKenzie, struck out seventeen batters in six innings.

A lot of the Sox struck out, too, and a lot of players on both teams walked — more than I could count, in fact. The big hit of the game was a triple to left center by the White Sox catcher, David Blass, who is ten years old. His eight-year-old brother, Chris, played second, and their father, Steve Blass, in old green slacks and a green T-shirt, coached at third. This was a late-afternoon date in the Upper St. Clair (Pennsylvania) Recreation League schedule, played between the White Sox and the Orioles on a field behind the Dwight D. Eisenhower Elementary School — Little League baseball, but at a junior and highly informal level. The low, *low* minors. Most of the action, or inaction, took place around home plate, since there was not much bat-on-ball contact, but there was a shrill nonstop piping of encouragement from the fielders, and disappointed batters were complimented on their overswings by a small, chilly assemblage of mothers, coaches, and dads. When Chris Blass went down swinging in the fourth, his father came over and said, "The sinker down and away is *tough*." Steve Blass has a longish, lightly freckled face, a tilted nose, and an alert and engaging expression. At this ball game, he looked like any young suburban father who had caught an early train home from the office in order to see his kids in action. He looked much more like a commuter than like a professional athlete.

Blass coached quietly, moving the fielders in or over a few steps, asking the shortstop if he knew how many outs there were, reminding someone to take his hands out of his pockets. "Learning the names of all the kids is the hard part," he said to me. It was his second game of the spring as a White Sox coach, and between innings one of the young outfielders said to him, "Hey, Mr. Blass, how come you're not playing with the Pirates at Three Rivers today?"

"Well," Blass said equably, "I'm not *in* baseball anymore."

"Oh," said the boy.

Twilight and the end of the game approached at about the same speed, and I kept losing track of the count on the batters. Steve Blass, noticing my confusion, explained that, in order to avert a parade of walked batters in these games, any strike thrown by a pitcher was considered to have wiped out the balls he had already delivered to the same batter; a strike on the 3–0 count reconverted things to 0–1. He suddenly laughed. "Why didn't they have that rule in the NL?" he said. "I'd have lasted until I was fifty."

Then it was over. The winning (and undefeated) White Sox and the losing Orioles exchanged cheers, and Karen Blass, a winning and clearly undefeated mother, came over and introduced me to the winning catcher and the winning second baseman. The Blasses and I walked slowly along together over the thick new grass, toting gloves and helmets and Karen's fold-up lawn chair, and at the parking lot the party divided into two cars — Karen and the boys homeward bound, and Steve Blass and I off to a nearby shopping center to order one large cheese-and-peppers-and-sausage victory pizza, to go.

Blass and I sat in his car at the pizza place, drinking beer and waiting for our order, and he talked about his baseball beginnings. I said I had admired the relaxed, low-key tenor of the game we had just seen, and he told me that his own Little League coach, back in Connecticut — a man named Jerry Fallon — had always seen to it that playing baseball on his club was a pleasure. "On any level, baseball is a tough game if it isn't really fun," Blass said. "I think most progress in baseball comes from enjoying it and then wanting to extend yourself a little, wanting it to become more. There should be a feeling of 'Let's go! Let's keep on with this!'"

He kept on with it, in all seasons and circumstances. The Blasses' place in Falls Village included an old barn with an interestingly angled roof, against which young Steve Blass played hundreds of one-man games (his four brothers and sisters were considerably younger) with a tennis ball. "I had all kinds of games, with different, very complicated ground rules," he said. "I'd throw the ball up, and then I'd be diving into the weeds for pop-ups or running back and calling for the long fly balls, and all. I'd always play a full game — a made-up game, with two big-league teams — and I'd write down the line score as I went along, and keep the results. One of the teams always had to be the Indians. I was a *total* Indians fan, completely buggy. In the summer of '54, when they won that record one hundred and eleven games, I managed to find every single Indians box score in the newspapers and clip it, which took some doing up where we lived. I guess Herb Score was my real hero — I actually pitched against him once in Indianapolis, in '63, when he was trying to make a comeback — but I knew the whole team by heart. Not just the stars but all the guys on the bench, like George Strickland and Wally Westlake and Hank Majeski and the backup third baseman, Rudy Regalado. My first big-league autograph was Hank Majeski."

Blass grew up into an athlete — a good sandlot football player, a second-team All-State Class B basketball star, but most of all a pitcher, like his father. ("He was wilder than hell," Blass said. "Once, in a Canaan game, he actually threw a pitch over the backstop.") Steve Blass pitched two no-hitters in his junior year at Housatonic Regional High School, and three more as a senior, but there were so many fine pitchers on the team that he did not get to be a starter until his final year. (One of the stars just behind him was John Lamb, who later pitched for the Pirates; Lamb's older sister, Karen, was a classmate of Steve's, and in time she found herself doubly affiliated with the Pirate mound staff.)

The Pittsburgh organization signed Steve Blass right out of Housatonic High in 1960, and he began moving up through the minors. He and Karen Lamb were married in the fall of 1963, and they went to the Dominican Republic that winter, where Steve played for the Cibaeñas Eagles and began working on a slider. He didn't quite make the big club when training ended in the spring, and was sent down to the Pirates' Triple A club in Columbus, but the call came three weeks later. Blass said, "We got in the car, and I floored it all the way across Ohio. I remember it was raining as we came out of the tunnel in Pittsburgh, and I drove straight to Forbes Field and went in and found the attendant and put my uniform on, at two in the afternoon. There was no *game* there, or anything — I just had to see how it looked."

We had moved along by now to the Blasses' house, a medium-sized brick structure on a hillside in Upper St. Clair, which is a suburb about twelve miles southeast of Pittsburgh. The pizza disappeared rapidly, and then David and Chris went off upstairs to do their homework or watch TV. The Blass family room was trophied and comfortable. On a wall opposite a long sofa there was, among other things, a plaque remembering the J. Roy Stockton Award for Outstanding Baseball Achievement, a Dapper Dan Award for meritorious service to Pittsburgh, a shiny metal bat with the engraved signatures of the National League All-Stars of 1972, a 1971 Pittsburgh Pirates World Champions bat, a signed photograph of President Nixon, and a framed, decorated proclamation announcing Steve Blass Day in Falls Village, Connecticut: "Be it known that this twenty-second day of October in the year of our Lord 1971, the citizens of Falls Village do set aside and do honor with pride Steve Blass, the tall skinny kid from Falls Village, who is now the hero of baseball and will be our hero always." It was signed by the town's three selectmen. The biggest picture in the room hung over the sofa — an enlarged color photograph of the Blass family at the Father-and-Sons Day at Three Rivers Stadium in 1971. In the photo, Karen Blass looks extremely pretty in a large straw hat, and all three male Blasses are wearing Pirate uniforms; the boys' uniforms look a little funny, because in their excitement each boy had put on the other's pants. Great picture.

Karen and Steve pointed this out to me, and then they went back to their arrival in the big time on that rainy long-ago first day in Pittsburgh and Steve's insisting on trying on his Pirate uniform, and they leaned back in their chairs and laughed about it again.

"With Steve, everything is right out in the open," Karen said. "Every accomplishment, every stage of the game — you have no idea how much he loved it, how he enjoyed the game."

That year, in his first outing, Blass pitched five scoreless innings in relief against the Braves, facing, among others, Hank Aaron. In his first start, against the Dodgers in Los Angeles, he pitched against Don Drysdale and won, 4–2. "I thought I'd died and gone to Heaven," Blass said to me.

He lit a cigar and blew out a little smoke. "You know, this thing that's happened has been painted so bad, so tragic," he said. "Well, I don't go along with that. I know what I've done in baseball, and I give myself all the credit in the world for it. I'm not bitter about this. I've had the greatest moments a person could ever want. When I was a boy, I used to make up those fictitious games where I was always pitching in the bottom of the ninth in the World Series. Well, I really *did* it. It went on and happened to me. Nobody's ever enjoyed winning a big-league game more than I have. All I've ever wanted to do since I was six years old was to keep on playing baseball. It didn't even have to be major-league ball. I've never been a goal-planner — I've never said I'm going to do this or that. With me, everything was just a continuation of what had come before. I think that's why I enjoyed it all so much when it did come along, when the good things did happen."

All this was said with an air of summing up, of finality, but at other times that evening I noticed that it seemed difficult for Blass to talk about his baseball career as a thing of the past; now and then he slipped into the present tense — as if it were still going on. This was understandable, for he was in limbo. The Pirates had finally released him late in March ("out-righted" him, in baseball parlance), near the end of the spring-training season, and he had subsequently decided not to continue his attempts to salvage his pitching form in the minor leagues. Earlier in the week of my visit, he had accepted a promising job with Josten's, Inc., a large jewelry concern that makes, among other things, World Series rings and high-school graduation rings, and he would go to work for them shortly as a traveling representative in the Pittsburgh area. He was out of baseball for good.

\* \* \*

Pitching consistency is probably the ingredient that separates major-league baseball from the lesser levels of the game. A big-league fastball comes in on the batter at about eighty-five or ninety miles an hour, completing its prescribed journey of sixty feet six inches in less than half a second, and, if it is a strike, generally intersects no more than an inch or two of the seventeen-inch-wide plate, usually near the upper or lower limits of the strike zone; curves and sliders arrive a bit later but with intense rotation, and must likewise slice off only a thin piece of the black if they are to be effective. Sustaining this kind of control over a stretch of, say, one hundred and thirty pitches in a seven- or eight-inning appearance places such excruciating demands on a hurler's body and psyche that even the most successful pitchers regularly have games when they simply can't get the job done. Their fastball comes in high, their curves hang, the rest of their prime weapons desert them. The pitcher is knocked about, often by an inferior rival team, and leaves within a few innings; asked about it later, he shrugs and says, "I didn't have it today." He seems unsurprised. Pitching, it sometimes appears, is too hard for *anyone*. Occasionally, the poor performance is repeated, then extended. The pitcher goes into a slump. He sulks or rages, according to his nature; he asks for help; he works long hours on his motion. Still he cannot win. He worries about his arm, which almost always hurts to some degree. Has it gone dead? He worries about his stuff. Has he lost his velocity? He wonders whether he will ever win again or whether he will now join the long, long list — the list that awaits him, almost surely, in the end — of suddenly slow, suddenly sore-armed pitchers who have abruptly vanished from the big time, down the drain to oblivion. Then, unexpectedly, the slump ends — most of the time, that is — and he is back where he was: a winning pitcher. There is rarely an explanation for this, whether the slump has lasted for two games or a dozen, and managers and coaches, when pressed for one, will usually mutter that "pitching is a delicate thing," or — as if it explained anything — "he got back in the groove."

In spite of such hovering and inexplicable hazards, every big-league pitcher knows exactly what is expected of him. As with the other aspects of the game, statistics define his work and — day by day, inning by inning — whether he is getting it done. Thus, it may be posited as a rule that a major-league hurler who gives up an average of just over three and a half runs per game is about at the middle of his profession — an average pitcher. (Last year, the National League and the American League both wound up with a per-game earned-run average of 3.62.) At contract-renewal time, earned-run averages below 3.30 are invariably mentioned by pitchers; an ERA close to or above the 4.00 level will always be brought up by management. The select levels of pitching proficiency (and salary) begin below the 3.00 line; in fact, an ERA of less than 3.00 certifies true quality in almost exactly the same fashion as an over-.300 batting average for hitters. Last year, both leagues had ten pitchers who finished below 3.00, led by Buzz Capra's NL mark of 2.28 and Catfish Hunter's 2.49 in the AL. The best season-long earned-run average of the modern baseball era was Bob Gibson's 1.12 mark, set in 1968.

Strikeouts are of no particular use in defining pitching effectiveness, since there are other, less vivid ways of retiring batters, but bases on balls matter. To put it in simple terms, a good, middling pitcher should not surrender more than three or four walks per game — unless he is also striking out batters in considerable clusters. Last year, Ferguson Jenkins, of the Texas Rangers, gave up only 45 walks in 328 innings pitched, or an average of 1.19 per game. Nolan Ryan, of the Angels, walked 202 men in 333 innings, or 5.4 per game; however, he helped himself considerably by fanning 367, or just under ten men per game. The fastball is a great healer.

At the beginning of the 1973 season, Steve Blass had a lifetime earned-run average of 3.25 and was averaging 1.9 walks per game. He was, in short, an extremely successful and useful big-league pitcher, and was understandably enjoying his work. Early that season, however, baseball suddenly stopped being fun for him. He pitched well in spring training in Bradenton, which was unusual, for he has always been a very slow starter. He pitched on opening day, against the Cards, but threw poorly and was relieved, although the Pirates eventually won the game. For a time, his performance was borderline, but his few wins were in sloppy, high-scoring contests, and his bad outings were marked by streaks of uncharacteristic wildness and ineffectuality. On April 22, against the Cubs, he gave up a walk, two singles, a homer, and a double in the first inning, sailed through the second inning, and then walked a man and hit two batsmen in the third. He won a complete game against the Padres, but in his next two appearances, against the Dodgers and the Expos, he survived for barely half the distance; in the Expos game, he threw three scoreless innings, and then suddenly gave up two singles, a double, and two walks. By early June, his record was three wins and three losses, but his earned-run average suggested that his difficulties were serious. Bill Virdon, the Pirate manager, was patient and told Blass to take all the time he needed to find himself; he reminded Blass that once — in 1970 — he had had an early record of two and eight but had then come back to finish the season with a mark of ten and twelve.

What was mystifying about the whole thing was that Blass still had his stuff, especially when he warmed up or threw on the sidelines. He was in great physical shape, as usual, and his arm felt fine; in his entire pitching career, Blass never experienced a sore arm. Virdon remained calm, although he was clearly puzzled. Some pitching mechanics were discussed and worked on; Blass was sometimes dropping his elbow as he threw; often he seemed to be hurrying his motion, so that his arm was not in synchronization with his body; perhaps he had exaggerated his peculiar swoop toward first base and thus was losing his power. These are routine pitching mistakes, which almost all pitchers are guilty of from time to time, and Blass worked on them assiduously. He started again against the Braves on June 11, in Atlanta; after three and one-third innings he was gone, having given up seven singles, a home run, two walks, and a total of five runs. Virdon and Blass agreed that a spell in the bullpen seemed called for; at least he could work on his problems there every day.

Two days later, the roof fell in. The team was still in Atlanta, and Virdon called Blass into the game in the fifth inning, with the Pirates trailing by 8–3. Blass walked the first two men he faced, and gave up a stolen base and a wild pitch and a run-scoring single before retiring the side. In the sixth, Blass walked Darrell Evans. He walked Mike Lum, throwing one pitch behind him in the process, which allowed Evans to move down to second. Dusty Baker singled, driving in a run. Ralph Garr grounded out. Davey Johnson singled, scoring another run. Marty Perez walked. Pitcher Ron Reed singled, driving in two more runs, and was wild-pitched to second. Johnny Oates walked. Frank Tepedino singled, driving in two runs, and Steve Blass was finally relieved. His totals for the one and one-third innings were seven runs, five hits, six bases on balls, and three wild pitches.

"It was the worst experience of my baseball life," Blass told me. "I don't think I'll ever forget it. I was embarrassed and disgusted. I was totally unnerved. You can't imagine the feeling that you suddenly have no *idea* what you're doing out there, performing that way as a major-league pitcher. It was kind of scary."

None of Blass's appearances during the rest of the '73 season were as dreadful as the Atlanta game, but none of them were truly successful. On August 1, he started against the Mets and Tom Seaver at Shea Stadium and gave up three runs and five walks in one and two-thirds innings. A little later, Virdon gave him a start in the Hall of Fame game at Cooperstown; this is a meaningless annual exhibition, played that year between the Pirates and the Texas Rangers, but Blass was as wild as ever and had to be relieved after two and one-third innings. After that, Bill Virdon announced that Blass would probably not start another game; the Pirates were in a pennant race, and the time for patience had run out.

Blass retired to the bullpen and worked on fundamentals. He threw a lot, once pitching a phantom nine-inning game while his catcher, Dave Ricketts, called the balls and strikes. At another point, he decided to throw every single day in the bullpen, to see if he could recapture his groove. "All it did was to get me very, very tired," Blass told me. He knew that Virdon was not going to use him, but whenever the Pirates fell behind in a game, he felt jumpy about the possibility of being called upon. "I knew I wasn't capable of going in there," he said. "I was afraid of embarrassing myself again, and letting down the club."

On September 6, the Pirate front office announced that Danny Murtaugh, who had served two previous terms as the Pirates' manager, was replacing Bill Virdon at the helm; the Pirates were caught up in a close, four-team division race, and it was felt that Murtaugh's experience might bring them home. One of Murtaugh's first acts was to announce that Steve Blass would be given a start. The game he picked was against the Cubs, in Chicago, on September 11. Blass, who had not pitched in six weeks, was extremely anxious about this test; he walked the streets of Chicago on the night before the game, and could not get to sleep until after five in the morning. The game went well for him. The Cubs won, 2–0, but Steve gave up only two hits and one earned run in the five innings he worked. He pitched with extreme care, throwing mostly sliders. He had another pretty good outing against the Cardinals, for no decision, and then started against the Mets, in New York, on September 21, but got only two men out, giving up four instant runs on a walk and four hits. The Mets won, 10–2, dropping the Pirates out of first place, but Blass, although unhappy about his showing, found some hope in the fact that he had at least been able to get the ball over the plate. "At that point," he said, "I was looking for even a little bit of success — one good inning, a few real fastballs, anything to hold on to that might halt my negative momentum. I wanted to feel I had at least got things turned around and facing in the right direction."

The Mets game was his last of the year. His statistics for the 1973 season were three wins and nine defeats, and an earned-run average of 9.81. That figure and his record of eighty-four walks in eighty-nine innings pitched were the worst in the National League.

I went to another ball game with Steve Blass on the night after the Little League affair — this time at Three Rivers Stadium, where the Pirates were meeting the Cardinals. We sat behind home plate, down near the screen, and during the first few innings a lot of young fans came clustering down the aisle to get Steve's autograph. People in the sections near us kept calling and waving to him. "Everybody has been great to me, all through this thing," Blass said. "I don't think there are too many here who are thinking, 'Look, there's the wild man.' I've had hundreds and hundreds of letters — I don't know how many — and not one of them was down on me."

In the game, Bob Gibson pitched against the Pirates' Jerry Reuss. When Ted Simmons stood in for the visitors, Blass said, "He's always hit me pretty good. He's really developed as a hitter." Then there was an error by Richie Hebner, at third, on a grounder hit by Ken Reitz, and Blass said, "Did you notice the batter take that big swing and then hit it off his hands? It was the swing that put Richie back on his heels like that." Later on, Richie Zisk hit a homer off Gibson, on a three-and-two count, and Blass murmured, "The high slider is one of *the* hittable pitches when it isn't just right. I should know."

The game rushed along, as games always do when Gibson is pitching. "You know," Blass said, "before we faced him we'd always have a team meeting and we'd say, 'Stay out of the batter's box, clean your spikes — anything to make him slow up.' But it never lasted more than an inning or two. He makes you play his game."

A little later, however, Willie Stargell hit a homer, and then Manny Sanguillen drove in another run with a double off the left-field wall ("*Get* out of here!" Steve said while the ball was in flight), and it was clear that this was not to be a Gibson night. Blass was enjoying himself, and it seemed to me that the familiarities and surprises of the game had restored something in him. At one point, he leaned forward a little and peered into the Pirate dugout and murmured, "Is Dock Ellis over in his regular corner there?" but for the most part he kept his eyes on the field. I tried to imagine what it felt like for him not to be down in the dugout.

I had talked that day to a number of Blass's old teammates, and all of them had mentioned his cheerfulness and his jokes, and what they had meant to the team over the years. "Steve's humor in the clubhouse was unmatched," relief pitcher Dave Giusti said. "He was a terrific mimic. Perfect. He could do Robert Kennedy. He could do Manny Sanguillen. He could do Roberto Clemente — not just the way he moved but the way he talked. Clemente loved it. He could do rat sounds — the noise a rat makes running. Lots of other stuff. It all made for looseness and togetherness. Because of Steve, the clubhouse was never completely silent, even after a loss." Another Pirate said, "Steve was about ninety percent of the good feeling on this club. He was always up, always agitating. If a player made a mistake, Steve knew how to say something about it that would let the guy know it was OK. Especially the young guys — he really understood them, and they put their confidence in him because of that. He picked us all up. Of course, there was a hell of a lot less of that from him, the last couple of years. We sure missed it."

For the final three innings of the game, Blass and I moved upstairs to general manager Joe Brown's box. Steve was startled by the unfamiliar view. "Hey, you can really see how it works from here, can't you?" he said. "Down there, you've got to look at it all in pieces. No wonder it's so hard to play this game right."

In the Pirates' seventh, Bill Robinson pinch-hit for Ed Kirkpatrick, and Blass said, "Well, *that* still makes me wince a little." It was a moment or two before I realized that Robinson was wearing Blass's old uniform number. Robinson fanned, and Blass said, "Same old twenty-eight."

The Pirates won easily, 5–0, with Jerry Reuss going all the way for the shutout, and just before the end Steve said, "I always had trouble sleeping after pitching a real good game. And if we were home, I'd get up about seven in the morning, before anybody else was up, and go downstairs and make myself a cup of coffee, and then I'd get the newspaper and open it to the sports section and just — just soak it all in."

We thanked Joe Brown and said good night, and as we went down in the elevator I asked Steve Blass if he wanted to stop off in the clubhouse for a minute and see his old friends. "Oh, no," he said. "No, I couldn't do that."

After the end of the 1973 season, Blass joined the Pirates' team in the Florida Instructional League (an autumn institution that exists mostly to permit the clubs to look over their prime minor-league prospects), where he worked intensively with a longtime pitching coach, Don Osborn, and appeared in three games. He came home feeling a little hopeful (he was almost living on such minimal nourishments), but when he forced himself to think about it he had to admit that he had been too tense to throw the fastball much, even against rookies. Then, in late February, 1974, Blass reported to Bradenton with the other Pirate pitchers and catchers. "We have a custom in the early spring that calls for all the pitchers to throw five minutes of batting practice every day," he told me. "This is before the rest of the squad arrives, you understand, so you're just pitching to the other pitchers. Well, the day before that first workout I woke up at four-thirty in the morning. I was so worried that I couldn't get back to sleep — and all this was just over going out and throwing to *pitchers*. I don't remember what happened that first day, but I went out there very tense and anxious every time. As you can imagine, there's very little good work or improvement you can do under those circumstances."

The training period made it clear that nothing had altered with him (he walked twenty-five men in fourteen innings in exhibition play), and when the club went north he was left in Bradenton for further work. He joined the team in Chicago on April 16, and entered a game against the Cubs the next afternoon, taking over in the fourth inning, with the Pirates down by 10–4. He pitched five innings and gave up eight runs (three of them unearned), five hits, and seven bases on balls. The Cubs batted around against him in the first inning he pitched, and in the sixth he gave up back-to-back home runs. His statistics for the game, including an ERA of 9.00, were also his major-league figures for the year, because late in April the Pirates sent him down to the Charleston (West Virginia) Charlies, their farm team in the Class AAA International League. Blass did not argue about the decision; in fact, as a veteran with more than eight years' service in the majors, he had to agree to the demotion before the parent club could send him down. He felt that the Pirates and Joe Brown had been extraordinarily patient and sympathetic in dealing with a baffling and apparently irremediable problem. They had also been generous, refusing to cut his salary by the full twenty percent permissible in extending a major-league contract. (His pay, which had been ninety thousand dollars in 1973, was cut to seventy-five thousand for the next season, and then to sixty-three thousand this spring.) In any case, Blass wanted to go. He needed continuous game experience if he was ever to break out of it, and he knew he no longer belonged with a big-league club.

The distance between the minors and the majors, always measurable in light-years, is probably greater today than ever before, and for a man making the leap in the wrong direction the feeling must be sickening. Blass tries to pass off the experience lightly (he is apparently incapable of self-pity), but one can guess what must have been required of him to summon up even a scrap of the kind of hope and aggressive self-confidence that are prerequisites, at every level, of a successful athletic performance. He and Karen rented an apartment in Charleston, and the whole family moved down when the school year ended; David and Chris enjoyed the informal atmosphere around the ball park, where they were permitted to shag flies in batting practice. "It wasn't so bad," Blass told me.

But it was. The manager of the Charlies, Steve Demeter, put Blass in the regular starting rotation, but he fared no better against minor-leaguers than he had in the big time. In a very brief time, his earned-run average and his bases-on-balls record were the worst in the league. Blass got along well with his teammates, but there were other problems. The mystery of Steve Blass's decline was old stuff by now in most big-league-city newspapers, but as soon as he was sent down, there was a fresh wave of attention from the national press and the networks; and sportswriters for newspapers in Memphis and Rochester and Richmond and the other International League cities looked on his arrival in town as a God-given feature story. Invariably, they asked him how much money he was earning as a player; then they asked if he thought he was worth it.

The Charlies did a lot of traveling by bus. One day, the team made an eight-hour trip from Charleston to Toledo, where they played a night game. At eleven that same night, they reboarded the bus and drove to Pawtucket, Rhode Island, for their next date, arriving at about nine in the morning. Blass had started the game in Toledo, and he was so disgusted with his performance that he got back on the bus without having showered or taken off his uniform. "We'd stop at an all-night restaurant every now and then, and I'd walk in with a two-day beard and my old Charleston Charlies uniform on, looking like go-to-hell," Blass said. "It was pretty funny to see people looking at me. I had some books along, and we had plenty of wine and beer on the bus, so the time went by somehow." He paused and then shook his head. "*God,* that was an awful trip," he said.

By early August, Blass's record with Charleston was two and nine, and 9.74. He had had enough. With Joe Brown's permission, he left the Charlies and flew West to consult Dr. Bill Harrison, of Davis, California. Dr. Harrison is an optometrist who has helped develop a system of "optometherapy," designed to encourage athletes to concentrate on the immediate physical task at hand — hitting a ball, throwing a strike —

by visualizing the act in advance; his firm was once retained by the Kansas City Royals baseball team, and his patients have included a number of professional golfers and football players. Blass spent four days with him and then rejoined the Pirates, this time as a batting-practice pitcher. He says now that he was very interested in Dr. Harrison's theories but that they just didn't seem to help him much.

In truth, nothing helped. Blass knew that his case was desperate. He was almost alone now with his problem — a baseball castaway — and he had reached the point where he was willing to try practically anything. Under the guidance of pitching coach Don Osborn, he attempted some unusual experiments. He tried pitching from the outfield, with the sweeping motion of a fielder making a long peg. He tried pitching while kneeling on the mound. He tried pitching with his left foot tucked up behind his right knee until the last possible second of his delivery. Slow-motion films of his delivery were studied and compared with films taken during some of his best games of the past; much of his motion, it was noticed, seemed extraneous, but he had thrown exactly the same way at his peak. Blass went back and corrected minute details, to no avail.

The frustrating, bewildering part of it all was that while working alone with a catcher Blass continued to throw as well as he ever had; his fastball was alive, and his slider and curve shaved the corners of the plate. But the moment a batter stood in against him he became a different pitcher, especially when throwing a fastball — a pitcher apparently afraid of seriously injuring somebody. As a result, he was of very little use to the Pirates even in batting practice.

Don Osborn, a gentle man in his mid-sixties, says, "Steve's problem was mental. He had mechanical difficulties, with some underlying mental cause. I don't think anybody will ever understand his decline. We tried everything — I didn't know anything else to do. I feel real bad about it. Steve had a lot of guts to stay out there as long as he did. You know, old men don't dream much, but just the other night I had this dream that Steve Blass was all over his troubles and could pitch again. I said, 'He's ready, we can use him!' Funny . . ."

It was probably at this time that Blass consulted a psychiatrist. He does not talk about it — in part out of a natural reticence but also because the Pirate front office, in an effort to protect his privacy, turned away inquiries into this area by Pittsburgh writers and persistently refused to comment on whether any such therapy was undertaken. It is clear, however, that Blass does not believe he gained any profound insights into possible unconscious causes of his difficulties. Earlier in the same summer, he also experimented briefly with transcendental meditation. He entered the program at the suggestion of Joe Brown, who also enrolled Dave Giusti, Willie Stargell, pitcher Bruce Kison, and himself in the group. Blass repeated mantras and meditated twice a day for about two months; he found that it relaxed him, but it did not seem to have much application to his pitching. Innumerable other remedies were proposed by friends and strangers. Like anyone in hard straits, he was deluged with unsolicited therapies, overnight cures, naturopathies, exorcisms, theologies, and amulets, many of which arrived by mail. Blass refuses to make jokes about these nostrums. "Anyone who takes the trouble to write a man who is suffering deserves to be thanked," he told me.

Most painful of all, perhaps, was the fact that the men who most sympathized with his incurable professional difficulties were least able to help. The Pirates were again engaged in a close and exhausting pennant race fought out over the last six weeks of the season; they moved into first place for good only two days before the end, won their half-pennant, and then were eliminated by the Dodgers in a four-game championship playoff. Steve Blass was with the team through this stretch, but he took no part in the campaign, and by now he was almost silent in the clubhouse. He had became an extra wheel. "It must have been hell for him," Dave Giusti says. "I mean *real* hell. I never could have stood it."

When Blass is asked about this last summer of his baseball career, he will only say that it was "kind of a difficult time" or "not the most fun I've had." In extended conversations about himself, he often gives an impression of an armored blandness that suggests a failure of emotion; this apparent insensitivity about himself contrasts almost shockingly with his subtle concern for the feelings of his teammates and his friends and his family, and even of strangers. "My overriding philosophy is to have a regard for others," he once told me. "I don't want to put myself over other people." He takes pride in the fact that his outward, day-to-day demeanor altered very little through his long ordeal. "A person lives on," he said more than once, smiling. "The sun will come up tomorrow." Most of all, perhaps, he sustained his self-regard by not taking out his terrible frustrations on Karen and the boys. "A ballplayer learns very early that he can't bring the game home with him every night," he said once. "Especially when there are young people growing up there. I'm real proud of the fact that this thing hasn't bothered us at home. David and Chris have come through it all in fine shape. I think Karen and I are closer than ever because of this."

Karen once said to me, "Day to day, he hasn't changed. Just the other morning, he was out working on the lawn, and a couple of neighbors' children came over to see him. Young kids — maybe three or four years old. Then I looked out a few minutes later, and there was a whole bunch of them yelling and rolling around on the grass with him, like puppies. He's always been that way. Steve has worked at being a man and being a father and a husband. It's something he has always felt very strongly about, and I have to give him all the credit in the world. Sometimes I think I got to hate the frustration and pain of this more than he did. He always found something to hold on to — a couple of good pitches that day, some little thing he had noticed. But I couldn't always share that, and I didn't have his ability to keep things under control."

I asked if maintaining this superhuman calm might not have damaged Steve in some way, or even added to his problems.

"I don't know," she said. "Sometimes in the evening — once in a great while — we'd be sitting together, and we'd have a couple of drinks and he would relax enough to start to talk. He would tell me about it, and get angry and hurt. Then he'd let it come out, and yell and scream and pound on things. And I felt that even this might not be enough for him. He would never do such a thing outside. Never." She paused, and then she said, "I think he directed his anger toward making the situation livable here at home. I've had my own ideas about Steve's pitching, about the mystery, but they haven't made much difference. You can't force your ideas on somebody, especially when he is doing what he thinks he has to do. Steve's a very private person."

Steve Blass stayed home last winter. He tried not to think much about baseball, and he didn't work on his pitching. He and Karen had agreed that the family would go back to Bradenton for spring training, and that he would give it one more try. One day in January, he went over to the field house at the University of Pittsburgh and joined some other Pirates there for a workout. He threw well. Tony Bartirome, the Pirate trainer, who is a close friend of Steve's, thought he was pitching as well as he ever had. He told Joe Brown that Steve's problems might be over. When spring training came, however, nothing had altered. Blass threw adequately in brief streaks, but very badly against most batters. He hit Willie Stargell and Manny Sanguillen in batting practice; both players told him to forget it. They urged him to cut loose with the fastball.

Joe Brown had told Blass that the end of the line might be approaching. Blass agreed. The Pirate organization had been extraordinarily patient, but it was, after all, in the business of baseball.

On March 24, Steve Blass started the second game of a doubleheader against the White Sox at Bradenton. For three innings, he escaped serious difficulty. He gave up two runs in the second, but he seemed to throw without much tension, and he even struck out Bill Melton, the Chicago third baseman, with a fastball. Like the other Pirates, Dave Giusti was watching with apprehensive interest. "I really thought he was on his way," he told me. "I was encouraged. Then, in the fourth, there were a couple of bases on balls and maybe a bad call by the ump on a close pitch, and suddenly there was a complete reversal. He was a different man out there."

Blass walked eight men in the fourth inning and gave up eight runs. He threw fifty-one pitches, but only seventeen of them were strikes. Some of his pitches were close to the strike zone, but most were not. He worked the count to 3–2 on Carlos May, and then threw the next pitch behind him. The booing from the fans, at first scattered and uncomfortable, grew louder. Danny Murtaugh waited, but Blass could not get the third out. Finally, Murtaugh came out very slowly to the mound and told Blass that he was taking him out of the game; Dave Giusti came in to relieve his old roommate. Murtaugh, a peaceable man, then charged the home-plate umpire and cursed him for the bad call, and was thrown out of the game. Play resumed. Blass put on his warm-up jacket and trotted to the outfield to run his wind sprints. Roland Hemond, the general manager of the White Sox, was at Bradenton that day, and he said, "It was the most heartbreaking thing I have ever seen in baseball."

Three days later, the Pirates held a press conference to announce that they had requested waivers from the other National League clubs, with the purpose of giving Blass his unconditional release. Blass flew out to California to see Dr. Bill Harrison once more, and also to visit a hypnotist, Arthur Ellen, who has worked with several major-league players, and has apparently helped some of them, including Dodger pitcher Don Sutton, remarkably. Blass made the trip mostly because he had promised Maury Wills, who is now a base-running consultant to several teams, that he would not quit the game until he had seen Mr. Ellen.

Blass then returned to Bradenton and worked for several days with the Pirates' minor-league pitching coach, Larry Sherry, on some pitching mechanics. He made brief appearances in two games against Pirate farmhands, and threw well. He struck out some players with his fastball.

After the second game, he showered and got into his Volkswagen and started north to join his family, who had returned to Pittsburgh. It was a good trip, because it gave him time to sort things out, and somewhere along the way he decided to give it up. The six-day waiver period had expired, and none of the other clubs had claimed him. He was encouraged about his pitching, but he had been encouraged before. This time, the fastball had been much better, and at least he could hold on to that; maybe the problem had been mechanical all along. If he came back now, however, it would have to be at the minor-league level, and even if he made it back to the majors, he could expect only three or four more years before his effectiveness would decline because of age and he would have to start thinking about retirement. At least *that* problem could be solved now. He didn't want to subject Karen to more of the struggle. It was time to get out.

Of all the mysteries that surround the Steve Blass story, perhaps the most mysterious is the fact that his collapse is unique. There is no other player in recent baseball history — at least none with Blass's record and credentials — who has lost his form in such a sudden and devastating fashion and been totally unable to recover. The players and coaches and fans I talked to about Steve Blass brought up a few other names, but then they quickly realized that the cases were not really the same. Some of them mentioned Rex Barney, a Dodger fastball pitcher of the nine-teen-forties, who quit baseball while still a young man because of his uncontrollable wildness; Barney, however, had only one good year, and it is fair to say he never did have his great stuff under control. Dick Radatz, a very tall relief pitcher with the Red Sox a decade ago, had four good years, and then grew increasingly wild and ineffective. (He is said to have once thrown twenty-seven consecutive balls in a spring-training game.) His decline, however, was partially attributable to his failure to stay in shape. Von McDaniel, a younger brother of Lindy McDaniel, arrived suddenly as a pitcher with the Cardinals, and disappeared just as quicky, but two years' pitching hardly qualifies as a record. There have been hundreds of shiningly promising rookie pitchers and sluggers who, for one reason or another, could not do their thing once they got up to the big time. Blass's story is different. It should also be understood that this was not at all the somewhat commonplace experience of an established and well-paid major-league star who suffers through one or two mediocre seasons. Tom Seaver went through such a slump last summer. But Seaver's problems were only relatively serious (his record for 1974 was 11–11), and were at least partly explicable (he had a sore hip), and he has now returned to form. Blass, once his difficulties commenced, was helpless. Finally, of course, one must accept the possibility that a great many players may have suffered exactly the same sort of falling off as Blass for exactly the same reasons (whatever they may be) but were able to solve the problem and continue their athletic careers. Sudden and terrible batting and pitching slumps are mysterious while they last; the moment they end, they tend to be forgotten.

What happened to Steve Blass? Nobody knows, but some speculation is permissible — indeed, is perhaps demanded of anyone who is even faintly aware of the qualities of the man and the depths of his suffering. Professional sports have a powerful hold on us because they display and glorify remarkable physical capacities, and because the artificial demands of games played for very high rewards produce vivid responses. But sometimes, of course, what is happening on the field seems to speak to something deeper within us; we stop cheering and look on in uneasy silence, for the man out there is no longer just another great athlete, an idealized hero, but only a man — only ourself. We are no longer at a game. The enormous alterations of professional sport in the past three decades, especially the prodigious inflation of franchises and salaries, have made it evident even to the most thoughtless fan that the play he has come to see is serious indeed, and that the heart of the game is not physical but financial. Sport is no longer a release from the harsh everyday American business world but its continuation and apotheosis. Those of us (fans and players alike) who return to the ball park in the belief that the game and the rules are unchanged — merely a continuation of what we have known and loved in the past — are deluding ourselves, perhaps foolishly, perhaps tragically.

Blass once told me that there were "at least seventeen" theories about the reason for his failure. A few of them are bromides: He was too nice a guy. He became smug and was no longer hungry. He lost the will to win. His pitching motion, so jittery and unclassical, at last let him down for good. His eyesight went bad. (Blass is myopic, and wears glasses while watching television and driving. He has never worn glasses when pitching, which meant that Pirate catchers had to flash him signals with hand gestures rather than with finger waggles; however, he saw well enough to win when he was winning, and his vision has not altered in recent years.) The other, more serious theories are sometimes presented alone, sometimes in conjunction with others. Answers here become more gingerly.

*He was afraid of injury — afraid of being struck by a line drive.*

Blass was injured three times while on the mound. He cracked a thumb while fielding a grounder in 1966. He was struck on the right forearm by a ball hit by Joe Torre in 1970, and spent a month on the disabled list. While trying for his twentieth victory in his last start in 1972, he was hit on the point of the elbow of his pitching arm by a line drive struck by the Mets' John Milner; he had to leave the game, but a few days later he pitched that first playoff game for the Pirates and won it handily. (Blass's brother-in-law, John Lamb, suffered a fractured skull when hit by a line drive in spring training in 1971, and it was more than a year before he recovered, but Blass's real pitching triumphs all came after that.)

*He was afraid of injuring someone — hitting a batter with a fastball.*

Blass did hit a number of players in his career, of course, but he never caused anyone to go on the disabled list or, for that matter, to miss even one day's work. He told me he did not enjoy brushing back hitters but had done so when it was obviously called for. The only real criticism of Blass I ever heard from his teammates was that he would not always "protect" them by retaliating against enemy hitters after somebody had been knocked down. During his decline, he was plainly unable to throw the fastball effectively to batters — especially to Pirate batters in practice. He says he hated the idea of hitting and possibly sidelining one of his teammates, but he is convinced that this anxiety was the result of his control problems rather than the cause.

*He was seriously affected by the death of Roberto Clemente.*

There is no doubt but that the sudden taking away of their most famous and vivid star affected all the Pirates, including Steve Blass. He and Clemente had not been particularly close, but Blass was among the members of the team who flew at once to Puerto Rico for the funeral services, where Blass delivered a eulogy in behalf of the club. The departure of a superstar leaves an almost visible empty place on a successful team, and the leaders next in line — who in this case would certainly include Steve Blass — feel the inescapable burden of trying to fill the gap. A Clemente, however, can never be replaced. Blass never pitched well in the majors after Clemente's death. This argument is a difficult one, and is probably impossible to resolve. There are Oedipal elements here, of course, that are attractive to those who incline in such a direction.

*He fell into a slump, which led to an irreparable loss of confidence.*

This is circular, and perhaps more a description of symptoms than of the disability itself. However, it is a fact that a professional athlete — and most especially a baseball player — faces a much more difficult task in attempting to regain lost form than an ailing businessman, say, or even a troubled artist; no matter how painful his case has been, the good will of his associates or the vagaries of critical judgment matter not at all when he tries to return. All that matters is his performance, which will be measured, with utter coldness, by the stats. This is one reason that athletes are paid so well, and one reason that fear of failure — the unspeakable "choking" — is their deepest and most private anxiety. Steve Blass passed over my questions about whether he had ever felt this kind of fear when on the mound. "I don't think pitchers, by their nature, allow themselves to think that way," he said. "To be successful, you turn that kind of thought away." On the other hand, he often said that two or three successive well-pitched games probably would have been all he needed to dissipate the severe tension that affected his per-formances once things began to go badly for him. They never came.

The remaining pieces of evidence (if, indeed, they have any part in the mystery) have been recounted here. Blass is a modest man, both in temperament and in background, and his success and fame were quite sudden and, to some degree, unexpected. His salary at the beginning of 1971 — the year of his two great Series wins — was forty thousand dollars; two years later it was ninety thousand, and there were World Series and playoff checks on top of that. Blass was never thought of as one of the great pitchers of his time, but in the late sixties and early seventies he was probably the most consistent starter on the Pirate staff; it was, in fact, a staff without stars. On many other teams, he would have been no more than the second- or third-best starter, and his responsi-bilities, real and imagined, would have been less acute.

I took some of these hard questions to Blass's colleagues. Danny Murtaugh and Bill Virdon (who is now the Yankees' pilot) both ex-pressed their admiration for Blass but said they had no idea what had happened to him. They seemed a bit brusque about it, but then I realized, of course, that ballplayers are forever disappearing from big-league dugouts; the manager's concern is with those who remain — with today's lineup. "I don't know the answer," Bill Virdon told me in the Yankee clubhouse. "If I did, I'd go get Steve to pitch for me. He sure won a lot of big games for us on the Pirates."

Joe Brown said, "I've tried to keep my distance and not to guess too much about what happened. I'm not a student of pitching and I'm not a psychologist. You can tell a man what to do, but you can't *make* him do it. Steve is an outstanding man, and you hate to quit on him. In this business, you bet on character. Big-league baseball isn't easy, yet you can stand it when things are going your way. But Steve Blass never had a good day in baseball after this thing hit him."

Blass's best friends in baseball are Tony Bartirome, Dave Giusti, and Nelson King (who, along with Bob Prince, was part of the highly regarded radio-and-television team that covered the Pirate games).

Tony Bartirome *(He is forty-three years old, dark-haired, extremely neat in appearance. He was an infielder before he became a trainer, and played one season in the majors — with the Pirates, in 1952):* "Steve is unique physically. He has the arm of a twenty-year-old. Not only did he never have a sore arm but he never had any of the stiffness and pain that most pitchers feel on the day after a game. He was always the same, day after day. You know, it's very important for a trainer to know the state of mind and the feelings of his players. What a player is thinking is about eighty percent of it. The really strange thing is that after this trouble started, Steve never showed any feelings about his pitching. In the old days, he used to get mad at himself after a bad showing, and sometimes he threw things around in the clubhouse. But after this began, when he was taken out of a game he only gave the impression that he was happy to be out of there — relieved that he no longer had to face it that day. Somehow, he didn't show any emotion at *all.* Maybe it was like his never having a sore arm. He never talked in any detail about his different treatments — the psychiatry and all. I think he felt he didn't need any of that — that at any moment he'd be back where he was, the Blass of old, and that it all was up to him to make that happen."

Dave Giusti *(He is one of the great relief pitchers in baseball. He earned a BA and an MA in physical education at Syracuse. He is thirty-five — dark hair, piercing brown eyes, and a quiet manner):* "Steve has the perfect build for a pitcher — lean and strong. He is remarkably open to all kinds of people, but I think he has closed his mind to his inner self. There are central areas you can't infringe on with him. There is no doubt that during the past two years he didn't react to a bad performance the way he used to, and you have to wonder why he couldn't apply his competitiveness to his problem. Karen used to bawl out me and Tony for not being tougher on him, for not doing more. Maybe I should have come right out and said he seemed to have lost his will to fight, but it's hard to shock somebody, to keep bearing in on him. You're afraid to lose a friend, and you want to go easy on him because he is your friend.

"Last year, I went through something like Steve's crisis. The first half of the season, I was atrocious, and I lost all my confidence, especially in my fastball. The fastball is my best pitch, but I'd get right to the top of my delivery and then something would take over, and I'd know even before I released the ball that it wasn't going to be in the strike zone. I began worrying about making big money and not performing. I worried about not contributing to the team. I worried about being traded. I thought it might be the end for me. I didn't know how to solve my problem, but I knew I *had* to solve it. In the end, it was talking to people that did it. I talked to everybody, but mostly to Joe Brown and Danny and my wife. Then, at some point, I turned the corner. But it was talking that did it, and my point is that Steve can't talk to people that way. Or won't.

"Listen, it's tough out there. It's hard. Once you start maintaining a plateau, you've got to be absolutely sure what your goals are."

Nellie King *(A former pitcher with the Pirates. He is friendly and informal, with an attractive smile. He is very tall — six-six. Forty-seven years old):* "Right after that terrible game in Atlanta, Steve told me that it had felt as if the whole world was pressing down on him while he was out there. But then he suddenly shut up about it, and he never talked that way again. He covered it all up. I think there *are* things weighing on him, and I think he may be so angry inside that he's afraid to throw the ball. He's afraid he might kill somebody. It's only nickel psychology, but I think there's a lost kid in Steve. I remembered that after the '71 Series he said, 'I didn't think I was as good as this.' He seemed truly surprised at what he'd done. The child in him is a great thing — we've all loved it — and maybe he was suddenly afraid he was losing it. It was being forced out of him.

"Being good up here is *so* tough — people have no idea. It gets much worse when you have to repeat it: 'We know you're great. Now go and do that again for me.' So much money and so many people depend on you. Pretty soon you're trying so hard that you can't function."

I ventured to repeat Nellie King's guesses about the mystery to Steve Blass and asked him what he thought.

"That's pretty heavy," he said after a moment. "I guess I don't have a tendency to go into things in much depth. I'm a surface reactor. I tend to take things not too seriously. I really think that's one of the things that *helped* me in baseball."

A smile suddenly burst from him.

"There's one possibility nobody has brought up," he said. "I don't think anybody's ever said that maybe I just lost my control. Maybe your control is something that can just go. It's no big thing, but suddenly it's gone." He paused, and then he laughed in a self-deprecating way. "Maybe that's what I'd like to believe," he said.

On my last morning with Steve Blass, we sat in his family room and played an imaginary ball game together — half an inning of baseball. It had occurred to me that in spite of his enforced and now permanent exile from the game, he still possessed a rare body of precise and hard-won pitching information. He still knew most of the hitters in his league, and probably as well as any other pitcher around, he knew what to pitch to them in a given situation. I had always wanted to hear a pitcher say exactly what he would throw next and why, and now I invited Blass to throw against the Cincinnati Reds, the toughest lineup of hitters anywhere. I would call the balls and strikes and hits. I promised he would have no control problems.

He agreed at once. He poured himself another cup of coffee and lit up a Garcia y Vega. He was wearing slacks and a T-shirt and an old sweater (he had a golfing date later that day), and he looked very young.

"OK," he said. "Pete Rose is leading off — right? First of all, I'm going to try to keep him off base if I can, because they have so many tough hitters coming up. They can bury you before you even get started. I'm going to try to throw strikes and not get too fine. I'll start him off with a slider away. He has a tendency to go up the middle and I'll try to keep it a bit away."

Rose, I decided, didn't offer. It was ball one.

"Now I'll throw him a sinking fastball, and still try to work him out that way. The sinking fastball tends to tail off just a little."

Rose fouled it into the dirt.

"Well, now we come back with another slider, and I'll try to throw it inside. That's just to set up another slider *outside*."

Rose fouled that one as well.

"We're ahead one and two now — right?" Blass said. "Well, this early in the game I wouldn't try to throw him that slow curve — that big slop off-speed pitch. I'd like to work on that a couple of times first, because it's early and he swings so well. So as long as I'm ahead of him, I'll keep on throwing him sliders — keep going that way."

Rose took another ball, and then grounded out on a medium-speed curveball.

Joe Morgan stood in, and Blass puffed on his cigar and looked at the ceiling.

"Joe Morgan is strictly a fastball hitter, so I want to throw him a *bad* fastball to start him off," he said. "I'll throw it in the dirt to show it to him — get him geared to that kind of speed. Now, after ball one, I'll give him a medium-to-slow curveball and try to get it over the plate — just throw it for a strike."

Morgan took: one and one.

"Now I throw him a *real* slow curveball — a regular rainbow. I've had good luck against him with that sort of stuff."

And so it went. Morgan, I decided, eventually singled to right on a curve in on the handle — a lucky hit — but then Blass retired his next Cincinnati hitter, Dan Driessen, who popped out on a slider. Blass laid off slow pitches here, so Sanguillen would have a chance to throw out Morgan if he was stealing.

Johnny Bench stood in, with two out.

"Morgan won't be stealing, probably," Blass said. "He won't want to take the bat out of Bench's hands." He released another cloud of cigar smoke, thinking hard. "Well, I'll start him out with a good, tough fastball outside. I've got to work very carefully to him, because when he's hot he's capable of hitting it out anytime."

Ball one.

"Well, the slider's only been fair today. . . . I'll give him a slider, but away — off the outside."

Swinging strike. Blass threw another slider, and Bench hit a line single to left, moving Morgan to second. Tony Perez was the next batter.

"Perez is not a good high, hard fastball hitter," Blass said. "I'll begin him with that pitch, because I don't want to get into any more trouble with the slider and have him dunk one in. A letter-high fastball, with good mustard on it."

Perez took a strike.

"Now I'll do it again, until I miss — bust him up and in. He has a tendency to go after that kind of pitch. He's an exceptional offspeed hitter, and will give himself up with men on base — give up a little power to get that run in."

Perez took, for a ball, and then Blass threw him an intentional ball — a very bad slider inside. Perez had shortened up on the bat a little, but he took the pitch. He then fouled off a fastball, and Blass threw him another good fastball, high and inside, and Perez struck out, swinging, to end the inning.

"Pretty good inning," I said. "Way to go." We both laughed.

"Yes, you know that *exact* sequence has happened to Perez many times," Blass said. "He shortens up and then chases the pitch up here."

He was animated. "You know, I can almost *see* that fastball to Perez, and I can see his bat going through it, swinging through the pitch and missing," he said. "That's a good feeling. That's one of the concepts of Dr. Harrison's program, you know — visualization. When I was pitching well, I was doing that very thing. You get so locked in, you see yourself doing things before they happen. That's what people mean when they say you're in the groove. That's what happened in that World Series game, when I kept throwing that big slop curveball to Boog Powell, and it really ruined him. I must have thrown it three out of four pitches to him, and I just *knew* it was going to be there. There's no doubt about it — no information needed. The crowd is there, this is the World Series, and all of a sudden you're locked into something. It's like being plugged into a computer. It's 'Gimme the ball, *boom!* Click, click, click . . . *shoom!*' It's that good feeling. You're just flowing easy."

## 1975

## Wells Twombly

...........................................................................................................................................

# There Was Only One Casey

FROM *The San Francisco Examiner*

ON CASUAL INSPECTION, the old man looked like a woodcarver's first attempt at a gargoyle. The face was crude and drooping, even when it was new. The eyes were watery and mournful, like a human basset hound. The ears were large and foolish. The hands were hopelessly gnarled. The legs looked like two Christmas stockings stuffed with oranges.

Luckily, greatness doesn't necessarily come in attractive wrappings. Up close, the old man was genuinely beautiful, not exactly in the category of Robert Redford, but beautiful just the same. It was the beauty of a rare antique, tenderly rendered and gracefully aged. It was the beauty of a three-hundred-year-old handcrafted pipe, rubbed by a thousand hands and redolent of a thousand aromatic tobaccos. This was a precious original and, of the millions of words that will be written about Charles Dillon Stengel in the next few days, none of them will quite do him justice.

He was one of a handful of baseball characters whose reputations did not exceed their true personalities. The fact is that Yogi Berra was never anything but a quiet, humorless, somewhat grumpy New Jersey businessman, whose humor was largely created by Joe Garagiola anyway. Bo Belinsky was just another charming scoundrel who liked girls, which made him about as kooky as five-sixths of America's male population. Dizzy Dean was a big depression-era redneck who loved beer. As a young man he was bumptious. As a senior citizen, he was a bore.

But the Casey Stengel of real life was better than the Casey Stengel of the printed page. The problem was a mechanical one, which was never solved. He could not be properly transmitted. However, the best literary men of his time worked on it. Oh, how they worked. Still, it never came out quite right, especially the rambling, shattered syntax of his speech, which was a flagrant put-on. Only a very few people understood what Stengel was doing. He led them through a merry maze built entirely of semantic disgraces. He did it on purpose.

Early one morning when he was between jobs, he sat in the tower at Wrigley Field in Los Angeles trying to make Gene Autry a pauper by sucking up so much free booze that the singing cowboy would have to get his guitar and make a comeback. The more he tucked away, the more lucid he became. A twenty-five-year-old baseball writer who covered the Los Angeles Angels and delivered a column nobody read out in the San Fernando Valley was utterly amazed. "That jargon of yours is just a joke," he gasped.

"Son," said Casey in that gravel-driveway voice of his. "This is gonna be our little secret, isn't it?"

The man was a clever and articulate comic who spoke two languages. When he was unguarded he would talk in this straightforward, highly lucid English, which nobody paid any attention to. When there were reporters and other assorted individuals present he spoke in tongues. It was a tangled rat's nest of verbiage that bore only a scanty resemblance to the Mother Tongue so heartily endorsed by the queen of England. Even the mightiest of journalists cowed when he turned on the juice.

When he was managing the wretched New York Mets of the early 1960s he attempted to describe what the fans were like. It was a fine, feathered piece of literature. "These fans are very rabid like they were very collegiate or something because it takes four hours for us to leave our dressing room after a game, which is good because the concession people sell a lot of hot dogs, which is good for our business and I like that. I expect that very soon they will carry one of my players out on their shoulders like he just caught a touchdown for Yale. They are very patient and that's good. These fellows of ours are going to keep right on improving because they are better than most folks think and not as bad as they used to be, because it would be hard to be as bad as that."

There were people who thought Charles Dillon Stengel was a bad manager, just because he had wretched teams in Boston, Brooklyn, and New York. They said that Harpo Marx could have won ten pennants in 12 years with the Yankee clubs that Casey had. That was a mistake. Oh, occasionally he would fall asleep on the bench during night games when he was fronting for the Mets, but that was strictly an epilogue to his years with the Yankees. Even that most cynical of athletes-turned-author, Jim Bouton, said that Stengel knew exactly what he was doing when he had Mickey Mantle and Whitey Ford working for him.

There was this pitcher named Hal Stowe who thought that all he had to do to make the major-league roster was to act like he belonged. He did none of the things other rookies were asked to do. He drank and went to dinner with Mantle and Ford. He did not run in the outfield and he made no overt attempt to impress Stengel. There was one place open on the roster, but Stowe failed to qualify.

"It's true that Hal Stowe pitched pretty good this spring," said Stengel in straight language. "But I noticed that he never ran in the outfield, that he never did all the things he was supposed to do. He never really hustled and he never really worked at it. That's why he didn't make the squad cut, he could bull-bleep everybody but the manager."

Just two years later, Stowe used the same act and managed to put a move on Ralph Houk, the hand-clapping, cigar-chewing militarist who replaced Stengel. The pitcher went north and opened the season with the Yankees because Houk thought he looked and acted like a big leaguer and that was very, very important. Stengel was not so easily confused. When he worked for the Mets the club came up with a nineteen-year-old first baseman named Greg Goossen, whom everybody gurgled about.

"In ten years, Greg Goossen has a great chance of being twenty-nine years old," he said. It wasn't cruel. It was accurate. Sure enough, just ten years later, Goossen did turn twenty-nine, but not with any major-league baseball club.

One afternoon before a World Series game, Stengel took a young Mickey Mantle out to right field at the old ball park in Brooklyn and started to explain how to play caroms off the concave wall. Mantle wanted to know how his manager knew so much about it.

"I used to play right field for the Dodgers!" growled Stengel. "Do you think I was born old?"

So there will be a World Series this year and Casey Stengel will not be present. He was always good for a story. One afternoon it was raining in Baltimore and there he stood with a foot on the rail. "Pardon me, Casey," said a columnist, "it's lousy outside and I need help." He went on for an hour.

Standing nearby was a slim, quivering journalist from a small-town paper. When he was through rescuing the veteran, he turned to the rookie, gave him about 15 minutes and ended up with: "Listen, I got a secret, exclusive story I don't want to give to nobody else. I go to bed late and get up early. You gotta meet me at 6 A.M., but bring some Scotch and we'll break things together."

The man was beautiful. If he's dead, it is only a rumor. Don't bother to print it.

# Tom Boswell

....................................................................................................................................

# Pain

FROM *The Washington Post*

BOXING AT ITS BEST is beastly.

If that assumption holds no appeal, then you cannot relish the stirring and horrid spectacle of Roberto Duran's public assault on Sugar Ray Leonard here on Friday.

Boxing is about pain. It is a night out for the carnivore in us, the hidden beast who is hungry. Few men have ever become world champion without facing that dark side of their game; Leonard was one.

Leonard might even have arrived in this cosmopolitan city to defend his WBC welterweight crown still believing, at twenty-four, that his profession was a sport rather than a disturbing, paradoxical arena where vice and virtue sometimes exchange roles once they enter the ring. Duran, who has been the quintessential creature of the ring in his time, acquainted Leonard with the true facts about his business.

After a lifetime of hard work but almost effortless success inside the ropes, Leonard finally came face to face with the core of boxing: suffering. He passed the test of personal courage but, because he was so intent on that examination of character, he neglected the tactics of his art and lost a crown. Someday, if the '80s turn out to be a decade of Leonard evolution, this fight may prove to be historic because it brought a great young fighter face to face with fear.

Duran, only the third man ever to be both lightweight and welterweight champion, won a unanimous decision over Leonard by a slim and controversial margin. Leonard won a unanimous and incontrovertible decision over fear. This defeat was his letter of credit to a doubting world that thought him a likable boxer but not necessarily a heroic fighter.

Few nights in history, certainly very few in the last twenty years, have met boxing's highest and most dubious standard of greatness: the constant, relentless and mutual inflicting of the maximum tolerable amount of pain. By that measure, the Leonard-Duran conflagration was worth every penny of the $30 million that it probably will gross. No one who is fascinated by watching men under extreme duress was cheated.

Duran, given his choice, would fight fifteen rounds in a telephone booth without any intermissions. Only the Panamanian brawler, among current fighters, can monopolize 399 square feet of a 400-square-foot ring. Duran's victims sometimes wonder if they have room to fall. That was the case for the first five and the last five rounds of Friday night's classic, which was as riveting as boxing can be without knockdowns or copious blood.

Experts will argue interminably over why Leonard fought what appeared to be a brave but hopelessly stupid fight. Why didn't he jab? Why didn't he dance? Why didn't he circle? Why didn't he slide when Duran tried to cut the ring? Why didn't he clinch or push off more to avoid the infighting? Why did he stand toe to toe countless times and exchange hooks to the head and uppercut digs to the gut? Only Leonard had the absolute and unarguable answer. "I had no other alternative," he said.

Early in the fight, when Duran was fresh, and late in the fight, when Leonard was tired, Duran made certain that the fight would be conducted only one way — his way. Wherever Leonard was, there was Duran — less than arm's reach away and throwing leather without surcease. In such circumstances, no man can dance, or jab or slide. Once Duran is within the parameters of an opponent's defense, and both his hands of stone are moving, a fighter has only one choice: exchange punches or call for Mama.

The tone of a brutal and elemental evening was established quickly when prelim lightweight Cleveland Denny was carried out unconscious in convulsive paroxysms so strong that doctors could not get the mouthpiece out of his clenched jaw. Denny is in intensive care. [Note: Denny later died.] For any in the crowd of 46,317 — the once-a-year boxing fans like Jack Nicklaus — who might doubt, that twitching body on the stretcher was a declaration of boxing's basic nature.

When Gaetan Hart, the man who knocked out Denny, was told that his last punch hardly seemed powerful enough for such damage, he was offended. His last opponent left the ring in a coma and required eight hours of brain surgery, so Hart, with his matted hair, tattoos and rearranged features, is proud of his punch. In his life, it is what he has. "When I hit Denny with the right hand," explained Hart, "his eyes go around backwards like this."

And Hart twirled his forefingers as though illustrating how the cherries on a slot machine revolve.

That is boxing. And Duran, the man who, in the ring, has the hands and the heart of stone, knows it better than any fighter of his generation.

Other boxing eras would not have found Duran unique. His personality type would have seemed comfortably familiar: a fatherless street urchin who stole to feed his brothers and sisters, dropped out of school in the third grade at the age of thirteen, turned pro at sixteen, became the athletic pet of a Latin military dictator, won a world title at age twenty-one, and now has a fleet of gaudy cars and a 680-pound pet lion which he walks on a leash.

In any period, Duran would have stood out. But in the '60s and '70s, when Muhammad Ali brought footwork, defense, an unmarked face and poetry to fighting, Duran seemed almost an embarrassing anachronism, a stage in boxing's evolution that the game seemed anxious to act as though it had passed. Duran, with his 71–1 record, seldom got his due. Or if he did, it was done with a shudder as though Heathcliff were being introduced in polite society and might smash the china in a rage.

But boxing never changes. One central truth lies at its heart and it never alters: pain is the most powerful and tangible force in life. The threat of torture, for instance, is stronger than the threat of death. Execution can be faced, but pain is corrosive, like an acid eating at the personality. Pain, as anyone with a toothache knows, drives out all other emotions and sensations before it. Pain is priority. It may even be man's strongest and most undeniable reality. And that is why the fight game stirs us, even as it repels us.

For at least ten of their fifteen rounds, Leonard and Duran set as intense a pace as any fan could wish — they looked like Ali and Smokin' Joe Frazier in the first round in Manila, but because they weigh only 147 pounds, their speed and frequency of violence did not dwindle nearly so much as the fight wore on.

"He threw his best. I threw my best," said Leonard. What landed? he was asked. "Everything," said Leonard.

In the early rounds, there was defense, slipping and blocking of the fiercest punches. In the late rounds, when the blows still carried pain but insufficient force for a blessed unconsciousness, every third swing seemed to land flush.

Only in the middle rounds, starting late in the fifth, when Leonard finally landed enough consecutive punches to make Duran back off for the first time, and extending through the tenth, did Leonard achieve a painless modus vivendi. Then, Leonard still had his speed and Duran had his doubts. The Sugar Man struck and escaped, dealt fire for fire, then had breathing time to regroup.

After those early rounds of perplexity bordering on fear, Leonard gradually gained confidence — more's the pity for him — until, by the eleventh, he thought he was Duran's better. He thought he could reach into the furnace and save the crown that he saw melting there.

The eleventh round was meant for the film archives. Everything that gives boxing undeniable dimension and emotional authority was wrought to white heat then. Money, glory of the search for identity may get a man into the ring, but only facing and surmounting pain can keep him there. Only that act of creating a brutal art in the presence of suffering can bring nobility to man's oldest and most visceral competition.

Boxing has the cleanest line, the fewest rules and the most self-evident objective of any endeavor that people gather to watch. When shabbily done, like the third meeting of their careers between Denny and Hart — a pair of lifelong plodders — few things are so worthless and destructive. Life and death on the undercard is as depressing as the sporting life gets.

However, at certain heights of skill and will, fighters like Duran and Leonard begin to carry with them a symbolic nimbus. They seem a distillation of their backgrounds, their time and place and the people out of which they sprang. Only when Duran is seen in this way does that eleventh round, and what he did after it, seem inevitable.

Here in Montreal, this town of boutiques and glass-and-neon malls where an obsession with the latest imported European fashion is everywhere, Duran's fans and followers have looked as alien as Martians. In swanky hotels like the Meridien, the Regency and the Bonaventure, these people who chant "Cholo" — the word for a Panamanian of Indian descent — and talk constantly with animated delight are distinguished by more than their old, clean, one-suit-per-lifetime clothes. Their hands and faces, like Duran's, have been weathered by eternal forces — the erosion of work, age and the rub of stubborn necessities. In Olympic Stadium on a cool Canadian night, with salsa music in the upper deck, Duran's people — his true kin or those here who have adopted him — cheered with raw conviction.

Out of our pestilential sump holes of social unconsciousness rise up a few strong, if lopsided personalities who create much of our public collective mythology. Duran is a sample of that up-from-under caste that seems simple, unified and forceful. In the eleventh, that absence of complexity proved useful.

Leonard had mustered both his confidence and his resolve. "Sugar Ray is like the rain," said Leonard's sparring partner Mike James before the fight. "Once he gets started, you can't make him stop." Leonard had clouded up and was in full thunderclap. Just as Duran had had Leonard deeply worried and near trouble in his second-round blitz, Leonard now was sure he was going for a kill. "I hit Duran some tremendous shots with left hooks, right hooks and overhand rights," said Leonard.

Instead of covering up, Duran met the pain directly, almost welcomed it. The more his head was battered from side to side, the most his fists flew in return. By midround, Leonard was so arm weary from punching that his gloves slipped to his waist. Duran took the initiative in the assault and battery until, by round's end, Leonard was in another desperate retaliatory rage, storming down punches on Duran after the bell sounded.

The net effect of this sustained firestorm was not a new balance of terror, but merely a change in exhaustion levels. Leonard had gambled and lost. The fight reverted to its early-round syndrome with Duran boring inside against a game but stationary Leonard. Had Leonard resisted the impulse to knock out this taunter, had he stayed with his midround style as long as his energy lasted, those ever-so-close judges' cards (146–144, 145–144 and 148–147) might have been reversed.

It is appropriate that in such a morally ambiguous sport, one of boxing's great fights should leave behind it a mood of nagging paradox. A view of the world — usually unspoken — often hangs around the edges of major sports. Certainly it always has with boxing. The notion that life is a fight is inescapable in this subculture of leather and liniment. The search for glory through taking advantage, the constant pursuit of getting the better of someone, are precepts so ingrained that no one would think to preach them.

As a consequence, those who tend to see the world that way are drawn here: politicians, mobsters, business millionaires, junkies of all persuasions, entertainers, athletes and journalists. It is a night for those who have sharp teeth, or think they do; vegetarians and saints need not apply. However, this shark ethic may have been carried further — reduced really to the absurd — in boxing than in any other corner of our culture. The big eating the little is gospel.

That is why Leonard entered this scene as such a refreshing anomaly. Essentially, he was a world champion who had none of boxing's shabby back-room entanglements. It was no accident that this fight could gross more money ($30 million predicted) and bring more to the fighters themselves (at least $8 to Leonard and $1.5 million to Duran) than any fight in history. Leonard's lawyer, Mike Trainer, set a precedent of squeezing out middlemen and promoters, keeping the financial books aboveboard and making no private deals.

But as soon as this beastly good fight ended, the big sharks of boxing began circling.

Duran, as devoid of *duende* — that indefinable Latin mixture of style and class — out of the ring as he is chocked with it inside the ropes, sat beside his boxing godfather, Don King, the promoter.

As Duran attacked an orange — spitting seeds and rind in any direction as he held a surly, gloating, graceless press conference — King, his hair electrified and his vanity in full bloom, took out a huge roll of big bills. With great pretense, King began slapping the money in Duran's palm of stone as the photographers clicked.

Not only Sugar Ray Leonard had been beaten but Sugar Ray Leonard, Inc., too. That great perennial enemy of boxing — an honest fighter — had been removed from the game's top rung.

And that, on one of boxing's best nights, was a beastly development indeed.

1980

# Tom Boswell

..........................................................................................................

# No Más

FROM *The Washington Post*

BULLIES CAN DISH it out, but they just can't take it. This is an ancient boxing rule of thumb: a seeming psychological paradox that really is a straightforward truth. Sugar Ray Leonard proved the verity of this maxim again tonight as he humiliated Roberto Duran with flashing combinations, glorious boxing skills and audacious courage.

For almost eight rounds, Leonard made a fool of Manos de Piedra, taunting him, beating him to the punch, disdaining him, laughing in his face, then smashing him with lightning blows from both hands.

Finally, with sixteen seconds left in the eighth round, Duran could not take it anymore. His face, although a bit puffy, was unmarked. He had not been knocked down or even severely hurt. But, far more important than that, his Panamanian macho had been slain. The man who had been feared more than any other brawler of his era, the man who had been both lightweight and welterweight champion and brought a 72–1 record into this fight, had been treated as though he were a pathetic little boy in a rage who needed to be cuffed about the head.

So, at 2:44 of that eighth round, Duran did what no one in the entire world of prizefighting ever dreamed him capable of doing: he quit. Later, he said he was retiring from the ring. "I had no idea what happened," said referee Octavio Meyran. "I said to Duran, 'What happened? Go in [and fight].' He said, 'No . . . no more.'"

The Louisiana State Athletic Commission, presumably displeased with the manner in which this fight ended, decided to hold up Duran's purse (a reported $10 million) until he could undergo a complete medical examination.

Truly, Duran had enough tonight. "I will never fight again," Duran said, after losing the WBC welterweight championship that he had taken from Leonard just five months and five days ago in Montreal. "I got cramps in the fifth round in my right arm and side. They got worse and worse. I was weakening."

The lion had quit with a thorn in his paw. The man they said could be stopped only with an elephant gun had thrown in the towel because a faster, younger and smarter man was giving him a boxing lesson and mocked him in the process.

Typically, Duran was brutish to the end. "I feel I am a thousand times a better man than Leonard," said Duran after the fight. "Just because he beat me once doesn't mean I have to respect him. . . . I am going home and count money."

Anyone searching for the cause of Duran's cramps can consider this. They may well have come from the bile when a bully's heart burst.

Leonard, who depended on a complete change of tactics to regain his crown — and prove himself to be a fighter for the ages in the process — was ecstatic, but gracious in his greatest moment. "I beat Duran more mentally than physically," said Leonard accurately. "The things I did, especially in the seventh round, demoralized him. But don't knock Duran. He will always be a great champion."

Told that Duran had made light of him, Leonard said quietly, "That's just Duran's nature. He wouldn't say anything else. I still respect the man."

Asked repeatedly about the shocking moment in the eighth when Duran simply backed away, turned his back and waved a glove dismissively at Leonard as he quit, Leonard showed the spark of genuine feeling. "Maybe Duran had heartburn," said Leonard critically. "Don't talk about Duran quitting. Talk about how badly I beat him. Duran's back, Duran's cramps . . . It's going to take a lot for people to accept that I beat the Macho Man, the Hands of Stone, a legend.

"It's simple. In the first fight [a unanimous fifteen-round decision] I learned Duran. I could change. He couldn't."

None of the roughly 40,000 in the Superdome for this Super Fight could doubt Leonard's word. By thoroughly licking the twenty-nine-year-old Duran while he was still in his prime, Leonard established himself as a great champion in his own right. And, certainly, one of the most versatile champions in history, at the least.

Every trap was laid for Duran here tonight. The American crowd booed his introduction as much as the Canadian crowd had cheered him. Who should sing "America the Beautiful" but Ray Charles, the blues singer for whom Sugar Ray Charles Leonard was named. Even Leonard's costume was a surprise. Both fighters claimed to want to wear white trunks, with Duran, as champ, getting his way. However, instead of wearing red, as he said he would, Leonard entered the ring all in black (with gold trim) right down to his black socks.

Duran's surprises started immediately. In Montreal, Leonard had proved his courage, his ability to take Duran's best punch. So, tonight, he didn't need to. In Montreal, Leonard started fearfully, losing the first four rounds as Duran swarmed him. Tonight, Leonard danced the whole first round, letting Duran stalk and stalk, then, when he finally struck, nailing the Panamanian with a vicious left hook.

Seldom has any fighter done a more splendid job of going to school between one fight and another. Leonard measured Duran from long range and by the fourth round was stinging him several times a round with clean snakelike hooks to the forehead. When Duran bored inside, Leonard snapped his head back time and again with the uppercuts that he neglected until the late rounds in Montreal.

Most impressive of all, Leonard turned all Duran's stalking and bulling tactics against him. Once, Duran used every ring-cutting technique, got Leonard seemingly pinned and leaped in with a left hook. But Leonard, with a shimmy of his hips like a football halfback, ruined Duran's timing, side-stepped him and popped him in the temple with the jab as he danced away laughing.

Once, Duran lunged so desperately that he went through the middle of the ropes and almost fell out of the ring. The only embarrassing moment all night for Leonard was when Duran once tackled him like a linebacker and knocked him on the seat of his pants with a push.

For Duran, the psychological Waterloo came in the seventh round. "I don't know why," said a grinning Leonard. "I just figured it was showtime."

Leonard stuck out his chin, inches from Duran's gloves, as Ali once had done to Liston, and when Duran lunged, Leonard retracted the chin and extended the gloves, smashing Duran in the mouth with a combination. Leonard did this not once but repeatedly, dancing all around Duran, tempting him, then punishing him. Once Leonard faked a straight right, then swatted Duran with a left hook.

The crowd was in an ecstasy of laughter and cheers as Leonard landed significant, if not crushing, blows throughout the round. "Just keep up the pace, and he's dead," yelled Dundee between rounds. The Sugar Man, however, knew even more. "I watched his eyes between rounds," said Leonard, "and they changed. He tried to sneer and leer. But I knew the truth. What punch paralyzed him? All of 'em."

Just as Liston stayed on his stool for an eighth-round TKO, so Duran's worst moment as a fighter will go into the books the same way — TKO in the eighth.

For the record, his cramps, if they existed, did not appear to damage his ability to fight. His face showed no pain. Between rounds, he did not dramatically favor his side. Certainly, he was in nothing like the pain that Ali, for instance, endured when he fought the last thirteen rounds of a fifteen-round defeat with a broken jaw against Kenny Norton.

Boxing has a long history of champions fighting gamely until the end, even if they have injuries far more severe than cramps, which, at worst, can go away after a couple of rounds. Duran, however, was in no mood to go from bad to worse. His stamina was dwindling, while Leonard was as fresh as in the early rounds. On the three judges' cards, Leonard was ahead, 4–2–1, 4–2–1 and 4–3 — margins which probably should have been even greater since only in the third round did Duran seem to score better. Duran knew that the first eight rounds were just prologue; worse awaited him and he ducked it.

"I have been fighting a long time," said Duran through his translator. "I have gotten tired of it. I want to retire."

Are you embarrassed? he was asked.

"No, why should I be? This happens to everybody."

For Leonard, just twenty-four, a long reign may be ahead. Certainly, his confidence should take a quantum leap forward after this night. In Montreal, he seemed dazed and almost lost as he entered the ring. Tonight, Leonard was so together, so relaxed, so confident that he was loose and smiling during the introductions. He was so delighted by Ray Charles singing, and the hug and kiss that the blind musician gave him just before the first bell, that he almost seemed euphoric. With each round, Leonard seemed more delighted with himself as those long hours of gym lessons were paying off in trumps.

On Basin Street here, in the St. Louis Cemetery, the names of many Lou'siana men are on the aboveground tombs. The epitaph on many reads: "Killed in a duel."

That is the epitaph for Duran tonight. This evening, Sugar Ray Leonard had the feet of a Bourbon Street tap dancer, the blended combinations of a fine Dixieland jazz band and the punch of Ramos gin fizz.

It only took Roberto Duran eight rounds to see enough of this demoralizing mixture. For the rest of the boxing world, which has years more of the developing saga of the Sugar Man ahead of it, this night was just the delicious first course in the long championship feast of Sugar Ray Leonard's career.

1981

George Plimpton

....................................................................................

# Medora Goes to The Game

FROM *Sports Illustrated*

LAST FALL, thinking of it as a kind of Christmas present given in advance, I offered to take my nine-year-old daughter, Medora, to her first Harvard-Yale football game. Actually, it was a selfish idea — an excuse to see my alma mater play against the Yales — and, as I expected, her enthusiasm was guarded. She has other ideas about Christmas. She has seen *The Black Stallion* six or seven times, and a horse, steaming in the winter air out on the lawn, is what she hopes to see through her window when she awakens on Christmas morning. It was easy to tell the Harvard-Yale game wasn't even on her "list." She looked at me gravely through the gray-green eyes she has inherited from her mother and asked, "What is it?"

"It's a football game," I explained, "so important that it's called The Game. There is no other The Game. A Yale coach named Ted Coy once told his players before The Game that they would never do anything quite as important in their lives as what they would be doing that afternoon." I went on to say that Percy Haughton, the Harvard coach from 1908 to 1916, had tried to get his players pepped up before The Game by hauling a bulldog, the Yale symbol, into the locker room and actually strangling the animal.

"He did *what?* Killed a dog?" Medora's eyes blazed. I had made a bad error.

I explained that it was just a legend. "He never actually *did* that," I said. "He couldn't. A bulldog hasn't got a neck." I went on to say that what Haughton had done was ride around Cambridge dragging a papier-mâché bulldog from the rear bumper of his car. That was how the legend had started.

Medora wasn't placated in the least. "That's even grosser," she said, "pulling a dog around from the back of a car!"

"More gross," I corrected her, and tried hurriedly to explain that papier-mâché — a word she had apparently not heard in her young life — wasn't the name of a bulldog breed, as she suspected, but meant that the dog was fake.

I assumed that was the end of things. The Harvard-Yale game as a Christmas present was out. But the night before The Game, just after her supper, Medora appeared at my study door and announced, "I'm ready. I've packed."

I was delighted. I retrieved the two tickets I was planning to give away, and early next morning we took the shuttle to Boston. The plane was crowded — many aboard, judging from the heavy coats and the predominance of blue and red in their attire, on their way to The Game. Medora and I sat together. She was wearing a yellow jumpsuit, but the rest of her outfit, somewhat to my dismay, was blue — the Yale color. Her woolen hat was blue, and so were her parka, scarf, socks, shoulder bag, and sneakers. "My favorite color is blue," she said simply.

It worried me. I had ulterior motives (besides the chance to see The Game) in taking Medora to Cambridge. My vague hope was that she would become impressed enough with Harvard to think about working hard at her studies so she might go there one day. I knew it wasn't important *where* she went as long as she approved of the choice herself. But I hoped it wasn't going to be Yale. After all, it would be one thing to sit in the stands and root for her as she performed for the Smith College field hockey team, or the Rutgers gymnastic squad, or whatever, but to think of her across the football field joyfully waving a blue pennant and yelling "Bowwow-wow!" with the Yale team poised on the Harvard goal line, while I raised a feeble "Hold 'em!" across the way, is a possibility too intolerable to consider.

"I should tell you something," Medora was saying beside me in the plane. She pointed to a tall blue feather a man a few seats in front of us sported from his hatband. It had a white *Y* on it. "There's my favorite letter." When I asked her why, she said it was because the yacht club where she is learning to sail has a blue pennant with a *Y* in the center and she likes to see it snapping in the wind from the bow of the club launch.

"What's wrong with an *H?*" I asked.

"Well, it looks like a house with two chimneys that are too tall," she said as she produced a note pad from her shoulder bag and with her brown hair brushing the paper as she bent to her work fashioned an *H*. She finished it with some squiggles of smoke emerging from both chimneys.

"See?"

"Yes," I said.

Her interest in yachting is another vague worry. Medora spends her summers on the water. Her lips are pale from the salt. Her yellow slicker lies discarded on the lawn when she comes home exhausted; retrieved, it is flung over a shoulder as she heads for Gardiners Bay the next morning. I keep hoping she'll spend more time on the tennis court. She can hit a tennis ball with authority, although she seems slightly hesitant about how the game is scored. Surely that will come. I see myself, like John McEnroe's father, peering out from under a white tennis hat, arms folded on the balustrade overlooking some exotic court, in Monte Carlo, say, and watching Medora move to the net under a high, kicking serve to Pam Shriver's backhand.

Medora was looking out the plane window. I interrupted her reverie. "When we get to Cambridge, would you mind if I bought you a Harvard hat?" I asked her. "We're going to be sitting among a lot of Harvards and there'll be confusion with all this blue you're wearing."

She nodded vaguely. She had some things she wanted to show me from her shoulder bag. She produced a four-page handwritten "newspaper." "Sherman Reddy and I are the editors," she told me. The front page dealt with the November election. CARTER IS DEFEETED the headline read in my daughter's recognizable penmanship. The subhead announced RAGEN WON THE ELECTION BY FAR. The news story was brief. It read: "Carter worked very hard but he was defeeted. In 1981 Ragen will be Presedent. Let us hope he is good." Underneath this story was a poll on whether Ragen would be good. He got one yes and one no — the two editors apparently being not only the pollsters but also the sole respondents as well. I asked Medora, who was the only girl in her class to "vote" for Carter, what was wrong with President Reagan. "He laughs too much. He thinks everything is funny," she said. The rest of the paper was made up of "advertisements," most of them for restaurants (*Dining out tonight? Have a fish . . .*). There was one recently added story.

MEDORA TO SEE THE GAM.

"It has an *e* on the end of it," I said.

She brought out her pencil to make the correction.

"Perhaps you could do an extra on the Harvard-Yale game," I suggested as Medora returned the newspaper to the bag. She said she would discuss it with her coeditor.

She had brought along some good-luck tokens she showed me — a stuffed koala bear in a miniature straw basket suspended by a ribbon from her neck. The bear was nestled on crumpled-up pieces of tissues — "to make him comfortable," Medora said. She took him out to show him to me, revolving him solemnly between thumb and forefinger before returning him to the basket. "I hope he's the right one," she said. "I have another one, which looks exactly the same, who is bad luck."

"How do you tell them apart?" I asked.

"If I have really bad luck," she explained, "I know I've got the wrong one with me."

"Perhaps you could throw that one away," I suggested.

"It's better not to," she replied. "In case the other is *really* bad luck."

She then showed me an ivory whistle made of two intertwined fish. She said if the Yale players heard it they would, as she put it, "shrivel."

The day in Boston was brilliant and cold; the wind ruffled the surface of the Charles as we drove beside it in a taxi from the airport. I said that in the spring the crews came out on the river — "Eight men in a line, one rowing behind the other. The boats they row in are as thin as pencils," I said, trying to be graphic. "They're called shells." Medora tried to look suave at this explanation. What an enormous amount of odd pursuits there were in the world, I thought, and how difficult it was to make sense of them to a nine-year-old. We saw a number of sights that required my saying something about them — the scrum of a rugby game on the lawn of the Harvard Business School, the tailgaters along the banks of the river — "drinking cocktails out of the back of their cars," was how I tried to describe it — the gay activist contingents chanting at the gates of Soldier's Field, the first raccoon coats she had ever seen.

We got out at Harvard Square. I had time before the game to show her part of the college. We wandered along the walks. I tried to think what would give her a sense of the history and the character of the university and yet would be interesting to someone infatuated with horses and sailboats. As we walked through the gates into Harvard Yard I said that I remembered that the Boylston Professor of Rhetoric was by tradition allowed to graze a cow in the Yard, though no holder of that position had been known to avail himself of the privilege. Professors rarely came with cows. Medora seemed especially interested. Was it possible to graze a *horse* in the Yard? she wished to know. "And what about birds?" she asked. "If I go to Harvard will I be able to bring Tiffany?" Tiffany is her parakeet. My heart jumped at her mention of the college. I said I was sure it could be arranged.

We started for Harvard Stadium. I bought her a wool Harvard cap and a large red Beat Yale button. She exchanged the red hat for the blue one she had been wearing, but she dropped the button into her shoulder bag. I shrugged. Perhaps it was too big for her tastes. Outside the stadium I bought a Harvard banner and a game program.

We found our seats and Medora almost immediately came down with an acute case of the hiccups. "Am I going to hiccup for the entire game?" she asked me.

"I don't know," I replied. "What do you think?"

She said she wasn't sure.

As the teams came out onto the field I opened up the program to see who was who and discovered I had been gulled by a vendor into buying a *Harvard Lampoon* parody of the official program. The lead story was about a headless Yale player — Aemon Bonderchuk: "the horrible freak who hopes to lead the Elis to victory" — and, sure enough, there were some photographs doctored so that it indeed looked as if Yale had a headless player. According to the story, Carmen Cozza, the Yale coach, had been asked about him: "Aemon? Sure. Nice boy. Good hands. Big heart. No head."

I showed a picture of Bonderchuk to Medora. "Look at this. Yale has somebody out there with no head."

"How awful," she said. "Was it a Harvard person who did that to him?"

After a while she said that she thought seeing the headless player in the program had startled away her hiccups. "I'm cured," she said. She gave a sigh of relief and looked out on the field.

"Does Yale have its bulldog over there?" she asked, squinting toward the opposite sideline. When I said I thought so, she asked what the Harvard mascot was.

"A Puritan."

"What's a Puritan?" Medora asked.

"He's a man with knee britches and a tall conical hat with a buckle on it. People like him founded Harvard."

As I brooded in the stands it occurred to me that there seemed to be so much more that Yale had to offer an impressionable young girl. Their songs were better. The bulldog, while hardly a comfy sort of animal, was infinitely more pleasant to have around than a Puritan, and he enabled the Yale songs to have catchy lines like "Bow-wow-wow." Why couldn't Cole Porter (Yale '13), who had written so many of those gems while an undergraduate, have gone to Harvard? Why had Leonard Bernstein (Harvard '39) waited until *West Side Story* before doing his best? The Yale band was playing one of Cole Porter's most memorable tunes, "March on Down the Field," and I realized with a start that I was singing along, my lips moving involuntarily.

It didn't turn out to be much of a day for Harvard. The wind, which remained brisk and into which yellow biplanes towing advertising messages above the stadium barely made headway, played havoc with the football — especially, it seemed to me, when Brian Buckley, the left-handed Harvard quarterback, tried to pass or when the Crimson's kicker, Steve Flach, went back to punt. On the whole, the brand of football was spotty, as symbolized by a play midway in the game when Flach, back to punt, took a snap that skittered along the ground like a dog running for him, leaping at the last second for his chest and bouncing off. By the time Flach had the ball under control, the Yale line was on him. He took a feeble swipe at the ball — the kind an elderly aunt might aim at a terrier nipping at her feet — and missed it. The Yale middle guard, Kevin Czinger, picked up the ball and started for the goal line. There wasn't a Harvard man within yards. A number of Yale men raced up to join Czinger, and it was while this pack of players was running unencumbered by anything more serious than a scrap of wind-blown paper scuttling across the field that Czinger suddenly went down as if he had run into a trip wire, apparently having stumbled over the heels of one of his teammates. A gasp went up in the stadium — not really of dismay from Yale fans or relief from Harvard rooters, but at the realization, I think, that because the game was being telecast throughout the East, this dreadful pratfall was being beamed into any number of places — bars in Hoboken, New Jersey, or Erie, Pennsylvania, perhaps — where people were quite likely scornful of Ivy League football to begin with and where now, peering up at the TV screen at the end of the bar, they saw a Yale player, racing for the Harvard goal line with a football under his arm, surrounded by his fellows, suddenly stumble and collapse as if poleaxed. And they would never know that after the game it would be discovered that Czinger, far from having been tripped, had torn a back muscle.

The enormity of this, of course, was lost on Medora. I kept an eye on her. Every once in a while I caught her staring at the field in deep thought, lost in some internal consideration. Sometimes her lips moved slightly — a recitation of some sort — and when she caught me looking at her, she would start and smile quickly, her eyes sparkling. Once she said, "Gee, Dad, that's great!" though I hadn't said anything to elicit such a remark. She had her mind on something.

"What do you think of it?" I asked.

"I think my hiccups are coming back," she said, but she seemed to offer it as an afterthought, rather than what was really on her mind.

I had spent much of the first half attempting to explain the meaning of third down and ten. My father has always said that there are two things that women, however brilliant, fail with great charm to understand: one is the International Date Line, the other is third and ten. "Ask Lillian Hellman about third and ten," he once said abruptly at lunch. "See what you get." I never did that, but Medora certainly did nothing to suggest my father's theory was in error. "I like it better when they kick," she said. "Why can't they kick all the time? My friend at school told me that they have sixty footballs for each game. They keep them in sacks."

Could she have been thinking of baseballs? I said, "That seems like an awful lot of footballs."

"Oh, no," she said positively. "You wait and see."

In the middle of the second quarter Medora said that she really liked the blue *Y*s on the Yale helmets. She announced it with a faint sigh, as if she had been making comparisons and had come to a decision. As I brooded over this disaffection, I was reminded that Alex Karras, the great Detroit Lion defensive tackle, had once told me that at the end of his illustrious career he had discovered his children were all Los Angeles Rams fans. They liked the way the horns curled up the side of the Rams' helmets. "To think," Alex said sorrowfully, "that I went out and slaved in the trenches all those Sundays to send my kids through school, getting my thumbs bent back so that I went like this in pain — 'AIEEE!' — while all the time the kids were rooting for these guys across the line because they had nice-looking logos on their helmets designed by some interior decorator in Pasadena."

The wind didn't let up. Before the half, Yale scored, and then again just after the third quarter began. Medora and I didn't see the second score. We spent the third quarter standing in line for a hot dog. The facilities at Harvard Stadium are notorious. The rest rooms were described in the game program parody as being "located under sections 6, 7 and 31 of the Loeb Drama Center on Brattle Street." It went on to call the stadium itself: "The oldest standing concrete structure in the United States since the collapse of a similar arena sixteen years ago. In its present condition, the Stadium is capable of supporting virtually two thousand people."

When we got back to our seats Medora discovered that she had lost her good-luck koala bear. Apparently it had tumbled out of its tiny wicker basket. She didn't seem especially put out by its loss. "It was probably the bad-luck bear anyway," she said. She reached in her bag and produced the backup charm — the intertwined ivory fish — and in the hubbub around us I heard the faint whistle that was supposed to make the Yale players shrivel.

Medora's mittens had disappeared, too. I felt her shivering. She curled up against the sheepskin coat I was wearing. I took her bare hands and rubbed them. On one of her thumbs I noticed a face she had drawn with a ballpoint pen; the back of her hand was decorated with a button with the word PUSH above it.

"What's this?"

She was embarrassed. "A push button," she said.

"What happens when you push it?"

She shrugged. "It starts engines and things," she said. She was still trembling.

I suggested, "Start up the heaters. Your mother will think I'm trying to kill you out here. Jiggle your feet. Then push the button for Harvard. They're not doing very well."

"Are they losing?" she asked.

"I'm afraid so."

"How much longer will it take them to lose?"

"About ten minutes," I said. "When you see the white handkerchiefs come out on the Yale side — then you'll know."

I tried to entertain her. We watched individual players to see what happened to them when the ball was snapped. I took another crack at third and ten. I told her about the pigeon that had caught the attention of the huge crowd one year — a pigeon that had settled down a yard or so from the goal line. A number of people in the stands noticed that in pecking here and there in the grass, the pigeon seemed to go right to the brink of the goal line and then back away, as if forced to do so by some psychic power. The stands took sides. Megaphones were raised. Cries began to go up, "Go, bird, go!" erupting from the far side and "Hold that pigeon!" from the Harvard supporters. At the opposite end of the stadium the football players toiled on in what must have seemed a

bewildering maelstrom of sound — standing in the huddle as a crescendo of pleading would give way to shouts of triumph as the pigeon,
unbeknownst to the players, had turned toward or away from the goal
line. Medora wanted to know if the pigeon had crossed the goal line. I
said I couldn't remember.

Medora began making a paper airplane from a page torn from the
*Lampoon* parody. "I'm going to fly this down to the field with a message
on it," she said. With her hands trembling from the cold she laboriously
wrote a sentence across the inner folds of the airplane; after creasing it
and preparing it for flight, she wrote "Open, open" along its length to
indicate it should be read by whoever picked it up.

"What did you say in it?" I asked.

She spread the airplane apart. The message read: "Yale stinks. Right?"

How odd, I thought, as she showed it to me, that she should add that
demure *right?*

She refolded it and asked me to throw it for her. She wanted it to
reach the Yale huddle. So I tried to do it for her, half standing and
attempting to sail it into the wind. The airplane stalled and crashed into
the hat brim of a man two rows down from us and fell off into his lap.
He turned and could see from my expression, and the fact that my arm
was still extended, that I was the one who had thrown the paper airplane. He looked, from the glimpse I had of him, like a professor or
perhaps a Harvard overseer. He opened the airplane and read the message. He didn't look at me again. From the heavy set of his shoulders, I
sensed that he was gloomily reflecting on an educational system that
had produced a grown man capable of setting down such an infantile
thought and in such execrable handwriting. I kept hoping he would
turn around again and catch sight of Medora, who was giggling into the
folds of my sheepskin coat.

From our side of the field the Harvard undergraduates began a
melancholy chant of "We're Number Two! We're Number Two!" Across
the way the handkerchiefs began to flutter in the Yale stands. Medora
said she felt sorry for the Harvard team. I wondered vaguely if it was
healthy to decide to go to a college because you "felt sorry" for its football team.

The game ended. The spectators in the Yale stands counted down the
last seconds and the gun went off. I took Medora down to the field so we
could hear the Harvard band and see what the field was like after it had
been kicked up by the players' cleats, and I eased her up to a Harvard
player standing with his parents so she could see how large he was. A

faint odor of liniment and grass drifted off him. She peered at the eyeblack above his cheekbones as if she were inspecting a painting. He must have felt embarrassed under her scrutiny. He turned away. I heard him say to one of his group, "Thank God, Priscilla didn't come here. You say she's up at Dartmouth? What's she doing up *there?*"

Medora asked about his eyes. I told her that athletes often wore eyeblack to cut down the sun's glare. She said it made them look neat, like Indians. Did the Yale players wear the stuff, too? Oh yes, I said. She announced that she thought she might wear it out on her Sunfish — the glare was just terrific off the water.

We slowly headed out of the stadium, Medora holding my hand. I commented to her that at times during the game she had seemed distracted. Was something on her mind? Had she had a good time?

"Oh, Dad, it was great," she said. "I liked the story about the pigeon. I wish you could remember if he went across the goal line."

We crossed the Anderson Bridge and walked up Boylston Street past the Houses. I pointed out the windows of the Elliot House room where I had lived. Someone had hung a hastily lettered sheet out of the row of windows below. SO WHAT IF YOU WON, the message read. YOU STILL GO TO YALE.

"Six U.S. presidents went to Harvard," I found myself saying to Medora as we strolled along. "William Howard Taft was the only one to come out of Yale, if you don't count Gerald Ford, who went to the law school there, and Taft was such an enormously fat man that they had to enlarge the doors of the White House to get his bathtub inside. Did I tell you that Harvard was founded a hundred and forty years before the Declaration of Independence?"

"Yes, Dad, you did."

I took her to some postgame parties. We went to the *Lampoon* building where in the crowded Gothic hall I pointed to a suit of Japanese armor hanging on the wall and told her I had worn it in a curious baseball game against the *Harvard Crimson,* the undergraduate newspaper. The *Lampoon* was famous for its high jinks. A couple of years after I'd left, the editors had plotted to steal a battleship out of Boston Harbor. "They only had men on the board then," I told Medora. "Now they accept women. You could be the editor. You could plot to steal a battleship." I twirled the ice in my drink. It was my third. She stood, a diminutive form beside me, in the crush of the cocktail party. An undergraduate editor of the *Lampoon* turned up. I told him that I had admired the game-program parody; I had been reminded that we had done one like it when I was an undergraduate. In fact, I could remember editing an article entitled, *Why Harvard Will Not Go to the Rose Bowl This Year,* one of the reasons being, as I recalled, that California was "in some kind of time zone."

The undergraduate looked at me gravely over his plastic glass. "Funny," he said without a smile.

It was dark when we left. We walked past Lowell House. I pointed up to the belfry. I told her the bells would be pealing if Harvard had won. They made a wonderful racket. In fact, the bells were something of a neighborhood nuisance because they were so loud; the person playing them sometimes got mixed up so that it sounded as if the bells were tumbling down a rock slide. The Cambridge citizens complained. In fact, they threatened to shut down the bells. I told Medora that in revenge the great Lowell House legend was that all the people who lived there synchronized their watches and simultaneously flushed every toilet in the place.

"Why did they do that?" Medora asked.

"It apparently puts a terrific strain on the plumbing system," I said. "Floods things all over town. So it was a kind of weapon. It was to tell the Cambridge citizens and the college administration not to fool around with their bells."

"I would like to have heard them," Medora suddenly said.

I thought she was referring to the Lowell House plumbing, but it turned out to be the bells. "I wish Harvard had won," she said wistfully, "so that you could stand here and listen to them."

Impossible to tell about Medora. Didn't she want to listen to them too?

Not long after our trip I wandered into her room when she wasn't there. Tiffany, her parakeet, was scrabbling around in its cage. Her room has always been an irresistible place to visit from time to time to see what is new in there — to check on the detritus of her complicated schoolgirl life. A "secret" note from a school chum pinned up on the cork bulletin board. What she has dropped into her fish tank lately. The newest of the mice figurines she has added to a fearsome array on a shelf.

On her desk was a draft of a newspaper that she was apparently putting together as a Christmas present. Green holly leaves were pasted at each corner. The headline read YALE BEATS HARVARD BY FAR, the subhead, SCORE IS 14–0 YALE ON FREEZING DAY. Involuntarily, I glanced back over my shoulder, to make certain I wouldn't be caught prying in her room, and then turned back to read: "Harvard fans had little to cheer about yesterday as Yale handkerchiefs fluttered in the air. There was lots of cheering coming from the Yale stands. Harvard players slipped too much on the grass. At the end of the game the two gold posts were torn down by Yale fans. The Harvard fans went off to partys to drown their sorrows."

A pile of photographs from newspaper sports sections were waiting to be pasted in. I recognized Earl Campbell of the Houston Oilers in one of the pictures, vaulting into a dense pile of tacklers, the distinction of what team Campbell actually played on being of little significance to the young editor. I couldn't resist browsing through the paper. On the second page was a large advertisement for cats illustrated with a dozen silhouette studies of cats with their tails hanging down, as though the cats were sitting on an imaginary shelf. Medora does a great many of these studies.

What caught my eye was a story on the same page under the large headline (with a line through the second word, the spelling of which had apparently stumped her): BLACK ~~STAL~~ HORSE BUYED. The text, again with a number of words crossed out, read as follows: "The black horse arrived in a truck shortly after nightfall. It was dark outside. His name was ~~Abraham Lincoln Tom, Blueboy~~ Prince!" I suspected I knew then what those thoughtful silences I had detected on that chilly November afternoon were all about — not about whether she was going to hiccup or whether a pigeon had crossed a goal line, or even whether she preferred Harvard, or Yale, or even Princeton. Names were under consideration but not the names of colleges.

A small story caught my eye on the last page of the paper. The headline read, HARVARD NOT DISCORAGED.

The story underneath, in its entirety, read: "Harvard is not discoraged."

1982

## Frank Deford

......................................................................................................

# The Rabbit Hunter

FROM *Sports Illustrated*

> Success is feminine and like a woman; if you cringe before her, she will override you. So the way to treat her is to show her the back of your hand. Then maybe she will do the crawling.
>
> WILLIAM FAULKNER

### I. Rabbits

AS BOBBY KNIGHT is the first to say, a considerable part of his difficulty in the world at large is the simple matter of appearance. "What do we call it?" he wonders. "Countenance. A lot of my problem is just that too many people don't go beyond countenances."

That's astute — Bobby Knight is an astute man — but it's not so much that his appearance is unappealing. No, like so much of him, his looks are merely at odds. Probably, for example, no matter how well you know Coach Knight, you have never been informed — much less noticed yourself — that he's dimpled. Well, he is, and invariably when anyone else has dimples, a great to-do is made about them. But, in Bobby's case, being dimpled just won't fly.

After all: DIMPLED COACH RAGES AGAIN. No. But then, symbolically, Knight doesn't possess dimples, plural, as one would expect. He has only the prize one, on his left side. Visualize him, standing in line, dressed like the New Year's Baby, when they were handing out dimples. He gets the one on his left side. "What the bleep is this?" says little Bobby, drawing away.

"Wait, wait!" cries the Good Fairy or the Angel Gabriel or whoever's in charge of distributing dimples. But it's too late. Bobby has no time for this extraneous crap with dimples. He's already way down the line, taking extras on bile.

"Countenances," Knight goes on, woefully. "I just don't have the personality that connotes humor. It kills me. I get castigated just for screaming at some official. And the other coach? Oh, he's perfect, he's being deified, and I know he's one of the worst cheaters in the country. It's like I tell my players: your biggest opponent isn't the other guy. It's human nature."

Knight happens to be a substance guy in a style world. Hey, he could look very good in polyester and boots and one of those teardrop hair-cuts that anchormen and male stewardesses wear. Very good: he's tall, 6'5", and dimpled (as we know) and handsome, and the gray hair and embryonic potbelly that have come to him as he crosses into his 41st winter are pleasant modifying effects.

In the early '60s, when Knight was a big-talking substitute on the famous Jerry Lucas teams at Ohio State, he was known as Dragon. Most people think it was in honor of his fire-snorting mien, with the bright and broken nose that wanders down his face and makes everything he says appear to have an exclamation mark. Only this was not so. He was called Dragon because when he came to Ohio State, he told everybody he was the leader of a motorcycle gang called the Dragons. This was pure fabrication, of course, but all the fresh-scrubbed crew cuts on the team lapped it up. It was easy. People have always been charmed by him; or conned: anyway, he gets in the last word.

It's never neat, of a piece. When Knight stands up, coaching, with his hands in his pockets, he looks like a street-corner guy. But with his tousled hair, the tie forever undone, there's also a childish aspect to his appearance:

*Wear your tie, Bobby.*

*All right, Mom, I'll put it on, but I won't tie it tight.*

The boy-coach who got his first major-college head-coaching job at 24 may be middle-aged now, but still, every day, in some way, adolescence must be conquered again. "Listen to me," Woody Hayes pleaded with him once. "Listen to me, Bobby, because I've made a lot of mistakes and you don't have to repeat mine."

The real issue isn't the countenance, anyway. The real issue is the rabbits. And Knight knows that. In the Indiana locker room before a game earlier this season, Knight was telling his players to concentrate on the important things. He said, "How many times I got to tell you? Don't fight the rabbits. Because, boys, if you fight the rabbits, the elephants are going to kill you." But the coach doesn't listen to himself. He's always chasing after the incidental; he's still a prodigy in search of proportion. "There are too many rabbits around," he says. "I know that. But it doesn't do me any good. Instead of fighting the elephants, I just keep going after the rabbits." And it's the rabbits that are doing him in, ruining such a good thing.

Pete Newell, the former Cal coach, a mentor: "There are times Bobby comes so close to self-destructing." Edwin Cady, a Duke University professor, after the Indiana Athletics Committee he chaired recommended Knight's hiring in 1971: "He's in a race now between overcoming immaturity and disaster. And even the warmest, most benign observers of the man offer variations of these themes.

Others are much more critical — especially since the sad events of July 1979 at the Pan American Games in Puerto Rico when Knight, the U.S. basketball coach, was arrested for aggravated assault on a police officer (and subsequently convicted *in absentia* and sentenced to six months in prison). "Bobby's so intelligent, but he has tunnel vision," says another Midwestern coach. "None of that stuff in Puerto Rico had to happen. On the contrary, he could've come out of there a hero. But he's a bully, always having to put people down. Someday, I'm afraid, he's going to be a sad old man." Says an Eastern coach, "He'll get away with the bullying and the vulgarity only so long as he wins. But the shame is, he's so smart, and he's so faithful to his principles, so why can't he understand that other people have principles too?"

Such criticism doesn't necessarily affect Knight in the ways and to the extent that most people imagine. In a sense, he enjoys being misunderstood, so no one can get a fix on him. It's like the effect Indiana's good defense has on the coaches of its opponents. "The average coach wants his team to score points," Knight says. "It's his character, his machismo, whatever you want to call it, that's at stake. So if I make a coach concerned enough about my defense stopping his offense, then he'll forget about *my* offense."

Though Knight may not give a hoot whether most people like him, it genuinely upsets him that anyone might think he's impulsive, much less berserk. "Hey, I'm not dumb, and too many people look at our operation as if we're all dumb here," he says. "Only people really involved here know what the hell we're doing. See, I don't think people understand what I can or can't do. They're not cognizant of my situation and *what I know about myself.* I always know what I'm doing."

Yet as intelligent as Knight is about most things, as searching as his mind is, he's also encumbered by a curious parochialism that too often brings him to grief. When all is said and done, his difficulties in Puerto Rico resulted mostly from his inability to concede that San Juan isn't just another Chicago, or that the Pan Am Games aren't another Mideast Regional — and it's their own fault that they're not. Knight's mind is too good to be wasted on a mere game — and he probably recognizes that — but he's personally not comfortable away from the precisely circumscribed environment in which college basketball is played. Therein lies the great conflict in him.

Does anybody else in this universe of shifting sands still have the control of a coach? No wonder it's difficult for a person like Knight, who tends toward prepossession anyway, to be confused about the limits of his dominion. Puerto Rico, women, writers, shoe salesmen, NCAA bigwigs . . . all of them are just more Rubicons to cross. He's in command; an awful lot of what you see is a good act. Says Harold Andreas, the high school coach who first hired Bobby as an assistant, "He can be as charming as anybody in the world or he can be the biggest horse's ass in the world. But *he* makes that decision, and he does it in a split second." Everyone identifies Knight with bad language, but the fact is that he can talk for hours, if he chooses to, using much less profanity than the average Joe. He doesn't have a foul mouth; he simply deploys bad language when it can be a weapon.

Knight is forever putting people back on their heels, testing them, making them uncomfortable in some way. Stop them from scoring points, and they won't be prepared to stop you. Although it's fashionable to say Knight rules by intimidation, he actually rules more by derision. He abuses the people he comes into contact with, taking the license to treat them as he does his players.

"O.K., it's true sometimes I intimidate a kid," Knight says. "Usually when I first get him. That sets up the best conditions for teaching. But that's only true with basketball players, not with anyone else. I don't think I'm overbearing with people, but look, that's an awfully hard thing for a man to judge of himself."

Most find him guilty. But, here, you judge. Here's five minutes of typical Bobby Knight. This isn't extreme Bobby Knight. This isn't Puerto Rico Bobby Knight. This is just some everyday stuff, the way he keeps an edge, even over people he likes.

It's practice time, and two of Knight's acquaintances are sitting at the scorer's table. One is a black man, Joby Wright, who starred on Knight's first Hoosier team in 1971–72. Six years after his athletic eligibility ran out, Wright returned to Indiana to get his degree; now he's going for a master's in counseling and guidance. All along, Knight helped Wright and encouraged him with his academics, as he has many of his players. In Knight's nine years, only one Hoosier among those who have played out their eligibility has failed sooner or later to get a degree.

The other person at the table is a white woman, Maryalyce Jeremiah, the Indiana women's basketball coach. Now it's an accepted fact of life — disputed, perhaps, only by Nancy Knight, Bobby's wife — that Knight is a misogynist, but Jeremiah he at least abides. She's a coach, after all.

Knight advances on Wright, and says, "Hey, Joby. Do me a favor."

"Sure, Coach."

"I want you to get my car and go downtown." Wright nods, taken in. Knight slams the trap: "And I want you to go to a pet shop and buy me a collar and a leash to put on that dog out there." And he points to one of his players, a kid Wright has been working with.

O.K., it's a harmless enough dig, and Wright laughs, easily. But Knight won't quit: "Because if you don't start to shape him up, I'll have to get some white guys working on him. You guys don't show any leadership, you don't show any incentive since you started getting too much welfare."

Wright smiles again, though uneasily. Now, understand, Knight isn't anti-black. Just anti-tact. That's the point. One of his former black stars once recalled a halftime against Michigan when Knight singled out two of his white regulars as gutless, and then went over as they cowered and slapped their cheeks, snarling, "Maybe this'll put some color in your faces." It isn't *racial* prejudice. Still, still. . . .

Knight walks down to the other end of the scorer's table. "Hey, Maryalyce."

Brightly: "Yes, Bobby?"

"You know what a dab is?"

"A what?"

"A dab — D-A-B."

"No, what's that?"

"It's a dumb-assed broad," he says, smirking.

"I don't know any of those," she replies — a pretty quick comeback.

But he won't leave it alone. The edge, again: "Yeah, you know one more than you think you do."

And he moves on. The white woman shrugs. It's just Bobby. The black man shrugs. It's just Bobby. But why is it just Bobby? Why does he do this to himself? He's smart enough to know that, in this instance, he isn't hurting his two friends nearly so much as he hurts himself, cumulatively, by casting this kind of bread upon the waters, day after day. Why? Why, Bobby, why?

What a setup he has. Forty years old, acknowledged to be at the top of his profession. Says the very coach who disparages Knight for being a bully, "Any coach who says Bobby's not the best is just plain jealous." Knight has already won 317 games, and nobody, not even Adolph Rupp, achieved that by his age.

Someday Knight could even surpass Rupp's record 874 wins, a seemingly insurmountable total. Knight has won one NCAA championship, in 1976, and five Big Ten titles in nine seasons; he was twice national coach of the year; he's the only man ever to both play on and coach an NCAA champion. He's the coach at one of America's great basketball schools, one that's also an academic institution of note. The state worships him; Hoosier politicians vie for his benediction. His contemporaries in coaching not only revere him for his professional gifts, but some of his esteemed predecessors — mythic men of basketball lore — see Knight as the very keeper of the game. The torch is in his hands.

He's also a clever man and delightful company when he chooses to be. Beyond all that he has an exemplary character, without any of the vices of the flesh that so often afflict men in his station and at his time of life. He's devoted to his family, Nancy and their two sons, Timothy, 16, and Patrick, 10. His supporters fall over themselves relating tales of his civic and charitable good works, a light that Knight humbly hides under a basket. In this era of athletic corruption Knight stands foursquare for the values of higher education that so many coaches and boot-lickers in the NCAA only pay lip service to. His loyalty is as unquestioned as his integrity. He is the best and brightest . . . and the most honorable, too. He has it all, every bit of it. Just lying there on the table. He has only to lean down, pick it up and let the chip fall off. But he can't. For Knight to succeed at basketball — not only to win, you understand, but to succeed because "That's much harder," he says — all the world must be in the game. All the people are players, for or against, to be scouted, tested, broken down, built back up if they matter. Life isn't lived; it's played. And the rabbits are everywhere.

## II. Coaches

Perhaps the most revealing statement that Knight makes about himself is this: "You know why Havlicek became such a great pro? Just because he wanted to beat Lucas, that's why." Yes, of course, Knight hasn't even mentioned himself, but that's the trick. Obviously, if only subconsciously, he's not really talking about John Havlicek superseding Lucas; he's talking about himself superseding Havlicek and Lucas both.

The best thing that ever happened to Knight was that after high school — he's still the greatest star ever to come out of Orrville, Ohio — he didn't amount to a hill of beans as a player. Knight the failed hero has not only served as the challenge for Knight the coach, but also Knight the disappointed hero is the model for the Everyplayer Knight coaches. That boy was limited, self-centered, frustrated, a pouter, then a bitcher, ultimately a back-biter against his coach, Fred Taylor, who once called Knight "the Brat from Orrville."

The one thing Knight could do was shoot, a strange low-trajectory shot that was deadly against zones when he had the time to get it off. To this day, no Knight team has ever set up in a zone defense. It's like Groucho Marx, who once said he didn't want to be part of any club that would have him as a member.

Although Knight only started two games in three years on the Buckeye varsity, he was a major figure on the team, something of a clubhouse lawyer and a practical joker (which he still is). Dragon and a roommate led the Buckeyes in hustling tickets, and he stunned his wide-eyed teammates with his brash high jinks. On a trip to New York he boldly swiped a couple of bottles of wine from Mamma Leone's restaurant, and not only pilfered a few ties from a midtown shop, but with the contraband under his coat, he went over to a cop who entered the store at that moment and started chatting him up.

There is little Knight's players can put over on him because he did just about all of it himself. Taylor wasn't the only coach Knight challenged, either. In his senior year at Orrville, he defied the school's new coach by refusing to leave a game for a substitute and was booted off the squad. Although subsequently reinstated, he found that season so unsatisfying that he gave up his baseball eligibility to barnstorm with an all-star basketball team in the spring. "I regret that more than anything I've ever done," he says, because he could hit a baseball and hit with power. Knight probably would've been better at baseball than he was at basketball.

Knight was also a pretty fair football end, and as he should've been a baseball player, so, by temperament, he would have made a better football coach. Wilkinson, Bryant, Hayes, Schembechler, Paterno and Royal are all friends and/or models of his, and he has a tape of Lombardi exhortations, plus a Lombardi polemic hanging on his office wall. And, like football coaches, Knight devotes himself to studying film, back and forth, over and over, like some Buddhist monk with his prayer wheel.

In the dazzle of the tight arena, basketball coaches tend to be popinjays, ruling by force of personality, glint of teeth, while football coaches are distant, solid sorts, administrators, with scores of lieutenants and troops. Being a basketball coach doesn't seem to prepare you for anything else in life, but even football coaches who can't win get bumped upstairs to assistant athletic director (a football coach who wins becomes athletic director). "I've always thought there's a greater depth to football coaches," Knight says.

But that's subsidiary to the main point: Knight loves all coaches. He will ask people who knew Rupp well to tell him about the old man. What made the Baron tick? Why did he do this? How? He has spent many hours listening to Sparky Anderson. He calls in the old basketball masters and studies at their feet. In his office, the only photographs (apart from those of his teams) are of Pete Newell and Clair Bee. Even as a boy, he would go off on scouting trips with coaches. Bill Shunkwiler, his football coach at Orrville, remembers that after school, when other kids were hanging out, chasing, Bobby would come by Shunkwiler's house and the two of them would sit and have milk and cookies and talk coach talk. Knight still keeps in touch with many of his old coaches, still calls them "Mister," and there is, in Coach Knight, almost a tribal sense of heritage and tradition.

"I just love the game of basketball so," he says. "The game! I don't need the 18,000 people screaming and all the peripheral things. To me, what's most enjoyable is the practice and preparation."

The ultimate contradiction is that Bobby Knight, of all people, profane as he is, seeks after purity. What troubles him is that the game must be muddied by outlanders and apostates — the press, for example. In fact, Knight has studied the subject, and he understands the press better than some writers who cover him understand basketball. He even numbers several writers as friends, and sometimes he will actually offer a grudging admiration beyond his famous institutional assessment: "All of us learn to write by the second grade, then most of us go on to other things." But his truest feelings were probably revealed one day recently when he blurted out, "How do they know what it's like if they've never played? How? *How?* Tell me: How can they know?"

At the base of everything, this is it: if you're not part of basketball, you can't really belong, you can only distort. He has taken over the microphone at Assembly Hall, the Hoosiers' arena, and told his own fans to back off, be good sports, even to stop using dirty words. Imagine, Knight telling people to improve their language. "It showed no bleeping class," he snapped afterward.

He just always wanted to be Coach Knight, officially expressing this desire in an autobiography he wrote when he was a junior in high school. It was entitled *It's Been a Great Life (So Far)*. Nancy Knight remembers nothing otherwise: "All Bobby ever wanted was to be a coach, in the Big Ten." Even now, when Knight deliberates on the rest of his life, he doesn't go much beyond his one love. "I hope," he says, "that when I retire I'll have enough assistants in head jobs so I can live anywhere I want and still have a place nearby where I can go over and help out and watch some films." As much as there is such a thing, he's a natural-born coach.

## III: Older People

Knight's father — his square name was Carroll, but everyone called him Pat — was a railroad man from Oklahoma, who came to Orrville because it was a railroad town, a division point. The main Pennsy line passed through, and the city slickers from Cleveland and Akron had to journey down on a spur to little Orrville to catch the Broadway Limited. So, despite having only about 5,000 folks when Bobby was growing up, Orrville was not quite as closed and homogeneous as you would expect of a Midwest coloring-book place, set in a dell, with a water tower.

Knight was born there, one of the last of the Depression Babies, on Oct. 25, 1940, a couple of weeks before FDR won his third term over Wendell Willkie and the objections of the Orrville electorate. He was reared in the '50s. Actually, the '50s were not much different in attitudes and values from the two decades that preceded them, but what sets the '50s apart is that they came right before the upheaval of the '60s. But just as the '60s flowered, Knight went off to coach at West Point, where his '50s just kept on going, even becoming sort of a badge of separation.

The '50s are too often disparaged for being simple, everyone in lockstep. But more accurately, what the '50s offered, in spades, was definition. In analyzing pre-'60s coaches like the unrepentant Knight, observers tend to confuse definition with discipline. Knight most of all wants to know where people stand — and that they do stand for something. Here's an example of how rigidly lines were drawn when Knight was growing up.

Shunkwiler takes out a copy of the 1958 *MemORRies*, the high school yearbook when Knight was a senior, and peruses the photographs of the boys, skipping the ones with pompadours, stopping on the ones who, like Bobby, wore crew cuts: "Athlete . . . athlete . . . athlete . . . ," he says. He comes to yet another boy with short hair. "Not an athlete." And hastily, "But a good kid." It was that easy then. More than one-third of the 200 or so boys were involved in athletics. Many of these were also involved in girls, too, but only *in their place*. If a coach so much as saw one of his players holding hands, he would bark out: "Hey, no skin-to-skin!"

The coach, you see, was a giant of a man in this well-defined culture. Shunkwiler recalls that if a coach was notified by a teacher that one of his players was causing a problem, the coach would take the boy aside and, presto, "That would be the end of the trouble." Jack Graham, another of Knight's Orrville basketball coaches, once kicked Bobby out of practice. Knight didn't head to the locker room, though; he waited patiently in the hallway so he could see Coach as soon as practice ended. "Bobby understood," Graham says. "I told him, 'There's only one man who can be the boss out there, and, Bobby, that's the coach.'"

Early this season Knight purposely overreacted one day so that he could boot his star, sophomore Guard Isiah Thomas, out of practice. He needed to show the kid, and the whole team, that there can be no exceptions. Some things don't change. Coach Knight can throw his star out at Indiana University as sure as Coach Graham could at Orrville High. On the team, on the court, time is frozen; *it's been a great life (so far)*.

What Knight didn't learn from his coaches came by example from his father, though theirs was an unusual relationship. The father and son weren't buddies, which has led some people to conclude that Knight's deep affection for older coaches is a manifestation of a perpetual search for a father figure. To some extent this analysis may be true, but the relationships in the Knight household were more complex than that analysis suggests.

Bobby was born six years into a marriage that had come late in life.

Though he was an only child, he had a companion at home — his maternal grandmother, Sarah Henthorne. "A classy lady — the love of Bobby's life," says Pauline Boop, who was Knight's childhood next-door neighbor and remains his friend. No wonder he gets along so well with older people; he grew up in a house full of them.

Both of Knight's parents worked — Pat on the railroad, Hazel as an elementary school teacher — and although they were loving, they weren't enthusiastic about the thing their only son loved the most, basketball. But at least Knight always had an ally in his grandmother. She was the one who followed his basketball closely. No matter what the hour, when Bobby came home he would go and kiss her good night. "I think he was closer to his grandmother than he ever was to me or his father," says the widowed Hazel Knight, who still lives in the house on North Vine Street, across the field from the high school where Bobby starred for the Orrville Red Riders.

Knight came home for spring vacation of his sophomore year at Ohio State, right after the Buckeyes had won the national championship. One day he returned to the house in the afternoon, and his grandmother was sitting there in her favorite chair. She had gone shopping in the morning and was tired. It took a while before Bobby realized that she wasn't napping, that she was dead. He remembers it very well: "She was just sitting there. Her legs were crossed at the ankles." Knight's grandmother had been sick all winter, and there are those in Orrville who say she willed herself to stay alive until the season was over and her beloved Bobby could come home from his basketball to see her. It was during the next two seasons he had all the trouble with Fred Taylor.

Knight's father died a decade later, when Bobby was 29. In those 29 years, Pat Knight owned only three automobiles. Most places, he walked. He rarely tipped; "Nobody tips me," he would say. The only thing he ever bought on time was the house on North Vine Street. And he hated to do that. He took out a 20-year mortgage and paid it off in 4½ years. He gave up golf and many other pleasures until he could square accounts. Now, you see, now we are talking about discipline. "My father was the most disciplined man I ever saw," Bobby Knight says. "Most people, they hear the word discipline, and right away they think about a whip and a chair. I've worked up my own definition. And this took a long time. Discipline: doing what you have to do, and doing it as well as you possibly can, and doing it that way all the time."

Pat Knight was very hard-of-hearing, which limited his communications with his son. He would turn off his hearing aid every night and read the evening paper, front to back. "And he believed every word he read," Knight says emphatically, explaining why he becomes so distraught when the press fails to meet his expectations. Pat also introduced his son to hunting and fishing, and to this day that's Bobby's escape. There are no outsiders to louse it up; it's as pure, God willing, as basketball should be.

"People are always surprised when they hear about my fishing," he says. "Everybody thinks I'm going to get so wound up I'm going to have to leave in five minutes. But I don't carry over that stuff you see on the court. There's nothing I enjoy more than winding down some river, floating along, watching for deer, counting the squirrels." A warm smile, a pause, and then: "And nobody knows what you've done that day except you and the guys involved."

### IV: Women

This particular day, he had been away, hunting down in southern Indiana with some of the guys. Nancy had a meeting to attend in the evening, but she passed it up, because Bobby was late getting back. She cooked a huge, scrumptious dinner, but apparently that's standard fare at the Knights'.

Whatever other ambiguities Knight has to deal with in these cloudy times, Nancy isn't one of them. "She's just a great coach's wife," he says. She knows her man, too, knows not to intrude on the game. When Indiana won the NCAA in Philadelphia in 1976, Knight and some old friends from basketball and Orrville went out to dinner afterward — the victory celebration, the culmination of his career. Neither Nancy nor any other woman was included.

Says Steve Green, one of Knight's better players, who graduated in 1975, "He feels women are just an obstacle that must be overcome. Players' girl friends didn't really exist for him. Just didn't exist. If he heard me talking to someone about my wedding, he'd be yelling, 'Don't do it! Don't do it!'"

It is instructive that Knight's language seldom goes beyond the anal stage. In the course of a day, he describes an incredible number of things being done to the derriere: it's burned, chewed out, kicked, frosted, blistered, chipped at, etc. Plus, almost every time he loses his temper, there is invariably a literal bottom line, involving the suggestion that the posterior be used as a depot — for money, a whistle, the Time and Life Building, what have you. But, when addressing the fairer sex, Knight has a reputation for purposely expanding his anatomical vocabulary to include graphic references to the male genitalia. This curious proclivity has offended people of both sexes and, perhaps more than anything, has tarnished his personal reputation.

One of Knight's heroes is Harry S. Truman, which is why Give-'em-hell Harry is conspicuously honored by bric-a-brac in Knight's office. But this graphic assessment of another President, Lyndon Johnson, by columnist William S. White, is eerily applicable to Knight: "His shortcomings were not the polite, pleasant little shortcomings, but the big ones — high temper, of course, too driving a personality, both of others and himself, too much of a perfectionist by far. . . . Curiously enough I think one of the reasons he didn't go down better . . . was that his faults were highly masculine faults and that our society is becoming increasingly less masculine; that there's a certain femininity about our society that he didn't fit into."

On the subject of Bobby and women, Nancy Knight demurs: "I certainly couldn't have been married more than 17 years to a man who hates women. But I can understand how Bobby feels about some of them. I believe a woman should try and stay in the home. I've never been anything but very happy and satisfied to spend my life raising a family."

Nancy is, really, the only woman who ever came from the outside into Knight's life. She isn't pretentious, and their sprawling house, hidden in the woods just outside of Bloomington, is warm and comfortable. But those who would deal glibly in harsh housewife stereotypes must be careful. Everyone who knows the Knights well has the same one secret: Nancy influences Bobby *more than you ever would guess.*

Like many coaches, she often speaks for her husband in the first person plural — "We got the job at West Point" — but in neither a proprietary nor insecure way. He has the court, she has the home. It's defined.

Nancy acknowledges that Bobby's disputes with the press may well be exacerbated by her overreaction to criticism of him. "I read about this ogre," she says, "and he's the gentlest, kindest person to his family. He does so much good everywhere. I just can't stand to see the man I love being torn apart."

It would also seem that Bobby is equally protective of Nancy. His seemingly exaggerated responses in two major controversies may be traced in part to the fact that Nancy was involved peripherally in each. His protracted altercation with this magazine centers on disputes he has had with Senior Writer Curry Kirkpatrick, who did a piece on the Hoosiers in 1975. But Nancy was also personally wounded by a throwaway line of Kirkpatrick's, just as she had been by a passing reference another SI writer, Barry McDermott, made in an earlier article. In trying to humorously mock Knight's martinetism, McDermott suggested that the Hoosier players had gone over to the coach's house for a holiday meal of bread and water. Nancy, who prides herself on being a gracious hostess and accomplished cook, took the crack literally. "I cried and cried," she says.

Then there were the 1979 Pan Am Games. Puerto Rico was, in many respects, an accident waiting to happen. Those who know Knight best say the episode traumatized him, and while he's a chatterbox, he talks compulsively on this subject. And he still won't give an inch. "There is no way I was going down there and turn the other cheek," he says. "If there was trouble, I was ready to give it right back to them. The first day we were down there, they burned some American flags. There was tremendous resentment toward the United States, tremendous hostility. Listen, America means a lot to me. If the guy . . ."

What guy?

"The *Guy.* If The Guy says tomorrow, hey, this country is in trouble and it needs you in this position or that one, then I give up coaching tomorrow and go."

So, even before the officious San Juan policeman threatened him — cursing him, poking at him — Knight was simmering. Then he became concerned for the safety of Nancy and his two sons. "It was terrifying," she says. "We had to change apartments. I couldn't sit in my seat at the games. I had to stay at the press table. I feared for my life and my children's."

However Knight behaved in Puerto Rico — "You have no respect for anybody. You treat us like dirt. You are an embarrassment to America, our country. You are an Ugly American," a Puerto Rican sports official snapped at him after the Pan Am basketball final — it must be understood that Knight perceived, correctly or not, that the three things he values most in his life were being menaced — his family, his country and his team.

## V: Players

Late in his senior year at Ohio State, Knight considered a job at a high school in Celina, Ohio, as the coach of basketball and an assistant in football. He liked the place, but walking back across the school's gridiron, he kicked at the turf and shook his head. "I thought, if I'm going to be a basketball coach, I can't be diverted," he says. "I wanted vertical concentration. That's still the essence of my coaching." So he took a lesser job as a basketball assistant, without any football responsibility, in Cuyahoga Falls, Ohio. In his first game as head coach of the 10th-graders, he broke a clipboard.

Intensity?

A year later, with Taylor's help, the Brat from Orrville got the assistant's post at West Point under Tates Locke, enlisting in the Army to qualify for the job. When Locke left in 1965, the brass stunned everybody by giving Pfc. Knight the job. "I've never had any apologies for being a head coach at 24," he says. "I was making $99 a month then. I have no sympathy for people who don't make progress because they won't accept the pay somewhere."

Money has never motivated Knight. He has turned down raises, preferring that the money go to his assistants, and he professes not even to know what his salary is — except that, relative to what other teachers at Indiana make, it's too much. This is not to say, of course, that Knight wears a hair shirt. He has a television show, a summer basketball camp, the free use of a car, and, he volunteers, Checkers-like, "I did take a fishing rod once." Also, it's an absolute point of pride with him that he must be paid as much as the Hoosier football coach, Lee Corso. But just as pointedly he has advised alumni and the commercial camp-followers who grubstake coaches on the side to take a wide berth. Recently, however, Knight decided he was a fool to look a gift horse in the mouth, so he solicited bids from shoe companies that were willing to pay him in the hope that his players would wear their sneakers. Adidas won, but instead of sticking this "pimp money," as he calls it, in his own pocket, Knight is turning it over to the university.

This isn't going to endear Knight to the coach who's looking to put a new Florida room on the house, just as a lot of Knight's colleagues weren't thrilled two years ago when he kicked three players off his team for abuses of training rules (drugs, obviously), and then trumpeted that he was the only coach extant with the "guts" to live up to his principles.

But his honor even exceeds his smugness. "He just doesn't cheat," says Newell. "Never. Bobby doesn't even rationalize. Instead, what he does do is the single most important thing in coaching: he turns out educated kids who are ready for society."

Now Knight is on an even broader crusade, trying to impose on others, by legislation, his devotion to academics. He would like the NCAA to pass a regulation that would deny a college some of its allotment of athletic scholarships if its players don't graduate within a year after their eligibility ends. That is, if a coach has five so-called student-athletes finishing up on the team in 1981 and only two graduate by 1982, then the coach can only replace the five with two new recruits. "With this, you're making the faculty a police department for the NCAA," Knight says. "Even if you can get a few professors to pimp for a coach, you can't buy a whole damn faculty." He laughs, devilishly. "And how can a coach vote against this plan? How can anyone vote publicly against education?"

Nothing pleases Knight as much as the success his players have had off the court. Indeed, he uses their accomplishments to justify the controversial "way we operate," saying, "Look, if all our players were losing jobs, I'd have to reassess my way. And if I heard some of my old players blistering my ass for the way I run things, I'd have to reassess. But, you see, despite all the crap you read, the only ones who've ever complained are the kids who didn't play, got frustrated and quit."

But, tit for tat, it may also be true that Knight's players have a high success rate because only success-oriented types would select Indiana basketball in the first place. In other words, the twigs only grow as they were bent a long time ago.

Knight's honesty extends to his recruiting. When a recruit is brought to Bloomington, he's introduced to the whole squad, and not merely sequestered with a happy star, a Mr. Personality and a pretty cheerleader. Parents of recruits are encouraged to talk with parents of present squad members. Knight doesn't have a missionary instinct. He isn't, he says, "an animal trainer. Recruit jackasses, they play like jackasses." Instead: "We've drawn up a personality profile, and you might even say it's a narrow-minded thing."

So, black or white, rich or poor, the neatly groomed Indiana players tend to be well-intentioned young things, upwardly mobile, serious about education and so well adjusted that they can endure Coach

Knight's wrath in fair exchange for the bounty of his professional genius. Calculated coach, calculated players.

The hand-picked Hoosiers are expected to speak to the press, even in defeat, the better to mature and cope. They dress in coats and ties on game days, and during the season must wear trim haircuts, without beards or mustaches.

Significantly, things have gone awry only since the national championship season, soon after which a number of players quit, some castigating Knight, and two seasons after that when the coach bounced the three players for disciplinary reasons. "All of a sudden I won, and I thought I could be a social worker, too," he says. "I thought I could take a guy off death row at Sing Sing and turn him into a basketball player." Never again. The prime result of that convulsion has been an even more careful weeding-out process. A single blackball from a team member can eliminate a prospect from consideration, and as a consequence, a sort of natural selection of the species has occurred. The system has become so inbred that, as contradictory as this sounds, rough-tough Knight's team now includes a bunch of nice Nellys. The Hoosier basketball coaches all worried about this even before this rather disappointing season — Indiana was 10–6 at the end of last week — confirmed their fears. Knight himself, like a grizzled old soldier, waxes nostalgic about the single-minded roughnecks who chopped their way to victory for him at the Point.

Had Knight never won a game at Indiana, he would have secured a lasting reputation for his work at Army, where he succeeded with little talent and no height. At Indiana, as well, the mark of Knight as coach goes far beyond his mere W-L totals. When he arrived in Bloomington, the entire Big Ten played run-and-gun, in the image of Indiana, the conference's traditional lodestar: racehorse ball, the Hurryin' Hoosiers. It wasn't just a catchy sports nickname. It was a real statement. The Hurryin' Hoosiers. The Bronx Bombers. The Monsters of the Midway. There aren't many of them. But no matter how much the old alumni whined at the loss of tradition and hittin' a hundred, Knight went his own way. From Knight's arrival through last week, Indiana has gone 215–65, but, more significantly, the average Big Ten score has declined from 74.0 to 67.5 in that span.

His strategic axioms are firm — no zones, disciplined offense — but he exercises latitude year by year, permitting himself to be dictated to by his material and the state of the art. He has such consummate confidence in his ability as a coach that he suffers no insecurity about crediting the sources of his handiwork. It all came from other coaches, didn't it? His defense is based on the old Ohio State pressure game, which Taylor had borrowed from Newell. His offense is an amalgam of the freelancing style used at Princeton in the early '60s, by Butch van Breda Kolff ("The best college coach I ever saw"), intertwined with the passing game that the venerable Hank Iba employed at Oklahoma State.

This season Knight was willing to modify some of his most cherished tenets to permit Isiah Thomas more artistic freedom. But, ultimately, those who would survive at Indiana, much less succeed, must subjugate themselves to the one man and his one way. Incredibly, 10 of Knight's former assistants are head coaches at major colleges, but those who coach under him are strictly that: underlings. Among other things, they aren't allowed to utter so much as a word of profanity before the players. Only Bobby.

He prowls the practice court, slouched, belly out, usually with a sour, disbelieving expression upon his visage. He is dressed in Indiana red and white, but of a different mix-and-match from his assistants'. Except for a few instructions barked out by these subordinates, the place is silent as a tomb. Only the most privileged visitors are permitted to watch this class.

The chosen few watch on two levels of consciousness: what they see before them, and what they anticipate Coach Knight might do next. If he really contrives to make a point, he will perhaps merely rage, or pick up a chair and slam it against the wall, or dismiss a hopeless athlete. It's like technical fouls — you don't ever get them, you take them. And, like every good coach, Knight knows how to deal with the unexpected. One day a few years ago Knight kicked a ball in anger. He caught it perfectly on his instep and the ball soared toward the very heavens, straight up. More miraculously, when it plummeted back to earth, it fell into a wastebasket, lodging there. It was a million-to-one shot, something from a Road Runner cartoon. But nobody dared change his expression. Finally, Knight began to grin, then to laugh, and only at that point did everyone else break up.

"I've always said, all along, that if I ever get to a point where I can't control myself, I'll quit," Knight says stoutly, though unmindful, perhaps, that he can drive things out of control even as he skirts the edge himself.

## VI: More Rabbits

John Havlicek once said, "Bobby was quite a split personality. There were times when we were good friends and, then, like that, times when he wouldn't even talk to me." Knight says, "My manners set me apart in a little cocoon, and that's something that's very beneficial to me." Maybe, but too many people humor Knight instead of responding to him, and that may be the single real deprivation of his life.

The one group of people who can still treat him honestly are the older coaches, Dutch uncles, who have earned his respect. A few years ago he took on as an assistant Harold Andreas, the man who had first hired him as an assistant at Cuyahoga Falls. What a wonderful gesture! Andreas retired from coaching in 1977, and so, in Andreas' place as the father/grandmother figure, Knight hired Roy Bates, who used to coach one of Orrville High's rivals. Bates, who recently took a leave of absence because of poor health, is a no-nonsense fellow with a crippled left arm, whose teams were 441–82 in basketball and 476–52 in baseball. Bates adored Knight, and though Knight had three younger assistants, it was the older man he was closest to, literally and otherwise. Bates always sat next to him on the bench.

Still Bates had to be tested, like everyone else. He has had a radio show in Ohio since 1949, and one time a while ago, when he was staying at the Knights', he asked Bobby to do a five-minute tape with him. Bobby said sure, but then he put Bates off and put him off. Finally, one day Bates said, "You know, Bobby, I've had that radio show for 30 years without you on it." And with that, he put on his coat and headed for the car. By the time Bates had started up the driveway, Knight was out there, waving for him to come back, and as soon as Bates arrived back at his home in Ohio, Bobby was on the phone to him. Knight was still in control of himself. But not of events.

"Bobby has got so much," Bates says. "And nobody can ever get him. He doesn't cheat. He doesn't drink. He doesn't even chase women. But for some reason he thinks he has been a bad boy, and no matter how successful he becomes, he thinks he must be punished."

This may be the best clue of all. Certainly, Knight accepts success defensively, if not suspiciously. His office celebrates underdogs like Truman and Lombardi, who weren't expected to triumph but, given the chance, thrived on their own sweet terms. And Patton is in evidence, as you might expect. A mean-spirited quote of his hangs on the wall, keynoting a display — an anthology — of paranoid sentiments.

Patton warns ominously that if you strive for a goal, "your loyal friends [will do] their hypocritical Goddamndest to trip you, blacken you and break your spirit." A flanking prayer advises, "If man thwart you pay no heed/If man hate you have no care. . . ." And an essay entitled "The Penalty of Leadership" warns, "The reward is widespread recognition, the punishment fierce denial and detraction."

Is it really that lonely at the top?

Knight also passes out copies of *If* to visitors.

And yet, as wary as he is of the hypocritical rabbits all around him, Knight is, in many respects, even more unsparing of himself. The game, we hear so often, has passed so-and-so by. With Knight, it may be the reverse; he may have passed it by. But he loves it so, and therefore he must concoct hurdles so that he can still be challenged by it. He even talks a lot about how nobody is really capable of playing the game well. Ultimately, it may be the final irony that the players themselves must become interlopers, separating him from the game.

Already he has gone so far that at age 40 winning is no longer the goal. "Look, I know this," he says. "If you're going to play the game, you're going to get more out of it winning. I know that, sure. Now, at West Point I made up my mind to win — *gotta win*. Not at all costs. Never that. But winning was the hub of everything I was doing. And understand, I've never gotten over West Point. Winning had to be more important there, and I had a point to prove. I was just coming off a playing career during which I didn't do as well as I'd hoped. I had to win. And so, to some extent, I won't ever change.

"But somewhere I decided I was wrong. You could win and still not succeed, not achieve what you should. And you can lose without really failing at all. But it's harder to coach this way, with this, uh, approach. I'm sure I'd be easier on myself and on other people if just winning were my ultimate objective." He pauses; he is in his study at home, amid his books, away from all the basketball regalia. "I never said much about this before."

It was a good secret. Now, Bobby Knight is one step closer to utter control of his game. Now all those dim-witted rabbits cannot touch him. They'll be looking at the scoreboard and the AP poll, judging him by those, but they won't have a clue, not the foggiest. Nobody holds a mortgage on him. Now, you see, now we are talking about definition.

Nancy says: "People keep asking me if Bobby is mellowing. We're not mellowing. What we are, we're growing up with the game. You've got to remember that not many people get a chance to start coaching in their 20s. We're not mellowing. Growing up is still more of the word for us."

There is still so much time for the Knights to take what is theirs and enjoy it. It can be a great life (someday).

1985

## Frank Deford

......................................................................................................

# The Boxer and the Blonde

FROM *Sports Illustrated*

THE BOXER and the blonde are together, downstairs in the club cellar. At some point, club cellars went out, and they became family rooms instead. This is, however, very definitely a club cellar. Why, the grand-children of the boxer and the blonde could sleep soundly upstairs, clear through the big Christmas party they gave when everybody came and stayed late and loud down here. The boxer and the blonde are sitting next to each other, laughing about the old times, about when they fell hopelessly in love almost half a century ago in New Jersey, at the beach. *Down the shore* is the way everyone in Pennsylvania says it. This club cellar is in Pittsburgh.

The boxer is going on 67, except in *The Ring* record book, where he is going on 68. But he has all his marbles; and he has his looks (except for the fighter's mashed nose); and he has the blonde; and they have the same house, the one with the club cellar, that they bought in the summer of 1941. A great deal of this is about that bright ripe summer, the last one before the forlorn simplicity of a Depression was buried in the thick-braided rubble of blood and Spam. What a fight the boxer had that June! It might have been the best in the history of the ring. Certainly, it was the most dramatic, all-time, any way you look at it. The boxer lost, though. Probably he would have won, except for the blonde — whom he loved so much, and wanted so much to make proud of him. And later, it was the blonde's old man, the boxer's father-in-law (if you can believe this), who cost him a rematch for the heavyweight championship of the world. Those were some kind of times.

The boxer and the blonde laugh again, together, remembering how they fell in love. "Actually, you sort of forced me into it," she says.

"I did you a favor," he snaps back, smirking at his comeback. After a couple of belts, he has been known to confess that although he fought twenty-one times against world champions, he has never yet won a decision over the blonde — never yet, as they say in boxing, *outpointed* her. But you can sure see why he keeps on trying. He still has his looks? Hey, you should see her. The blonde is past 60 now, and she's still cute as a button. Not merely beautiful, you understand, but schoolgirl cute, just like she was when the boxer first flirted with her down the shore in Jersey. There is a picture of them on the wall. Pictures cover the walls of the club cellar. This particular picture was featured in a magazine, the boxer and the blonde running, hand in hand, out of the surf. Never in your life did you see two better-looking kids. She was Miss Ocean City, and Alfred Lunt called him "a Celtic god," and Hollywood had a part for him that Errol Flynn himself wound up with after the boxer said no thanks and went back to Pittsburgh.

The other pictures on the walls of the club cellar are mostly of fighters. Posed. Weighing in. Toe to toe. Bandaged. And ex-fighters. Mostly in Las Vegas, it seems, the poor bastards. And celebrities. Sinatra, Hope, Bishop Sheen. Politicians. Various Kennedys. Mayor Daley. President Reagan. Vice-President Bush. More fighters. Joe Louis, whom the boxer loved so much, is in a lot of the pictures, but the largest single photograph belongs to Harry Greb, the Pittsburgh Windmill, the middleweight champeen, the only man ever to beat Gene Tunney. When the boxer's mother died that summer of '41, one of the things that mattered most then was to get her the closest possible plot in Calvary Cemetery to where Harry Greb already lay in peace.

But then, down on the far wall, around the corner from Greb, behind the bar, there's another big photograph, and it's altogether different from the others, because this one is a horizontal. Boxing pictures are either square, like the ring itself, or vertical, the fighter standing tall, fists cocked high. If you see a horizontal, it's almost surely not a boxing photograph. More than likely it's from another sport; it's a team picture, all the players spread out in rows. And sure enough, the photograph on the far wall is of the 1917 New York Giants, winners of the National League pennant, and there in the middle of the back row, with a cocky grin hung on his face, is Greenfield Jimmy Smith. The story really starts with him. He was the one who introduced the boxer and the blonde down the shore.

The book on Greenfield Jimmy Smith as a ballplayer was good mouth, no hit (.219 lifetime). His major talent earned him another nickname up in the bigs, Serpent Tongue. Muggsy McGraw, the Giants' manager, kept Smith around pretty much as a bench jockey. But after the Giants lost to the White Sox in the '17 Series, four games to two, McGraw traded him. That broke Smith's heart. He loved McGraw. They were both tough cookies.

"Ah, rub it with a brick," Greenfield Jimmy would say whenever anybody complained of an injury. He was just a little guy, maybe 5'9", a banty rooster, but one time he went over to the Dodger dugout and yelled, "All right, you so-and-sos, I'll fight you one at a time or in groups of five." Not a single Dodger took up the offer.

Greenfield Jimmy's grandchildren remember a day in Jimmy's sixties when he took them out for a drive. A truck got behind him coming up Forbes Avenue and sat on his tail, and Greenfield Jimmy slowed down. The truck driver rested on his horn until finally the grandfather pulled his car over and got out. Livid, the big truck driver came over and started hollering down at the little old guy. Softly Greenfield Jimmy cut in, "Oh, I'm so sorry, but my neighbor over there saw the whole thing."

"What neighbor?" the big truck driver asked, twisting his head to catch a glimpse of this witness. That was his mistake. As soon as he turned to the side, Greenfield Jimmy reared back and popped him flush on the chin. The old man wasn't anything but a banjo hitter on the diamond, but he could sure slug off it.

Greenfield Jimmy played in the bigs as late as '22, but by then the Eighteenth Amendment was the law of the land, and he was discovering that his playing baseball was getting in the way of a more lucrative new career, which was providing alcoholic beverages to those who desired them, notwithstanding their legal unavailability. Sometimes, he would even carry the hooch about in the big trunks that held the team's uniforms and equipment.

Back in Pittsburgh, where he hailed from — the Greenfield section, as you might imagine — Greenfield Jimmy Smith became a man of substance and power. He consorted with everybody, priests and pugs and politicians alike. He ran some speakeasies and, ultimately, the Bachelor's Club, which was the classiest joint in town — a "city club," so-called, as opposed to the numerous neighborhood clubs, which would let in anybody with a couple of bucks' annual dues and the particularly correct European heritage. But the Bachelor's Club was a plush place, and some of Pittsburgh's finest made a great deal of walking-around money by overlooking its existence. Even after repeal, the Bachelor's Club offered games of chance for those so inclined. It helped that, like so much of the Steel City constabulary, Greenfield Jimmy Smith was Irish.

The Bachelor's Club was located in the East Liberty section of Pittsburgh — or 'Sliberty, as it's pronounced in the slurred argot of the community. In a city of neighborhoods, before automobiles begat suburbs, 'Sliberty was known as a very busy place; people came to shop there. For action, though, it was probably not the match of Oakland, a couple of miles away. Most neighborhoods in Pittsburgh were parochial, with a single ethnic legacy, but Oakland had more of a mix and stronger outside influences as well, inasmuch as it embraced the University of Pittsburgh and Forbes Field (where the Pirates played), and the Duquesne Gardens, which must surely be the only boxing arena that was ever set right across the street from a cathedral, which, in this particular case, was St. Paul's.

The Gardens was an old converted carbarn — which, once upon a time, was a place where streetcars were kept when they were sleeping. Pittsburgh was strictly a streetcar town. That was how everybody got to the steel mills. Only in Pittsburgh, nobody ever said "carbarn." They said "coreborn." In Pittsburgh, even now, they don't know how to correctly pronounce any of the vowels and several of the consonants. Even more than the *a*'s, they mess up the *o*'s. A cawledge, for example, is what Pitt is; a dawler is legal tender; and, at that time, the most popular bawxer at the Duquesne Gardens was a skinny Irish contender from 'Sliberty named Billy Cawn, which, despite the way everybody said it, was, curiously, spelled Conn.

Greenfield Jimmy took a real liking to the kid. They had a lot in common. Somebody asked Conn once if he had learned to fight in the streets; no, he replied, it was a long time before he got to the streets from the alleys. Early in '39, after fifty fights around Pittsburgh and West Virginia and two in San Francisco, Conn finally got a shot in New York. "Uncle" Mike Jacobs, the promoter, brought him to Gotham in order to get beat up by a popular Italian fighter, a bellhop out of San Francisco named Freddie Apostoli. Only it was Conn who beat Apostoli in ten, and then, in a rematch a month later, with 19,000 fans packed to the rafters of the old Madison Square Garden on Eighth Avenue, he beat Apostoli in a fifteen-round bloodbath. As much as possible, then, the idea was to match the ethnic groups, so after Conn had beat the Italian twice, Uncle Mike sent him up against a Jew named Solly Krieger. And when the Irish boy beat Krieger in twelve, he was signed to fight Melio Bettina for the world light-heavyweight title the following July.

Suddenly, Conn was the hottest thing in the ring. "Matinee-idol looks," they all said, curly-haired, quick with a quip, full of fun, free, white, and (almost) 21. Money was burning a hole in his pocket, and the dames were chasing him. Right at the time, he took up with an older woman, a divorcée, and remember, this was back in the days when divorcée meant Look Out. He left her for a couple of days and came to Greenfield Jimmy's summer place down the shore in a Cadillac driven by a chauffeur.

Billy Conn was the cat's meow, and Smith was anxious for his wife and kids to meet him, too. Greenfield Jimmy wasn't just a provider, you understand, but also a great family man, and, they said, he never missed Mass. He thought it was really swell when Billy volunteered to take Mary Louise, his little daughter, out to dinner that evening. She was only 15, and for her to be able to go over to Somers Point and have a meal out with Sweet William, the Flower of the Monongahela, would sure be something she could tell the other girls back at Our Lady of Mercy Academy.

How would Greenfield Jimmy ever know that before the evening was over, Billy Conn would turn to the pretty little 15-year-old kid and say right out, "I'm going to marry you."

Mary Louise managed to stammer back, "You're crazy." She remembered what her father had advised her — that all prizefighters were punchy — only it surprised her that one so young and good-looking could be that way. Only, of course, he wasn't punchy. He had just fallen for the kid doll like a ton of bricks.

So now you see: It is Billy Conn who is the boxer in the club cellar and Mary Louise who is the blonde. By the time Greenfield Jimmy Smith (who prided himself on knowing everything) found out what was going on right under his nose, it was too late.

The Conn house is in the Squirrel Hill district. It has long been mostly a Jewish area, but the house was a good bargain at $17,500 when Billy bought it forty-four years ago because he wanted to stay in the city. Billy is a city guy, a Pittsburgh guy. Billy says, "Pittsburgh is the town you can't wait to leave, and the town you can't wait to get back to." They loved him in Gotham, and they brought him to Tinseltown to play the title role in *The Pittsburgh Kid,* and later he spent a couple of years in Vegas, working the Stardust's lounge as a greeter, like Joe Louis at the Dunes down the Strip. His son Timmy remembers the time a high roller gave the boxer $9,000, just for standing around and being Billy Conn.

But soon the boxer grew tired of that act and came back to the house in Squirrel Hill, where, in the vernacular, he "loafs with" old pals like Joey Diven, who was recognized as the World's Greatest Street Fighter.

Pittsburgh may be a metropolitan area of better than two million souls, but it still has the sense of a small town. "Everybody's closely knitted," Diven explains. "A guy hits a guy in 'Sliberty, everybody knows about it right away, all over." Or it's like this: One time the boxer was trying to get a patronage job with the county for a guy he loafs with. But everybody was onto the guy's act. "Billy," the politician said, "I'd like to help you. I really would. But everybody knows, he just don't ever come to work."

Conn considered that fact. "Look at it this way," he said at last. "Do you *want* him around?" The guy got the job.

Pittsburgh, of course, like everyplace else, has changed . . . only more so. The mills are closed, the skies are clear, and Rand McNally has decreed that it is the very best place to live in the United States. Oakland is just another cawledge town; the warm saloons of Forbes Avenue have become fast-food "outlets." Where Forbes Field once stood is Pitt's Graduate School of Business, and in place of Duquesne Gardens is an apartment house.

It was so different when Conn was growing up. Then it was the best of capitalism, it was the worst of capitalism. The steel came in after the Civil War — Bessemer and his blasts — and then came the immigrants to do the hard, dirty work of making ore into endless rolls of metal. Then the skies were so black with smoke that the office workers had to change their white shirts by lunchtime, and the streetlights seldom went off during the day, emitting an eerie glow that turned downtown Pittsburgh into a stygian nightmare. At the time Conn was a kid, taking up space at Sacred Heart School, H. L. Mencken wrote of Pittsburgh that it was "so dreadfully hideous, so intolerably bleak and forlorn that it reduced the whole aspiration of a man to a macabre and depressing joke."

The people coughed and wheezed, and those who eschewed the respiratory nostrums advertised daily in the newspapers would, instead, repair to the taprooms of Pittsburgh, there to try to cut the grime and soot that had collected in their dusty throats. The Steel City was also know as "the wettest spot in the United States," and even at seven in the morning the bars would be packed three deep, as the night-shift workers headed home in the gloom of another graying dawn, pausing to toss down the favored local boilermaker — a shot of Imperial whiskey chased by an Iron City beer. An Iron and an Imp.

And then another. Can't expect someone to fly on one wing.

Conn's father, Billy, Sr., was such a man. He toiled at Westinghouse for forty years. Eventually, Billy would come to call his old man Westinghouse instead of Dad. But even in the worst of the Depression, Billy, Sr., kept his job as a steam fitter, and he was proud of it, and one day he took his oldest boy down to the plant, and he pointed to it and said, "Here's where you're gonna work, son."

Billy, Jr., was aghast. "That scared the shit out of me," he says. Shortly thereafter he began to apprentice as a prizefighter, and when he got to New York and began to charm the press, he could honestly boast that his greatest achievement in life was never having worked a day.

The mills meant work, but it was a cruel living, and even so recently as the time when Conn was growing up, two-thirds of the work force in Pittsburgh was foreign-born. "People think you gotta be nuts to be a fighter," he says now.

Well?

"Yeah, they're right. I *was* nuts. But it beats working in those mills."

The immigrants who were shipped in from Europe to work in the mills mostly stayed with their own — the Galway Irish on the North Side, the Italians in the Bloomfield section, the Poles and Balkans on the South Side, the Irish in 'Sliberty, the Germans on Troy Hill. Harry Greb was German, but his mother was Irish, which mattered at the gate. Promoters liked Irishers. A good little lightweight named Harry Pitler, Jewish boy, brother of Jake Pitler, who would play for the Pirates and later become a Brooklyn Dodger coach, took the Irish handle of Johnny Ray to fight under. Jawnie Ray, one of Erin's own.

Everybody fought some in Pittsburgh. It was a regular activity, like dancing or drinking. It wasn't just that the men were tough and the skies were mean; it was also a way of representing your parish or your people. It wasn't just that Mr. Art Rooney, promoter, or Mr. Jake Mintz, matchmaker, would pit an Irishman against a Jew or a Pole versus an Italian, or bring in a colored boy the white crowds could root against at Duquesne Gardens. No, it was every mother's son scuffling, on the streets or at the bar rail. It was a way of life. It was also cheap entertainment.

Greenfield Jimmy Smith, as we know, enjoyed fighting all his life. So did Billy Conn, Sr., Westinghouse. Nearing 50, he was arrested and fined a five-spot for street-fighting only a few weeks before his son fought for the heavyweight title. Just for kicks, Westinghouse used to fight Billy all the time. When Westinghouse came to New York to watch his boy in the ring one time, Billy told the press, "My old man is a fighting mick. Give him a day or two here, and he'll find some guys to slug it out with."

Billy fought even more with his younger brother Jackie, who was an absolutely terrific street fighter. One time Jimmy Cannon wrote that "if the ring in Madison Square Garden were made of cobblestones," it would be Jackie Conn, not Billy, who would be the champion of the world. A night or so after Cannon's tribute appeared in the paper, Jackie came strolling into Toots Shor's. He was dressed to the nines, as usual. Jackie fancied himself a fashion plate, and he regularly rifled his brother's wardrobe. So Jackie took a prominent seat at the bar, and he was sitting there, accepting compliments and what-have-you from the other patrons, when a stranger came over to him and asked if he was Jackie Conn, the street-fighting champion of the world.

Jackie puffed up and replied that indeed he was, whereupon the stranger coldcocked him, sending Jackie clattering to the floor of Toots Shor's Saloon. "Now I'm the champion," the guy said.

Still, everybody says that Joey Diven was the best street fighter who ever lived. There are stories that he would, for amusement, take on and beat up the entire Pitt football team. Joey is a decade younger than Billy, in his fifties now, working as an assistant to the Allegheny County commissioner. He is a big, red-faced Irishman. That's unusual because most ace street fighters are little guys. Does Billy Martin come to mind? Big guys grow up figuring nobody will challenge them, so they don't learn how to fight. Big guys break up fights. Little guys are the ones who learn to fight because they figure they had better. Billy always told his three sons, "Don't fight on the streets, because you'll only find out who's good when it's too late."

But Joey Diven was good and big. So first the other Irish pretenders in the neighborhood — the champion of this street or that bar — would come by to find him at the Oakland Cafe, where he loafed, and when he was done beating all those comers, the champs from the other neighborhoods would come over and insult him, so as to get into an inter-ethnic fight.

Insults were automatic. People routinely referred to one another, face to face, with the racial epithets we find so offensive today. For fighting, it was the dagos and the Polacks, the micks and the jigs, and so forth. Sticks and stones. Before a fight with Gus Dorazio, when Dorazio was carrying on at the weigh-in about what color trunks he would wear, Conn cut the argument short by snapping, "Listen, dago, all you're going to need is a catcher's mitt and a chest protector." It was late in Conn's career before he took to using a mouthpiece, because, like his hero Greb, he got a kick out of insulting the people he fought.

On the street, stereotypes prevailed all the more. Usually that meant that everybody (your own group included) was dim-witted, everybody else practiced poor hygiene, everybody else's women were sluts, and everybody but the Jews drank too much and had the most fun. Were the Irish the best fighters? Joey Diven says, "Ah, they just stayed drunk more and stayed louder about it."

One time Joey Diven was working as a doorman over at the AOH on Oakland Avenue. The AOH is the Ancient Order of Hibernians. You needed a card to get into the place, which was located on the third floor, or, as Joey explains it, "Up twenty-eight steps if you accidentally fell down them." This particular night, a guy showed up, but he didn't have a card, so Joey told him to take off. "Come on, let me in, I'm Irish," the guy said. Joey said no card, no admittance, and when the guy persisted, Joey threw him down the steps.

Pretty soon there was a knock on the door again. Joey opened it. Same guy. Same thing: no card. "Come on, let me in, I'm Irish." Joey threw him down the steps again.

A few more minutes and another knock. And get this: It was the same guy. What did Joey do? He ushered him in, and said, "You're right. You must be Irish."

What made Joey Diven such a good street fighter was that he held no illusions. Poor Jackie Conn (who is dead now) was different. He thought he could be as good as his brother in the prize ring. Jackie was on the undercard a night in '39 when Billy defended against Gus Lesnevich, but the kid brother lost a four-rounder. The failure ate him up so, he came apart afterward in the locker room. Just before Billy went off to fight Lesnevich, he had to soothe Jackie and make sure the brother would be taken to the hospital and sedated. Diven was different. "Ah, I didn't ever have the killer instinct like Billy in the ring," he says. "You see, even though Billy's such a God-fearing man, he could be ruthless in the ring. That's why Billy was so good."

Still, Joey will razz Billy good. For example, he says that Conn always was a rotten drinker — "Three drinks, and he's talking about the Blessed Mother or Thomas Aquinas." He also kids Conn that, when he travels, he still sleeps with all his valuables tucked into his pillowcase.

Once when they were staying together in Vegas, Billy got up in the middle of the night to take a leak, and Joey was awakened by the sound of change rattling in the pillowcase. Billy was taking his nickels and dimes with him to the bathroom.

"Hey, Billy," Joey said. "You didn't have to take the pillow to the toilet. There's nobody here."

Conn stopped. "*You're* here," he said.

Joey had a lot of fun with Billy. They had a lot of fun street-fighting. It wasn't ever vicious. In those days, nobody ever drew guns or knives or even clubs. Nobody was loco with drugs. You could do all the same stuff Billy did in the ring — gouging and biting and that type of thing, plus the friendly name-calling — all the things that made up what used to be known as *a fair fight.* "No booting, though," says Joey.

"And it never took more than four or five minutes. Somebody would get in one good shot, and that would wear you out pretty quick, and after that there'd be a lot of mauling and rassling, and then it was history." It wasn't at all like in the movies, where the fights go on forever no matter how many times people get clobbered. "As soon as a guy said he'd had enough, that was it. No more," Joey says. That was the code. "Then you'd go back into the joint together and buy each other a drink, maybe even end up getting fractured together." An Iron and an Imp, twice. Do this again for both of us. One more time.

That was the sort of environment young Billy grew up in in 'Sliberty — scrapping with everyone in the neighborhood, running errands for the bootleggers over on Station Street, filching pastries from the bakery wagon to put a little something extra on the family table. There were four younger brothers and sisters. To help make ends meet, Billy's father didn't altogether shy away from working with the bootleggers; the authorities estimated there were 10,000 stills in the Pittsburgh area during Prohibition. Westinghouse sometimes brewed beer in the family bathtub. For Mrs. Conn, the former Marguerite McFarland, the most devout of Catholic women, this made it nearly impossible to ensure that cleanliness would take its assigned runner-up spot to godliness. "Be patient, woman, the beer'll be ready in a few days," Westinghouse would chide his wife as she fretted over her dirty-necked tykes.

Billy adored his mother. He was the one who named her Maggie, and it was that — not Mother or Mom — he called her as he grew older. He always gives nicknames to the people he loves the most. Maggie had come over in steerage from County Cork when she was a young girl, and she never did lose all of her brogue. She grew plump, but with her magnificent skin and blue eyes in a beautiful face framed by black hair, she was a colleen to the day she died. She lavished all that she could upon her oldest, and she was not frightened when he told her he wanted to be a boxer. She knew how hard it was in the mills, and when Westinghouse gave the boy gloves one Christmas, Maggie made him some fine, Celtic green trunks.

Billy Conn leans back in his chair in the club cellar and takes a deep drag on his cigarette, and this is what he says: "Your mother should be your best friend."

Maggie's boy did have one other talent besides boxing and loafing, and that was art. He could draw, and if he were growing up in Pittsburgh today, when Irish boys stay in school and don't lace on gloves, no doubt he would become an artist or a draftsman of some sort. But he never pursued drawing, never even played team sports. His children — Timmy, Billy, Susan, and Mike — all had to learn games from their granddad Greenfield Jimmy, and they still like to laugh at their old man, the former champion of the world, because he throws like a girl.

He stayed two years in the eighth grade at Sacred Heart before one of the sisters suggested that he give up his seat to someone who might use it to greater advantage. He departed school then, but it didn't matter because already, as he puts it, "I was going to cawledge at Jawnie Ray's." That was in 'Sliberty. Ray had retired from fighting, but he ran a gym so he could keep himself in bootleg whiskey. It came in milk bottles and cost 15 cents a pint.

The first time Billy ventured into the gym, Ray was amazed at how tiny and smooth the boy's face was. And Billy couldn't have weighed more than 80, maybe 85, pounds. But Jawnie let him audition in the ring, and he saw the instincts and the courage right off. So he let Billy work around the gym, tidying the place up, fetching him his booze, earning the occasional chance to spar.

One day a bunch of older neighborhood toughs confronted Billy as he came back to the gym toting a pint of moonshine. "What are you, a messenger boy for the rummy?" one of them said, and they jostled and taunted Billy.

He pulled himself up as tall as he could, and he hollered back, "You bums! Someday, I'm gonna be a champeen!"

They laughed, and he went on inside and gave Ray the moonshine. Billy came to call him Moonie for his addiction, and Moonie called him Junior. "All right now, Junior," Moonie would say, swilling the rotgut, "keep your hands up and punch straight." This was the shell defense

Jawnie Ray taught. "Moonie was quiet, but he was a Michelangelo as a teacher. Hell, I didn't know he drank until one day I saw him sober. You know how it is — no Jews drink. I get the one who does. Only I tell you one thing, Jawnie Ray knew more about bawxing drunk than anybody else did sober."

Conn stayed with Ray in the gym three years but never was allowed to engage in an official fight. That was because Ray didn't believe in amateur fisticuffs. If you were going to chance being busted in the kisser, then you should make a dawler off it. Also, what could you learn from some amateur? During one period in the late thirties and early forties, the Pittsburgh area gave the world five champions, and Conn got to practice against a lot of talent in the gym. When Joe Louis came to town to fight Hans Birkie, Conn made a buck holding the spit box for the Brown Bomber. It was the first time he ever saw the man with whom he would be linked forever in boxing history.

Finally, when he was 17 years old, Ray drove him down to Fairmont, West Virginia, where he went four rounds against an experienced 24-year-old named Dick Woodwer. There were probably 300 fans at the armory, and Woodwer outpointed the novice. Conn's share was $2.50.

Ray gave him four bits. "Hey, Moon, what is this?" Billy said. "I get two and a half."

"We gotta eat," Ray said.

"Yeah, but how come we're both eating out of my share?"

"You were the one who lost," said Ray.

They never had a contract, but no other man ever managed Billy Conn. He even told the mob to back off when it tried to muscle in.

In the beginning, Ray had Billy fighting somebody somewhere every two weeks or so. Fairmont, Charleston, Wheeling, Johnstown. It was nickel hamburgers, 15-cent moonshine, and 16-cent-a-gallon gas that kept them going. "You tell kids that nowadays, they're sure you ran into too many of Joe Louis's blows," Billy says. And nowadays it's not just the prices that are different. A prospect is brought along against handpicked roundheels on Sunday afternoon TV. After ten bouts everybody gets to fight for the championship of something or other. Conn was barely out of West Virginia after ten fights, and even after fourteen he was hardly .500; then he had to win or draw thirteen in a row before he was allowed a ten-rounder. It was against Honeyboy Jones.

But he was learning. Always, he learned. Even when he fought for championships, he seldom won any of the early rounds. "They don't matter," he says. They counted, but they didn't matter, because that was the time you picked up the other guy's style. And Ray put him in against everybody, every style.

Near the end of 1936, when Conn was still only 18, Ray threw the boy in against the older Fritzie Zivic. "He put an awful face on me," Billy says, and he still honors Zivic, a Pittsburgh guy, by calling him the dirtiest fighter he ever met. But Billy outpointed Zivic and moved out of the welterweights.

A few months later, he won his twenty-third in a row over a red-haired black powerhouse named Oscar Rankins, who knocked Billy down in the eight with such a stiff blow that, says Conn, "I didn't know I'd won till I read it the next day in the paper." Years later, when Joe Louis heard that Conn had fought Rankins, he said to Billy, "The people who managed you must not have liked you very much. Nobody would let *me* fight that sonuvabitch."

Conn's favorite photograph in the club cellar is a wirephoto of himself bandaged and stitched after he won the rematch with Freddie Apostoli. The headline reads: IF THIS IS THE WINNER, WHAT DOES THE LOSER LOOK LIKE? Conn howls at that, and to this day he speaks with greatest affection about the fighters who did him the most damage.

Damn, it was fun. After he beat Zivic and made big money, $2,180, Conn bought himself a brand new Chevy for $600. When he whipped Bettina for the title, he said, "Gee, I'm champion. Now I can eat regular." Then he went back home to Pittsburgh and out to 'Sliberty. "I hadn't been around the corner for a long time," he says. But now he made a point of going back, and he found the guys who had ridiculed him when he had just been starting out, running errands for Jawnie Ray. They were loafing in a bar. "Remember the messenger boy you laughed at?" he asked, and they nodded, cowering. Billy brought his hands up fast, and they ducked away, but all he did was lay a lot of big bills on the hardwood. "Well, all right," Billy said, "stay drunk a long time on the light-heavyweight champeen of the world."

He bought Maggie anything she wanted. He gave her champagne, the real stuff. She loved champagne. He bought presents for his younger brothers and sisters, and for the dames he found and who found him. He was even interviewed by a New York fashion editor on the subject of how a woman should be turned out.

"I guess these women's fashions are O.K.," Conn declared. "That is, except those dizzy hats and the shoes some of them wear. . . . I wouldn't wear a boxing glove for a hat, but some girls do. . . . Plaid dresses are pips. I think plaid looks swell on any woman, and I like any color as long as it's red. . . . Some evening dresses are pretty nice, if they're lacy and frilly and with swoopy skirts. But most girls look too much like China dolls when they're dressed in evening dresses. But what the hell! They're going to dress up the slightest chance you give 'em. And I'm for giving 'em every chance."

"We're just a bunch of plain, ordinary bums having a good time," Jawnie Ray explained. He and Billy would scream at each other and carry on constantly. "I'm glad we ain't got a contract, you dumb mick sonuvabitch," Jawnie would holler, "because maybe I'll get lucky and somebody even dumber than you will steal you from me." "Yeah, you rummy Jew bastard," Billy would coo back. It was like that, right to the end. The last time Billy saw him, Jawnie was at death's door in the hospital, and Joey Diven and Billy were visiting him.

"C'mon, you guys, sneak me outta here for some drinks," Jawnie Ray pleaded from the hospital bed.

"Moonie," Billy replied, "the only way you're gettin' outta this place is with a tag tied on your big toe."

Sometimes Westinghouse joined the traveling party, too, and on one occasion, coming back from Erie, he and Jawnie Ray got into a first-class fight. As Conn described it in a contemporary account, "My old man swung, Jawnie swung. When it was finished, Pop had a broken nose and Jawnie had lost a tooth. That made them pals."

Yes, sir, it was a barrelful of monkeys. They all loved to throw water on one another, too, and to play practical jokes with the telephone and whatnot. Eventually, when Jackie had grown up enough to come on board, it made it even more fun because then Billy had a partner to scuffle with. Billy would always go after Jackie when he caught him wearing his clothes. One time Billy was voted Best-Dressed Sportsman of the Year, so, Billy chuckled, that must have made Jackie the Second-Best-Dressed Sportsman of the Year.

The day before Conn defended his crown in Forbes Field against Bettina in September of '39, Billy found out that Jackie had been joyriding with his pals in Billy's new black Cadillac, so he put out a $300 bounty on his brother, and when he caught up with him he thrashed him bare-knuckled in the garage. "OK, get it over," Jackie said when he had positively had enough, and he laid out his chin for Billy to paste him square on it. Billy popped him a right, and Jackie was sliding down the wall clear across the garage when Jawnie Ray and Uncle Mike Jacobs and the cops burst in, all of them in disbelief that Billy would get into a fraternal dustup right before a championship fight. They were much relieved to discover that the blood all over Billy was only Jackie's.

Billy wiped himself clean and outpointed Bettina in fifteen. He was the toast of Pittsburgh and the world, as well. The *New York Daily News* rhapsodized: "The Irishman is indeed a beauteous boxer who could probably collect coinage by joining the ballet league if he chose to flee the egg-eared and flattened-nose fraternity." When Conn fought in New York, Owney McManus, who ran a saloon in Pittsburgh, would charter trains, and hundreds of the Irish faithful would follow Conn to Gotham — the Ham and Cabbage Special, they called it — and loaf on Broadway, even if it meant that maybe when they went back to the mills in Pittsburgh they'd be handed a DCM.

A DCM is a Don't Come Monday, the pink slip.

When Conn fought in Oakland, at the Gardens, the streetcars would disgorge fans from all over the Steel City. Pittsburgh's streetcar lines were almost all laid out east-west, except for one, which ran north from the mills along the river. It was called the Flying Fraction because it was number 77/54 — a combination of two east-west lines, the 77 and the 54 — and it went right past both the Gardens and Forbes Field. Three rides to a quarter, and if you were getting off for the fights you got a transfer anyhow and sold it for a nickel to the people waiting, so they could save 3 cents on their ride home.

Photos of Conn went up in all the bars where those of Greb and Zivic were to be seen, and in a lot of other places where the Irish wanted strictly their own hero. And now that Billy had grown into a light heavyweight and had beaten all of them, it seemed like the only one left for him to fight was the heavyweight champion, the Brown Bomber himself. There wasn't anybody Irish in the country who wasn't looking forward to that. And by this point, there probably wasn't anybody Irish in Pittsburgh who hadn't seen Billy Conn fight, except for Mary Louise Smith.

"I've never seen a prizefight in my life," she said just the other day. Mary Louise just never cared very much for Billy's business, even when he was earning a living at it.

"You didn't miss anything," Billy replied.

But even if she hadn't seen him work, she was in love with him. She had fallen in love with the boxer. He gave her a nickname, too: Matt — for the way her hair became matted on her brow when she went swimming down the Jersey shore. She was still only a kid, still at Our Lady of Mercy, but she had become even more beautiful than she had been at that first dinner, and the sheltered life Greenfield Jimmy had imposed upon her was backfiring some. Billy had the lure of forbidden fruit. "I was mature for my age," Mary Louise says, "something of a spitfire. And I guess you'd have to say that when my father didn't want me to see Billy, I turned out to be a good prevaricator, too." She sighs. "Billy just appealed to me so."

"Ah, I told her a lot of lies," he says.

They would sneak off, mostly for dinners, usually at out-of-town roadhouses, hideaways where they could be alone, intimate in their fashion, staring into each other's blue eyes. It was so very innocent. He was always in training, and she was too young to drink, and kisses are what they shared. That and their song, "A Pretty Girl Is Like a Melody." Well, Billy made it their song, and he would request it from the big band on Saturdays when they would get all gussied up and go dancing downtown at the William Penn Hotel, which was the fanciest spot in Pittsburgh. And he was the champion of the world, and she was the prettiest girl, dressed all *lacy and frilly and with swoopy skirts.*

Even if Greenfield Jimmy didn't know the half of it, he could sense that it was getting out of hand. Mary Louise played Jo in *Little Women* at Our Lady of Mercy, and he liked that; he wanted her to be an actress, to be something, to move up. He liked Billy, he really did, and he thought he was as good a boxer as he had ever seen, but he didn't want his daughter, his firstborn, marrying a pug. So Greenfield Jimmy sent Mary Louise to Philadelphia, to a classy, cloistered college called Rosemont, and he told the mother superior never to let his daughter see the likes of Mr. Billy Conn.

So Billy had to be content sending letters and presents. When he came into Philly for a fight, he had twenty ringside tickets delivered to Rosemont so that Mary Louise could bring her friends. The mother superior wouldn't let any of the young ladies go, though, and when Billy climbed into the ring and looked down and saw the empty seats, he was crestfallen. His opponent that night was Gus Dorazio, and despite Billy's lipping off at the weigh-in, Billy was even slower than usual to warm up, and the fight went eight rounds before Billy won on a KO.

Greenfield Jimmy was pleased to learn about these events and that Mary Louise was going out with nice young men from the Main Line, who went to St. Joseph's and Villanova, who called for her properly and addressed her as Mary Louise, and not anything common like Matt. Greenfield Jimmy sent her off to Nassau for spring vacation with a bunch of her girlfriends, demure young ladies all.

As for Billy, he went into the heavies, going after Louis. "We're in this racket to make money," Jawnie Ray said. Billy had some now. He rented Maggie and the family a house on Fifth Avenue, an address that means as much in Pittsburgh as it does in New York. One of the Mellons had a mansion on Fifth with sixty-five rooms and eleven baths. "The days of no money are over, Maggie," Billy told his mother. She said fine, but she didn't know anybody on Fifth Avenue. Couldn't he find something in 'Sliberty? "Bring your friends over every day," Billy told her.

Maggie was 40 that summer, a young woman with a son who was a renowned champion of the world. But she began to feel a little poorly and went for some tests. The results were not good. Not at all. So now, even if Billy Conn was a champion, what did it mean? Of the two women he loved, one he almost never got to hold, and now the other was dying of cancer.

Conn's first fight against a heavyweight was with Bob Pastor in September of 1940. Pastor irritated him. "I hit him low one time," Billy recalls. "All right, all right. But he just kept on bitching. So now, I'm *really* gonna hit him low. You know, you were supposed to do everything to win." He knocked Pastor out in thirteen, then he outpointed Al McCoy in ten and Lee Savold in twelve, even after Savold busted his nose in the eighth.

All too often now, though, Conn wasn't himself. He couldn't get to see Mary Louise, and worse, Maggie was becoming sicker and weaker, and almost every cent he made in the ring went to pay for the treatment and the doctors and the round-the-clock nurses he ordered. "His mother's illness has Billy near crazy at times," Jawnie Ray explained after one especially lackluster bout. Between fights Billy would head back to Pittsburgh and slip up to see Maggie, and, against doctor's orders, he would bring her champagne, the finest, and the two of them would sit there on an afternoon, best friends, and get quietly smashed together. They were the happiest moments Maggie had left.

June 18, 1941, was the night set for the Louis fight at the Polo Grounds, and Uncle Mike Jacobs began to beat the biggest drums for Conn, even as Louis kept trooping the land, beating up on what became known as the Bums-of-the-Month. Incredibly, 27,000 people — most of them coming off the Flying Fraction — showed up at Forbes Field to watch Conn's final tune-up in May, against a nobody named Buddy Knox.

Everywhere, the world was swirling, and that seemed to make even everyday events larger and better and more full of ardor. Even if Americans didn't know what lay ahead, even if they told themselves it couldn't happen here, that foreign wars wouldn't engage us, there may have been deeper and truer instincts that inspired and drove them as the year of 1941 rushed on. It was the last summer that a boy hit .400. It was the only summer that anyone hit safely in fifty-six straight games. A great beast named Whirlaway, whipped by Eddie Arcaro, the little genius they called Banana Nose, ran a Derby so fast that the record would stand for more than twenty years, and he finished up with the Triple Crown in June. That was when the Irishman and the Brown Bomber were poised to do battle in what might have been the most wonderful heavyweight final there ever was. And all this as the Nazis began their move toward Russia and Yamamoto was okaying the attack on Pearl Harbor.

The pace was quickening. Mary Louise was as impetuous now as the boy she loved. It couldn't go on this way anymore. On May 28, a couple of days after he beat Knox, Billy drove her to Brookville, way north out of Pittsburgh, and took out a marriage license. DiMaggio got a triple in Washington that day, at Griffith Stadium, to raise his streak to thirteen. Mary Louise was 18 now, and Greenfield Jimmy couldn't change her plans any more than he could her heart, but she and Billy were good Catholic kids, and they wanted to be married in the Church, and that meant the banns had to be posted.

So Greenfield Jimmy heard, and he fulminated, "I'm just trying to raise a decent family, and I know where these boxers end up." He said he would punch Billy's lights out, and Westinghouse said he would rattle Greenfield Jimmy's cage first. Greenfield Jimmy went directly to the rectory where the bishop lived in Pittsburgh. He banged on the door and said there had better not be any priest anywhere in Pennsylvania who would marry his flesh and blood to the pug.

It worked, too. The next Saturday, Billy left his training camp and went to a nearby parish named St. Philomena's. He and Mary Louise had someone who had promised to marry them at the altar at 9:30 A.M., and an excited crowd had gathered. But the priests wouldn't buck Greenfield Jimmy, and, after a couple of hours of bickering, somebody came out and told the people there wouldn't be any June wedding this day.

Billy went back to prepare to fight the heavyweight champion. Di-Maggio got three singles against the Brownies that afternoon.

The next time Billy left camp, a few days before the bout, he flew to Pittsburgh to see his mother. He probably didn't realize how close to the end she was, because she kept the news from him. "Listen, I've got to live a little longer," Maggie told everyone else in the family. "I can't worry Billy."

He couldn't bring her champagne this time. Instead, he brought her a beautiful diamond bracelet, and he gave it to her. "Maggie," he said, "this is for you." She was so sick, so weak, so in pain that she could barely work up a smile, but she thanked him the best she could. And then she pushed it back.

"Oh, it's so beautiful, Billy," she said. "But don't give it to me. Give it to Mary Louise." And Maggie told him then that he was to marry her, no matter what Greenfield Jimmy said, because he was her boy and a good boy and as good as any boy, and because he loved Mary Louise more than anyone else in the world.

Billy nodded. He kept his hand wrapped around the bracelet. He couldn't stay much longer. Just these few minutes had tired Maggie so. He kissed her and got ready to leave. "Maggie," Billy said, "I gotta go now, but the next time you see me, I'll be the heavyweight champion of the world."

Maggie smiled one more time. "No, son," she said, "the next time I see you will be in Paradise."

Tuesday, the seventeenth, the day before the fight, DiMaggio made it an even thirty in a row, going 1 for 4 against the Chisox across the river in the Bronx. That night, Billy slept hardly at all. And he always slept. Sometimes he would even lie down in the locker room while the under-card bouts were being fought and doze right off just minutes before he had to go into the ring. But this whole night he barely got forty winks. And he wasn't even worrying about getting in the ring with Joe Louis. He was worrying about Maggie and Matt.

At the weigh-in the next morning Louis, who had trained down because of Conn's speed, came in at 200. Conn tipped 169. That made Uncle Mike a bit nervous. It was already 17 to 5 for the champion in the betting, and this weight spread was making the bout look like homicide. Uncle Mike announced Conn's weight at a more cosmetic 174 and Louis at 199½.

Conn went back to his hotel to rest, but the Ham and Cabbage Special had just got in, and all the fans, wearing leprechaun hats and carrying paper shamrocks and clay pipes, came over to see him, and when a bunch of them barged right into his room, Billy went outside and loafed with them.

Finally, Jawnie got him back to his room, but who should come storming in, wearing a zoot suit and smoking a big cigar, but Jackie. Naturally, he and Billy started wrestling each other all over the suite, driving the trainer, Freddie Fierro, nuts. People can get hurt wrestling. At last Fierro was able to separate them, but Billy still couldn't sleep, so he looked in on Jackie and saw him snoring with his mouth open. He called down to room service, ordered a seltzer bottle, and squirted it right into Jackie's mouth. You can bet that woke Jackie up.

Jackie chased Billy into the hall. Billy was laughing, and he wasn't wearing anything but his shorts. That was how Billy spent the day getting ready for the Brown Bomber. Just a few miles away, at the Stadium, DiMaggio went 1 for 3 to stretch it to thirty-one.

Back in Pittsburgh the Pirates had scheduled one of their few night games for this evening, June 18. They knew everybody wanted to stay home to listen to the fight on the radio, so the Pirates announced that when the fight began, the game would be suspended and the radio broadcast would go out over the PA. Baseball came to a halt. Most of America did. Maybe the only person not listening was Maggie. She was so sick the doctors wouldn't let her.

Billy crossed himself when he climbed into the ring that night.

And then the Pirates stopped, and America stopped, and the fight began. Louis's eighteenth defense, his seventh in seven months.

Conn started slower than even he was accustomed to. Louis, the slugger, was the one who moved better. Conn ducked a long right so awkwardly that he slipped and fell to one knee. The second round was worse, Louis pummeling Conn's body, trying to wear the smaller man down. He had thirty pounds on him, after all. Unless you knew the first rounds didn't matter, it was a rout. This month's bum.

In his corner, Conn sat down, spit, and said, "All right, Moon, here we go." He came out faster, bicycled for a while, feinted with a left, and drove home a hard right. By the end of the round he was grinning at the champ, and he winked to Jawnie Ray when he returned to the corner. The spectators were up on their feet, especially the ones who had bet Conn.

The fourth was even more of a revelation, for now Conn chose to slug a little with the slugger, and he came away the better for the exchange. When the bell rang, he was flat out laughing as he came back to his corner. "This is a cinch," he told Jawnie.

But Louis got back on track in the fifth, and the fight went his way for the next two rounds as blood flowed from a nasty cut over the challenger's right eye. At Forbes Field in Pittsburgh the crowd grew still, and relatives and friends listening downstairs from where Maggie lay worried that Billy's downfall was near.

But Conn regained command in the eighth, moving back and away from Louis's left, then ripping into the body or the head. The ninth was all the more Conn, and he grew cocky again. "Joe, I got you," he popped off as he flicked a good one square on the champ's mouth, and then, as Billy strode back to his corner at the bell, he said, "Joe, you're in a fight tonight."

"I knows it," Louis replied, confused and clearly troubled now.

The tenth was something of a lull for Conn, but it was a strategic respite. During the eleventh, Conn worked Louis high and low, hurt the champ, building to the crescendo of the twelfth, when the *New York Herald Tribune* reported in the casual racial vernacular of the time that Conn "rained left hooks on Joe's dusky face." He was a clear winner in this round, which put him up 7–5 on one card and 7–4–1 on another; the third was 6–6. To cap off his best round, Conn scored with a crushing left that would have done in any man who didn't outweigh him by thirty pounds. And it certainly rattled the crown of the world's heavyweight champion. The crowd was going berserk. Even Maggie was given the report that her Billy was on the verge of taking the title.

Only later would Conn realize the irony of striking that last great blow. "I miss that, I beat him," he says. It was that simple. He was nine minutes from victory, and now he couldn't wait. "He wanted to finish the thing as Irishmen love to," the *Herald Tribune* wrote.

Louis was slumped in his corner. Jack Blackburn, his trainer, shook his head and rubbed him hard. "Chappie," he said, using his nickname for the champ, "you're *losing*. You gotta knock him out." Louis didn't have to be told. Everyone understood. Everyone in the Polo Grounds. Everyone listening through the magic of radio. Everyone. There was bedlam. It was wonderful. Men had been slugging it out for eons, and there had been 220 years of prizefighting, and there would yet be Marciano and the two Sugar Rays and Ali, but this was it. This was the best it had ever been and ever would be, the twelfth and thirteenth rounds of Louis and Conn on a warm night in New York just before the world went to hell. The people were standing and cheering for Conn, but it was really for the sport and for the moment and for themselves that they cheered. They could be a part of it, and every now and then, for an instant, *that* is it, and it can't ever get any better. This was such a time in the history of games.

Only Billy Conn could see clearly — the trouble was, what he saw was different from what everybody else saw. What he saw was himself walking with Mary Louise on the boardwalk at Atlantic City, down the shore, and they were the handsomest couple who ever lived, and people were staring, and he could hear what they were saying. What they were saying was: "There goes Billy Conn with his bride. He just beat Joe Louis." And he didn't want to hear just that. What he wanted to hear was: "There goes Billy Conn with his bride. He's the guy who just *knocked out* Joe Louis." Not for himself: That was what Mary Louise deserved.

Billy had a big smile on his face. "This is easy, Moonie," he said. "I can take this sonuvabitch out this round."

Jawnie blanched. "No, no, Billy," he said. "Stick and run. You got the fight won. Stay away, kiddo. Just stick and run, stick and run. . . ." There was the bell for the thirteenth.

And then it happened. Billy tried to bust the champ, but it was Louis who got through the defenses, and then he pasted a monster right on the challenger's jaw. "Fall! Fall!" Billy said to himself. He knew if he could just go down, clear his head, he would lose the round, but he could still save the day. "But for some reason, I couldn't fall. I kept saying, 'Fall, fall,' but there I was, still standing up. So Joe hit me again and again, and when I finally did fall, it was a slow, funny fall. I remember that." Billy lay flush out on the canvas. There were two seconds left in the round, 2:58 of the thirteenth, when he was counted out. *The winnah and still champeen. . . .*

"It was nationality that cost Conn the title," the *Herald Tribune* wrote. "He wound up on his wounded left side, trying to make Irish legs answer an Irish brain."

On the radio, Billy said, "I just want to tell my mother I'm all right."

Back in the locker room, Jawnie Ray said not to cry because bawxers don't cry. And Billy delivered the classic: "What's the sense of being Irish if you can't be dumb?"

Maggie lasted a few more days. "She held on to see me leading Joe Louis in the stretch," Billy says.

He and Mary Louise got married the day after the funeral. The last time they had met with Greenfield Jimmy, he said that Billy had to "prove he could be a gentleman," but what did a father-in-law's blessing matter anymore after the twelfth and thirteenth rounds and after Maggie's going?

They found a priest in Philly, a Father Schwindlein, and he didn't care from Greenfield Jimmy or the bishop or whoever. As Mary Louise says,

"He just saw two young people very much in love." They had a friend with them who was the best man, and the cleaning lady at the church stood in as the maid of honor. DiMaggio got up to forty-five that day in Fenway, going 2 for 4 and then 1 for 3 in a twin bill. Greenfield Jimmy alerted the state police and all the newspapers when he heard what was going on, but Billy and Mary Louise were on their honeymoon in Jersey, man and wife, by the time anybody caught up with them.

"They're more in love than ever today, forty-four years later," Michael Conn says. He is their youngest child. The Conns raised three boys and a girl at the house they bought that summer in Squirrel Hill.

That was it, really. DiMaggio's streak ended the night of July 17 in Cleveland. Churchill and Roosevelt signed the Atlantic Charter four weeks later, and on November 26 the first subs pulled away from Japan on the long haul to Pearl Harbor. By then Billy was shooting a movie. It was called *The Pittsburgh Kid*, and in it he played (in an inspired bit of casting) an Irish fighter from the Steel City. Mary Louise was so pretty the producers wanted at least to give her a bit part as a cigarette girl, but she was too bashful, and Billy wasn't crazy about the idea himself. Billy did so well that the moguls asked him to stay around and star in the life story of Gentleman Jim Corbett, but the house in Squirrel Hill was calling. And Mary Louise was pregnant. "We were just a couple of naive young kids from Pittsburgh, and we didn't like Hawllywood," she says.

Joey Diven says that if Billy doesn't care for somebody a whole lot, he'll have them over to the house, take them down to the club cellar, and make them watch *The Pittsburgh Kid*.

After Pearl Harbor, Conn fought three more times. Nobody knew it then, but he was done. Everything ended when he hit Louis that last big left. The best he beat after that was Tony Zale, but even the fans in the Garden booed his effort, and he only outpointed the middleweight. It didn't matter, though, because all anybody cared about was a rematch with Louis — even if both fighters were going into the service.

The return was in the works for the summer, a year after the first meeting. It was looked upon as a great morale builder and diversion for a rattled America. The victories at Midway and Guadalcanal were yet to come.

Then, in the middle of May, Private First Class Conn got a three-day pass to come home to the christening of his firstborn, Timmy. Art Rooney was the godfather, and he thought it would be the right time to patch things up between Greenfield Jimmy and his son-in-law; and so he and Milton Jaffe, Conn's business adviser, arranged a christening party at Smith's house and they told Billy that his father-in-law was ready to smoke the peace pipe.

On Sunday, at the party, Greenfield Jimmy and Conn were in the kitchen with some of the other guests. That is where people often congregated in those days, the kitchen. Billy was sitting up on the stove, his legs dangling, when it started. "My father liked to argue," Mary Louise says, "but you can't drag Billy into an argument." Greenfield Jimmy gave it his best, though. Art Rooney says, "He was always the boss, telling people what to do, giving orders." On this occasion he chose to start telling Conn that if he was going to be married to his daughter and be the father of his grandson, he damn sight better attend church more regularly. Then, for good measure, he also told Billy he could beat him up. Finally, Greenfield Jimmy said too much.

"I can still see Billy come off that stove," Rooney says.

Just because it was family, Billy didn't hold back. He went after his father-in-law with his best, a left hook, but he was mad, he had his Irish up, and the little guy ducked like he was getting away from a brushback pitch, and Conn caught him square on the top of his skull. As soon as he did it, Billy knew he had broken his hand. He had hurt himself worse against his own father-in-law than he ever had against any bona fide professional in the prize ring.

Not only that, but when the big guys and everybody rushed in to break it up, Milton Jaffe fractured an ankle and Mary Louise got herself all cut and bruised. Greenfield Jimmy took advantage of the diversion to inflict on Conn additional scratches and welts — around the neck, wrists, and eyes. Billy was so furious about blowing the rematch with Louis that he busted a window with his good hand on the way out and cut himself more. The New York Times, ever understated, described Conn's appearance the next day "as if he had tangled with a half-dozen alley cats."

Greenfield Jimmy didn't have a single mark on him.

Years later, whenever Louis saw Conn, he would usually begin, "Is your old father-in-law still beating the shit out of you?"

In June, Secretary of War Henry Stimson announced there would be no more public commercial appearances for Louis, and the champ began a series of morale-boosting tours. The fight at the christening had cost Louis and Conn hundreds of thousands of dollars and, it turned out, any real chance Conn had for victory. Every day the war dragged on diminished his skills.

The legs go first.

Conn was overseas in Europe for much of the war, pulling punches in exhibition matches against regimental champs. One time, the plane he was on developed engine trouble over France, and Billy told God he would do two things if the plane landed safely.

It did, and he did. Number one, he gave $5,000 to Dan Rooney, Art's brother, who was a missionary in the Far East. And number two, he gave $5,000 to Sacred Heart, his old parish in 'Sliberty, to build a statue of the Blessed Virgin. It is still there, standing prominently by the entrance.

Conn was with Bob Hope at Nuremberg when V-E day came. There is a picture of that in the club cellar.

Then he came home and patched up with Greenfield Jimmy and prepared for the long-awaited rematch with Louis. It was on June 19, 1946, and such was the excitement that, for the first time, ringside seats went for $100, and a $2 million gate was realized. This was the fight — not the first one — when Louis observed, "He can run, but he can't hide." And Joe was absolutely right. Mercifully, the champion ended the slaughter in the eighth. In the locker room Conn himself called it a "stinkeroo," and it was Jawnie Ray who cried, because, he said, "Billy's finished."

As Conn would tell his kids, boxing is bad unless you happen to be very, very good at it. It's not like other sports, where you can get by. If you're not very, very good, you can get killed or made over into a vegetable or what-have-you. Now Billy Conn, he had been very, very good. Almost one-third of his seventy-five fights had been against champions of the worlds, and he had beaten all those guys except Louis, and that was as good a fight as there ever was. Some people still say there never has been a better fighter, a stylist, than Sweet William, the Flower of the Monongahela. But, of course, all anybody remembers is the fight that warm June night in the year of '41 and especially that one round, the thirteenth.

One time, a few years ago, Art Rooney brought the boxer into the Steelers' locker room and introduced him around to a bunch of white players standing there. They obviously didn't have the foggiest idea who Billy Conn was. Conn saw some black players across the way. "Hey, blackies, you know who Joe Louis was?" They all looked up at the stranger and nodded. Conn turned back to the whites and shook his head. "And you sonsuvbitches don't know me," he said.

But really he didn't care. "Everything works out for the best," he says in the club cellar. "I believe that." He's very content. They can't ever get him to go to sports dinners so they can give him awards and stuff. "Ah, I just like being another bum here," he says. "I just loaf around, on the corner, different places." Then Mary Louise comes around, and he falls into line. He never moved around much, Billy Conn. Same town, same house, same wife, same manager, same fun. "All the guys who know me are dead now, but, let me tell you, if I drop dead tomorrow, I didn't miss anything."

He's standing over by the photograph of Louis and him, right after their first fight. He still adores Louis, they became fast friends, and he loves to tell stories about Louis and money. Some guys have problems with money. Some guys have, say, problems with fathers-in-law. Nobody gets off scot-free. Anyway, in the picture Louis has a towel wrapped around a puzzled, mournful countenance. Conn, next to him, is smiling to beat the band. He was the loser?

Billy says, "I told Joe later, 'Hey, Joe, why didn't you just let me have the title for six months?' All I ever wanted was to be able to go around the corner where the guys are loafing and say, 'Hey, I'm the heavyweight champeen of the world.'

"And you know what Joe said back to me? He said, 'I let you have it for twelve rounds, and you couldn't keep it. How could I let you have it for six months?'"

A few years ago Louis came to Pittsburgh, and he and Conn made an appearance together at a union hall. Roy McHugh, the columnist for the *Pittsburgh Press*, was there. Billy brought the film of the '41 fight over from Squirrel Hill in a shopping bag. As soon as the fight started, Louis left the room and went into the bar to drink brandy. Every now and then Louis would come to the door and holler out, "Hey, Billy, have we got to the thirteenth yet?" Conn just laughed and watched himself punch the bigger man around, until finally, when they did come to the thirteenth, Joe called out, "Good-bye, Billy."

Louis knocked out Conn at 2:58, just like always, but when the lights went on, Billy wasn't there. He had left when the thirteenth round started. He had gone into another room, to where the buffet was, after he had watched the twelve rounds when he was the heavyweight champeen of the world, back in that last indelible summer when America dared yet dream that it could run and hide from the world, when the handsomest boy loved the prettiest girl, when streetcars still clanged and fistfights were fun, and the smoke hung low when Maggie went off to Paradise.

1987

David Remnick

........................................................................................................................

# The September Song
# of Mr. October

FROM *The New Yorker*

IN THE LAST WEEKS before spring training, Reggie Jackson drove down the freeway from his home in the Oakland hills to the ballpark where he began his career in 1968. He ran sprints across the outfield, fielded fungoes, and took batting practice with players half his age, boys who looked at him with the same slack-jawed regard he once had for Mantle, Maris, and Mays. They studied his easy looping warm-up swings, his murderous slashes at the ball, even the vicious way he spit through his teeth after every pitch, and as they watched him, they may have remembered seeing the same motions a decade ago on television or, if they were lucky, from a seat in the upper deck. Jackson was a part of their boyhood. Now they were professional ballplayers and an audience for the September song of Mr. October.

The youngest of them could hardly imagine Reggie Jackson in gold, green, and white; for them, he was born in pinstripes. But all knew him as a man of swaggering qualities, a name as resonant in their imagination as Ali, Elvis, or even the Babe. At least a dozen players in Reggie's era, from Clemente to Schmidt to Mattingly, were better players, more complete and consistent, but he was the Promethean among them. He defined an Age of Jackson.

Statistically, he is king only of strikeouts, the all-time leader in that category, but his legacy is the big stroke, the electric moment. He won three championships with the Athletics, two with the Yankees. He played in the postseason in eleven of his nineteen years. No player ever had a single day greater than his October 18, 1977. On the cool night when the Yankees won their first World Series in fifteen years, Jackson hit three home runs on three swings. No one else had ever done that. Likely, no one would again. "I have been to the mountaintop, and I have seen the promised land," he said. "I've seen it more than any man alive."

The brilliant light was out. It was like watching the movements of a shadow on the grass. His swing — which often left him screwed into the clay, his helmet falling over his eyes, his number, 44, stretched grotesquely across his back — his swing still had the old ferocious look. But something was wrong. The eyes, the concentration, the reflexes, something. Jackson was not past heroics — he could still send the ball screaming into the outer dark — but he was past the *expectation* of heroics. His home runs now had the quality only of nostalgia and accident. He was forty years old.

In the fall of 1986, he seemed sure to play in another World Series. "I might have gone out on that," he said. His California Angels were one strike away from beating the Boston Red Sox. Horribly, the Angels let go their grip, and the Red Sox advanced instead. It mattered little to Jackson that in the Series against the Mets, Boston would imitate California's collapse, and, somehow, surpass it. Only one thing resonated in his mind. His last at-bat had been a strikeout, and his team had lost. "Of course, you can't blame the Angels," he said. "They'd never won anything. They didn't know how. I was a different story. I'd been there." When it was over, California no longer wanted him. They had already forced one of the game's most superb batsmen, Rod Carew, into a ragged, undignified end. Now to the sixth-leading home-run hitter of all time, the Angels said, in no uncertain terms, find another team, quit. Suddenly, Reggie Jackson was just an overpaid .240 hitter without a glove. Jackson waited for offers. Thirty-six hours after the owners of the A's called him, he signed a one-year contract with them for $525,000, little more than half his old salary. He was already worth millions in stocks, real estate, and other investments. He had homes in Carmel, Oakland, and Los Angeles; his own Cessna jet; and a car collection worth two and a half million dollars. He had a china collection featuring a six-hundred-dollar teacup. The money was meaningless. He would not go out on strike three. "It wouldn't be right," he said. "Someone like me is supposed to leave the game in a different way. That's not how it ends for Reggie Jackson."

A couple of days before his next workout at the Coliseum, Jackson flew in his private plane to Las Vegas. A Canadian auto-painting-supply company called Spraybake had invited him to the auto show there, where they were displaying Jackson's favorite, a 1955 Chevrolet Bel Air. The license plate read R JAX 55. Normally Jackson gets ten to fifteen thousand dollars to lend what he himself calls the Reggie aura, but Spraybake was one of his "best relationships," he said, and he would do it for expenses. "They like me. They're Reggie guys."

Jackson walked in a half-hour late, wearing a blue sweatshirt and faded, pressed jeans. His hair, which he used to wear in a woolly Afro style, now had the patchy look of a putting green on an abandoned course. There were flecks of gray in his beard. More than one visitor noted that he seemed shorter than his "official height" of six feet. "I thought he'd be a giant," said one young girl. "He's just plain."

Jackson found a central spot on the carpet, spread his legs, folded his arms over his chest, and waited. Warily, all the Spraybake men formed a circle around the star. They made small talk about Jackson's hundred or so cars, about his feelings on having just joined the Oakland A's. And as their nerve increased and their imagined sense of fraternity took hold, they asked his opinion of a passing girl in silver tights. They had seen the photographs through the years of Reggie with dozens of beautiful women, mostly blondes. "Not bad," Jackson allowed. "Not bad."

Clubhouse talk with Reggie: even fifteen thousand dollars would have been a small price to pay. Still, the men were uncomfortable. They appeared to concentrate very hard on what they said before they said it. If Jackson does not care for a question, he will often ignore it. If he thinks a query too obvious, he will say, "You mean you don't know?" Disgust is one of his moods. They shift easily, inexplicably. But he was in a good mood now, and he received even banalities with cheer.

After a while, the crowd thinned out and Reggie was almost alone. There were no balls to sign, no absurdities to answer. And so he picked up a soft towel and began polishing the fingerprints off his Chevrolet. "I hate fingerprints," he said. "Why do people put their fingers all over something like this?" As he buffed the chrome, he said, "It's like I've lived a dream. If you're talking about a standard for success, they're Steve Jobs in computers, Lee Iacocca in cars, and Reggie Jackson in baseball. I was the standard in clutch situations for ten years. I wasn't the best hitter, but I was the most feared. I was the baddest motherfucker on the block. I was Jesse James, Wyatt Earp. But even they slow down. Even they deteriorate.

"From 1972 to 1979, when you needed a home run in the ninth, and the pennant was riding on it, I was going to the plate to hit that cocksucker over the fence. And not just hit it over. I mean, like forty rows deep. You know what I'm saying? But it didn't last forever. It wasn't just last year or the year before that. It goes as far back as the 1981 Series against the Dodgers. I was out hurt at the beginning. I got back in it, but I couldn't turn it around. I couldn't do it anymore."

Jackson sat down on a couch and drank a cup of orange juice. The crowds returned as quickly as they had gone.

"Hi! I'm a Ziebart girl!" said an almost-blonde in a pair of white hot pants. "I thought you were giving balls out."

"Reggie. Hey, Reggie! I just want to shake your hand. No questions asked. Is that okay?"

"Hey, Reggie Jackson. You're always selling something, aren't you?"

One after another. The strangeness of being Reggie. In public, he is like a ferocious animal in a zoo cage: people admire him, poke him, measure themselves against him. Then they go away, perhaps frightened, disappointed, or thrilled. Usually Jackson endures it. Sometimes he snaps back. It depends on his mood.

Once, when all of New York wanted to know when Reggie would recover from an injury and return to right field, a young boy said to him in an elevator, "Hey, when are you gonna play, Reg?"

Jackson grabbed himself by the crotch and said, "Play with this."

Sometimes it is not his fault. In bars, people try to pick a fight. In New York, someone took a shot at him with a pistol. It is part of the idiocy of being that famous.

Finally, Jackson rose from the sofa and told the Spraybake men, "The crowds are a little thick. I'll be back in fifteen minutes." He said he'd take a walk and let them thin out. He was gone for hours. When he finally returned, it was time to go.

Jackson left the convention center that evening with Everett Moss and Ted Kay, two of his buddies from California. Moss is Jackson's closest friend and one of six people on the Reggie payroll. Ted Kay is a scarred former football player from Kent State who met Jackson in a pickup basketball game. Ted told Reggie he was out of work, and the next day he had a job caring for the "L.A. division" of Reggie's car collection. "Reggie saved me," Ted said. "Now I live over the garage."

As they left the hall, 1984 Playmate of the Year Barbara Edwards, who was at the convention selling Snap-on tools, caught up to Jackson. A calendar photo of Edwards wearing a farmer's-daughter outfit and clutching a Snap-on tool hangs near the desk in his L.A. garage. In Las Vegas she wore fur.

"You ever see anything that gorgeous?" Ted said to Everett as they kept a respectable distance behind their man.

"Yes, I have," Everett said. He has been with Jackson for twenty years. "Sometimes even a bit better," Everett added.

The streets were clogged with conventioneers, and Jackson and Barbara Edwards could not get a cab. One cabdriver slowed, as if in response to Jackson's signal, but then he drove away. All he wanted was a closer look.

"My Gawd," said Barbara Edwards. "What kinda town is this?" Jackson ran across the street in an attempt to flag a cab, but it was filled, and defiantly sped away. Finally, he gave up and took a place in line at a nearby hotel. He was reduced to the sort of patience required of bunters and long relievers. It hurt. When Barbara Edwards climbed into her cab, Reggie leaned into the backseat and kept his face very close to hers for almost a minute. Then he said goodbye.

Someone mentioned that perhaps her beauty exceeded her intellectual strengths. "It's true. She doesn't seem too sharp," Reggie said, "but it's probably the whole thing of meeting Reggie Jackson for the first time. If I spent time with her, she'd get over it."

The next cab was supposed to be Jackson's, but a woman in the line insisted otherwise. Exasperated, he offered to split the ride with the woman, who called herself Roxanne. In the front seat, Roxanne turned to Jackson and said, "I drive eighteen-wheelers. Whadda you do?"

Ted and Everett laughed nervously. Then Reggie laughed, too. He knew it was just a joke, but when he dropped her off he made no motion to let her skip the fare. As the cab rode toward the airport he said, "Fuck her. She wasn't too impressed with me."

Then, to the driver, he said, "You like this job? It's not bad, is it? Six months from now I'll be out here in Vegas with a checker cab, cigarette breath, and a T-shirt. I'll be great. Won't I?"

As the car pulled up to the airport gate, Reggie had one more question for the driver. "Hey, you ever get a blowjob in the cab?"

The walls of Reggie's plane are covered with Ultrasuede. The seats are deep and embracing. Before he fell asleep, Reggie put his feet up on a seat and said, "This plane doesn't make economic sense. It's seven thousand eight hundred dollars an hour. But I'm buying time. I'm buying solitude."

That winter he needed quiet more than ever. His father was very sick. Several times in the weeks before spring training, Reggie flew to Philadelphia to visit him in the hospital. "For a while we weren't sure if he was gonna make it," Reggie said.

Martinez Jackson ran a cleaning store when Reggie was growing up, and brewed corn liquor in the basement to make a little extra money. To keep the cold out of the house, they draped blankets across the doors.

One day when Reggie was around six, he was riding with his father in the delivery truck when he noticed his father was crying.

"What's wrong?" Reggie asked.

"Your mom and I are splitting up," he said. "She's leaving today." In his autobiography, written with Mike Lupica, Jackson put it this way: "The next thing I knew, my mother was just kind of gone. Her other three natural children went with her. I stayed with my dad. . . . There are things that happen to you in your life that you don't question, maybe because you're afraid of what the answer will be. My mom leaving me behind is one of those things. I never asked her why."

Martinez and Reggie grew closer. Then, when he was a senior at Cheltenham High School and the best athlete in the Philadelphia area, Reggie saw police cars parked in front of his house. A court sentenced Martinez Jackson to six months in jail for making liquor illegally. For a while, Reggie was as alone as a boy can be. With his father gone, Reggie helped run the business, finished school, handled the recruiters, and, finally, left for Arizona State. He visited his father only once in prison. He could not stand the sight of the old man in prison grays.

And now Martinez Jackson was worn out. Reggie did not know what more he could do for his father. He had been a good and grateful son. Long ago, when times were tough, his father dreamed of owning a red Cadillac. Reggie bought him one. He helped him build his cleaning business. So his dad could make some extra money, Reggie even got him a "job" as a scout for the Angels. ("The only scouting he's got to do is scout the mailbox for his check every month.") He had always done for his father what every son hopes he will be in the position to do. But he could not make it all right, not with fame or money or words.

In feeling his own decline, Jackson was himself learning a little of what it is to grow old. "You don't retire at your convenience. You don't die when you're ready," he said. Below, the lights of Los Angeles blurred through the fog. "It's an inconvenience to die. You don't retire at the top. There are no announcements. There are no invitations. You're just gone."

*  *  *

He had a date in town that night, but by morning he was alone. He woke at 6:00 A.M., made a few business calls, and rode a stationary bike for twenty minutes. At seven-thirty he drove his garnet Porsche to Super Bodies, a storefront gym near Newport Beach. Another "Reggie guy," a hulking blond named Walt Harris, met Jackson on the sidewalk, and the two men went inside to stretch. "I used to tear my muscles up all the time," Reggie said. "Now I don't run fast enough to tear nothing."

Jackson worked harder than anyone else in the gym. "When I quit I'll become a body builder," he said with a load of weights on his back. "Just for the hell of it. For vanity." He worked his quadriceps, his calves, his triceps and biceps. Between sets, he ran in place with the quick, short steps of a shadowboxer. He wore a baseball cap, sweatpants, and a blue rubber shirt. Sweat washed over his face and dripped off the point of his chin. He had always looked more like a heavyweight fighter than a ball-player.

To strengthen the muscles that power his baseball swing, Jackson took a twenty-five-pound barbell and mimicked the motions of batting. Many players disdain heavy weight training, saying it makes them bulky, but Reggie was not lifting for singles or doubles to the opposite field. He was training his muscles for a last season of all-or-nothing.

Jackson climbed on a computerized exercise bike to get his heart beating faster. "When I was twenty-eight years old I didn't have any of this," he said over the whir. "I did nothing. I did, like, a million five hundred thousand dollars in the off-season just hustling business."

He finished his workout with a series of abdominal exercises. Some days he did thirteen hundred sit-ups.

At last he rested and drank a glass of blended fruits. A few friends dropped by the gym to say hello, including a young woman named Anne Appleby, who brought her one-month-old daughter, Kimberley Nicole. Reggie cradled the baby in his arms and stood in front of a mirror. "How do I look?" he said. "Like a daddy?" The mother laughed. Kimberley cried. Reggie gave the baby back to Anne. "Hey, so it's only Reggie Jackson," he said. "Who cares, right?"

Before every game at Yankee Stadium, old clips of Ruth and Gehrig, DiMaggio and Mantle flicker on the big screen above the bleachers.

When he visits the stadium, Jackson sometimes tries to take his batting practice while his own image — younger, faster, reliably heroic — is on the screen. Once, while warming up on an August afternoon with the Angels, he belted one ball straight at his own looming icon.

Afterward he told *The Washington Post,* "I'm still Reggie, but not as often."

Inevitably, the stadium's film shows Jackson's performance against the Dodgers in the sixth and final game of the 1977 World Series. As he hits his three home runs, the PA system plays the old rock standard "Lightnin' Strikes (again and again and again)."

"It was the worst year of my life," Jackson said behind the wheel of a van. "I was a walking-around mental case." It began with a disastrous interview in which he said that he, and not the team's gritty catcher, Thurman Munson, was the "straw that stirs the drink." Every morning in the *Times,* the *Post,* and the *News,* the protagonists continued their *opéra bouffe.* Billy and George and Reggie. Thurman and Graig and Sparky. That one season generated more books than the Korean War. Though he never avoided the clubhouse and dugout madness, Jackson would spend hour after hour that year sitting on the terrace of his Fifth Avenue apartment, depressed and weary. "I used to read the Bible and take little sayings out of it because I needed support, I needed help," he said. "Sounds like I was nuts, huh?"

Then the autumn came. In the postseason most hitters do not perform nearly as well as they do in the spring or summer. It is not only the pressure that oppresses them, it is the cold air, the truncated and superior pitching staffs, the constant night games.

Reggie Jackson lived for October. That he could focus so clearly on a speeding ball amid all the turbulence — that was always his gift. After five games, the Yankees had a 3–2 lead over the Dodgers. Reggie left Los Angeles on his second homer of the Series, a long shot off Don Sutton. He wanted the season to end, and, somehow, he had an idea of just how it would.

Driving toward a body shop where he often hangs out, Jackson turned down the oldies station he listens to and let it all roll back over him like a wave.

"The day of game six, well, everybody has asked me, what did you do? And I just kinda said I relaxed and listened to the radio. The truth is I spent the afternoon relaxing with a lady. Relaxing, baby, I was relaxed.

"I knew I was swinging the bat good in batting practice. I probably hit two dozen balls out. The crowd in right field was going crazy.

"I was on the money. I was like a guy rolling a three hundred game. I was like a basketball shooter, and when he lets go you know it's gonna be all net. So I was ready. Sometimes you just know.

"The first time up against Burt Hooton, I didn't get to swing. Got walked on four pitches. The next time up, Thurman was on base and they had to give me a ball to hit. It was the first pitch he threw. It felt like I'd hit it hard enough to go five hundred feet, but I hit over the ball because I thought it was going to sink. But Yankee Stadium has a short right field, and the ball stayed up just long enough.

"The next time up, in the fifth, Hooton was out of the game and Elias Sosa was in. Sosa was a hard thrower, and I knew he was going to try to bust me with a pitch inside. That's always been the thing to do. Even when I was on deck I was saying to myself, Please, dear God, let him hurry up and get ready so I can get it.

"I knew as soon as Sosa let go of the ball I was going to hit it out of the ballpark. It was the best ball I hit all night, like a one-iron shot. Now I could hear the crowd starting to chant my name, '*Reg*-gie. *Reg*-gie.' Jesus.

"I knew I was going to get up again, and I figured I might as well go for another one. It wouldn't matter even if I struck out. No matter what I did I'd still get another ovation.

"And so they brought in Charlie Hough. We were up seven-three in the bottom of the eighth. A knuckler! I probably have more career home runs off knucklers than any pitchers I'd ever faced. I couldn't lose. All I wanted him to do was throw a strike. And, man, he threw a cookie."

The second-base umpire, Ed Sudol, could not believe it. "Hough threw him a tremendous knuckleball," he said. "I don't know how Reggie even got his bat on it, let alone hit it about four hundred and twenty feet." The Dodger first baseman, Steve Garvey, began to applaud in his glove. In the dugout, all the year's tensions melted. Munson hugged Reggie, and so did Martin. Graig Nettles, who would later get in a fistfight with Jackson at a party, said, "It was magic. And it didn't matter in the slightest whether you liked him or detested him. After the third home run, I walked out to the on-deck circle as the crowd was cheering and cheering, and I took my helmet off and waved at everybody as though they were cheering me, and I enjoyed my little fantasy as the noise swirled over the whole stadium."

When Jackson trotted out to right field, they chanted his name, louder and louder, *Reg*-gie . . . *Reg*-gie . . . *Reg*-gie. Confetti, most of it torn flecks of programs, napkins, and toilet paper, showered over him. For once, the sound was clear and unanimous. No one who appreciated the difficulty of what he had done could withhold his admiration or affection.

He never grew bored remembering his perfect night. He pulled the van off the highway, turned off the engine, and gripped the wheel with both hands. A hard sun shone through the window, and Reggie put his face in the light. He was quiet awhile. Then he said, "When all is said and done, people like me. They like me. That's something."

Reggie drove back home. His condominium was packed with Reggie memorabilia: a wood clock with Reggie's image carved into the face; a gilt baseball, a tribute to the home run that propelled Reggie past Mickey Mantle; two copies of his autobiography, *Reggie;* a videotape labeled REGGIE JACKSON, POSITIVE AT-BATS, 1985; a batch of Reggie clips stacked on a director's chair emblazoned with its owner's name.

Earlier he had read with evident sadness a story about George Foster, a once-extraordinary hitter for the Reds and Mets who had squandered his fortune. "You see it all the time," Reggie said. "Sometimes it's the player, sometimes it's these agents who are telling them what to do. They're just a bunch of white guys with Samsonite briefcases and bad suits." He was in his bedroom, dressing while he watched the Financial News Network on cable. His eyes fixed on the stock ticker that ran across the bottom of the screen. Every few minutes or so he stopped to place a call to his lawyer in Oakland, his agent in New York, his real estate partner in Phoenix, a car dealer in Los Angeles. He seemed to love this part of being him.

"Are you in?" he asked his broker. They were talking about a "very hot" jeans company. "It was up to three and heading toward four. You in? Hang in there, at least today. If it gets hairy, I'll call you."

He got up from the bed and began to sway to the electronic bounce of FNN's theme song. "I'm a capitalist," he said. "And I'm a Reagan supporter. But mostly in politics I'm a fence-sitter. I don't want to put myself in a position to say too many controversial things, because a lot of the people I'm in contact with are CEOs. They can affect my future." He shimmied during the bond report, hopped during the NASDAQ index. When the report on the top ten stocks of the day came on, Reggie sat perched on the edge of his bed and watched every second.

"I think you're getting to see that there are all sides to Reggie," he said after it was over. "I may not necessarily be better than anyone, but I'm unique. There's Reggie the ballplayer and Reggie the media guy and Reggie who's into cars. But Reggie's also meeting with the main players of the eighties. I call Boone Pickens for advice on high-end economics.

I look hard at what Steve Jobs is doing. Tonight I'm supposed to have dinner with John Sculley, the head of Apple. You think I won't come away with any wisdom?"

A report came on the television about the scandals on Wall Street. "Boesky just got caught," Reggie said. "I'm not condoning what he did. It's just not wrong. They say that pigs get fat, hogs go to market."

Jackson made a few more calls. Then he pulled out his suitcases. The next morning he had practice at the Coliseum in Oakland. He stepped into a walk-in closet filled with dozens of shirts, and fingered sleeve after sleeve. When he emerged with the chosen shirts draped across his arm, Jackson's whole expression had changed. "Let me ask you some-thing," he said. "What kind of story are you doing?" There was a painful, nervous pause. "Is it a Reggie profile? A 'Reggie retires' kind of thing? See, I think the media get some kind of weird enjoyment out of asking, 'What are you going to do when you're not the center of attention anymore? What are you going to do when all the adulation is dried up and all the cheers die down? Huh?' It's like they want you to say, 'I'll collapse. I won't be able to make it in society. I'll end up in a halfway house.' Well, you can see that baseball is just a part of me. Reggie Jack-son is not your average baseball player."

Reggie cannot get over the completeness of himself, his multifaceted self. "I guess I underestimated the magnitude of me," he has said. No one, he is convinced, has told his story adequately. He has already written two autobiographies and is considering a third. When he con-tracted Lupica to write *Reggie* with him, there were hermeneutic de-bates of every sort. *Reggie,* Jackson believed, did not contain all that is Reggie. "It was on the best-seller list, but it could have been a huge book, you know what I'm saying? It could have been something. It could have been another fucking Hemingway, but for that I would've needed a . . . James Michener."

He checked his watch, a chunky gold Rolex. "It's getting late," he said. "We've got a couple of things to do before we fly to Oakland, and I've got that dinner with John Sculley tonight. Did I mention that? He's the head of Apple."

At lunch, Reggie, Ted, and Walt stood in front of a big-screen TV that was playing old baseball highlights. As the tape rolled they quizzed each other on averages, plays, nicknames — all the ephemera of the game. Jackson never missed a question.

"You're the king," Walt said.

"Yes," Reggie said.

They drove back to the garage — Ted and Walt on motorcycles, Jackson in one of his vintage "muscle" cars. There to greet them was one of Reggie's girlfriends — a young, blond student from Golden West College. ("About the ladies. Keep the names out of it," Reggie said. "I don't want one of them getting mad about another. I mean, they know, but, well, you understand.")

"I thought we were going to lunch," she complained. "I've been here for like an hour."

"I said one o'clock, didn't I?" Reggie said.

"I was here early," she said. "You guys were gone."

"*Ahh*, well," Reggie said, and he enveloped her in his arms.

For the next hour or so Reggie watched Ted hose down a buddy's Oldsmobile. They talked carburetors and camshafts. Jackson walked from one car to the next, admiring the Corniche, perusing the Corvette, checking out the "fat fender" on the custom Mercedes-Benz. The blonde looked for something to do. She helped Ted polish the hood of the Oldsmobile. Reggie watched her while he spoke once more on the phone to his broker.

"Honey!" he said when he hung up. "It's long strokes. Not across. Not short. *Looong* strokes."

"I didn't — "

"I know, honey, you're learning."

Reggie and the blonde drove back to his condominium, leaving Walt and Ted to work in the garage. "I've got the plane set to go in a couple of hours," he told them. "I've got some packing to do."

Jackson was once married to a woman named Jennie Campos. They were divorced, after four years, in 1972. Since then he has come close to marrying once, lived with at least one other woman, and has dated "a lot." "Reggie's girls all look pretty much the same," Walt said. "Blond, pretty, twenty-one or twenty-two, perfect bods, kind of beachy." He said he wants a family "after baseball sometime," but for the moment one of the biggest portraits in his house is of Reggie and his Chevrolet. "So I'm not married," he said. "Whoopee shit. The only thing about not being married is I don't have children, or I don't have someone to share my life with all the time. So I'm missing a couple of things, but I'm not exactly . . . I don't need a goddam psychoanalyst."

Walt checked his watch, smiled, and said, "That should be enough time." He drove Jackson's van back to the condominium. When Walt arrived, Reggie was standing outside surrounded by his bags. He was fidgety, scowling. He was in a panic. Once more the mood had shifted.

"You see a little white sack?" he asked Walt.

"No, what's in it? What are you talking about?"

"I can't find the thing," Reggie said, louder now. "I hid it and now I don't know where I put it."

"What's in it? How big is it?"

"It's a little bank sack with ten thousand dollars in it, that's what it is, and now I can't find it. Jesus."

"Maybe you hid it in the garage."

For the next couple of hours, Reggie, Ted, and Walt looked everywhere in the garage, in the condominium. They shuttled back and forth following one false lead after another. Finally Jackson went back home and emptied his bags all over his driveway. A neighbor named Heather walked over from the condominium next door.

"Hi! What's goin' on?" she chirped through her gum.

"Oh, I just misplaced something," he said. The sun was getting dim, and the appointment four hundred miles away with John Sculley, one of the main players of the 1980s, was drawing close. "It's driving me crazy," he said.

Then Heather began laughing. "Hah, hah, hah." It was inexplicable.

"Yeah, well . . ." Reggie said, containing himself.

"How's that ball team up in California?"

Reggie blinked. Wasn't he in California?

"Oh, they're all right," he said.

Heather just stood there.

"Well . . ." Reggie said hopefully.

"Well," Heather replied. Then, after a cruel silence, she added, ". . . see ya 'round."

"See ya 'round, Heather."

Reggie drove once more to the garage, where he leaned on his Chevrolet. "Ten thousand bucks," he said. "Ten thousand bucks." He called San Francisco and canceled his dinner with John Sculley.

"All right, now, we're not going home until we find it," he announced. Ted and Walter never stopped looking, no doubt out of good fellowship, but also, one could not help thinking, in an effort to obliterate suspicion. They were Reggie guys.

"Wait," Jackson said. "I think I know where it is." Jackson's relief was considerable, though nothing compared with Ted's and Walt's. Walt drove Jackson back to the condominium. Reggie opened the trunk of his garnet Porsche and found a black box used for holding compact disks. Inside was the sack, and inside that was the ten thousand dollars.

On February 26, 1935, the Yankees released Babe Ruth. He played two months for the Boston Braves, hitting just .181. Fat, tired, and looking for an exit line, he hit three home runs one afternoon at Forbes Field. But those home runs had the quality of nostalgia and accident. Ruth retired that June at the age of forty. For the rest of his life he tried to win a job as a manager. No one would hire him.

Twelve years later, Ruth was dying of throat cancer. Commissioner Happy Chandler declared a "Babe Ruth Day" at Yankee Stadium. Wearing a camel's-hair coat, Ruth stepped slowly up to the microphone and spoke in a rasp. "You know, this baseball game of ours comes up from the youth," he said to the crowd. "That means the boys. The only real game in the world, I think, is baseball."

Yogi Berra was there, and he later said, "When he finished talking, the Babe waved a salute and turned around and walked back to the dugout. Nobody made a move to help him. I remember one of the ballplayers saying, 'Do you think we ought to go out and give him a hand?' And somebody said, 'Leave him alone. He knows where the dugout is.'"

In his last days, Ruth still had a strong appetite, but he could no longer chew. Some days Babe would eat a mound of chopped meat. As he grew worse he ate soft-boiled eggs. At least the cancer had not robbed him of his memory. He could summon pleasure in an instant. One day shortly before he died Ruth looked down at his egg and said, "To think of the steaks . . ."

"You compare me to Babe Ruth and I'll look silly," Reggie said, driving the Oakland freeway. In athletic terms, he is right. It is as a folk hero, not as a player, that Reggie reaches across time to Babe.

Now Reggie was trying to end a little better than the Babe. He would be a designated hitter, he would play first base. He would change if he had to. But he could not humiliate himself. He would not go out on .181. That would be torture to him. "I'm not going to embarrass myself," he said. "You talk about the way Ted Williams went out on a home run. Who wouldn't want that?"

As he sat now in the Coliseum's dim and tiny clubhouse, Jackson looked around at all the kids. Who had worked as hard as he had? Who among them understood the importance of the game, and the short time they had to play it? Jackson saw players with better reflexes but with rolls of fat around their middles; he saw young men charged by the pleasures of their game but ignorant of its subtleties. Even their lack of financial savvy annoyed him. He saw young Tony Phillips dressing and joking about the "great salary deal" he was going to make. That did it.

"'Great'? How great?" Reggie said. "What did you make last year?"

"Three-fifty, four hundred thou with incentives," Phillips said.

"And now you're in arbitration?"

"Yeah."

"What are your numbers? How many hits did you have last year?"

"I don't know exactly."

"How many runs?"

"I'm not sure."

"You don't know?"

"Not sure."

"You've *gotta* know," Reggie said. "If you're in arbitration how can you *not* know? You have an agent?"

"Yeah, sure I do." Phillips was getting more and more defensive. He wanted out, he wanted to hit and run and get out of the jaws of Reggie Jackson.

"Who is he? Your brother? Your best friend? Why don't you do your own deal?"

To Phillips's astonishment, Reggie began to explain the way "agents can cut you," the sort of studying he'd better do, the interest-free loans he could ask for. "You have to make the deal that's good for you," Jackson said. "Are you gonna have any left when you're done? Can you buy your own home? Can you structure a bank loan? I'm giving you the third degree, man, because you gotta know what you're doing."

Phillips was silent. Vaguely, he understood that Jackson, of all people, knew what he was talking about. Still, he wanted out.

Reggie smiled. "Hey, man, don't listen to me. I'm just an old shit. I don't know nothing."

"No, brother, what have you been around? Twenty years?"

"Don't mean nothing. I'm just an old man."

The other players left for the field, Phillips included. Reggie waited until the others were gone before he put on his jade-colored Athletics jacket, his shades, and his shoes.

"You think Phillips will listen?" someone asked him.

Jackson spit through his teeth as he walked through the shadowy hall toward the field. His spikes clicked on the concrete. "I don't give a shit if he listens or not, to be honest," he said. "I just don't care."

The morning was clear and cool, and the grass brilliant in the hard winter light. So direct was the sun that it burned off the previous day's rain in a couple of hours. Only twenty players came to the optional workout. The manager, Tony LaRussa, was out of town, and most of the veterans had better things to do. Spring training was still weeks away. The emptiness of the seats made an echo chamber of the Coliseum, so that a sharp line drive sounded like the report from a .22.

In the dugout, a young outfielder named Michael Williams slammed a ball into his glove. He played awhile for the Cleveland Indians in 1986, but they released him. Now he was hoping to land a job in the A's system. "Class A would be fine with me," he said. "I've gotta start somewhere." Williams grew up in Hayward, California, just a short drive from the Coliseum, and when he was six or seven years old he and a friend came to the ballpark to see their first game.

"Just about the second I walked into the park, Reggie put one over the fence. Right over there," Williams said, pointing to left center field. "It was incredible, the way he hit it, and he'd just drop his bat at home plate and watch the ball and admire it going over the wall. Man! I followed every move he made. I didn't watch anyone else."

After the players did a few stretching exercises and ran laps around the grass, Jackson seized the privilege of seniority and took the first turn at bat. His own bats had not yet arrived in Oakland, so he selected a thirty-four-ounce Adirondack of white ash from a heap on the grass. "I used to use a thirty-six or a thirty-seven. Biggest bat in the league for five years," he said, taking a few warm-up swings. "Now I use a thirty-three or a thirty-four."

With his old Yankee teammate Bob Watson watching him, with nearly everyone in the park watching him, Jackson stepped into the cage. He tapped his bat on home plate, then bunted three pitches to the left, three more to the right.

"Okay now, Reg, let it rip," Watson said. It was unlikely that the A's would ask him to do any bunting.

Jackson took the first pitch, then hit three pop flies to short right field. They were too shallow for the outfielders to bother with them.

Jackson tapped once more on the plate, then cracked a line drive to center field.

"Better," Watson said. "But you're lifting that back foot."

"It's February," Jackson said, and he stepped in once more. He hit another drive, which echoed through the empty park, then a dozen pops to center and right. He smacked a foul back into the cage. At the finish of his swing his body had dropped close to the dirt and his arms and bat described a pretzel. "Damn," he said.

Jackson unwound himself and took on a more determined air. Sweating freely now, he kicked the dirt and nodded to the pitcher. He hit a couple of drives that would have been singles, then another series of shallow fly balls that were sure outs. "That's slow hands right there," he grumbled. The big hits were just not coming: foul, foul, fly, single, fly, single, single. No numbers on the board. "It takes a while for my hands to get ready," he said.

"Keep that back foot down," Watson said.

Then the pitcher grooved one in, chest-high, medium-fast. Reggie cocked his elbows and lunged at the pitch. The ball exploded off the bat, arcing into the cloudless sky and sailing over a group of fielders who were chatting in center field. Reggie dropped his bat and, along with everyone else, followed the flight of the ball. It was beautiful what the man could do. Finally, the ball cleared the fence and smacked sharply off the empty seats. A lovely, lonely sound. A home run in wintertime.

1989

## Mike Lupica

............................................................................................

# A Brother's Keeper

FROM *Esquire*


THE SUN THROWS a morning light that covers the Atlantic like a blanket both soft and warm. Out the back window you can see Egg Rock sitting in the middle of the water like a piece of God's sculpture, and beyond that, on Massachusetts' North Shore, Lynn Harbor and Marblehead. Fresh cookies are on the kitchen table. There is the smell of coffee.

And suddenly, from another part of the house, like thunder signaling the coming of a storm and a darkening morning, there is the terrible sound of the coughing.

"That's him," Billy Conigliaro, the middle brother, says at the kitchen table. He stares out at the water and clasps his fingers tightly.

"He can't keep his lungs clear. The threat of pneumonia is something we fight continually."

He gets up from the table. "C'mon," he says. "I'll show you around." We go into the bar area of the beautiful house in Nahant. Here, on the walls, are the plaques and photographs that tell of the brief, shining career of Billy's older brother, Tony Conigliaro. Tony C.

Here is Tony C., young and lean and dark and handsome, with Willie Mays. Here is Tony with his two brothers, Billy and Richie. Tony was in the big leagues by then, with the Red Sox. Billy and Richie were still kids. But they were ballplayers, too. Here is Tony C. in a Red Sox uniform, crossing home plate. He was the youngest American League home-run champ in history. Even after a terrible beaning in 1967 that took a season and two months out of his career and nearly cost him the sight in his left eye, Tony C. had 164 home runs by the time he was twenty-six.

Those of us who grew up in New England in the '60s and loved baseball thought that even with all the bad luck he had seen — two broken arms with the Sox, a fractured wrist, the eye — he still was going to hit six hundred home runs for the Boston Red Sox. That was long before Tony C. and everybody found out he didn't know anything about bad luck, anything at all.

Down the hall from the plaques and the pictures, a woman is chattering on, almost musically, nonstop.

"You just a big phony." She laughs. There is more coughing, a man's coughing. "You wanna go out in the car today? Maybe we'll go to the mall. Dress you right up and take you to the mall."

Billy Conigliaro says, "That's Yvonne Baker. We call her the Big E. She's one of his nurses. We gotta go around the clock with him."

Then from down the hall comes Yvonne Baker, a pretty, wide-faced black woman pushing a wheelchair into the morning.

Seated in the wheelchair, hands forgotten in his lap, wearing a white T-shirt, the pants from a red jogging suit, and white sneakers, no longer the boy from Swampscott who hit those balls over the wall at Fenway, a forty-three-year-old man trapped in his own body since his heart stopped beating in Billy's car for several terrible minutes seven years ago, unable to feed himself or walk without help or say more than a couple of words, too much of his brain lost for good, is Tony Conigliaro. Tony C.

Billy squeezes his brother's hand and kneels in front of him. "Hey, pal," he says. "How're you doin' today?"

"He was a natural home-run hitter," Billy Conigliaro says. Billy's own big-league career, which began with the Red Sox, was cut short by a knee injury. "Tony grew up with one dream: hitting home runs for the Boston Red Sox."

He was doing it by the age of nineteen. He hit twenty-four home runs in 1964, in just 111 games; he had broken his arm in the spring and gotten a late start. In 1965 he hit thirty-two and won the home-run title. By August 1967, more than halfway through the Red Sox's Impossible Dream season, when magic came back into the storied little ball park, Tony had twenty more.

He was twenty-two years and seven months old on the August night at Fenway in '67 when a Jack Hamilton fastball hit him in the temple and shattered his cheekbone. The Red Sox's dream continued, but Tony C.'s abruptly halted.

"He had been in a little slump before that," Billy remembers. "Before the game that night he told me, 'You gotta get up on the plate to hit home runs. I'm gonna stand a little closer and stand in a little longer.'"

He did not play again in 1967. The damage to the retina was worse than the doctors had originally thought. They told Tony C. the headaches would go away eventually, but he would never see well enough to hit a baseball again.

But he came back. He hit twenty homers in 1969 and was Comeback Player of the Year. In 1970 it was as if Tony, still only twenty-five, had never been away. He hit thirty-six home runs and knocked in 116. Billy was a rookie center fielder with the Red Sox that season. Richie was playing a hot shortstop at Swampscott High.

But Tony still had some trouble seeing the ball in the outfield as late afternoon became night. This he confided to coaches late in the season. Billy believes it got Tony traded to the California Angels. "After everything, they decided to get as much for him as they could before the eye went bad," Billy says today. "Nice business, huh?"

The eye did get worse; he hit four home runs for the Angels in 1971 and retired. He made one more comeback with the Red Sox, in 1975. Only the Conigliaro family and the most lunatic of trivia buffs know that he opened that World Series season as the Red Sox's designated hitter, and even hit his last two home runs. But, really, the vision was no better. It was Conigliaro's heart that kept bringing him back.

The Red Sox sent him to the minor leagues. The last time I saw him in a baseball uniform was at McCoy Stadium in Pawtucket, Rhode Island, in his final baseball summer. After he retired for good, he drifted into television work.

"He never once said, 'Why me?'" Billy Conigliaro says. "He never once complained about his luck."

Yvonne Baker, the Big E, helps Tony C. into the red jacket that goes with the red pants. She positions the wheelchair in front of the large Panasonic television screen. Geraldo Rivera's talk show comes on.

Billy returns to the kitchen. He stares through the doorway at his brother, who stares at Geraldo Rivera. "You can't even ask him how's he feeling," Billy says. "He can't respond."

Yvonne Baker goes over to the kitchen counter and makes fresh coffee. In the living room, Tony Conigliaro's head has dropped to his shoulder in front of the screen. He is asleep.

"It's not Tony," Billy says. "If he could fight, he would fight, because he fought his whole life. Tony could overcome anything, if he just had the chance."

*    *    *

On January 9, 1982, Billy was driving Tony to Logan Airport, only fifteen minutes away from their Nahant home. Tony had been home for the Christmas holidays and stayed to audition for a job as the Red Sox's TV analyst on Boston's Channel 38. According to Billy Conigliaro, Tony had been told the night before that the job was his. "He said, 'I'm finally coming home,'" Billy remembers. It was two days after Tony Conigliaro's thirty-seventh birthday. He still looked like a movie star. He was going to be very big on Channel 38.

In a voice made of stone, Billy Conigliaro says, "We were just talking about the new job and how great it was that he was coming home. We were about two miles from the airport when it happened. A girl had called looking for him a few days before, and I said, 'You ever think of who that girl was that called?' And he didn't answer me right away. So I looked over. And his face was twitching. I thought he was fooling, making fun of the girl or something. He was a great mimic. Now I said, 'Tony, what are you doing?' He didn't answer me. Then his head fell to the side, and tears started coming out of his eyes. I thought to myself, Geez, he's passed out. But he was breathing still, so I didn't think he was having a heart attack. I thought about pulling over to the side and calling for help. But Mass General was close-by, so I pushed down on the gas and started goin' about eighty for the emergency entrance. It couldn't have taken me more than five minutes. But it seemed like an hour. By the time we got there, he had no pulse."

Billy Conigliaro stops here, remembering again what he cannot forget. There is just the sound of the television from the other room. Then he tells of the doctors performing the tracheotomy, and getting the heartbeat back, and how he, Billy, had to go fetch his father, Sal, from the Suffolk Downs racetrack nearby. Sal Conigliaro, dead now, had just had a bypass operation himself. Billy Conigliaro got nitroglycerin pills for his father before leaving Mass General and made him take the pills at Suffolk Downs before telling him about Tony.

They drove back to the hospital. Tony Conigliaro was in the coma from which he would not emerge for three weeks. The sudden cardio-pulmonary arrest had cut off oxygen to the brain's cells. The brain damage, of course, was irreversible.

"My brother was dead for five minutes," Billy says. "How was he going to be normal after that?"

In the room where Tony C. does physical therapy, there is an elevated exercise mat as big as a queen-size bed. There is a table, to which he is attached and turned upside down to help his blood circulate. With the help of a walker, his feet being picked up and laid down by the nurses, Tony C. can be taken outside to walk around the swimming pool that overlooks the Atlantic.

"Sometimes," Billy says, "in the summer, I'll come by and they'll have him lying out by the pool and he'll look, in that split second, like . . . Tony."

A few friends still come by to see him. Tony Athanas, who owns the famous Anthony's Pier 4 restaurant in Boston, comes by, and so does Bill Bates, another friend, and Ben Davidson, the former Oakland Raider whom Tony met in California, will call from a trip to Maine and say he is driving down. Baseball teammates like Rico Petrocelli and Mike Andrews used to come by, but not so much lately, as the years move everybody except his family and closest friends away from the Tony Conigliaro everybody remembers.

"You have to prod him," Billy says. "But sometimes if you give him the first name of a teammate, he'll give you the last. You say 'Rico' and he'll say 'Petrocelli.' If somebody he knows comes over, he'll look up and laugh. Or cry. Really, not many people come by anymore. It's been so long. I think they feel funny."

Billy Conigliaro shrugs.

"Don't you?" he says.

In the living room, Yvonne Baker talks Tony C. awake and tells him they're going to the mall soon. Above him, over the fireplace, is a portrait, a lovely portrait, of Tony C. swinging a bat, done by his cousin.

"I just keep pushing him," Billy says. "But it's not even like teaching someone how to talk, because he can't retain anything." He walks into the living room and kneels in front of his brother. He says, "Where you going with the Big E? C'mon. Talk to me. You're going for a . . ." Tony C. says, "Ride." With love that the house can barely contain, Billy, his brother, touches him on the cheek.

Teresa Conigliaro, the mother, has come back from morning errands and immediately offers a plate of cookies. She is sixty-eight years old. She lost her husband to his bad heart in 1987. Half an hour with her tells you she has had a certain marvelous strength her whole life. We have been talking at her kitchen table about this passage in the Bible, from First Corinthians, one promising that God will give no person more burden than he or she can bear.

"I used to believe that," she says. "And the part about seek and you shall find, and ask and you shall receive. I've been asking for five years."

She takes a breath and tries building another smile. "There I go. You can't look back. If I did, I'd cry all the time."

The care of Tony C. is expensive, more than $100,000 a year according to Billy. As I write this, the Conigliaro family is still fighting with Equitable about insurance money through the Major League Baseball Players Association. A 1983 benefit at Boston's Symphony Hall, at which Frank Sinatra and Dionne Warwick performed, raised $230,000, but, as Teresa Conigliaro says, "That was a long time ago."

Yvonne Baker comes into the kitchen for another cup of coffee. Tony C. has gone back to sleep. At forty-three, going on forty-four, he has gray hair and is quite skinny; you already see what he will look like at sixty-four.

In the kitchen, I tell the Big E she has a lot of energy. "It doesn't help if I come in every day with a sad face," she says. "All I do then is drag him down."

In the living room she shuts off the television and pokes Tony C. on the shoulder.

"C'mon fella," the Big E says, "we got interesting things to do today."

Billy Conigliaro drives me to where my rented car is parked. We shake hands. I tell him I will pray for his brother.

"We just don't want people to forget," he says. "You know?"

People shouldn't forget. Sometime this season there should be a big night for the Conigliaro family, a big fundraising night, maybe at the All-Star Dinner, something to put on television. The commissioner-elect of baseball, A. Bartlett Giamatti, has been a Red Sox fan his whole life. He should organize it, so that baseball can remember, so everybody can remember, just once more, on a fine summer night, what it was like when Tony C. was young and he was going to hit balls over the wall forever.

1990

## William Nack

....................................................................................................

# Pure Heart

FROM *Sports Illustrated*

JUST BEFORE NOON the horse was led haltingly into a van next to the stallion barn, and there a concentrated barbiturate was injected into his jugular. Forty-five seconds later there was a crash as the stallion collapsed. His body was trucked immediately to Lexington, Kentucky, where Dr. Thomas Swerczek, a professor of veterinary science at the University of Kentucky, performed the necropsy. All of the horse's vital organs were normal in size except for the heart.

"We were all shocked," Swerczek said. "I've seen and done thousands of autopsies on horses, and nothing I'd ever seen compared to it. The heart of the average horse weighs about nine pounds. This was almost twice the average size, and a third larger than any equine heart I'd ever seen. And it wasn't pathologically enlarged. All the chambers and the valves were normal. It was just larger. I think it told us why he was able to do what he did."

In the late afternoon of Monday, October 2, 1989, as I headed my car from the driveway of Arthur Hancock's Stone Farm onto Winchester Road outside of Paris, Kentucky, I was seized by an impulse as beckoning as the wind that strums through the trees there, mingling the scents of new grass and old history.

For reasons as obscure to me then as now, I felt compelled to see Lawrence Robinson. For almost thirty years, until he suffered a stroke in March of 1983, Robinson was the head caretaker of stallions at Claiborne Farm. I had not seen him since his illness, but I knew he still lived on the farm, in a small white frame house set on a hill overlooking the lush stallion paddocks and the main stallion barn. In the first stall of that barn, in the same space that was once home to the great Bold Ruler, lived Secretariat, Bold Ruler's greatest son.

It was through Secretariat that I had met Robinson. On the bright, cold afternoon of November 12, 1973, he was one of several hundred people gathered at Blue Grass Airport in Lexington to greet the horse on his flight from New York into retirement in Kentucky. I flew with the horse that day, and as the plane banked over the field, a voice from the tower crackled over the airplane radio: "There's more people out here to meet Secretariat than there was to greet the governor."

"Well, he's won more races than the governor," pilot Dan Neff replied.

An hour later, after a van ride out the Paris Pike behind a police escort with blue lights flashing, Robinson led Secretariat onto a ramp at Claiborne and toward his sire's old stall — out of racing and into history. For me, that final walk beneath a grove of trees, with the colt slanting like a buck through the autumn gloaming, brought to a melancholy close the richest, grandest, damnedest, most exhilarating time of my life. For eight months, first as the racing writer for Long Island, New York's *Newsday* and then as the designated chronicler of the horse's career, I had a daily front-row seat to watch Secretariat. I was at the barn in the morning and the racetrack in the afternoon for what turned out to be the year's greatest show in sports, at the heart of which lay a Triple Crown performance unmatched in the history of American racing.

Sixteen years had come and gone since then, and I had never attended a Kentucky Derby or a yearling sale at Keeneland without driving out to Claiborne to visit Secretariat, often in the company of friends who had never seen him. On the long ride from Louisville, I would regale them with stories about the horse — how on that early morning in March of 1973 he had materialized out of the quickening blue darkness in the upper stretch at Belmont Park, his ears pinned back, running as fast as horses run; how he had lost the Wood Memorial and won the Derby, and how he had been bothered by a pigeon feather at Pimlico on the eve of the Preakness (at the end of this tale I would pluck the delicate, mashed feather out of my wallet, like a picture of my kids, to pass around the car); how on the morning of the Belmont Stakes he had burst from the barn like a stud horse going to the breeding shed and had walked around the outdoor ring on his hind legs, pawing at the sky; how he had once grabbed my notebook and refused to give it back, and how he had seized a rake in his teeth and begun raking the shed; and, finally, I told about that magical, unforgettable instant, frozen now in time, when he had turned for home, appearing out of a dark drizzle at Woodbine, near Toronto, in the last race of his career, twelve in front and steam puffing from his nostrils as from a factory whistle, bounding like some mythical beast out of Greek lore.

Oh, I knew all the stories, knew them well, had crushed and rolled them in my hand until their quaint musk lay in the saddle of my palm. Knew them as I knew the stories of my children. Knew them as I knew the stories of my own life. Told them at dinner parties, swapped them with horseplayers as if they were trading cards, argued over them with old men and blind fools who had seen the show but missed the message. Dreamed them and turned them over like pillows in my rubbery sleep. Woke up with them, brushed my aging teeth with them, grinned at them in the mirror. Horses have a way of getting inside of you, and so it was that Secretariat became like a fifth child in our house, the older boy who was off at school and never around but who was as loved and true a part of the family as Muffin, our shaggy, epileptic dog.

The story I now tell begins on that Monday afternoon last October on the macadam outside of Stone Farm. I had never been to Paris, Kentucky, in the early fall, and I only happened to be there that day to begin an article about the Hancock family, the owners of Claiborne and Stone farms. There wasn't a soul on the road to point the way to Robinson's place, so I swung in and out of several empty driveways until I saw a man on a tractor cutting the lawn in front of Marchmont, Dell Hancock's mansion. He yelled back to me: "Take a right out the drive. Go down to Claiborne House. Then a right at the driveway across the road. Go up a hill to the big black barn. Turn left and go down to the end. Lawrence had a stroke a few years back, y'know."

The house was right where he said. I knocked on the front door, then walked behind and knocked on the back, and called through a side window into a room where music was playing. No one answered. But I had time to kill, so I wandered over to the stallion paddock, just a few yards from the house. The stud Ogygian, a son of Damascus, lifted his head inquiringly. He started walking toward me, and I put my elbows on the top of the fence and looked down the gentle slope toward the stallion barn.

And suddenly there he was, Secretariat, standing outside the barn and grazing at the end of a lead shank held by Groom Bobby Anderson, who was sitting on a bucket in the sun. Even from a hundred yards away, the horse appeared lighter than I had seen him in years. It struck me as curious that he was not running free in his paddock — why was Bobby grazing him? — but his bronze coat reflected the October light, and it never occurred to me that something might be wrong. But something was terribly wrong. On Labor Day, Secretariat had come down with laminitis, a life-threatening hoof disease, and here, a month later, he was still suffering from its aftershocks.

Secretariat was dying. In fact, he would be gone within forty-eight hours.

I briefly considered slipping around Ogygian's paddock and dropping down to visit, but I had never entered Claiborne through the back door, and so I thought better of it. Instead, for a full half hour I stood by the paddock waiting for Robinson and gazing in the distance at Secretariat. The gift of reverie is a blessing divine, and it is conferred most abundantly on those who lie in hammocks or drive alone in cars. Or lean on hillside fences in Kentucky. The mind swims, binding itself to whatever flotsam comes along, to old driftwood faces and voices of the past, to places and scenes once visited, to things not seen or done but only dreamed.

It was July 4, 1972, and I was sitting in the press box at Aqueduct with Clem Florio, a former prizefighter turned Baltimore handicapper, when I glanced at the *Daily Racing Form*'s past performances for the second race, a 5½-furlong buzz for maiden two-year-olds. As I scanned the pedigrees, three names leaped out: By Bold Ruler–Somethingroyal, by Princequillo. Bold Ruler was the nation's preeminent sire, and Somethingroyal was the dam of several stakes winners, including the fleet Sir Gaylord. It was a match of royalty. Even the baby's name seemed faintly familiar: Secretariat. Where had I heard it before? But of course! Lucien Laurin was training the colt at Belmont Park for Penny Chenery Tweedy's Meadow Stable, making Secretariat a stablemate of that year's Kentucky Derby and Belmont Stakes winner, Riva Ridge.

I had seen Secretariat just a week before. I had been at the Meadow Stable barn one morning, checking on Riva, when exercise rider Jimmy Gaffney took me aside and said, "You wanna see the best-lookin' two-year-old you've ever seen?"

We padded up the shed to the colt's stall. Gaffney stepped inside. "What do you think?" he asked. The horse looked magnificent, to be sure, a bright red chestnut with three white feet and a tapered white marking down his face. "He's gettin' ready," Gaffney said. "Don't forget the name: Secretariat. He can run." And then, conspiratorially, Gaffney whispered, "Don't quote me, but this horse will make them all forget Riva Ridge."

So that is where I had first seen him, and here he was in the second at

Aqueduct. I rarely bet in those days, but Secretariat was 3–1, so I put $10 on his nose. Florio and I fixed our binoculars on him and watched it all. Watched him as he was shoved sideways at the break, dropping almost to his knees, when a colt named Quebec turned left out of the gate and crashed into him. Saw him blocked in traffic down the back side and shut off again on the turn for home. Saw him cut off a second time deep in the stretch as he was making a final run. Saw him finish fourth, obviously much the best horse, beaten by only 1¼ lengths after really running but an eighth of a mile.

You should have seen Clem. Smashing his binoculars down on his desk, he leaped to his feet, banged his chair against the wall behind him, threw a few punches in the air, and bellowed, "Secretariat! That's my Derby horse for next year!"

Two weeks later, when the colt raced to his first victory by six, Florio announced to all the world, "Secretariat will win the Triple Crown next year." He nearly got into a fistfight in the Aqueduct press box that day when Mannie Kalish, a New York handicapper, chided him for making such an outrageously bold assertion: "Ah, you Maryland guys, you come to New York and see a horse break his maiden and think he's another Citation. We see horses like Secretariat all the time. I bet he don't even *run* in the Derby." Stung by the put-down "you Maryland guys," Florio came forward and stuck his finger into Kalish's chest, but two writers jumped between them and they never came to blows.

The Secretariat phenomenon, with all the theater and passion that would attend it, had begun. Florio was right, of course, and by the end of Secretariat's two-year-old season, everyone else who had seen him perform knew it. All you had to do was watch the Hopeful Stakes at Saratoga. I was at the races that August afternoon with Arthur Kennedy, an old-time racetracker and handicapper who had been around the horses since the 1920s, and even he had never seen anything quite like it. Dropping back to dead last out of the gate, Secretariat trailed eight horses into the far turn, where jockey Ron Turcotte swung him to the outside. Three jumps past the half-mile pole the colt exploded. "Now he's runnin'!" Kennedy said.

You could see the blue-and-white silks as they disappeared behind one horse, reappeared in a gap between horses, dropped out of sight again, and finally reemerged as Secretariat powered to the lead off the turn. He dashed from last to first in 290 yards, blazing through a quarter in :22, and galloped home in a laugher to win by six. It was a performance with style, touched by art. "I've never seen a two-year-old do that," Kennedy said quietly. "He looked like a four-year-old out there."

So that was when I knew. The rest of Secretariat's two-year-old campaign — in which he lost only once, in the Champagne Stakes when he was disqualified from first to second after bumping Stop the Music at the top of the stretch — was simply a mopping-up operation. At year's end, so dominant had he been that he became the first two-year-old to be unanimously voted Horse of the Year.

Secretariat wintered at Hialeah, preparing for the Triple Crown, while I shoveled snow in Huntington, New York, waiting for him to race again. In February, twenty-three-year-old Seth Hancock, the new president of Claiborne Farm, announced that he had syndicated the colt as a future breeding stallion for a then world record $6.08 million, in thirty-two shares at $190,000 a share, making the 1,154-pound horse worth more than three times his weight in gold. (Bullion was selling at the time for $90 an ounce.) Like everyone else, I thought Secretariat would surely begin his campaign in Florida, and I did not expect to see him again until the week before the Kentucky Derby. I was browsing through a newspaper over breakfast one day when I saw a news dispatch whose message went through me like a current. Secretariat would be arriving soon to begin his Triple Crown campaign by way of the three New York prep races: the Bay Shore, the Gotham, and the Wood Memorial Stakes.

"Hot damn!" I blurted to my family. "Secretariat is coming to New York!"

At the time, I had in mind doing a diary about the horse, a chronicle of the adventures of a Triple Crown contender, which I thought might one day make a magazine piece. The colt arrived at Belmont Park on March 10, and the next day I was there at 7 A.M., scribbling notes in a pad. For the next forty days, in what became a routine, I would fall out of bed at 6 A.M., make a cup of instant coffee, climb into my rattling green Toyota, and drive the twenty miles to Belmont Park. I had gotten to know the Meadow Stable family — Tweedy, Laurin, Gaffney, groom Eddie Sweat, assistant trainer Henny Hoeffner — in my tracking of Riva Ridge the year before, and I had come to feel at home around Belmont's Barn 5, particularly around stall 7, Secretariat's place. I took no days off, except one morning to hide Easter eggs, and I spent hours sitting on the dusty floor outside Secretariat's stall, talking to Sweat as he turned a rub rag on the colt, filled his water bucket, bedded his stall with straw, kept him in hay and oats. I took notes compulsively, endlessly, feeling for the texture of the life around the horse.

A typical page of scribblings went like this: "Sweat talks to colt . . . easy, Red, I'm comin' in here now . . . stop it, Red! You behave now . . . Sweat moves around colt. Brush in hand. Flicks off dust. Secretariat sidesteps and pushes Sweat. Blue sky. Henny comes up. 'How's he doin', Eddie?' 'He's gettin' edgy.' . . . Easy Sunday morning."

Secretariat was an amiable, gentlemanly colt with a poised and playful nature that at times made him seem as much a pet as the stable dog was. I was standing in front of his stall one morning, writing, when he reached out, grabbed my notebook in his teeth, and sank back inside, looking to see what I would do. "Give the man his notebook back!" yelled Sweat. As the groom dipped under the webbing, Secretariat dropped the notebook on the bed of straw.

Another time, after raking the shed, Sweat leaned the handle of the rake against the stall webbing and turned to walk away. Secretariat seized the handle in his mouth and began pushing and pulling it across the floor. "Look at him rakin' the shed!" cried Sweat. All up and down the barn, laughter fluttered like the pigeons in the stable eaves as the colt did a passable imitation of his own groom.

By his personality and temperament, Secretariat became the most engaging character in the barn. His own stable pony, a roan named Billy Silver, began an unrequited love affair with him. "He loves Secretariat, but Secretariat don't pay any attention to him," Sweat said one day. "If Billy sees you grazin' Secretariat, he'll go to hollerin' until you bring him out. Secretariat just ignores him. Kind of sad, really." One morning, I was walking beside Hoeffner through the shed, with Gaffney and Secretariat ahead of us, when Billy stuck his head out of his jerry-built stall and nuzzled the colt as he went by.

Hoeffner did a double take. "Jimmy!" he yelled. "Is that pony botherin' the big horse?"

"Nah," said Jimmy. "He's just smellin' him a little."

Hoeffner's eyes widened. Spinning around on his heels, jabbing a finger in the air, he bellowed, "Get the pony out of here! I don't want him smellin' the big horse."

Leaning on his rake, Sweat laughed softly. "Poor Billy Silver. He smelled the wrong horse!"

I remember wishing that those days could breeze on forever — the mornings over coffee and doughnuts at the truck outside the barn, the hours spent watching the red colt walk to the track and gallop once around, the days absorbing the rhythms of the life around the horse. I had been following racehorses since I was twelve, back in the days of Native Dancer, and now I was an observer on an odyssey, a quest for the Triple Crown. It had been twenty-five years since Citation had won racing's holy grail. For me, the adventure really began in the early morning of March 14, when Laurin lifted Turcotte aboard Secretariat and said, "Let him roll, Ronnie."

The colt had filled out substantially since I had last seen him under tack, in the fall, and he looked like some medieval charger — his thick neck bowed and his chin drawn up beneath its mass, his huge shoulders shifting as he strode, his coat radiant and his eyes darting left and right. He was walking to the track for his final workout, a three-eighths-of-a-mile drill designed to light the fire in him for the seven-furlong Bay Shore Stakes three days later. Laurin, Tweedy, and I went to the clubhouse fence near the finish line, where we watched and waited as Turcotte headed toward the pole and let Secretariat rip. Laurin clicked his stopwatch.

The colt was all by himself through the lane, and the sight and sound of him racing toward us is etched forever in memory: Turcotte was bent over him, his coat blown up like a parachute, and the horse was reaching out with his forelegs in that distinctive way he had, raising them high and then, at the top of the lift, snapping them out straight and with tremendous force, the snapping hard as bone, the hooves striking the ground and folding it beneath him. Laurin clicked his watch as Secretariat raced under the wire. "Oh my god!" he cried. "Thirty-three and three fifths!" Horses rarely break thirty-four seconds in three-furlong moves.

Looking ashen, fearing the colt might have gone too fast, Laurin headed for the telephone under the clubhouse to call the upstairs clocker, Jules Watson. "Hello there, Jules. How fast did you get him?"

I watched Laurin's face grow longer as he listened, until he looked thunderstruck: *Thirty-two and three fifths?* A full second faster than Laurin's own clocking, it was the fastest three-furlong workout I had ever heard of. Tweedy smiled cheerily and said, "Well, that ought to open his pipes!"

Oh, it did that. Three days later, blocked by a wall of horses in the Bay Shore, Secretariat plunged through like a fullback, 220 yards from the wire, and bounded off to win the race by 4½ lengths. I could hear a man screaming behind me. I turned and saw Roger Laurin, Lucien's son, raising his arms in the air and shouting, "He's too much horse! They can't stop him. They can't even stop him with a wall of horses!"

I had ridden horses during my youth in Morton Grove, Illinois, and I remember one summer I took a little black bullet of a thoroughbred filly out of the barn and walked her to the track that rimmed the polo field across Golf Road. I had been to the races a few times, had seen the jockeys ride, and I wanted to feel what it was like. So I hitched up my stirrups and galloped her around the east turn, standing straight up. Coming off the turn, I dropped into a crouch and clucked to her. She took off like a sprinter leaving the blocks — swooooosh! — and the wind started whipping in my eyes. I could feel the tears streaming down my face, and then I looked down and saw her knees pumping like pistons. I didn't think she would make the second turn, the woods were looming ahead, big trees coming up, and so I leaned a little to the left and she made the turn before she started pulling up. No car ever took me on a ride like that. And no roller coaster, either. Running loose, without rails, she gave me the wildest, most thrilling ride I had ever had.

And there was nothing like the ride that Secretariat gave me in the twelve weeks from the Bay Shore through the Belmont Stakes. Three weeks after the Bay Shore, Turcotte sent the colt to the lead down the backstretch in the one-mile Gotham. It looked like they were going to get beat when Champagne Charlie drove to within a half length at the top of the stretch — I held my breath — but Turcotte sent Secretariat on, and the colt pulled away to win by three, tying the track record of 1:33²/₅.

By then I had begun visiting Charles Hatton, a columnist for the *Daily Racing Form,* who the previous summer had proclaimed Secretariat the finest physical specimen he had ever seen.At sixty-seven, Hatton had seen them all. After my morning work was over, I would trudge up to Hatton's private aerie at Belmont Park and tell him what I had learned. I was his backstretch eyes, he my personal guru. One morning, Hatton told me that Secretariat had galloped a quarter mile past the finish line at the Gotham, and the clockers had timed him pulling up at 1:59²/₅, three fifths of a second faster than Northern Dancer's Derby record for 1¼ miles.

"This sucker breaks records pulling up," Hatton said. "He might be the best racehorse I ever saw. Better than Man o' War."

Those were giddy, heady days coming to the nine-furlong Wood

Memorial, the colt's last major prep before the Kentucky Derby. On the day of the Wood, I drove directly to Aqueduct and spent the hour before the race in the receiving barn with Sweat, exercise rider Charlie Davis, and Secretariat. When the voice over the loudspeaker asked the grooms to ready their horses, Sweat approached the colt with the bridle. Secretariat always took the bit easily, opening his mouth when Sweat moved to fit it in, but that afternoon it took Sweat a full five minutes to bridle him. Secretariat threw his nose in the air, backed up, shook his head. After a few minutes passed, I asked, "What's wrong with him, Eddie?"

Sweat brushed it off: "He's just edgy."

In fact, just that morning, Dr. Manuel Gilman, the track veterinarian, had lifted the colt's upper lip to check his identity tattoo and had discovered a painful abscess about the size of a quarter. Laurin decided to run Secretariat anyway — the colt needed the race — but he never told anyone else about the boil. Worse than the abscess, though, was the fact that Secretariat had had the feeblest workout of his career four days earlier, when Turcotte, seeing a riderless horse on the track, had slowed the colt to protect him from a collision. Secretariat finished the mile that day in 1:42²/₅, five seconds slower than Laurin wanted him to go. Thus he came to the Woody doubly compromised.

The race was a disaster. Turcotte held the colt back early, but when he tried to get Secretariat to pick up the bit and run, he got no response. I could see at the far turn that the horse was dead. He never made a race of it, struggling to finish third, beaten by four lengths by his own stablemate, Angle Light, and by Sham. Standing near the owner's box, I saw Laurin turn to Tweedy and yell, "Who won it?"

"You won it!" Tweedy told him.

"Angle Light won it," I said to him.

"Angle Light?" he howled back. But of course! Laurin trained him, too, and so Laurin had just won the Wood, but with the wrong horse.

I was sick. All those hours at the barn, all those early mornings at the shed, all that time and energy for naught. And in the most important race of his career, Secretariat had come up as hollow as a gourd. The next two weeks were among the most agonizing of my life. As great a stallion as he was, Bold Ruler had been essentially a speed sire and had never produced a single winner of a Triple Crown race. I couldn't help but suspect that Secretariat was another Bold Ruler, who ran into walls beyond a mile. In the next two weeks, Churchill Downs became a nest of rumors that Secretariat was unsound. Jimmy (the Greek) Snyder caused an uproar when he said the colt had a bum knee that was being treated with ice packs. I *knew* that wasn't true. I had been around him all spring, and the most ice I had seen near him was in a glass of tea.

All I could hope for, in those final days before the Derby, was that the colt had been suffering from a bellyache on the day of the Wood and had not been up to it. I remained ignorant of the abscess for weeks, and I had not yet divined the truth about Secretariat's training: he needed hard, blistering workouts before he ran, and that slow mile before the Wood had been inadequate. The night before the Derby, I made my selections, and the next day, two hours before post time, I climbed the stairs to the Churchill Downs jockeys' room to see Turcotte. He greeted me in an anteroom, looking surprisingly relaxed. Gilman had taken him aside a few days earlier and told him of the abscess. Turcotte saw that the boil had been treated and had disappeared. The news had made him euphoric, telling him all he needed to know about the Wood.

"You nervous?" he asked.

I shrugged. "I don't think you'll win," I said. "I picked My Gallant and Sham one-two, and you third."

"I'll tell you something," Turcotte said. "He'll beat these horses if he runs his race."

"What about the Wood?" I asked.

He shook me off. "I don't believe the Wood," he said. "I'm telling you. Something was wrong. But he's O.K. now. That's all I can tell you."

I shook his hand, wished him luck, and left. Despite what Turcotte had said, I was resigned to the worst, and Secretariat looked hopelessly beaten as the field of thirteen dashed past the finish line the first time. He was dead last. Transfixed, I could not take my eyes off him. In the first turn, Turcotte swung him to the outside and Secretariat began passing horses, and down the back side I watched the jockey move him boldly from eighth to seventh to sixth. Secretariat was fifth around the far turn and gaining fast on the outside. I began chanting: "Ride him, Ronnie! Ride him!" Sham was in front, turning for home, but then there was Secretariat, joining him at the top of the stretch. Laffit Pincay, on Sham, glanced over and saw Secretariat and went to the whip. Turcotte lashed Secretariat. The two raced head and head for 100 yards, until gradually Secretariat pulled away. He won by 2½ lengths. The crowd roared, and I glanced at the tote board: 1:59²/₅! A new track and Derby record.

Throwing decorum to the wind, I vaulted from my seat and dashed madly through the press box, jubilantly throwing a fist in the air. Handicapper Steve Davidowitz came racing toward me from the other end.

We clasped arms and spun a jig in front of the copy machine. "Unbelievable!" Davidowitz cried.

I bounded down a staircase, three steps at a time. Turcotte had dismounted and was crossing the racetrack when I reached him. "What a ride!" I yelled.

"What did I tell you, Mr. Bill?" he said.

I had just witnessed the greatest Kentucky Derby performance of all time. Secretariat's quarter-mile splits were unprecedented — :25⅕, :24, :23⅘, :23⅖, and :23. He ran each quarter faster than the preceding one. Not even the most veteran racetracker could recall a horse who had done this in a mile-and-a-quarter race. As quickly as his legions (I among them) had abandoned him following the Wood, so did they now proclaim Secretariat a superhorse.

We all followed him to Pimlico for the Preakness two weeks later, and he trained as if he couldn't get enough of it. He thrived on work and the racetrack routine. Most every afternoon, long after the crowds of visitors had dispersed, Sweat would graze the colt on a patch of grass outside the shed, then lead him back into his stall and while away the hours doing chores. One afternoon I was folded in a chair outside the colt's stall when Secretariat came to the door shaking his head and stretching his neck, curling his upper lip like a camel does. "What's botherin' you, Red?" Sweat asked. The groom stepped forward, plucked something off the colt's whiskers, and blew it in the air. "Just a pigeon feather itchin' him," said Sweat. The feather floated into the palm of my hand. So it ended up in my wallet, along with the $2 mutuel ticket that I had on Secretariat to win the Preakness.

In its own way, Secretariat's performance in the 1³/₁₆-mile Preakness was even more brilliant than his race in the Derby. He dropped back to last out of the gate, but as the field dashed into the first turn, Turcotte nudged his right rein as subtly as a man adjusting his cuff, and the colt took off like a flushed deer. The turns at Pimlico are tight, and it had always been considered suicidal to take the first bend too fast, but Secretariat sprinted full-bore around it, and by the time he turned into the back side, he was racing to the lead. Here Turcotte hit the cruise control. Sham gave chase in vain, and Secretariat coasted home to win by 2½. The electric timer malfunctioned, and Pimlico eventually settled on 1:54⅖ as the official time, but two *Daily Racing Form* clockers caught Secretariat in 1:53⅖, a track record by three fifths of a second.

I can still see Florio shaking his head in disbelief. He had seen thousands of Pimlico races and dozens of Preaknesses over the years, but never anything like this. "Horses don't *do* what he did here today," he kept saying. "They just don't *do* that and win."

Secretariat wasn't just winning. He was performing like an original, making it all up as he went along. And everything was moving so fast, so unexpectedly, that I was having trouble keeping a perspective on it. Not three months before, after less than a year of working as a turf writer, I had started driving to the racetrack to see this one horse. For weeks I was often the only visitor there, and on many afternoons it was just Sweat, the horse, and me, in the fine dust with the pregnant stable cat. And then came the Derby and the Preakness, and two weeks later the colt was on the cover of *Time, Sports Illustrated,* and *Newsweek,* and he was a staple of the morning and evening news. Secretariat suddenly transcended being a racehorse and became a cultural phenomenon, a sort of undeclared national holiday from the tortures of Watergate and the Vietnam War.

I threw myself with a passion into that final week before the Belmont. Out to the barn every morning, home late at night, I became almost manic. The night before the race, I called Laurin at home and we talked for a long while about the horse and the Belmont. I kept wondering, What is Secretariat going to do for an encore? Laurin said, "I think he's going to win by more than he has ever won in his life. I think he'll win by ten."

I slept at the *Newsday* offices that night, and at 2 A.M. I drove to Belmont Park to begin my vigil at the barn. I circled around to the back of the shed, lay down against a tree, and fell asleep. I awoke to the crowing of a cock and watched as the stable workers showed up. At 6:07, Hoeffner strode into the shed, looked at Secretariat, and called out to Sweat, "Get the big horse ready! Let's walk him about fifteen minutes."

Sweat slipped into the stall, put the lead shank on Secretariat and handed it to Davis, who led the colt to the outdoor walking ring. In a small stable not thirty feet away, pony girl Robin Edelstein knocked a water bucket against the wall. Secretariat, normally a docile colt on a shank, rose up on his hind legs, pawing at the sky, and started walking in circles. Davis cowered below, as if beneath a thunderclap, snatching at the chain and begging the horse to come down. Secretariat floated back to earth. He danced around the ring as if on springs, his nostrils flared and snorting, his eyes rimmed in white.

Unaware of the scene she was causing, Edelstein rattled the bucket again, and Secretariat spun in a circle, bucked and leaped in the air, kicking and spraying cinders along the walls of the pony barn. In a panic, Davis tugged at the shank, and the horse went up again, higher and higher, and Davis bent back yelling, "Come on down! Come on down!"

I stood in awe. I had never seen a horse so fit. The Derby and Preakness had wound him as tight as a watch, and he seemed about to burst out of his coat. I had no idea what to expect that day in the Belmont, with him going a mile and a half, but I sensed we would see more of him than we had ever seen before.

Secretariat ran flat into legend, started running right out of the gate and never stopped, ran poor Sham into defeat around the first turn and down the backstretch and sprinted clear, opening two lengths, four, then five. He dashed to the three-quarter pole in 1:09⅘, the fastest six-furlong clocking in Belmont history. I dropped my head and cursed Turcotte: *What is he thinking about? Has he lost his mind?* The colt raced into the far turn, opening seven lengths past the half-mile pole. The timer flashed his astonishing mile mark: 1:34⅕!

I was seeing it but not believing it. Secretariat was still sprinting. The four horses behind him disappeared. He opened ten. Then twelve. Halfway around the turn, he was fourteen in front . . . fifteen . . . sixteen . . . seventeen. Belmont Park began to shake. The whole place was on its feet. Turning for home, Secretariat was twenty in front, having run the mile and a quarter in 1:59 flat, faster than his Derby time.

He came home alone. He opened his lead to twenty-five . . . twenty-six . . . twenty-seven . . . twenty-eight. As rhythmic as a rocking horse, he never missed a beat. I remember seeing Turcotte look over to the timer, and I looked over too. It was blinking 2:19, 2:20. The record was 2:26⅗. Turcotte scrubbed on the colt, opening thirty lengths, finally thirty-one. The clock flashed crazily: 2:22 . . . . 2:23. The place was one long, deafening roar. The colt seemed to dive for the finish, snipping it clean at 2:24.

I bolted up the press box stairs with exultant shouts and there yielded a part of myself to that horse forever.

I didn't see Lawrence Robinson that day last October. The next morning, I returned to Claiborne to interview Seth Hancock. On my way through the farm's offices, I saw one of the employees crying at her desk. Treading lightly, I passed farm manager John Sosby's office. I stopped, and he called me in. He looked like a chaplain whose duty was to tell the news to the victim's family.

"Have you heard about Secretariat?" he asked quietly.

I felt the skin tighten on the back of my neck. "Heard what?" I asked. "Is he all right?"

"We might lose the horse," Sosby said. "He came down with laminitis last month. We thought we had it under control, but he took a bad turn this morning. He's a very sick horse. He may not make it.

"By the way, why are you here?"

I had thought I knew, but now I wasn't sure.

Down the hall, sitting at his desk, Hancock appeared tired, despairing and anxious, a man facing a decision he didn't want to make. What Sosby had told me was just beginning to sink in. "What's the prognosis?" I asked.

"Ten days to two weeks," Hancock said.

"Two weeks? Are you serious?" I blurted.

"You asked me the question," he said.

I sank back in my chair. "I'm not ready for this," I told him.

"How do you think I feel?" he said. "Ten thousand people come to this farm every year, and all they want to see is Secretariat. They don't give a hoot about the other studs. You want to know who Secretariat is in human terms? Just imagine the greatest athlete in the world. The greatest. Now make him six foot three, the perfect height. Make him real intelligent and kind. And on top of that, make him the best-lookin' guy ever to come down the pike. He was all those things as a horse. He isn't even a horse anymore. He's a legend. So how do you think I feel?"

Before I left, I asked Hancock to call me in Lexington if he decided to put the horse down. We agreed to meet at his mother's house the next morning. "By the way, can I see him?" I asked.

"I'd rather you not," he said. I told Hancock I had been to Robinson's house the day before and I had seen Secretariat from a distance, grazing. "That's fine," Hancock said. "Remember him how you saw him, that way. He doesn't look good."

I did not know it then, but Secretariat was suffering the intense pain in the hooves that is common to laminitis. That morning, Anderson had risen at dawn to check on the horse, and Secretariat had lifted his head and nickered very loudly. "It was like he was beggin' me for help," Anderson would later recall.

I left Claiborne stunned. That night, I made a dozen phone calls to friends, telling them the news, and I sat up late, dreading the next day. I woke up early and went to breakfast and came back to the room. The message light was dark. It was Wednesday, October 4. I drove out to Waddell Hancock's place in Paris. "It doesn't look good," she said. We had talked for more than an hour when Seth, looking shaken and pale, walked through the front door. "I'm afraid to ask," I said.

"It's very bad," he said. "We're going to have to put him down today."

"When?"

He did not answer. I left the house, and an hour later I was back in my room in Lexington. I had just taken off my coat when I turned and saw it, the red blinking light on my phone. I knew. I walked around the room. Out the door and down the hall. Back into the room. Out the door and around the block. Back into the room. Out the door and down to the lobby. Back into the room. I called sometime after noon. "Claiborne Farm called," said the message operator.

I phoned Annette Couvault, an old friend who is the mare booker at Claiborne, and she was crying when she read the message: "Secretariat was euthanized at 11:45 A.M. today to prevent further suffering from an incurable condition. . . ."

The last time I remember really crying was on St. Valentine's Day of 1982, when my wife called to tell me that my father had died. At the moment she called, I was sitting in a purple room in Caesars Palace, in Las Vegas, waiting for an interview with the heavyweight champion, Larry Holmes. Now here I was, in a different hotel room in a different town, suddenly feeling like a very old and tired man of forty-eight, leaning with my back against a wall and sobbing for a long time with my face in my hands.

1990

## Johnette Howard

·····································································································

# The Making of a Goon

FROM *The National Sports Daily*

HE WENT FROM nobody to notorious with a cudgel of a fist, and there was no rung of hockey to which it couldn't take him. Once he got to the NHL and stayed, the job then became one of maintaining his niche — even after the bone showed through the sliced skin of his knuckles and he had to soak his punching hand in ice between periods, even after doctors nearly had to amputate his right arm.

Joe Kocur, the Detroit Red Wings enforcer, is sometimes referred to by the rabid cult of fight-video collectors around the league as "the Mike Tyson of the NHL." But earning that reputation was one thing; maintaining it led to a frightening night against Pittsburgh when Kocur's whistling right hand dropped Jim Kyte, a six foot five Penguin defenseman, to the ice unconscious; it led to a night against Quebec when he shattered Terry Karkner's jaw and the shaken Nordique team took a week to recover; and it led to a game last February when Kocur flattened New York Islanders winger Brad Dalgarno with a single wallop, then watched Dalgarno teeter off the ice, only to learn later that he'd fractured Dalgarno's left eye orbit, his cheekbone, and — people now whisper — his resolve to go on.

In the beginning, it wasn't Kocur's idea to fistfight his way to the NHL. His first fight? He was just fourteen, playing in his first exhibition game with a new team, and an older kid cornered him and dared him to go. He says he was just fifteen when his coach was Gerry James, a sort of Bo Jackson of Canada, who had dual careers with the Toronto Maple Leafs and Winnipeg Blue Bombers. James pulled Kocur aside and told him that if he wanted to make hockey a paying career, he had better start fighting with his fists.

"So I did," Kocur recalls. "I had about ten penalty minutes in the first twenty games. In the last forty games, I had two hundred fifty."

But Kocur's start — his real start — came at age seventeen, the night he knocked out a kid named Bruce Holloway in a Western League game in Kamloops, British Columbia. Not every man can recognize a peek at his destiny when he gets it, and even then, not everyone accepts it. But there was no question in young Joe Kocur's mind that he had done both after he saw Holloway collapse with a suddenness that was astounding.

Word of his savagery preceded him — "like wildfire," Kocur says — in stops at Seattle and Portland, in Swift Current and Moose Jaw and Victoria, too. At every arena, scouts with wizened eyes and sharp pencils secretly began pulling Kocur's Saskatoon coach aside, all wanting to know: "Was it a lucky punch or the real thing? Can the kid really fight? How hard does he throw?"

Holloway's coach, a celebrated tough guy named Bill LaForge, said back then: "Kocur took a couple real tough shots that didn't faze him, then he came back and threw a bomb that, I'm sure, Bruce will remember the rest of his life." The other guys on Kocur's team remarked later how he seemed changed as he lunged after Holloway. At that moment, the Saskatoon kids said, Joey Kocur was someone they did not know.

"I never really remembered this myself — I mean, the other guys had to tell me — but I just clicked . . . I mean, something inside of me just snapped," Kocur says today. "I just remember I was coming across the neutral ice and he high-sticked me. And I remember saying something — screaming — that I was going to get him.

"Up to that point I'd been fighting before, but I never really got mad because I guess I was just enjoying it. But right then, against that guy, I just got mad. After that, it was odd because I didn't really know what had happened to him, didn't know what to do — it was the first time, you know? I just remember standing there, thinking, 'Geez, what do I do? Do I hold him up? Do I hit him again? Should I just keep fighting or let him go?' But the refs jumped in quick and the trainers came out running."

And Kocur's teammates were right — he was changed.

"After that, I just threw caution to the wind," Kocur says. "After that, I just felt that I could fight and not get hurt. That I would never lose."

It was a far cry from his first hockey fight two years earlier. "That one, I didn't throw too many punches but I sure received a lot," Kocur says. "As I skated off I just thought, 'What a way to make a living.'"

\* \* \*

When the NHL All-Star game convened in Pittsburgh last month, Joe Kocur was not one of the skaters who glided out for a pre-game bow. In fact, in his six NHL seasons, his name has never even appeared on the ballot. But if you were to take a poll among the NHL's players and coaches, you would certainly find Kocur, twenty-five, mentioned among the league's top five "heavyweights" — NHL parlance for players whose main role is to police the ice, always ready to punch a nose when the team needs a boost or to mete out retaliatory justice as seems fitting. In his particular case, Kocur says, that especially means "keeping the flies off Stevie" (Yzerman, that is, the Red Wings superstar center and Kocur's sometime line mate).

Any poll would show one other thing, too, says St. Louis Blues center Adam Oates: "No one in our league punches harder. In that regard Joe's the absolute best at what he does."

If any pangs of conscience come with the job, if Kocur feels a measure of regret on those mornings when he wakes up and finds blood on his pillow from his mangled right hand, he will not confess them. Doctors have told him to expect arthritis and calcium deposits in his punching fist. "Put it this way," Kocur says drolly, "I'll never play piano."

Detroit General Manager Jimmy Devellano hopes to find Kocur a job with the Red Wings after his playing days are through because "he's given his hand for the organization."

Devellano's assessment of Kocur's contribution is closer to the literal truth than perhaps he intended.

Along the back side of Kocur's always bloated right hand, a three-inch red scar carves a crooked path from the middle knuckle toward the wrist. He split the hand open during a 1985 minor league game in Halifax, when he knocked out a six-three, two-hundred-pound Nova Scotia defenseman named Jim Playfair.

In the dressing room later, a doctor needed forty stitches to close the gash. But when the rest of the team came off the ice, Kocur got some good news, too: The Red Wings had called him up to the NHL.

The next morning, Kocur took the first plane out and flew all day. He checked into a hotel in Detroit, then spent an excruciating, sleepless night watching his right arm balloon to three times its normal size. When sunrise finally came, he got to the rink early for the Wings' morning skate. But a trainer noticed the new kid was wearing only one glove. The team doctor was summoned, then a hand surgeon, too.

"This was about two P.M.," Kocur says, "and the next thing I knew, they got me a hospital room, got me an IV. I was in major surgery by five P.M."

Because doctors in Halifax didn't realize Kocur had cut his hand on Playfair's teeth, they sewed the wound shut, preventing it from draining and allowing infection to take hold. Just a day and a half later, the poisoned tendons and tissue between Kocur's third and fourth knuckles had already begun to rot.

When he emerged from a morphine-induced cloud two weeks after surgery, doctors explained what had happened. "If I'd waited even one more day, they might have had to amputate my whole right arm," Kocur says.

And how did that make him feel?

"Well," Kocur says, "it made me realize how bad I want to play hockey."

When asked if he ever dreamed of being a goal scorer — maybe a star center who glided along the ice, protected by guys like him — Kocur won't commit. "Maybe," he says. Then he adds, "I also know what got me here and how I'm going to stay.

"I know the day I start playing a fancy hockey game without hitting anyone, without fighting, is the day I'll either get sent down or released from the game," Kocur says. "It's put food in my belly. It's what has kept me in this game. And I wouldn't give up this lifestyle for anything else in the world. So I'm not about to trade in my boxing gloves for a, for a . . . a wand."

But what about that year in the juniors, that year he scored a career-high forty goals?

"That," Kocur says with a sardonic smile, "was also the year I knocked out Holloway. Guys tend to give you a little more room."

On the surface, the fighting and machismo that abound in hockey may seem like an archaic ritual, the folly of men in oversize shorts. But hockey's insiders — men like Kocur — shake their heads and explain not only why intimidation works but why they believe that policing the ice is necessary. Their reasoning also explains why hockey's tough guys are almost as celebrated as the great scorers.

First remember, they will tell you, that hockey would be a violent game even without fighting. Players wear heavy padding. They carry sticks they're unafraid to use, and their skate blades are so sharp that several NHL players have nearly died from gashes suffered in pileups.

The danger is multiplied even further at the NHL level by the sheer speed of the game and the inevitability of collisions. Today's swiftest skaters hit speeds around thirty miles per hour in rinks just 200 feet long and 85 feet wide. And every hockey trainer's black bag contains a pair of forceps, just in case the impact of a collision causes a player to swallow his tongue.

In a game like this, the indecisive and the fearful cannot survive. On rinks this small, there is nowhere to hide. And perhaps it's no wonder that hockey's past is dotted with instances of players retiring because of "nerves" and goalies who suddenly begin to suffer from agoraphobia. Once the puck starts ricocheting around, says Kocur, "you have to be absolutely fearless out there. You have to think that you can't be hurt and never will."

Then, once you have that conviction, hockey also asks that you hold on to it, even when it doesn't make sense.

"Outsiders look at these guys and marvel at how they keep coming back, coming back, playing with broken noses and their jaws wired shut," Red Wings Coach Jacques Demers says. "But it's funny — as a coach, you almost get used to it. They skate off and take stitches and sometimes they just miss one or two shifts. You look and they're back in there. They're tough."

Like no other sport, hockey celebrates its toughest players. Gone are legends like Detroit's Ted (Scarface) Lindsay and savage Eddie Shore, the Boston defenseman of the 1930s who ended his career with a total of 978 stitches. But inside the current edition of *The Hockey Register,* an annual compilation of NHL players' career stats, there appears below each man's name a sort of living lore, a boldface paragraph recounting calamitous injuries or noteworthy fights.

DEAN CHYNOWETH (October 27, 1988) — Left eye injured by Rick Tocchet vs. Philadelphia and missed nearly two months.

BRUCE DRIVER (December 8, 1988) — Broke right leg in three places when checked by Lou Franceschetti vs. Washington and had surgery to implant a plate and 10 screws.

The *Register's* grisly cataloguing sometimes includes fetishistic detail. Under Guy LaFleur's name it reads: "(March 24, 1981) — Fell asleep at the wheel of his car, hit a fence and a metal sign post, sliced off the top part of his right ear after the fence post went through his windshield." But there's some unintended humor, too. Take Larry Robinson's entry:

"(January 1, 1987) — Broken nose. (November 9, 1988) — Sinus problem."

Though the NHL has taken steps, especially in the last fifteen years, to limit the bench-clearing brawls and dangerous stick-swinging incidents that fatten those boldface paragraphs in the *Register*, no one foresees the game's unique nightly phenomenon — legal, bare-knuckle fistfighting — being banned anytime soon.

Not as long as NHL President John Zeigler, like his predecessors, continues to define fighting as "the spontaneous combat which comes out of the frustrations of the game." Not while league executives are buoyed by modestly increasing attendance and a discernible statistical decline in violent incidents. And not in the absence of any serious uprising among the players.

Before the 1974–75 season, the players' union asked owners to ban fighting for one year and were flatly refused. But in a survey taken last season, players were "divided about fifty-fifty" when asked about abolishing fighting, says Sam Simpson, director of operations for the NHLPA.

Salaries are now the hot issue among NHL players, who see major league baseball's average climbing to $500,000 and the NBA median approaching $1 million a year. Against those numbers, the NHL average of $180,000 seems paltry.

"To be honest," says Cliff Fletcher, general manager of the Stanley Cup champion Calgary Flames, "the only real debate going on about fighting is in a couple of magazines and a few newspapers now and then."

As a result, tough guys remain not only legal but important enough to a team that the Red Wings' Demers candidly admits, "I know we wouldn't trade Joey Kocur for a thirty-goal scorer even though Joey has never scored thirty goals."

Why?

"Intimidation," Demers says, shrugging his shoulders. "It works."

"It works," says New York Rangers General Manager Neil Smith.

"It works," says Calgary's Fletcher.

Evidently, it works.

Fearless hockey fighters, like fearless hockey players, are not so much born as they are made. There's a very good reason for that, too, says Demers: "No one enjoys getting punched in the head."

Though Kocur's father, Joe Senior, is a strong, sturdy man — he's got "a handshake you remember for days," says Demers — Kocur says his dad "never fought in his life." And that was pretty much true of Joe Senior's only boy as young Joey was growing up with two sisters on a Kelvington, Saskatchewan, farm.

Fighting on ice never occurred to Kocur back then. But once he started looking beyond his small town, Kocur also understood that hockey requires players to grow up fast. By age fifteen or sixteen, most Canadian prospects leave home and live with foster families while they play fifty- or sixty-game schedules for traveling teams. These prospects, who often don't finish high school, encounter such concepts as "career advancement" early.

Besides, once Kocur started scuffling, he discovered something unexpected: "After the first couple times I got hit, I just thought, 'This ain't so bad.'"

When he looks at his role now, Kocur says, "I guess I enjoy it. But I don't want to sound like an animal, like my sole intention is to hurt somebody permanently. I just look at it as a job that I'm paid to do. And my job is not to lose. I won't fight dirty. I won't jump someone from behind. But when I go to hit someone, I want to hit him in the face. I'm trying to hit as hard as I can. And a few times it has happened that someone got hurt."

That's partly because fighting on skates changes things. "See, hockey fighting is different than boxing," says Kocur, who once visited the training camp of Detroit's Thomas Hearns — courtesy of Red Wings owner Mike Illitch — to pick up a few tips. "In hockey, fighting is pulling and punching. If you just stand there and hold a guy out and hit him, you won't faze him. But if you can pull him into you and punch at the same time, that's when you start hurting people."

How to hit hard is just one of the lessons an enforcer must learn. There's also an unwritten and often unspoken code of honor that governs who hits whom, and under what circumstances. Kocur also likes to do research of his own; knowing other fighters' tendencies helps him avoid surprises. But nothing, Kocur says, supersedes the most basic fighter's rule: Never, ever lose.

"You've got to understand some things about the fighter's job," says Demers. "Tough guys in this league are under a tremendous amount of pressure. Unfortunately, many of them are untalented except for fighting, and they've gotten here the hard way. And once you're recognized as a tough guy in this league, you go from having targets to becoming one.

"As long as you're beating up somebody, the fans are cheering and shouting your name. But the first time you lose one, everyone gets down on you. You have to be fearless. I've seen guys lose just once, and pretty soon they just sort of fade away."

Though coaches and other players all say that Kocur has good all-around hockey talent and that Demers encourages him to use it, Kocur considers himself a fighter first. He believes that preserving his aura of invincibility is essential because "it pays off down the line. Maybe I'll be going into the corner to get the puck and the guy going with me will think, 'Uh-oh, it's Joe Kocur. This guy's crazy. I won't give him the elbow in the face. I'll give him that extra step and poke at the puck instead of trying to take the body. And then maybe I can make a play, make a good pass. And maybe we'll put the puck in the net.'"

Or maybe, as in Brad Dalgarno's case, Kocur will go after the guy who follows him into the corner anyway.

Dalgarno has heard the explanations of why Kocur stalked him for two shifts during that game last February: that the Red Wings thought the six foot three, 215-pound Dalgarno had earlier put too aggressive a cross-check on Gilbert Delorme, that the penalty Dalgarno received wasn't enough.

"In the first place, I thought the penalty was a rather questionable call," Dalgarno says. "But sure enough, two shifts later, Kocur was out on the ice every time I came out. I was kind of, well, nervous. I knew he was tough, and the guys on my team kept skating by and telling me, 'Be careful, be careful Brad. He's out to get you. He's a dangerous guy.' And sure enough, after two shifts, we were fighting."

Before that single punch from Kocur shattered his cheekbone and eye socket, Dalgarno had always had nagging questions about the ethos of the game and prickly doubts about the coaches who kept trying, futilely, to turn him into a fighter because of his size. After Kocur's punch, that chasm grew deeper.

While recuperating at his parents' home in Hamilton, Ontario, a letter arrived. "Someone sent me a newspaper article from Detroit," Dalgarno says. "In it, Delorme was interviewed after I was hurt, and he made it look like, 'Oh, he deserved it.' And I remember I just thought, 'Wait a minute. Who deserved what?' Where's the justice, the value, in that?

"The doctors had to drill a hole in the side of my head [during surgery]. I could've lost my left eye, or my eye could've sunk into my orbital bone and I would've lost my vision. The nerves in the left side of my face might never have rematerialized. Fortunately they have, or I'd look like I had a stroke. I thought, 'Deserves it, deserves it? Who deserves *that?*'"

Knowing hockey wasn't going to change, Dalgarno decided that he would. He says he holds no grudges toward the game and doesn't blame Kocur for triggering his dissatisfaction. Dalgarno says other players feel "trapped by the game," just as he did.

"Ninety-nine percent of the guys in the NHL have been playing since they were five and have no idea what else they would do, or could do," he says. "It's tough for intelligent men to try to put things in hockey into perspective, because you're never told the answers. Hockey doesn't have them."

And so, for Brad Dalgarno, it all came down to this: On the eve of the 1989–90 regular season, with people whispering that his game wasn't the same, Dalgarno — age twenty-two, a former number one draft pick, a potential twenty-five-goals-a-year scorer — officially retired.

There is a TV on in a Red Wings coach's office, and one shelf below it a VCR whirs and sighs. Joe Kocur, who is pushing buttons on a remote control, says he didn't see a small classified ad in *The Hockey News* touting "The Bruise Brothers," a two-hour bootleg tape of every fight between 1983 and 1989 involving Kocur and ex-Wing Bob Probert. Kocur can hardly believe there is such a tape. But, he says, he'd like to see it.

Five days later, courtesy of a reporter, Kocur has the tape. As he fast forwards past fights he doesn't care to see, the combatants swirl on the screen at a comic, Keystone Kops pace. At one point he hits Play, and the announcer suddenly shouts, "Kocur's pulling some hair now!"

"Aw, shaaaaddup," Kocur says, scowling sheepishly, hitting Fast Forward, then Play again.

Announcer: "If Kocur's going to be a fighter in this league, he's going to have to avoid turning sideways!"

"Awwwww, what does he know?" Kocur says, restarting the fast-forward frenzy but hitting the Mute button to kill the voices, too. In a few seconds it becomes clear that the entire tape consists of nothing but fights spliced end to end. For $45, there are 170 fights in all, 84 of them Kocur's.

Most of the time, Kocur watches quietly, looking serious. When other Red Wings players begin to straggle into the room, their faces are serious, too. Sometimes they wince.

In time, the crowd grows to nine. And suddenly Kocur pipes up and says, "Hey, did any of you guys see 'Sports Final Edition' last night on TV? They had this story about people in sports who've injured other athletes. And one of the guys was this NFL linebacker that got hurt by Freeman McNeil, this running back for the Jets who had to block him and blew out the guy's knee."

Eyes remain on the screen. But Kocur continues: The linebacker said McNeil called to apologize later, but he said he felt sorry for McNeil, too. Once he saw what he'd done, McNeil was so distraught he could no longer play effectively that day. For that, Jets Coach Joe Walton publicly criticized McNeil's sensitivity.

"In the end," Kocur says, "this linebacker says that, to him, that makes Freeman McNeil a good guy, you know? A real person."

Later, when the office has cleared and the door is shut, Kocur is asked if the linebacker's story made him think. Reluctantly, Kocur says, "Well, yeah. I thought about it."

There is a long pause. When he doesn't continue he is asked, "Would you like to share what you thought?"

Without looking away from the TV or the silent fighting still going on, Joe Kocur says, "No."

1991

## Paul Solotaroff

......................................................................................................................

# The Power and the Gory

FROM *The Village Voice*

HALF THE WORLD was in mortal terror of him. He had a sixty-inch chest, twenty-three-inch arms, and when the Anadrol and Bolasterone backed up in his bloodstream, his eyes went as red as the laser scope on an Uzi. He threw people through windows, and chased them madly down Hempstead Turnpike when they had the temerity to cut him off. And in the gym he owned in Farmingdale, the notorious Mr. America's, if he caught you looking at him while he trained, you generally woke up, bleeding, on the pavement outside. Half out of his mind on androgens and horse steroids, he had this idea that being looked at robbed him of energy, energy that he needed to leg-press two thousand pounds.

Nonetheless, one day a kid walked up to him between sets and said, "I want to be just like you, Steve Michalik. I want to be Mr. America and Mr. Universe."

"Yeah?" said Michalik in thick contempt. "How bad do you think you want it?"

"Worse than anything in the world," said the kid, a scrawny seventeen-year-old with more balls than biceps. "I can honestly say that I would die for a body like yours."

"Well, then you probably will," snorted Michalik. "Meet me down at the beach tomorrow at six A.M. sharp. And if you're like even half a minute late . . ."

The kid was there at six A.M. pronto, freezing his ass off in a raggedy hood and sweats. "What do we do first?" he asked.

"Swim," grunted Michalik, dragging him into the ocean. Twenty yards out, Michalik suddenly seized the kid by his scalp and pushed him under a wave. The kid flailed punily, wriggling like a speared eel. A half minute, maybe forty-five seconds, passed before Michalik let the kid up, sobbing out sea water. He gave the kid a breath, then shoved him down again, holding him under this time until the air bubbles stopped, whereupon he dragged him out by the hood and threw him, gasping, on the beach.

"When you want the title as bad as you wanted that last fucking breath," sneered Michalik, "then and only then can you come talk to me."

For himself, Michalik only wanted two things anymore. He wanted to walk on stage at the Beacon Theater on November 15, 1986, professional bodybuilding's Night of Champions, and just turn the joint out with his 260 pounds of ripped, stripped, and shrink-wrapped muscle. And then, God help him, he wanted to die. Right there, in front of everybody, with all the flashbulbs popping, he wanted to drop dead huge and hard at the age of thirty-nine, and leave a spectacular corpse behind.

The pain, you see, had become just unendurable. Ten years of shot-gunning steroids had turned his joints into fish jelly and spiked his blood pressure so high he had to pack his nose to stop the bleeding. He'd been pissing blood for months, and what was coming out of him now was *brown*, pure protoplasm that his engorged liver hadn't the wherewithal to break down. And when he came home from the gym at night, his whole body was in spasm. His eight-year-old boy, Steve Junior, had to pack his skull in ice, trying to take the top 10 percent off his perpetual migraine.

"I knew it was all over for me," Michalik says. "Every system in my body was shot, my testicles had shrunk to the size of cocktail peanuts. It was only a question of which organ was going to explode on me first.

"See, we'd all of us [professional bodybuilders] been way over the line for years, and it was like, suddenly, all the bills were coming in. Victor Faizowitz took so much shit that his brain exploded. The Aldactazone [a diuretic] sent his body temperature up to one hundred twelve degrees, and he literally melted to death. Another guy, an Egyptian bodybuilder training for the Mr. Universe contest, went the same way, a massive hemorrhage from head to toe — died bleeding out of every orifice. And Tommy Sansone, a former Mr. America who'd been my very first mentor in the gym, blew out his immune system on Anadrol and D-ball [Dianabol], and died of tumors all over his body.

"As for me, I couldn't wait to join 'em. I had so much evil in me from all the drugs I was taking that I'd go home at night and ask God why he hadn't killed me yet. And then, in the next breath, I'd say, 'Please, I know

I've done a lot of terrible things — sold steroids to kids, beaten the shit out of strangers — but please don't let me go out like a sucker, God. Please let me die hitting that last pose at the Beacon, with the crowd on its feet for a second standing O.'"

Michalik's prayers might better have been addressed to a liver specialist. Two weeks before the show, he woke up the house at four in the morning with an excruciating pain beneath his rib cage. His wife, Thomasina, long since practiced at such emergencies, ran off to fetch some ice.

"Fuck the ice," he groaned. "Call Dr. Ludwig."

Dr. Arthur Ludwig, a prominent endocrinologist who had been treating Michalik on and off for a number of years, was saddened but unsurprised by the call. "Frankly," he told Michalik, "I've been expecting it now for ages. Your friends have been telling me lately how bad you've been abusing the stuff, especially for the last five years."

That he certainly had. Instead of cycling on and off of steroids, giving his body here and there a couple months' recuperation, Michalik had been juicing pretty much constantly since 1976, shooting himself with fourteen different drugs and swallowing copious amounts of six or seven others. Then there was all the speed he was gulping — bennies, black beauties — to get through his seven-hour workouts, and the handful of downs at night to catch four hours of tortuous sleep.

There, at any rate, Michalik was, doubled over in bed at four in the morning, his right side screaming like a bomb had gone off in it.

You'd better get him to New York Hospital as fast as you can," Ludwig told Michalik's wife over the phone. "They've got the best liver specialist on the East Coast there. I'll meet you in his office in an hour."

At the hospital, they pumped Michalik full of morphine and took a hasty sonogram upstairs. The liver specialist, a brusque Puritan who'd been apprised of Michalik's steroid usage, called him into his office.

"See this?" he pointed to the sonogram, scarcely concealing a sneer. "This is what's left of your liver, Mr. Michalik. And these" — indicating the four lumps grouped inside it, one of them the size of a ripe grapefruit — "these are hepatic tumors. You have advanced liver cancer, sir."

"I do?" grinned Michalik, practically hugging himself for joy. "How long you think I've got?"

"Mr. Michalik, do you understand what I'm telling you?" snapped the doctor, apparently miffed that his news hadn't elicited operatic grief. "You have cancer, and will be dead within weeks or days if I don't operate immediately. And frankly, your chances of surviving surgery are — "

"Surgery!" blurted Michalik, looking at the man as if he were bonkers. "You're not coming near me with a knife. That would leave a *scar*."

The doctor was with perfect justice about to order Michalik out of his office when Ludwig walked in. He took a long look at the sonogram and announced that surgery was out of the question. Michalik's liver was so compromised, he would undoubtedly die on the table. Besides, Ludwig adjudged, those weren't tumors at all. They were something rarer by far but no less deadly: steroid-induced cysts, or thick sacs of blood and muscle, that were full to bursting — and growing.

He ordered Michalik strapped down — the least movement now could perforate the cysts — and wheeled upstairs to intensive care. The next twenty-four hours, he declared, would tell the tale. If, deprived of steroids, the cysts stopped growing, there was a small chance that Michalik might come out of this. If, on the other hand, they fed on whatever junk he'd injected the last couple of days — well, he'd get his wish, at any rate, to die huge.

Michalik knew it was the liver, of course. He might have been heedless, but he was hardly uninformed. In fact, he knew so much about steroids that he'd written a manual on their use, and gone on the *Today* show to debate doctors about their efficacy. Like the steroid gurus of southern California, Michalik was a self-taught sorcerer whose laboratory was his body. From the age of eleven, he'd read voraciously in biochemistry, obsessed about finding out what made people big. He walked the streets of Brooklyn as a teenager, knocking on physicians' doors, begging to be made enlightened about protein synthesis. And years later he scoured the *Physicians' Desk Reference* from cover to cover, searching not for steroids but for other classes of drugs whose secondary function was to grow muscle.

Steroids, Michalik knew, were a kind of God's play, a way of rewriting his own DNA. He'd grown up skinny and hating himself to his very cell level. According to Michalik, his father, a despotic drunk with enormous forearms, beat him with whatever was close to hand, and smashed his face, for fun, into a plate of mashed potatoes.

"I was small and weak, and my brother Anthony was big and graceful, and my old man made no bones about loving him and hating me," Michalik recalls. "The minute I walked in from school, it was, 'You worthless little shit, what are you doing home so early?' His favorite way to torture me was to tell me he was going to put me in a *home*. We'd be driving along in Brooklyn somewhere, and we'd pass a building with iron bars on the windows, and he'd stop the car and say to me, 'Get out. This is the home we're putting you in.' I'd be standing there, sobbing on the curb — I was maybe eight or nine at the time — and after a while he'd let me get back into the car and drive off laughing at his little joke."

Fearful and friendless throughout childhood — even his brother was leery of being seen with him — Michalik hid out in comic books and Steve Reeves movies, burning to become huge and invulnerable. At thirteen, he scrubbed toilets in a Vic Tanny spa just to be in the presence of that first generation of iron giants — Eddie Juliani and Leroy Colbert, among others. At twenty, stationed at an Air Force base in Southeast Asia, he ignored sniper fire and the 120-degree heat to bench-press a cinder-block barbell in an open clearing, telling the corps psychiatrist that he couldn't be killed because it was his destiny to become Mr. America. And at thirty-four, years after he'd forgotten where he put all his trophies, he was still crawling out of bed at two in the morning to eat his eighth meal of the day because he *still* wasn't big enough. As always, there was that fugitive inch or two missing, that final heft without which he wouldn't even take his shirt off on the beach — for fear that everyone would laugh.

And so, of course, there were steroids. They'd been around since at least the mid-1930s, when Hitler had them administered to his SS thugs to spike their bloodlust. By the fifties, the eastern bloc nations were feeding them to school kids, creating a generation of bioengineered athletes. And in the late sixties, anabolics hit the beaches of California, as U.S. drug companies discovered that there was a vast new market out there of kids who'd swallow anything to double their pecs and their pleasure.

The dynamics of anabolic steroids have been pretty well understood for years. Synthetic variations of the male hormone testosterone, they enter the bloodstream as chemical messengers and attach themselves to muscle cells. Once attached to these cells, they deliver their twofold message: grow, and increase endurance.

Steroids accomplish the first task by increasing the synthesis of protein. In sufficient quantities, they turn the body into a kind of fusion engine, converting everything, including fat, into mass and energy. A chemical bodybuilder can put on fifty pounds of muscle in six months because most of the 6,000 to 10,000 calories he eats a day are incorporated, not excreted.

The second task — increasing endurance — is achieved by stimulating the synthesis of a molecule called creatine phosphate, or CP. CP is essentially hydraulic fluid for muscles, allowing them to do more than just a few seconds' work. The more CP you have in your tank, the more power you generate. Olympic weightlifters and defensive linemen have huge stockpiles of CP, some portion of which is undoubtedly genetic. The better part of it, though, probably comes out of a bottle of Anadrol, a popular oral steroid that makes you big, strong, and savage — and not necessarily in that order.

Over the course of eleven years, Michalik had taken ungodly amounts of Anadrol. If his buddies were taking two 50 mg tablets a day, he took four. Six weeks later, when he started to plateau, he jacked the ante to eight. So, too, with Dianabol, another brutal oral steroid. Where once a single 5 mg pill sufficed, inevitably he was gulping ten or twelve of them a day, in conjunction with the Anadrol.

The obstacle here was his immune system, which was stubbornly going on about its business, neutralizing these poisons with antibodies and shutting down receptor sites on the muscle cells. No matter. Michalik, upping the dosage, simply overwhelmed his immune system, and further addled it by flooding his bloodstream with other drugs.

All the while, of course, he was cognizant of the damage done. He knew, for instance, that Anadrol, like all oral steroids, was utter hell on the liver. An alkylated molecule with a short carbon chain, it had to be hydralized, or broken down, within twenty-four hours. This put enormous stress on his liver, which had thousands of other chemical transactions to carry out every day, not the least of which was processing the waste from his fifty pounds of new muscle. The *Physicians' Desk Reference* cautions that the smallest amounts of Anadrol may be toxic to the liver, even in patients taking it for only a couple of months for anemia:

WARNING: MAY CAUSE PELIOSIS HEPATIS, A CONDITION IN WHICH LIVER TISSUE IS REPLACED WITH BLOOD-FILLED CYSTS, OFTEN CAUSING LIVER FAILURE. . . . OFTEN NOT RECOGNIZED UNTIL LIFE-THREATENING LIVER FAILURE OR INTRA-ABDOMINAL HEMORRHAGE OCCURS. . . . FATAL MALIGNANT LIVER TUMORS ARE ALSO REPORTED.

As lethal as it was, however, Anadrol was like a baby food compared to some of the other stuff Michalik was taking. On the bodybuilding black market, where extraordinary things are still available, Michalik and some of his buddies bought the skulls of dead monkeys. Cracking them open with their bare hands, they drank the hormone-rich fluid that poured out of the hypothalamus gland. They filled enormous syringes with a French supplement called Triacana and, aiming for the elusive thyroid gland, *shot it right into their necks*. They took so much Ritalin before workouts to psych themselves up that one of Michalik's training partners, a former Mr. Eastern USA, ran out of the gym convinced that he could stop a car with his bare hands. He stood in the passing lane of the Hempstead Turnpike, his feet spread shoulder-width apart, bracing for the moment of impact — and got run over like a dog by a Buick Skylark, both his legs and arms badly broken.

Why, knowing what he knew about these poisons, did Michalik continue taking them? Because he, as well as his buddies and so many thousands of other bodybuilders and football players, were fiercely and progressively addicted to steroids. The American medical community is currently divided about whether or not the stuff is addictive. These are the same people who declared, after years of thorough study, that *steroids do not grow muscle*. Bodybuilders are still splitting their sides over that howler. Michalik, however, is unamused.

"First, those morons at the AMA say that steroids don't work, which anyone who's ever been inside a gym knows is bullshit," he snorts. "Then, ten years later, they tell us they're deadly. Oh, now they're deadly? Shit, that was like the FDA seal of approval for steroids. C'mon, everybody, they *must* be good for you — the AMA says they'll kill you!

"Somehow, I don't know how, I escaped getting addicted to them the first time, when I was training for the Mr. America in 1972. Maybe it was because I was on them for such a short stretch, and went relatively light on the stuff. Mostly, all it amounted to was a shot in the ass once a week from a doctor in Roslyn. I never found out what was in that shot, but Jesus, did it make me crazy. Here I was, a churchgoing, gentle Catholic, and suddenly I was pulling people out of restaurant booths and threatening to kill them just because there were no other tables open. I picked up a three-hundred-pound railroad tie and caved in the side of some guy's truck with it because I thought he'd insulted my wife. I was a nut, a psycho, constantly out of control — and then, thank God, the contest came, and I won it and got off the juice, and suddenly became human again. I retired, and devoted myself entirely to my wife for all the hell I'd put her through, and swore I'd never go near that shit again."

A couple of years later, however, something happened that sent him back to the juice, and this time there was no getting off it. "I'd bought Thomasina a big house in Farmingdale, and filled it with beautiful things, and was happier than I'd ever been in my life. And then one day I found out she'd been having an affair. I was worse than wiped out, my soul was ripped open. It had taken me all those years to finally feel like I was a man, to get over all the things my father had done to me . . . and she cut my fucking heart out."

Michalik went back to the gym, where he'd always solved all his problems, and started seeing someone we'll call Dr. X. A physician and insider in the subculture, for two decades Dr. X had been supplying bodybuilders with all manner of steroids in exchange for sexual favors. Michalik hit him up for a stack of prescriptions, but made it clear that he couldn't accommodate the doctor sexually, to the latter's keen disappointment. The two, however, worked out a satisfactory compromise. Michalik, the champion bodybuilder who was constantly being consulted by young wannabes, directed some of them posthaste to the tender governance of Dr. X.

"They had to find out sooner or later that the road to the title went through Dr. X's office," Michalik shrugs. "Nobody on this coast was gonna get to be competition size unless they put out for him — that, or they had a daddy in the pharmaceutical business. The night Dr. X first tried to seduce me, he showed me pictures of five different champions that he said he'd had sex with. I checked it out later and found out it was all true. Nice business, isn't it, professional bodybuilding? More pimps and whores than Hollywood."

Michalik didn't care about any of that, however. Nor did he care if he went crazy or got addicted to steroids. "I didn't care if I fucking died from 'em. All I cared about was getting my body back. I was down to one hundred fifty pounds, which was my natural body weight, and no one in the gym even knew who I was. Big guys were screaming at me, 'Get off that bench, you little punk, I wanna use it!' Three months later, I'm two hundred pounds and bench-pressing four hundred, and the same guys are coming over to me, going, 'Hey, aren't you Steve Michalik? When did you get here?' And I'd tell 'em, 'I've been here for the last three months, motherfucker. I'm the guy you pushed offa that bench over there, remember?'"

By that third month, he recalls, he was hopelessly hooked on steroids, unable to leave the house without "gulping three of something, and taking a shot of something else. I'd get out of bed in the morning feeling weak and sick, and stagger around, going, 'Where's my shit?' I was a junkie and I knew it and I hated myself for it. But what I hated much, much more was not getting to Dr. X's office. He had the *real* hot shit —

Primobolan, Parabolin — that you couldn't get anywhere else. They were so powerful you felt them *immediately* in your muscles, and tasted them for hours on your lips. My heart would start pounding, and the blood would come pouring out of my nose, but he'd just pack it with cotton and send me on my way.

"Suddenly, all I was doing was living and dying for those shots. I was totally obsessed about seeing him, I'd have terrible panic attacks on the subway, my brain would be racing — was I going to make it up to his office before I fell down? I was throwing people out of my way, shoving 'em into poles, practically knocking the door down before we pulled into the station.

"Understand, there was no justification for the things I did; not my wife's affair, not what had happened to me as a kid — nothing. I was an adult, I knew what I was doing, at least at the beginning, and when you add it all up, I deserve to have died from it.

"But I want you to understand what it's like to just completely lose yourself. To get buried in something so deep that you think the only way out is to die. Those ten years, it was like I was trapped inside a robot body, watching myself do horrible things, and yelling, 'Stop! Stop!' but I couldn't even slow down. It was always *more* drugs, and *more* side effects, and *more* drugs for the side effects. For ten years, I was just an animal on stimulus-response."

He flew to London in the fall of 1975 for the Mr. Universe show, already so sick from the steroids and the eight meals a day that he could scarcely make it up the stairs to the stage. "I had a cholesterol level of over 400, my blood pressure was 240 over 110 — but, Jesus Christ, I was a great-looking corpse. No one had ever seen anything like me on stage before, I had absolutely *perfect* symmetry: nineteen-inch arms, nineteen-inch calves, and a fifty-four-inch chest that was exactly twice the size of my thighs. The crowd went bazongo, the judges all loved me — and none of it, not even the title, meant shit to me. Joy, pride, any sense of satisfaction — the drugs wiped all of that out of me. The only feeling I was capable of anymore was deep, deep hatred."

Michalik went home, threw his trophy into a closet, and began training maniacally for the Mr. Olympia show, bodybuilding's most prestigious event. He'd invented a training regimen called "Intensity/Insanity," which called for *seventy* sets per body part instead of the customary ten. This entailed a seven-hour workout and excruciating pain, but the steroids, he found, turned that pain into pleasure, "a huge release of all the pressure built up inside me, the rage and the energy."

And with whatever rage and energy he had left, he ran his wife's panicked lover out of town, and completed his revenge by impregnating her "so that there'd be *two* Steve Michalik's in the world to oppress her." Spotlessly faithful to her for the first ten years of their marriage, he began nailing everyone he could get his hands on now, thanks in no small part to his daily dosage of Halotestin, a steroid whose chief side effect was a constant — and conspicuous — erection. He was also throwing down great heaps of Clomid and HCG, two fertility drugs for women that, in men, stimulate the production of testosterone.

"Bottom line, I was insatiable, and acting it out all over the place. I had girlfriends in five different towns in Long Island, and one day I was so hormone-crazed I fucked 'em all, one right after the other. Suddenly, I saw why there was so much rampant sex in this business, why the elite bodybuilders always had two or three girls in their hotel room, or were making thousands of dollars a weekend at private gay parties. In fact, one of my friends in the business, a former Mr. America, used to get so horny on tour that he'd fuck the Coke machine in his hotel. Swear to God, he'd stick his dick right in the change slot and bang it for all he was worth. I'm telling you, my wife saw him do this, she can vouch for it. He fucked those machines from coast to coast, and even had ratings for them. I seem to remember the Chicago Hyatt's being pretty high up there on the list."

Hot, in any event, off his win in the Mr. Universe, and absolutely galactic now at 250 pounds, he was the consensus pick among his peers to put an end to Arnold Schwarzenegger's reign as Mr. Olympia and begin a five- or six-year run of his own. He had even prepped himself to follow Ahnuld into show business, taking two years of acting lessons and a year of speech at Weiss-Baron Studios in Manhattan. One of the networks approached him about hosting a science show. George Butler and Charles Gaines filmed him extensively for *Pumping Iron,* the definitive bodybuilding flick that put Schwarzenegger on the map in Hollywood.

And then, driving himself to the airport for the Mr. Olympia show that November, Michalik suddenly ran into something bigger than steroids. A tractor-trailer driver, neglecting to check his mirror, veered into Michalik's lane on Route 109 and ran right over the hood of his Mustang. Michalik was dragged twenty yards into an embankment; the Mustang crumpled up around him. When they finally sawed him out of it two hours later, he had four cracked discs and a torn sciatic nerve, and was completely paralyzed from the waist down.

The bad news, said the surgeon after a battery of X-rays, was that Michalik would never walk again. The good news was that with a couple of operations, the pain could be substantially mitigated. Michalik told him to get the fuck out of his room. For months he lay in traction, refusing medication, and with his free arm went on injecting himself with testosterone, which he'd had with him in a black bag at the time of the accident, and which the hospital had so thoughtfully put on his bedside table.

"It was hilarious. The idiot doctors kept coming in and going. 'Gee, your blood pressure seems awfully high, Mr. Michalik,' and I'd just lay there with a straight face and go, 'Well, I *have* been very tense, you know, since the accident.'

"Meanwhile, for the one and only time in my life, the steroids were actually helping me. They speeded up the healing, which is actually their medical purpose, and kept enough size on me so that the nurses used to fight over who was supposed to wash me every day. I started getting a little sensation back in my right leg, enough so that when the doctor told me he'd send me home if I could stand up, I managed to fake it by standing on one leg."

There, however, the progress halted, and Michalik, unspeakably depressed, lay in bed for a year, bloating on steroids and chocolate chip cookies. He got a call from the TV people, telling him that they'd hired Leonard Nimoy to replace him on the science show. He got another one from the producers of *Pumping Iron,* informing him that he'd been all but cut out of the film. Worst of all, his friends and training partners jumped ship on him, neither calling nor coming by to see him.

"So typical of bodybuilders," he sneers. "'Hey, Michalik's crippled, I gotta go see him — nah, it's Tuesday, chest-and-back day. Fuck him.' But the *real* reason, I think, was they couldn't stand to see one of their own hurt. In order to keep on doing what they're doing — the drugs, the binge eating, the sex-for-money — they've gotta keep lying to themselves, saying, 'I can't be hurt, I can't get sick. I'm Superman. Cancer is *afraid* to live in my body.'"

About the only person who didn't abandon him was his kid brother, Paulie, an adopted eight-year-old who utterly worshipped Michalik. "He used to come into my room every day and massage my legs, going, 'You feel anything yet? You feel it?' He's stubborn like me. He just refused to give up, he kept saying, 'You're a *champion*, Steve, you're my hero, you're gonna be back.'

"And then one day we're watching TV, and a pro bodybuilding show comes on. This was 1978, and the networks had started up a Grand Prix tour to cash in on the fad after *Pumping Iron*. I'm watching all the guys and just going crazy, wishing I could just get up on stage against 'em one more time, and Paulie goes, 'You *can* do it, Steve. You can come back and whip those guys. I'll help you in the gym.'"

Aroused, Michalik called an old friend, Julie Levine, and begged him for the keys to his new gym in Amityville. The next night, he got out of bed at 2 A.M. and scuttled to the window, where Paulie assisted him over the sash. Crawling across the lawn to his wife's car, Michalik got in the driver's seat and pushed his dead legs back, making room for his little brother beneath the steering wheel. As he steered, Paulie worked the gas and brake pedals with his hands, and in this manner they accomplished the ten miles to Amityville.

In the gym, Paulie dragged him from machine to machine, helping him push the weight stacks up. Michalik's upper body responded quickly — muscle had remarkable memory — but his legs, particularly the left one, lay there limp as old celery. After several months, however, the pain started up in them. Sharp and searing, it was as if someone had stuck a fork in his sciatic nerve. Michalik, a self-made master of pain, couldn't have been happier if he'd hit the lottery.

"The doctors all told me it would be ten years, if ever, for the nerve to come back, and here it was howling like a monster. I kicked up the dosages of all the stuff I was taking, and started *attacking* the weights instead of just lifting 'em. Six months later, the pain was so bad I still could barely straighten up — but I was leg-pressing seven hundred and eight hundred pounds, and my thighs were as big as a bear's."

And a year after that, he walked on stage in Florida, an unadvertised guest poser at the end of a Grand Prix show. The crowd, recognizing a miracle when it saw one, went berserk as Michalik modeled those thirty-four-inch thighs, each of which was considerably wider than his twenty-seven-inch waist. Schwarzenegger, in the broadcast booth doing color for ABC, was overwhelmed. "I don't believe what I am seeing," he gasped. "It's Steve Michalik, the phantom bodybuilder!"

There Michalik should have left it. He was alive, and ambulatory, and his cult status was set. Thanks to Arnie, he would be forever known as the Phantom Bodybuilder, a tag he could have turned into a merchandising gold mine, and retired.

But like a lot of other steroid casualties, Michalik couldn't stop pushing his luck. He had to keep going, had to keep *growing*, testing the limits of his skeleton and the lining of his liver. If he'd gotten galactic, he figured, on last year's drugs, there was no telling how big he could get on this year's crop. A new line of killer juice was coming out of southern California — Hexalone, Bolasterone, Dehydralone — preposterously toxic compounds that sent the liver into warp drive but which grew hard, mature muscle right before your very eyes. Sexier still, there was that new darling of the pro circuit, human growth hormone, and who knew where the ceiling even *began* on that stuff?

Instead of pulling over, then, Michalik put the hammer down. He joined the Grand Prix tour immediately after the show in Florida and began the brutal grind of doing twelve shows annually. Before the tour, top bodybuilders did five shows a year, tops — the Mr. Olympia, the Night of Champions, and two or three others in Europe — which gave them several months to recuperate from the drugs and heavy training. Now, thanks to TV, they had to do a show a month. The pace was quite literally murderous.

"Not only did guys have to peak every month, they had to keep getting *better* as the year went on. No downtime, no rest from the binging and fasting — you could see guys turning green from all the shit in their systems. As you might expect, some of them were falling by the wayside, one guy from arrythmia, another guy from heart attacks.

"As for me, all I knew was that I was spending every dime I had on drugs. It cost me $25,000 that first year just to keep up, and that was *without* human growth hormone, which I couldn't even afford. The sport had become like an arms race now. If you heard that some guy was using Finajet, then *you* had to have it, no matter what it cost or where you had to go to get it. It actually paid to fly back and forth to France every couple of months, where you could buy the crap off the shelves of some country pharmacy and save yourself thousands of bucks.

"Needless to say, those five years on the tour were the most whacked-out of my life. My cognitive mind went on like a permanent stroll, and I became an enormous, lethal caveman. The only reason I didn't spend most of that time in jail was because two thirds of the cops in town were customers of mine. They belonged to my gym, and bought their steroids from me, and when I got into a little beef, which was practically every other day, they took care of it on the QT for me.

"Once I was on Hempstead Turnpike, on my way to the gym, when some guy in a pickup gave me the finger. That's it, lights out. I chased him doing ninety in my new Corvette, and did a three-sixty in heavy traffic right in front of him. I jumped out, ripped the door off his truck, and caved in his face with one punch. The other guy in the cab, who had done nothing to me, jumps out and starts running down the divider to get away from me. I chased him on foot and was pounding the shit out of him on the side of the road when the cops pulled up in two cruisers. 'Michalik, get outta here, ya crazy fuck,' they go, 'this is the last goddamn time we're lettin' you slide.'"

Word quickly got around town that Michalik was to be avoided at all costs. That went double for the wild-style gym he opened, which did everything but hang a sign out saying, STEROIDS FOR SALE HERE. There were plaques on the walls that proclaimed, UP THE DOSAGE! and pictures not of stars but of twenty-gauge syringes.

As for the clientele, it ran heavily toward the highly crazed. There was the seven-foot juice freak who stomped around muttering, "I'll kill you all. I'll rip your guts out and eat them right here." There was the mob hit man who drove up in a limo every day and checked his automatic weapons at the door. There was the herpetologist who came in with a python wrapped around him, trailing a huge sea turtle, for good measure, on a leash. There was the former Mr. America who was so distraught when his dog died that he had it stuffed, and dragged it around the gym from station to station.

"I had every freak and psycho within a 300-mile radius," Michalik recalls. "At night, there'd be all these animals hanging around outside my gym, slurping protein shakes and twirling biker chains — and every single one of 'em was afraid of me. That was the only way I kept 'em in line. As crazy as they all were, they knew I was crazier, and that I'd just as soon kill 'em as re-enroll 'em."

If that sounds like dubious business practice, consider that a year after opening, Michalik was so successful that he had to move to a location twice the size. But for all the money he was making, and for all the scams he was running — selling "Banana Packs," a worthless mixture of rotten bananas and egg powder, as his "secret muscle formula" for $25 a pop; passing himself off as a veterinarian to get cases of human growth hormone at wholesale for his "clinical experiments" — he was still being bankrupted by his skyrocketing drug bills.

The federal heat had begun to come down on the steroid racket, closing out the pill-mill pharmacies where Michalik was filling his

scrips. The national demand, moreover, for the high-octane stuff —
Hexalone, Bolasterone, etc. — was going through the roof, which
meant that Michalik, like everybody else, had to get on line, and pay
astronomical prices for his monthly package from Los Angeles.

Constantly broke, and going nowhere fast on the Grand Prix tour —
"where in the beginning I'd been finishing third or fourth in the shows,
by 1983 I was coming in like eleventh or twelfth" — Michalik began
caving in emotionally and physically. He'd come home from the gym at
night, dead-limbed and nauseous, and suddenly burst into tears without warning. Cut off from everyone, even the stouthearted Thomasina,
who had finally thrown up her hands and stopped caring what he did to
himself, he sat alone in a dark room, hearing his joints howl, and
dreamed about killing himself.

"I was just lost, gone, in a constant state of male PMS — the hormones flying around inside, my mood going yoyo. I just wanted an end
to it; an end to all the pain I was in, and to the pain I was causing others.

"I mean, of course I had tried to get off the drugs, and always it just
got worse. The depression got deeper, the craving was incredible, and
those last couple of years, I was worse than any crackhead. As crazed as
I was, I'd've killed to keep on going, to get my hands on that next ship-
ment of Deca or Maxibolin."

As for his body, it was finally capitulating to all the accumulated
toxins. By 1983, he was bleeding from everywhere: his gums, kidneys,
colon, and sinuses. The headaches started up, so piercing and obdurate
that he developed separate addictions to Percodan and Demerol. And
worst of all (by Michalik's lights), his muscles suddenly went soft on
him. No matter how he worked them or what he shot into them, they
lost their gleaming, osmotic hardness, and began to pooch out like $20
whitewalls.

His last two years on the tour were a run-on nightmare. He almost
dropped dead at a show in Toronto, collapsing on stage in head-to-toe
convulsions; the promoters, disgraced, hauled him off by the ankles.
There was a desperate attempt in 1985, after his cholesterol hit 500, to
wean himself from steroids once and for all. His testosterone level
plummeted, however, his sperm count went to zero, and all the estrogen
in his body, which had been accruing for years, turned his pecs into soft,
doughy breasts. Such friends as he still had pointed out that his ass was
plumping like a woman's, and tweaked him for his sexy new hip-swish-
ing walk.

He ran to one endocrinologist after another, begging them for something to reverse the condition. To a man, each pointed to Michalik's liver reading and showed him out of his office. Leaving, he had the distinct feeling that they were laughing at him.

And so, after weighing his options — a bleak, emasculated life off steroids or a slam-bang, macho death on them — Michalik emphatically chose the latter. He packed a bag, grabbed his weight belt, and caught a plane for L.A., winding up for nine months in the valley, where all the chemical studs were training.

Just up the freeway, a cartel of former med students were minting drugs so new they scarcely had names for them yet. The stuff ran $250, $300 a bottle, but pumped you up like an air hose and kept you that way. It also made you violently sick to your stomach, but Michalik didn't have time to worry about that. He simply ran to the bathroom to heave up his guts, then came back and ripped off another thirty sets.

His hair fell out in heavy clumps; a dry cough emanated from his liver, wracking him. Every joint was inflamed; it was excruciating even to walk now. But at night, in bed and in too much pain to sleep, it cheered him to think that he would finally be dead soon, and that it would take eight men to carry his casket.

He came back to New York in the fall of 1986, on his last legs but enormous and golden brown. All along, he'd targeted the Night of Champions, to be held that November at the Beacon Theater, as his swan song. It was the Academy Awards show of bodybuilding. Everyone would be there, all the stars and cognoscenti, and it would consolidate his legend to show up one last time, coming out of a coffin to the tune of Elton John's "Funeral for a Friend." Of course, it would *really* help matters if he could drop dead on stage, but that seemed too much to hope for. All that mattered, finally, was that he go out with twenty-five hundred people thundering their approval, drowning out, once and for all, his old man's malediction that he'd never amount to shit.

And then, two weeks before the show, he woke up at four in the morning with his liver on fire, and that was the end of all that.

Happily afloat on morphine and Nembutol, Michalik drifted for seventy-two hours, dreaming that he was dead. In the course of those three days, however, his extraordinary luck held up. The huge cysts in his liver stabilized and began to shrink, though they'd so eviscerated the organ already that there was practically nothing left of it. Short of a transplant, it would be months before he could so much as sit up and take nourishment. His bodybuilding career, in any case, was finished.

When Michalik awoke in intensive care, he was inconsolable. Not only was he still unaccountably alive, his beautiful body was dissolving and going away from him. His muscles, bereft of steroids and the five pounds of chicken he ate a day, decomposed and flowed into his blood-stream as waste. In three weeks, he lost more than 100 pounds, literally pissing himself down to 147 from a steady weight of 255.

Predictably, his kidneys began to fail, functioning at 60 percent, then 40, then 20. His black hair turned gray, and the skin hung off him in folds. His father came in and told him, with all his customary tact, that he looked like an eighty-five-year-old man.

In the few hours a day that he was lucid, Michalik wept uncon-trollably. Out of the unlikeliest materials — bad genes, a small bone structure, and a thoroughly degraded ego — he had assembled this utterly remarkable thing, a body that no less than Arnold Schwarzeneg-ger once venerated as the very best in the world. Now he was too weak to lift his head off the pillow. He lay there inert for months and months, the very image, it seemed to him, of his old man's foretelling.

"I was just like Lyle Alzado, who I went to high school in Brooklyn with: weak and broken-down, leaning on my wife to keep me alive. She came and fed me every day through a straw, and swiped the huge bunch of pills I was saving to kill myself. To thank her for still being there after everything, I sold the gym and gave her all the money from it. I didn't want any of it, I didn't want anything. I just wanted to lie in bed and be miserable by myself. I was so depressed I could hardly move my jaws to speak."

Finally, by the spring of 1988, he'd recovered sufficiently to get out of bed for short stretches. Possessed by the sudden urge to atone for his sins, Michalik called every promoter he knew, begging them to let him go on stage in his condition and dramatize the wages of steroids. Surprisingly, several of them agreed to the idea. They brought Michalik out, a bag of bones in a black shirt, and let him turn the place into a graveyard for ten minutes.

"All these twenty-year-olds would be staring up at me with their jaws hanging open, and I'd get on the mike and say, 'You think this can't happen to you, tough guy? You think you know more about steroids than I do? Well, I wrote the book on 'em, buddy, and they *still* ate me up. I'm forty years old and I'm finished. Dead.'"

The former proselytizer for steroids got some grim satisfaction out of spreading the gospel against them. He dragged himself out to high schools and hard-core juice gyms, using himself as a walking cautionary tale. But whatever his good works were doing for his soul, they weren't doing a damn thing for his body. He still woke up sick in every cell, poisoned by the residue of all the drugs. The liver cysts, shrunk to the size of golf balls but no further, sapped his strength and forced him to eat like a sparrow, subsisting on farina and chicken soup. His hormones were wildly scrambled — a blood test revealed he had the testosterone level of a twelve-year-old *girl* — and it had been two years since he'd had even a twinge of an erection. Indeed, his moods were so erratic that he had his wife commit him to a stretch in a Long Island nut bin.

"I wasn't crazy, but I didn't know what else to do. All day long I just sat there, consumed with self-hatred: 'Why did you do this? Why did you do that?' I mean, even when I was huge, I never had what you would call the greatest relationship with myself, but now it was, 'You're *weak!* You're *tiny!* You're *stupid!* You're *worthless!*' — and what the hell was I going to say to shut it up? The only thing I'd ever valued about myself was my body, and I'd totally, systematically fucked it up. My life, as you can probably guess, was intolerable."

It was here, however, that fate stepped in and cut Michalik a whopping break. Halfway across the world, an Australian rugby player named Joe Reesh somehow heard about Michalik's plight and called to tell him about a powerful new detox program. It was a brutally arduous deal — an hour of running, then five hours straight in a 180-degree sauna, for a minimum of twenty-one days — but infallibly, it leeched the poisons out of your fat cells, where they'd otherwise sit, crystallized, for the rest of your life.

Utterly desperate, Michalik gave it a shot. He could scarcely jog around the block that first day, but in the sauna, it all started coming out of him: a viscous, green paste that oozed out of his eyes and nostrils. By the end of the first week, he reports, he was running two miles; by the end of the second, his ex-wife verifies, his gray hair had turned black again. And when he stepped out of the sauna after the twenty-third and final day, his skin was as pink and snug as a teenager's. Liver and kidney tests confirmed the wildly improbable: he was perfectly healthy again.

"Everything came back to me: my sense of humor, my lust for life — hell, my lust, *period.* Don't forget, it'd been almost three years since I'd gotten it up — I had some serious business to take care of. But the greatest thing by far was what *wasn't* there anymore. All the biochemical hatred I'd been walking around with for twelve years, it was like that all bled out of me with the green stuff, and I had this overpowering need to be with people again, especially my son, Stevie. I had tons of making up to do with him, and I've loved every minute of it. It kills me that I could've let myself get so sick that I was ready to die and leave him."

Michalik went to his wife and told her he was going back to body-building. It was his life, his art, he couldn't leave it alone — only this time, he swore on heaven, he was going to do it clean. She understood, or at least tried to, but said she couldn't go through with it again: the 2 A.M. feedings, the $500-a-week grocery bills. They parted amicably, and Michalik returned to the gym, as zealous and single-minded as a monk. In the last two years he's put on 60 pounds, and looks dense and powerful at 225, though he's sober about the realities.

"There are *nineteen-year-olds* clocking in now at two sixty-five," he says, shaking his head. "The synthetic HGH [human growth hormone] has evolved a new species in five years. By the end of the decade, the standard will be three-hundred-pounders, with twenty-three-inch necks that are almost as big as their waists.

"But all around the country, kids'll be dropping dead from the stuff, and getting diabetes because it burns out their pancreas. I don't care what those assholes in California say, there's no such thing in the world as a 'good' drug. There's only bad drugs and sick bastards who want to sell them to you."

Someone ought to post those words in every high school in the country. The latest estimate from a *USA Today* report is that there are half a million teenagers on juice these days, almost half of whom, according to a University of Kentucky study, are so naïve they think that steroids *without exercise* will build muscle. In this second stone age, the America of Schwarzkopf and Schwarzenegger, someone needs to tell them that bigger isn't necessarily better. Sometimes, bigger is deader.

1992

Peter Richmond

## Tangled Up in Blue

FROM *GQ*

NIGHTTIME IN LOS ANGELES, on a quiet street off Melrose Avenue. An otherwise normal evening is marked by an oddly whimsical celestial disturbance: Baseballs are falling out of the sky.

They are coming from the roof of a gray apartment building. One ball pocks an adjacent apartment. Another bounces to the street. A third flies off into the night, a mighty shot.

This is West Hollywood in the early eighties, where anything is not only possible but likely. West Hollywood shakes its head and drives on by.

But if a passerby's curiosity had been piqued and he'd climbed to the roof of a neighboring building to divine the source of the show, he would have been rewarded by a most unusual sight: a man of striking looks, with long blond hair, startlingly and wincingly thin, hitting the ball with a practiced swing — a flat, smooth, even stroke developed during a youth spent in minor-league towns from Pocatello to Albuquerque.

This is not Tommy Lasorda, Jr.'s, routine nighttime activity. A routine night is spent in the clubs, the bright ones and dark ones alike.

Still, on occasion, here he'd be, on the roof, clubbing baseballs into the night. Because there were times when the pull was just too strong. Of the game. Of the father. He could never be what his father was — Tommy Lasorda's own inner orientation made that impossible — but he could fantasize, couldn't he? That he was ten, taking batting practice in Ogden, Utah, with his dad, and Garvey, and the rest of them?

And so, on the odd night, on a night he was not at Rage, or the Rose Tattoo, he'd climb to the roof, the lord of well-tanned West Hollywood, and lose himself in the steady rhythm of bat hitting ball — the reflex ritual that only a man inside the game can truly appreciate.

"Junior was the better hitter," recalls Steve Garvey. "He didn't have his father's curveball, but he was the better hitter."

"I cried," Tom Lasorda says quietly. He is sipping a glass of juice in the well-appointed lounge of Dodgertown, the Los Angeles baseball team's green-glorious oasis of a spring-training site. It's a place that heralds and nurtures out-of-time baseball and out-of-time Dodgers. A place where, each spring, in the season of illusion's renewal, they are allowed to be the men they once were.

On this February weekend, Dodgertown is crowded with clearly affluent, often out-of-shape white men, each of whom has parted with $4,000 to come to Dodgers fantasy camp. In pink polo shirts and pale-pink slacks — the pastels of privilege — they are scattered around the lounge, flirting with fantasy lives, chatting with the coaches.

"I cried. A lot of times. But I didn't cry in the clubhouse. I kept my problems to myself. I never brought them with me. I didn't want to show my family — that's my family away from my house. What's the sense of bringing my problems to my team?

". . . I had him for thirty-three years. Thirty-three years is better than nothing, isn't it? If I coulda seen God and God said to me 'I'm going to give you a son for thirty-three years and take him away after thirty-three years,' I'd have said 'Give him to me.'"

His gaze skips about the room — he always seems to be looking around for someone to greet, a hand to shake, another camper to slap another anecdote on. Tom Lasorda floats on an ever-flowing current of conversation.

"I signed that contract [to manage the Dodgers] with a commitment to do the best of my ability," he says. "If I'm depressed, what good does it do? When I walk into the clubhouse, I got to put on a winning face. A happy face. If I go in with my head hung down when I put on my uniform, what good does it do?"

These are words he has said before, in response to other inquiries about Tommy's death. But now the voice shifts tone and the words become more weighted; he frames each one with a new meaning.

And he stops looking around the room and looks me in the eye.

"I could say 'God, why was I dealt this blow? Does my wife — do I — deserve this?' [But] then how do I feel, hunh? Does it change it?" Now the voice grows even louder, and a few fantasy campers raise their eyebrows and turn their heads toward us.

"See my point?"

The words are like fingers jabbed into my chest.

"Hunh?"

Then his eyes look away and he sets his face in a flat, angry look of defiance.

"You could hit me over the head with a fucking two-by-four and you don't knock a tear out of me," he says.

"Fuck," he says.

The word does not seem to be connected to anything.

He was the second of five sons born, in Norristown, Pennsylvania, a crowded little city-town a half-hour north of Philadelphia, to Sabatino Lasorda, a truckdriver who'd emigrated from Italy, and Carmella Lasorda.

By the age of twenty-two, Tom Lasorda was a successful minor league pitcher by trade, a left-hander with a curveball and not a lot more. But he was distinguished by an insanely dogged belief in the possibility of things working out. His father had taught him that. On winter nights when he could not turn the heat on, Sabatino Lasorda would nonetheless present an unfailingly optimistic face to his family, and that was how Tom Lasorda learned that nothing could stomp on the human spirit if you didn't let it.

Tom Lasorda played for teams at nearly every level of professional ball: in Concord, New Hampshire; Schenectady, New York; Greenville, South Carolina; Montréal; Brooklyn (twice, briefly); Kansas City, Missouri; Denver; and Los Angeles. Once, after a short stay in Brooklyn, he was sent back to the minors so the Dodgers could keep a left-handed pitcher with a good fastball named Sandy Koufax, and to this day Lasorda will look you in the eye and say "I still think they made a mistake" and believe it.

The Dodgers saw the white-hot burn and made it into a minor-league manager. From 1965 to 1972, Lasorda's teams — in Pocatello, Ogden, Spokane, then Albuquerque — finished second, first, first, first, second, first, third and first. Sheer bravado was the tool; tent-preaching thick with obscenities the style.

In 1973, the Dodgers called him to coach for the big team, and he summoned his wife and his son and his daughter from Norristown, and they moved to Fullerton, California, a featureless sprawl of a suburb known for the homogeneity of its style of life and the conservatism of its residents.

In 1976, he was anointed the second manager in the Los Angeles Dodgers' nineteen-year history. His managing style was by instinct, not by the book, and his instincts were good enough to pay off more often than not. In his first two years, the Dodgers made the World Series. In 1981, they won it. In 1985, they didn't make it because Lasorda elected to have Tom Niedenfuer pitch to St. Louis's Jack Clark in the sixth game of the playoffs, against the odds, and Jack Clark hit a three-run home run. In 1988, though, he sent a limping Kirk Gibson to the plate and gave us a moment for history.

From the first, Lasorda understood that he had to invent a new identity for this team, the team that Walter O'Malley had yanked out of blue-collar-loyal Brooklyn-borough America and dropped into a city whose only real industry was manufacturing the soulless stuff of celluloid fantasy. His clubhouse became a haunt for show-business personalities, usually of distinctly outsized demeanor — Sinatra, Rickles — and he himself became the beacon of a new mythology, leader of the team that played in a ballpark on a hill on a road called Elysian, perched above the downtown, high and imperious. Because, really, aren't there too many theme parks to compete with in Los Angeles to manage your baseball team as anything other than another one?

In sixteen years, the tone of the sermon has seldom faltered, at least not before this year. This year, through no fault of Tom Lasorda's, his fielders have forgotten how to field, in a game in which defense has to be an immutable; and if this is anyone's fault, it's that of the men who stock the farm system. His pitching is vague, at best. So the overwhelming number of one-run games — most of which the Dodgers lost — is, in fact, testament, again, to Lasorda's management. No one has questioned his competence.

His spirit has flagged considerably, but his days, in season and out, are as full of Dodger Blue banquet appearances as ever, with impromptu Dodgers pep rallies in airport concourses from Nashville to Seattle. Unlike practitioners of Crystal Cathedral pulpitry, Lasorda the tent-preacher believes in what he says, which, of course, makes all the difference in the world. Because of his faith, Dodger Blue achieves things, more things than you can imagine. The lights for the baseball field in Caledonia, Mississippi; the fund for the former major leaguer with cancer in Pensacola: Tom showed up, talked Dodger Blue, raised the money. Tom's word maintains the baseball field at Jackson State and upgraded the facilities at Georgia Tech.

"I was in Nashville," Tom says, still sitting in the lounge, back on automatic now, reciting. "Talking to college baseball coaches, and a buddy told me nine nuns had been evicted from their home. I got seven or eight dozen balls [signed by Hall of Fame players], we auctioned them, and we built them a home. They said, 'We prayed for a miracle, and God sent you to us.'"

Nine nuns in Nashville.

In the hallway between the lounge and the locker room hang photographs of Brooklyn Dodgers games. Lasorda has pored over them a thousand times, with a thousand writers, a thousand campers, a thousand Dodgers prospects — identifying each player, re-creating each smoky moment.

But on this day, a few minutes after he's been talking about Tommy, he walks this gauntlet differently.

"That's Pete Reiser," Tom Lasorda says. "He's dead." He points to another player. He says, "He's dead." He walks down the hallway, clicking them off, talking out loud but to himself.

"He's dead. He's dead. He's dead. He's dead. He's dead. He's dead."

Back in his suite, in the residence area of Dodgertown, I ask him if it was difficult having a gay son.

"My son wasn't gay," he says evenly, no anger. "No way. No way. I read that in a paper. I also read in that paper that a lady gave birth to a fuckin' monkey, too. That's not the fuckin' truth. That's not the truth."

I ask him if he read in the same paper that his son had died of AIDS.

"That's not true," he says.

I say that I thought a step forward had been taken by Magic Johnson's disclosure of his own HIV infection, that that's why some people in Los Angeles expected him to . . .

"Hey," he says. "I don't care what people . . . I know what my son died of. I know what he died of. The doctor put out a report of how he died. He died of pneumonia."

He turns away and starts to brush his hair in the mirror of his dressing room. He is getting ready to go to the fantasy-camp barbecue. He starts to whistle. I ask him if he watched the ceremony on television when the Lakers retired Johnson's number.

"I guarantee you one fuckin' thing," he says. "I'll lay you three to one Magic plays again [in the NBA]. Three to one. That Magic plays again."

As long as he's healthy, I say. People have lived for ten years with the right medication and some luck. Your quality of life can be good, I say.

Lasorda doesn't answer. Then he says, "You think people would have cared so much if it had been Mike Tyson?"

On death certificates issued by the state of California, there are three lines to list the deceased's cause of death, and after each is a space labeled TIME INTERVAL BETWEEN ONSET AND DEATH.

Tom Lasorda, Jr.'s, death certificate reads:

IMMEDIATE CAUSE: A) PNEUMONITIS — 2 WEEKS DUE TO: B) DE-HYDRATION — 6 WEEKS DUE TO: C) PROBABLY ACQUIRED IM-MUNE DEFICIENCY SYNDROME — 1 YEAR.

At Sunny Hills High School, in Fullerton, California — "the most horrible nouveau riche white-bread high school in the world," recalls Cat Gwynn, a Los Angeles photographer and filmmaker and a Sunny Hills alumna — Tommy Lasorda moved through the hallways with a style and a self-assurance uncommon in a man so young; you could see them from afar, Tommy and his group. They were all girls, and they were all very pretty. Tommy was invariably dressed impeccably. He was as beautiful as his friends. He had none of his father's basset-hound features; Tommy's bones were carved, gently, from glass.

"It was very obvious that he was feminine, but none of the jocks nailed him to the wall or anything," Gwynn says. "I was enamored of him because he wasn't at all uncomfortable with who he was. In this judgmental, narrow-minded high school, he strutted his stuff."

In 1980, at the Fashion Institute of Design and Merchandising, Cindy Stevens and Tommy Lasorda shared a class in color theory. Tommy, Stevens recalls, often did not do his homework. He would spend a lot of his time at Dodgers games or on the road with the team. At school, they shared cigarettes in the hallway. Tommy would tell her about the latest material he'd bought to have made into a suit. She'd ask him where the money came from. Home, he'd say.

"He talked lovingly about his father and their relationship — they had a very good relationship," Stevens says now. "I was surprised. I didn't think it'd be like that. You'd think it'd be hard on a macho Italian man. This famous American idol. You'd figure it'd be [the father saying] 'Please don't let people know you're my son,' but it was the opposite. I had new respect for his father. There had to be acceptance from his mom and dad. Tommy had that good self-esteem — where you figure that [his] parents did something right."

In the late seventies, Tommy left Fullerton, moving only an hour northwest in distance — though he might as well have been crossing the border between two sovereign nations — to West Hollywood, a pocket of gay America unlike any other, a community bound by the shared knowledge that those within it had been drawn by its double distinction: to be among gays, and to be in Hollywood. And an outrageous kid from Fullerton, ready to take the world by storm, found himself dropped smack into the soup — of a thousand other outrageous kids, from Appleton, and Omaha, and Scranton.

But Tommy could never stand to be just another anything. The father and the son had that in common. They had a great deal in common. Start with voice: gravelly, like a car trying to start on a cold morning. The father, of course, spends his life barking and regaling, never stopping; he's baseball's oral poet, an anti-Homer. It's a well-worn voice. Issuing from the son, a man so attractive that men tended to assume he was a woman, it was the most jarring of notes. One of his closest friends compared it to Linda Blair's in *The Exorcist* — the scenes in which she was possessed.

More significantly, the father's world was no less eccentric than the son's: The subset of baseball America found in locker rooms and banquet halls is filled with men who have, in large part, managed quite nicely to avoid the socialization processes of the rest of society.

Then, the most obvious similarity: Both men were so outrageous, so outsized and surreal in their chosen persona, that, when it came down to it, for all of one's skepticism about their sincerity, it was impossible not to like them — not to, finally, just give in and let their version of things wash over you, rather than resist. Both strutted an impossibly simplistic view of the world — the father with his gospel of fierce optimism and blind obeisance to a baseball mythology, and the son with a slavery to fashion that he carried to the point of religion.

But where the illusion left off and reality started, that was a place hidden to everyone but themselves. In trying to figure out what each had tucked down deep, we can only conjecture. "You'd be surprised what agonies people have," Dusty Baker, the former Dodger, reminds us, himself a good friend of both father and son, a solid citizen in a sport that could use a few more. "There's that old saying that we all have something that's hurting us."

In the case of the son, friends say the West Hollywood years were born of a Catch-22 kind of loneliness: The more bizarre the lengths to which he went to hone the illusion, the less accessible he became. In his last years, friends say, everything quieted down, markedly so. The flamboyant life gave way to a routine of health clubs and abstinence and sobriety and religion. But by then, of course, the excesses of the earlier years had taken their inexorable toll.

As for the father, there's no question about the nature of the demon he's been prey to for the past two years. Few in his locker room saw any evidence of sadness as his son's illness grew worse, but this should come as no surprise: Tom Lasorda has spent most of four decades in the same baseball uniform. Where else would he go to get away from the grief?

"Maybe," Baker says, "his ballpark was his sanctuary."

In a plague town now, there's no way around it. At brunch at the French Quarter, men stop their conversations to lay out their pills on the tables, and take them one by one with sips of juice. A mile west is Rage, its name having taken on a new meaning. Two blocks away, on Santa Monica Boulevard, at A Different Light, atop the shelves given over to books on how to manage to stay alive for another few weeks, sit a dozen clear bottles, each filled with amber fluid and a rag — symbolic Molotovs, labeled with the name of a man or a woman or a government agency that is setting back the common cause, reinforcing the stereotypes, driving the social stigmata even deeper into West Hollywood's already weakened flesh.

But in the late seventies, it was a raucous, outrageous and joyous neighborhood, free of the pall that afflicted hetero Los Angeles, thronged as it was with people who'd lemminged their way out west until there was no more land, fugitives from back east.

In the late seventies and the early eighties, say his friends and his acquaintances and those who knew him and those who watched him, Tommy Lasorda was impossible to miss. They tell stories that careen from wild and touching to sordid and scary; some ring true, others fanciful. Collected, they paint a neon scar of a boy slashing across the town. They trace the path of a perfect, practiced, very lonely shooting star.

His haunt was the Rose Tattoo, a gay club with male strippers, long closed now. One night, he entered — no, he made an entrance — in a cape, with a pre-power ponytail and a cigarette holder: Garbo with a touch of Bowie and the sidelong glance of Veronica Lake. He caught the eye of an older man. They talked. In time, became friends. In the early eighties, they spent a lot of time together. Friends is all they were. They were very much alike.

"I'm one of those gentlemen who liked him," says the man. "I was his Oscar Wilde. He liked me because I was an older guy who'd tasted life. I was his Mame. I showed him life. Art. Theater. I made him a little more sophisticated. [Showed him] how to dress a little better."

They spent the days poolside at a private home up behind the perfect pink stucco of the Beverly Hills Hotel, Tommy lacquering himself with a tan that was the stuff of legend. The tan is de rigueur. The tan is all. It may not look like work, but it is; the work is to look as good as you can.

He occasionally held a job, never for long. Once, he got work at the Right Bank, a shoe store, to get discounts. His father bought him an antique-clothing store. He wearied of it. Tommy, says one friend, wanted to be like those women in soap operas who have their own businesses but never actually work at them.

Tommy's look was his work. If there were others who were young and lithe and handsome and androgynous, none were as outré as Tommy. Tommy never ate. A few sprouts, some fruit, a potato. Tommy spent hours at the makeup table. Tommy studied portraits of Dietrich and Garbo to see how the makeup was done. Tommy bleached his hair. On his head. On his legs. Tommy had all of his teeth capped. Tommy had a chemabrasion performed on his face, in which an acid bath removes four of the skin's six layers. Then the skin is scrubbed to remove yet another layer. It is generally used to erase scars or wrinkles. Tommy had two done.

But he smoked, and he drank. Champagne in a flute, cigarette in a long holder, graceful and vampish at the same time: This was Tommy at the Rose Tattoo. His friend also remembers how well Tommy and his father got along. His friend would drive Tommy to the Italian restaurant where he'd meet his father for Sunday dinners.

"He loved his father, you know. They got along perfectly well." His friend was never his lover. Only his friend. That was all. That was enough. "He was very lonely."

On occasion, the nighttime ramble led him far from the stilted elegance of Santa Monica Boulevard. In the punk clubs, amid the slam-dancing and the head-butting, Tommy parted the leathered seas, a chic foil for all the pierced flesh and fury, this man who didn't sweat. The man who crossed himself when someone swore in public.

Penelope Spheeris met him at Club Zero. She would go on to direct the punk documentary *The Decline of Western Civilization* and, years later, *Wayne's World*. They became friends. They met at punk clubs — the blond man in custom-made suits, the striking woman in black cocktail dresses and leather boots. In 1981, she interviewed Tommy for a short-lived underground paper called *No Mag*.

PENELOPE: Have you been interviewed very much before?

TOMMY: No, but I'm very . . . *oral.* . . .

PENELOPE: People who would see you around town, they would probably think you were gay.

TOMMY: *I don't care.*

PENELOPE: What do you do when you get that reaction from them?

TOMMY: I like all people. And it's better having comments, be it GOOD, BAD or WHATEVER. I don't mind at all, but I dress quite . . . well, I wouldn't say it's FLAMBOYANT because it's not intentional. *It's just intentionally ME.*

PENELOPE: O.K., but you understand, when somebody looks at a picture of you, they're going to say, *this guy's awfully feminine.*

TOMMY: I'm there for anyone to draw any conclusions.

PENELOPE: Are you?

TOMMY: Well, I mean, I've done different things . . . of course. . . . I have *no label on myself* because then I have restrictions. I would really hate to state anything like that.

PENELOPE: When you were young did your dad say, "Come on, Tommy, Jr., *let's go play baseball*"?

TOMMY: *Never.* They always allowed me to do exactly what I pleased. I don't know how they had the sense to be that way. As parents they're both so . . . well, very straitlaced and conservative. I don't know how I was allowed to just be ME, but I think it was because I was so strongly ME that I don't think they thought they could ever STOP IT. . . .

PENELOPE: Do you feel like you should be careful in the public eye?

TOMMY: *I feel like I should,* but I don't.

PENELOPE: Do you think the press would be mean to you if they had the chance?

TOMMY: I'm sure they would, but I'll take ANY PUBLICITY.

PENELOPE: Why?

TOMMY: Because that's what I want. . . . I do everything TO BE SEEN.

"I found him totally fascinating. He was astoundingly beautiful, more than most women," Spheeris says now. "I became interested in . . . the blatant contrast in lifestyles. Tommy Lasorda, Sr., was so involved in that macho sports world, and his son was the opposite. . . ."

She laughs.

"I was astounded at how many clothes he had. I remember walking into the closet. The closet was as big as my living room. Everything was organized perfectly. Beautiful designer clothes he looked great in."

Often in the early eighties, when fashion photographer Eugene Pinkowski's phone would ring, it would by Tommy. Tommy wanting to shop or Tommy wanting Eugene to photograph his new look.

When they went shopping, they would fly down Melrose in Tommy's Datsun 280Z, much, much too fast, Tommy leaning out of the driver's window, hair flying in the wind, like some Valley Girl gone weird, hurling gravelly insults ("Who did your hair? It looks awful") at the pedestrians diving out of the way.

He was a terrible driver. Once he hit a cat. He got out of the car, knelt on the street and cried. He rang doorbells up and down the street, trying to find the owner.

Tommy would call to tell Eugene he was going to buy him a gift. Then Tommy would spend all his money on himself. Then, the next day, Tommy would make up for it. He would hand him something. A pair of porcelain figures, babies, a boy and a girl, meant to be displayed on a grand piano — very difficult to find, very expensive.

Then the phone would ring. It'd be Eugene's mother, saying she just got a bracelet. From his friend Tommy.

"He was a character," Pinkowski says at breakfast in a Pasadena coffee shop. "He was a case. He was a complete and total case."

Then he looks away.

"He was really lonely," Pinkowski says. "He was sad."

When he was being photographed, Tommy was always trying to become different people.

Eugene captured them all. Tommy with long hair. With short hair. With the cigarette. Without it. With some of his exceptionally beautiful women friends. Tommy often had beautiful women around him, Pinkowski recalls — vaguely European, vaguely models. Sometimes Tommy had Pinkowski take pictures of them.

Mostly he took pictures of Tommy. Tommy with a stuffed fox. Lounging on the floor. In the piano. Sitting in a grocery cart.

In red. In green. In white. In blue. In black and gray.

His four toes. Tommy had four toes on his right foot, the fifth lost in a childhood accident. He posed the foot next to a gray boot on the gray carpet. Then he posed it next to a red shoe on the gray carpet. The red looked better.

Tommy and his foot were a regular subject of conversation, often led by Tommy.

"Tommy was a great storyteller, and he'd tell you stories of his dad in the minor leagues," Pinkowski says. "Everybody'd like him. He was very much like the old boy. He could really hold his own in a group of strangers. And he'd do anything to keep it going. To be the center of attention. He'd just suddenly take his shoe and sock off at dinner and say 'Did you know I was missing my toe?'"

One day, Tommy wanted to pose wrapped in a transparent shower curtain. Tommy was wearing white underwear. For forty-five minutes they tried to light the shot so that the underwear was concealed, to no avail. Tommy left, and returned in flesh-colored underwear.

There was nothing sexual about Tommy's fashion-posing. Tommy's fashion-posing was designed to get Tommy into fashion magazines. Tommy was forever bugging the editors of *Interview* to feature him, but they wouldn't.

"As beautiful as he was, as famous as his father was, he thought he should be in magazines," Pinkowski says now. "He was as hungry as Madonna. But Bowie and Grace [Jones] could do something. He couldn't do anything. He could never see any talent in himself."

The closest Tommy came was when he bought himself a full page in *Stuff* magazine, in 1982, for a picture of himself that Eugene took.

He would pay Eugene out of the house account his parents had set up for him. On occasion, Eugene would get a call from Tommy's mother: We don't need any more pictures this year. Still, Tommy would have several of his favorites printed for his parents. One is from the blue period.

At the Duck Club, down behind the Whiskey, in 1985, Tommy sat in a corner drinking Blue Hawaiians. To match his blue waistcoat. Or his tailored blue Edwardian gabardine jacket. This was during his blue period. In his green period, he was known to wear a green lamé wrap and drink crème de menthe. But the blue period lasted longer. The good thing about the blue period was that on the nights he didn't want to dress up, he could wear denim and still match his drink. And, sometimes, his mood.

"He walked around with a big smile on his face, as if everything was great because he had everything around him to prove it was great," Spheeris says. "But I don't think it was. . . . When you're that sad, you have to cover up a lot of pain. But he didn't admit it."

The nature of the pain will forever be in debate. Few of his friends think it had to do with the relationship with his parents. "The parents — both of them — were incredibly gracious and kind to everyone in Tommy's life," says a close friend of the family's.

Alex Magno was an instructor at the Voight Fitness and Dance Center and became one of Tommy's best friends. Tommy was the godfather of his daughter. "We used to ask him, 'You're thirty-three, what kind of life is that — you have no responsibilities. Why don't you work?'" says Magno. "You lose your identity when you don't have to earn money, you know what I mean? Everything he owns, his parents gave him. I never heard him say 'I want to do my own thing.' When you get used to the easy life, it's hard to go out there. I don't think he appreciated what he had."

He loved the Dodgers. He attended many games each season. His father regularly called him from the road. In his office at Dodger Stadium, the father kept a photograph of Tommy on his desk.

Tommy loved the world of the Dodgers. He loved the players. To friends who were curious about his relationship with his father's team — and all of them were — he said it was great. He told Spheeris they were a turn-on.

"He was a good, sensitive kid," says Dusty Baker, now a coach with the San Francisco Giants. "There was an article one time. Tommy said I was his favorite player because we used to talk music all the time. He loved black female artists. He turned me on to Linda Clifford. He loved Diana Ross. He loved Thelma Houston.

"Some of the guys kidded me. Not for long. Some of the guys would say stuff — you know how guys are — but most were pretty cool. That's America. Everybody's not going to be cool. Most people aren't going to be. Until they have someone close to them afflicted. Which I have."

Baker spent last Christmas Eve distributing turkey dinners with the Shanti Foundation, an AIDS-education group in California.

"There are a lot of opinions about Tom junior, about how [his father] handled his relationship with his son," says Steve Garvey, who more than anyone was the onfield embodiment of Dodger Blue. "Everyone should know that there is this Tom [senior] who really loved his son and was always there for him. The two loving parents tried to do as much for him as he chose to let them do. . . . Junior chose a path in life, and that's his prerogative. That's every individual's right."

Garvey attended the memorial service for Alan Wiggins, his former teammate on the San Diego Padres, who died of an AIDS-related illness last year, after a seven-year career in the majors.

"He was a teammate, we always got along well, he gave me one hundred percent effort, played right next to me. I think the least you can do, when you go out and play in front of a million people and sweat and pull muscles and bleed and do that as a living, when that person passes away, is be there. It's the right thing to do."

Garvey was the only major league baseball player at Wiggins's service. I ask him if he was surprised that he was alone.

"Not too much surprises me in life anymore," Garvey says.

In the mid-1980s, Tommy's style of life changed. It may have been because he learned that he had contracted the human immunodeficiency virus. According to Alex Magno, he knew he was infected for years before his death. It may have been that he simply grew weary of the scene. It may have been that he grew up.

He entered a rehabilitation program. He became a regular at the Voight gym, attending classes seven days a week. Henry Siegel, the Voight's proprietor, was impressed by Tommy's self-assurance and generosity. Tommy moved out of his West Hollywood place into a new condo in Santa Monica, on a quiet, neat street a few blocks from the beach—an avenue of trimmed lawns and stunning gardens displayed beneath the emerald canopies of old and stalwart trees. "T. L. JR." reads the directory outside the locked gate; beyond it, a half-dozen doorways open onto a carefully tiled courtyard. The complex also features Brooke Shields on its list of tenants.

He was a quiet tenant, a thoroughly pleasant man. He had a new set of friends—whom he regaled, in his best raconteurial fashion, with tales of the past.

"Tommy used to tell us incredible stuff about how he used to be . . . everything he'd done—drugs, sleeping with women, sleeping with men," says Magno.

"He went through the homosexual thing and came out of it," Magno continues. "Gay was the thing to be back when he first came to L.A. Tommy used to tell his friends he had been gay. He didn't pretend. He let people know he had been this wild, crazy guy who had changed. He was cool in that. When you got to meet him, you got to know everything about him."

Including that he slept with guys?

"Yes. But . . . he didn't want to admit he had AIDS because people would say he was gay."

This apparent contradiction surfaces regularly in the tale of Tommy Lasorda.

"I think he wanted to make his father happy," says his Oscar Wilde. "But he didn't know how to. He wanted to be more macho but didn't know how to. He wanted to please his dad. He wished he could have liked girls. He tried."

No one who knew Tommy in the seventies and the early eighties recalls him having a steady romantic relationship. Pinkowski remarks on the asexual nature of the masks his friend kept donning—and about how his friend kept some sides of himself closed off. "He'd never talk about being gay. He'd never reveal himself that way. He'd never say anything about anybody that way."

"Of course he was gay," says Jeff Kleinman, the manager of a downtown restaurant who used to travel the same club circuit as Lasorda in the early eighties. "No, I never saw him with another guy as a couple. [But] just because a man doesn't have a date doesn't mean he isn't gay! To say he wasn't gay would be like saying Quentin Crisp isn't gay. How could you hide a butterfly that was so beautiful?"

"Please," says his Oscar Wilde. "He was gay. He was gay. He was gay."

"Gay," of course, is not a word that describes sexual habits. It speaks of a way of living. No one interviewed for this story thought that Tommy wasn't gay; reactions to his father's denial range from outrage and incredulity to laughter and a shake of the head. Former major league umpire Dave Pallone, who revealed his own homosexuality in an autobiography two years ago, knows the father well, and also knew his son.

"Tommy senior is, as far as I'm concerned, a tremendous man," says Pallone. "I consider him a friend. I have a lot of empathy for what he's going through. [But] as far as I'm concerned, I don't think he ever accepted the fact that his son was a gay man. I knew him to be a gay man, and I knew a lot of people who knew him as a gay man.

"We don't want to be sexual beings. We just want to be human beings."

"If nothing else, his father should be proud that he repented," Alex Magno says. "He'd come a long way—denying what he used to be, so happy with what he'd become."

I tell him his father denies the illness.

"He died of AIDS," Magno says. "There's no question. But what difference does it make? He was a good man. He was a great man. You shouldn't judge. He had had no sex for a long time. We didn't know how he could do that. I mean . . . but he was incredible. He gave up everything. That's what he said, and there was no reason not to believe him. He was totally like a normal man. He was still feminine—that gets in your system—but there was no lust after men."

In the last two years of his life, Tommy's illness took its toll on his looks. He was not ashamed, though. The surface self-assurance remained. One night, he made an entrance into Rage—thinner, not the old Tommy, but acting every bit the part. He still showed up at Dodger Stadium, too, with his companion, a woman named Cathy Smith, whom Tom senior said was Tommy's fiancée. When he did, he was as elegant and debonair as ever: wide-brimmed hats, tailored suits.

"Nobody in their right mind is going to say it's not difficult—I know how difficult it is for them to try and understand their son," Dave Pallone says. "And to accept the fact he's not with them and what the real reason is. But . . . here was a chance wasted. The way you get rid of a fear is by attacking it. . . . Can you imagine if the Dodgers, who are somewhat conservative, could stand up and say, 'We understand this is a problem that needs to be addressed. . . . We broke down the barriers from the beginning with Jackie Robinson. Why can't we break down the barriers with the AIDS epidemic?'"

A close friend who was with Tommy the day before his death vehemently disagrees.

"If his father has to accept his son's death right now in that way, let him do it," she says. "If he can't accept things yet, he may never be able to . . . but what good does it do? [Tom's] world is a different world. We should all do things to help, yes, but at the same time, this is a child who someone's lost. Some people have the fortitude, but they simply don't have the strength. . . . There comes a point, no matter how public they may be, [at which] we need to step back and let them be. You can't force people to face what they don't want to face without hurting them."

"There's something wrong with hiding the truth," Penelope Spheeris says. "It's just misplaced values. It is a major denial. People need to know these things. Let's get our values in the right place. That's all."

"I'm in a position where I can help people, so I help people," Tom Lasorda says. We are strolling through the night in Dodgertown, toward the fantasy-camp barbecue. "You don't realize the enjoyment I got with those nuns in that convent. I can't describe how good that made me feel."

I ask him what his dad would say if he were alive.

"I think he'd have been so proud of me. My father was the greatest man."

He tells me that his winters are so busy with appearances that "you wouldn't believe it." I ask him why he doesn't slow down.

"I don't know," he says. "I like to help people. I like to give something back."

On Valentine's Day, 1991, Eugene Pinkowski's phone rang. It was Tommy. His voice was weak.

"He was typical Tommy. He was really noble about it. He was weak, you could tell. I was so sad. He said, in that voice, 'I'm sure you've read that I'm dying. Well, I am.'

"Then he said, 'Thank you for being so nice to me during my lifetime.' He said, 'I want to thank you, because you made me look good.'"

On June 3, 1991, with his parents and his sisters at his bedside, in the apartment on the cool, flower-strewn street, Tommy Lasorda died.

His memorial service was attended by Frank Sinatra and Don Rickles. Pia Zadora sang "The Way We Were," one of Tommy junior's favorite songs.

Tom Lasorda asked that all donations go to the Association of Professional Ball Players of America, a charity that helps former ballplayers in need, one of two charities to which baseball players in trouble can turn for help. It is a conservative group, known for its refusal to offer assistance to ballplayers who fall into the trap of substance abuse.

\* \* \*

In the coffee shop in Pasadena, it is late morning, and Eugene Pink-owski is lingering, remembering. His Tommy portfolio is spread across the table. Tommy is smiling at us from a hundred pictures.

I ask Eugene if Tommy would have wanted this story written.

"Are you kidding?" he says. "If there's any sort of afterlife, Tommy is looking down and cheering. There is something he wanted. To be remembered like this. He'd be in heaven."

1996

## Gary Smith

# The Chosen One

FROM *Sports Illustrated*

IT WAS ORDINARY. It was oh so ordinary. It was a salad, a dinner roll, a steak, a half potato, a slice of cake, a clinking fork, a podium joke, a ballroom full of white-linen-tablecloth conversation. Then a thick man with tufts of white hair rose from the head table. His voice trembled and his eyes teared and his throat gulped down sobs between words, and everything ordinary was cast out of the room.

He said, "Please forgive me . . . but sometimes I get very emotional . . . when I talk about my son. . . . My heart . . . fills with so . . . much . . . joy . . . when I realize . . . that this young man . . . is going to be able . . . to help so many people. . . . He will transcend this game . . . and bring to the world . . . a humanitarianism . . . which has never been known before. The world will be a better place to live in . . . by virtue of his existence . . . and his presence. . . . I acknowledge only a small part in that . . . in that I know that I was personally selected by God himself . . . to nurture this young man . . . and bring him to the point where he can make his contribution to humanity. . . . This is my treasure . . . Please accept it . . . and use it wisely. . . . Thank you."

Blinking tears, the man found himself inside the arms of his son and the applause of the people, all up on their feet.

In the history of American celebrity, no father has ever spoken this way. Too many dads have deserted or died before their offspring reached this realm, but mostly they have fallen mute, the father's vision exceeded by the child's, leaving the child to wander, lost, through the sad and silly wilderness of modern fame.

So let us stand amidst this audience at last month's Fred Haskins Award dinner to honor America's outstanding college golfer of 1996, and take note as Tiger and Earl Woods embrace, for a new manner of celebrity is taking form before our eyes. Regard the 64-year-old African-American father, arm upon the superstar's shoulder, right where the chip is so often found, declaring that this boy will do more good for the world than any man who ever walked it. Gaze at the 20-year-old son, with the blood of four races in his veins, not flinching an inch from the yoke of his father's prophecy but already beginning to scent the complications. The son who stormed from behind to win a record third straight U.S. Amateur last August, turned pro and rang up scores in the 60s in 21 of his first 27 rounds, winning two PGA Tour events as he doubled and tripled the usual crowds and dramatically changed their look and age.

Now turn. Turn and look at us, the audience, standing in anticipation of something different, something pure. Quiet. Just below the applause, or within it, can you hear the grinding? That's the relentless chewing mechanism of fame, girding to grind the purity and the promise to dust. Not the promise of talent, but the bigger promise, the father's promise, the one that stakes everything on the boy's not becoming separated from his own humanity and from all the humanity crowding around him.

It's a fitting moment, while he's up there at the head table with the audience on its feet, to anoint Eldrick (Tiger) Woods — the rare athlete to establish himself immediately as the dominant figure in his sport — as *Sports Illustrated*'s 1996 Sportsman of the Year. And to pose a question: Who will win? The machine . . . or the youth who has just entered its maw?

Tiger Woods will win. He'll fulfill his father's vision because of his mind, one that grows more still, more willful, more efficient, the greater the pressure upon him grows.

The machine will win because it has no mind. It flattens even as it lifts, trivializes even as it exalts, spreads a man so wide and thin that he becomes margarine soon enough.

Tiger will win because of God's mind. Can't you see the pattern? Earl Woods asks. Can't you see the signs? "Tiger will do more than any other man in history to change the course of humanity," Earl says.

Sports history, Mr. Woods? Do you mean more than Joe Louis and Jackie Robinson, more than Muhammad Ali and Arthur Ashe? "More than any of them because he's more charismatic, more educated, more prepared for this than anyone."

Anyone, Mr. Woods? Your son will have more impact than Nelson Mandela, more than Ghandi, more than Buddha?

"Yes, because he has a larger forum than any of them. Because he's playing a sport that's international. Because he's qualified through his ethnicity to accomplish miracles. He's the bridge between the East and the West. There is no limit because he has the guidance. I don't know yet exactly what form this will take. But he is the Chosen One. He'll have the power to impact nations. Not people. Nations. The world is just getting a taste of his power."

Surely this is lunacy. Or are we just too myopic to see? One thing is certain: we are witnessing the first volley of an epic encounter, the machine at its mightiest confronting the individual groomed all his life to conquer it and turn it to his use. The youth who has been exposed to its power since he toddled onto *The Mike Douglas Show* at 3, the set of *That's Incredible!* at 5, the boy who has been steeled against the silky seduction to which so many before him have succumbed. The one who, by all appearances, brings more psychological balance, more sense of self, more consciousness of possibility to the battlefield than any of his predecessors.

This is war, so let's start with war. Remove the images of pretty putting greens from the movie screen standing near the ballroom's head table. Jungle is what's needed here, foliage up to a man's armpits, sweat trickling down his thighs, leeches crawling up them. Lieut. Col. Earl Woods, moving through the night with his rifle ready, wondering why a U.S. Army public information officer stationed in Brooklyn decided in his mid-30s that he belonged in the Green Berets and ended up doing two tours of duty in Vietnam. Wondering why his first marriage has died and why the three children from it have ended up without a dad around when it's dark like this and it's time for bed — just as Earl ended up as a boy after his own father died. Wondering why he keeps plotting ways to return to the line of fire — "creative soldiering," he calls it — to eyeball death once more. To learn once again about his dark and cold side, the side that enables Earl, as Tiger will remark years later, "to slit your throat and then sit down and eat his dinner."

Oh, yes, Earl is one hell of a cocktail. A little Chinese, a little Cherokee, a few shots of African-American; don't get finicky about measurements, we're making a vat here. Pour in some gruffness and a little intimidation, then some tenderness and some warmth and a few jiggers of old anger. Don't hold back on intelligence. And stoicism. Add lots of stoicism, and even more of responsibility — "the most responsible son of a bitch you've ever seen in your life" is how Earl himself puts it. Top it all with "a bucket of whiskey," which is what he has been known to order when he saunters into a bar and he's in the mood. Add a dash of hyperbole, maybe two, and to hell with the ice, just whir. This is one of those concoctions you're going to remember when morning comes.

Somewhere in there, until a good fifteen years ago, there was one other ingredient, the existential Tabasco, the smoldering why? The Thai secretary in the U.S. Army office in Bangkok smelled it soon after she met Earl, in 1967. "He couldn't relax," says Kultida (Tida) Woods. "Searching for something, always searching, never satisfied. I think because both his parents died when he was young, and he didn't have Mom and Dad to make him warm. Sometimes he stayed awake till three or four in the morning, just thinking."

In a man so accustomed to exuding command and control, in a Green Beret lieutenant colonel, *why?* has a way of building up power like a river dammed. Why did the Vietcong sniper bracket him that day (first bullet a few inches left of one ear, second bullet a few inches right of the other) but never fire the third bullet? Why did Earl's South Vietnamese combat buddy, Nguyen Phong — the one Earl nicknamed Tiger, and in whose memory he would nickname his son — stir one night just in time to awaken Earl and warn him not to budge because a viper was poised inches from his right eye? What about that road Earl's jeep rolled down one night, the same road on which two friends had just been mutilated, the road that took him through a village so silent and dark that his scalp tingled, and then, just beyond it . . . hell turned inside-out over his shoulder, the sky lighting up and all the huts he had just passed spewing Vietcong machine-gun and artillery fire? He never understands what is the purpose of Lieutenant Colonel Wood's surviving again and again. He never quite comprehends what is the point of his life, until . . .

Until the boy is born. He will get all the time that Earl was unable to devote to the three children from his first marriage. He will be the only child from Earl's second marriage, to the Thai woman he brought back to America, and right away there are signs. What other 6-month-old, Earl asks, has the balance to stand in the palm of his father's hand and remain there even as Daddy strolls around the house? Was there another 11-month-old, ever, who could pick up a sawed-off club, imitate his father's golf swing so fluidly, and drive the ball so wickedly into the nylon net across the garage? Another 4-year-old who could be dropped off at the golf course at 9 A.M. on a Saturday and picked up at 5 P.M., pockets bulging with money he had won from disbelievers ten and twenty years older, until Pop said, "Tiger you can't do that"? Earl starts to get a glimmer. He is to be the father of the world's most gifted golfer.

But why? What for? Not long after Tiger's birth, when Earl has left the military to become a purchaser for McDonnell Douglas, he finds himself in a long discussion with a woman he knows. She senses the power pooling inside him, the friction. "You have so much to give," she tells him, "but you're not giving it. You haven't even scratched the surface of your potential." She suggests he try EST, Erhard Seminars Training, an intensive self-discovery and self-actualizing technique, and it hits Earl hard, direct mortar fire to the heart. What he learns is that his overmuscular sense of responsibility for others has choked his potential.

"To the point," says Earl, "that I wouldn't even buy a handkerchief for myself. It went all the way back to the day my father died, when I was 11, and my mother put her arm around me after the funeral and said, 'You're the man of the house now.' I became the father that young, looking out for everyone else, and then she died two years later.

"What I learned through EST was that by doing more for myself, I could do much more for others. Yes, be responsible, but love life, and give people the space to be in your life, and allow yourself room to give to others. That caring and sharing is what's most important, not being responsible for everyone else. Which is where Tiger comes in. What I learned led me to give so much time to Tiger, and to give him the space to be himself, and not to smother him with dos and don'ts. I took out the authority aspect and turned it into companionship. I made myself vulnerable as a parent. When you have to earn respect from your child, rather than demanding it because it's owed to you as the father, miracles happen. I realized that, through him, the giving could take a quantum leap. What I could do on a limited scale, he could do on a global scale."

At last, the river is undammed, and Earl's whole life makes sense. At last, he sees what he was searching for, a pattern. No more volunteering for missions — he has his. Not simply to be a great golfer's father. To be destiny's father. His son will change the world.

"What the hell had I been doing in public information in the army, posted in Brooklyn?" he asks. "Why, of course, what greater training can there be than three years of dealing with the New York media to prepare me to teach Tiger the importance of public relations and how to handle the media?"

Father: Where were you born, Tiger?

Son, age 3: I was born on December 30, 1975, in Long Beach, California.

Father: No, Tiger, only answer the question you were asked. It's important to prepare yourself for this. Try again.

Son: I was born in Long Beach, California.

Father: Good, Tiger, good.

The late leap into the Green Berets? "What the hell was that for?" Earl says. "Of course, to prepare me to teach Tiger mental toughness."

The three children by the first marriage? "Not just one boy the first time," says Earl, "but two, along with a girl, as if God was saying, 'I want this son of a bitch to really have previous training.'"

The Buddhist wife, the one who grew up in a boarding school after her parents separated when she was 5, the girl who then vowed that her child would know nothing but love and attention? The one who will preach inner calm to Tiger simply by turning to him with that face — still awaiting its first wrinkle at 52? Whose eyes close when she speaks, so he can almost see her gathering and sifting the thoughts? The mother who will walk every hole and keep score for Tiger at children's tournaments, adding a stroke or two if his calm cracks? "Look at this stuff!" cries Earl. "Over and over you can see the plan being orchestrated by someone other than me because I'm not this damn good! I tried to get out of that combat assignment to Thailand. But Tida was meant to bring in the influence of the Orient, to introduce Tiger to Buddhism and inner peace, so he would have the best of two different worlds. And so he would have the knowledge that there were two people whose lives were totally committed to him."

What of the heart attack Earl suffered when Tiger was 10 and the way the retired lieutenant colonel felt himself floating down the gray tunnel toward the light before he was wrenched back? "To prepare me to teach Tiger that life is short," Earl says, "and to live each day to the maximum, and not worry about the future. There's only now. You must understand that time is just a linear measurement of successive increments of now. Anyplace you go on that line is now, and that's how you have to live it."

No need to wonder about the appearance of the perfect childhood coach, John Anselmo: the perfect sports psychologist, Jay Brunza; the perfect agent, Hughes Norton; the perfect attorney, John Merchant; and the perfect pro swing instructor, Butch Harmon. Or about the great tangle of fate that leads them all to Tiger at just the right junctures in his development. "Everything," says Earl, "right there when he needs it. Everything. There can't be this much coincidence in the world. This is a directed scenario, and none of us involved in the scenario has failed to accept the responsibility. This is all destined to be."

His wife ratifies this, in her own way. She takes the boy's astrological chart to a Buddhist temple in Los Angeles and to another in Bangkok and is told by monks at both places that the child has wondrous powers. "If he becomes a politician, he will be either a president or a prime minister," she is told. "If he enters the military, he will be a general."

Tida comes to a conclusion. "Tiger has Thai, African, Chinese, American Indian, and European blood," she says. "He can hold everyone together. He is the Universal Child."

This is in the air the boy breathes for twenty years, and it becomes bone fact for him, marrow knowledge. When asked about it, he merely nods in acknowledgment of it, assents to it; of course he believes it's true. So failure, in the rare visits it pays him, is not failure. It's just life pausing to teach him a lesson he needs in order to go where he's inevitably going. And success, no matter how much sooner than expected it comes to the door, always finds him dressed and ready to welcome it. "Did you ever see yourself doing this so soon?" a commentator breathlessly asks him seconds after his first pro victory, on October 6 in Las Vegas, trying to elicit wonder and awe on live TV. "Yeah," Tiger responds. "I kind of did." And sleep comes to him so easily; in the midst of conversation, in a car, in a plane, off he goes, into the slumber of the destined. "I don't see any of this as scary or a burden," Tiger says. "I see it as fortunate. I've always known where I wanted to go in life. I've never let anything deter me. This is my purpose. It will unfold."

No sports star in the history of American celebrity has spoken this way. Maybe, somehow, Tiger can win.

The machine will win. It must win because it too is destiny, 5 billion destinies leaning against one. There are ways to keep the hordes back, a media expert at Nike tells Tiger. Make broad gestures when you speak. Keep a club in your hands and take practice swings, or stand with one foot well out in front of the other, in almost a karate stance. That will give you room to breathe. Two weeks later, surrounded by a pen-wielding mob in La Quinta, California, in late November, just before the Skins Game, the instruction fails. Tiger survives, but his shirt and slacks are ruined, felt-tip-dotted to death.

The machine will win because it will wear the young man down, cloud his judgment, steal his sweetness, the way it does just before the Buick Challenge in Pine Mountain, Georgia, at the end of September. It will make his eyes drop when the fans' gaze reaches for his, his voice growl at their clawing hands, his body sag onto a sofa after a practice round and then rise and walk across the room and suddenly stop in bewilderment. "I couldn't even remember what I'd just gotten off the couch for, two seconds before," he says. "I was like mashed potatoes. Total mush."

So he walks. Pulls out on the eve of the Buick Challenge, pulls out of the Fred Haskins Award dinner to honor him, and goes home. See, maybe Tiger can win. He can just turn his back on the machine and walk. Awards? Awards to Tiger are like echoes, voices bouncing off the walls, repeating what a truly confident man has already heard inside his own head. The Jack Nicklaus Award, the one Jack himself was supposed to present to Tiger live on ABC during the Memorial tournament last spring? Tiger would have blown it off if Wally Goodwin, his coach at Stanford during the two years he played there before turning pro, hadn't insisted that he show up.

The instant Tiger walks away from the Buick Challenge and the Haskins dinner, the hounds start yapping. See, that's why the machine will win. It's got all those damn heel-nippers. Little mutts on the PGA Tour resenting how swiftly the 20-year-old was ordained, how hastily he was invited to play practice rounds with Nicklaus and Arnold Palmer, with Greg Norman and Ray Floyd and Nick Faldo and Fred Couples. And big dogs snapping too. Tom Kite quoted as saying, "I can't ever remember being tired when I was twenty," and Peter Jacobsen quoted, "You can't compare Tiger to Nicklaus and Palmer anymore because they never [walked out]."

He rests for a week, stunned by the criticism — "I thought those people were my friends," he says. He never second-guesses his decision to turn pro, but he sees what he surrendered. "I miss college," he says. "I miss hanging out with my friends, getting in a little trouble. I have to be so guarded now. I miss sitting around drinking beer and talking half the night. There's no one my own age to hang out with anymore because almost everyone my age is in college. I'm a target for everybody now, and there's nothing I can do about it. My mother was right when she said that turning pro would take away my youth. But golfwise, there was nothing left for me in college."

He reemerges after the week's rest and rushes from four shots off the lead on the final day to win the Las Vegas Invitational in sudden death. The world's waiting for him again, this time with reinforcements. Letterman and Leno want him as a guest; *GQ* calls about a cover; Cosby, along with almost every other sitcom you can think of, offers to write an episode revolving around Tiger, if only he'll appear. Kids dress up as Tiger for Halloween — did anyone ever dress up as Arnie or Jack? — and Michael Jordan declares that his only hero on earth is Tiger Woods. Pepsi is dying to have him cut a commercial for one of its soft drinks aimed at Generation Xers; Nike and Titleist call in chits for the $40 million and $20 million contracts he signed; money managers are eager to know how he wants his millions invested; women walk onto the course during a practice round and ask for his hand in marriage; kids stampede over and under ropes and chase him from the 18th hole to the clubhouse; piles of phone messages await him when he returns to his hotel room. "Why," Tiger asks, "do so many people want a piece of me?"

Because something deeper than conventional stardom is at work here, something so spontaneous and subconscious that words have trouble going there. It's a communal craving, a public aching for a superstar free of anger and arrogance and obsession with self. It's a hollow place that chimes each time Tiger and his parents strike the theme of father and mother and child love, each time Tiger stands at a press conference and declares, "They have raised me well, and I truly believe they have taught me to accept full responsibility for all aspects of my life." During the making of a Titleist commercial in November, a makeup woman is so moved listening to Earl describe his bond with Tiger that she decides to contact her long-estranged father. "See what I mean?" cries Earl. "Did you affect someone that way today? Did anyone else there? It's destiny, man. It's something bigger than me."

What makes it so vivid is context. The white canvas that the colors are being painted on — the moneyed, mature, and almost minority-less world of golf — makes Tiger an emblem of youth overcoming age, have-not overcoming have, outsider overcoming insider, to the delight not only of the 18-year-olds in the gallery wearing nose rings and corn-rows, but also — of all people — of the aging insider haves.

So Tiger finds himself, just a few weeks after turning pro at the end of August, trying to clutch a bolt of lightning with one hand and steer an all-at-once corporation — himself — with the other, and before this he has never worked a day in his life. Never mowed a neighbor's lawn, never flung a folded newspaper, never stocked a grocery shelf; Mozarts just don't, you know. And he has to act as if none of this is new or vexing because he has this characteristic — perhaps from all those years of hanging out with his dad at tournaments, all those years of mixing with and mauling golfers five, ten, twenty, thirty years older than he is — of never permitting himself to appear confused, surprised, or just generally a little squirt. "His favorite expression," Earl says, "is, 'I knew that.'" Of course Pop, who is just as irreverent with Tiger as he is reverent, can say, "No, you didn't know that, you little s — ." But Earl, who has always been the filter for Tiger, decides to take a few steps back during his son's first few months as a pro because he wishes to encourage Tiger's independence and because he is uncertain of his own role now that the International Management Group (IMG) is managing Tiger's career.

Nobody notices it, but the inner calm is beginning to dissolve. Earl enters Tiger's hotel room during the Texas Open in mid-October to ask him about his schedule, and Tiger does something he has never done in his twenty years. He bites the old man's head off.

Earl blinks. "I understand how you must feel," he says.

"No, you don't," snaps Tiger.

"And I realized," Earl says later, "that I'd spent twenty years planning for this, but the one thing I didn't do was educate Tiger to be the boss of a corporation. There was just no vehicle for that, and I thought it would develop more slowly. I wasn't presumptuous enough to anticipate this. For the first time in his life, the training was behind the reality. I could see on his face that he was going through hell."

The kid is fluid, though. Just watch him walk. He's quick to flow into the new form, to fit the contour of necessity. A few hours after the outburst he's apologizing to his father and hugging him. A few days later he's giving Pop the O.K. to call a meeting of the key members of Tiger's new corporation and establish a system, Lieutenant Colonel Woods in command, chairing a two-and-a-half-hour teleconference with the team each week to sift through all the demands, weed out all the chaff, and present Tiger five decisions to make instead of five hundred. A few days after that, the weight forklifted off his shoulders, at least temporarily, Tiger wins the Walt Disney World/Oldsmobile Classic. And a few weeks later, at the Fred Haskins Award dinner, which has been rescheduled at his request, Tiger stands at the podium and says, "I should've attended the dinner [the first time]. I admit I was wrong, and I'm sorry for any inconvenience I may have caused. But I have learned from that, and I will never make that mistake again. I'm very honored to be part of this select group, and I'll always remember, for both good and bad, this Haskins Award; for what I did and what I learned, for the company I'm now in and I'll always be in. Thank you very much." The crowd surges to its feet, cheering once more.

See, maybe Tiger can win. He's got the touch. He's got the feel. He never writes down a word before he gives a speech. When he needs to remember a phone number, he doesn't search his memory or a little black book; he picks up a phone and watches what number his fingers go to. When he needs a 120-yard shot to go under an oak branch and over a pond, he doesn't visualize the shot, as most golfers would. He looks at the flag and pulls everything from the hole back, back, back . . . not back into his mind's eye, but into his hands and forearms and hips, so they'll do it by feel. Explain how he made the preposterous shot? He can't. Better you interview his knuckles and metacarpals.

"His handicap," says Earl, "is that he has such a powerful creative mind. His imagination is too vivid. If he uses visualization, the ball goes nuts. So we piped into his creative side even deeper, into his incredible sense of feel."

"I've learned to trust the subconscious," says Tiger. "My instincts have never lied to me."

The mother radiates this: the Eastern proclivity to let life happen, rather than the Western one to make it happen. The father comes to it in his own way, through fire. To kill a man, to conduct oneself calmly and efficiently when one's own death is imminent — a skill Earl learns in Green Beret psychological training and then again and again in jungles and rice paddies — one removes the conscious mind from the task and yields to the subconscious. "It's the more powerful of the two minds," Earl says. "It works faster than the conscious mind, yet it's patterned enough to handle routine tasks over and over, like driving a car or making a putt. It knows what to do.

"Allow yourself the freedom of emotion and feeling. Don't try to control them and trap them. Acknowledge them and become the beneficiary of them. Let it all outflow."

Let it all because it's all there: the stability, almost freakish for a close-of-the-millennium California child — same two parents, same house all his twenty years, same best friends, one since second grade, one since eighth. The kid, for god's sake, never once had a baby-sitter. The conditioning is there as well, the two years of psychological boot camp during which Earl dropped golf bags and pumped cart brakes during Tiger's backswings, jingled change and rolled balls across his line of vision to tests his nerves, promising him at the outset that he only had to say "Enough" and Earl would cut off the blowtorch, but promising too that if Tiger graduated, no man he ever faced would be mentally stronger than he. "I am the toughest golfer mentally," Tiger says.

The bedrock is so wide that opposites can dance upon it: the cautious man can be instinctive, the careful man can be carefree. The bedrock is

622

GARY SMITH

so wide that it has enticed Tiger into the habit of falling behind — as he did in the final matches of all three U.S. Junior Amateur and all three U.S. Amateur victories — knowing in his tissue and bones that danger will unleash his greatest power. "Allow success and fame to happen," the old man says. "Let the legend grow."

To hell with the Tao. The machine will win, it has to win, because it makes everything happen before a man knows it. Before he knows it, a veil descends over his eyes when another stranger approaches. Before he knows it, he's living in a walled community with an electronic gate and a security guard, where the children trick-or-treat in golf carts, a place like the one Tiger just moved into in Orlando to preserve some scrap of sanity. Each day there, even with all the best intentions, how can he help but be a little more removed from the world he's supposed to change, and from his truest self?

Which is . . . who? The poised, polite, opaque sage we see on TV? No, no, no; his friends hoot and haze him when they see that Tiger on the screen, and he can barely help grinning himself. The Tiger they know is perfectly a fast-food freak who never remembers to ask if anyone else is hungry before he bolts to Taco Bell or McDonald's for the tenth time of the week. The one who loves riding roller coasters, spinning out golf carts, and winning at cards no matter how often his father accuses him of "reckless eyeballing." The one who loves delivering the dirty joke, who owns a salty barracks tongue just a rank or two beneath his father's. The one who's flip, who's downright cocky. When a suit walks up to him before the Haskins Award dinner and says, "I think you're going to be the next great one, but those are mighty big shoes to fill," Tiger replies, "Got big feet."

A typical exchange between Tiger and his agent, Norton:

"Tiger, they want to know when you can do that interview."

"Tell them to kiss my ass!"

"All right, and after that, what should I tell them?"

"Tell them to kiss my ass again!"

"O.K., and after that . . ."

But it's a cockiness cut with humility, the paradox pounded into his skull by a father who in one breath speaks of his son with religious awe and in the next grunts, "You weren't s — then, Tiger. You ain't s — now. You ain't never gonna be s — ."

"That's why I know I can handle all this," Tiger says, "no matter how big it gets. I grew up in the media's eye, but I was taught never to lose sight of where I came from. Athletes aren't as gentlemanly as they used to be. I don't like that change. I like the idea of being a role model. It's an honor. People took the time to help me as a kid, and they impacted my life. I want to do the same for kids."

So, if it's a clinic for children instead of an interview or an endorsement for adults, the cynic in Tiger gives way to the child who grew up immersed in his father's vision of an earth-altering compassion, the 7-year-old boy who watched scenes from the Ethiopian famine on the evening news, went right to his bedroom and returned with a $20 bill to contribute from his piggy bank. Last spring busloads of inner-city kids would arrive at golf courses where Tiger was playing for Stanford, spilling out to watch the Earl and Tiger show in wonder. Earl would talk about the dangers of drugs, then proclaim, "Here's Tiger Woods on drugs," and Tiger would stagger to the tee, topping the ball so it bounced crazily to the side. And then, presto, with a wave of his arms Earl would remove the drugs from Tiger's body, and his son would stride to the ball and launch a 330-yard rocket across the sky. Then Earl would talk about respect and trust and hard work and demonstrate what they can all lead to by standing ten feet in front of his son, raising his arms and telling Tiger to smash the ball between them — and, *whoosh,* Tiger would part not only the old man's arms but his haircut too.

They've got plans, the two of them, big plans, for a Tiger Woods Foundation that will fund scholarships across the country, set up clinics and coaches and access to golf courses for inner-city children. "I throw those visions out there in front of him," Earl says, "and it's like reeling in a fish. He goes for the bait, takes it, and away he goes. This is nothing new. It's been working this way for a long time."

"That's the difference," says Merchant, Tiger's attorney and a family friend. "Other athletes who have risen to this level just didn't have this kind of guidance. With a father and mother like Tiger's, he has to be real. It's such a rare quality in celebrities nowadays. There hasn't been a politician since John Kennedy whom people have wanted to touch. But watch Tiger. He has it. He actually listens to people when they stop him in an airport. He looks them in the eye. I can't ever envision Tiger Woods selling his autograph."

See, maybe Tiger can win.

Let's be honest. The machine will win because you can't work both sides of this street. The machine will win because you can't transcend wearing sixteen Nike swooshes, you can't move human hearts while you're busy pushing sneakers. Gandhi didn't hawk golf balls, did he?

Jackie Robinson was spared that fate because he came and went while Madison Avenue was still teething. Ali became a symbol instead of a logo because of boxing's disrepute and because of the attrition of cells in the basal ganglia of his brain. Who or what will save Tiger Woods?

Did someone say Buddha?

Every year near his birthday, Tiger goes with his mother to a Buddhist temple and makes a gift of rice, sugar, and salt to the monks there who have renounced all material goods. A mother-of-pearl Buddha given to Tiger by his Thai grandfather watches over him while he sleeps, and a gold Buddha hangs from the chain on his neck. "I like Buddhism because it's a whole way of being and living," Tiger says. "It's based on discipline and respect and personal responsibility. I like Asian culture better than ours because of that. Asians are much more disciplined than we are. Look how well behaved their children are. It's how my mother raised me. You can question, but talk back? Never. In Thailand, once you've earned people's respect, you have it for life. Here it's, What have you done for me lately? So here you can never rest easy. In this country I have to be very careful. I'm easygoing, but I won't let you in completely. There, I'm Thai, and it feels very different. In many ways I consider that home.

"I believe in Buddhism. Not every aspect, but most of it. So I take bits and pieces. I don't believe that human beings can achieve ultimate enlightenment, because humans have flaws. I don't want to get rid of all my wants and desires. I can enjoy material things, but that doesn't mean I need them. It doesn't matter to me whether I live in a place like this" — the golf club in his hand makes a sweep of the Orlando villa — "or in a shack. I'd be fine in a shack, as long as I could play some golf. I'll do the commercials for Nike and for Titleist, but there won't be much more than that. I have no desire to be the king of endorsement money."

On the morning after he decides to turn pro, there's a knock on his hotel room door. It's Norton, bleary-eyed but exhilarated after a late-night round of negotiations with Nike. He explains to Tiger and Earl that the benchmark for contract endorsements in golf is Norman's reported $2½ million-a-year deal with Reebok. Then, gulping down hard on the yabba-dabba-doo rising up his throat, Norton announces Nike's offer: $40 million for five years, 8 mil a year. "Over three times what Norman gets!" Norton exults.

Silence.

"Guys, do you realize this is more than Nike pays any athlete in salary, even Jordan?"

Silence.

"Finally," Norton says now, recalling that morning, "Tiger says 'Mmmm-hmmm,' and I say, 'That's it? Mmmm-hmmm?' No 'Omigod.' No slapping five or 'Ya-hooo!' So I say, 'Let me go through this again, guys.' Finally Tiger says, 'Guess that's pretty amazing.' That's it. When I made the deal with Titleist a day later, I went back to them saying, 'I'm almost embarrassed to tell you this one. Titleist is offering a little more than $20 million over five years.'"

On the Monday morning after his first pro tournament, a week after the two megadeals, Tiger scans the tiny print on the sports page under Milwaukee Open money earnings and finds his name. Tiger Woods: $2,544. "That's my money," he exclaims. "I earned this!"

See, maybe Tiger can win.

How? How can he win when there are so many insects under so many rocks? Several more death threats arrive just before the Skins Game, prompting an increase in his plainclothes security force, which is already larger than anyone knows. His agent's first instinct is to trash every piece of hate mail delivered to IMG, but Tiger won't permit it. Every piece of racist filth must be saved and given to him. At Stanford he kept one letter taped to his wall. Fuel comes in the oddest forms.

The audience, in its hunger for goodness, swallows hard over the Nike ad that heralds Tiger's entrance into the professional ranks. The words that flash on the screen over images of Tiger — "There are still courses in the United States I am not allowed to play because of the color of my skin. I've heard I'm not ready for you. Are you ready for me?" — ooze the very attitude from which many in the audience are seeking relief. The media backlash is swift: the Tiger Woods who used to tell the press "The only time I think about race is when the media ask me" — whoa, what happened to him?

What happened to him was a steady accretion of experiences, also known as a life. What happened, just weeks before he was born, was a fusillade of limes and BBs rattling the Woods house in Cypress, California, one of the limes shattering the kitchen window, splashing glass all around the pregnant Tida, to welcome the middle-class subdivision's first non-Caucasian family.

What happened was a gang of older kids seizing Tiger on his first day of kindergarten, tying him to a tree, hurling rocks at him, calling him monkey and nigger. And Tiger, at age 5, telling no one what happened for several days, trying to absorb what this meant about himself and his world.

What happened was the Look, as Tiger and Earl came to call it, the uneasy, silent stare they received in countless country-club locker rooms and restaurants. "Something a white person could never understand," says Tiger, "unless he went to Africa and suddenly found himself in the middle of a tribe." What happened was Tiger's feeling pressured to leave a driving range just two years ago, not far from his family's California home, because a resident watching Tiger's drives rocket into the nearby protective netting reported that a black teenager was trying to bombard his house.

What happened was the cold shoulder Earl got when he took his tyke to play at the Navy Golf Course in Cypress — "a club," Earl says, "composed mostly of retired naval personnel who knew blacks only as cooks and servers, and along comes me, a retired lieutenant colonel outranking 99 percent of them, and I have the nerve to take up golf at 42 and immediately become a low handicap and beat them, and then I have the audacity to have this kid. Well, they had to do something. They took away Tiger's playing privileges twice, said he was too young, even though there were other kids too young who they let play. The second time it happened, I went up to the pro who had done it and made a bet. I said, 'If you'll spot my 3-year-old just one stroke a hole, nine holes, playing off the same tees, and he beats you, will you certify him?' The pro started laughing and said, 'Sure.' Tiger beat him by two strokes, got certified, then the members went over the pro's head and kicked him out again. That's when we switched him to another course."

Beat them. That was his parents' solution for each banishment, each Look. Hold your tongue, hew to every rule, and beat them. Tiger Woods is the son of the first black baseball player in the Big Seven, a catcher back in the early '50s, before the conference became the Big Eight. A man who had to leave his Kansas State teammates on road trips and travel miles to stay in motels for blacks; who had to go to the back door of restaurant kitchens to be fed while his teammates dined inside; who says, "This is the most racist society in the world — I know that." A man who learned neither to extinguish his anger nor spray it but to quietly convert it into animus, the determination to enter the system and overcome it by turning its own tools against it. A Green Beret explosives expert whose mind naturally ran that way, whose response, upon hearing Tiger rave about the security in his new walled community, was, "I could get in. I could blow up the clubhouse and be gone before they ever knew what hit them." A father who saw his son, from the beginning, as the one who would enter one of America's last Caucasian bastions, the PGA Tour, and overthrow it from within in a manner that would make it smile and ask for more. "Been planning that one for twenty years," says Earl. "See, you don't turn it into hatred. You turn it into something positive. So many athletes who reach the top now had things happen to them as children that created hostility, and they bring that hostility with them. But that hostility uses up energy. If you can do it without the chip on the shoulder, it frees up all that energy to create."

It's not until Stanford, where Tiger takes an African-American history course and stays up half the night in dormitories talking with people of every shade of skin, that his experiences begin to crystallize. "What I realized is that even though I'm mathematically Asian — if anything — if you have one drop of black blood in the United States, you're black," says Tiger. "And how important it is for this country to talk about this subject. It's not me to blow my horn, the way I come across in that Nike ad, or to say things quite that way. But I felt it was worth it because the message needed to be said. You can't say something like that in a polite way. Golf has shied away from this for too long. Some clubs have brought in tokens, but nothing has really changed. I hope what I'm doing can change that."

But don't overestimate race's proportion in the fuel that propels Tiger Woods. Don't look for traces of race in the astonishing rubble at his feet on the Sunday after he lost the Texas Open by two strokes and returned to his hotel room and snapped a putter in two with one violent lift of his knee. Then another putter. And another. And another and another — eight in all before his rage was spent and he was ready to begin considering the loss's philosophical lesson. "That volcano of competitive fire, that comes from me," says Earl. A volcano that's mostly an elite athlete's need to win, a need far more immediate than that of changing the world.

No, don't overestimate race, but don't overlook it, either. When Tiger is asked about racism, about the effect it has on him when he senses it in the air, he has a golf club in his hands. He takes the club by the neck, his eyes flashing hot and cold at once, and gives it a short upward thrust. He says, "It makes me want to stick it right up their asses." Pause. "On the golf course."

The machine will win because there is so much of the old man's breath in the boy . . . and how long can the old man keep breathing? At 2 A.M., hours before the second round of the Tour Championship in

GARY SMITH

Tulsa on October 25, the phone rings in Tiger's hotel room. It's Mom. Pop's in an ambulance, on his way to a Tulsa hospital. He's just had his second heart attack.

The Tour Championship? The future of humanity? The hell with 'em. Tiger's at the old man's bedside in no time, awake most of the night. Tiger's out of contention in the Tour Championship by dinnertime, with a second-round 78, his worst till then as a pro. "There are things more important than golf," he says.

The old man survives — and sees the pattern at work, of course. He's got to throw away the cigarettes. He's got to quit ordering the cholesterol special for breakfast. "I've got to shape up now, God's telling me," Earl says, "or I won't be around for the last push, the last lesson." The one about how to ride the tsunami of runaway fame.

The machine will win because no matter how complicated it all seems now, it is simpler than it will ever be. The boy will marry one day, and the happiness of two people will lie in his hands. Children will follow, and it will become his job to protect three or four or five people from the molars of the machine. Imagine the din of the grinding in five, ten, fifteen years, when the boy reaches his golfing prime.

The machine will win because the whole notion is so ludicrous to begin with, a kid clutching an eight-iron changing the course of humanity. No, of course not, there won't be thousands of people sitting in front of tanks because of Tiger Woods. He won't bring about the overthrow of a tyranny or spawn a religion that one day will number 300 million devotees.

But maybe Pop is onto something without quite seeing what it is. Maybe it has to do with timing: the appearance of his son when America is turning the corner to a century in which the country's faces of color will nearly equal those that are white. Maybe, every now and then, a man gets swallowed by the machine, but the machine is changed more than he is.

For when we swallow Tiger Woods, the yellow-black-red-white man, we swallow something much more significant than Jordan or Charles Barkley. We swallow hope in the American experiment, in the pell-mell jumbling of genes. We swallow the belief that the face of the future is not necessarily a bitter or bewildered face; that it might even, one day, be something like Tiger Wood's face: handsome and smiling and ready to kick all comers' asses.

We see a woman, 50-ish and Caucasian, well-coiffed and tailored — the woman we see at every country club — walk up to Tiger Woods before he receives the Haskins Award and say, "When I watch you taking on all those other players, Tiger, I feel like I'm watching my own son"... and we feel the quivering of the cosmic compass that occurs when human beings look into the eyes of someone of another color and see their own flesh and blood.

1996

Jon Krakauer

...........................................................................................................

# Into Thin Air

FROM *Outside*

STRADDLING THE TOP of the world, one foot in Tibet and the other in Nepal, I cleared the ice from my oxygen mask, hunched a shoulder against the wind, and stared absently at the vast sweep of earth below. I understood on some dim, detached level that it was a spectacular sight. I'd been fantasizing about this moment, and the release of emotion that would accompany it, for many months. But now that I was finally here, standing on the summit of Mount Everest, I just couldn't summon the energy to care.

It was the afternoon of May 10. I hadn't slept in fifty-seven hours. The only food I'd been able to force down over the preceding three days was a bowl of Ramen soup and a handful of peanut M&M's. Weeks of violent coughing had left me with two separated ribs, making it excruciatingly painful to breathe. Twenty-nine thousand twenty-eight feet up in the troposphere, there was so little oxygen reaching my brain that my mental capacity was that of a slow child. Under the circumstances, I was incapable of feeling much of anything except cold and tired.

I'd arrived on the summit a few minutes after Anatoli Boukreev, a Russian guide with an American expedition, and just ahead of Andy Harris, a guide with the New Zealand–based commercial team that I was a part of and someone with whom I'd grown to be friends during the last six weeks. I snapped four quick photos of Harris and Boukreev striking summit poses, and then turned and started down. My watch read 1:17 P.M. All told, I'd spent less than five minutes on the roof of the world.

After a few steps, I paused to take another photo, this one looking down the Southeast Ridge, the route we had ascended. Training my lens on a pair of climbers approaching the summit, I saw something that until that moment had escaped my attention. To the south, where the sky had been perfectly clear just an hour earlier, a blanket of clouds now hid Pumori, Ama Dablam, and the other lesser peaks surrounding Everest.

Days later — after six bodies had been found, after a search for two others had been abandoned, after surgeons had amputated the gangrenous right hand of my teammate Beck Weathers — people would ask why, if the weather had begun to deteriorate, had climbers on the upper mountain not heeded the signs? Why did veteran Himalayan guides keep moving upward, leading a gaggle of amateurs, each of whom had paid as much as $65,000 to be ushered safely up Everest, into an apparent death trap?

Nobody can speak for the leaders of the two guided groups involved, for both men are now dead. But I can attest that nothing I saw early on the afternoon of May 10 suggested that a murderous storm was about to bear down on us. To my oxygen-depleted mind, the clouds drifting up the grand valley of ice known as the Western Cwm looked innocuous, wispy, insubstantial. Gleaming in the brilliant midday sun, they appeared no different than the harmless puffs of convection condensation that rose from the valley almost daily. As I began my descent, I was indeed anxious, but my concern had little to do with the weather. A check of the gauge on my oxygen tank had revealed that it was almost empty. I needed to get down, fast.

The uppermost shank of the Southeast Ridge is a slender, heavily corniced fin of rock and wind-scoured snow that snakes for a quarter-mile toward a secondary pinnacle known as the South Summit. Negotiating the serrated ridge presents few great technical hurdles, but the route is dreadfully exposed. After fifteen minutes of cautious shuffling over a 7,000-foot abyss, I arrived at the notorious Hillary Step, a pronounced notch in the ridge named after Sir Edmund Hillary, the first Westerner to climb the mountain, and a spot that does require a fair amount of technical maneuvering. As I clipped into a fixed rope and prepared to rappel over the lip, I was greeted by an alarming sight.

Thirty feet below, some twenty people were queued up at the base of the Step, and three climbers were hauling themselves up the rope that I was attempting to descend. I had no choice but to unclip from the line and step aside.

The traffic jam comprised climbers from three separate expeditions: the team I belonged to, a group of paying clients under the leadership of the celebrated New Zealand guide Rob Hall; another guided party headed by American Scott Fischer; and a nonguided team from Taiwan. Moving at the snail's pace that is the norm above 8,000 meters, the throng labored up the Hillary Step one by one, while I nervously bided my time.

Harris, who left the summit shortly after I did, soon pulled up behind me. Wanting to conserve whatever oxygen remained in my tank, I asked him to reach inside my backpack and turn off the valve on my regulator, which he did. For the next ten minutes I felt surprisingly good. My head cleared. I actually seemed less tired than with the gas turned on. Then, abruptly, I felt like I was suffocating. My vision dimmed and my head began to spin. I was on the brink of losing consciousness.

Instead of turning my oxygen off, Harris, in his hypoxically impaired state, had mistakenly cranked the valve open to full flow, draining the tank. I'd just squandered the last of my gas going nowhere. There was another tank waiting for me at the South Summit, 250 feet below, but to get there I would have to descend the most exposed terrain on the entire route without benefit of supplemental oxygen.

But first I had to wait for the crowd to thin. I removed my now useless mask, planted my ice ax into the mountain's frozen hide, and hunkered on the ridge crest. As I exchanged banal congratulations with the climbers filing past, inwardly I was frantic: "Hurry it up, hurry it up!" I silently pleaded. "While you guys are screwing around here, I'm losing brain cells by the millions!"

Most of the passing crowd belonged to Fischer's group, but near the back of the parade two of my teammates eventually appeared: Hall and Yasuko Namba. Girlish and reserved, the 47-year-old Namba was forty minutes away from becoming the oldest woman to climb Everest and the second Japanese woman to reach the highest point on each continent, the so-called Seven Summits.

Later still, Doug Hansen — another member of our expedition, a postal worker from Seattle who had become my closest friend on the mountain — arrived atop the Step. "It's in the bag!" I yelled over the wind, trying to sound more upbeat than I felt. Plainly exhausted, Doug mumbled something from behind his oxygen mask that I didn't catch, shook my hand weakly, and continued plodding upward.

The last climber up the rope was Fischer, whom I knew casually from Seattle, where we both lived. His strength and drive were legendary — in 1994 he'd climbed Everest without using bottled oxygen — so I was surprised at how slowly he was moving and how hammered he looked when he pulled his mask aside to say hello. "Bruuuuuuce!" he wheezed with forced cheer, employing his trademark, fratboyish greeting. When I asked how he was doing, Fischer insisted he was feeling fine: "Just dragging ass a little today for some reason. No big deal." With the Hillary Step finally clear, I clipped into the strand of orange rope, swung quickly around Fischer as he slumped over his ice ax, and rappelled over the edge.

It was after 2:30 when I made it down to the South Summit. By now tendrils of mist were wrapping across the top of 27,890-foot Lhotse and lapping at Everest's summit pyramid. No longer did the weather look so benign. I grabbed a fresh oxygen cylinder, jammed it onto my regulator, and hurried down into the gathering cloud. Moments after I dropped below the South Summit, it began to snow lightly and the visibility went to hell.

Four hundred vertical feet above, where the summit was still washed in bright sunlight under an immaculate cobalt sky, my compadres were dallying, memorializing their arrival at the apex of the planet with photos and high-fives — and using up precious ticks of the clock. None of them imagined that a horrible ordeal was drawing nigh. None of them suspected that by the end of that long day, every minute would matter.

In May of 1963, when I was 9 years old, Tom Hornbein and Willi Unsoeld made the first ascent of Everest's daunting West Ridge, one of the great feats in the annals of mountaineering. Late in the day on their summit push, they climbed a stratum of steep, crumbly limestone — the infamous Yellow Band — that they didn't think they'd be able to descend. Their best shot for getting off the mountain alive, they reckoned, was to go over the top and down the Southeast Ridge, an extremely audacious plan, given the late hour and the unknown terrain. Reaching the summit at sunset, they were forced to spend the night in the open above 28,000 feet — at the time, the highest bivouac in history — and to descend the Southeast Ridge the next morning. That night cost Unsoeld his toes, but the two survived to tell their tale.

Unsoeld, who hailed from my hometown in Oregon, was a close friend of my father's. I climbed my first mountain in the company of my dad, Unsoeld, and his oldest son, Regon, a few months before Unsoeld departed for Nepal. Not surprisingly, accounts of the 1963 Everest epic resonated loud and long in my preadolescent imagination. While my friends idolized John Glenn, Sandy Koufax, and Johnny Unitas, my heroes were Hornbein and Unsoeld.

Secretly, I dreamed of climbing Everest myself one day; for more than a decade it remained a burning ambition. It wasn't until my mid 20s that I abandoned the dream as a preposterous boyhood fantasy. Soon thereafter I began to look down my nose at the world's tallest mountain. It had become fashionable among alpine cognoscenti to denigrate Everest as a "slag heap," a peak lacking sufficient technical challenge or aesthetic appeal to be a worthy objective for a "serious" climber, which I desperately aspired to be.

Such snobbery was rooted in the fact that by the early 1980s, Everest's easiest line — the South Col/Southeast Ridge, or the so-called Yak Route — had been climbed more than a hundred times. Then, in 1985, the floodgates were flung wide open when Dick Bass, a wealthy 55-year-old Texan with limited climbing experience, was ushered to the top of Everest by an extraordinary young climber named David Breashears. In bagging Everest, Bass became the first person to ascend all of the so-called Seven Summits, a feat that earned him worldwide renown and spurred a swarm of other amateur climbers to follow in his guided bootprints.

"To aging Walter Mitty types like myself, Dick Bass was an inspiration," Seaborn Beck Weathers explained during the trek to Everest Base Camp last April. A 49-year-old Dallas pathologist, Weathers was one of eight paying clients on my expedition. "Bass showed that Everest was within the realm of possibility for regular guys. Assuming you're reasonably fit and have some disposable income, I think the biggest obstacle is probably taking time off from your job and leaving your family for two months."

For a great many climbers, the record shows, stealing time away from the daily grind has not been an insurmountable obstacle, nor has the hefty outlay of cash. Over the past half-decade, the traffic on all of the Seven Summits, and especially Everest, has grown at an astonishing rate. And to meet demand, the number of commercial enterprises peddling guided ascents of these mountains has multiplied correspondingly. In the spring of 1996, thirty separate expeditions were on the flanks of Everest, at least eight of them organized as moneymaking ventures.

Even before last season's calamitous outcome, the proliferation of commercial expeditions was a touchy issue. Traditionalists were offended that the world's highest summit was being sold to rich parvenus who, if denied the services of guides, would have difficulty making it to the top of a peak as modest as Mount Rainier. Everest, the purists sniffed, had been debased and profaned.

Such critics also point out that, thanks to the commercialization of Everest, the once hallowed peak has now even been dragged into the swamp of American jurisprudence. Having paid princely sums to be escorted up Everest, some climbers have then sued their guides after the summit eluded them. "Occasionally you'll get a client who thinks he's bought a guaranteed ticket to the summit," laments Peter Athans, a highly respected guide who's made eleven trips to Everest and reached the top four times. "Some people don't understand that an Everest expedition can't be run like a Swiss train."

Sadly, not every Everest lawsuit is unwarranted. Inept or disreputable companies have on more than one occasion failed to deliver crucial logistical support — oxygen, for instance — as promised. On some expeditions guides have gone to the summit without any of their clients, prompting the bitter clients to conclude that they were brought along simply to pick up the tab. In 1995, the leader of one commercial expedition absconded with tens of thousands of dollars of his clients' money before the trip even got off the ground.

To a certain degree, climbers shopping for an Everest expedition get what they pay for. Expeditions on the northern, Tibetan side of the mountain are considerably cheaper — the going rate there is $20,000 to $40,000 per person — than those on the south, in part because China charges much less for climbing permits than does Nepal. But there's a tradeoff: until 1995, no guided client had ever reached the summit from Tibet.

This year, Hall charged $65,000 a head, not including airfare or personal equipment, to take people up the South Col/Southeast Ridge route. Although no commercial guide service charged more, Hall, a lanky 35-year-old with a biting Kiwi wit, had no difficulty booking clients, thanks to his phenomenal success rate: He'd put thirty-nine climbers on the summit between 1990 and 1995, which meant that he was responsible for three more ascents than had been made in the first twenty years after Hillary's inaugural climb. Despite the disdain I'd expressed for Everest over the years, when the call came to join Hall's expedition, I said yes without even hesitating to catch my breath. Boyhood dreams die hard, I discovered, and good sense be damned.

On April 10, after ten days of hiking through the steep, walled canyons and rhododendron forests of northern Nepal, I walked into Everest Base Camp. My altimeter read 17,600 feet.

Situated at the entrance to a magnificent natural amphitheater formed by Everest and its two sisters, Lhotse and Nuptse, was a small city of tents sheltering 240 climbers and Sherpas from fourteen expeditions, all of it sprawled across a bend in the Khumbu Glacier. The escarpments above camp were draped with hanging glaciers, from which calved immense serac avalanches that thundered down at all hours of the day and night. Hard to the east, pinched between the Nuptse wall and the West Shoulder of Everest, the Khumbu Icefall spilled to within a quarter-mile of the tents in a chaos of pale blue shards.

In stark contrast to the harsh qualities of the environment stood our campsite and all its creature comforts, including a nineteen-person staff. Our mass tent, a cavernous canvas structure, was wired with a stereo system and solar-powered electric lights; an adjacent communications tent housed a satellite phone and fax. There was a hot shower. A cook boy came to each client's tent in the mornings to serve us steaming mugs of tea in our sleeping bags. Fresh bread and vegetables arrived every few days on the backs of yaks.

In many ways, Rob Hall's Adventure Consultants site served as a sort of town hall for Base Camp, largely because nobody on the mountain was more respected than Hall, who was on Everest for his eighth time. Whenever there was a problem — a labor dispute with the Sherpas, a medical emergency, a critical decision about climbing strategy — people came to him for advice. And Hall, always generous, dispensed his accumulated wisdom freely to the very rivals who were competing with him for clients, most notably Fischer.

Fischer's Mountain Madness camp, distinguished by a huge Starbucks Coffee banner that hung from a chunk of granite, was a mere five minutes' walk down the glacier. Fischer and Hall were competitors, but they were also friends, and there was a good deal of socializing between the two teams. His mess tent wasn't as well appointed as ours, but Fischer was always quick to offer a cup of fresh-brewed coffee to any climber or trekker who poked a head inside the door.

The 40-year-old Fischer was a strapping, gregarious man with a blond ponytail and manic energy. He'd grown up in New Jersey and had fallen in love with climbing after taking a NOLS course as a 14-year-old. In his formative years, during which he became known for a damn-the-torpedoes style, he'd survived a number of climbing accidents, including twice cratering into the ground from a height of more than 70 feet. Fischer's infectious, seat-of-the-pants approach to his own life was reflected in his improvisational approach to guiding Everest. In striking contrast to Hall — who insisted that his clients climb as a group at all times, under the close watch of his guides — Fischer encouraged his clients to be independent, to move at their own pace, to go wherever they wanted, whenever they wanted.

Both men were under considerable pressure this season. The previous year, Hall had for the first time failed to get anybody to the top. Another dry spell would be very bad for business. Meanwhile Fischer, who had climbed the peak without oxygen but had never guided the mountain, was still trying to get established in the Everest business. He needed to get clients to the summit, especially a high-profile one like Sandy Hill Pittman, the Manhattan boulevardier-cum-writer who was filing daily diaries on an NBC World Wide Web site.

Despite the many trappings of civilization at Base Camp, there was no forgetting that we were more than three miles above sea level. Walking to the mess tent at mealtime left me wheezing to catch my breath. If I sat up too quickly, my head reeled and vertigo set in. I developed a dry, hacking cough that would steadily worsen over the next six weeks. Cuts and scrapes refused to heal. I was rarely hungry, a sign that my oxygen-deprived stomach had shut down and my body had begun to consume itself for sustenance. My arms and legs gradually began to wither to toothpicks, and by expedition's end I would weigh twenty-five pounds less than when I left Seattle.

Some of my teammates fared even worse than I in the meager air. At least half of them suffered from various intestinal ailments that kept them racing to the latrine. Hansen, 46, who'd paid for the expedition by working at a Seattle-area post office by night and on construction jobs by day, was plagued by an unceasing headache for most of his first week at Base Camp. It felt, as he put it, "like somebody's driven a nail between my eyes." This was Hansen's second time on Everest with Hall. The year before, he'd been forced to turn around 330 vertical feet below the summit because of deep snow and the late hour. "The summit looked *sooooo* close," Hansen recalled with a painful laugh. "Believe me, there hasn't been a day since that I haven't thought about it." Hansen had been talked into returning this year by Hall, who felt sorry that Hansen had been denied the summit and who had significantly discounted Hansen's fee to entice him to give it another try.

A rail-thin man with a leathery, prematurely furrowed face, Hansen was a single father who spent a lot of time in Base Camp writing faxes to his two kids, ages 19 and 27, and to an elementary school in Kent,

Washington, that had sold T-shirts to help fund his climb. Hansen bunked in the tent next to mine, and every time a fax would arrive from his daughter, Angie, he'd read it to me, beaming. "Jeez," he'd announce, "how do you suppose a screw-up like me could have raised such a great kid?"

As a newcomer to altitude — I'd never been above 17,000 feet — I brooded about how I'd perform higher on the mountain, especially in the so-called Death Zone above 25,000 feet. I'd done some fairly extreme climbs over the years in Alaska, Patagonia, Canada, and the Alps. I'd logged considerably more time on technical rock and ice than most of the other clients and many of the guides. But technical expertise counted for very little on Everest, and I'd spent less time at high altitude — none, to be precise — than virtually every other climber here. By any rational assessment, I was singularly unqualified to attempt the highest mountain in the world.

This didn't seem to worry Hall. After seven Everest expeditions he'd fine-tuned a remarkably effective method of acclimatization. In the next six weeks, he would make three trips above Base Camp, climbing about two thousand feet higher each time. After that, he insisted, our bodies would be sufficiently adapted to the altitude to permit safe passage to the 29,028-foot summit. "It's worked thirty-nine times so far, pal," Hall assured me with a wry grin.

Three days after our arrival in Base Camp, we headed out on our first acclimatization sortie, a one-day round-trip to Camp One, perched at the upper lip of the Icefall, two thousand vertical feet above. No part of the South Col route is more feared than the Icefall, a slowly moving jumble of huge, unstable ice blocks: We were all well aware that it had already killed nineteen climbers. As I strapped on my crampons in the frigid predawn gloom, I winced with each creak and rumble from the glacier's shifting depths.

Long before we'd even got to Base Camp, our trail had been blazed by Sherpas, who had fixed more than a mile of rope and installed about sixty aluminum ladders over the crevasses that crisscross the shattered glacier. As we shuffled forth, three-quarters of the way to Camp One, Hall remarked glibly that the Icefall was in better shape than he'd ever seen it: "The route's like a bloody freeway this season."

But only slightly higher, at about 19,000 feet, the fixed ropes led us beneath and then over a twelve-story chunk of ice that leaned precariously off kilter. I hurried to get out from beneath its wobbly tonnage and reach its crest, but my fastest pace was no better than a crawl. Every four or five steps I'd stop, lean against the rope, and suck desperately at the thin, bitter air, searing my lungs.

We reached the end of the Icefall about four hours after setting out, but the relative safety of Camp One didn't supply much peace of mind: I couldn't stop thinking about the ominously tilted slab and the fact that I would have to pass beneath its frozen bulk at least seven more times if I was going to make it to the top of Everest.

Most of the recent debate about Everest has focused on the safety of commercial expeditions. But the least experienced, least qualified climbers on the mountain this past season were not guided clients; rather, they were members of traditionally structured, noncommercial expeditions.

While descending the lower Icefall on April 13, I overtook a pair of slower climbers outfitted with unorthodox clothing and gear. Almost immediately it became apparent that they weren't very familiar with the standard tools and techniques of glacier travel. The climber in back repeatedly snagged his crampons and stumbled. Waiting for them to cross a gaping crevasse bridged by two rickety ladders lashed end to end, I was shocked to see them go across together, almost in lockstep, a needlessly dangerous act. An awkward attempt at conversation revealed that they were members of a Taiwanese expedition.

The reputation of the Taiwanese had preceded them to Everest. In the spring of 1995, the team had traveled to Alaska to climb Mount McKinley as a shakedown for their attempt on Everest in 1996. Nine climbers reached the summit of McKinley, but seven of them were caught by a storm on the descent, became disoriented, and spent a night in the open at 19,400 feet, initiating a costly, hazardous rescue by the National Park Service.

Five of the climbers — two of them with severe frostbite and one dead — were plucked from high on the peak by helicopter. "If we hadn't arrived right when we did, two others would have died, too," says American Conrad Anker, who with his partner Alex Lowe climbed to 19,400 feet to help rescue the Taiwanese. "Earlier, we'd noticed the Taiwanese group because they looked so incompetent. It really wasn't any big surprise when they got into trouble."

The leader of the expedition, Ming Ho Gau — a jovial photographer who answers to "Makalu" — had to be assisted down the upper mountain. "As they were bringing him down," Anker recalls, "Makalu was yelling, 'Victory! Victory! We made summit!' to everyone he passed, as if the disaster hadn't even happened." When the survivors of the McKinley debacle showed up on Everest in 1996, Makalu Gau was again their leader.

In truth, their presence was a matter of grave concern to just about everyone on the mountain. The fear was that the Taiwanese would suffer a calamity that would compel other expeditions to come to their aid, risking further lives and possibly costing climbers a shot at the summit. Of course, the Taiwanese were by no means the only group that seemed egregiously unqualified. Camped beside us at Base Camp was a 25-year-old Norwegian climber named Petter Neby, who announced his intention to make a solo ascent of the Southwest Face, an outrageously difficult route, despite the fact that his Himalayan experience consisted of two easy ascents of neighboring Island Peak, a 20,270-foot bump.

And then there were the South Africans. Lavishly funded, sponsored by a major newspaper, the source of effusive national pride, their team had received a personal blessing from Nelson Mandela prior to their departure. The first South African expedition ever to be granted a permit to climb Everest, they were a mixed-race group that hoped to put the first black person on the summit. They were led by a smooth-talking former military officer named Ian Woodall. When the team arrived in Nepal it included three very strong members, most notably a brilliant climber named Andy de Klerk, who happened to be a good friend of mine.

But almost immediately, four members, including de Klerk, defected. "Woodall turned out to be a total control freak," said de Klerk. "And you couldn't trust him. We never knew when he was talking bullshit or telling the truth. We didn't want to put our lives in the hands of a guy like that. So we left."

Later de Klerk would learn that Woodall had lied about his climbing record. He'd never climbed anywhere near 8,000 meters, as he claimed. In fact, he hadn't climbed much of anything. Woodall had also allegedly lied about expedition finances and even lied about who was named on the official climbing permit.

After Woodall's deceit was made public, it became an international scandal, reported on the front pages of newspapers throughout the Commonwealth. When the editor of the Johannesburg *Sunday Times,* the expedition's primary sponsor, confronted Woodall in Nepal, Woodall allegedly tried to physically intimidate him and, according to de Klerk, threatened, "I'm going to rip your fucking head off!"

In the end, Woodall refused to relinquish leadership and insisted that the climb would proceed as planned. By this point none of the four climbers left on the team had more than minimal alpine experience. At least two of them, says de Klerk, "didn't even know how to put their crampons on."

The solo Norwegian, the Taiwanese, and especially the South Africans were frequent topics of discussion around the dinner table in our mess tent. "With so many incompetent people on the mountain," Hall frowned one evening in late April, "I think it's pretty unlikely that we'll get through this without something bad happening."

For our third and final acclimatization excursion, we spent four nights at 21,300-foot Camp Two and a night at 24,000-foot Camp Three. Then on May 1 our whole team descended to Base Camp to recoup our strength for the summit push. Much to my surprise, Hall's acclimatization plan seemed to be working: After three weeks, I felt like I was finally adapting to the altitude. The air at Base Camp now seemed deliciously thick.

From the beginning, Hall had planed that May 10 would be our summit day. "Of the four times I've summited," he explained, "twice it was on the tenth of May. As the Sherps would put it, the tenth is an 'auspicious' date for me." But there was also a more down-to-earth reason for selecting this date: The annual ebb and flow of the monsoon made it likely that the most favorable weather of the year would fall on or near May 10.

For all of April, the jet stream had been trained on Everest like a fire hose, blasting the summit pyramid with nonstop hurricane-force winds. Even on days when Base Camp was perfectly calm and flooded with sunshine, an immense plume of wind-driven snow was visible over the summit. But if all went well, in early May the monsoon approaching from the Bay of Bengal would force the jet stream north into Tibet. If this year was like past years, between the departure of the wind and the arrival of the monsoon storms we would be presented with a brief window of clear, calm weather during which a summit assault would be possible.

Unfortunately, the annual weather patterns were no secret, and every expedition had its sights set on the same window. Hoping to avoid dangerous gridlock on the summit ridge, Hall held a powwow in the mess tent with leaders of the expeditions in Base Camp. The council, as it were, determined that Göran Kropp, a young Swede who had ridden a bicycle all the way to Nepal from Stockholm, would make the first attempt, alone, on May 3. Next would be a team from Montenegro. Then, on May 8 or 9, it would be the turn of the IMAX expedition, headed by David Breashears, which hoped to wrap up a large-format film about Everest with footage from the top.

Our team, it was decided, would share a summit date of May 10 with Fischer's group. An American commercial team and two British-led commercial groups promised to steer clear of the top of the mountain on the tenth, as did the Taiwanese. Woodall, however, declared that the South Africans would go to the top whenever they pleased, probably on the tenth, and anyone who didn't like it could "bugger off."

Hall, ordinarily extremely slow to rile, flew into a rage over Woodall's refusal to cooperate. "I don't want to be anywhere near the upper mountain when those punters are up there," he seethed.

"It feels good to be on our way to the summit, yeah?" Harris inquired as we pulled into Camp Two. The midday sun was reflecting off the walls of Nuptse, Lhotse, and Everest, and the entire ice-coated valley seemed to have been transformed into a huge solar oven. We were finally ascending for real, headed straight toward the top, Harris and me and everybody else.

Harris — Harold to his friends — was the junior guide on the expedition and the only one who'd never been to Everest (indeed, he'd never been above 23,000 feet). Built like an NFL quarterback and preternaturally good-natured, he was usually assigned to the slower clients at the back of the pack. For much of the expedition, he had been laid low with intestinal ailments, but he was finally getting his strength back, and he was eager to prove himself to his seasoned colleagues. "I think we're actually gonna knock this big bastard off," he confided to me with a huge smile, staring up at the summit.

Harris worked as a much-in-demand heli-skiing guide in the antipodal winter. Summers he guided climbers in New Zealand's Southern Alps and had just launched a promising heli-hiking business. Sipping tea in the mess tent back at Base Camp, he'd shown me a photograph of Fiona McPherson, the pretty, athletic doctor with whom he lived, and described the house they were building together in the hills outside Queenstown. "Yeah," he'd marveled, "it's kind of amazing, really. My life seems to be working out pretty well."

Later that day, Kropp, the Swedish soloist, passed Camp Two on his way down the mountain, looking utterly worked. Three days earlier, under clear skies, he'd made it to just below the South Summit and was no more than an hour from the top when he decided to turn around. He had been climbing without supplemental oxygen, the hour had been late — 2 P.M., to be exact — and he'd believed that if he'd kept going, he'd have been too tired to descend safely.

"To turn around that close to the summit," Hall mused, shaking his head. "That showed incredibly good judgment on young Göran's part. I'm impressed." Sticking to your predetermined turn-around time — that was the most important rule on the mountain. Over the previous month, Rob had lectured us repeatedly on this point. Our turn-around time, he said, would probably be 1 P.M., and no matter how close we were to the top, we were to abide by it. "With enough determination, any bloody idiot can get up this hill," Hall said. "The trick is to get back down alive."

Cheerful and unflappable, Hall's easygoing facade masked an intense desire to succeed — which to him was defined in the fairly simple terms of getting as many clients as possible to the summit. But he also paid careful attention to the details: the health of the Sherpas, the efficiency of the solar-powered electrical system, the sharpness of his clients' crampons. He loved being a guide, and it pained him that some celebrated climbers didn't give his profession the respect he felt it deserved.

On May 8 our team and Fischer's team left Camp Two and started climbing the Lhotse Face, a vast sweep of steel-hard ice rising from the head of the Western Cwm. Hall's Camp Three, two-thirds of the way up this wall, was set on a narrow ledge that had been chopped into the face by our Sherpas. It was a spectacularly perilous perch. A hundred feet below, no less exposed, were the tents of most of the other teams, including Fischer's, the South Africans, and the Taiwanese.

It was here that we had our first encounter with death on the mountain. At 7:30 A.M. on May 9, as we were pulling on our boots to ascend to Camp Four, a 36-year-old steelworker from Taipei named Chen Yu-Nan crawled out of his tent to relieve himself, with only the smooth-soled liners of his mountaineering boots on his feet — a rather serious lapse of judgment. As he squatted, he lost his footing on the slick ice and went hurtling down the Lhotse Face, coming to rest, headfirst, in a crevasse. Sherpas who had seen the incident lowered a rope, pulled him out of the slot, and carried him back to his tent. He was bruised and badly rattled, but otherwise he seemed unharmed. Chen's teammates left him in a tent to recover and departed for Camp Four. That afternoon, as Chen tried to descend to Camp Two with the help of the Sherpas, he keeled over and died.

Over the preceding six weeks there had been several serious accidents: Tenzing Sherpa, from our team, fell 150 feet into a crevasse and injured a leg seriously enough to require helicopter evacuation from Base Camp. One of Fischer's Sherpas nearly died of a mysterious illness at Camp Two. A young, apparently fit British climber had a serious heart attack near the top of the Icefall. A Dane was struck by a falling serac and broke several ribs. Until now, however, none of the mishaps had been fatal.

Chen's death cast a momentary pall over the mountain. But 33 climbers at the South Col would be departing for the summit in a few short hours, and the gloom was quickly shoved aside by nervous anticipation of the challenge to come. Most of us were simply wrapped too tightly in the grip of summit fever to engage in thoughtful reflection about the death of someone in our midst. There would be plenty of time for reflection later, we assumed, after we all had summited — and got back down.

Climbing with oxygen for the first time, I had reached the South Col, our launching pad for the summit assault, at one o'clock that afternoon. A barren plateau of bulletproof ice and windswept boulders, the Col sits at 26,000 feet above sea level, tucked between the upper ramparts of Lhotse, the world's fourth-highest mountain, and Everest. Roughly rectangular, about four football fields long by two across, the Col is bounded on the east by the Kangshung Face, a 7,000-foot drop-off, and on the west by the 4,000-foot Lhotse Face. It is one of the coldest, most inhospitable places I have ever been.

I was the first Western climber to arrive. When I got there, four Sherpas were struggling to erect our tents in a 50-mph wind. I helped them put up my shelter, anchoring it to some discarded oxygen canisters wedged beneath the largest rocks I could lift. Then I dove inside to wait for my teammates.

It was nearly 5 P.M. when the last of the group made camp. The final stragglers in Fischer's group came in even later, which didn't augur well for the summit bid, scheduled to begin in six hours. Everyone retreated to their nylon domes the moment they reached the Col and did their best to nap, but the machine-gun rattle of the flapping tents and the anxiety over what was to come made sleep out of the question for most of us.

Surrounding me on the plateau were some three dozen people, huddled in tents pitched side by side. Yet an odd sense of isolation hung over the camp. Up here, in this godforsaken place, I felt distressingly disconnected from everyone around me — emotionally, spiritually, physically. We were a team in name only, I'd sadly come to realize. Although we would leave camp in a few hours as a group, we would ascend as individuals, linked to one another by neither rope nor any deep sense of loyalty. Each client was in it for himself or herself, pretty much. And I was no different: I really hoped Doug Hansen would get to the top, for instance, yet if he were to turn around, I knew I would do everything in my power to keep pushing on. In another context this insight would have been depressing, but I was too preoccupied with the weather to dwell on it. If the wind didn't abate, the summit would be out of the question for all of us.

At 7 P.M. the gale abruptly ceased. The temperature was 15 below zero, but there was almost no wind. Conditions were excellent; Hall, it appeared, had timed our summit bid perfectly. The tension was palpable as we sipped tea, delivered to us in our tents by Sherpas, and readied our gear. Nobody said much. All of us had suffered greatly to get to this moment. I had eaten little and slept not at all since leaving Camp Two two days earlier. Damage to my thoracic cartilage made each cough feel like a stiff kick between the ribs and brought tears to my eyes. But if I wanted a crack at the summit, I had no choice but to ignore my infirmities as much as possible and climb.

Finally, at 11:35, we were away from the tents. I strapped on my oxygen mask and ascended into the darkness. There were fifteen of us in Hall's team: guides Hall, Harris, and Mike Groom, an Australian with impressive Himalayan experience; Sherpas Ang Dorje, Lhakpa Chhiri, Nawang Norbu, and Kami; and clients Hansen, Namba, Weathers, Stuart Hutchison (a Canadian doctor), John Taske (an Australian doctor), Lou Kasischke (a lawyer from Michigan), Frank Fischbeck (a publisher from Hong Kong), and me.

Fischer's group — guides Fischer, Boukreev, and Neal Beidleman; five Sherpas; and clients Charlene Fox, Tim Madsen, Klev Schoening, Sandy Pittman, Lene Gammelgaard, and Martin Adams — left the South Col at midnight. Shortly after that, Makalu Gau started up with three Sherpas, ignoring his promise that no Taiwanese would make a summit attempt on May 10. Thankfully, the South Africans had failed to make it to Camp Four and were nowhere in sight.

The night had a cold, phantasmal beauty that intensified as we ascended. More stars than I had ever seen smeared the frozen sky. Far to the southeast, enormous thunderheads drifted over Nepal, illuminating the heavens with surreal bursts of orange and blue lightning. A gibbous moon rose over the shoulder of 27,824-foot Makalu, washing the slope beneath my boots in ghostly light, obviating the need for a headlamp. I broke trail throughout the night with Ang Dorje — our *sirdar,* or head Sherpa — and at 5:30, just as the sun was edging over the horizon, I reached the crest of the Southeast Ridge. Three of the world's five highest peaks stood out in jagged relief against the pastel dawn. My altimeter read 27,500 feet.

Hall had instructed us to climb no higher until the whole group gathered at this level roost known as the Balcony, so I sat down on my pack to wait. When Hall and Weathers finally arrived at the back of the herd, I'd been sitting for more than ninety minutes. By now Fischer's group and the Taiwanese team had caught and passed us. I was peeved over wasting so much time and at falling behind everybody else. But I understood Hall's rationale, so I kept quiet and played the part of the obedient client. To my mind, the rewards of climbing come from its emphasis on self-reliance, on making critical decisions and dealing with the consequences, on personal responsibility. When you become a client, I discovered, you give up all that. For safety's sake, the guide always calls the shots.

Passivity on the part of the clients had thus been encouraged throughout our expedition. Sherpas put in the route, set up the camps, did the cooking, hauled the loads; we clients seldom carried more than daypacks stuffed with our personal gear. This system conserved our energy and vastly increased our chances of getting to the top, but I found it hugely unsatisfying. I felt at times as if I wasn't really climbing the mountain — that surrogates were doing it for me. Although I had willingly accepted this role in order to climb Everest, I never got used to it. And I was happy as hell when, at 7:10 A.M., Hall gave me the O.K. to continue climbing.

One of the first people I passed when I started moving again was Fischer's sirdar, Lobsang Jangbu, kneeling in the snow over a pile of vomit. Both Lobsang and Boukreev had asked and been granted permission by Fischer to climb without supplemental oxygen, a highly questionable decision that significantly affected the performance of both men, but especially Lobsang. His feeble state, moreover, had been compounded by his insistence on "short-roping" Pittman on summit day.

Lobsang, 25, was a gifted high-altitude climber who'd summited Everest twice before without oxygen. Sporting a long black ponytail and a gold tooth, he was flashy, self-assured, and very appealing to the clients, not to mention crucial to their summit hopes. As Fischer's head Sherpa, he was expected to be at the front of the group this morning, putting in the route. But just before daybreak, I'd looked down to see Lobsang hitched to Pittman by her three-foot safety tether; the Sherpa, huffing and puffing loudly, was hauling the assertive New Yorker up the steep slope like a horse pulling a plow. Pittman was on a widely publicized quest to ascend Everest and thereby complete the Seven Summits. She'd failed to make it to the top on two previous expeditions; this time she was determined to succeed.

Fischer knew that Lobsang was short-roping Pittman, yet did nothing to stop it; some people have thus concluded that Fischer ordered Lobsang to do it, because Pittman had been moving slowly when she started out on summit day, and Fischer worried that if Pittman failed to reach the summit, he would be denied a marketing bonanza. But two other clients on Fischer's team speculate that Lobsang was short-roping her because she'd promised him a hefty cash bonus if she reached the top. Pittman has denied this and insists that she was hauled up against her wishes. Which begs a question: Why didn't she unfasten the tether, which would have required nothing more than reaching up and unclipping a single carabiner?

"I have no idea why Lobsang was short-roping Sandy," confesses Beidleman. "He lost sight of what he was supposed to be doing up there, what the priorities were." It didn't seem like a particularly serious mistake at the time. A little thing. But it was one of many little things — accruing slowly, compounding imperceptibly, building steadily toward critical mass.

A human plucked from sea level and dropped on the summit of Everest would lose consciousness within minutes and quickly die. A well-acclimatized climber can function at that altitude with supplemental oxygen — but not well, and not for long. The body becomes far more vulnerable to pulmonary and cerebral edema, hypothermia, frostbite. Each member of our team was carrying two orange, seven-pound oxygen bottles. A third bottle would be waiting for each of us at the South Summit on our descent, stashed there by Sherpas. At a conservative flow rate of two liters per minute, each bottle would last between five and six hours. By 4 or 5 P.M., about eighteen hours after starting to climb, everyone's gas would be gone.

Hall understood this well. The fact that nobody had summited this season prior to our attempt concerned him, because it meant that no fixed ropes had been installed on the upper Southeast Ridge, the most exposed part of the climb. To solve this problem, Hall and Fischer had agreed before leaving Base Camp that on summit day the two sirdars — Ang Dorje from Hall's team and Lobsang from Fischer's — would leave Camp Four 90 minutes ahead of everybody else and put in the fixed lines before any clients reached the upper mountain. "Rob made it very clear how important it was to do this," recalls Beidleman. "He wanted to avoid a bottleneck at all costs."

For some reason, however, the Sherpas hadn't set out ahead of us on the night of May 9. When Ang Dorje and I reached the Balcony, we were an hour in front of the rest of the group, and we could have easily moved on and installed the ropes. But Hall had explicitly forbidden me to go ahead, and Lobsang was still far below, short-roping Pittman. There was nobody to accompany Ang Dorje.

A quiet, moody young man who regarded Lobsang as a showboat and a goldbrick, Ang Dorje had been working extremely hard, well beyond the call of duty, for six long weeks. Now he was tired of doing more than his share. If Lobsang wasn't going to fix ropes, neither was he. Looking sullen, Ang Dorje sat down with me to wait.

Sure enough, not long after everybody caught up with us and we continued climbing up, a bottleneck occurred when our group encountered a series of giant rock steps at 28,000 feet. Clients huddled at the base of this obstacle for nearly an hour while Beidleman, standing in for the absent Lobsang, laboriously ran the rope out.

Here, the impatience and technical inexperience of Namba nearly caused a disaster. A businesswoman who liked to joke that her husband did all the cooking and cleaning, Namba had become famous back in Japan for her Seven Summits globe-trotting, and her quest for Everest had turned into a minor cause célèbre. She was usually a slow, tentative climber, but today, with the summit squarely in her sights, she seemed energized as never before. She'd been pushing hard all morning, jostling her way toward the front of the line. Now, as Beidleman clung precariously to the rock one hundred feet above, the overeager Namba clamped her ascender onto the dangling rope before the guide had anchored his end of it. Just as she was about to put her full body weight on the rope — which would have pulled Beidleman off — guide Mike Groom intervened and gently scolded her.

The line continued to grow longer, and so did the delay. By 11:30 A.M., three of Hall's clients — Hutchison, Taske, and Kasischke — had become worried about the lagging pace. Stuck behind the sluggish Taiwanese team, Hutchison now says, "It seemed increasingly unlikely that we would have any chance of summiting before the 1 P.M. turn-around time dictated by Rob."

After a brief discussion, they turned their back on the summit and headed down with Kami and Lhakpa Chhiri. Earlier, Fischbeck, one of Hall's strongest clients, had also turned around. The decision must have been supremely difficult for at least some of these men, especially Fischbeck, for whom this was a fourth attempt on Everest. They'd each spent as much as $70,000 to be up here and had endured weeks of misery. All were driven, unaccustomed to losing and even less to quitting. And yet, faced with a tough decision, they were among the few who made the right one that day.

There was a second, even worse, bottleneck at the South Summit, which I reached at about 11 A.M. The Hillary Step was just a stone's throw away, and slightly beyond that was the summit itself. Rendered dumb with awe and exhaustion, I took some photos and sat down with Harris, Beidleman, and Boukreev to wait for the Sherpas to fix ropes along the spectacularly corniced summit ridge.

A stiff breeze raked the ridge crest, blowing a plume of spindrift into Tibet, but overhead the sky was an achingly brilliant blue. Lounging in the sun at 28,700 feet inside my thick down suit, gazing across the Himalayas in a hypoxic stupor, I completely lost track of time. Nobody paid much attention to the fact that Ang Dorje and Nawang Norbu were sharing a thermos of tea beside us and seemed to be in no hurry to go higher. Around noon, Beidleman finally asked, "Hey, Ang Dorje, are you going to fix the ropes, or what?"

Ang Dorje's reply was a quick, unequivocal "No" — perhaps because neither Lobsang nor any of Fischer's other Sherpas was there to share the work. Shocked into doing the job ourselves, Beidleman, Boukreev, Harris, and I collected all the remaining rope, and Beidleman and Boukreev started stringing it along the most dangerous sections of the summit ridge. But by then more than an hour had trickled away.

Bottled oxygen does not make the top of Everest feel like sea level. Ascending above the South Summit with my regulator delivering two liters of oxygen per minute, I had to stop and draw three or four heaving lungfuls of air after each ponderous step. The systems we were using delivered a lean mix of compressed oxygen and ambient air that made 29,000 feet feel like 26,000 feet. But they did confer other benefits that weren't so easily quantified, not the least of which was keeping hypothermia and frostbite at bay.

Climbing along the blade of the summit ridge, sucking gas into my ragged lungs, I enjoyed a strange, unwarranted sense of calm. The world beyond the rubber mask was stupendously vivid but seemed not quite real, as if a movie were being projected in slow motion across the front of my goggles. I felt drugged, disengaged, thoroughly insulated from external stimuli. I had to remind myself over and over that there was seven thousand feet of sky on either side, that everything was at stake here, that I would pay for a single bungled step with my life.

Plodding slowly up the last few steps to the summit, I had the sensation of being underwater, of moving at quarter-speed. And then I found myself atop a slender wedge of ice adorned with a discarded oxygen cylinder and a battered aluminum survey pole, with nowhere higher to climb. A string of Buddhist prayer flags snapped furiously in the wind. To the north, down a side of the mountain I had never seen, the desiccated Tibetan plateau stretched to the horizon.

Reaching the top of Everest is supposed to trigger a surge of intense elation; against long odds, after all, I had just attained a goal I'd coveted since childhood. But the summit was really only the halfway point. Any impulse I might have felt toward self-congratulation was immediately extinguished by apprehension about the long, dangerous descent that lay ahead. As I turned to go down, I experienced a moment of alarm when a glance at my regulator showed that my oxygen was almost gone. I started down the ridge as fast as I could move but soon hit the traffic jam at the Hillary Step, which was when my gas ran out. When Hall came by, I masked my rising panic and thanked him for getting me to the top of Everest. "Yeah, it's turned out to be a pretty good expedition," he replied. "I only wish we could have gotten more clients to the top." Hall was clearly disappointed that five of his eight clients had turned back earlier in the day, while all six of Fischer's clients were still plugging toward the summit.

Soon after Hall passed, the Hillary Step finally cleared. Dizzy, fearing that I would black out, I made my way tenuously down the fixed lines. Then, fifty feet above the South Summit, the rope ended, and I balked at going farther without gas.

Over at the South Summit I could see Harris sorting through a pile of oxygen bottles. "Yo, Andy!" I yelled. "Could you bring me a fresh bottle?"

"There's no oxygen here!" the guide shouted back. "These bottles are all empty!" I nearly lost it. I had no idea what to do. Just then, Groom came past on his way down from the summit. He had climbed Everest in 1993 without supplemental oxygen and wasn't overly concerned about going without. He gave me his bottle, and we quickly scrambled over to the South Summit.

When we got there, an examination of the oxygen cache revealed right away that there were six full bottles. Harris, however, refused to believe it. He kept insisting that they were all empty, and nothing Groom or I said could convince him otherwise. Right then it should have been obvious that Harris was acting irrationally and had slipped well beyond routine hypoxia, but I was so impeded myself that it simply didn't register. Harris was the invincible guide, there to look after me and the other clients; the thought never entered my own crippled mind that he might in fact be in dire straits — that a guide might urgently need help from me.

As Harris continued to assert that there were no full bottles, Groom looked at me quizzically. I looked back and shrugged. Turning to Harris, I said, "No big deal, Andy. Much ado about nothing." Then I grabbed a new oxygen canister, screwed it onto my regulator, and headed down the mountain. Given what unfolded over the next three hours, my failure to see that Harris was in serious trouble was a lapse that's likely to haunt me for the rest of my life.

At 3 P.M., within minutes of leaving the South Summit, I descended into clouds ahead of the others. Snow started to fall. In the flat, diminishing light, it became hard to tell where the mountain ended and where the sky began. It would have been very easy to blunder off the edge of the ridge and never be heard from again. The lower I went, the worse the weather became.

When I reached the Balcony again, about 4 P.M., I encountered Beck Weathers standing alone, shivering violently. Years earlier, Weathers had undergone radial keratotomy to correct his vision. A side effect, which he discovered on Everest and consequently hid from Hall, was that in the low barometric pressure at high altitude, his eyesight failed. Nearly blind when he'd left Camp Four in the middle of the night but hopeful that his vision would improve at daybreak, he stuck close to the person in front of him and kept climbing.

Upon reaching the Southeast Ridge shortly after sunrise, Weathers had confessed to Hall that he was having trouble seeing, at which point Hall declared, "Sorry, pal, you're going down. I'll send one of the Sherpas with you." Weathers countered that his vision was likely to improve as soon as the sun crept higher in the sky; Hall said he'd give Weathers thirty minutes to find out — after that, he'd have to wait there at 27,500 feet for Hall and the rest of the group to come back down. Hall didn't want Weathers descending alone. "I'm dead serious about this," Hall admonished his client. "Promise me that you'll sit right here until I return."

"I crossed my heart and hoped to die," Weathers recalls now, "and promised I wouldn't go anywhere." Shortly after noon, Hutchison, Taske, and Kasischke passed by with their Sherpa escorts, but Weathers elected not to accompany them. "The weather was still good," he explains, "and I saw no reason to break my promise to Rob."

By the time I encountered Weathers, however, conditions were turning ugly. "Come down with me," I implored. "I'll get you down, no problem." He was nearly convinced, until I made the mistake of mentioning that Groom was on his way down, too. In a day of many mistakes, this would turn out to be a crucial one. "Thanks anyway," Weathers said. "I'll just wait for Mike. He's got a rope; he'll be able to short-rope me." Secretly relieved, I hurried toward the South Col, 1,500 feet below.

These lower slopes proved to be the most difficult part of the descent. Six inches of powder snow blanketed outcroppings of loose shale. Climbing down them demanded unceasing concentration, an all but impossible feat in my current state. By 5:30, however, I was finally within two hundred vertical feet of Camp Four, and only one obstacle stood between me and safety: a steep bulge of rock-hard ice that I'd have to descend without a rope. But the weather had deteriorated into a full-scale blizzard. Snow pellets borne on 70-mph winds stung my face; any exposed skin was instantly frozen. The tents, no more than two hundred horizontal yards away, were only intermittently visible through the whiteout. There was zero margin for error. Worried about making a critical blunder, I sat down to marshal my energy.

Suddenly, Harris appeared out of the gloom and sat beside me. At this point there was no mistaking that he was in appalling shape. His cheeks were coated with an armor of frost, one eye was frozen shut, and his speech was slurred. He was frantic to reach the tents. After briefly discussing the best way to negotiate the ice, Harris started scooting down on his butt, facing forward. "Andy," I yelled after him, "it's crazy to try it like that!" He yelled something back, but the words were carried off by the screaming wind. A second later he lost his purchase and was rocketing down on his back.

Two hundred feet below, I could make out Harris's motionless form. I was sure he'd broken at least a leg, maybe his neck. But then he stood up, waved that he was O.K., and started stumbling toward camp, which was for the moment in plain sight, 150 yards beyond.

I could see three or four people shining lights outside the tents. I watched Harris walk across the flats to the edge of camp, a distance he covered in less than ten minutes. When the clouds closed in a moment later, cutting off my view, he was within 30 yards of the tents. I didn't see him again after that, but I was certain that he'd reached the security of camp, where Sherpas would be waiting with hot tea. Sitting out in the storm, with the ice bulge still standing between me and the tents, I felt a pang of envy. I was angry that my guide hadn't waited for me.

Twenty minutes later I was in camp. I fell into my tent with my crampons still on, zippered the door tight, and sprawled across the frost-covered floor. I was drained, more exhausted than I'd ever been in my life. But I was safe. Andy was safe. The others would be coming into camp soon. We'd done it. We'd climbed Mount Everest.

It would be many hours before I learned that everyone had in fact not made it back to camp — that one teammate was already dead and that twenty-three other men and women were caught in a desperate struggle for their lives.

Neil Beidleman waited on the summit from 1:25 until 3:10 as Fischer's clients appeared over the last rise, one by one. The lateness of the hour worried him. After Gammelgaard, the last of them, arrived with Lobsang, "I decided it was time to get the hell out of there," Beidleman says, "even though Scott hadn't shown yet." Twenty minutes down the ridge, Beidleman — with Gammelgaard, Pittman, Madsen, and Fox in tow — passed Fischer, still on his way up. "I didn't really say anything to him," Beidleman recalls. "He just sort of raised his hand. He looked like he was having a hard time, but he was Scott, so I wasn't particularly worried. I figured he'd tag the summit and catch up to us pretty quick to help bring the clients down. But he never showed up."

When Beidleman's group got down to the South Summit, Pittman collapsed. Fox, the most experienced client on the peak, gave her an injection of a powerful steroid, dexamethasone, which temporarily negates the symptoms of altitude sickness. Beidleman grabbed Pittman by her harness and started dragging her down behind him.

"Once I got her sliding," he explains, "I'd let go and glissade down in front of her. Every fifty meters I'd stop, wrap my hands around the fixed rope, and brace myself to arrest her slide with a body block. The first time Sandy came barrelling into me, the points of her crampons sliced into my down suit. Feathers went flying everywhere." Fortunately, after about twenty minutes the injection revived Pittman, and she was able to resume the descent under her own power.

As darkness fell and the storm intensified, Beidleman and five of Fischer's clients overtook Groom, who was bringing down Weathers, on a short rope, and Namba. "Beck was so hopelessly blind," Groom reports, "that every ten meters he'd take a step into thin air and I'd have to catch him with the rope. It was bloody nerve-racking."

Five hundred feet above the South Col, where the steep shale gave way to a gentler slope of snow, Namba's oxygen ran out and the diminutive Japanese woman sat down, refusing to move. "When I tried to take her oxygen mask off so she could breathe more easily," says Groom, "she'd insist on putting it right back on. No amount of persuasion could convince her that she was out of oxygen, that the mask was actually suffocating her."

Beidleman, realizing that Groom had his hands full with Weathers, started dragging Namba down toward Camp Four. They reached the broad, rolling expanse of the South Col around 8 P.M., but by then it was pitch black, and the storm had grown into a hurricane. The windchill was in excess of 70 below. Only three or four headlamps were working, and everyone's oxygen was long gone. Visibility was down to a few meters. No one had a clue how to find the tents. Two Sherpas materialized out of the darkness, but they were lost as well.

For the next two hours, Beidleman, Groom, the two Sherpas, and seven clients staggered blindly around in the storm, growing ever more exhausted and hypothermic, hoping to blunder across the camp. "It was total chaos," says Beidleman. "People are wandering all over the place; I'm yelling at everyone, trying to get them to follow a single leader. Finally, probably around ten o'clock, I walked over this little rise, and it felt like I was standing on the edge of the earth. I could sense a huge void just beyond."

The group had unwittingly strayed to the easternmost edge of the Col, the opposite side from Camp Four, right at the lip of the 7,000-foot Kangshung Face. "I knew that if we kept wandering in the storm, pretty soon we were going to lose somebody," says Beidleman. "I was exhausted from dragging Yasuko. Charlotte and Sandy were barely able to stand. So I screamed at everyone to huddle up right there and wait for a break in the storm."

The climbers hunkered in a pathetic cluster on a windswept patch of ice. "By then the cold had about finished me off," says Fox. "My eyes were frozen. The cold was so painful, I just curled up in a ball and hoped death would come quickly."

Three hundred and fifty yards to the west, while this was going on, I was shivering uncontrollably in my tent, even though I was zipped into my sleeping bag and wearing my down suit and every other stitch of clothing I had. The gale was threatening to blow the tent apart. Oblivious to the tragedy unfolding outside and completely out of bottled oxygen, I drifted in and out of fitful sleep, delirious from exhaustion, dehydration, and the cumulative effects of oxygen depletion.

At some point, Hutchison shook me and asked if I would go outside with him to bang on pots and shine lights, in the hope of guiding any lost climbers in, but I was too weak and incoherent to respond. Hutchison, who had got back to camp at 2 P.M. and was less debilitated than those of us who'd gone to the summit, then tried to rouse clients and Sherpas in the other tents. Everybody was too cold, too exhausted. So Hutchison went out into the storm alone.

He left six times that night to look for the missing climbers, but the blizzard was so fierce that he never dared to venture more than a few yards from the tents. "The winds were ballistically strong," says Hutchison. "The blowing spindrift felt like a sandblaster or something."

Just before midnight, out among the climbers hunkered on the Col, Beidleman noticed a few stars overhead. The wind was still whipping up a furious ground blizzard, but far above, the sky began to clear, revealing the hulking silhouettes of Everest and Lhotse. From these reference points, Klev Schoening, a client of Fischer's, thought he'd figured out where the group was in relation to the tents. After a shouting match with Beidleman, Schoening convinced the guide that he knew the way.

Beidleman tried to coax everyone to their feet and get them moving in the direction indicated by Schoening, but Fox, Namba, Pittman, and Weathers were too feeble to walk. So Beidleman assembled those who were ambulatory, and together with Groom they stumbled off into the storm to get help, leaving behind the four incapacitated clients and Tim Madsen. Madsen, unwilling to abandon Fox, his girlfriend, volunteered to look after everybody until a rescue party arrived.

The tents lay about 350 yards to the west. When Beidleman, Groom, and the clients got there, they were met by Boukreev. Beidleman told the Russian where to find the five clients who'd been left out in the elements, and then all four climbers collapsed in their tents.

Boukreev had returned to Camp Four at 4:30 P.M., before the brunt of the storm, having rushed down from the summit without waiting for clients — extremely questionable behavior for a guide. A number of Everest veterans have speculated that if Boukreev had been present to help Beidleman and Groom bring their clients down, the group might not have got lost on the Col in the first place. One of the clients from that group has nothing but contempt for Boukreev, insisting that when it mattered most, the guide "cut and ran."

Boukreev argues that he hurried down ahead of everybody else because "it is much better for me to be at South Col, ready to carry up oxygen if clients run out." This is a difficult rationale to understand. In fact, Boukreev's impatience on the descent more plausibly resulted from the fact that he wasn't using bottled oxygen and was relatively lightly dressed and therefore *had* to get down quickly: Without gas, he was much more susceptible to the dreadful cold. If this was indeed the case, Fischer was as much to blame as Boukreev, because he gave the Russian permission to climb without gas in the first place.

Whatever Boukreev's culpability, however, he redeemed himself that night after Beidleman staggered in. Plunging repeatedly into the maw of the hurricane, he single-handedly brought back Fox, Pittman, and Madsen. But Namba and Weathers, he reported, were dead. When Beidleman was informed that Namba hadn't made it, he broke down in his tent and wept for forty-five minutes.

Stuart Hutchison shook me awake at 6:00 A.M. on May 11. "Andy's not in his tent," he told me somberly, "and he doesn't seem to be in any of the other tents, either. I don't think he ever made it in."

"Andy's missing?" I asked. "No way. I saw him walk to the edge of camp with my own eyes." Shocked, horrified, I pulled on my boots and rushed out to look for Harris. The wind was still fierce, knocking me down several times, but it was a bright, clear dawn, and visibility was perfect. I searched the entire western half of the Col for more than an hour, peering behind boulders and piking under shredded, long-abandoned tents, but found no trace of Harris. A surge of adrenaline seared my brain. Tears welled up in my eyes, instantly freezing my eyelids shut. How could Andy be gone? It couldn't be so.

I went to the place where Harris had slid down the ice bulge and methodically retraced the route he'd taken toward camp, which followed a broad, almost flat ice gully. At the point where I last saw him when the clouds came down, a sharp left turn would have taken Harris forty or fifty feet up a rocky rise to the tents.

I saw, however, that if he hadn't turned left but instead had continued straight down the gully — which would have been easy to do in a whiteout, even if one wasn't exhausted and stupid with altitude sickness — he would have quickly come to the westernmost edge of the Col and a four-thousand-foot drop to the floor of the Western Cwm. Standing there, afraid to move any closer to the edge, I noticed a single set of faint crampon tracks leading past me toward the abyss. Those tracks, I feared, were Harris's.

After getting into camp the previous evening, I'd told Hutchison that I'd seen Harris arrive safely in camp. Hutchison had radioed this news to Base Camp, and from there it was passed along via satellite phone to the woman with whom Harris shared his life in New Zealand, Fiona McPherson. Now Hall's wife back in New Zealand, Jan Arnold, had to do the unthinkable: call McPherson back to inform her that there had been a horrible mistake, that Andy was in fact missing and presumed dead. Imagining this conversation and my role in the events leading up to it, I fell to my knees with dry heaves, retching as the icy wind blasted my back.

I returned to my tent just in time to overhear a radio call between Base Camp and Hall — who, I learned to my horror, was up on the summit ridge and calling for help. Beidleman then told me that Weathers and Namba were dead and that Fischer was missing somewhere on the peak above. An aura of unreality had descended over the mountain, casting the morning in a nightmarish hue.

Then our radio batteries died, cutting us off from the rest of the mountain. Alarmed that they had lost contact with us, climbers at Camp Two called the South African team, which had arrived on the South Col the previous day. When Ian Woodall was asked if he would loan his radio to us, he refused.

After reaching the summit around 3:30 P.M. on May 10, Scott Fischer had headed down with Lobsang, who had waited for Fischer on the summit while Beidleman and their clients descended. They got no farther than the South Summit before Fischer began to have difficulty standing and showed symptoms of severe hypothermia and cerebral edema. According to Lobsang, Fischer began "acting like crazy man. Scott is saying to me, 'I want to jump down to Camp Two.' He is saying many times." Pleading with him not to jump, Lobsang started short-roping Fischer, who outweighed him by some seventy pounds, down the Southeast Ridge. A few hours after dark, they got into some difficult mixed terrain 1,200 feet above the South Col, and Lobsang was unable to drag Fischer any farther.

Lobsang anchored Fischer to a snow-covered ledge and was preparing to leave him there when three tired Sherpas showed up. They were struggling to bring down Makkalu Gua, who was as debilitated as Fischer. The Sherpas sat the Taiwanese leader beside the American leader, tied the two semiconscious men together, and around 10 P.M. descended into the night to get help.

Meanwhile, Hall and Hansen were still on the frightfully exposed summit ridge, engaged in a grim struggle of their own. The 46-year-old Hansen, whom Hall had turned back just below this spot exactly a year ago, had been determined to bag the summit this time around. "I want to get this thing done and out of my life," he'd told me a couple of days earlier. "I don't want to have to come back here."

Indeed, Hansen had reached the top this time, though not until after 3 P.M., well after Hall's predetermined turn-around time. Given Hall's conservative, systematic nature, many people wonder why he didn't turn Hansen around when it became obvious that he was running late. It's not far-fetched to speculate that because Hall had talked Hansen into coming back to Everest this year, it would have been especially hard for him to deny Hansen the summit a second time — especially when all of Fischer's clients were still marching blithely toward the top.

"It's very difficult to turn someone around high on the mountain," cautions Guy Cotter, a New Zealand guide who summited Everest with Hall in 1992 and was guiding the peak for him in 1995 when Hansen made his first attempt. "If a client sees that the summit is close and they're dead-set on getting there, they're going to laugh in your face and keep going up."

In any case, for whatever reason, Hall did not turn Hansen around. Instead, after reaching the summit at 2:10 P.M., Hall waited for more than an hour for Hansen to arrive and then headed down with him. Soon after they began their descent, just below the top, Hansen apparently ran out of oxygen and collapsed. "Pretty much the same thing happened to Doug in '95," says Ed Viesturs, an American who guided the peak for Hall that year. "He was fine during the ascent, but as soon as he started down he lost it mentally and physically. He turned into a real zombie, like he'd used everything up."

At 4:31 P.M., Hall radioed Base Camp to say that he and Hansen were above the Hillary Step and urgently needed oxygen. Two full bottles were waiting for them at the South Summit; if Hall had known this he could have retrieved the gas fairly quickly and then climbed back up to give Hansen a fresh tank. But Harris, in the throes of his oxygen-starved dementia, overheard the 4:31 radio call while descending the South-east Ridge and broke in to tell Hall — incorrectly, just as he'd told Groom and me — that all the bottles at the South Summit were empty. So Hall stayed with Hansen and tried to bring the helpless client down without oxygen, but could get him no farther than the top of the Hillary Step.

Cotter, a very close friend of both Hall and Harris, happened to be a few miles from Everest Base Camp at the time, guiding an expedition on Pumori. Overhearing the radio conversations between Hall and Base Camp, he called Hall at 5:36 and again at 5:57, urging his mate to leave Hansen and come down alone. "I know I sound like the bastard for telling Rob to abandon his client," confesses Cotter, "but by then it was obvious that leaving Doug was his only choice." Hall, however, wouldn't consider going down without Hansen.

There was no further word from Hall until the middle of the night. At 2:46 A.M. on May 11, Cotter woke up to hear a long, broken transmission, probably unintended: Hall was wearing a remote microphone clipped to the shoulder strap of his backpack, which was occasionally keyed on by mistake. In this instance, says Cotter, "I suspect Rob didn't even know he was transmitting. I could hear someone yelling — it might have been Rob, but I couldn't be sure because the wind was so loud in the background. He was saying something like 'Keep moving! Keep going!' presumably to Doug, urging him on."

If that was indeed the case, it meant that in the wee hours of the morning Hall and Hansen were still struggling from the Hillary Step toward the South Summit, taking more than twelve hours to traverse a stretch of ridge typically covered by descending climbers in half an hour.

Hall's next call to Base Camp was at 4:43 A.M. He'd finally reached the South Summit but was unable to descend farther, and in a series of transmissions over the next two hours he sounded confused and irrational. "Harold was with me last night," Hall insisted, when in fact Harris had reached the South Col at Sunset. "But he doesn't seem to be with me now. He was very weak."

Mackenzie asked him how Hansen was doing. "Doug," Hall replied, "is gone." That was all he said, and it was the last mention he ever made of Hansen.

On May 23, when Breashears and Viesturs, of the IMAX team, reached the summit, they found no sign of Hansen's body but they did find an ice ax planted about fifty feet below the Hillary Step, along a highly exposed section of ridge where the fixed ropes came to an end. It is quite possible that Hall managed to get Hansen down the ropes to this point, only to have him lose his footing and fall 7,000 feet down the sheer Southwest Face, leaving his ice ax jammed into the ridge crest where he slipped.

During the radio calls to Base Camp early on May 11, Hall revealed that something was wrong with his legs, that he was no longer able to walk and was shaking uncontrollably. This was very disturbing news to the people down below, but it was amazing that Hall was even alive after spending a night without shelter or oxygen at 28,700 feet in hurricane-force wind and minus-100-degree windchill.

At 5 A.M., Base Camp patched through a call on the satellite telephone to Jan Arnold, Hall's wife, seven months pregnant with their first child in Christchurch, New Zealand. Arnold, a respected physician, had summited Everest with Hall in 1993 and entertained no illusions about the gravity of her husband's predicament. "My heart really sank when I heard his voice," she recalls. "He was slurring his words markedly. He sounded like Major Tom or something, like he was just floating away. I'd been up there; I knew what it could be like in bad weather. Rob and I had talked about the impossibility of being rescued from the summit ridge. As he himself had put it, 'You might as well be on the moon.'"

By that time, Hall had located two full oxygen bottles, and after struggling for four hours trying to deice his mask, around 8:30 A.M. he finally started breathing the life-sustaining gas. Several times he announced that he was preparing to descend, only to change his mind and remain at the South Summit. The day had started out sunny and clear, but the wind remained fierce, and by late morning the upper mountain was wrapped with thick clouds. Climbers at Camp Two reported that the wind over the summit sounded like a squadron of 747s, even from 8,000 feet below.

About 9:30 A.M., Ang Dorje and Lhakpa Chhiri ascended from Camp Four in a brave attempt to bring Hall down. At the same time, four other Sherpas went to rescue Fischer and Gau. When they reached Fischer, the Sherpas tried to give him oxygen and hot tea, but he was unresponsive. Though he was breathing — barely — his eyes were fixed and his teeth were clenched. Believing he was as good as dead, they left him tied to the ledge and started descending with Gau, who after receiving tea and oxygen, and with considerable assistance, was able to move to the South Col.

Higher on the peak, Ang Dorje and Lhakpa Chhiri climbed to 28,000 feet, but the murderous wind forced them to turn around there, still 700 feet below Hall.

Throughout that day, Hall's friends begged him to make an effort to descend from the South Summit under his own power. At 3:20 P.M., after one such transmission from Cotter, Hall began to sound annoyed. "Look," he said, "if I thought I could manage the knots on the fixed ropes with me frostbitten hands, I would have gone down six hours ago, pal. Just send a couple of the boys up with a big thermos of something hot — then I'll be fine."

At 6:20 P.M., Hall was patched through a second time to Arnold in Christchurch. "Hi, my sweetheart," he said in a slow, painfully distorted voice. "I hope you're tucked up in a nice warm bed. How are you doing?"

"I can't tell you how much I'm thinking about you!" Arnold replied. "You sound so much better than I expected. . . . Are you warm, my darling?"

"In the context of the altitude, the setting, I'm reasonably comfortable," Hall answered, doing his best not to alarm her.

"How are your feet?"

"I haven't taken me boots off to check, but I think I may have a bit of frostbite."

"I'm looking forward to making you completely better when you come home," said Arnold. "I just know you're going to be rescued. Don't feel that you're alone. I'm sending all my positive energy your way!" Before signing off, Hall told his wife, "I love you. Sleep well, my sweetheart. Please don't worry too much."

These would be the last words anyone would hear him utter. Attempts to make radio contact with Hall later that night and the next day went unanswered. Twelve days later, when Breashears and Viesturs climbed over the South Summit on their way to the top, they found Hall lying on his right side in a shallow ice-hollow, his upper body buried beneath a drift of snow.

Early on the morning of May 11, when I returned to Camp Four after searching in vain for Harris, Hutchison, standing in for Groom, who was unconscious in his tent, organized a team of four Sherpas to locate the bodies of our teammates Weathers and Namba. The Sherpa search party, headed by Lhakpa Chhiri, departed ahead of Hutchison, who was so exhausted and befuddled that he forgot to put his boots on and left camp in his light, smooth-soled liners. Only when Lhakpa Chhiri pointed out the blunder did Hutchison return for his boots. Following Boukreev's directions, the Sherpas had no trouble locating the two bodies at the edge of the Kangshung Face.

The first body turned out to be Namba, but Hutchison couldn't tell who it was until he knelt in the howling wind and chipped a three-inch-thick carapace of ice from her face. To his shock, he discovered that she was still breathing. Both her gloves were gone, and her bare hands appeared to be frozen solid. Her eyes were dilated. The skin on her face was the color of porcelain. "It was terrible," Hutchison recalls. "I was overwhelmed. She was very near death. I didn't know what to do."

He turned his attention to Weathers, who lay 20 feet away. His face was also caked with a thick armor of frost. Balls of ice the size of grapes were matted to his hair and eyelids. After clearing the frozen detritus from his face, Hutchison discovered that he, too, was still alive: "Beck was mumbling something, I think, but I couldn't tell what he was trying to say. His right glove was missing and he had terrible frostbite. He was as close to death as a person can be and still be breathing."

Badly shaken, Hutchison went over to the Sherpas and asked Lhakpa Chhiri's advice. Lhakpa Chhiri, an Everest veteran respected by Sherpas and sahibs alike for his mountain savvy, urged Hutchison to leave Weathers and Namba where they lay. Even if they survived long enough to be dragged back to Camp Four, they would certainly die before they could be carried down to Base Camp, and attempting a rescue would needlessly jeopardize the lives of the other climbers on the Col, most of whom were going to have enough trouble getting themselves down safely.

Hutchison decided that Chhiri was right. There was only one choice, however difficult: Let nature take its inevitable course with Weathers and Namba, and save the group's resources for those who could actually be helped. It was a classic act of triage. When Hutchison returned to camp at 8:30 A.M. and told the rest of us of his decision, nobody doubted that it was the correct thing to do.

Later that day a rescue team headed by two of Everest's most experienced guides, Pete Athans and Todd Burleson, who were on the mountain with their own clients, arrived at Camp Four. Burleson was standing outside the tents about 4:30 P.M. when he noticed someone lurching slowly toward camp. The person's bare right hand, naked to the wind and horribly frostbitten, was outstretched in a weird, frozen salute. Whoever it was reminded Athans of a mummy in a low-budget horror film. The mummy turned out to be none other than Beck Weathers, somehow risen from the dead.

A couple of hours earlier, a light must have gone on in the reptilian core of Weathers's comatose brain, and he regained consciousness. "Initially I thought I was in a dream," he recalls. "Then I saw how badly frozen my right hand was, and that helped bring me around to reality. Finally I woke up enough to recognize that I was in deep shit and the cavalry wasn't coming so I better do something about it myself."

Although Weathers was blind in his right eye and able to focus his left eye within a radius of only three or four feet, he started walking into the teeth of the wind, deducing correctly that camp lay in that direction. If he'd been wrong he would have stumbled immediately down the Kangshung Face, the edge of which was a few yards in the opposite direction. Ninety minutes later he encountered "some unnaturally smooth, bluish-looking rocks," which turned out to be the tents of Camp Four.

The next morning, May 12, Athans, Burleson, and climbers from the IMAX team short-roped Weathers down to Camp Two. On the morning of May 13, in a hazardous helicopter rescue, Weathers and Gau were evacuated from the top of the icefall by Lieutenant Colonel Madan Kahtri Chhetri of the Nepalese army. A month later, a team of Dallas surgeons would amputate Weathers's dead right hand just below the wrist and use skin grafts to reconstruct his left hand.

After helping to load Weathers and Gau into the rescue chopper, I sat in the snow for a long while, staring at my boots, trying to get some grip, however tenuous, on what had happened over the preceding seventy-two hours. Then, nervous as a cat, I headed down into the Icefall for one last trip through the maze of decaying seracs.

I'd always known, in the abstract, that climbing mountains was a dangerous pursuit. But until I climbed in the Himalayas this spring, I'd never actually seen death at close range. And there was so much of it: Including three members of an Indo-Tibetan team who died on the north side just below the summit in the same May 10 storm and an Austrian killed some days later, 11 men and women lost their lives on Everest in May 1996, a tie with 1982 for the worst single-season death toll in the peak's history.

Of the six people on my team who reached the summit, four are now dead — people with whom I'd laughed and vomited and held long, intimate conversations. My actions — or failure to act — played a direct role in the death of Andy Harris. And while Yasuko Namba lay dying on the South Col, I was a mere 350 yards away, lying inside a tent, doing absolutely nothing. The stain this has left on my psyche is not the sort of thing that washes off after a month or two of grief and guilt-ridden self-reproach.

Five days after Namba died, three Japanese men approached me in the village of Syangboche and introduced themselves. One was an interpreter, the other was Namba's husband, the third was her brother. They had many questions, few of which I could answer adequately. I flew back to the States with Doug Hansen's belongings and was met at the Seattle airport by his two children, Angie and Jaime. I felt stupid and utterly impotent when confronted by their tears.

Stewing over my culpability, I put off calling Andy Harris's partner, Fiona McPherson, and Rob Hall's wife, Jan Arnold, so long that they finally phoned me from New Zealand. When Fiona called, I was able to say nothing to diminish her anger or bewilderment. During my conversation with Jan, she spent more time comforting me than vice versa.

With so many marginally qualified climbers flocking to Everest these days, a lot of people believe that a tragedy of this magnitude was overdue. But nobody imagined that an expedition led by Hall would be at the center of it. Hall ran the tightest, safest operation on the mountain, bar none. So what happened? How can it be explained, not only to the loved ones left behind, but to a censorious public?

Hubris surely had something to do with it. Hall had become so adept at running climbers of varying abilities up and down Everest that he may have become a little cocky. He'd bragged on more than one occasion that he could get almost any reasonably fit person to the summit, and his record seemed to support this. He'd also demonstrated a remarkable ability to manage adversity.

In 1995, for instance, Hall and his guides not only had to cope with Hansen's problems high on the peak, but they also had to deal with the complete collapse of another client, the celebrated French Alpinist Chantal Mauduit, who was making her seventh stab at Everest without oxygen. Mauduit passed out stone cold at 28,700 feet and had to be dragged and carried all the way from the South Summit to the South Col "like a sack of spuds," as Guy Cotter put it. After everybody came out of that summit attempt alive, Hall may well have thought there was little he couldn't handle.

Before this year, however, Hall had had uncommonly good luck with the weather, and one wonders whether it might have skewed his judgment. "Season after season," says David Breashears, who has climbed Everest three times, "Rob had brilliant weather on summit day. He'd never been caught by a storm high on the mountain." In fact, the gale of May 10, though violent, was nothing extraordinary; it was a fairly typical Everest squall. If it had hit two hours later, it's likely that nobody would have died. Conversely, if it had arrived even one hour earlier, the storm could easily have killed 18 or 20 climbers — me among them.

Indeed, the clock had as much to do with the tragedy as the weather, and ignoring the clock can't be passed off as an act of God. Delays at the fixed lines could easily have been avoided. Predetermined turn-around times were egregiously and willfully ignored. The latter may have been influenced to some degree by the rivalry between Fischer and Hall. Fischer had a charismatic personality, and that charisma had been brilliantly marketed. Fischer was trying very hard to eat Hall's lunch, and Hall knew it. In a certain sense, they may have been playing chicken up there, each guide plowing ahead with one eye on the clock, waiting to see who was going to blink first and turn around.

Shocked by the death toll, people have been quick to suggest policies and procedures intended to ensure that the catastrophes of this season won't be repeated. But guiding Everest is a very loosely regulated business, administered by a byzantine Third World bureaucracy that is spectacularly ill-equipped to assess qualifications of guides or clients, in a nation that has a vested interest in issuing as many climbing permits as the market will support.

Truth be told, a little education is probably the most that can be hoped for. Everest would without question be safer if prospective clients truly understood the gravity of the risks they face — the thinness of the margin by which human life is sustained above 25,000 feet. Walter Mittys with Everest dreams need to keep in mind that when things go wrong up in the Death Zone — and sooner or later they always do — the strongest guides in the world may be powerless to save their clients' lives. Indeed, as the events of 1996 demonstrated, the strongest guides in the world are sometimes powerless to save even their own lives.

Climbing mountains will never be a safe, predictable, rule-bound enterprise. It is an activity that idealizes risk-taking; its most celebrated figures have always been those who stuck their necks out the farthest and managed to get away with it. Climbers, as a species, are simply not distinguished by an excess of common sense. And that holds especially true for Everest climbers: When presented with a chance to reach the planet's highest summit, people are surprisingly quick to abandon prudence altogether. "Eventually," warns Tom Hornbein, thirty-three years after his ascent of the West Ridge, "what happened on Everest this season is certain to happen again."

For evidence that few lessons were learned from the mistakes of May 10, one need look no farther than what happened on Everest two weeks later. On the night of May 24, by which date every other expedition had left Base Camp or was on its way down the mountain, the South Africans finally launched their summit bid. At 9:30 the following morning, Ian Woodall radioed that he was on the summit, that teammate Cathy O'Dowd would be on top in fifteen minutes, and that his close friend Bruce Herrod was some unknown distance below. Herrod, whom I'd met several times on the mountain, was an amiable 37-year-old with little climbing experience. A freelance photographer, he hoped that making the summit of Everest would give his career a badly needed boost.

As it turned out, Herrod was more than seven hours behind the others and didn't reach the summit until 5 P.M., by which time the upper mountain had clouded over. It had taken him 21 hours to climb from the South Col to the top. With darkness fast approaching, he was out of oxygen, physically drained, and completely alone on the roof of the world. "That he was up there that late, with nobody else around, was crazy," says his former teammate, Andy de Klerk. "It's absolutely boggling."

Herrod had been on the South Col from the evening of May 10 through May 12. He'd felt the ferocity of that storm, heard the desperate radio calls for help, seen Beck Weathers crippled with horrible frostbite. Early on his ascent of May 24–25, Herrod had climbed right past the frozen body of Scott Fischer. Yet none of that apparently made much of an impression on him. There was another radio transmission from Herrod at 7 P.M., but nothing was heard from him after that, and he never appeared at Camp Four. He is presumed to be dead — the eleventh casualty of the season.

As I write this, fifty-four days have passed since I stood on top of Everest, and there hasn't been more than an hour or two on any given day in which the loss of my companions hasn't monopolized my thoughts. Not even in sleep is there respite: Imagery from the climb and its sad aftermath permeates my dreams.

There is some comfort, I suppose, in knowing that I'm not the only survivor of Everest to be so affected. A teammate of mine from Hall's expedition tells me that since he returned, his marriage has gone bad, he can't concentrate at work, his life has been in turmoil. In another case, Neal Beidleman helped save the lives of five clients by guiding them down the mountain, yet he is haunted by a death he was unable to prevent, of a client who wasn't on his team and thus wasn't really his responsibility.

When I spoke to Beidleman recently, he recalled what it felt like to be out on the South Col, huddling with his group in the awful wind, trying desperately to keep everyone alive. He'd told and retold the story a hundred times, but it was still as vivid as the initial telling. "As soon as the sky cleared enough to give us an idea of where camp was," he recounted, "I remember shouting, 'Hey, this break in the storm may not last long, so let's *go!*' I was screaming at everyone to get moving, but it became clear that some of them didn't have enough strength to walk or even stand.

"People were crying. I heard someone yell, 'Don't let me die here!' It was obvious that it was now or never. I tried to get Yasuko on her feet. She grabbed my arm, but she was too weak to get up past her knees. I started walking and dragging her for a step or two. Then her grip loosened and she fell away. I had to keep going. Somebody had to make it to the tents and get help, or everybody was going to die."

Beidleman paused. "But I can't help thinking about Yasuko," he said when he resumed, his voice hushed. "She was so little. I can still feel her fingers sliding across my biceps and then letting go. I never even turned to look back."

1997

## J. R. Moehringer

# Resurrecting the Champ

FROM *The Los Angeles Times Magazine*

### 1.

I'M SITTING IN A HOTEL room in Columbus, Ohio, waiting for a call from a man who doesn't trust me, hoping he'll have answers about a man I don't trust, which may clear the name of a man no one gives a damn about. To distract myself from this uneasy vigil — and from the phone that never rings, and from the icy rain that never stops pelting the window — I light a cigar and open a forty-year-old newspaper. • "Greatest puncher they ever seen," the paper says in praise of Bob Satterfield, a ferocious fighter of the 1940s and 1950s. "The man of hope — and the man who crushed hope like a cookie in his fist." Once again, I'm reminded of Satterfield's sorry luck, which dogged him throughout his life, as I'm dogging him now. • I've searched high and low for Satterfield. I've searched the sour-smelling homeless shelters of Santa Ana. I've searched the ancient and venerable boxing gyms of Chicago. I've searched the eerily clear memory of one New York City fighter who touched Satterfield's push-button chin in 1946 and never forgot the panic on Satterfield's face as he fell. I've searched cemeteries, morgues, churches, museums, slums, jails, courts, libraries, police blotters, scrapbooks, phone books and record books. Now I'm searching this dreary, sleet-bound Midwestern city, where all the streets look like melting Edward Hopper paintings and the sky like a storm-whipped sea. • Maybe it's fatigue, maybe it's caffeine, maybe it's the fog rolling in behind the rain, but I feel as though Satterfield has become my own 180-pound Moby Dick. Like Ahab's obsession, he casts a harsh light on his pursuer. Stalking him from town to town and decade to decade, I've learned almost everything there is to know about him, along with valuable lessons about boxing, courage and the eternal tension between fathers and sons. But I've learned more than I bargained for about myself, and for that I owe him a debt. I can't repay the debt unless the phone rings.

## 2.

We met because a coworker got the urge to clean. It was early January, 1996. The cop reporter who sits near me at the Orange County edition of the *Times* was straightening her desk when she came across an old tip, something about a once-famous boxer sleeping on park benches in Santa Ana. Passing the tip along, she deflected my thank-you with an off-the-cuff caveat, "He might be dead."

The tipster had no trouble recalling the boxer when I phoned. "Yeah, Bob Satterfield," he said. "A contender from the 1950s. I used to watch him when I watched the fights on TV." Forty years later, though, Satterfield wasn't contending anymore, except with cops. When last seen, the old boxer was wandering the streets, swilling whiskey and calling himself Champ. "Just a guy that lived too long," the tipster said, though he feared this compassion might be outdated. There was a better-than-ever chance, he figured, that Satterfield was dead.

If Satterfield was alive, finding him would require a slow tour of Santa Ana's seediest precincts. I began with one of the city's largest men's shelters. Several promising candidates lingered inside the shelter and out, but none matched my sketchy notion of an elderly black man with a boxer's sturdy body. From there I drove to 1st Street, a wide boulevard of taco stands and bus stops that serves as a promenade for homeless men. Again, nothing. Next I cruised the alleys and side streets of nearby McFadden Avenue, where gutters still glistened with tinsel from discarded Christmas trees. On a particularly lively corner I parked the car and walked, stopping passersby and asking where I might find the fighter from the 1950s, the one who called himself Champ, the one who gave the cops all they could handle. No one knew, no one cared, and I was ready to knock off when I heard someone cry out, "Hiya, Champ!"

Wheeling around, I saw an elderly black man pushing a grocery cart full of junk down the middle of the street. Rancid clothes, vacant stare, sooty face, he looked like every other homeless man in America. Then I noticed his hands, the largest hands I'd ever seen, each one so heavy and unwieldy that he held it at his side like a bowling ball. Hands such as these were not just unusual, they were natural phenomena. Looking closer, however, I saw that they complemented the meaty plumpness of his shoulders and the brick-wall thickness of his chest, exceptional attributes in a man who couldn't be getting three squares a day. To maintain such a build on table scraps and handouts, he must have been immense back when.

More than his physique, what distinguished him was a faint sugges-tion of style. Despite the cast-off clothes, despite the caked-on dirt, there was a vague sense that he clung to some vestigial pride in his appearance. Under his grimy ski parka he wore an almost professorial hound's-tooth vest. Atop his crown of graying hair was a rakish brown hat with a pigeon feather tucked jauntily in its brim.

His skin was a rich cigar color and smooth for an ex-boxer's, except for one bright scar between his eyebrows that resembled a character in the Chinese alphabet. Beneath a craggy five-o'clock shadow, his face was pleasant: dark eyes and high cheekbones sat astride a strong, well-formed nose, and each feature followed the lead of his firm, squared-off chin. He was someone's heartthrob once. His teeth, however, were long gone, save for some stubborn spikes along the mandible.

I smiled and strolled toward him.

"Hey, Champ," I said.

"Heyyy, Champ," he said, looking up and smiling as though we were old friends. I half expected him to hug me.

"You're Bob Satterfield, aren't you?" I said.

"Battlin' Bob Satterfield!" he said, delighted at being recognized. "I'm the Champ, I fought 'em all, Ezzard Charles, Floyd Patterson—"

I told him I was a reporter from the *Los Angeles Times*, that I wanted to write a story about his life.

"How old are you?" I asked.

"I count my age as 66," he said. "But *The Ring Record Book*, they say 72."

"Did you ever fight for the title?"

"They just didn't give me the break to fight for the title," he said woefully. "If they'd given me the break, I believe I'd be the champ."

"Why didn't they give you the break?"

"You got to be in the right clique," he said, "to get the right fight at the right time."

His voice was weak and raspy, no more than a child's whisper, his words filled with the blurred vowels and squishy consonants of someone rendered senseless any number of times by liquor and fists. He stuttered slightly, humming his "m," gargling his "l," tripping over his longer sentences. By contrast, his eyes and memories were clear. When I asked about his biggest fights, he rattled them off one by one, naming every opponent, every date, every arena. He groaned at the memory of all those beatings, but it was a proud noise, to let me know he'd held his own with giants. He'd even broken the nose of Rocky Marciano, the only undefeated heavyweight champion in history. "He was strooong, I want to tell you," Champ said, chuckling immodestly.

It happened during a sparring session, Champ said, demonstrating how he moved in close, slipping an uppercut under Marciano's left. Marciano shivered, staggered back, and Champ pressed his advantage with another uppercut. Then another. And another. Blood flowed.

"I busted his nose!" Champ shouted, staring at the sidewalk where Marciano lay, forever vanquished. "They rushed in and called off the fight and took Rock away!"

Now he was off to get some free chow at a nearby community center. "Would you care for some?" he asked, and I couldn't decide which was more touching, his largess or his mannerly diction.

## 3.

"I was born Tommy Harrison," he said, twirling a chicken leg in his toothless mouth. "That's what you call my legal name. But I fought as Bob Satterfield." His handlers, he explained, didn't want him confused with another fighter, Tommy "Hurricane" Jackson, so they gave him an alias. I asked how they chose Bob Satterfield and he shrugged.

As a boy in and around Chicago, he built his shoulders by lifting ice blocks, a job that paid pennies at first but huge dividends years later in the ring. At 15, he ran away from home, fleeing a father who routinely whipped him. For months he rode the rails as a hobo, then joined the army. Too young to enlist, he pretended to be his older brother, George, paying a prostitute to pose as his mother at the induction center.

He learned to box in the Army as a way of eating better and avoiding strenuous duty. Faced with older and tougher opponents, he developed a slithery, punch-and-move style, which must have impressed Marciano, who was collecting talented young fighters to help him prepare for a title shot against Jersey Joe Walcott. Upon his discharge, Champ became chief sparring partner to the man who would soon become the

Zeus of modern boxing. Flicking his big fists in the air, each one glimmering with chicken grease, Champ again recreated the sequence of punches that led to Marciano's broken nose, and we laughed about the blood, all that blood.

When he left Marciano's camp and struck out on his own, Champ won a few fights, and suddenly the world treated him like a spoiled prince. Women succumbed, celebrities vied to sit at his side. The mountaintop was within view. "I never really dreamed of being champ," he said, "but as I would go through life, I would think, if I ever get a chance at the title, I'm going to win that fight!"

Instead, he lost. It was February, 1953. Ezzard Charles, the formidable ex-champion, was trying to mount a comeback. Champ was trying to become the nation's top-ranked contender. They met in Detroit before a fair-sized crowd, and Champ proved himself game in the early going. But after eight rounds, his eye swollen shut and his mouth spurting blood, he crumbled under Charles's superior boxing skills. The fateful punch was a slow-motion memory four decades later. Its force was so great that Champ bit clean through his mouthpiece. At the bell, he managed to reach his corner. But when the ninth started, he couldn't stand.

Nothing would ever be the same. A procession of bums and semi-bums made him look silly. Floyd Patterson dismantled him in one round. One day he was invincible, the next he was retired.

As with so many fighters, he'd saved nothing. He got $34,000 for the Charles fight, a handsome sum for the 1950s, but he frittered it on good times and "tutti-frutti" Cadillacs. With no money and few prospects, he drifted to California, where he met a woman, raised a family and hoped for the best. The worst came instead. He broke his ankle on a construction job and didn't rest long enough for it to heal. The injury kept him from working steadily. Then, the punch he never saw coming. His son was killed.

"My son," Champ said, his voice darkening. "He was my heart."

"Little Champ" fell in with the wrong people. An angry teenager, he got on somebody's bad side, and one night he walked into an ambush. "My heart felt sad and broke," Champ said. "But I figured this happened because he was so hotheaded."

Racked with pain, Champ left the boy's mother, who still lived in the house they once shared, not far from where we sat. "Sometimes I go see her," he said. "It's kind of hard, but somehow I make it."

Park benches were his beds, though sometimes he slept at the shelter and sometimes in the backseat of a periwinkle and navy blue Cadillac he bought with his last bit of money. He missed the good life but not the riches, the fame or the women. He missed knowing that he was the boss, his body the servant. "The hard work," he whispered. "Sparring with the bags, skipping rope. Every night after a workout we'd go for a big steak and a half a can of beer. Aaah."

Finishing his lunch, Champ wrapped the leftovers in a napkin and carefully stowed them in a secret compartment of his grocery cart. We shook hands, mine like an infant's in his. When we unclasped, he looked at the five-dollar bill I'd slipped him.

"Heyyy," he said soulfully. "Thanks, amigo. All right, thank you."

My car was down the block. When I reached it, I turned to look over my shoulder. Champ was still waving his massive right hand, still groping for words. "Thank you, Champ!" he called. "All right? Thank you!"

4.

Like Melville's ocean, or Twain's Mississippi, boxing calls to a young man. Its victims are not only those who forfeit their wits and dive into the ring. The sport seduces writers, too, dragging them down with its powerful undertow of testosterone. Many die a hideous literary death, drowning in their own hyperbole. Only a few — Ernest Hemingway, Jimmy Cannon, A. J. Liebling — cross to safety. Awash in all that blood, they become more buoyant.

For most Americans, however, boxing makes no sense. The sport that once defined the nation now seems hopelessly archaic, like jousting or pistols at six paces. The uninitiated, the cultivated, the educated don't accept that boxing has existed since pre-Hellenic Greece, and possibly since the time of the pharaohs, because it concedes one musky truth about masculinity: hitting a man is sometimes the most satisfying response to *being* a man. Disturbing, maybe, but there it is.

Just the sight of two fighters belting each other around the ring triggers a soothing response, a womblike reassurance that everything is less complicated than we've been led to believe. From brutality, clarity. As with the first taste of cold beer on a warm day, the first kiss of love in the dark, the first meaningful victory over an evenly matched foe, the brain's simplest part is appeased. Colors become brighter, shapes grow deeper, the world slides into smoother focus. And focus was what I craved the day I went searching for Champ. Focus was what made a copy reporter's moth-eaten tip look to me like the Hope diamond. Focus was what I feared I'd lost on the job.

As a newspaper writer, you spend much of your time walking up dirty steps to talk to dirty people about dirty things. Then, once in a great while, you meet an antidote to all that dirt. Champ wasn't the cleanest of men — he may have been the dirtiest man I ever met — but he was pure of heart. He wasn't the first homeless heavyweight either, not by a long shot. Another boxer lands on Skid Row every day, bug-eyed and scrambled. But none has a résumé to compare with Champ's, or a memory. He offered a return to the unalloyed joy of daily journal-ism, not to mention the winning ticket in the Literary Lottery. He was that rarest of rare birds, a people-watcher's version of the condor: *Pugilisticum luciditas.* He was noble. He was innocent. He was all mine.

I phoned boxing experts throughout the nation. To my astonishment, they not only remembered Champ, they worshiped him. "Hardest hitter who ever lived." "Dynamite puncher." "One of the greatest punchers of all time." Boxing people love to exaggerate, but there was a persuasive sameness to their praise. Bob Satterfield was a beast who slouched toward every opponent with murder in his eye. He could have, should have, would have been champion, except for one tiny problem. He couldn't take a punch.

"He was a bomber," said boxing historian Burt Sugar. "But he had a chin. If he didn't take you out with the first punch, he was out with the second."

Every fighter, being human, has one glaring weakness. For some, it's a faint heart. For others, a lack of discipline. Satterfield's shortcoming was more comic, therefore more melodramatic. Nobody dished it out better, but few were less able to take it. He knocked out seven of his first twelve opponents in the first round, a terrifying boxing blitzkrieg. But over the course of his twelve-year professional career he suffered many first-round knockouts himself. The skinny on Satterfield spliced together a common male fantasy with the most common male fear: loaded with raw talent, he was doomed to fail because of one factory-installed flaw.

Rob Mainwaring, a researcher at boxing's publication of record, *The Ring* magazine, faxed me a fat Satterfield file, rife with vivid accounts of his fragility and prowess. Three times, Satterfield destroyed all comers and put himself in line for a title shot. But each time, before the big fight could be set, Satterfield fell at the feet of some nobody. In May, 1954, for instance, Satterfield tangled with an outsized Cuban fighter named Julio Mederos, banging him with five fast blows in the second round. When

Mederos came to, he told a translator: "Nobody ever hit me that hard before. I didn't know any man could hit that hard." Satterfield appeared unstoppable. Six months later, however, he was stopped by an also-ran named Marty Marshall, who found Satterfield's flukish chin before some fans could find their seats.

Viewed as a literary artifact, the Satterfield file was a lovely sampler of overwrought prose. "The Chicago sleep-inducer," one fight writer called him. "Embalming fluid in either hand," said another. Then, in the next breath, came the qualifiers: "Boxing's Humpty-Dumpty." "A chin of Waterford." "Chill-or-be-chilled." It was a prankish God who connected that dainty jaw and that sledgehammer arm to one man's body, and it was the same almighty jokester who put those Hemingway wannabes in charge of chronicling his rise and fall.

Mainwaring faxed me several photos of Satterfield and one of a wife named Iona, whom he divorced in 1952. The library at the *Times*, meanwhile, unearthed still more Satterfield clippings, including a brief 1994 profile by *Orange County Register* columnist Bill Johnson. ("Bob Satterfield, one of the top six heavyweight fighters in the world from 1950 to 1956, today is homeless, living in old, abandoned houses in Santa Ana.") From Chicago newspapers, the library culled glowing mentions of Satterfield, including one describing his nightmarish blood bath with middleweight Jake LaMotta, the fighter portrayed by Robert De Niro in Martin Scorsese's 1980 *Raging Bull*. Midway through the film, Satterfield's name fills the screen — then, as the name dissolves, LaMotta–De Niro smashes him in the face.

5.

"Mr. LaMotta," I said. "I'm writing a story about an old opponent of yours, Bob Satterfield."

"Hold on," he said. "I'm eating a meatball."

I'd phoned the former champion in Manhattan, where he was busy launching his new spaghetti sauce company, LaMotta's Tomatta. His voice was De Niro's from the film — nasal, pugnacious, phlegm-filled, a cross between Don Corleone and Donald Duck. At last he swallowed and said, "Bob Satterfield was one of the hardest punchers who ever lived."

Reluctantly, I told LaMotta the bad news. Satterfield was sleeping on park benches in Santa Ana.

"You sure it's him?" he said. "I heard he was dead."

"No," I assured him, "I just talked to him yesterday."

"Awww," he said, "that's a shame. He put three bumps on my head before I knocked him out. Besides Bob Satterfield, the only ones who ever hurt me were my ex-wives."

LaMotta began to reminisce about his old nemesis, a man so dangerous that no one dared spar with him. "He hit me his best punch," he said wistfully. "He hit me with plenty of lefts. But I was coming into him. He hit me with a right hand to the top of the head. I thought I'd fall down. Then he did it again. He did it three times, and when nothing happened he sort of gave up. I knocked him on his face. Flat on his face."

LaMotta asked me to say hello to Satterfield, and I promised that I would. "There but for the grace of God go I," he said. "God dealt me a different hand."

I visited Champ that day to deliver LaMotta's best wishes. I visited him many times in the days ahead, always with some specific purpose in mind. Flesh out the details of his life. Ask a few more questions. See how he was faring. Each time the drill was the same. I'd give him five dollars and he'd give me a big tumble, making such a fuss over me that I'd turn red.

"A boxer, like a writer, must stand alone," Liebling wrote, inadvertently explaining the kinship between Champ and me. To my mind, anyone who flattened Rocky Marciano and put three bumps on Jake LaMotta's melon ranked between astronaut and Lakota warrior on the delicately calibrated scale of bad asses, and thus deserved at least a Sunday profile. To Champ's mind, anyone willing to listen to forty-year-old boxing stories could only be a bored writer or a benevolent Martian. Still, there was something more basic about our connection. As a man, I couldn't get enough of his hyper-virile aura. As a homeless man, he couldn't get enough of my patient silence. Between his prattling and my scribbling, we became something like fast friends.

Our mutual admiration caused me to sputter with indignation when my editors asked what hard evidence I had that Champ was Satterfield. What more hard evidence do you need, I asked, besides Champ's being the man in these old newspaper photos — allowing for forty years of high living and several hundred quarts of cheap whiskey? Better yet, how about Champ's being able to name every opponent, and the dates on which he fought them — allowing for an old man's occasional memory lapses?

If the evidence of our senses won't suffice, I continued, let's use *common* sense: Champ is telling the truth because he has no reason to lie. For being Bob Satterfield, he gets no money, no glory, no extra chicken legs at senior centers and soup kitchens. Pretending to be a fighter forgotten by all but a few boxing experts? Pretending in such convincing fashion? He'd have to be crazy. Or brilliant. And I could say with some confidence that he was neither. Even so, the editors said, get something harder.

### 6.

Champ's old house in Santa Ana sat along a bleak cul-de-sac, its yard bursting with cowlick-shaped weeds, its walls shedding great slices of paint. It looked like a guard shack at the border crossing of some desolate and impoverished nation.

An unhappy young woman scowled when I asked to see Champ's ex-girlfriend. "Wait here," she said.

Minutes later, she returned with a message: go away. Champ's things have been burned, and no one has any interest in talking to you.

Next I tried the Orange County courthouse, hoping arrest records would authenticate Champ. Sure enough, plenty of data existed in the courthouse ledger. Finding various minor offenses under Thomas Harrison, alias Bob Satterfield, I rejoiced. Here was proof, stamped with the official seal of California, that Champ was Satterfield. A scoundrel, yes, but a truthful one.

Then I saw something bad. Two felony arrests, one in 1969, one in 1975. Champ had been candid about his misdemeanors, but he had never mentioned these more serious offenses. "Oh, God," I said, scanning the arrest warrant: "Thomas Harrison, also known as Bob Satterfield . . . lewd and lascivious act upon and with the body . . . child under the age of 14 years." Champ molesting his girlfriend's 10-year-old daughter. Champ punching the little girl's aunt in the mouth.

"Did you know [Champ] to be a professional prizefighter?" a prosecutor asked the aunt during a hearing.

"Yes," she said.

"Did you know that he was once a contender for the heavyweight boxing championship of the world?"

Before she could answer, Champ's lawyer raised an objection, which the judge sustained.

Champ pleaded guilty to assaulting the aunt — for which he received probation — and the molestation charge was dropped.

Then, six years later, it happened again. Same girlfriend, different daughter.

"Thomas Harrison, also known as Tommy Satterfield, also known as Bobby Satterfield . . . lewd and lascivious act."

Again, Champ avowed his innocence, but a jury found him guilty. In May 1976, Champ wrote the judge from jail, begging for a second chance. He signed the letter, "Yours truly, Thomas Harrison. Also Known as Bob Satterfield, Ex-Boxer, 5th in the World."

This is how it happens, I thought. This is how a newspaper writer learns to hate the world. I could feel the cynicism setting inside me like concrete. My reprieve from the dirtiness of everyday journalism had turned into a reaffirmation of everything I loathed and feared. My noble warrior, my male idol, my friend, was a walking, talking horror show, a homeless Humbert Humbert.

## 7.

He greeted me with his typical good cheer, doffing his hat.

"Hey, Champ, whaddya say!?" he cried. "Long time no see, amigo."

"Hey, Champ," I said, glum. "Let's sit down here and have a talk."

I led him over to some bleachers in a nearby baseball field. We passed the afternoon talking about all the major characters of his life — Marciano, Charles, Little Champ. Abruptly, I mentioned the ex-girlfriend.

"Now that I'm on the outside looking in," he mumbled, "I see she wasn't 100 percent in my corner."

"Because she accused you of doing those awful things to her baby?"

He lifted his head, startled. He was spent, punch drunk, permanently hung over, but he knew what I was saying. "They just took her word for it," he said of the jury. "The only regret I have in life is that case she made against me with the baby." Only a monster would hurt a child, Champ said. He begged his ex-girlfriend to recant those false accusations, which he blamed on her paranoia and jealousy. And she did recant, he said, but not to the judge.

More than this he didn't want to say. He wanted to talk about Chicago, sweet home, and all the other way-off places where he knew folks. How he yearned for friendly faces, especially his sister, Lily, with whom he'd left his scrapbook and other papers for safekeeping. He told me her address in Columbus, Ohio, and her phone number. He wanted to see her before he died. See anyone. "Get me some money and head on down the road," he said, eyes lowered, half to himself.

A cold winter night was minutes off, and Champ needed to find a bed, fast. This posed a problem, since taking leave of Champ was never fast. It was hard for him to overcome the inertia that crept into his bones while he sat, harder still to break away from anyone willing to listen. Watching him get his grocery cart going was like seeing an ocean liner off at the dock. The first movement was imperceptible. "See you later, Champ," I said, hurrying him along, shaking that catcher's mitt of a hand. Then I accidentally looked into his eyes, and I couldn't help myself. I believed him.

Maybe it was faith born of guilt. Maybe it was my way of atoning. After all, I was the latest in a long line of people — managers, promoters, opponents — who wanted something from Champ. I wanted his aura, I wanted his story, I wanted his friendship. As partial restitution, the least I could give him was the benefit of the doubt.

Also, he was right. Only a monster would commit the crimes described in those court files, and I didn't see any monster before me. Just a toothless boxer with a glass chin and a pigeon feather in his hat. Shaking his hand, I heard myself say, "Go get warm, Champ," and I watched myself slip him another five-dollar bill.

### 8.

LaMotta would not let up. He refused to let me write. Each time I tried, he swatted me around my subconscious. "Besides Bob Satterfield," he'd said, "the only ones who ever hurt me were my ex-wives." Men seldom speak of other men with such deference, such reverence, particularly men like LaMotta. One of the brashest fighters ever, he discussed Satterfield with all the bluster of a curtsy. "You sure it's him?" he'd asked, distressed. "I heard he was dead."

You sure it's him? The courts were sure, the cops were sure, the editors were pretty sure. But I was getting ready to tell several million people that Bob Satterfield was a homeless wreck and a convicted child molester. Was I sure?

I phoned more boxing experts and historians, promoters and managers, libraries and clubs, referees and retired fighters, and that's when

I found Ernie Terrell, former heavyweight champion. I reached him in Chicago at the South Side offices of his janitorial business.

"You remember Bob Satterfield?" I asked.

"One of the hardest punchers who ever lived," he said.

I've been hanging out with Satterfield, I said, and I need someone who can vouch for his identity. A long silence followed. A tingly silence, a harrowing silence, the kind of silence that precedes the bloodcurdling scream in a horror film. "Bob Satterfield is dead," Terrell said.

"No, he's not," I said, laughing. "I just talked to him."

"You talked to Bob Satterfield."

"Yes. He sleeps in a park not ten minutes from here."

"Bob Satterfield?" he said. "Bob Satterfield the fighter? Bob Satterfield's dead."

Now it was my turn to be silent. When I felt the saliva returning to my mouth, I asked Terrell what made him so sure.

"Did you go to his funeral?" I asked.

He admitted that he had not.

"Do you have a copy of his obituary?"

Again, no.

"Then how do you know he's dead?" I asked.

Suddenly, he seemed less sure.

"Hold on," he said. "We're going to get to the bottom of this."

He opened a third phone line and began conference-calling veteran corner men and trainers on the South Side. The voices that joined us on the line were disjointed and indistinct, as though recorded on scratchy vinyl records. Rather than a conference call, we were conducting a seance, summoning the spirits of boxing's past. He dialed a gym where the phone rang and rang. When someone finally answered, Terrell asked to speak with D.D. The phone went dead for what seemed a week. In the background, I heard speed bags being thrummed and ropes being skipped, a sound like cicadas on a summer day. At last, a scruffy and querulous voice came on the line, more blues man than corner man.

"Who's this?"

"It's Ernie."

"Ernie?"

"Ernie."

"Ernie?"

"Ernie!"

"Yeah, Ernie, yeah."

"I got a guy here on the other line from the *Los Angeles Times,* in

California, says he's writing a story about Bob Satterfield. You remember Bob Satterfield."

"Suuure."

"Says he just talked to Satterfield and Satterfield's sleeping in a park out there in Santa Ana."

"Bob Satterfield's dead."

"No," I said.

I told them about Champ's encyclopedic knowledge of his career. I told them about Champ's well-documented reputation among cops, judges, and reporters. I told them about Champ's face matching old Satterfield photos.

"Then I will come out there and shoot that dude," D.D. said. "Because Bob Satterfield is *dead*."

Ten minutes later I was in Santa Ana, where I found Champ sweeping someone's sidewalk for the price of a whiskey bottle. It was a hot spring day, and he looked spent from the hard work.

"Look," I said, "a lot of people say you're dead."

"I'm the one," he said, bouncing on his feet, shadowboxing playfully with me. "Battlin' Bob Satterfield. I fought 'em all. Ezzard Charles, Rocky Marciano—"

"Don't you have any identification?" I said, exasperated. "A birth certificate? A union card? A Social Security card?"

He patted his pockets, nothing. We'd been through this.

"In that case," I said, "I'm going to have to give you a test."

Far from offended, he couldn't wait. Leaning into me, he cocked his head to one side and closed his eyes, to aid concentration.

"Who was Jack Kearns?" I asked, knowing that "Doc" Kearns, who managed Jack Dempsey in the 1920s, briefly managed Satterfield's early career.

"Jack Kearns," Champ said. "He was the first manager I ever had."

"All right," I said. "Who's this?"

I held before his nose a 45-year-old wire photo of Iona Satterfield. Champ touched her face gingerly and said, "That's Iona. That's the only woman I ever loved."

## 9.

Asked to explain myself, I usually start with my father, who disappeared when I was seven months old, walked away from his only son the way some people leave a party that's grown dull. At precisely the moment I learned to crawl, he ran. An unfair head start, I always felt.

As a boy, I could repress all stirrings of curiosity about him, because I knew what he sounded like, and this seemed sufficient. A well-known radio man in New York City, he often came floating out of my grand-mother's olive-drab General Electric clock-radio, cracking jokes and doing bits, until an adult passing through the room would lunge for the dial. It was thought that The Voice upset me. No one realized that The Voice nourished me. My father was invisible, therefore mythic. He was whatever I wanted him to be, and his rumbling baritone inspired men-tal pictures of every male archetype, from Jesus to Joe Namath to Baloo the bear in *The Jungle Book.*

Over time, I grew impatient with the mystery surrounding him, the not knowing, particularly when he changed his name and vanished altogether. (Seeing fatherhood and child support as a maximum-secu-rity prison, he took a fugitive's pains to cover his tracks once he es-caped.) As his absence came to feel more like a constant presence, I spent long hours puzzling about the potential intersections between his identity and mine. My predecessor in the generational parade, my ac-cursed precursor, was a voice. It unnerved me. It unmanned me. One day, shortly before my seventeenth birthday, I made what felt like a conscious decision to find him. At least, that's what I thought until I met Champ, who forced me to see that no such conscious decision ever took place, that I'd been trying to find my father all my life, that every man is trying to find his father.

True, a love of boxing and a budding disenchantment with daily journalism sparked my original interest in Champ. Then a genuine fondness made me befriend him. But what made me study him like an insect under a microscope was my inescapable fascination with anyone who disappears, dissolves his identity, walks away from fame and family. When pushed to deconstruct my relationship with Champ, I saw that we were trading more than fivers and fellowship. Champ was using me as a surrogate for his dead son, and I was using him as a stand-in for my own deep-voiced demon, whom I met after a brief, furious search.

We sat in an airport coffee shop and talked like strangers. Strangers who had the same nose and chin. I remember random things. I remem-ber that he was the first man I ever made nervous. I remember that he wore a black leather coat, ordered eggs Benedict and flirted relentlessly with a waitress, asking like some fussy lord if the chef made his own

Hollandaise sauce. I remember that he was portly and jovial, with wild eyebrows that forked straight out from his head. I remember laughing at his stories, laughing against my will because he could be painfully funny. I remember breathing in his peppery scent, a uniquely male cocktail of rubbing alcohol, hair spray and Marlboro 100s. I remember the hug when we parted, the first time I ever hugged another man.

But what we said to each other over the hours we sat together, I don't know. The meeting was so emotionally high-watt that it shorted my memory circuits. My only other impression of that night is one of all-pervasive awe. My father, my mythic father, had boozed away his future and parlayed his considerable talents into a pile of unpaid bills. I saw none of that. If losing him was a hardship, losing my mythic idea of him would have been torture. So I chose to see him as a fallen god, an illusion he fostered with a few white lies. I loved him in the desperate way you love someone when you need to.

Now, months after meeting Champ, I asked myself if I wasn't viewing this poor homeless man through the same hopeful myopia. If so, why? The answer dawned one day while I was reading *Moby-Dick*, the bible of obsession, which provides a special sort of reading pleasure when you substitute the word "father" for "whale": "It is a thing most sorrowful, nay shocking, to expose the fall of valor in the soul. . . . That immaculate manliness we feel within ourselves . . . bleeds with keenest anguish at the undraped spectacle of a valor-ruined man."

When the valor-ruined man is your father, the anguish quadruples and the manliness hemorrhages. Sometimes the anguish reaches such a crescendo that you simply disobey your eyes. Anything to stanch the bleeding.

Because he recalled the specter of my father and his equally enigmatic cop-out, Champ might have revived that early talent I showed for self-deception. He also either benefited or suffered from the trinity of habits that constitutes my father's legacy. An obsession with questions of identity. A tendency to overestimate men. And an inability to leave the past alone.

### 10.

Not every homeless man can look nonchalant speaking into a cellular phone, but Champ acclimated himself to the technology, even if he did aim the phone at that part of the heavens where he imagined Ohio to be. He told his sister he was fine, getting by, and urged her to cooperate. "Please," he said, handing me the phone, "let this man look at my scrapbook."

Establishing Champ's credibility was one thing. Establishing mine with his sister was another. Lily couldn't imagine what I wanted from her poor brother, and I couldn't blame her. I tried to explain that Champ merited a newspaper story because he'd contended for the title.

"You remember your brother fighting," I said, "as Bob Satterfield?"

"Yes," she said casually.

"And you have a scrapbook with clippings and photos?"

"I've had that scrapbook for years."

I asked her to mail me the book, but she refused. She wasn't about to ship a family heirloom to someone she'd never met. Again, I couldn't blame her.

It was then that I heard from a former boxing writer. He'd been watching TV recently when he hit on something called the Classic Sports Network, which was airing a prehistoric episode of Rocky Marciano's TV show, wherein Marciano analyzed a 1951 bout at Madison Square Garden between Rex Layne and Bob Satterfield.

When the tape arrived the next morning, I cradled it like a newborn to the nearest VCR. There was Marciano, pudgy and past his prime, a real-life version of Fred Flintstone. Beside him sat his guest, comic Jimmy Durante. After several excruciating minutes of idle chitchat, Marciano turned to Durante and said, "I want to show you the Bob Satterfield–Rex Layne fight."

Durante's eyes widened.

"Satterfield?" he said.

"You remember him?" Marciano asked.

"So help me," Durante said, "he's my favorite. A great, great fighter. I thought he'd be a champion."

"He had the punch, Jim," Marciano said, shaking his head.

The screen went dark. A ring appeared. In the foreground stood a man in a hooded robe, his back to the camera. On either side of him stood corner men in cardigan sweaters, "SATTERFIELD" emblazoned across their backs. Doffing his robe, the fighter started forward, his torso atremble with muscles. Slowly he turned toward the camera, and I saw that he was not Champ. The resemblance was strong, as the resemblance between Champ and old photos of Satterfield had been strong. But they were different men.

My stomach tightened as the "real" Satterfield threw a walloping right. Layne dropped to one knee and shook his head, not knowing what hit him. I knew exactly how he felt.

Champ a fake. Somehow I felt less betrayed when I thought he was a child molester. It made me sick. It made no sense. He knew too much about Satterfield. He knew the record. He knew Doc Kearns. He recognized Iona. Plus, he was built like a fighter — that body, those hands. Yes, I thought, he's built like a fighter.

I phoned *The Ring* and asked Mainwaring to check his records for a heavyweight named Tommy Harrison. Minutes later, he faxed me the file. There, at long last, was Champ. This time, no allowance needed to be made for the passage of years and the corrosive effects of whiskey. That body, those hands.

Besides his name, it seemed, Champ was frequently telling the truth. Not only did he break Marciano's nose, the injury postponed a storied rematch with Walcott. Like Satterfield, he *had* been a highly touted contender, a guy within striking distance of the championship. Like Satterfield, he *had* fought Ezzard Charles. In fact, Harrison and Satterfield had fought many of the same men.

Opponents weren't the only thing they had in common. Both were Army veterans. Both were right-handers. Both were built like light-heavyweights. Both were anxious to break into the heavyweight division. Both were clobbered when they tried. Both retired in the mid-1950s. Both were born in November; their birthdays were one day apart.

"He's fast," Marciano said of Harrison in one clipping. "Has a great ring future. In a year or so, if I'm still champ, I expect trouble from him."

The file proved that Champ was a fraud, or delusional, or something in between. But it couldn't explain his motives, nor account for his corroborative sister. In fact, it raised more questions than it answered, including the most pressing question of all: if Champ wasn't Satterfield, who was?

Ernie Terrell said Satterfield was dead. But I couldn't find an obituary — not even in Chicago. How did a fighter of Satterfield's stature not rate a death notice in his native city?

Phone directories in scores of area codes listed hundreds of Satterfields, too many to dial. A search of databases throughout the Midwest found one Illinois death certificate in the name of Robert Satterfield, a truck driver buried in Restvale Cemetery, Worth, Illinois. Under next of kin, a son on the South Side of Chicago.

"Robert Satterfield Junior?" I asked when the son answered the phone.

"Yes?"

"I'm writing a story about Bob Satterfield, the heavyweight of the 1950s and I was wondering if you might be any—"

"That's my father," he said proudly.

## 11.

The neighborhood was dodgy, some houses well kept and others falling down. Few addresses were visible and some street signs were gone, so I drove in circles, getting lost twice, doubling back, and that's when I saw him. Bob Satterfield. In the flesh.

After staring at old newspaper photos and studying the tape of his fight with Rex Layne, I'd committed Satterfield's face to memory — never realizing he might have bequeathed that face to his son. Seeing Satterfield Jr. outside his house, the resemblance fooled me like a mirage, and I did what anyone in my shoes would have done: I backed straight into his neighbor's truck.

The first time I ever laid eyes on Bob Satterfield, therefore, he flinched, as though bracing for a punch.

After making sure I'd left no visible dent, we shook hands and went inside his brick house, the nicest on the block. The living room was neat and intensely bright, morning sunlight practically shattering the glass windows. He introduced me to his wife, Elaine, who took my hand somewhat timidly. Together, they waved me toward the couch, then sat far away, grimacing.

They were visibly afraid of me, but they did everything possible to make me feel welcome. She was all smiles and bottled-up energy; he was old-school polite, verging on courtly. He'd just finished a double shift at O'Hare, where he loaded cargo for a living, and he actually apologized for his exhaustion. I looked into his basset-hound eyes and cringed, knowing I'd soon add to his burdens.

I started by acknowledging their apprehension. As far as they knew, I'd come all the way from California to ask questions about a fighter few people remembered. It seemed suspicious.

"But the first time I heard the name Bob Satterfield," I said, "was when I met this man."

I dealt them several photos of Champ, like gruesome playing cards, then court papers and clippings describing Champ as Satterfield. Another profile had recently appeared in a college newspaper, and I laid this atop the pile. Lastly, I outlined Champ's criminal past. They looked at each other gravely.

"I hate this man," Elaine blurted.

Satterfield Jr. lit a cigarette and gazed at Champ. He murmured something about a resemblance, then walked to a sideboard, from which he pulled a crumbling scrapbook. Returning to his chair, he balanced the book on one knee and began assembling photos, clippings, documents, anything to help me recognize that Champ's impersonation was no victimless crime.

While I scrutinized the scrapbook, Satterfield Jr. talked about his father's life. He told me about his father's close friends, Miles Davis and Muhammad Ali, who met his first wife through Satterfield. He told me about his father's triumphs in the ring and the difficult decision to retire. (After suffering a detached retina in 1958, Satterfield fled to Paris and studied painting.) He told me about his father's ancestry, back, back, back, and I understood the desperation seeping into his voice, a desperation that made him stammer badly. He'd opened his door to a total stranger who repaid the hospitality by declaring that countless other strangers believed his beloved father was a "valor-ruined man." I'd walked up clean steps to talk to clean people and made them feel dirty.

Lastly, Satterfield Jr. produced his father's birth certificate, plus a 1977 obituary from a now-defunct Chicago newspaper. To these precious items he added a photo of his parents strolling arm in arm, kissing. When I told Satterfield Jr. about Champ pointing to Iona and calling her "the only woman I ever loved," I thought he might eat the coffee table.

"That somebody would intrude on his memory like this," Elaine said. "My father-in-law was a man. He was a man's man, nothing like the men of today. He was a prideful man. He continued to work up until his operation for cancer. If a person knows he's dying, and he still gets up to go to work, that says a lot about him as a man, and if he knew some homeless man sleeping on a park bench was impersonating him—"

She stopped herself and went to the window, struggling to keep her composure. Satterfield Jr. now began phoning family.

"I'm sitting here with a reporter from the *Los Angeles Times*," he shouted into the phone, "and he says there's a man in California who's telling everybody he's Bob Satterfield the fighter. He's homeless and he has a very bad record, and he's been molesting children and he's using Pop's name. Yeah. Uh huh. Now, now, don't cry . . ."

### 12.

An old boxing hand once said, "You never learn anything until you're tired," and by that criterion I'm capable of learning plenty right now. After the overnight flight, after the cab ride through the rainy dawn to this downtown Columbus hotel, I'm tired enough to understand why Champ's sister doesn't trust me, and why she's turned me over to Champ's nephew, Gregory Harrison, who trusts me even less. I left word for him two hours ago saying I'd arrived, but he seems like a guy who'd rather give me a stiff beating than a straight answer, so the chance of seeing Champ's scrapbook seems remote.

Above all, I'm tired enough to understand that Champ isn't Satterfield, never was Satterfield, never will be, no matter how hard I try. But I'm also tired enough to understand why he pretended to be Satterfield. He became Satterfield because he didn't like being Tommy Harrison.

It was Satterfield Jr. who made me appreciate how ripe his father was for imitation. Fast, stylish, pretty, Satterfield was Champ's superior in every way. He was the ballyhooed one, the better one. Yes, he had the famously weak chin. But he led with it, time after time, meaning he had one hellacious heart. Champ must have studied Satterfield from afar, longingly, as I did. He must have gone to school on Satterfield, devouring facts about his life, as I did. He must have viewed Satterfield as a model, an ideal, as I also did. One day, Champ must have spied Satterfield across a musty gym, perhaps with Doc Kearns, or a smoky nightclub, where Iona was the prettiest girl in the joint, and said, "Ah, to be him." From there, it was a short, dizzy trip to "I *am* him."

As a man, you need someone to instruct you in the masculine verities. Your father is your first choice, but when he drops out, you search for someone else. If you're careless, the search creeps into your psyche and everyone becomes a candidate, from homeless men to dead boxers. If you're careless and unlucky, the search devours you. That doppelganger eats you up.

"One of the primary things boxing is about is lying," Joyce Carol Oates writes in *On Boxing*. "It's about systematically cultivating a double personality: the self in society, the self in the ring."

What Champ did, I think, was sprout a third self, a combination of the two, which may be what Champ has been trying to tell me all along.

After Chicago, I wanted to scold him about the people his lies were hurting. But when I found him wearing a ten-gallon cowboy hat and a polo shirt with toothbrushes stuffed in the breast pocket, my anger drained away.

"Champ," I said, "when you pretended to be Bob Satterfield, weren't you afraid the other Bob Satterfield would find out?"

Without hesitating, he put a hand to his chin and said, "I always figured the other Bob Satterfield knew about me. As long as everyone got paid, I didn't think the other Bob Satterfield would mind."

"What?"

"This is just you and me talking," he said. "But my manager, George Parnassus, he told me like this here: 'If you go to fight in Sioux City, Iowa, and you say you is Bob Satterfield, then you get a big crowd, see? But if you say you is Tommy Harrison, and like that, you only get a medium-size crowd.'"

Champ's manager had been dead twenty years. But his son, Msgr. George Parnassus, was pastor of St. Victor's Roman Catholic Church in West Hollywood. I phoned Parnassus and told him about Champ, then asked if his father might have staged bogus fights in the 1950s. Before TV came along, I ventured, most fighters were faceless names in the dark, so it might have been easy, and it might have been highly profitable, to promote lookalike fighters in out-of-the-way places. Say, Sioux City.

"Why do you say Sioux City?" he demanded.

"Because Champ said Sioux City."

"My father moved to Sioux City in the 1950s and staged fights there for a number of years."

Which is why I'm in Columbus this morning. I owed it to Champ to take one last stab at the truth. I owed it to myself. More than anyone, I owed it to Satterfield, whose absence I've come to feel like a constant presence.

"I've had a lot of disappointments," Satterfield told a reporter in 1958, sitting in a hospital with his detached retina. "I don't remember all the disappointments I've had." Maybe, forty years later, he's still disappointed. Maybe he knows someone swiped the only shiny prize he ever had — his good name — and he can't rest until he gets it back. All this time, I've been casting Satterfield as Moby Dick, myself as Ahab. Now I'm wondering if Satterfield is the real Ahab, and Champ the whale. Which makes me the harpoon.

The phone rings.

"I'm downstairs."

## 13.

Champ's nephew is sitting in the middle of the lobby, unaware or pretending to be unaware that people are staring. It's not that he looks out of place, with his floor-length black leather overcoat and gold-rimmed sunglasses. It's that he looks famous. He also looks like a younger, fitter, toothier version of Champ.

He shakes my hand tentatively and we duck into the hotel restaurant. The place is closed, but a waiter says we're welcome to have coffee. We sit by a rain-streaked window. I thank him for meeting me, but he whips off his sunglasses and stares.

"I'm not here for you," he says. "I'm here for my uncle Tommy. And before I tell you anything you need to know, I need to know from you why you would get on a plane and fly all night, come all the way from California, to Columbus, Ohio, to write a story about *my uncle?*"

I try explaining my complicated relationship with his uncle, but the subject makes me more mumbly than Champ. Interrupting, he says softly: "Uncle Tommy was the father I should have had."

He tells me about the only time he met his uncle, a meeting so charged that it defined his life, and I wonder if he notices the strange look on my face.

"My uncle Tommy was like the Last Action Hero," he says. "I wanted to be just like him."

"You were a boxer," I say.

"I was a sparring partner of Buster Douglas," he says, sitting straighter.

His nickname was Capital City Lip, but everyone nowadays calls him Lip. With the waiters watching, he throws his right, jabs his left, bobs away from an invisible opponent, taking me through several hard-won fights, and I'm reminded of the many times his uncle broke Marciano's nose for my enjoyment.

"When you hit a guy," he says dreamily, "when you hit him in the body, you demean his manner, you know? You sap his strength, you impose your will on him. I was in the tippy-top physical shape of my life! No one could beat me! I was *good!*"

"What happened?"

He purses his lips. His story is Champ's story, Satterfield's story, every fighter's story. One day, there was someone he just couldn't beat.

"Now I race drag bikes," he says.

"Drag bikes? Why?"

"Because someday I want to be world champion of something."

His father got him interested, he says, mentioning the man in a curious way. "My father walks down the street, people part ways," he says. "Big George, that's what everyone in Columbus calls my father. He was a boxer, too, although he didn't go as far as Uncle Tommy."

Feeling an opening, I try to tell Lip about my father. He seems confused at first, then instantly empathetic. He understands the link between boxing and growing up fatherless. Maybe only a boxer can fathom that kind of fear.

"Have you ever heard the name Bob Satterfield?" I ask.

"Yes, I have heard that name."

As a boy, Lip often heard that Uncle Tommy fought as Bob Satterfield, but he never knew why.

He promises to bring me Champ's scrapbook tomorrow, then take me to meet his father. I walk him outside to his Jeep, which is double-parked in a tow zone, hazard lights flashing, just as he left it three hours ago.

### 14.

White shirt, white pants, white shoes, Lip comes for me the next morning looking like an angel of the streets. As we zoom away from the hotel, I scan the backseat, floor, dashboard. No scrapbook. The angel shakes his head.

"Aunt Lily just doesn't trust you," he says. "I was over there all morning, but she won't let that book out of her house."

I groan.

"I looked through the book myself, though," he says, lighting a cigarette, "and I don't think it has what you want. This Bob Satterfield, the book has lots of newspaper articles about his career, and there's a picture of him with my uncle — "

I wince.

" — and an article saying Satterfield and my uncle Tommy were scheduled to fight."

Disconsolate, I stare at the bullet hole in the windshield.

We drive to Lip's father's house, where a candy-apple red Cadillac the size of a fire engine sits outside, license plate "BIG GEO." Lip takes a deep breath, then knocks. Whole minutes crawl by before the door flies open and Champ's brother appears. He looks nothing like Champ, mainly because of old burn scars across his face. But wrapped in a baby blue bathrobe and glowering hard, he does look like an old boxer. He turns and disappears inside the house. Meekly, we follow.

Off to the left is a small room crammed with trophies and boxing memorabilia. To the right seems to be the living room, though it's impossible to tell because all the lights are off. Big George keeps moving until he reaches a high-backed chair. Despite the oceanic darkness of the place, he remains clearly visible, as if lit from within by his own anger. I can see why he's such a force in Lip's life. He scares the wits out of me.

Rubbing his palms together, Lip tells his father I'm writing a story about Uncle Tommy.

"Hmph," Big George scoffs. "Tommy. He's a stranger to me. He's my brother and I love him, but he's a stranger."

"Have you ever heard the name Bob Satterfield?" I ask.

"Bob Satterfield," Big George says, "was one of the hardest punchers of all time—"

He coughs, a horrifying cough, then adds:

"—but he couldn't take a punch."

"Do you remember Tommy ever fighting as Bob Satterfield?" I ask.

"Tommy never fought as nobody else."

He stands and goes to a sideboard, where he rifles through a stack of papers and bills. "Here," he says, yanking loose a yellowed newspaper account of the night in 1953 when Champ's life began its downward spiral.

"Tommy wasn't ready for Ezzard Charles," Big George says with sudden tenderness while Lip and I read over his shoulder. "They rushed him."

The three of us stand together, silently, as though saying a prayer for Champ. Then, without warning, Lip breaks the mood, mentioning a beef he's having with Big George. They start to argue, and I see that Lip brought me here for more than an interview. He's hoping I can play referee. As with Champ, I was too busy using him to notice that he was using me.

Father and son argue for five minutes, each landing heavy verbal blows. Then Big George makes it plain that these will be the final words spoken on the subject.

"The Bible say this," he bellows. "Honor your parents! Honor your mother and father! Regardless what they say, what they do, all mothers and dads love their children! All of them!"

"He's lying to you," Lip says when we get in the car.

I look at him, startled.

"About what?"

"He knows all about Satterfield."

We drive to a beloved old gym that former champion Buster Douglas helped rebuild after knocking down Mike Tyson. Inside, we find Douglas' father, Bill, training a young featherweight. When Lip tells Douglas that I'm writing about his uncle, "a former heavyweight con-TEN-der," Douglas nods his head several times, and I feel Lip's self-worth balloon with each nod.

We watch the featherweight work the heavy bag, a black, water-filled sack that hangs from the ceiling. Each time he snaps a hard right, the bag swings like a man in a noose. His name is Andre Cray, and he's 25. Rawboned and scowling, with a flat head and rubbery limbs, he looks like an angry Gumby. When his workout ends, we ask him why he chose boxing as a trade.

"To me it's like an art," he says quietly, unwinding the padded white tape from his fists.

But this isn't the real reason, he admits. Growing up without money, without a father, boxing was the only straight path to manhood. Many of his friends chose the crooked path, a choice they didn't always live to regret. Those who prospered in the crack trade often gave Cray money and begged him not to follow their lead. Some even bought him gloves and shoes, to make sure the streets didn't claim another boxer.

He remembers those early patrons, uses their fate as inspiration. His future is bright, he figures, if he can just protect his chin and not lose heart. In 19 fights, he's scored 17 wins. When he loses, he says, the anguish is more than he can stand.

"You have family?" Lip asks.

"Yeah," Cray says. "I have a son. He'll be 1 on Tuesday."

"What's his name?"

"Andre Cray *Junior*."

"I imagine he inspires you a lot."

"Yeah," Cray says, looking down at his oversize hands.

Lip nods, solemn. Douglas nods. I nod.

## 15.

Like a favorite movie, the one-reel *Satterfield Versus Layne* says something different every time I watch, each punch a line of multilayered dialogue. After several hundred viewings, the core theme emerges. It's about pressing forward, I think. Ignoring your pain. Standing.

"Satterfield is out of this world," Marciano says in his narrative voice-over. "He's one of the hardest hitters I've ever seen."

Satterfield lives up to his reputation in the very first minute, greeting Layne with a vicious second-clefter on the point of the chin. Kneeling, Layne takes the count, then staggers upright and hugs Satterfield until the bell.

Satterfield, in white trunks, with a pencil-thin mustache and muscles upon muscles, is a joy to look at. Decades before Nautilus, his biceps look like triple-scoop ice cream cones. By contrast, Layne looks like a soda jerk who's wandered mistakenly into the ring. Over the first three rounds he does little more than push his black trunks and flabby belly back and forth while offering his square head as a stationary target.

Still, Layne seems the luckier man. In the sixth, Satterfield puts every one of his 180 pounds behind a right hook. He brings the fist from behind his back like a bouquet of flowers, but Layne weaves, avoiding the punch by half an inch. "Just missed!" Marciano shouts. "That would have done it!"

Had that punch landed, everything would be different. Layne would be stretched out on the canvas, Satterfield would be looking forward to the title shot he craves. Instead, the eighth begins, and Satterfield's wondering what more he can do. It's LaMotta all over again. No matter what you do, the other guy keeps coming — obdurate, snarling, fresh.

Far ahead on points, Satterfield can still win a decision, as long as he protects himself, covers up, plays it safe. He does just the opposite, charging forward, chin high, the only way he knows. In the kind of punch-for-punch exchange that went out with fedoras, Satterfield and Layne stand one inch apart, winging at each other from all directions, Satterfield trying frantically to turn out Layne's dim bulb — until Layne lands a right hook on the magic chin.

"I don't think [he] can get up," Marciano says as Satterfield lies on his back, blinking at the house lights. "But look at this guy try."

Boxing's Humpty-Dumpty. The book on Satterfield proves true. Or does it? Always, this is the moment I hit the pause button and talk to

Satterfield while he tries to tap some hidden wellspring of strength. Somehow, he taps it every time, a display of pure grit that never fails to make my heart beat faster.

"He's hurt bad," Marciano says, as Satterfield stands and signals the referee that he's ready for another dose. Dutifully, Layne steps forward and sends a crashing left into Satterfield's head. Then a right. And another right. Finally, the referee rushes forward and removes Satterfield's mouthpiece. Corner men leap into the ring. Photographers with flashes the size of satellite dishes shoot the covers of tomorrow's sports pages. Amid all the commotion, Layne takes a mincing step forward and does something shocking.

It's hard to believe, in an age of end-zone dances and home-run trots, that boxers in a bygone era often hugged after their meanest fights. (Some actually kissed.) But Layne gives that postfight tenderness a new twist. As Satterfield sags against the ropes, dead-eyed, Layne reaches out to touch him ever so lightly on the cheek.

It's a haunting gesture, so intimate and unexpected that it begs imitation. Like Layne — like Champ — I want to reach out to Satterfield, to show my admiration. I want to tell him how glad I am to make his acquaintance, how grateful I am for the free instruction. More than all that, I suppose, I just want to thank him for the fight.

One day, after watching his greatest defeat, I visit his impostor.

"Heyyy," Champ says, beaming, waving hello. "What do you know about that? Hey, your picture ran through my mind many times, and then I'd say, well, my friend, he give me up."

He's wearing a white karate uniform, mismatched sneakers and a shirt from the Orange County Jail. Clouds of flies swarm around his head and grocery cart this warm November afternoon, Champ's sixty-seventh birthday. Tomorrow would have been Satterfield's seventy-third.

There are many things about Champ that I don't know, things I'll probably never know. He either got money to be Satterfield, then forgot to drop the con, or wished he were Satterfield, then let the wish consume him. Not knowing doesn't bother me as I feared it would. Not getting his scrapbook doesn't torment me as I thought it might. Every man is a mystery, because manhood itself is so mysterious; that's what Champ taught me. Maturity means knowing when to solve another man's mystery, and when to respect it.

"Been traveling," I tell him. "And guess where I went?"

He cocks his head.

"Columbus. And guess who I saw? Your nephew, Gregory."

"That's my brother's son!"

"Yep. And guess who else I met. Big George."

He pulls a sour face, like his brother's, and we both laugh.

We talk about George, Lily and Lip, and Champ grows heavy with nostalgia. He recalls his childhood, particularly his stern father, who hit him so hard one day that he flayed the muscle along Champ's left bicep. Champ rolls up his sleeve to show me the mark, but I look away.

To cheer him up, to cheer us both up, I ask Champ to tell me once more about busting Marciano's nose.

"Marciano and I were putting on an exhibition that day," he says, crouching. "We were going good. But he had that long overhand right, and every time I seen it coming, I'd duck it. And I'd come up, and I'd keep hitting him on the tip of his nose."

He touches my nose with a gentle uppercut, flies trailing in the wake of his fist.

"On the tip, on the tip, I kept hitting," he says. "Finally, his nose started bleeding, and they stopped the fight."

Smiling now, more focused than I've ever seen him, Champ says he needs my advice. He's been reviewing his life lately, wondering what next. Times are hard, he says, and maybe he should head on down the road, polish up the Cadillac and return to Columbus, though he fears the cold and what it does to an old boxer's bones.

"What do you think?" he says.

"I think you should go be with people who love you and care about you," I say.

"Yeah, that's true, that's true."

We watch the cars whizzing by, jets roaring overhead, strangers walking past.

"Well, Champ," I say, slipping him five dollars. "I've got to get going."

"Yeah, yeah," he says, stopping me. "Now, listen."

He rests one of his heavy hands on my shoulder, a gesture that makes me swallow hard and blink for some reason. I look into his eyes, and from his uncommonly serious expression, I know he's getting ready to say something important.

"I know you a long time," he says warmly, flashing that toothless smile, groping for the words. "Tell me your name again."

# The One and Only

1964

## Murray Kempton

...........................................................................................................................................................

# The Champ and the Chump

FROM *The New Republic*

JUST BEFORE THE bell for the seventh round, Cassius Clay got up to
go about his job. Suddenly, he thrust his arms straight up in the air in
the signal with which boxers are accustomed to treat victory and you
laughed at his arrogance. No man could have seen Clay that morning at
the weigh-in and believed that he could stay on his feet three minutes
that night. He had come in pounding the cane Malcolm X had given
him for spiritual support, chanting "I am the greatest, I am the champ,
he is a chump." Ray Robinson, that picture of grace who is Clay's ideal
as a fighter, pushed him against the wall and tried to calm him, and this
hysterical child turned and shouted at him, "I am a great *performer,* I
am a great *performer.*"

Suddenly almost everyone in the room hated Cassius Clay. Sonny
Liston just looked at him. Liston used to be a hoodlum; now he was our
cop; he was the big Negro we pay to keep sassy Negroes in line and he
was just waiting until his boss told him it was time to throw this kid out.

British journalists who were present remembered with comfort how
helpful beaters like Liston had been to Sanders of the River; Northern
Italian journalists were comforted to see on Liston's face the look that
*mafiosi* use to control peasants in Sicily; promoters and fight managers
saw in Clay one of their animals utterly out of control and were glad to
know that soon he would be not just back in line but out of the
business. There were two Catholic priests in attendance whose vocation
it is to teach Sonny Liston the values of organized Christianity, and one
said to the other: "Do you see Sonny's face? You *know* what he's going to
do to this fellow."

The great legends of boxing are of managers like Jack Hurley, who
had taken incompetent fighters and just by shouting their merits,

against all reason built them up for one big payday at which they disgraced themselves and were never heard from again. Clay had created himself the way Hurley created his paper tigers. His most conspicuous public appearance in the week before he was to fight had been a press conference with the Beatles. They were all very much alike — sweet and gay. He was an amateur Olympic champion who had fought twenty professional fights, some of them unimpressive, and he had clowned and blustered about how great he was until he earned his chance from a Liston who, if he could not respect him as an opponent, could recognize him as a propagandist skilled enough to fool the public. A reporter had asked Liston if he thought the seven to one odds against Clay were too long, and he answered: "I don't know. I'm not a bookmaker. I'm a fighter." But there was no hope Clay could win; there was barely the hope that he could go like a gentleman. Even Norman Mailer settled in this case for organized society. Suppose Clay won the heavyweight championship, he asked; it would mean that every loudmouth on a street corner could swagger and be believed. But if he lay down the first time Liston hit him, he would be a joke and a shame all his life. He carried, by every evidence unfit, the dignity of every adolescent with him. To an adult a million dollars may be worth the endurance of being clubbed by Sonny Liston; but nothing could pay an adolescent for just being picked up by the bouncer and thrown out.

On the night, Clay was late getting to the dressing room and he came to stand in back of the arena to watch his younger brother fight one of the preliminaries. He spoke no word and seemed to look, if those blank eyes could be said to look, not at the fighters but at the lights above them. There was a sudden horrid notion that just before the main event, when the distinguished visitors were announced, Cassius Clay in his dinner jacket might bounce into the ring, shout one more time that he was the greatest, and go down the steps and out of the arena and out of the sight of man forever. Bystanders yelled insults at him; his handlers pushed him toward his dressing room, stiff, his steps hesitant. One had thought him hysterical in the morning; now one thought him catatonic.

He came into the ring long before Liston and danced with the mechanical melancholy of a marathon dancer; it was hard to believe that he had slept in forty-eight hours. Liston came in; they met in the ring center with Clay looking over the head of that brooding presence; then Clay went back and put in his mouthpiece clumsily like an amateur and shadowboxed like a man before a mirror and turned around, still catatonic and the bell rang and Cassius Clay went forward to meet the toughest man alive.

He fought the first round as though without plan, running and slipping and sneaking punches, like someone killing time in a poolroom. But it was his rhythm and not Liston's; second by slow second, he was taking away the big bouncer's dignity. Once Liston had him close to the ropes — where fighters kill boxers — and Clay, very slowly, slipped sideways from a left hook and under the right and away, just grazing the ropes all in one motion, and cut Liston in the eye. For the first time there was the suspicion that he might know something about the trade.

Clay was a little ahead when they stopped it. Liston had seemed about to fall on him once; Clay was caught in a corner early in the fifth and worked over with the kind of sullen viciousness one cannot imagine a fighter sustaining more than four or five times in one night. He seemed to be hurt and walked back, being stalked, and offering only a left hand listlessly and unimpressively extended in Liston's face. We thought that he was done and asking for mercy, and then that he was tapping Liston to ask him to quiet down a moment and give the greatest a chance to speak, and then we saw that Clay's legs were as close together as they had been before the round started and that he was unhurt and Liston just wasn't coming to him. It ended there, of course, although we did not know it.

"I told ye," Cassius Clay cried to all of us who had laughed at him. "I told ye'. I just played with him. I whipped him so bad and wasn't that good. And look at me: I'm still pretty."

An hour later he came out dressed; a friend stopped him and the heavyweight champion of the world smiled and said he would be available in the morning. His eyes were wise and canny, like Ray Robinson's.

## Dick Schaap

..........................................................................................................

# Muhammad Ali Then and Now

FROM *Sport*

IN SOME WAYS it seems so long ago: John F. Kennedy was a handsome young Senator, starting to campaign for the Presidency of the United States.

In some ways, it seems like yesterday: Richard M. Nixon was starting to campaign for the presidency of the United States.

It was August, 1960, when I first met Cassius Marcellus Clay, when he was 18 years old and brash and wide-eyed and naive and shrewd, and now more than a decade has elapsed, and John F. Kennedy is dead, and Richard M. Nixon is President, and those two facts, as well as anything, sum up how much everything has changed, how much everything remains the same.

It is ridiculous, of course, to link Presidents and prize fighters, yet somehow, in this case, it seems strangely logical. When I think back to the late summer of 1960, my most persistent memories are of the two men who wanted to be President and of the boy who wanted to be heavyweight champion of the world.

And he was a boy — a bubbling boy without a serious thought in his head, without a problem that he didn't feel his fists or his wit would eventually solve.

He is so different now. He is so much the same.

We met a few days before he flew from New York to Rome to compete in the 1960 Olympic Games. I was sports editor of *Newsweek* then, and I was hanging around a Manhattan hotel where the American Olympic team had assembled, picking up anecdotes and background material I could use for my long-distance coverage of the Games. I spent a little time with Bob Boozer, who was on the basketball team, and with Bo Roberson, a broad jumper who later played football for the Oakland Raiders, and with Ira Davis, a hop-step-and-jump specialist who'd played on the same high school basketball team with Wilt Chamberlain and Johnny Sample. And then I heard about Cassius Clay.

He was a light-heavyweight fresh out of high school in Louisville, Kentucky, and he had lost only one amateur bout in two years, a decision to a southpaw named Amos Johnson. He was supposed to be one of the two best pro prospects on the boxing team, he and Wilbert McClure, a light-middleweight, a college student from Toledo, Ohio. I offered to show the two of them, and a couple of other American boxers, around New York, to take them up to Harlem and introduce them to Sugar Ray Robinson. Cassius leaped at the invitation, the chance to meet his idol, the man whose skills and flamboyance he dreamed of matching. Sugar Ray meant big money and fancy cars and flashy women, and if anyone had told Cassius Clay then he would someday deliberately choose a course of action that scorned those values, the boy would have laughed and laughed and laughed.

I wasn't just being hospitable, offering to show the boxers around. I figured I could maybe get lucky and pick up a story. I did. And more.

On the ride uptown, Cassius monopolized the conversation. I forget his exact words, but I remember the message: I'm great, I'm beautiful, I'm going to Rome and I'm gonna whip all those cats and then I'm coming back and turning pro and becoming the champion of the world. I'd never heard an athlete like him; he had no doubts, no fears, no second thoughts, not an ounce of false humility. "Don't mind him," said McClure, amiably. "That's just the way he is."

He was, even then, an original, so outrageously bold he was funny. We all laughed at him, and he didn't mind the laughter, but rode with it, using it to feed his ego, to nourish his self-image.

But there was one moment when he wasn't laughing, he wasn't bubbling. When we reached Sugar Ray's bar on Seventh Avenue near 124th Street, Robinson hadn't shown up yet, and Cassius wandered outside to inspect the sidewalks. At the corner of 125th Street, a black man, perched on a soap box, was preaching to a small crowd. He was advocating something that sounds remarkably mild today — his message, as I recall, was simply buy black, black goods from black merchants — but Cassius seemed stunned. He couldn't believe that a black man would stand up in public and argue against white America. He shook his head in wonderment. "How can he talk like that?" Cassius said. "Ain't he gonna get in trouble?"

A few minutes later, as a purple Lincoln Continental pulled up in front of the bar, Cassius literally jumped out of his seat. "Here he comes," he shouted. "Here comes the great man Robinson."

I introduced the two of them, and Sugar Ray, in his bored, superior way, autographed a picture of himself, presented it to Cassius, wished the kid luck in the Olympics, smiled and drifted away, handsome and lithe and sparkling.

Cassius clutched the precious picture. "That Sugar Ray, he's something," he said. "Someday *I'm* gonna own two Cadillacs — and a Ford for just getting around in."

I didn't get to Rome for the Olympics, but the reports from the *Newsweek* bureau filtered back to me: Cassius Clay was the unofficial mayor of the Olympic Village, the most friendly and familiar figure among thousands of athletes. He strolled from one national area to the next, spreading greetings and snapping pictures with his box camera. He took hundreds of photographs — of Russians, Chinese, Italians, Ethiopians, of everyone who came within camera range. Reporters from Europe and Asia and Africa tried to provoke him into discussions of racial problems in the United States, but this was eight years before John Carlos and Tommie Smith. Cassius just smiled and danced and flicked a few jabs at the air and said, as if he were George Foreman waving a tiny flag, "Oh, we got problems, man, but we're working 'em out. It's still the best country in the world."

He was an innocent, an unsophisticated good-will ambassador, filled with kind words for everyone. Shortly before he won the Olympic light-heavyweight title, he met a visitor to Rome, Floyd Patterson, the only man to win, lose and regain the heavyweight championship of the world, and Cassius commemorated Patterson's visit with one of his earliest poems:

> You can talk about Sweden,
> You can talk about Rome,
> But Rockville Centre's
> Floyd Patterson's home.
> A lot of people said
> That Floyd couldn't fight,

> But they should've seen him
> On that comeback night . . .

There was no way Cassius could have conceived that, five years later, in his most savage performance, he would taunt and torture and brutalize Floyd Patterson.

The day Cassius returned from Rome, I met him at New York's Idlewild Airport — it's now called JFK; can you imagine what the odds were against both the fighter and the airport changing their names within five years? — and we set off on a victory tour of the town, a tour that ranged from midtown to Greenwich Village to Harlem.

Cassius was an imposing sight, and not only for his developing light-heavyweight's build, 180 pounds spread like silk over a six-foot-two frame. He was wearing his blue American Olympic blazer, with USA embroidered upon it, and dangling around his neck was his gold Olympic medal, with PUGILATO engraved in it. For 48 hours, ever since some Olympic dignitary had draped the medal on him, Cassius had kept it on, awake and asleep. "First time in my life I ever slept on my back," he said. "Had to, or that medal would have cut my chest."

We started off in Times Square, and almost immediately a passerby did a double-take and said, "Say, aren't you Cassius Clay?"

Cassius's eyes opened wide. "Yeah man," he said. "That's me. How'd you know who I is?"

"I saw you on TV," the man said. "Saw you beat that Pole in the final. Everybody knows who you are."

"Really?" said Cassius, fingering his gold medal. "You really know who I is? That's wonderful."

Dozens of strangers spotted him on Broadway and recognized him, and Cassius filled with delight, spontaneous and natural, thriving on the recognition. "I guess everybody do know who I is," he conceded.

At a penny arcade, Cassius had a bogus newspaper headline printed: CASSIUS SIGNS FOR PATTERSON FIGHT. "Back home," he said, "they'll think it's real. They won't know the difference."

He took three copies of the paper, jammed them into his pocket, and we moved on, to Jack Dempsey's restaurant. "The champ around?" he asked a waiter.

"No, Mr. Dempsey's out of town," the waiter said.

Cassius turned and stared at a glass case, filled with cheesecakes. "What are them?" he asked the waiter.

"Cheesecakes."

"Do you have to eat the whole thing," Cassius said, "or can you just get a little piece?"

Cassius got a little piece of cheesecake, a glass of milk and a roast beef sandwich. When the check arrived and I reached for it, he asked to see it. He looked and handed it back; the three items came to something like two and a half dollars. "Man," he said. "That's too much money. We coulda gone next door" — there was a Nedick's hot dog stand down the block — "and had a lot more to eat for a whole lot less money."

From Dempsey's, we went to Birdland, a jazz spot that died in the 1960s, and as we stood at the bar — with Cassius holding a Coke "and put a drop of whisky in it" — someone recognized him. "You're Cassius Clay, aren't you?" the man said.

"*You* know who I is, too?" said Cassius.

Later, in a cab heading toward Greenwich Village, Cassius confessed, at great length, that he certainly must be famous. "Why," he said, leaning forward and tapping the cab driver on the shoulder, "I bet even you know that I'm Cassius Clay, the great fighter."

"Sure, Mac," said the cabbie, and Cassius accepted that as positive identification.

In Greenwich Village, in front of a coffeehouse, he turned to a young man who had a goatee and long hair and asked, "Man, where do all them beatniks hang out?"

In Harlem, after a stroll along Seventh Avenue, Cassius paused in a tavern, and some girl there knew who he was, too. She came over to him and twirled his gold medal in her fingers and said that she wouldn't mind if Cassius took her home. *We* took her home, the three of us in a cab. We stopped in front of her home, a dark building on a dark Harlem street, and Cassius went to walk her to her door. "Take your time," I said. "I'm in no hurry. I'll wait with the cab."

He was back in 30 seconds.

"That was quick," I said.

"Man," he said, "I'm in training. I can't fool around with no girls."

Finally, deep into the morning, we wound up at Cassius' hotel room, a suite in the Waldorf Towers, courtesy of a Louisville businessman who hoped someday to manage the fighter. We were roughly halfway between the suites of Douglas MacArthur and Herbert Hoover, and Cassius knew who one of them was.

For an hour, Cassius showed me pictures he had taken in Rome, and then he gave me a bedroom and said goodnight. "Cassius," I said, "you're gonna have to explain to my wife tomorrow why I didn't get home tonight."

"You mean," said Cassius, "your *wife* knows who I is, too?"

A few months later, after he turned professional, I traveled to Louisville to spend a few days with Cassius and write a story about him. In those days, we couldn't go together to the downtown restaurants in Louisville, so we ate each night at the same place, a small restaurant in the black section of town. Every night, Cassius ordered the same main course, a two-pound sirloin, which intrigued me because nothing larger than a one-pound sirloin was listed on the menu.

"How'd you know they served two-pound steaks?" I asked him the third or fourth night.

"Man," he said, "when I found out you were coming down here, I went in and told them to order some."

In the few months since Jack Dempsey's, Cassius had discovered the magic of expense accounts.

But he was still as ebullient, as unaffected, as cocky and as winning as he had been as an amateur. He was as quick with a needle as he was with his fists. One afternoon, we were driving down one of the main streets of Louisville and I stopped for a traffic light. There was a pretty white girl standing on the corner. I looked at her, turned to Cassius and said, "Hey, that's pretty nice."

Cassius whipped around. "You crazy, man?" he said. "You can get electrocuted for that! A Jew looking at a white girl in Kentucky!"

In 1961, his first year as a professional, while he was building a string of victories against unknowns, Cassius came to New York for a visit with his mother, his father and his younger brother, Rudolph. Rudy was the Clay the Louisville schoolteachers favored; he was quiet, polite, obedient. Later, as Rahaman Ali, he became the more militant, the more openly bitter, of the brothers.

I took the Clays to dinner at Leone's, an Italian restaurant that caters partly to sports people and mostly to tourists. To titillate the tourists, Leone's puts out on the dinner table a huge bowl filled with fruit. Cassius took one look at the bowl of fruit, asked his mother for the large pocketbook she was carrying and began throwing the fruit into the pocketbook. "Don't want to waste any of this," he said.

The first course was prosciutto and melon, and Cassius recoiled.

"Ham!" he said. "We don't eat ham. We don't eat any pork things." I knew he wasn't kosher, and I assumed he was stating a personal preference. Of course, Muslims don't eat pork, and perhaps his Muslim training had already begun. I still suspect, however, that he simply didn't like pork.

After dinner, we went out in a used Cadillac Cassius had purchased with part of the bonus he received for turning pro (sponsored by nine Louisville and one New York businessmen, all white), and Cassius asked me to drive around town. On Second Avenue, in the area that later became known as the East Village, I pulled into a gas station. It was a snowy night, and after the attendant, a husky black man, had filled the gas tank, he started to clean off the front window. "Tell him it's good enough, and we'll go," I said to Cassius.

"Hey, man," Cassius said. "It's good enough, and we'll go."

The big black man glowered at Cassius. "Who's doing this?" he said. "You or me?"

Cassius slouched down. "You the boss, man," he said. "You the boss."

The attendant took his time wiping off the front windshield and the back. "Hey, Cash," I said, "I thought you told me you were the greatest fighter in the world. How come you're afraid of that guy?"

"You kidding?" said Clay. "He looks like Sonny Liston, man."

During the middle 1960s, when Cassius soared to the top of the heavyweight division, I drifted away from sports for a while, covering instead politics and murders and riots and lesser diversions. I didn't get to see any of his title fights, except in theaters, and of course, I didn't see him. But our paths crossed early in 1964; by then, as city editor of the *New York Herald Tribune,* I was very much interested in the Black Muslim movement. At first, I didn't know that Cassius was, too.

Through a contact within the Muslim organization, I learned that Cassius, while training in Miami for his first title fight with Sonny Liston, had flown to New York with Malcolm X and had addressed a Muslim rally in Harlem. As far as anyone knew, that was his first commitment to the Muslims, although he had earlier attended a Muslim meeting with Bill White and Curt Flood, the baseball players (all three attended out of curiosity), and he had been seen in the company of Malcolm X (but so had Martin Luther King).

When the *Herald Tribune* decided to break the story of Clay's official connection with the Muslims, I tried to reach him by telephone half a dozen times for him to confirm or deny or withhold comment on the story. I left messages, explaining why I was calling, and I never heard from him. The story broke, and I heard from mutual acquaintances that Cassius was angry.

The first time I saw him after that — by then, he had adopted the name Muhammad Ali — he was cool, but the next time, in St. Louis, where he was addressing a Muslim group, he was as friendly as he had ever been. He quoted Allah, he paid tribute to the Honorable Elijah Muhammad, yet he still answered to the nickname "Cash." He even insulted me a few times, a sure sign that he was no longer angry.

He had been stripped of his heavyweight title, and he was fighting through the courts his conviction for refusing induction into the armed forces. I could see him changing, but it was never the words he mouthed that signified the change. His logic was often upside-down, his reasoning faulty, and yet, despite that, he had acquired a new dignity. The words didn't make any difference; the actions did. He had taken a dangerously costly step because of something he believed in. I might not share his belief or fathom the way he arrived at that belief, but still I had to respect the way he followed through on his beliefs, the way he refused to cry about what he was losing.

Yet it was during this period, when I sympathized with his stand, when I found that some segments of the sportswriting world were exhibiting more venom, more stupidity and more inaccuracies than I had thought even they were capable of, that Muhammad took the only step of his career I can really fault. He turned his back on Malcolm X.

I don't know the reasoning. I don't know why he chose Elijah Muhammad over Malcolm X in the dispute between the leader of the Muslims and his most prominent disciple. I can't, therefore, say flatly that he made the wrong choice, even though I believe he made the wrong choice; Malcolm was a gifted man, an articulate and compassionate man. But I can say that Muhammad showed, for the one time in his life, a totally brutal personal — away from the ring — side. It is brutal to turn on a friend without one word of explanation, without one word of regret, with only blind obedience to the whims of a leader. I have tried, since then, to bring up the subject of Malcolm X with Muhammad Ali several times, and, always, he has tuned out. His expressive face has turned blank. His enthusiasm has turned to dullness. Maybe he is embarrassed. He should be.

\*   \*   \*

During Muhammad's 43 months away from the ring, I bumped into him occasionally and found him still to be the only professional fighter who was personally both likable and exciting. (Floyd Patterson and Jose Torres, for example, are likable, but not often personally exciting; Ingemar Johansson was exciting.) At one point, David Merrick, the theatrical producer, professed an interest in sponsoring a legal battle to get Muhammad back his New York State boxing license; Merrick wanted to promote an Ali fight in New York for a worthy cause, which was not, in this case, David Merrick.

I arranged a meeting between the two, and Muhammad swept into Merrick's office and stopped, stunned by the decor, the entire room done in red-and-black. "Man," said Muhammad, "you got to be part-black to have a place like this. You sure you ain't black?"

It was the only time I ever saw David Merrick attempt to be charming.

The legal fight never materialized, not through Merrick, and Muhammad continued his road tour, speaking on college campuses, appearing in a short-lived Broadway play, serving as a drama critic, reviewing *The Great White Hope* for *Life*. One night, I accompanied him to a taping of *The Merv Griffin Show* — he was a regular on the talk-show circuit — and during the show, outlining his Muslim philosophy, he spoke of his belief in whites sticking with whites and blacks with blacks.

Afterward, as we emerged from the studio, he was engulfed by admirers, calling him "Champ" and pleading for his autograph. He stopped and signed and signed and signed, still soaking as happily in recognition as he had almost a decade earlier, and finally — because he was late for an appointment — I grabbed one arm and my wife grabbed the other and we tried to shepherd him away. He took about five steps and then looked at my wife and said, "Didn't you hear what I said about whites with whites and blacks with blacks?"

She dropped his arm and Muhammad laughed and danced away, like a man relishing a role.

In the fall of 1969, when the New York Mets finished their championship baseball season in Chicago, Muhammad and I and Tom Seaver had dinner one night at a quiet restaurant called the Red Carpet, a place that demanded a tie of every patron except the dethroned heavyweight champion.

The conversation was loud and animated, dominated by Muhammad as always, and about halfway through the meal, pausing for breath, he turned to Seaver and said, "Hey, you a nice fella. You a sportswriter?"

When we left the restaurant, we climbed into Muhammad's car, an Eldorado coupe, pink with white upholstery, with two telephones. Two telephones in a coupe! "C'mon, man," he said to Seaver. "Use the phone. Where's your wife? In New York? Well, call her up and say hello."

Seaver hesitated, and Muhammad said, "I'll place the call. What's your number?"

Seaver gave Muhammad the phone number, and Muhammad reached the mobile operator and placed the call, and when Nancy Seaver picked up the phone, she heard a deep voice boom. "This is the baddest cat in the world, and I'm with your husband and five hookers."

Nancy Seaver laughed. Her husband had told her he was having dinner with the champ.

Later, we returned to my hotel room, and after a few questions about his physical condition, Muhammad took off his suit jacket and his shirt and began shadow-boxing in front of a full-length mirror. For 15 straight minutes, he shadow-boxed, letting out "Whoosh, whoosh," the punches whistling, a dazzling display of footwork and stamina and sheer unbelievable speed, all the time telling Seaver his life story, his religious beliefs and his future plans.

"I never saw anything like that in my life," said Seaver afterward.

Neither had anyone else.

A few weeks later in the fall of 1969, Muhammad appeared as a guest on a sports-talk show, a show in which I served each week as sub-host and willing straight man for Joe Namath. For each show, we had one sports guest and one non-sports guest, and that week Muhammad was joined by George Segal, the actor.

After the interview with Muhammad, Joe and I began chatting with Segal, and the subject of nudity came up. Segal had just finished filming a nude or semi-nude scene with Barbra Streisand in *The Owl and the Pussycat*. As the conversation about nudity began, Muhammad visibly stiffened. "What's the matter?" Joe said. "How you feel about that, Muhammad?"

Muhammad's reaction was immediate. He was affronted and insulted. He was a minister, and he did not know that the show was going to deal with such blasphemy, and he was about to walk off the stage rather than join in, or even tolerate, such talk.

"Aw, c'mon," Joe said.

Muhammad sat uncomfortably through the remainder of the show, punctuating his distaste with winces and grimaces. It made for a very exciting show, and when it was over, Joe and I both sort of apologized to Muhammad for embarrassing him. "I gotta act like that," Muhammad explained. "You know, the FBI might be listening, or the CIA, or somebody like that."

He is now 29 years old. He has been a professional fighter for a full decade, and he has fought 31 times, and he has never been beaten.

On March 8, he faces Joe Frazier, who has also never been beaten, who is younger, who is considerably more single-minded. Logic is on Frazier's side. Reason is on Frazier's side.

But logic and reason have never been Muhammad Ali's strong suits. They were never Cassius Clay's either. His game always will be emotion and charm and vitality and showmanship.

Eight weeks before the night of the Frazier fight, the telephone rang in my bedroom late one night. I picked it up. "Hello," I said.

"The *champion* of the world," said the caller. "I'm back from the dead."

I hope so. The man-child should be the heavyweight champion of the world. It is the only role he was born to play.

1971

## Norman Mailer

......................................................................................

# Ego

FROM *Life*

IT IS THE GREAT WORD of the twentieth century. If there is a single word our century has added to the potentiality of language, it is ego. Everything we have done in this century, from monumental feats to nightmares of human destruction, has been a function of that extraordinary state of the psyche which gives us authority to declare we are sure of ourselves when we are not.

Muhammad Ali begins with the most unsettling ego of all. Having commanded the stage, he never pretends to step back and relinquish his place to other actors — like a six-foot parrot, he keeps screaming at you that he is the center of the stage. "Come here and get me, fool," he says. "You can't, 'cause you don't know who I am. You don't know *where* I am. I'm human intelligence and you don't even know if I'm good or evil." This has been his essential message to America all these years. It is intolerable to our American mentality that the figure who is probably most prominent to us after the president is simply not comprehensible, for he could be a demon or a saint. Or both! Richard Nixon, at least, appears comprehensible. We can hate him or we can vote for him, but at least we disagree with each other about him. What kills us about a.k.a. Cassius Clay is that the disagreement is inside us. He is *fascinating* — attraction and repulsion must be in the same package. So, he is obsessive. The more we don't want to think about him, the more we are obliged to. There is a reason for it. He is America's Greatest Ego. He is also, as I am going to try to show, the swiftest embodiment of human intelligence we have had yet, he is the very spirit of the twentieth century, he is the prince of mass man and the media. Now, perhaps temporarily, he is the fallen prince. But there still may be one holocaust of an urge to understand him, or try to, for obsession is a disease. Twenty little obsessions are twenty leeches on the mind, and one big obsession can become one big operation if we refuse to live with it. If Muhammad Ali defeats Frazier in the return bout, then he'll become the national obsession and we'll elect him president yet — you may indeed have to vote for any man who could defeat a fighter as great as Joe Frazier and still be Muhammad Ali. That's a great combination!

Yes, ego — that officious and sometimes efficient exercise of ignorance-as-authority — must be the central phenomenon of the twentieth century, even if patriotic Americans like to pretend it does not exist in their heroes. Which, of course, is part of the holy American horseball. The most monstrous exhibition of ego by a brave man in many a year was Alan Shepard's three whacks at a golf ball while standing on the moon. There, in a space suit, hardly able to stand, he put a club head on an omnipurpose tool shaft, and, restricted to swinging his one arm, dibbled his golf ball on the second try. On the third it went maybe half a mile — a nonphenomenal distance in the low gravitational field of the lunar sphere.

"What's so unpleasant about that?" asked a pleasant young jet-setter.

Aquarius, of the old book, loftily replied, "Would you take a golf ball into St. Patrick's and see how far you can hit it?"

The kid nodded his head. "Now that you put it that way, I guess I wouldn't, but I was excited when it happened. I said to my wife, 'Honey, we're playing golf on the moon.'"

Well, to the average fight fan, Cassius Clay has been golf on the moon. Who can comprehend the immensity of ego involved? Every fighter is in a whirligig with his ego. The fight game, for example, is filled with legends of fighters who found a girl in an elevator purposefully stalled between floors for two minutes on the afternoon of a main-event fight. Later, after he blew the fight, his irate manager blew his ears. "Were you crazy?" the manager asked. "Why did you do it?"

"Because," said the fighter, "I get these terrible headaches every afternoon, and only a chick who knows how, can relieve them."

Ego is driving a point through to a conclusion you are obliged to reach without knowing too much about the ground you cross between. You suffer for a larger point. Every good prizefighter must have a large ego, then, because he is trying to demolish a man he doesn't know too much about, he is unfeeling — which is the ground floor of ego; and he is full of techniques — which are the wings of ego. What separates the noble ego of the prizefighters from the lesser ego of authors is that the fighter goes through experiences in the ring which are occasionally immense, incommunicable except to fighters who have been as good, or to women who have gone through every minute of an anguish-filled birth, experiences which are finally mysterious. Like men who climb mountains, it is an exercise of ego which becomes something like soul — just as technology may have begun to have transcended itself when we reached to the moon. So, two great fighters in a great fight travel down subterranean rivers of exhaustion and cross mountain peaks of agony, stare at the light of their own death in the eye of the man they are fighting, travel into the crossroads of the most excruciating choice of karma as they get up from the floor against the appeal of the sweet swooning catacombs of oblivion — it is just that we do not see them this way, because they are not primarily men of words, and this is the century of words, numbers, and symbols. Enough.

We have come to the point. There are languages other than words, languages of symbol and languages of nature. There are languages of the body. And prizefighting is one of them. There is no attempting to comprehend a prizefighter unless we are willing to recognize that he speaks with a command of the body which is as detached, subtle, and comprehensive in its intelligence as any exercise of mind by such social engineers as Herman Kahn or Henry Kissinger. Of course, a man like Herman Kahn is by report gifted with a bulk of three hundred pounds. He does not move around with a light foot. So many a good average prizefighter, just a little punchy, does not speak with any particular éclat. That doesn't mean he is incapable of expressing himself with wit, style, and an esthetic flair for surprise when he boxes with his body, any more than Kahn's obesity would keep us from recognizing that his mind can work with strength. Boxing is a dialogue between bodies. Ignorant men, usually black, and next to illiterate, address one another in a set of *conversational* exchanges which go deep into the heart of each other's matter. It is just that they converse with their physiques. But unless you believe that you cannot receive a mortal wound from an incisive re-mark, you may be forced to accept the novel idea that men doing friendly boxing have a conversation on which they can often thrive. William Buckley and I in a discussion in a living room for an evening will score points on one another, but enjoy it. On television, where the stakes may be more, we may still both enjoy it. But put us in a debating hall with an argument to go on without cease for twenty-four hours, every encouragement present to humiliate each other, and months of preparation for such a debate hooplas and howlers of publicity, our tongues stuck out at one another on TV, and repercussions in Vietnam depending on which one of us should win, then add the fatigue of harsh lights, and a moderator who keeps interrupting us, and we are at the beginning of a conversation in which at least one of us will be hurt, and maybe both. Even hurt seriously. The example is picayune, however, in relation to the demands of a fifteen-round fight — perhaps we should have to debate nonstop for weeks under those conditions before one of us was carried away comatose. Now the example becomes clearer: Boxing is a rapid debate between two sets of intelligence. It takes place rapidly because it is conducted with the body rather than the mind. If this seems extreme, let us look for a connection. Picasso could never do arithmetic when he was young because the number seven looked to him like a nose upside down. So to learn arithmetic would slow him up. He was a future painter — his intelligence resided somewhere in the coordination of the body and the mind. He was not going to cut off his body from his mind by learning numbers. But most of us do. We have minds which work fairly well and bodies which sometimes don't. But if we are white and want to be comfortable we put our emphasis on learning to talk with the mind. Ghetto cultures, black, Puerto Rican, and Chicano cultures having less expectation of comfort tend to stick with the wit their bodies provide. They speak to each other with their bodies, they signal with their clothes. They talk with many a silent telepathic intelligence. And doubtless feel the frustration of being unable to express the subtleties of their states in words, just as the average middle-class white will feel unable to carry out his dreams of glory by the uses of his body. If black people are also beginning to speak our mixture of formal English and jargon-polluted American with real force, so white corporate America is getting more sexual and more athletic. Yet to begin to talk about Ali and Frazier, their psyches, their styles, their honor, their character, their greatness, and their flaws, we have to recognize that there is no way to comprehend them as men like ourselves — we can only guess at their insides by a real jump of our imagination into the science Ali invented — he was the first psychologist of the body.

Okay. There are fighters who are men's men. Rocky Marciano was one of them. Oscar Bonavena and Jerry Quarry and George Chuvalo and Gene Fullmer and Carmen Basilio, to name a few, have faces which would give a Marine sergeant pause in a bar fight. They look like they could take you out with the knob of bone they have left for a nose. They are all, incidentally, white fighters. They have a code — it is to fight until they are licked, and if they have to take a punch for every punch they give, well, they figure they can win. Their ego and their body intelligence are both connected to the same source of juice — it is male pride. They are substances close to rock. They work on clumsy skills to hone them finer, knowing if they can obtain parity, blow for blow with any opponent, they will win. They have more guts. Up to a far-gone point, pain is their pleasure, for their character in combat is their strength to trade pain for pain, loss of faculty for loss of faculty.

One can cite black fighters like them. Henry Hank and Rubin Carter, Emile Griffith and Benny Paret. Joe Frazier would be the best of them. But black fighters tend to be complex. They have veins of unsuspected strength and streaks when they feel as spooked as wild horses. Any fight promoter in the world knew he had a good fight if Fullmer went against Bailio, it was a proposition as certain as the wages for the week. But black fighters were artists, they were relatively moody, they were full of the surprises of Patterson or Liston, the virtuosities of Archie Moore and Sugar Ray, the speed, savagery, and curious lack of substance in Jimmy Ellis, the vertiginous neuroses of giants like Buster Mathis. Even Joe Louis, recognized by a majority in the years of his own championship as the greatest heavyweight of all time, was surprisingly inconsistent with minor fighters like Buddy Baer. Part of the unpredictability of their performances was due to the fact that all but Moore and Robinson were heavyweights. Indeed, white champions in the top division were equally out of form from fight to fight. It can, in fact, be said that heavyweights are always the most lunatic of prizefighters. The closer a heavyweight comes to the championship, the more natural it is for him to be a little bit insane, secretly insane, for the heavyweight champion of the world is either the toughest man in the world or he is not, but there is a real possibility he is. It is like being the big toe of God. You have nothing to measure yourself by. Lightweights, welterweights, middleweights can all be exceptionally good, fantastically talented — they are still very much in their place. The best lightweight in the world knows that an unranked middleweight can defeat him on most nights, and the best middleweight in the world will kill him every night. He knows that the biggest strongman in a tough bar could handle him by sitting on him, since the power to punch seems to increase quickly with weight. A fighter who weighs two-forty will punch more than twice as hard as a fighter who weighs one-twenty. The figures have no real basis, of course, they are only there to indicate the law of the ring: a good big man beats a good little man. So the notion of prizefighters as hardworking craftsmen is most likely to be true in the light and middle divisions.

Since they are fighters who know their limitations, they are likely to strive for excellence in their category. The better they get, the closer they have come to sanity, at least if we are ready to assume that the average fighter is a buried artist, which is to say a *body* artist with an extreme amount of violence in him. Obviously the better and more successful they get, the more they have been able to transmute violence into craft, discipline, even body art. That is human alchemy. We respect them and they deserve to be respected.

But the heavyweights never have such simple sanity. If they become champions they have to have inner lives like Hemingway or Dostoyevsky, Tolstoy or Faulkner, Joyce or Melville or Conrad or Lawrence or Proust. Hemingway is the example above all. Because he wished to be the greatest writer in the history of literature and still be a hero with all the body arts age would yet grant him, he was alone and he knew it. So are heavyweight champions alone. Dempsey was alone and Tunney could never explain himself and Sharkey could never believe himself nor Schmeling nor Braddock, and Carnera was sad and Baer an indecipherable clown; great heavyweights like Louis had the loneliness of the ages in their silence, and men like Marciano were mystified by a power which seemed to have been granted them. With the advent, however, of the great modern black heavyweights, Patterson, Liston, then Clay and Frazier, perhaps the loneliness gave way to what it had been protecting itself against — a surrealistic situation unstable beyond belief. Being a black heavyweight champion in the second half of the twentieth century (with black revolutions opening all over the world) was now not unlike being Jack Johnson, Malcolm X, and Frank Costello all in one. Going down the aisle and into the ring in Chicago was conceivably more frightening for Sonny Liston than facing Patterson that night — he was raw as uncoated wire with his sense of retribution awaiting him for years of prison pleasures and underworld jobs. Pools of paranoia must have reached him like different washes of color from different sides of the arena. He was a man who had barely learned to read and write — he had none of the impacted and mediocre misinformation of all the world of daily dull reading to clot the antenna of his senses — so he was keen to every hatred against him. He knew killers were waiting in that mob, they always were, he had been on speaking terms with just such subjects himself — now he dared to be king — any assassin could strike for his revenge upon acts Liston had long forgot; no wonder Liston was in fear going into the ring, and happier once within it.

And Patterson was exhausted before the fight began. Lonely as a monk for years, his daily gym work the stuff of his meditation, he was the first of the black fighters to be considered, then used, as a political force. He was one of the liberal elite, an Eleanor Roosevelt darling, he was political mileage for the NAACP. Violent, conceivably to the point of murder if he had not been a fighter, he was a gentleman in public, more, he was a man of the nicest, quietest, most private good manners. But monastic by inclination. Now, all but uneducated, he was appealed to by political blacks to win the Liston fight for the image of the Negro. Responsibility sat upon him like a comic cutback in a silent film where we return now and again to one poor man who has been left to hold a beam across his shoulders. There he stands, hardly able to move. At the end of the film he collapses. That was the weight put on Patterson. The responsibility to beat Liston was too great to bear. Patterson, a fighter of incorruptible honesty, was knocked out by punches hardly anybody saw. He fell in open air as if seized by a stroke. The age of surrealistic battles had begun. In the second fight with Liston, Patterson, obviously more afraid of a repetition of the first nightmare than anything else, simply charged his opponent with his hands low and was knocked down three times and out in the first round. The age of body psychology had begun and Clay was there to conceive it.

A kid as wild and dapper and jaybird as the president of a down-home college fraternity, bow tie, brown-and-white shoes, sweet, happy-go-lucky, *raucous*, he descended on Vegas for the second Patterson-Liston fight. He was like a beautiful boy surrounded by doting aunts. The classiest-looking middle-aged Negro ladies were always flanking him in Vegas as if to set up a female field of repulsion against any evil black magnetic forces in the offing. And from the sanctuary of his ability to move around crap tables like a kitten on the frisk, he taunted black majestic king-size Liston before the fight and after the fight. "You're so ugly," he would jeer, crap table safely between them, "that I don't know how you can get any uglier."

"Why don't you sit on my knee and I'll feed you your orange juice," Liston would rumble back.

"Don't insult me, or you'll be sorry. 'Cause you're just an ugly slow bear."

They would pretend to rush at one another. Smaller men would hold them back without effort. They were building the gate for the next fight. And Liston was secretly fond of Clay. He would chuckle when he talked about him. It was years since Liston had failed to knock out his opponent in the first round. His charisma was majestic with menace. One held one's breath when near him. He looked forward with obvious amusement to the happy seconds when he would take Clay apart and see the expression on that silly face. In Miami he trained for a three-round fight. In the famous fifth round when Clay came out with caustic in his eyes and could not see, he waved his gloves at Liston, a look of abject horror on his face, as if to say, "Your younger brother is now an old blind beggar. Do not strike him." And did it with a peculiar authority. For Clay looked like a ghost with his eyes closed, tears streaming, his extended gloves waving in front of him like a widow's entreaties. Liston drew back in doubt, in bewilderment, conceivably in concern for his new great reputation as an ex-bully; yes, Liston reached like a gentleman, and Clay was home free. His eyes watered out the caustic, his sight came back. He cut Liston up in the sixth. He left him beaten and exhausted. Liston did not stand up for the bell to the seventh. Maybe Clay had even defeated him earlier that day at the weigh-in when he had harangued and screamed and shouted and whistled and stuck his tongue out at Liston. The Champ had been bewildered. No one had been able ever to stare him in the eyes these last four years. Now a boy was screaming at him, a boy reported to belong to Black Muslims, no, stronger than that, a boy favored by Malcolm X who was braver by reputation than the brave, for he could stop a bullet any day. Liston, afraid only, as he put it, of crazy men, was afraid of the Muslims for he could not contend with their allegiance to one another in prison, their puritanism, their discipline, their martial ranks. The combination was too complex, too unfamiliar. Now, their boy, in a pain of terror or in a mania of courage, was screaming at him at the weigh-in. Liston sat down and shook his head, and looked at the press, now become his friend, and wound his fingers in circles around his ears, as if saying, Whitey to Whitey, "That black boy's nuts." So Clay made Liston Tom it, and when Liston missed the first jab he threw in the fight by a foot and a half, one knew the night would not be ordinary in the offing.

For their return bout in Boston, Liston trained as he had never before. Clay got a hernia. Liston trained hard. Hard training as a fighter grows older seems to speak of the dull deaths of the brightest cells in all the favorite organs; old fighters react to training like beautiful women to washing floors. But Liston did it twice, once for Clay's hernia, and again for their actual fight in Maine, and the second time he trained, he aged as a fighter, for he had a sparring partner, Amos Lincoln, who was one of the better heavyweights in the country. They had wars with one another every afternoon in the gym. By the day before the fight, Liston

was as relaxed and sleepy and dopey as a man in a steambath. He had
fought his heart out in training, had done it under constant pressure
from Clay who kept telling the world that Liston was old and slow and
could not possibly win. And their fight created a scandal, for Liston ran
into a short punch in the first round and was counted out, unable to
hear the count. The referee and timekeeper missed signals with one
another while Clay stood over fallen Liston screaming, "Get up and
fight!" It was no night for the fight game, and a tragedy for Clay since
he had trained for a long and arduous fight. He had developed his
technique for a major encounter with Liston and was left with a horde
of unanswered questions including the one he could never admit —
which was whether there had been the magic of a real knockout in his
punch or if Liston had made — for what variety of reasons! — a conscious decision to stay on the floor. It did him no good.

He had taken all the lessons of his curious life and the outrageously
deep comprehension he had of the motivations of his own people —
indeed, one could even approach the beginnings of a Psychology of the
Blacks by studying his encounters with fighters who were black — and
had elaborated that into a technique for boxing which was almost
without compare. A most cultivated technique. For he was no child of
the slums. His mother was a gracious pale-skinned lady, his father a
bitter wit pride-oriented on the family name of Clay — they were de-
scendants of Henry Clay, the orator, on the white side of the family,
nothing less, and Cassius began boxing at twelve in a police gym, and
from the beginning was a phenomenon of style and the absence of pain,
for he knew how to use his physical endowment. Tall, relatively light,
with an exceptionally long reach even for his size, he developed defensive skills which made the best use of his body. Working apparently on
the premise that there was something obscene about being hit, he boxed
with his head back and drew it further back when attacked, like a kid
who is shy of punches in a street fight, but because he had a waist which
was more supple than the average fighter's neck, he was able to box with
his arms low, surveying the fighter in front of him, avoiding punches by
the speed of his feet, the reflexes of his waist, the long spoiling deploy-
ment of his arms which were always tipping other fighters off balance.
Added to this was his psychological comprehension of the vanity and
confusion of other fighters. A man in the ring is a performer, as well as
a gladiator. Elaborating his technique from the age of twelve, Clay knew
how to work on the vanity of other performers, knew how to make

them feel ridiculous and so force them into crucial mistakes, knew how to set such a tone from the first round — later he was to know how to begin it a year before he would even meet the man. Clay knew that a fighter who had been put in psychological knots before he got near the ring had already lost half, three quarters, no, all of the fight could be lost before the first punch. That was the psychology of the body.

Now, add his curious ability as a puncher. He knew that the heaviest punches, systematically delivered, meant little. There are club fighters who look like armadillos and alligators — you can bounce punches off them forever and they never go down. You can break them down only if they are in a profound state of confusion, and the bombardment of another fighter's fists is never their confusion but their expectation. So Clay punched with a greater variety of mixed intensities than anyone around, he played with punches, was tender with them, laid them on as delicately as you put a postage stamp on an envelope, then cracked them in like a riding crop across your face, stuck a cruel jab like a baseball bat held head on into your mouth, next waltzed you in a clinch with a tender arm around your neck, winged away out of reach on flying legs, dug a hook with the full swing of a baseball bat hard into your ribs, hard pokes of a jab into the face, a mocking soft flurry of pillows and gloves, a mean forearm cutting you off from coming up on him, a cruel wrestling of your neck in a clinch, then elusive again, gloves snake-licking your face like a whip. By the time Clay had defeated Liston once and was training for the second fight, by the time Clay, now champion and renamed Muhammad Ali, and bigger, grown up quickly and not so mysteriously (after the potent ego soups and marrows of his trip through Muslim Africa) into a Black Prince, Potentate of his people, new Poombah of Polemic, yes, by this time, Clay — we will find it more natural to call him Ali from here on out (for the Prince will behave much like a young god) — yes, Muhammad Ali, Heavyweight Champion of the World, having come back with an amazing commitment to be leader of his people, proceeded to go into training for the second Liston fight with a commitment and then a genius of comprehension for the true intricacies of the Science of Sock. He alternated the best of sparring partners and the most ordinary, worked rounds of dazzling speed with Jimmy Ellis — later, of course, to be champion himself before Frazier knocked him out — rounds which displayed the high esthetic of boxing at its best, then lay against the ropes with other sparring partners, hands at his sides as if it were the eleventh or thirteenth round of an excruciating and exhausting fight with Liston where

Ali was now so tired he could not hold his hands up, could just manage to take punches to the stomach, rolling with them, smothering them with his stomach, absorbing them with backward moves, sliding along the ropes, steering his sparring partner with passive but off-setting moves of his limp arms. For a minute, for two minutes, the sparring partner — Shotgun Sheldon was his name — would bomb away on Ali's stomach much as if Liston were tearing him apart in later rounds, and Ali weaving languidly, sliding his neck for the occasional overhead punch to his face, bouncing from the rope into the punches, bouncing back away from the punches, as if his torso had become some huge boxing glove to absorb punishment, had penetrated through into some further conception of pain, as if pain were not pain if you accepted it with a relaxed heart, yes, Ali let himself be bombarded on the ropes by the powerful bull-like swings of Shotgun Sheldon, the expression of his face as remote, and as searching for the last routes into the nerves of each punch going in as a man hanging on a subway strap will search into the meaning of the market quotations he has just read on the activities of a curious stock. So Ali relaxed on the ropes and took punches to the belly with a faint disdain, as if, curious punches they did not go deep enough and after a minute of this, or two minutes, having offered his body like the hide of a drum for a mad drummer's solo, he would snap out of his communion with himself and flash a tattoo of light and slashing punches, mocking as the lights on water, he would dazzle his sparring partner, who, arm-weary and punched out, would look at him with eyes of love, complete was his admiration. And if people were ever going to cry watching a boxer in training, those were the moments, for Ali had the far-off concentration and disdain of an artist who simply cannot find anyone near enough or good enough to keep him and his art engaged, and all the while was perfecting the essence of his art, which was to make the other fighter fall secretly, helplessly, in love with him. Bundini, a special trainer, an alter ego with the same harsh, demoniac, witty, nonstop powers of oration as Ali himself — he even looked a little like Ali — used to weep openly as he watched the workouts.

Training session over, Ali would lecture the press, instruct them — looking beyond his Liston defense to what he would do to Patterson, mocking Patterson, calling him a rabbit, a white man's rabbit, knowing he was putting a new beam on Patterson's shoulders, an outrageously helpless and heavy beam of rage, fear, hopeless anger, and secret black admiration for the all-out force of Ali's effrontery. And in the next instant Ali would be charming as a movie star on the make speaking tenderly to a child. If he was Narcissus, so he was as well the play of mood in the water which served as mirror to Narcissus. It was as if he knew he had disposed of Patterson already, that the precise attack of calling him a rabbit would work on the weakest link — wherever it was — in Patterson's tense and tortured psyche and Patterson would crack, as indeed, unendurably for himself, he did, when their fight took place. Patterson's back gave way in the early rounds, and he fought twisted and in pain, half crippled like a man with a sacroiliac, for eleven brave and most miserable rounds before the referee would call it and Ali, breaking up with his first wife then, was unpleasant in the ring that night, his face ugly and contemptuous, himself well on the way to becoming America's most unpopular major American. That, too, was part of the art — to get a public to the point of hating him so much the burden on the other fighter approached the metaphysical — which is where Ali wanted it. White fighters with faces like rock embedded in cement would trade punch for punch. Ali liked to get the boxing where it belonged — he would trade metaphysic for metaphysic with anyone.

So he went on winning his fights and growing forever more unpopular. How he inflamed the temper of boxing's white establishment, for they were for the most part a gaggle of avuncular drunks and hard-bitten hacks who were ready to fight over every slime-slicked penny, and squared a few of their slippery crimes by getting fighters to show up semblance-of-sober at any available parish men's rally and charity church breakfast — "Everything I am I owe to boxing," the fighter would mumble through his dentures while elements of gin, garlic, and goddess-of-a-girlie from the night before came off in the bright morning fumes.

Ali had them psyched. He cut through moribund coruscated dirty business corridors, cut through cigar smoke and bushwah, hypocrisy and well-aimed kicks to the back of the neck, cut through crooked politicians and patriotic pus, cut like a laser, point of the point, light and impersonal, cut to the heart of the rottenest meat in boxing, and boxing was always the buried South Vietnam of America, buried for fifty years in our hide before we went there, yes, Ali cut through the flag-dragooned salutes of drunken dawns and said, "I got no fight with those Vietcongs," and they cut him down, thrust him into the three and a half years of his martyrdom. Where he grew. Grew to have a little fat around his middle and a little of the complacement muscle of the clam to his world-ego. And grew sharper in mind as well, and deepened and broadened physically. Looked no longer like a boy, but a sullen man, almost heavy, with the beginnings of a huge expanse across his shoulders. And developed the patience to survive, the wisdom to contemplate future nights in jail, grew to cultivate suspension of belief and the avoidance of disbelief — what a rack for a young man! As the years of hope for reinstatement, or avoidance of prison, came up and waned in him, Ali walked the tightrope between bitterness and apathy, and had enough left to beat Quarry and beat Bonavena, beat Quarry in the flurry of a missed hundred punches, ho! how his timing was off! beat him with a calculated whip, snake-like whip, to the corrugated sponge of dead flesh over Quarry's Irish eyes — they stopped it after the third on cuts — then knocked out Bonavena, the indestructible, never stopped before, by working the art of crazy mixing in the punches he threw at the rugged — some of the punches Ali threw that night would not have hurt a little boy — the punch he let go in the fifteenth came in like a wrecking ball from outer space. Bonavena went sprawling across the ring. He was a house coming down.

Yet it may have been the blow which would defeat him later. For Ali had been tired with Bonavena, lackluster, winded, sluggish, far ahead on points but in need of the most serious work if he were to beat Frazier. The punch in the last round was obliged, therefore, to inflame his belief that the forces of magic were his, there to be called upon when most in need, that the silent leagues of black support for his cause — since their cause was as his own — were like some cloak of midnight velvet, there to protect him by black blood, by black sense of tragedy, by the black consciousness that the guilt of the world had become the hinge of a door that they would open. So they would open the way to Frazier's chin, the blacks would open the aisle for his trip to the gods.

Therefore he did not train for Frazier as perhaps he had to. He worked, he ran three miles a day when he could have run five, he boxed some days and let a day and perhaps another day go, he was relaxed, he was confident, he basked in the undemanding winter sun of Miami, and skipped his rope in a gym crowded with fighters, stuffed now with working fighters looking to be seen, Ali comfortable and relaxed like the greatest of movie stars, he played a young fighter working out in a corner on the heavy bag — for of course every eye was on him — and afterward doing sit-ups in the back room and having his stomach rubbed with liniment, he would talk to reporters. He was filled with confidence there was no black fighter he did not comprehend to the root of the valve in the hard-pumping heart, and yes, Frazier, he assured everybody, would be easier than they realized. Like a little boy who had grown up to take on a mountain of responsibility he spoke in the deep relaxation of the wise, and teased two of the reporters who were present and fat. "You want to drink a lot of water," he said, "good cold water instead of all that liquor rot-your-gut," and gave the smile of a man who had been able to intoxicate himself on water (although he was, by re-pute, a fiend for soft drinks), "and fruit and good clean vegetables you want to eat and chicken and steak. You lose weight then," he advised out of kind secret smiling thoughts, and went on to talk of the impact of the fight upon the world. "Yes," he said, "you just think of a stadium with a million people, ten million people, you could get them all in to watch they would all pay to see it live, but then you think of the hundreds of millions and the billions who are going to see this fight, and if you could sit them all down in one place, and fly a jet plane over them, why that plane would have to fly for an hour before he would reach the end of all the people who will see this fight. It's the greatest event in the history of the world, and you take a man like Frazier, a good fighter, but a simple hardworking fellow, he's not built for this kind of pressure, the eyes," Ali said softly, "of that many people upon him. There's an experience to pressure which I have had, fighting a man like Liston in Miami the first time, which he has not. He will cave in under the pressure. No, I do not see any way a man like Frazier can whup me, he can't reach me, my arms are too long, and if he does get in and knock me down I'll never make the mistake of Quarry and Foster or Ellis of rushing back at him, I'll stay away until my head clears, then I begin to pop him again, pop! pop!" a few jabs, "no there is no way this man can beat me, this fight will be easier than you think."

There was one way in which boxing was still like a street fight and that was in the need to be confident you would win. A man walking out of a bar to fight with another man is seeking to compose his head into the confidence that he will certainly triumph — it is the most mysteri-ous faculty of the ego. For that confidence is a sedative against the pain of punches and yet is the sanction to punch your own best. The logic of the spirit would suggest that you win only if you deserve to win: the logic of the ego lays down the axiom that if you don't think you will win, you don't deserve to. And, in fact, usually don't; it is as if not believing you will win opens you to the guilt that perhaps you have not the right, you are too guilty.

So training camps are small factories for the production of one rare psychological item — an ego able to bear huge pain and administer drastic punishment. The flow of Ali's ego poured over the rock of every distraction, it was an ego like the flow of a river of constant energy fed by a hundred tributaries of black love and the love of the white left. The construction of the ego of Joe Frazier was of another variety. His manager, Yancey "Yank" Durham, a canny foxy light-skinned Negro with a dignified mien, a gray head of hair, gray mustache and a small but conservative worthy's paunch, plus the quick-witted look of eyes which could spot from a half mile away any man coming toward him with a criminal thought, was indeed the face of a consummate jeweler who had worked for years upon a diamond in the rough until he was now and at last a diamond, hard as the transmutation of black carbon from the black earth into the brilliant sky-blue shadow of the rarest shining rock. What a fighter was Frazier, what a diamond of an ego had he, and what a manager was Durham. Let us look.

Sooner or later, fight metaphors, like fight managers, go sentimental. They go military. But there is no choice here. Frazier was the human equivalent of a war machine. He had tremendous firepower. He had a great left hook, a left hook frightening even to watch when it missed, for it seemed to whistle; he had a powerful right. He could knock a man out with either hand — not all fighters can, not even very good fighters. Usually, however, he clubbed opponents to death, took a punch, gave a punch, took three punches, gave two, took a punch, gave a punch, high speed all the way, always working, pushing his body and arms, short for a heavyweight, up through the middle, bombing through on force, reminiscent of Jimmy Brown knocking down tacklers, Frazier kept on coming, hard and fast, a hang-in, hang-on, go-and-get him, got-him, got-him, slip and punch, take a punch, wing a punch, whap a punch, never was Frazier happier than with his heart up on the line against some other man's heart, let the bullets fly — his heart was there to stand up at the last. Sooner or later, the others almost all fell down. Undefeated like Ali, winner of twenty-three out of twenty-six fights by knockout, he was a human force, certainly the greatest heavyweight force to come along since Rocky Marciano. (If those two men had ever met, it would have been like two Mack trucks hitting each other head-on, then backing up to hit each other again — they would have kept it up until the wheels were off the axles and the engines off the chassis.) But this would be a different kind of fight. Ali would run, Ali would keep hitting Frazier with long jabs, quick hooks and rights while backing up, staying out of reach unless Frazier could take the punishment and get in. That was where the military problem began. For getting in against the punishment he would take was a question of morale, and there was a unique situation in this fight — Frazier had become the white man's fighter, Mr. Charley was rooting for Frazier, and that meant blacks were boycotting him in their heart. That could be poison to Frazier's morale, for he was twice as black as Clay and half as handsome, he had the rugged decent life-worked face of a man who had labored in the pits all his life, he looked like the deserving modest son of one of those Negro cleaning women of a bygone age who worked from six in the morning to midnight every day, raised a family, endured and occasionally elicited the exasperated admiration of white ladies who would kindly remark, "That woman deserves something better in her life." Frazier had the mien of the son, one of many, of such a woman, and he was the hardest-working fighter in training many a man had ever seen, he was conceivably the hardest-working man alive in the world, and as he went through his regimen, first boxing four rounds with a sparring partner, Kenny Norton, a talented heavyweight from the Coast with an almost unbeaten record, then working on the heavy bag, then the light bag, then skipping rope, ten to twelve rounds of sparring and exercise on a light day, Frazier went on with the doggedness, the concentration, and the pumped-up fury of a man who has had so little in his life that he can endure torments to get everything, he pushed the total of his energy and force into an absolute abstract exercise of will so it did not matter if he fought a sparring partner or the heavy bag, he lunged at each equally as if the exhaustion of his own heart and the clangor of his lungs were his only enemies, and the head of a fighter or the leather of the bag as it rolled against his own head was nothing but some abstract thunk of material, not a thing, not a man, but thunk! thunk! something of an obstacle, thunk! thunk! thunk! to beat into thunk! oblivion. And his breath came in rips and sobs as he smashed into the bag as if it were real, just that heavy big torso-sized bag hanging from its chain but he attacked it as if it were a bear, as if it were a great fighter and they were in the mortal embrace of a killing set of exchanges of punches in the middle of the eighth round, and rounds of exercise later, skipping rope to an inhumanly fast beat for this late round in the training day, sweat pouring like jets of blood from an artery, he kept swinging his rope, muttering, "Two-million-dollars-and-change, two-million-dollars-and-change," railroad train chugging into the terminals of exhaustion. And it was obvious that Durham, jeweler to his diamond, was working to make the fight as abstract as he could for Frazier, to keep Clay out of it — for they would not call him Ali in their camp — yes, Frazier was fortifying his ego by depersonalizing his opponent, Clay was, thunk! the heavy bag, thunk! and thunk! — Frazier was looking to get no messages from that cavern of velvet when black people sent their good wishes to Ali at midnight, no, Frazier would insulate himself with prodigies of work, hardest-working man in the hell-hole of the world, and on and on he drove himself into the depressions each day of killing daily exhaustion.

That was one half of the strategy to isolate Frazier from Ali, hard work and thinking of thunking on inanimate Clay; the other half was up to Durham who was running front relations with the blacks of North Philly who wandered into the gym, paid their dollar, and were ready to heckle on Frazier. In the four rounds he boxed with Norton, Frazier did not look too good for a while. It was ten days before the fight and he was in a bad mood when he came in, for the word was through the gym that they had discovered one of his favorite sparring partners, just fired that morning, was a Black Muslim and had been calling Ali every night with reports, that was the rumor, and Frazier, sullen and cold at the start, was bopped and tapped, then walloped by Norton moving fast with the big training gloves in imitation of Ali, and Frazier looked very easy to hit until the middle of the third round when Norton, proud of his something like twenty wins and one loss, beginning to get some ideas himself about how to fight champions, came driving in to mix it with Frazier, have it out man to man and caught a right which dropped him, left him looking limp with that half-silly smile sparring partners get when they have been hit too hard to justify any experience or any money they are going to take away. Up till then the crowd had been with Norton. There at one end of the Cloverlay gym, a street-level storefront room which could have been used originally by an automobile dealer, there on that empty, immaculate Lysol-soaked floor, designed when Frazier was there for only Frazier and his partners to train (as opposed to Miami where Ali would rub elbows with the people) here the people were at one end, the end off the street, and they jeered whenever Norton hit Frazier, they laughed when Norton made him look silly, they called out, "Drop the mother," until Durham held up a gentlemanly but admonishing finger in request for silence. Afterward, however, training completed, Durham approached them to answer questions, rolled with their sallies, jived the people back, subtly enlisted their sympathy for Frazier by saying,

"When I fight Clay, I'm going to get him somewhere in the middle rounds," until the blacks quipping back said angrily, "You ain't fighting him, Frazier is."

"Why you call him Clay?" another asked. "He Ali."

"His name is Cassius Clay to me," said Durham.

"What you say against his religion?"

"I don't say nothing about his religion and he doesn't say anything about mine. I'm a Baptist."

"You going to make money on this?"

"Of course," said Durham, "I got to make money. You don't think I work up this sweat for nothing."

They loved him. He was happy with them. A short fat man in a purple suit wearing his revival of the wide-brim bebop hat said to Durham, "Why don't you get Norton to manage? He was beating up on *your* fighter," and the fat man cackled for he had scored and could elaborate the tale for his ladies later how he had put down Yank, who was working the daily rite on the edge of the black street for his fighter, while upstairs, dressed, and sucking an orange, sweat still pouring, gloom of excessive fatigue upon him, Frazier was sitting through his two-hundredth or two-thousandth interview for this fight, reluctant indeed to give it at all. "Some get it some don't," he had said for refusal, but relented when a white friend who had done roadwork with him interceded, so he sat there now against a leather sofa, dark blue suit, dark T-shirt, mopping his brow with a pink-red towel, and spoke dispiritedly of being ready too early for the fight. He was waking up an hour too early for roadwork each morning now. "I'd go back to sleep but it doesn't feel good when I do run."

"I guess the air is better that hour of the morning."

He nodded sadly. "There's a limit to how good the air in Philly can get."

"Where'd you begin to sing?" was a question asked.

"I sang in church first," he replied, but it was not the day to talk about singing. The loneliness of hitting the bag still seemed upon him as if in his exhaustion now, and in the thoughts of that small insomnia which woke him an hour too early every day was something of the loneliness of all blacks who work very hard and are isolated from fun and must wonder in the just-awakened night how large and pervasive was the curse of a people. "The countdown's begun," said Frazier, "I get impatient about now."

*   *   *

For the fight, Ali was wearing red velvet trunks, Frazier had green. Before they began, even before they were called together by the referee for instructions, Ali went dancing around the ring and glided past Frazier with a sweet little-boy smile, as if to say, "You're my new playmate. We're going to have fun." Ali was laughing. Frazier was having nothing of this and turned his neck to embargo him away. Ali, having alerted the crowd by this first big move, came prancing in again. When Frazier looked ready to block him, Ali went around, evading a contact, gave another sweet smile, shook his head at the lack of high spirit. "Poor Frazier," he seemed to say.

At the weigh-in early that afternoon Ali looked physically resplendent; the night before in Harlem, crowds had cheered him; he was coming to claim his victory on the confluence of two mighty tides — he was the mightiest victim of injustice in America and he was also — the twentieth century was nothing if not a tangle of opposition — he was also the mightiest narcissist in the land. Every beard, dropout, homosexual, junkie, freak, swinger, and plain simple individualist adored him. Every pedantic liberal soul who had once loved Patterson now paid homage to Ali. The mightiest of the black psyches and the most filigreed of the white psyches were ready to roar him home, as well as every family-loving hardworking square American who genuinely hated the war in Vietnam. What a tangle of ribbons he carried on his lance, enough cross purposes to be the knight-resplendent of television, the fell hero of the medium, and he had a look of unique happiness on television when presenting his program for the course of the fight, and his inevitable victory. He would be as content then as an infant splashing the waters of the bathinette. If he was at once a saint and a monster to any mind which looked for category, any mind unwilling to encounter the thoroughly dread-filled fact that the twentieth century breed of man now in birth might be no longer half good and half evil — generous and greedy by turns — but a mutation with Cassius Muhammad for the first son — then that mind was not ready to think about Twentieth Century Man. (And indeed Muhammad Ali had twin poodles he called Angle and Demon.) So now the ambiguity of his presence filled the Garden before the fight was fairly begun, it was as if he had announced to that plural billion-footed crowd assembled under the shadow of the jet which would fly over them that the first enigma of the fight would be the way he would win it, that he would initiate his triumph by getting the crowd to laugh at Frazier, yes, first premise tonight was that the poor black man in Frazier's soul would go berserk if made a figure of roll-off-your-seat amusement.

The referee gave his instructions. The bell rang. The first fifteen seconds of a fight can be the fight. It is equivalent to the first kiss in a love affair. The fighters each missed the other. Ali blocked Frazier's first punches easily, but Ali then missed Frazier's head. That head was bobbing as fast as a third fist. Frazier would come rushing in, head moving like a fist, fists bobbing too, his head working above and below his forearm, he was trying to get through Ali's jab, get through fast and sear Ali early with the terror of a long fight and punches harder than he had ever taken to the stomach, and Ali in turn, backing up, and throwing fast punches, aimed just a trifle, and was therefore a trifle too slow, but it was obvious. Ali was trying to shiver Frazier's synapses from the start, set waves of depression stirring which would reach his heart in later rounds and make him slow, deaden nerve, deaden nerve went Ali's jab flicking a snake tongue, whoo-eet! whoo-eet! but Frazier's head was bobbing too fast, he was moving faster than he had ever moved before in that bobbing nonstop never-a-backward step of his, slogging and bouncing forward, that huge left hook flaunting the air with the confidence it was enough of a club to split a tree, and Ali, having missed his jabs, stepped nimbly inside the hook and wrestled Frazier in the clinch. Ali looked stronger here. So by the first forty-five seconds of the fight, each had surprised the other profoundly. Frazier was fast enough to slip through Ali's punches, and Ali was strong enough to handle him in the clinches. A pattern had begun. Because Ali was missing often, Frazier was in under his shots like a police dog's muzzle on your arm, Ali could not slide from side to side, he was boxed in, then obliged to go backward, and would end on the ropes again and again with Frazier belaboring him. Yet Frazier could not reach him. Like a prestidigitator Ali would tie the other's punches into odd knots, not even blocking them yet on his elbows or his arms, rather throwing his own punches as defensive moves, for even as they missed, he would brush Frazier to the side with his forearm, or hold him off, or clinch and wrestle a little of the will out of Frazier's neck. Once or twice in the round a long left hook by Frazier just touched the surface of Ali's chin, and Ali waved his head in placid contempt to the billions watching as if to say, "This man has not been able to hurt me at all."

The first round set a pattern for the fight. Ali won it and would win the next. His jab was landing from time to time and rights and lefts of no great consequence. Frazier was hardly reaching him at all. Yet it looked like Frazier had established that he was fast enough to get in on Ali and so drive him to the ropes and to the corners, and that spoke of a fight which would be determined by the man in better condition, in better physical condition rather than in perfect psychic condition, the kind of fight Ali could hardly want for his strength was in his pauses, his nature passed along the curve of every dialectic, he liked, in short, to fight in flurries, and then move out, move away, assess, take his time, fight again. Frazier would not let him. Frazier moved in with the snarl of a wolf, his teeth seemed to show through his mouthpiece, he made Ali work. Ali won the first two rounds but it was obvious he could not continue to win if he had to work all the way. And in the third round Frazier began to get to him, caught Ali with a powerful blow to the face at the bell. That was the first moment where it was clear to all that Frazier had won a round. Then he won the next. Ali looked tired and a little depressed. He was moving less and less and calling upon a skill not seen since the fight with Chuvalo when he had showed his old ability, worked on all those years ago with Shotgun Sheldon, to lie on the ropes and take a beating to the stomach. He had exhausted Chuvalo by welcoming attacks on the stomach but Frazier was too incommensurable a force to allow such total attack. So Ali lay on the ropes and wrestled him off, and moved his arms and waist, blocking punches, slipping punches, countering with punches — it began to look as if the fight would be written on the ropes, but Ali was getting very tired. At the beginning of the fifth round, he got up slowly from his stool, very slowly. Frazier was beginning to feel that the fight was his. He moved in on Ali jeering, his hands at his side in mimicry of Ali, a street fighter mocking his opponent, and Ali tapped him with long light jabs to which Frazier stuck out his mouthpiece, a jeer of derision as if to suggest that the mouthpiece was all Ali would reach all night.

There is an extortion of the will beyond any of our measure in the exhaustion which comes upon a fighter in early rounds when he is already too tired to lift his arms or take advantage of openings there before him, yet the fight is not a third over, there are all those rounds to go, contractions of torture, the lungs screaming into the dungeons of the soul, washing the throat with a hot bile that once belonged to the liver, the legs are going dead, the arms move but their motion is limp, one is straining into another will, breathing into the breath of another will as agonized as one's own. As the fight moved through the fifth, the sixth and the seventh, then into the eighth, it was obvious that Ali was into the longest night of his career, and yet with that skill, that research into the pits of every miserable contingency in boxing, he came up with odd somnambulistic variations, holding Frazier off, riding around Frazier with his arm about his neck, almost entreating Frazier with his arms extended, and Frazier leaning on him, each of them slowed to a pit-a-pat of light punches back and forth until one of them was goaded up from exhaustion to whip and stick, then hook and hammer and into the belly and out, and out of the clinch and both looking exhausted, and then Frazier, mouth bared again like a wolf, going in and Ali waltzing him, tying him, tapping him lightly as if he were a speed bag, just little flicks, until Frazier, like an exhausted horse finally feeling the crop, would push up into a trot and try to run up the hill. It was indeed as if they were both running up a hill. As if Frazier's offensive was so great and so great was Ali's defense that the fight could only be decided by who could take the steepest pitch of the hill. So Frazier, driving, driving, trying to drive the heart out of Ali, put the pitch of that hill up and up until they were ascending an unendurable slope. And moved like somnambulists slowly working and rubbing one another, almost embracing, next to locked in the slow moves of lovers after the act until, reaching into the stores of energy reaching them from cells never before so used, one man or the other would work up a contractive spasm of skills and throw punches at the other in the straining slow-motion hypnosis of a deepening act. And so the first eight rounds went by. The two judges scored six for Frazier, two for Ali. The referee had it even. Some of the press had Ali ahead — it was not easy to score. For if it were an alley fight, Frazier would win. Clay was by now hardly more than the heavy bag to Frazier. Frazier was dealing with a man, not a demon. He was not respectful of that man. But still! It was Ali who was landing the majority of punches. They were light, they were usually weary, but some had snap, some were quick, he was landing two punches to Frazier's one. Yet Frazier's were hardest. And Ali often looked as tender as if he were making love. It was as if he could now feel the whole absence of that real second fight with Liston, that fight for which he had trained so long and so hard, the fight which might have rolled over his laurels from the greatest artist of pugilism to the greatest brawler of them all — maybe he had been prepared on that night to beat Liston at his own, be more of a slugger, more of a man crude to crude than Liston. Yes, Ali had never been a street fighter and never a whorehouse knock-it-down stud, no, it was more as if a man with the exquisite reflexes of Nureyev had learned to throw a knockout punch with either hand and so had become champion of the world without knowing if he was the man of all men or the most delicate with special privilege endowed by God. Now with Frazier, he was in a sweat bath (a mudpile, a knee, elbow, and death-thumping chute of a pit) having in this late year the fight he had sorely needed for his true greatness as a fighter six and seven years ago, and so whether ahead, behind or even, terror sat in the rooting instinct of all those who were for Ali for it was obviously Frazier's fight to win, and what if Ali, weaknesses of character now flickering to the surface in a hundred little moves, should enter the valve of prizefighting's deepest humiliation, should fall out half conscious on the floor and not want to get up. What a death to his followers.

The ninth began. Frazier mounted his largest body attack of the night. It was preparations-for-Liston-with-Shotgun-Sheldon, it was the virtuosity of the gym all over again, and Ali, like a catcher handling a fast-ball pitcher, took Frazier's punches, one steamer, another steamer, wing! went a screamer, a steamer, warded them, blocked them, slithered them, winced from them, absorbed them, took them in and blew them out and came off the ropes and was Ali the Magnificent for the next minute and thirty seconds. The fight turned. The troops of Ali's second corps of energy had arrived, the energy for which he had been waiting long agonizing heartsore vomit-mean rounds. Now he jabbed Frazier, he snake-licked his face with jabs faster than he had thrown before, he anticipated each attempt of Frazier at counterattack and threw it back, he danced on his toes for the first time in rounds, he popped in rights, he hurt him with hooks, it was his biggest round of the night, it was the best round yet of the fight, and Frazier full of energy and hordes of sudden punishment was beginning to move into that odd petulant concentration on other rituals besides the punches, tappings of the gloves, stares of the eye, that species of mouthpiece-chewing which is the prelude to fun-strut in the knees, then Queer Street, then waggle on out, drop like a steer.

It looked like Ali had turned the fight, looked more like the same in the tenth, now reporters were writing another story in their minds where Ali was not the magical untried Prince who had come apart under the first real pressure of his life but was rather the greatest Heavyweight Champion of all time for he had weathered the purgatory of Joe Frazier.

But in the eleventh, that story also broke. Frazier caught him, caught him again and again, and Ali was near to knocked out and swayed and slid on Queer Street himself, then spent the rest of the eleventh and the longest round of the twelfth working another bottom of hell, holding off Frazier who came on and on, sobbing, wild, a wild honor of a beast, man of will reduced to the common denominator of the will of all of us back in that land of the animal where the idea of man as a tool-wielding beast was first conceived. Frazier looked to get Ali forever in the eleventh and the twelfth, and Ali, his legs slapped and slashed on the thighs between each round by Angelo Dundee, came out for the thirteenth and incredibly was dancing. Everybody's story switched again. For if Ali won this round, the fourteenth and the fifteenth, who could know if he could not win the fight? . . . He won the first half of the thirteenth, then spent the second half on the ropes with Frazier. They were now like crazy death-march-maddened mateys coming up the hill and on to home, and yet Ali won the fourteenth, Ali looked good, he came out dancing for the fifteenth, while Frazier, his own armies of energy finally caught up, his courage ready to spit into the eye of any devil black or white who would steal the work of his life, had equal madness to steal the bolt from Ali. So Frazier reached out to snatch the magic punch from the air, the punch with which Ali topped Bonavena, and found it and thunked Ali a hell and hit Ali a heaven of a shot which dumped Muhammad into 50,000 newspaper photographs — Ali on the floor! Great Ali on the floor was out there flat singing to the sirens in the mistiest fogs of Queer Street (same look of death and widowhood on his far-gone face as one had seen in the fifth blind round with Liston) yet Ali got up, Ali came sliding through the last two minutes and thirty-five seconds of this heathen holocaust in some last exercise of the will, some iron fundament of the ego not to be knocked out, and it was then as if the spirit of Harlem finally spoke and came to rescue and the ghosts of the dead in Vietnam, something held him up before arm-weary triumphant near-crazy Frazier who had just hit him the hardest punch ever thrown in his life and they went down to the last few seconds of a great fight, Ali still standing and Frazier had won.

The world was talking instantly of a rematch. For Ali had shown America what we all had hoped was secretly true. He was a man. He could bear moral and physical torture and he could stand. And if he could beat Frazier in the rematch we would have at last a national hero who was hero of the world as well, and who could bear to wait for the next fight? Joe Frazier, still the champion, and a great champion, said to the press, "Fellows, have a heart — I got to live a little. I've been working for ten long years." And Ali, through the agency of alter-ego Bundini, said — for Ali was now in the hospital to check on the possible fracture of a jaw — Ali was reported to have said, "Get the gun ready — we're going to set traps." Oh, wow. Could America wait for something so great as the Second Ali-Frazier?

1974

## Jim Murray

....................................................................................................

# Weird Site for a Fight

FROM *The Los Angeles Times*

EN ROUTE TO DARKEST AFRICA — All right, my good man, hand me my jodhpurs and pith helmet and polish my monocle. Get the elephant ready. Fire up the African Queen. Phone Berlitz and see what they have in the way of Swahili. Get Tarzan and Jane on the drum and see what they're doing Tuesday. See what you can find out about the tsetse fly. Call me Bwana. Let's hope Grace Kelly and Ava Gardner get to fight over me in the steaming jungle night.

They're holding the world heavyweight championship fight in the Congo, I guess because the top of Mt. Everest was busy. I don't know why they can't hold it in Yankee Stadium like everybody else. The only African word I know is "Cheetah." I always thought "Kinshasa" was one of the Gabor sisters. "Zaire" sounds like an NFL placekicker.

It took the Mann Act to run the Jack Johnson–Jess Willard fight to Havana. It took the governor of California, taken down with an attack of high-minded morality, to run the Johnson-Jeffries fight to Reno.

They have fought on barges, in Mississippi swamps. They ran the Muhammad Ali–Sonny Liston bout clear up to Lewiston, Maine, before they found somebody who wouldn't padlock it. But nobody ever thought of the equator before.

Dempsey and Gibbons fought in Shelby, Montana, because the state solons wanted to put Shelby on the map. When Dempsey's manager got through with it, they had put it off the map. Dempsey was the first fighter in history to knock out seven banks in one fight.

But, ordinarily, promoters from Tex Rickard to Mike Jacobs preferred to keep the thing on a subway . . . until lately when the "Have Fight, Will Travel" syndrome cropped up. George Foreman won his title in Jamaica, defended it in Tokyo and Venezuela. Ali picks Madison Square Garden only after he has exhausted all the other romantic places on the globe — like Frankfurt, Zurich, Houston, Lewiston and Las Vegas.

Here, perhaps, is a chance to top Dempsey, to break a country. Except that Swiss banks are putting up the line of credit and American pay-TV is almost sure to sell out — at $25 a seat tops.

For those with a stake in the Congo, it is viewed as a chance to prove it is not the 17th-century happy hunting ground of the gorilla, the tsetse fly, and asp, pygmy blowgun and purple people-eaters of the *Trader Horn* and *Africa Speaks* movies; not the Ernest Hemingway country where the hyenas prowl the expedition tents by night and the vultures circle by day and the jungle drums in the soundtrack mean that 8-foot warriors with rings through their noses and stone spears are coming.

It is a dark and bloody ground like Boone's Kentucky. Before the blood was off the walls, the UN, Kasavubu, Tshombe, Lumumba and Mobutu had warred over the land when they threw the Belgians out. Dag Hammerskjold died there.

It is worth fighting over. Tin and gold, copper and diamonds are found there. Madame Curie got her radium there. Pythons, tree cobras, puff adders, tigerfish, electric eels, gorillas, elephants, hippopotamus, rhinoceros, leopards and the dreaded tsetse are also found there. Dr. Livingstone, I presume, was found there.

It is a 200-tribe complex which lay comfortably in the Stone Age until the white man began the search for the headwaters of the Nile. The elephants' graveyard, theme of many Edgar Rice Burroughs ape-man movies, lies there.

It is an audacious idea, a heavyweight title bout in the shadow of the Ruwenzori. For ink-stained wretches, more used to the dark interior of Madison Square Garden whose only knowledge of Africa comes from reading *The Short Happy Life of Francis Macomber,* the experience may be unsettling enough so that many will never return and be found unshaven and delirious wandering the brush looking for the Eighth Avenue subway or Robinson Crusoe.

The fight will be held at the witching hour of 3:30 A.M., a time zone for millions of spontaneous fights over the years but never one contracted beforehand. Usually you have to steal someone's girl or drink to get in a fight at that hour. These guys are only going to steal $5 million apiece. This will be the first fight at that hour where the principals wore gloves.

Well, if you're sure Clyde Beatty and Cecil Rhodes and Martin and Osa Johnson got their start this way, hand me my quinine and I'll unlock the secrets of the Dark Continent — like, do they use the 5-point must system of scoring there? Do you stop a fight because of malaria? What language is the count in? Arthur Brisbane once said of a title fight, "A gorilla could lick both of them." Unless they post guards at the gate at Kinshasa, we may find out.

1975

## Mark Kram

....................................................................................................................

# "Lawdy, Lawdy, He's Great"

FROM *Sports Illustrated*

IT WAS only a moment, sliding past the eyes like the sudden shifting of light and shadow, but long years from now it will remain a pure and moving glimpse of hard reality, and if Muhammad Ali could have turned his eyes upon himself, what first and final truth would he have seen? He had been led up the winding, red-carpeted staircase by Imelda Marcos, the First Lady of the Philippines, as the guest of honor at the Malacañang Palace. Soft music drifted in from the terrace as the beautiful Imelda guided the massive and still heavyweight champion of the world to the long buffet ornamented by huge candelabra. The two whispered, and then she stopped and filled his plate, and as he waited the candles threw an eerie light across the face of a man who only a few hours before had survived the ultimate inquisition of himself and his art.

The maddest of existentialists, one of the great surrealists of our time, the king of all he sees, Ali had never before appeared so vulnerable and fragile, so pitiably unmajestic, so far from the universe he claims as his alone. He could barely hold his fork, and he lifted the food slowly up to his bottom lip, which had been scraped pink. The skin on his face was dull and blotched, his eyes drained of that familiar childlike wonder. His right eye was a deep purple, beginning to close, a dark blind being drawn against a harsh light. He chewed his food painfully, and then he suddenly moved away from the candles as if he had become aware of the mask he was wearing, as if an inner voice were laughing at him. He shrugged, and the moment was gone.

A couple of miles away in the bedroom of a villa, the man who has always demanded answers of Ali, has trailed the champion like a timber wolf, lay in semi-darkness. Only his heavy breathing disturbed the quiet as an old friend walked to within two feet of him. "Who is it?" asked Joe Frazier, lifting himself to look around. "Who is it? I can't see! I can't see! Turn the lights on!" Another light was turned on, but Frazier still could not see. The scene cannot be forgotten; this good and gallant man lying there, embodying the remains of a will never before seen in a ring, a will that had carried him so far — and now surely too far. His eyes were only slits, his face looked as if it had been painted by Goya. "Man, I hit him with punches that'd bring down the walls of a city," said Frazier. "Lawdy, Lawdy, he's a great champion." Then he put his head back down on the pillow, and soon there was only the heavy breathing of a deep sleep slapping like big waves against the silence.

Time may well erode that long morning of drama in Manila, but for anyone who was there those faces will return again and again to evoke what it was like when two of the greatest heavyweights of any era met for a third time, and left millions limp around the world. Muhammad Ali caught the way it was: "It was like death. Closest thing to dyin' that I know of."

Ali's version of death began about 10:45 a.m. on Oct. 1 in Manila. Up to then his attitude had been almost frivolous. He would simply not accept Joe Frazier as a man or as a fighter, despite the bitter lesson Frazier had given him in their first savage meeting. Esthetics govern all of Ali's actions and conclusions; the way a man looks, the way he moves is what interests Ali. By Ali's standards, Frazier was not pretty as a man and without semblance of style as a fighter. Frazier was an affront to beauty, to Ali's own beauty as well as to his precious concept of how a good fighter should move. Ali did not hate Frazier, but he viewed him with the contempt of a man who cannot bear anything short of physical and professional perfection.

Right up until the bell rang for Round One, Ali was dead certain that Frazier was through, was convinced that he was no more than a shell, that too many punches to the head had left Frazier only one more solid shot removed from a tin cup and some pencils. "What kind of man can take all those punches to the head?" he asked himself over and over. He could never come up with an answer. Eventually he dismissed Frazier as the embodiment of animal stupidity. Before the bell Ali was subdued in his corner, often looking down to his manager, Herbert Muhammad, and conversing aimlessly. Once, seeing a bottle of mineral water in front of Herbert, he said, "Watcha got there, Herbert? Gin! You don't need any of that. Just another day's work. I'm gonna put a whuppin' on this nigger's head."

Across the ring Joe Frazier was wearing trunks that seemed to have been cut from a farmer's overalls. He was darkly tense, bobbing up and down as if trying to start a cold motor inside himself. Hatred had never been a part of him, but words like "gorilla," "ugly," "ignorant" — all the cruelty of Ali's endless vilifications — had finally bitten deeply into his soul. He was there not seeking victory alone; he wanted to take Ali's heart out and then crush it slowly in his hands. One thought of the moment days before, when Ali and Frazier with their handlers between them were walking out of the Malacañang Palace, and Frazier said to Ali, leaning over and measuring each word, "I'm gonna whup your half-breed ass."

By packed and malodorous Jeepneys, by small and tinny taxis, by limousine and by worn-out bikes, 28,000 had made their way into the Philippine Coliseum. The morning sun beat down, and the South China Sea brought not a whisper of wind. The streets of the city emptied as the bout came on public television. At ringside, even though the arena was air-conditioned, the heat wrapped around the body like a heavy wet rope. By now, President Ferdinand Marcos, a small brown derringer of a man, and Imelda, beautiful and cool as if she were relaxed on a palace balcony taking tea, had been seated.

True to his plan, arrogant and contemptuous of an opponent's worth as never before, Ali opened the fight flat-footed in the center of the ring, his hands whipping out and back like the pistons of an enormous and magnificent engine. Much broader than he has ever been, the look of swift destruction defined by his every move, Ali seemed indestructible. Once, so long ago, he had been a splendidly plumed bird who wrote on the wind a singular kind of poetry of the body, but now he was down to earth, brought down by the changing shape of his body, by a sense of his own vulnerability, and by the years of excess. Dancing was for a ball-room; the ugly hunt was on. Head up and unprotected, Frazier stayed in the mouth of the cannon, and the big gun roared again and again.

Frazier's legs buckled two or three times in that first round, and in the second he took more lashing as Ali loaded on him all the meanness that he could find in himself. "He won't call you Clay no more," Bundini Brown, the spirit man, cried hoarsely from the corner. To Bundini, the fight would be a question of where fear first registered, but there was no fear in Frazier. In the third round Frazier was shaken twice, and looked as if he might go at any second as his head jerked up toward the hot lights and the sweat flew off his face. Ali hit Frazier at will, and when he chose to do otherwise he stuck his long left arm in Frazier's face. Ali would not be holding in this bout as he had in the second. The referee, a brisk workman, was not going to tolerate clinching. If he needed to buy time, Ali would have to use his long left to disturb Frazier's balance.

A hint of shift came in the fourth. Frazier seemed to be picking up the beat, his threshing-blade punches started to come into range as he snorted and rolled closer. "Stay mean with him, champ!" Ali's corner screamed. Ali still had his man in his sights, and whipped at his head furiously. But at the end of the round, sensing a change and annoyed, he glared at Frazier and said, "You dumb chump, you!" Ali fought the whole fifth round in his own corner. Frazier worked his body, the whack of his gloves on Ali's kidneys sounding like heavy thunder. "Get out of the goddamn corner," shouted Angelo Dundee, Ali's trainer. "Stop playin'," squawked Herbert Muhammad, wringing his hands and wiping the mineral water nervously from his mouth. Did they know what was ahead?

Came the sixth, and here it was, that one special moment that you always look for when Joe Frazier is in a fight. Most of his fights have shown this: you can go so far into that desolate and dark place where the heart of Frazier pounds, you can waste his perimeters, you can see his head hanging in the public square, may even believe that you have him, but then suddenly you learn that you have not. Once more the pattern emerged as Frazier loosed all of the fury, all that has made him a brilliant heavyweight. He was in close now, fighting off Ali's chest, the place where he was to be. His old calling card — that sudden evil, his left hook — was working the head of Ali. Two hooks ripped with slaughterhouse finality at Ali's jaw, causing Imelda Marcos to look down at her feet, and the President to wince as if a knife had been stuck in his back. Ali's legs seemed to search for the floor. He was in serious trouble, and he knew that he was in no-man's-land.

Whatever else might one day be said about Muhammad Ali, it should never be said that he is without courage, that he cannot take a punch. He took those shots by Frazier, and then came out for the seventh, saying to him, "Old Joe Frazier, why I thought you were washed up." Joe replied, "Somebody told you all wrong, pretty boy."

Frazier's assault continued. By the end of the 10th round it was an even fight. Ali sat on his stool like a man ready to be staked out in the sun. His head was bowed, and when he raised it his eyes rolled from the agony of exhaustion. "Force yourself, champ!" his corner cried. "Go down to the well once more!" begged Bundini, tears streaming down his face. "The world needs ya, champ!" In the 11th, Ali got trapped in

Frazier's corner, and blow after blow bit at his melting face, and flecks of spittle flew from his mouth. "Lawd have mercy!" Bundini shrieked.

The world held its breath. But then Ali dug deep down into whatever it is that he is about, and even his severest critics would have to admit that the man-boy had become finally a man. He began to catch Frazier with long right hands, and blood trickled from Frazier's mouth. Now, Frazier's face began to lose definition; like lost islands reemerging from the sea, massive bumps rose suddenly around each eye, especially the left. His punches seemed to be losing their strength. "My God," wailed Angelo Dundee. "Look at 'im. He ain't got no power, champ!" Ali threw the last ounces of resolve left in his body in the 13th and 14th. He sent Frazier's bloody mouthpiece flying into the press row in the 13th, and nearly floored him with a right in the center of the ring. Frazier was now no longer coiled. He was up high, his hands down, and as the bell for the 14th round sounded, Dundee pushed Ali out saying, "He's all yours!" And he was, as Ali raked him with nine straight right hands. Frazier was not picking up the punches, and as he returned to his corner at the round's end the Filipino referee guided his great hulk part of the way.

"Joe," said his manager, Eddie Futch, "I'm going to stop it."

"No, no, Eddie, ya can't do that to me," Frazier pleaded, his thick tongue barely getting the words out. He started to rise.

"You couldn't see in the last two rounds," said Futch. "What makes ya think ya gonna see in the 15th?"

"I want him, boss," said Frazier.

"Sit down, son," said Futch, pressing his hand on Frazier's shoulder. "It's all over. No one will ever forget what you did here today."

And so it will be, for once more had Frazier taken the child of the gods to hell and back. After the fight Futch said: "Ali fought a smart fight. He conserved his energy, turning it off when he had to. He can afford to do it because of his style. It was mainly a question of anatomy, that is all that separates these two men. Ali is now too big, and when you add those long arms, well . . . Joe has to use constant pressure, and that takes its toll on a man's body and soul." Dundee said: "My guy sucked it up and called on everything he had. We'll never see another one like him." Ali took a long time before coming down to be interviewed by the press, and then he could only say, "I'm tired of bein' the whole game. Let other guys do the fightin'. You might never see Ali in the ring again."

In his suite the next morning he talked quietly. "I heard somethin' once," he said. "When somebody asked a marathon runner what goes through his mind in the last mile or two, he said that you ask yourself why am I doin' this. You get so tired. It takes so much out of you mentally. It changes you. It makes you go a little insane. I was thinkin' that at the end. Why am I doin' this? What am I doin' here in against this beast of a man? It's so painful. I must be crazy. I always bring out the best in the men I fight, but Joe Frazier, I'll tell the world right now, brings out the best in me. I'm gonna tell ya, that's one helluva man, and God bless him."

1989

## Davis Miller

........................................................................................................

# My Dinner with Ali

I'D BEEN WAITING FOR YEARS. When it finally happened, it wasn't what I expected. But he's been fooling many of us for most of our lives.

Several people had been trying to connect me with him at his farm in Michigan for the previous six months. Yet when I finally got to see him, it wasn't in Michigan and I didn't have an appointment. I simply drove past his mother's house in Louisville. It was mid-afternoon on Good Friday, April 1st, two days before Resurrection Day. A block-long white Winnebago with Virginia plates was parked out front. Though he hadn't often been in town lately, I knew it was his vehicle.

I was certain it was him because I know his patterns and his style. Since 1962, when he has travelled unhurried in this country, he has driven either buses or RVs. And he owns another farm in Virginia. The connections were obvious. Some people study faults in the earth's crust or the habits of storms or of galaxies, hoping to make sense of the world and of their own lives. Others meditate on the life and work of only one social movement or one man. Since I was 10 years old, I have been a Muhammad Ali scholar.

I parked my car behind the Winnebago and grabbed a few old magazines and a special stack of papers I'd been storing under the front seat, waiting for the meeting with Ali that I'd been sure would come. Like everyone else, I wondered in what shape I would find The Champ. I'd heard all about his condition and had watched him stumble through the ropes when introduced at recent big fights. But when I thought of Ali, I remembered him as I'd seen him several times years before, when he was luminous. I was in my early twenties, trying to make a living as a kickboxer and, on one occasion, was fortunate enough to spar with him.

I later wrote a couple of stories about the experience and had copies of those with me today, hoping he would sign them.

Yes, in those days he had shone. There was an aura of light and confidence around him. He had told the world of his importance: "I am the center of the universe," he had said, and we almost believed him. But recent reports had Ali sounding like a turtle spilled onto his back.

It was his brother Rahaman who opened the door. He saw the stack of papers and magazines under my arm, smiled an understanding smile and said, "He's out in the Winnebago. Just knock on the door. He'll be happy to sign those for you." Rahaman looked pretty much the way I remembered him, a little like a black, aging Errol Flynn. There was no indication in his voice or on his face that I would find his brother less than healthy.

I re-crossed the yard, climbed the couple of steps on the side of the Winnebago and prepared to knock. Ali opened the door before I got the chance. He is, of course, a huge man. His presence filled the doorway. He had to lean under the frame to see me.

I felt no nervousness. Ali's face, in many ways, is as familiar to me as my father's. His skin remains unmarked, his countenance has a nearly perfect symmetry. Yet something is different: Ali is no longer the world's prettiest man. This has little relationship to his sickness; it is largely because he is heavier than he needs to be. He remains handsome, but in the way of a youngish granddad who likes to tell stories about how he could have been a movie star, if he'd wanted.

"Come on in," he said and waved me past him. His voice had a gurgle to it, like he needed to clear his throat. He offered his massive hand. His grip was not a grip at all — his touch was gentle, almost feminine. His palm was cool and uncalloused, his fingers were the long, tapered digits of a hypnotist, his knuckles large and slightly swollen. They looked like he had recently been punching the heavy bag.

He was dressed in white: new leather tennis shoes, cotton socks, custom-tailored linen slacks and short-sleeved safari-style shirt crisp with starch. I told him I thought white was a better color for him than the black he often wears.

He motioned for me to sit, but didn't speak. His mouth was a little tense at the corners; it looked like a kid's who has been forced by a parent or teacher to keep it closed. He slowly lowered himself into a chair beside the window. I took a seat across from him and laid my magazines on a table between us. He immediately picked them up, produced a pen and began signing them. He asked, "What's your name?" without looking up and when I told him, he continued writing. His eyes were not glazed, as I'd heard, but they looked tired. A wet cough rattled in his throat. His left hand tremored continuously. In the silence around us, I felt a need to tell him some of the things I'd been wanting to say for years.

"Champ, you changed my life," I said. It was true. "When I was a kid, I was messed up, couldn't even talk to people."

He raised his eyes from an old healthy image of himself on a magazine cover.

"You made me believe I could do anything," I said. "Now I'm a writer, I've sold several stories about you. And I've just finished a first novel that you're in."

He was watching me while I talked, not judging, just watching. I picked up a magazine from the stack in front of him. "This is a story I wrote about the ways you've influenced my life."

"What's your name?" he asked again, this time looking right at me. I told him. He nodded. "I'll finish signing these for you in a little while," he said. He put his pen on the table. "Read me your story."

"You have a good face," he said when I was through. "I like your face."

He'd listened seriously as I'd read, laughing at the funny lines and when I'd tried to imitate his voice. He had not been bored. It was a lot more than I could have expected — Muhammad Ali doesn't like to read, but he had listened to, and seemed to enjoy, my story.

"You ever seen any magic?" he asked. "You like magic?"

"Not in years," I said.

He stood and walked to the back of his RV. He moved mechanically. It was my great-grandfather's walk. He motioned for me to follow. There was a sad, yet lovely, noble and intimate quality to his movements.

He did about 10 tricks. The one that interested me the most required no props. It was a very simple deception. "Watch my feet," he said. He was standing about eight feet in front of me, with his back to me and his arms perpendicular to his sides. Then, though he has real trouble walking and talking, he seemed to levitate about four inches off of the floor. He turned to me and in his thick, slow voice said, "I'm *baadd,*" and gave me the old easy Ali smile.

I laughed and asked him to do it again; it was a good one. I thought I might like to try it myself, just as 20 years earlier I had stood in front of the mirror in my dad's hallway for hours, pushing my worm of a left arm out at the reflection, trying feebly to imitate Ali's cobra jab. And I had found an old laundry bag, filled it with rags, and hung it from a ceiling beam in the basement. I pushed my left hand into that 20-pound marshmallow 200, 300, 500 times a day, concentrating on speed: dazzling, crackling speed, in pursuit of godly speed — *zing, ting, ding* went the punches on the bag, and I strove to make the three sounds as one (like Ali's), strove to make my fists move quicker than thought, and then I would try to spring up on my toes, as I had watched Ali do; I would try to fly like Ali, bouncing away from the bag and to my left.

After the levitation trick, Ali grabbed an empty plastic milk jug from beside a sink. He asked me to examine it. "What if I make this jug rise up from the sink about this high and sit there? Will you believe?"

"I'm not much of a believer these days, Champ," I said. I wasn't exactly sure what he was selling.

"Watch," he said, pointed at the plastic container, and took three or four steps back. I was trying to see both the milk jug and Ali. He waved his hands a couple of times in front of his body, said, "Arise, ghost, arise," in a foggy-sounding voice. The plastic container did not move from the counter.

"April Fools," Ali said. We both chuckled and he walked over and slipped his arm around my shoulders.

He autographed the stories and wrote a special note on a page of my book-length manuscript I'd asked him to take a look at. "To Davis Miller, The Greatest Fan of All Times," he wrote, "From Muhammad Ali, King of Boxing." I felt my stories were finally complete, now that he had confirmed their existence. He handed me the magazines and asked me into his mother's house. We left the Winnebago. I unlocked my car and leaned across the front seat, carefully placing the magazines and manuscript on the passenger's side, not wanting to take a chance on damaging them or leaving them behind. Suddenly there was a chirping, insect-like noise in my ear. I jumped back, swatted the air, turned around. It had been Ali's hand. He was standing right behind me, still the practical joker.

"How'd you do that?" I wanted to know. It was a question I'd find myself asking several times that day.

He didn't answer, but raised both fists to shoulder height and motioned me out into the yard. We walked about five paces, I put up my hands, and he tossed a slow jab at me. I blocked and countered with my own. Fighters and ex-fighters are always throwing punches at each other or at the air or at whatever happens to be around. It's the way we play. I'd bet Ali must still toss over a hundred lefts a day. He and I had both thrown our punches a full half-foot away from the other, but my adrenal gland was pumping at high gear from being around Ali and my jab had come out fast — it had made the air sing. He slid back a half-step and took a serious look at me. A couple of kids were riding past on bikes; they recognized Ali and stopped.

"He doesn't understand I'm the greatest boxer of all times," he yelled to the kids. He pulled his watch from his arm, stuck it in his pants pocket; he'd get down to business now. He danced to his left a little, loosening up his legs. Just a couple of minutes before, climbing down the steps of his RV, he'd moved so awkwardly that he'd almost lost his balance. I'd wanted to give him a hand, but knew not to. I'd remembered seeing old Joe Louis "escorted" in that fashion by lesser mortals, and I couldn't do that to Muhammad Ali. But now that Ali was on his toes and boxing, he was moving fluidly.

He flung another jab in my direction, a second, a third. He wasn't one-fifth as fast as he had been in 1975, when I'd first sparred with him, but his eyes were alert, shining like black electric marbles, and he saw everything and was real relaxed. That's precisely why old fighters keep making comebacks: We are more alive when boxing than at any other time. The grass around us was green and was already getting high; it would soon need its first cutting. A jay squawked from an oak tree to the left. There were five or six robins around us in the yard. I instinctively blocked all three of his blows, or slid to the side of them, then immediately felt guilty about it, like being 14 years old and knowing for the first time that you can beat your dad at ping-pong. I wished I could stop myself from slipping Ali's jabs, but I couldn't. Reflexive training runs faster and deeper than thought. I zipped a jab to his nose, one to his body, a straight right to the chin, and was dead certain all three would have scored. A couple of cars stopped in front of the house. His mom's is on a corner lot. Two or three more were parked on the side.

"Check out the left," I heard a young-sounding voice say from somewhere. I knew the owner of the voice was talking about mine, not Ali's.

"He's in with the triple greatest of all times," Ali was shouting. "Gonna let him tire himself out. He'll get tired soon."

I didn't, but pretended to, anyway.

"You're right, Champ," I told him and dropped my hands. "I'm 35. I can't go like I used to."

I held my right hand to my chest, acting out of breath. I looked at Ali; his hand was in exactly the same position. We were both smiling, but he was sizing me up a little.

"He got scared," he shouted. All of the onlookers laughed from their bicycles or through their car windows. Some of them blew their horns and yelled, "Hey, Champ!"

"Come on in the house," he said softly in my ear. We walked toward the door, Ali in the lead, moving woodenly through the new grass, while all around us people rolled up their car windows and started their engines.

Ali's family easily accepted me. They were not surprised to have a visitor and handled me with ritualistic grace and charm. It was obvious that many people still come to see Ali when he is in Louisville. Rahaman told me to make myself at home, offered a root beer, and went to get it. I took a seat on the sofa beside Ali's mother, Mrs. Odessa Clay. Mrs. Clay must be in her early seventies, yet her face has few wrinkles. Short, her hair nearly as orange as a hazy Louisville sunset, she is freckled, fragile-looking, and pretty. Ali's face is shaped much like his mother's. When he was fighting she was quite heavy, but she has lost what looks to be about 75 pounds over the last 10 years.

Mrs. Clay was watching Oprah Winfrey on TV. Ali had disappeared from the room and I was wondering where he had gone. Rahaman brought the drink and a paper napkin and a coaster. Mrs. Clay patted me on the hand. "Don't worry," she said. "Ali hasn't left you here. I'm sure he's just gone upstairs to say his prayers." I hadn't realized my anxiety had shown. But Ali's mother has watched him bring home puppies many times during his 46 years. "He's always been a restless man. Can't ever sit still." She spoke carefully, with a mother's sweet sadness about her. The dignified clip to her voice must have once been affected, but after cometing all over the globe with Ali, it now sounds genuinely British and Virginian in its inflections.

"Have you met Lonnie, Ali's new wife?" she asked. "He's known her since she was a baby. I'm so happy for him. She's my best friend's daughter, we used to all travel to his fights together. She's a smart girl, has a master's degree in business. She's so good to him, doesn't use him. He told me, 'Mom, Lonnie's better to me than all the other three put together.' She treats him so good. He needs somebody to take care of him."

Just then, Ali came back into the room, carrying himself high and with statesmanly dignity, though his footing was ever-so-slightly unsteady. He fell deep into a chair on the other side of the room.

"You tired, baby?" Mrs. Clay asked.

"Tired, I'm always tired," he said, then rubbed his face a couple of times and closed his eyes.

He must have felt me watching him or was simply conscious of someone other than family being in the room. His eyes weren't closed 10 seconds before he shook himself awake, balled his hands into fists again and started making typical Ali faces and noises at me — grimacing, growling, other playful cartoon kid stuff. After a few seconds he asked, "Y-Y-You okay?" He was so difficult to understand that I didn't so much hear him as I conjectured what he must have been saying. "Y-Y-You need anything? They taking care of you?" I assured him I was fine.

He made a loud clicking noise by pressing his tongue against the roof of his mouth. Rahaman came quickly from the kitchen. Ali motioned him close and whispered a brief message in his ear. Rahaman went back to the kitchen. Ali turned to me. "Come sit beside me," he said, patting a bar stool just to his right. He waited for me to take my place, then said, "You had any dinner? Sit and eat with me."

"Can I use the phone? I need to call home and let my wife know."

"You got kids?" he asked. I told him I had two. He asked how old. I told him the ages.

"They know me?" he asked.

"Even the two-year-old. He throws punches at the TV whenever I play your old fights."

He nodded, satisfied. "Bring 'em over Sunday," he said, matter-of-factly. "I'll do my magic for 'em. Here's Mom's number. Be sure to phone first."

I called Lynn and told her where I was and what I was doing. She didn't seem surprised. She asked me to pick up a gallon of milk on the way home. I knew she was excited for me but she wouldn't show it in her voice on the phone. In September, 1977, when Lynn and I were in college, we skipped class, took most of the money from our bank accounts, drove to New York and attended the Ali–Earnie Shavers fight at Madison Square Garden. For the rest of the year, we had to live off what little money I was making teaching karate at the university two nights a week. But it was worth it to both of us to have seen Ali in what we knew would be one of his last fights.

Rahaman brought two large bowls of chili and two enormous slices of bread from the kitchen. Ali and I sat at our chairs and ate. He put his face down close to the bowl and the food was gone. Three minutes tops.

The entire time I continued to eat, the telephone was ringing. It was always for Ali. He spent only a few seconds with each caller; he no longer likes to talk to most people on the phone, having to frequently repeat himself to be understood. He handles calls, other than from his immediate family, the same way he deals with being expected to speak in public — he says what he has to say in as few words as possible. His situation is similar to that of a person with a stuttering problem in that he performs much better when he doesn't feel pressured to perform. Between calls, he spoke easily to me.

"Do you know how many people in the world would like to have the opportunity you're getting, how many people would like to come into my house and spend the day with me?" he said. "Haven't fought in seven years and I still get over 400 letters a week."

I asked how people got his address.

"I don't know," he answered. "Sometimes they come addressed 'Muhammad Ali, Los Angeles, California, U.S.A.' I don't have a house in L.A. anymore, but the letters still get to me.

"I want to get me a place, a coffee shop, where I can give away free coffee and doughnuts and people can just sit around and talk, people of all races, and I can go and talk to people. Have some of my old robes and trunks and gloves around, show old fight films, call it 'Ali's Place.'"

"I'd call it 'Ali's,'" I said, not believing there would or ever could be such a place, but enjoying sharing his dream with him. "Just 'Ali's,' that's enough. People would know what it was."

"'Ali's?'" he repeated, and his eyes focused inward, visualizing the dream.

"Do you have copies of your old fights?" I asked. He shook his head no. "Well, look," I said, "why don't I go to a video place and see if I can rent some and we can watch them tonight. Would you like that? You want to ride with me?"

"I'll drive," Ali said.

There was a rubber monster mask in the Winnebago and I wore it on my hand on the way to the video store. I pressed the mask against the window at stop lights. A couple of times people in the cars would see the mask, then recognize Ali. Ali wears glasses when he reads and when he drives. When he saw someone looking at him, he'd carefully remove his glasses, place them in his lap, make his hands into fists and put them up beside his head. People would lay on their horns and wave and cheer and shriek and lean out of their car windows.

We rented a tape of his fights and interviews called *Ali: Skill, Brains and Guts* that was directed by Jimmy Jacobs, the great handball champ and fight historian and Mike Tyson's co-manager. Jacobs had died of a deteriorative illness. Ali hadn't known of Jacobs' death until I told him. "He was a good man," Ali said. His voice had that same quality that an older person's takes on who daily reads obituaries.

I stopped by my car again on the way back into Mrs. Clay's house. There was one more picture I hoped Ali would sign, but earlier I'd felt I might be imposing on him. It was a facial shot in a biography by Wilfrid Sheed that features hundreds of wonderfully reproduced color plates. I grabbed the book from the car and followed Ali into the house.

When we were seated, I handed him the book and he signed the picture on the title page. I was about to ask if he'd mind autographing the photo I especially wanted, but he turned to page two, signed that picture, then the next page and the next. He continued to sign photographs for about 15 minutes, writing notes about opponents, wives, parents, Elijah Muhammad, Malcolm X, Howard Cosell, then passing the book to his mother and brother to sign a family portrait. Ali autographed nearly every photo in the book, pointing out special comments as he signed.

I carefully placed the book on a table and excused myself to the bathroom. I locked the door behind me. A pair of Ali's huge black shoes were beside the toilet. The toe of one had been crushed, the other was lying on its side. When I unlocked the door to leave, it wouldn't budge. I couldn't even turn the handle. I knocked. There was laughter from the other room. I yanked fairly hard on the door a couple of times. Nothing.

Finally it easily opened. I caught just a glimpse of Ali bounding into a side room to the right, laughing and high-stepping like some oversized, out-of-shape Nubian leprechaun. I peeked around the corner into the room. He was standing with his back flat against the wall. He saw me, jumped from the room and began tickling me. Next thing I knew, he had me on the floor, balled-up in a fetal position, with tears flowing down both sides of my face, laughing. Then he stopped tickling me and helped me to my feet.

Everybody kept laughing. Mrs. Clay's face was round and wide with laughter. She looked like the mom of a leprechaun. "What'd you think happened to the door?" Rahaman asked. I told him I figured it was Ali. "Then why are you turning red?" he wanted to know.

"It's not every day," I said, "that I go to Muhammad Ali's, he locks me in the bathroom, then tickles me into submission." Everyone laughed again.

Suddenly I realized the obvious, that all day I'd been acting like a teenage admirer again. And that Muhammad Ali has not yet lost perhaps his highest talent — the ability to transport people past thoughts and words to a world of play. Being around Ali, or watching him perform on TV, has always made me feel genuinely childlike.

We finally slipped the Ali tape into the VCR. Rahaman brought everyone another root beer and we settled back to watch, Rahaman to my left, Ali beside me on the right and Mrs. Clay beside Ali. The family's reactions to the tape were not dissimilar to those you or I would have looking at old home movies or high school annuals. Everyone sighed and their mouths arced at tender angles. "Oh, look at Bundini," Mrs. Clay would say or, "Hey, there's Otis," Rahaman would offer. Whenever there was a film clip of Ali reciting verse, we'd all recite with him. "Those were the days," Rahaman said several times, to which Mrs. Clay would respond, "Yes, yes they were," in a high, lamentative lilt. After a half-hour or so, she left the room. Rahaman continued to watch the tape with us for a while, but then said he needed to be going.

It was just Ali and me. On the TV, it was 1963 and he was framed on the left by Jim Jacobs and on the right by Drew "Bundini" Brown. "They're both dead now," he said, an acute awareness of his own mortality in his tone.

For a time he continued to smile at the old Ali on the screen, but eventually he lost interest in peering at the distant mountains of his youth. "Did my mom go upstairs? Do you know?" he asked.

"Yeah, I think she's probably asleep."

He nodded, stood, and left the room to check on her. When he came back he was moving heavily. His shoulder hit the side of the doorway to the kitchen. He went in and brought out two fistfuls of cookies. Crumbs were all over his mouth. He sat beside me on the sofa. Our knees were touching. Usually when a man gets this close I pull away. He offered me a couple of cookies. When he was through eating, he yawned a giant's yawn, closed his eyes and seemed to go dead asleep.

"Champ, you want me to leave?" I said. "Am I keeping you up?"

He slowly opened his eyes and was back to our side of The Great Mystery.

The pores on his face suddenly looked huge, his features elongated, distorted, like someone's in an El Greco. He rubbed his face the way I rub mine when I haven't shaved in a week.

"No, stay," he said. His voice was very gentle.

"You'd let me know if I was staying too late?"

"I go to bed at eleven," he said.

With the volume turned this low on the TV, you could hear the videotape's steady whir. "Can I ask you a serious question?" I said. He nodded okay.

"You're still a great man, Champ, I see that, but a lot of people think your mind is fried. Does that bother you?"

He didn't hesitate before he answered. "No, there are ignorant people everywhere," he said. "Even educated people can be ignorant."

"Does it bother you that you're a great man who's not being allowed to be great?"

"Wh-Wh-What do you mean, 'not allowed to be great'?" he said.

"I mean . . . let me think about what I mean . . . I mean the things you seem to care most about, the things you really enjoy doing, the things the rest of us think of as *being* Muhammad Ali, those are exactly the things that have been taken from you. It just doesn't seem fair."

"You don't question God," he said.

"Okay, I respect that, but . . . Aw, man, I don't have any business talking to you about this."

"No, no, go on," he said.

"It just bothers me," I told him. I was thinking about the obvious ironies, thinking about Ali continuing to invent, and be invented by, his own late-20th-century mythology. About how he used to talk more easily, maybe better, than anybody in the world; how he often still *thinks* with speed and dazzle, but it takes serious effort for him to communicate even with the people closest to him. About how he may have been the world's best athlete — when just walking he used to have the grace of a cat turning corners; now, at night, he stumbles around the house. About how it's his left hand, the most visible source of his boxing greatness, the hand that won more than 150 fights, it's *his left hand*, not his right, that shakes almost continuously. And I was thinking how his major source of pride, his "prettiness," remains more or less intact. If Ali lost 30 pounds, he would still look classically Greek. Despite not expecting to encounter the miraculous any more than any other agnostic, I'm sort of spooked by the seeming precision with which things have been excised from Ali's life.

"I know why this has happened," Ali said. "God is showing me, and showing *you*," he pointed his shaking index finger at me and widened his eyes, "that I'm just a man, just like everybody else."

We sat a long quiet time then, and watched Ali's flickering image on the television screen. It was now 1971 and there was footage of him in training for the first Joe Frazier fight. Our Most Public Figure was then The World's Most Beautiful Man and The Greatest Athlete of All Time, his tight, copper-colored skin glowing under the fluorescents, secret rhythms springing in loose firmness from his fingertips.

"Champ, I think it's time for me to go," I said and made an effort to stand.

"No, stay. You my man," he says and pats my leg. It seems almost tragic that he needs company this badly, but it has nothing to do with his illness; he's always been this way, and I take his accolade as the greatest compliment of my life.

"I'll tell you a secret," he says and leans close. "I'm gonna make a comeback."

*"What?"* I think he's joking, hope he is, but something in the way he's speaking makes me uncertain. "You're not serious."

And suddenly there is musk in his voice. "I'm gonna make a comeback," he repeats louder, more firmly.

"Are you serious?"

"The timing is perfect. They'd think it was a miracle, wouldn't they?" He's speaking in a distinct, familiar voice; he is very easy to understand. It is almost the voice I remember from when I first met him in 1975, the one that seemed to come rolling up from deep in his abdomen. In short, Ali sounds like Ali.

"Wouldn't they?" he asks again.

"It *would* be a miracle," I say.

"Nobody'll take me serious at first. But then I'll get my weight down to 215 and have an exhibition at Yankee Stadium or someplace. Then they'll believe. I'll fight for the title. It'll be bigger than the Resurrection." He stands and walks out to the center of the room.

"It'd be good for you to get your weight down," I say.

"Watch this," he says and begins dancing to his left. He is watching himself in the mirror above the TV. His clean white shoes bounce around the room; I marvel at how easily he moves. His white clothing accentuates his movements in the dark room. The white appears to make him glow. Then he starts throwing punches, not the kind he'd tossed at me earlier, but now really letting them zing. I'd honestly thought what he'd thrown in the yard was indicative of what he had left. But what he'd done was allow me to play; he'd wanted me to enjoy myself.

"Look at the TV. That's 1971 and I'm just as fast now." It's true, the old man can still do it. He can still make the fire appear in the air. One second, two seconds, sixteen punches flash in the night. Actually, he looks faster standing in front of me than does the ghost-like Ali images still running on the screen. God, I wish I had a video camera to tape this. Nobody would believe me.

"And I'll be even faster when I get my weight down," he tells me.

"You know more now, too," I find myself admitting. Jesus, what am I saying? This is a sick man.

"Do you believe?" he asks.

"Well . . ." I say. Is this Parkinson's syndrome affecting his sanity? Look at the gray shining in his hair. And Ali throws another three dozen punches at the gods of mortality — he springs a *triple* hook off of a jab, drops straight right leads in multiples, explodes into a blur of upper-cuts, and the air pops, and his fists and feet whir. This was his best work. His highest art. When Ali was fighting, he typically held back a little; this is the stuff he seldom chose to use against opponents.

"Do you believe?" he asks, breathing no harder than I would if I'd thrown the punches he's just thrown.

They wouldn't let you, even if you could do it, I'm thinking. There's too much concern everywhere for your health. Everybody thinks they see old Mr. Thanatos waiting for you.

"Do you *believe?*" he asks again.

"I believe," I hear myself say.

He stops dancing and points a magician's finger at me. Then I get the look, the smile, that has closed 10,000 interviews. "April Fools," he says and sits down beside me yet again. He looks confident, relaxed, satisfied, alive. We sit in silence for several minutes. I look at my watch. It's 11:18. I hadn't realized it was that late. I'd told Lynn I'd be in by eight.

"Champ, I better go home. I have a wife and kids waiting."

"Okay," he says almost inaudibly and yawns the kind of long uncovered yawn people usually do only among family and friends.

He's bone-tired, I'm tired, too, but I want to leave him by saying something that will mean something to him, something that will set me apart from the two billion other people he's met, that will imprint me indelibly in his memory and will make the kind of impact on his life he has made on mine. I want to say the words that will cure his Parkinson's.

Instead I say, "We'll see you Easter, Champ."

He coughs and gives me his hand. "Be cool and look out for the ladies." His words are so volumeless and full of fluid that I don't realize what he's said until I'm halfway out the door.

I don't recall picking up the book he signed, but I must have; it's sitting beside my typewriter now. I can't remember walking across his mom's yard and don't remember starting the car.

I didn't forget Lynn's gallon of milk. The doors to the grocery store whooshed closed behind me. For this time of night, there were quite a few customers in the store. They seemed to move more as floating shadows than as people. An old feeling came across me that I immediately recognized. The sensation was much like going out into the day-to-day world soon after making love for the first time. It was the same sense of having landed in a lesser reality. And of having a secret that the rest of the world can't see. I'd have to wake Lynn and share the memory of this feeling with her.

I reached to grab a milk jug and caught a reflection of myself in the chrome at the dairy counter. There was a half-smile on my face and I hadn't realized it.

# Biographical Notes
## Notable Sports Writing and Sports Writers of the Century

# Biographical Notes

**Roger Angell** has served as fiction editor and contributor at *The New Yorker* since 1956, where his elegant essays on baseball have gained a loyal following. His baseball writing has been compiled in several collections, including *The Summer Game* (1972), *Five Seasons* (1977), *Late Innings* (1982), *Season Ticket* (1988), and *Once More Around the Park* (1991).

**Ira Berkow** is a sports columnist and feature writer for the *New York Times*. A graduate of Miami (Ohio) University, he began his career with the *Minneapolis Tribune* in 1965. He was a runner-up for the Pulitzer Prize for distinguished commentary in 1987. He is the author of *Red: A Biography of Red Smith*, a collection of his columns and features, *Pitchers Do Get Lonely* (1988), and *To the Hoop: Seasons of a Basketball Life* (1997).

**Tom Boswell** has covered baseball and other sports for the *Washington Post* since graduating from Amherst College in 1969. A sports commentator on National Public Radio since 1984, he served as guest editor for *The Best American Sports Writing 1994*. His books include *How Life Imitates the World Series: An Inquiry into the Game* (1982) and *Why Time Begins on Opening Day* (1984).

**Jimmy Breslin** is a native of Jamaica, New York. His journalism career began with the *Long Island Press* in 1948. He later joined the *New York Journal-American* and became a columnist for the *New York Herald Tribune*, which merged to become the *World Journal Tribune* before folding in 1969. Breslin then joined the *New York Post* before taking his column to the *New York Daily News* in 1978. He is the author of *Can't Anybody Here Play This Game? The Improbable Saga of the New York Mets' First Year* (1963), *The Gang That Couldn't Shoot Straight* (1969), *How the Good Guys Finally Won: Notes From an Impeachment Summer* (1975), *The World According to Jimmy Breslin* (1984), *Damon Runyon* (1991), and *I Want to Thank My Brain for Remembering Me: A Memoir* (1996).

**Heywood Broun** (1888–1939) began his career as a reporter with the *New York Morning Telegraph,* writing about baseball and Broadway. He joined the *New York Telegraph* in 1911 and served in a variety of capacities; he was a war correspondent during World War I before becoming the paper's literary editor and columnist. He moved to the *New York World* in 1921, authored the column "It Seems to Me," and achieved notoriety for his writing on the Sacco and Vanzetti trial. He then joined the *New York Telegram,* ran for Congress in 1930 on the Socialist ticket, and served as the first president of the Newspaper Guild in 1933. After writing one column for the *New York Post* in 1939, he fell ill with pneumonia and died shortly thereafter. A collection of his work, *It Seems to Me,* appeared in 1935. *The Collected Edition of Heywood Broun* was published in 1941.

**Jimmy Cannon** (1909–1963) was born in New York and grew up in Greenwich Village. He began his journalism career as a copy boy with the *New York Daily News,* and he eventually moved on to the *World-Telegram* and *PM.* In 1946 he began to author a syndicated column for the *New York Post* before moving once again to the *Journal-American.* He was the author of *Nobody Asked Me* (1950) and *Who Struck John?* (1956).

**Bob Considine** (1906–1975) became a journalist after his name was misspelled in a *Washington Herald* report on his victory in a tennis match. He complained, and was hired. He moved to the *Washington Post* before returning to the *Herald,* where he eventually served as sports editor. His daily column, "On the Line with Considine" was syndicated in more than one hundred newspapers, which he continued writing after joining the *New York American* and the *New York Daily Mirror.* At the same time, he wrote for Hearst International News Service, for which he served as a war correspondent in World War II. Considine authored or edited twenty-five books and five screenplays, among them *MacArthur the Magnificent* (1942) and *Thirty Seconds over Tokyo* (1943). His biography, *It's All News to Me,* was published in 1967.

**Richard Ben Cramer,** a graduate of Columbia University, won a Pulitzer Prize for international reporting for the *Philadelphia Inquirer* in 1979, which he joined after beginning his career with the *Baltimore Sun* in 1973. He has since worked as a freelance journalist and writer and served as a contributing editor for *Esquire.* He is the author of *What It Takes,* a chronicle of the 1988 presidential race, and *Bob Dole* (1995). His profile of Ted Williams also appeared in book form in *Ted Williams: Seasons of the Kid* (1991).

**Brad Darrach** (1921–1997) may well have been the most prolific magazine writer of all time. For fifty years he wrote for a variety of Time Inc. publications before retiring in 1996. He was noted for his movie reviews in *Time,* his profiles in *People,* and his writing on a wide variety of topics for *Life,* for which he served as contributing editor. He is the author of *Bobby Fischer vs. the Rest of the World* (1974).

**Frank Deford** is the author of eleven books. From 1962 to 1989 he served on the staff of *Sports Illustrated,* to which he returned in 1998. He also served as editor-in-chief of the *National Sports Daily* and was guest editor of *The Best American Sports Writing 1993.* His features have been collected in the book *The World's Tallest Midget.*

**Stan Fischler** is a leading authority on hockey and has written more than fifty books on the sport, including *The Hockey Encyclopedia* (1983) and *Stan Fischler's Illustrated History of Hockey* (1993). He has contributed stories on a variety of topics to such periodicals as *Sport* and *Sports Illustrated,* and authored weekly hockey columns for the *Sporting News* and *Hockey News.*

**Frank Graham** (1893–1965) was credited by Red Smith with revolutionizing the approach of writing a sports column, changing it from a forum of editorial opinion to one of reporting. He was particularly noted for his adept use of conversation and dialogue. Graham, a columnist for the *New York Sun* and the *New York Journal-American,* was one of the most respected boxing writers in the country. His books include *Lou Gehrig* (1942), *The New York Yankees* (1942), *McGraw of the Giants* (1944), and *The New York Giants: An Informal History* (1952).

**W. C. Heinz** was born in Mount Vernon, New York, and graduated from Middlebury College. He began his career with the *New York Sun,* working his way up from copy boy to war correspondent and sports reporter before laving to devote himself to magazine work and books in 1950. His work was honored a number of times in *Best Sports Stories,* and he is the author of *The Professional* (1958), *The Surgeon* (1963), *Once They Heard the Cheers* (1979), and *American Mirror* (1982).

**Gerald Holland** (1907–1974) was a founding editor of *Sports Illustrated,* for which he served as an associate and senior editor from the magazine's inception through 1966. In a varied career, Holland also worked as public relations director for the St. Louis Browns in the 1930s, when he first made the acquaintance of Branch Rickey. His work appeared in a variety of publications in the 1950s and 1960s. "Mr. Rickey and the Game" was included in both Charles Einstein's *Fireside Book of Baseball* (1956) and Herbert Warren Wind's collection *The Realm of Sport* (1966).

**Johnette Howard** is a sports columnist at *New York Newsday* and a former senior writer at *Sports Illustrated* and the *National Sports Daily.* "The Making of a Goon" appeared in the inaugural edition of *The Best American Sports Writing.*

**Murray Kempton** (1918–1997) was a native of Baltimore and a 1939 graduate of Johns Hopkins University. He then went to work as a political activist for the Socialist party and union organizer before joining the *New York Post* as a labor reporter in 1942. After serving with the United States Army in the Pacific, he returned to the *Post,* becoming labor editor in 1949 and a columnist, focusing primarily on civil rights and politics. He left the *Post* in 1963 to write for the *New Republic,* then returned to New York as a columnist for the *New York World-Telegram* and *Sun* before rejoining the *Post,* where he remained until 1981, when he became a columnist for *New York Newsday.* His columns were collected in *America Comes of Middle Age: Columns 1950–1962* (1963) and *Rebellions, Perversities and Main Events* (1994).

**Jon Krakauer** won a National Magazine Award for his *Outside* magazine story "Into Thin Air," which later became a best-selling book of the same name. A contributing editor to *Outside,* Krakauer is also the author of *Eiger Dreams: Ventures Among Men and Mountains* (1990) and *Into the Wild* (1996).

**Mark Kram** is a contributing editor to *Esquire* and a screenwriter. His work has previously been featured in several editions of *The Best American Sports Writing.*

**Arthur Kretchmer** is a senior vice president, editorial director, and associate publisher of *Playboy.* In 1963 he graduated from City College of New York with a degree in creative writing. In 1964 he joined *Cavalier* magazine as associate editor, and he became the managing editor there in 1966. He joined *Playboy* in 1966 as associate editor.

**John Lardner** (1913–1960) was one of four sons born to Ring Lardner. He joined the *New York Herald Tribune* in 1931 after attending Harvard for one year; by 1933 his column for the North American Newspaper Syndicate was appearing nationwide. In 1939 he joined *Newsweek* as a columnist, then served as one of the magazine's war correspondents. After the war his work also began to appear in *The New Yorker* and numerous other publications. His books include *The Crowning of Technology* (1933), *Southwest Passage* (1943), *It Beats Working* (1947), *White Hopes and Other Tigers* (1951), and *Strong Cigars and Lovely Women* (1951).

**Ring Lardner** (1885–1933) began his writing career as a sports writer for the *South Bend Times,* before joining, in turn, the *Chicago Inter Ocean,* the *Chicago*

*Examiner,* and the *Chicago Tribune,* where his lively accounts of baseball first drew attention. After briefly working for the *Sporting News* and the *Boston American,* he returned to Chicago, and in 1913 took over the column "In the Wake of the News" for the *Chicago Tribune.* Lardner soon discovered his writing interests extended beyond his column, and he began writing short stories and sketches for a number of magazines. After serving as a war correspondent for the *Tribune* during World War I, he left the *Tribune* and covered sports for the Bell Syndicate. He is the author of twenty books, and his work has since been collected in *The Portable Lardner* (1946), *Shut Up, He Explained* (1962), *The Ring Lardner Reader* (1963), and *Some Champions* (1976).

**Mike Lupica** was a correspondent for the *Boston Globe* and a columnist for the *Boston Phoenix* and *Boston* magazine while still an undergraduate at Boston College. After graduating in 1974, he joined the *Washington Star* as a feature writer, then moved to the *New York Post* and the *New York News* before settling in as a columnist for the *New York Daily News* in 1980. In 1990 he also authored a column for the *National Sports Daily* and for a number of years wrote the sports column in *Esquire.* Lupica has also worked as both a radio and television commentator and host. An author of several mystery novels, his work appears in *Shooting from the Lip: Essays, Columns, Quips and Gripes in the Grand Tradition of Dyspeptic Sports Writing* (1988). His most recent book is *Mad as Hell: How Sports Got Away from the Fans — And How We Get It Back* (1997). Lupica is presently a contributing writer for *ESPN: The Magazine.*

**Norman Mailer,** a native of Brooklyn and graduate of Harvard, is one of America's best-known authors and commentators whose fiction, reportage, and essays have won numerous awards. After first achieving success with his war novel *The Naked and the Dead* (1948), Mailer then wrote two more novels, *Barbary Shore* (1951) and *Deer Park* (1955), before co-founding the *Village Voice* in 1955, for which he also served as a contributor. His output of fiction and essays has continued ever since, most notably in *Armies of the Night* (1968), which won both the National Book Award and the Pulitzer Prize, *Miami and the Siege of Chicago* (1968), *The Fight* (1975), *The Executioner's Song (1979),* *Ancient Evenings* (1983), and *Oswald's Tale: An American Mystery* (1995).

**Thomas McGuane** is the author of *Nothing but Blue Skies* and *Ninety-two in the Shade.* His essays on sport appear in the collection *An Outside Chance: Classic and New Essays on Sport* (1992). A frequent contributor to *Sports Afield,* McGuane served as guest editor for *The Best American Sports Writing 1992.*

**John McPhee** has served as a staff writer for *The New Yorker* since 1965 and as the Ferris Professor of Journalism at Princeton University since 1975. He is the author of more than twenty books, including *A Sense of Where You Are* (1965), about the basketball star Bill Bradley, and *Levels of the Game* (1970), about Arthur Ashe. His shorter works have been collected in several volumes, including *The John McPhee Reader* (1977) and *Table of Contents* (1985). He received the Award in Literature from the American Academy of Arts and Letters in 1977 and the John Burroughs Medal in 1990.

**Davis Miller** is the author of *The Tao of Muhammad Ali* (1997), a personal memoir that traces the role Ali has played in the author's life. "My Dinner with Ali," Miller's first published story, was voted by the Sunday Magazine Editors Association as the best essay published in a newspaper magazine in 1989. Also the author of *The Tao of Bruce Lee* (1999) and *Sleighbed* (1999), he has written for numerous publications, including *Sport, Men's Journal, Esquire,* and *Sports Illustrated.*

**J. R. Moehringer** is the Atlanta bureau chief for the *Los Angeles Times.* His story "Resurrecting the Champ," was a finalist for the 1998 Pulitzer Prize for feature reporting.

**Jim Murray** (1919–1998) of the *Los Angeles Times* won virtually every award available to sports writers, including the 1990 Pulitzer Prize for commentary. Murray spent his formative years as a reporter for the *New Haven Register* and the *Los Angeles Examiner* before joining *Time* in 1948. In 1954, Murray helped launch *Sports Illustrated,* and he joined the *Times* in 1961. Murray is a member of both the Baseball Hall of Fame and the National Sportscasters and Sportswriters Hall of Fame. His work can be found in *The Best of Jim Murray* and *The Sporting World of Jim Murray.*

**William Nack,** a Chicago native, grew up working at the Arlington Race Track in suburban Chicago. He attended the University of Illinois, then served in General Westmoreland's command headquarters in Vietnam. In 1968 he joined *Newsday,* where he served as a reporter and sports columnist, then joined *Sports Illustrated* as a senior writer in 1979. Nack, one of America's leading thoroughbred-racing writers, is the author of *Secretariat: The Making of a Champion* (1988).

**Westbrook Pegler** (1894–1969) was perhaps the foremost columnist of his era. His sports coverage for the United Press from 1919 to 1925 earned him his reputation, and he joined the *Chicago Tribune* as a sports columnist in 1925. In 1932 he was sent to Washington to write about politics and the next year was hired by Scripps Howard to write the syndicated column "Fair Enough," which earned him a Pulitzer Prize in 1941. In 1944 he joined the *New York Journal-American,* and in his column "As Pegler Sees It" invented the character George Spelvin, whom he used as a foil for his satiric, sometimes acerbic commentary.

After losing a libel suit filed by fellow writer Quentin Reynolds, Pegler's career went into decline. In 1962 he was fired by the Hearst organization after he charged the organization was censoring his columns.

**George Plimpton** pioneered participatory sports journalism, for at various times he has played NFL quarterback, boxed Archie Moore, played tennis against Pancho Gonzalez, swam against Don Schollander, golfed in a pro tournament, and competed in a variety of other events. A founder of the *Paris Review*, Plimpton has served as a contributing editor at *Sports Illustrated*, an associate editor at *Harper's*, and a contributing editor for *Esquire*. His books include *Out of My League* (1961), *Paper Lion* (1966), *The Bogey Man* (1968), *Open Net* (1985), and *The Best of Plimpton* (1991). He also served as guest editor of *The Best American Sports Writing 1997*.

**David Remnick** is a 1981 graduate of Princeton. He joined the *Washington Post* in 1982, for which he covered sports from 1984 to 1985. He later spent four years in Moscow as one of the *Post*'s foreign correspondents, where he witnessed the fall of the Soviet Union. This resulted in his book *Lenin's Tomb: The Last Days of the Soviet Empire*, which won the Pulitzer Prize in 1993. A staff writer for *The New Yorker* since 1992, he became editor in 1998. His features have been collected in *The Devil Problem (and Other True Stories)*.

**Grantland Rice** (1880–1954) was easily the best-known and most prolific sports writer of his generation. After graduating from Vanderbilt University in 1901, he worked as a reporter for the *Nashville News* before joining the *Atlanta Journal* in 1902. After several brief stops at other papers, he went to New York in 1910 and joined the *New York Mail*, then moved to the *New York Tribune*, where he gained a national reputation and remained until 1930. After leaving the *Tribune* he authored a syndicated column, "The Spotlight," wrote features, and produced radio programs and sports films, for which he won an Academy Award in 1943. Rice worked until the day of his death; he claimed that he wrote more than one million words per year for fifty years, a heady pace of more than three thousand words per day. His autobiography, *The Tumult and the Shouting: My Life in Sport*, appeared in 1954.

**Peter Richmond**'s work has appeared in many publications, including *Rolling Stone* and the *New York Times Magazine*, and he served on the staff of the *National Sports Daily*. His work has appeared in *The Best American Sports Writing* several times. A special correspondent for *GQ*, he is the author of *Ballpark: Camden Yards and the Building of an American Dream* (1996).

**Mike Royko** (1932–1997), a native of Chicago, began his career in the air force, working on the base newspaper. After leaving the service he joined the *North*

*Side Newspapers* in 1956 as a reporter, then moved to the *Chicago Daily News* in 1959 as a columnist and reporter, where his streetwise background and grasp of Chicago politics served him well. He achieved national notoriety with his best-selling book *Boss: Richard J. Daley of Chicago* (1971). When the *News* folded in 1978, he joined the *Chicago Sun-Times,* then left in protest when Rupert Murdoch purchased the paper, joining the *Chicago Tribune.* His work was collected in a number of books, including *Up Against It* (1967), *I May Be Wrong, But I Doubt It* (1968), *Slats Grobnik and Other Friends* (1973), *Sez Who? Sez Me!* (1982), *Like I Was Sayin'* (1984), and *Dr. Kookie, You're Right!* (1990). A posthumous collection, *One More Time: The Best of Mike Royko,* is scheduled to appear in 1999.

**Dick Schaap** is the host of ESPN's "The Sports Reporters" and ESPN Classic's "One on One." The former city editor of the *New York Herald Tribune,* Schaap later became senior editor with *Newsweek* and editor of *Sport* magazine. His thirty-two books include the classic *Instant Replay* (1968), which he wrote in collaboration with Jerry Kramer and was at the time the best-selling sports book ever. His most recent books are *Green Bay Replay: The Packers' Return to Glory* (1998) and his autobiography, *Namedropping* (1999).

**Diane K. Shah** became the first woman to write a regularly scheduled sports column when her column appeared in the *Los Angeles Herald Examiner* in 1981. Since leaving the *Examiner* she has been a frequent contributor to a variety of publications, writing on sports, entertainment, and police issues. She is the coauthor of *Chief: My Life in the LAPD* (1993) with Darryl Gates and a series of mystery novels, including *High Heel Blue* (1996). Shah is presently a contributing writer for *ESPN: The Magazine.*

**Gary Smith** is a senior writer for *Sports Illustrated.* This is his third appearance in *The Best American Sports Writing.* His story about high school basketball on a Crow reservation won the 1992 National Magazine Award for feature writing.

**Red Smith** (1905–1982) worked as a sports writer for more than five decades, beginning in 1928 with the *St. Louis Star* and continuing with the *Philadelphia Record,* the *New York Herald Tribune* and the *New York Times,* with whom he won a Pulitzer Prize for distinguished commentary in 1976. He was unquestionably the most influential and respected sports writer of his time, as well as the most widely syndicated newspaper sports columnist in the world. His work is available in several collections, including *The Red Smith Reader, Strawberries in Wintertime,* and *To Absent Friends.*

**Paul Solotaroff,** a graduate of the State University of New York at Stony Brook, served on the staff of the *National Sports Daily.* He is the author of *House of*

*Purple Hearts: Stories of Vietnam Vets Who Find Their Way Back* (1995) and *Group: Six People in Search of a Life* (1999).

**Al Stump** is a freelance writer whose work has appeared in numerous publications. More than thirty years after it was written, Stump's story "Fight to Live," which was based on his experience as Cobb's ghostwriter for his autobiography *Ty Cobb: The True Record*, was the inspiration for the motion picture *Cobb*.

**Gay Talese** was hired by the *New York Times* after graduating from the University of Alabama in 1953. He soon became a human-interest reporter and his work began to appear in magazines as well, most notably the *New York Times Magazine* and *Esquire*, where his celebrity profiles earned him a national reputation. A contributing editor for *Esquire*, he is the author of *The Bridge* (1964), *Honor Thy Father* (1971), *Thy Neighbor's Wife* (1980), and *Unto the Sons* (1992).

**Hunter S. Thompson** started writing in the air force and then embarked on a brief newspaper career that ended following repeated clashes with his editors. He moved to the Caribbean and began writing for a bowling magazine and penning freelance dispatches for the *New York Herald Tribune* and the *National Observer*. After he moved to California, his freewheeling, personal reportage, dubbed "gonzo" journalism, found favor in magazines. One particular story on the Hell's Angels that he wrote for *The Nation* made him a celebrity. In 1970 he joined *Rolling Stone*, and his articles have made more or less regular appearance in that and several other publications ever since. He is the author of several collections, including *Hell's Angels* (1966), *Fear and Loathing in Las Vegas* (1971), *Fear and Loathing on the Campaign Trail '72* (1973), *The Great Shark Hunt* (1979), *Generation of Swine* (1988), *Songs of the Doomed* (1991), and *Better Than Sex* (1994).

**Wells Twombly** (1936–1977) was a graduate of the University of Connecticut and began his career with the *Willimantic Daily Chronicle* before moving to the *Pasadena Star News* and *North Hollywood Valley Times Today*. He then worked as a columnist for the *Houston Chronicle*, the *Detroit Free Press*, and the *San Francisco Examiner*. He is the author of *Shake Down the Thunder, Blanda Alive and Kicking, Fireworks and Fury,* and *200 Years of Sport in America*. A profile by David Klein of the *Newark Star-Ledger* titled "Wells Twombly, 41, The Laughter Still Echoes," appeared in *Best Sports Stories 1977* after Twombly's death.

**John Updike** is one of the nation's most honored authors. After graduating from Harvard, he joined the staff of *The New Yorker* in 1955. His first book, a volume of poetry titled *The Carpentered Hen and Other Tame Creatures* (1958), appeared shortly after he left the magazine to focus his efforts on fiction and poetry. His first novel, *Rabbit Run,* was published in 1960. Both *Rabbit Is Rich* (1981) and *Rabbit at Rest* (1990) won the Pulitzer Prize for fiction. His most recent book is the novel *Bech at Bay* (1998), and he is guest editor of *The Best American Short Stories of the Century* (1999).

**Tom Wolfe** graduated from Yale in 1957 and for the next six years worked for the *Springfield Union* and *Washington Post.* After leaving the *Post* he joined the *New York Herald Tribune.* Frustrated with a magazine assignment from *Esquire* on California's fetish with customized cars, Wolfe typed up his notes in an overnight marathon session, and *Esquire* published the groundbreaking story as is. Wolfe became identified as the major proponent of what later became known as "the new journalism." Over the next year and a half he wrote forty more such pieces, which were collected in the best-selling *The Kandy-Kolored Tangerine-Flake Streamline Baby* (1965). Several similar collections followed, and Wolfe has remained one of the most popular and influential contemporary journalists. His other books include *The Electric Kool-Aid Acid Test* (1968), *The Painted Word* (1975), *The Right Stuff* (1979), and the novels *The Bonfire of the Vanities* (1987) and *A Man in Full* (1998).

**Stanley Woodward** (1895–1965) served as sports editor of the *New York Herald Tribune* from 1938 to 1948, during which time he assembled perhaps the greatest staff of sports writers in the history of the newspaper, including Red Smith, Joe Palmer, Al Laney, and Roger Kahn. After graduating from Amherst College, he served in the merchant marine, and in 1919 he was hired by the *Worcester Evening Gazette.* Three years later he became the paper's city editor. Following a stint with the *Boston Herald* he joined the *Herald Tribune* in 1930; there he became well known as a football writer before becoming sports editor. During World War II, Woodward worked as a war correspondent. In 1948 he was fired following a dispute with management, and then he served as editor of the original *Sports Illustrated.* Woodward then wrote for the *New York Daily Compass,* the *Miami Herald,* and the *Newark Star Ledger* before returning to the *Herald Tribune* in 1959. His work is found in the books *Sports Page* (1949), *Paper Tiger* (1964), and *Sportswriter* (1967).

**Dick Young** (1918–1987) first gained notoriety as a sports reporter for the *New York Daily News,* for which he covered the Brooklyn Dodgers. After the Dodgers moved to Los Angeles, Young became a columnist; his column "Young Ideas" was syndicated nationally and became a regular feature in the *Sporting News.* In 1982 Young had a dispute with the paper's management and moved to the *New York Post.* The *News* promptly filed a $1.5 million breach-of-contract suit, which was later dismissed by the courts. Known for his unapologetic, combative style, Young was elected to the writers' wing of the Baseball Hall of Fame in 1978.

# Notable Sports Writing and Sports Writers of the Century

Selected by Glenn Stout and David Halberstam

MITCH ALBOM
  Mark Messner. *Detroit Free Press,*
  1989
  A Tragedy Too Easy to Ignore. *De-troit Free Press,* 1993
DAVE ANDERSON
ROGER ANGELL
  Agincourt and After. *The New Yorker,* 1975
PETE AXTHELM

JAMES BALDWIN
  The Fight: Patterson vs. Liston.
  *Playboy,* 1962
IRA BERKOW AND MURRAY
  OLDERMAN
  An American Tragedy. *Inside Sports,* 1980
IRA BERKOW
  A Killing in Omaha. *Inside Sports,*
  February 1982
FURMAN BISHER
JENNIFER BRIGGS
  My Life in the Locker Room. *Dal-las Observer,* 1992

BRUCE BUSCHEL
  Lips Gets Smacked. *Philadelphia Magazine,* 1993

COLIN CAMPBELL
  The Sharkers. *Sports Afield,* 1978
JIMMY CANNON
  The Beautiful Racket. *New York Post,* 1956
  Club Fighter. *True,* 1948
BUD COLLINS
MYRON COPE
  Feats of Clay. *True,* 1962
BARNABY CONRAD
  The Death of Manolete. *True,* 1950
KYLE CHRICHTON
  Hot Tamale Circuit. *Collier's,* 1946

ARTHUR DALEY
ALLISON DANZIG
DAVID DAVIS
  The 13th Round. *L.A. Reader,* 1996
MICHAEL DISEND
  Painter on a Planet of Blind Peo-ple. *Sports Illustrated,* 1991

RICHARD DONOVAN
The Fabulous Satchel Paige. *Collier's,* 1953
JOHN DREBINGER

JOHN FEINSTEIN
DAVID FINKEL
Golf's Saving Grace. *Washington Post Magazine,* 1997
JOE FLAHERTY
Sympathy for the Devil. *Inside Sports,* 1982
HUGH FULLERTON

PAUL GALLICO
PETER GAMMONS
PETER GOLDMAN
Requiem for a Globetrotter. *Sport,* 1977

DAVID HALBERSTAM
A Hero for the Wired World. *Sports Illustrated,* 1991
W. C. HEINZ
The Day of the Fight. *Cosmopolitan,* 1947
MARK HEISLER
ED HINTON
Forever Fighting the War for Lost Pride. *Atlanta Journal Constitution,* 1993
AL HIRSHBERG
JEROME HOLTZMAN

DAN JENKINS
SALLY JENKINS
PAT JORDAN
Going Nowhere, Fast. *Inside Sports,* 1982
PAT JORDAN
War of the Roses. *GQ,* 1989

ROGER KAHN
STEVE KELLEY
JOHN KIERAN
STEPHEN KING
Head Down. *The New Yorker,* 1990
CURRY KIRKPATRICK
How King Rat Became the Big Cheese. *Sports Illustrated,* 1983
TONY KORNHEISER
Body and Soul. *Inside Sports,* 1979
MABREY "DOC" KOUNTZE

SAM LACY
AL LANEY
A Dark Man Laughs. *New York Herald Tribune,* 1944
RING LARDNER
Oddities of Bleacher Bugs. *Boston American,* 1908
FRED LIEB
A.J. LIEBLING
Ahab and Nemesis. *The New Yorker,* 1955
ED LINN
The Sad End of Big Daddy. *Saturday Evening Post,* 1963
ROBERT LIPSYTE
JACK LONDON
Jack Johnson v. Jim Jeffries. *New York Herald,* 1908

NORMAN MAILER
The Crazy One. *Playboy,* 1967
DAVID MAMET
The Buck Passes. *Men's Journal,* 1995
TEX MAULE
Here's Why It Was the Best Football Game Ever. *Sports Illustrated,* January 19, 1959
W. O. MCGEEHAN

THOMAS MCGUANE
The Heart of the Game. *Outside,*
1977
THOMAS MCINTYRE
Buff. *Sports Afield,* 1981
JOHN MCNULTY
LEIGH MONTVILLE
Triumph on Sacred Ground.
*Sports Illustrated,* 1992

JOYCE CAROL OATES
On Boxing. *The Ontario Review,*
1987
JOE H. PALMER
CHARLES P. PIERCE
The Man. Amen. *GQ,* 1997
SHIRLEY POVICH

SCOTT RAAB
Asphalt Junkie. *GQ,* 1992
RON RAPPAPORT
RICK REILLY
The Mourning Anchor. *Sports
Illustrated,* 1988
A Ring and a Prayer. *Sports Illus-
trated,* 1987
GRANTLAND RICE
Notre Dame Cyclone Beats Army
13-7, 1927
LINDA ROBERTSON
BOB RYAN
JOAN RYAN
DAMON RUNYON
Bred for Battle. *New York Ameri-
can,* 1925
The Havana Affair. *New York Jour-
nal,* 1915
Undertaker Song. *Collier's,* 1934
STEVE RUSHIN
1954–1994: How We Got Here.
*Sports Illustrated,* 1995

LE ANNE SCHREIBER
The Long Light. *Independent,* 1989
BUDD SCHULBERG
DAN SHAUGHNESSY
DALE SHAW
Anatomy of a Pool Hustler. *Saga,*
1961
LEONARD SHECTER
BLACKIE SHERROD
BUD SHRAKE
AL SILVERMAN
CLAIRE SMITH
SUSAN STERLING
The Soccer Parents. *North Ameri-
can Review,* 1997
ASHTON STEVENS
Old Man Britt. *San Francisco Ex-
aminer,* 1905
GARY SMITH
Shadow of a Nation. *Sports Illus-
trated,* 1991
GARY SMITH
Tyson, the Timid. *Sports Illus-
trated,* 1988
WENDELL SMITH
It was a Great Day in Jersey. *Pitts-
burgh Courier,* 1945
SHELBY STROTHER
A Home Town Mourns Joe De-
laney. *Denver Post,* 1983

RICK TELANDER
HUNTER S. THOMPSON
Fear and Loathing at the Super
Bowl. *Rolling Stone,* 1974
MIKE TRIMBLE
Memoirs of a Miner. *Arkansas
Times Magazine,* 1985
JOHN R. TUNIS

GEORGE VECSEY

MICHAEL WILBON

TOM WOLFE

TURNLEY WALKER
  Fighting Man. *Pageant,* 1957

HERBERT WARREN WIND
  Jack, the Giant Killer. *Sports Illustrated,* 1955